A New Star-Rat[illegible] & Other Exciting News from Frommer's!

In our continuing effort to publish the savviest, most up-to-date, and most appealing travel guides available, we've added some great new features.

Frommer's guides now include a new **star-rating system.** Every hotel, restaurant, and attraction is rated from 0 to 3 stars to help you set priorities and organize your time.

We've also added **seven brand-new features** that point you to the great deals, in-the-know advice, and unique experiences that separate travelers from tourists. Throughout the guide, look for:

Finds Special finds—those places only insiders know about

Fun Fact Fun facts—details that make travelers more informed and their trips more fun

Kids Best bets for kids—advice for the whole family

Moments Special moments—those experiences that memories are made of

Overrated Places or experiences not worth your time or money

Tips Insider tips—some great ways to save time and money

Value Great values—where to get the best deals

We've also added a **"What's New"** section in every guide—a timely crash course in what's hot and what's not in every destination we cover.

Here's what the critics say about Frommer's:

"Amazingly easy to use. Very portable, very complete."

—*Booklist*

"Detailed, accurate, and easy-to-read information for all price ranges."

—*Glamour Magazine*

"Hotel information is close to encyclopedic."

—*Des Moines Sunday Register*

"Frommer's Guides have a way of giving you a real feel for a place."

—*Knight Ridder Newspapers*

Other Great Guides for Your Trip:

Frommer's Barcelona, Madrid & Seville

Spain For Dummies

Frommer's Spain's Best-Loved Driving Tours

Frommer's Europe

Frommer's Road Atlas Europe

Frommer's®

Barcelona, Madrid & Seville

4th Edition

by Darwin Porter & Danforth Prince

Wiley Publishing, Inc.

About the Authors

Veteran travel writers **Darwin Porter** and **Danforth Prince** have written numerous bestselling Frommer's guides, notably to France, Italy, England, Germany, and Spain. Porter, who was bureau chief for the *Miami Herald* when he was 21, wrote the first-ever Frommer's guide to Spain while still a student. Prince, who began writing with Porter in 1982, worked for the Paris bureau of the *New York Times.*

Published by:

Wiley Publishing, Inc.

909 Third Ave.
New York, NY 10022

ISBN 0-7645-6713-6
ISSN 1090-5499

Editor: John Vorwald
Production Editor: Suzanna R. Thompson
Cartographer: Nick Trotter
Photo Editor: Richard Fox
Production by Wiley Indianapolis Composition Services

Front cover photo: Antoni Gaudí's Casa Batlló in Barcelona
Back cover photo: Girls in traditional Spanish dress

For information on our other products and services or to obtain technical support, please contact our Customer Care Department within the U.S. at 800-762-2974, outside the U.S. at 317-572-3993 or fax 317-572-4002.

Wiley also publishes its books in a variety of electronic formats. Some content that appears in print may not be available in electronic formats.

Manufactured in the United States of America

5 4 3 2

Contents

5 Settling into Madrid 136

6 Exploring Madrid 190

7 Side Trips from Madrid 224

8 Seville 251

Appendix: Barcelona, Madrid & Seville in Depth 295

Index 300

List of Maps

An Invitation to the Reader

In researching this book, we discovered many wonderful places—hotels, restaurants, shops, and more. We're sure you'll find others. Please tell us about them, so we can share the information with your fellow travelers in upcoming editions. If you were disappointed with a recommendation, we'd love to know that, too. Please write to:

Frommer's Barcelona, Madrid & Seville, 4th Edition
Wiley Publishing, Inc. • 909 Third Ave. • New York, NY 10022

An Additional Note

Please be advised that travel information is subject to change at any time—and this is especially true of prices. We therefore suggest that you write or call ahead for confirmation when making your travel plans. The authors, editors, and publisher cannot be held responsible for the experiences of readers while traveling. Your safety is important to us, however, so we encourage you to stay alert and be aware of your surroundings. Keep a close eye on cameras, purses, and wallets, all favorite targets of thieves and pickpockets.

New! Frommer's Star Ratings & Icons

Every hotel, restaurant, and attraction listing in this guide has been ranked for quality, value, service, amenities, and special features using a star-rating scale. In country, state, and regional guides, we also rate towns and regions to help you narrow down your choices and budget your time accordingly. Hotels and restaurants in the Very Expensive and Expensive categories are rated on a scale of one (highly recommended) to three stars (exceptional). Those in the Moderate and Inexpensive categories rate from zero (recommended) to two stars (very highly recommended). Attractions, towns, and regions are rated according to the following scale: zero stars (recommended), one star (highly recommended), two stars (very highly recommended), and three stars (must-see).

In addition to the rating system, we also use seven icons to highlight insider information, useful tips, special bargains, hidden gems, memorable experiences, kid-friendly venues, places to avoid, and other useful information:

Finds *Fun Fact* *Kids* *Moments* *Overrated* *Tips* *Value*

The following abbreviations are used for credit cards:

AE	American Express	DISC	Discover	V	Visa
DC	Diners Club	MC	MasterCard		

FROMMERS.COM

Now that you have the guidebook to a great trip, visit our website at **www.frommers.com** for travel information on nearly 2,500 destinations. With features updated regularly, we give you instant access to the most current trip-planning information available. At Frommers.com, you'll also find the best prices on airfares, accommodations, and car rentals—and you can even book travel online through our travel booking partners. At Frommers.com, you'll also find the following:

- Online updates to our most popular guidebooks
- Vacation sweepstakes and contest giveaways
- Newsletter highlighting the hottest travel trends
- Online travel message boards with featured travel discussions

What's New in Barcelona, Madrid & Seville

As Spain—along with France and the United States—moves into the forefront of world tourism, here is a roundup of some late-breaking developments in its most populous cities.

BARCELONA

ACCOMMODATIONS The hotel building boom that swept Barcelona when it hosted the Olympics has long since dissipated, although new hotels keep cropping up. Just off Les Rambles, **Hotel Peninsular,** Sant Pau 34–36 (© **93-302-31-38**), has been converted into a budget inn in the Art Nouveau style. Thoroughly overhauled in an evocative Modernist style, it is imbued with a Spanish colonial aura. See chapter 3 for more details.

RESTAURANTS The restaurant explosion continues unabated in Barcelona, the city having overtaken Madrid as a destination for world gourmets. Some of the most exciting developments include the opening of **Coses de Menjar,** Plaza de Palau 5 (© **93-310-60-01**), bringing fusion cuisine to the Catalán capital. A hip hangout for New Age Barcelona, the restaurant serves a superb cuisine. For a *Kama Sutra*–like dining experience, head for **Jean Luc Figueras,** Santa Teresa 10 (© **93-415-28-77**), serving top-of-the-line viands in a Gràcia town house that was once the studio of Balenciaga. The cookery is both innovative and traditional, each dish imbued with a personal touch. For one of the greatest restaurants of Spain, you take a 30-minute drive north to reach **El Racó de Can Fabes,** Sant Joan 6, in Sant Celoni (© **93-867-28-51**), a gourmet citadel offering the finest Mediterranean cuisine along Spain's eastern coastline. Refined, elegant, yet rustic, it is run with dedication and care. See chapter 3 for more details.

ATTRACTIONS In the heart of Barcelona, **Fundación Francisco Godia,** Valencia 284 (© **93-272-31-80**), showcases a fabled art collection of a wealthy Catalán collector who amassed one of the largest and most exquisite private collections in the country. He had a keen insight for purchasing great art, especially paintings, as a visit here will quickly reveal. See chapter 4 for more details.

MADRID

ACCOMMODATIONS The hotel map of Spain's capital keeps constantly changing. One of the city's newest hotels, **Preciados,** Preciados 37 (© **91-454-44-00**), has been carved from a historic 1861 structure, with many of its original architectural details retained. Otherwise, one of Madrid's most centrally located hotels is as modern as the millennium. Even better is **Hotel Adler,** Calle Velázquez (© **91-548-78-84**), lying at a location called "the golden triangle of art" (near El Prado, Reina Sofía, and the Thyssen-Bornemisza collections). A classic 1880s building has been painstakingly restored and imbued with modern comforts. See chapter 5 for more details.

RESTAURANTS A dining oddity and a former members-only club, **Café del Círculo de Bellas Artes,** Calle Alcalá 42 (© **91-521-69-42**), now attracts the general public to an atmospheric choice lying within an arts center. You get culture and good food served in a palatial hall. Only tapas (hors d'oeuvres) are featured at night. See chapter 5 for more details.

SEVILLE

ACCOMMODATIONS In the city of Carmen, the so-called "world's best small hotel" has opened, the beautifully restored **Casa Número 7,** Vírgenes 7 (© **95-422-15-18**), in a 19th-century town house mansion. There's even a butler to serve you breakfast at this elegant inn that is like living in grandeur in the palace of an Andalusian don. The prices are reasonable, too. See chapter 8 for more details.

1

Introducing Barcelona, Madrid & Seville

Although these three cities are remarkably different in texture and attractions, each is evocative of the region it presides over: Barcelona, capital of Catalonia; Madrid, capital of Castile (and the entire country); and Seville, capital of Andalusia. To walk their streets, to sample their cuisine, to view their monuments, to taste and observe their daily life: These are reasons enough to visit Spain. If you do miss the rest of the country, it would be a pity; but if you at least manage the cities covered in this guide, you'll have found a window on the three different worlds that best exemplify Spain: Catalonia, Castile, and Andalusia.

Barcelona, progressive and industrial, is the most European of Spanish cities, yet also Mediterranean in both climate and atmosphere. Cataláns often speak of their "schizophrenia"—that is, the tension caused by their desires both to maintain the traditional and to embrace the new.

Though the city's palm tree-lined streets may seem languid, there's activity aplenty as Barcelona races to keep up with other major cities in Europe. Economic vigor is one part of the mix—one-fourth of the country's goods are manufactured here—but 21st-century Barcelona is also a place to have fun and relax. Never before have there been so many good restaurants, hotels, nightclubs, and new attractions.

Since the 1992 Olympics, the city has undergone a veritable renaissance, sprucing up its buildings and improving its tourist facilities at a rate equaled by no other city in Spain, not even Madrid.

Speaking of the capital city: Once staid, almost seedy in its decay, Madrid has burst upon the European scene with newfound enthusiasm for the modern world. Lively at all hours, the city appears to be recovering from a long and dreary sleep, determined to stay up every minute of the day and night for fear of missing out on anything.

It's true that Madrid doesn't match the great attractions and architecture of London, Paris, or Rome, but it does have the Prado and its other stellar art galleries. It offers visitors a fascinating nightlife scene, great restaurants, and deluxe hotels, and it's within striking distance of some of the country's best day trips, including Toledo, Segovia, and El Escorial. Neither Barcelona nor Seville can be used as a base for such a diverse array of attractions. Heading south, the temperature rises and the pace slows as we approach Seville, center of world attention during the 1992 Expo. It doesn't boast the great art museums of Barcelona or Madrid, but it does possess a stunning cathedral, along with truly incomparable Moorish architecture. Orange and palm trees line its streets, where panoramic vistas await at every turn. Chances are you won't be singing in the rain, as Seville is dry, dusty, and hot—in fact, it's the hottest city in Iberia.

Famed for its Easter festivities, when hooded and robed penitents march through the streets, Seville follows those events with its April Fair, a week of celebrations. Sevillanos ride on horseback looking like stage extras from *Carmen,* and the entire city celebrates with food, wine, and bullfights, followed by nightly flamenco dancing and the region's own special dance, the *sevillanas.* Almost any time of the year is ideal for a visit to Andalusia's capital, although we prefer the spring or fall. Seville's cathedral is one of the finest in Spain; the Alcazar evokes memories of a great Moorish civilization; and the Museo de Bellas Artes has one of the country's best art collections. But Seville offers much more: Visitors can enjoy the sensory pleasures of Andalusia itself.

1 Frommer's Favorite Barcelona Experiences

- **Wandering the Crooked Streets of the Gothic Quarter.** Long before Madrid was founded, the kingdom of Catalonia was a bastion of art and architecture. Whether the Barri Gòtic, as it's called in Catalán, is truly Gothic is the subject of endless debate, but the Ciutat Vella, or old city, of Barcelona is one of the most evocative sites in Spain. Its richly textured streets, with their gurgling fountains, vintage stores, and ancient fortifications, inspired such artists as Pablo Picasso (a museum of whose work is found here) and Joan Miró (who was born in this neighborhood). Stop in at Sala Parés, Spain's oldest art gallery, at Carrer Petritxol 5 (© **93-318-70-20**)—one of the birthplaces of Catalán modernismo. See chapter 4.
- **Watching the Sardana.** The national dance of Catalonia is performed at noon in the Plaça de Sant Jaume, in front of the cathedral. Nothing is more folkloric than this street dance played out against the backdrop of a *cobla,* or brass band. The dance may have originated in one of the Greek islands, and then been brought to Barcelona by sailors. It may even have come from Sardinia (hence the name). But regardless of its point of origin, the *Sardana* remains uniquely Catalán. See chapter 4.
- **Strolling Along Les Rambles.** Les Rambles cuts through the heart of Barcelona's oldest district, beginning at the Plaça de Catalunya and running toward the sea. A tree-lined boulevard, it's the most famous street in Spain—and a lot more intriguing than Madrid's dull Gran Vía. The street is democratic, bringing together buskers, shop owners, tourists, drag queens, and drug dealers—mixed in with hotels, cafes, porno houses, newsstands, and flower stalls. It's composed of five different Ramblas or Rambles (either term is correct). Late at night, the scene on Spain's most charismatic street evokes the writings about Barcelona by Jean Genet. See chapter 4.
- **Drinking Cava in a *Xampanyería.*** Enjoy a glass of bubbly, Barcelona style. Cataláns swear that their *cavas* taste better than French champagne. After the staid Franco years, *xampanyerías* (champagne bars) literally burst onto the Barcelona nightlife scene; many stay open until the wee hours of the morning. You can select *brut* or *brut nature* (brut is slightly sweeter). Try any of these popular brands, which also happen to be the best: Mestres, Parxet, Torello, Recaredo, Gramona, or Mont-Marçal. See chapter 4.
- **Exploring the Museu Picasso.** Barcelona's most popular attraction, housed in three Gothic mansions, spans Picasso's long, multifaceted career, taking in the blue period, cubism, and beyond. Of special interest are the

paintings in the Barcelona section from the years 1895 to 1897, when he lived in the Catalán capital. See works by Picasso-as-copyist (he re-created Velázquez's famous portrait of Philip IV) and admire the portraits, especially the one he painted of his aunt, *Retrato de la Tía Pepa* (*Portrait of Aunt Pepa*). In the *Caballo Corneado* (*Gored Horse*) charcoal drawing, you can see the beginnings of cubism. See chapter 4.

- **Going Gaga Over Gaudí.** No architect in Europe was as fantastical as Antoni Gaudí y Cornet, the foremost proponent of Catalán modernismo. Barcelona is studded with the works of this extraordinary artist—in fact, UNESCO now lists all his creations among the World Trust Properties. This eccentric genius conceived buildings as "visions." A recluse and a celibate bachelor, as well as a fervent Catalán nationalist, he lived out his own fantasy. Nothing is more stunning than his Sagrada Família, Barcelona's best-known landmark, a cathedral on which Gaudí labored for the last 43 years of his life, before he was tragically killed by a tram in 1926. The landmark cathedral was never completed. In Barcelona, the question is not "to be or not to be," but "to finish or not to finish." Believe it or not, they're still working on it. If it's ever finished, "The Sacred Family" will be Europe's largest cathedral. See chapter 4.
- **Boozing at the Bars.** No city in Spain, and few others in Europe, can match Barcelona when it comes to barhopping. Many of its more celebrated bars are fashion statements, on the see-and-be-seen circuit, and the later you go the better. Ranging from rustic to the most avant-garde modern, these bars attract the young and fashionable, a social elite that would not even think of patronizing a bar in some other city. For the hottest, hippest nights in Barcelona, head for the city's bars. See chapter 4.
- **Walking the Harbor Front.** A major port of call for international cruise ships, Spain's largest port boasts a pedestrian promenade with benches, contemporary bridges, palm trees, and some of the city's finest (and priciest) restaurants. Begin at the Moll de la Fusta, or "Wooden Wharf," where the Barri Gòtic meets the harbor. Continue along the beach of Barceloneta to the Port Vell, or Olympic port. This is the site of Platja Barcelona, a beach constructed for the 1992 Olympic games. If you're hungry, head for one of the several excellent restaurants at the yacht basin, or one of the modest cafes serving Spanish tapas (hors d'oeuvres). Panoramic views of the sea unfold before you. It's a great way to spend an afternoon or early evening. See the accompanying walking tour in chapter 4.

2 Frommer's Favorite Madrid Experiences

- **Sitting in *Sol* or *Sombra* at the Bullfights.** With origins as old as pagan Spain, the art of bullfighting is the expression of Iberian temperament and passions. Detractors object to the sport as cruel, bloody, violent, hot, and savage. Aficionados, however, understand bullfighting as a microcosm of death, catharsis, and rebirth. These philosophical underpinnings may not be immediately apparent, but if you strive to understand the bullfight, it can be one of the most evocative and memorable events in Spain. Head for the *plaza de toros* (bullring) in Madrid. Tickets are either *sol* (sunny side) or *sombra* (in the shade); you'll pay more to get out of the sun. Observe how the feverish crowds appreciate the ballet of the *banderilleros,* the thundering fury of the bull, the arrogance of the matador—all leading to "death in the afternoon." See chapter 6.

- **Seeing the Masterpieces at the Prado.** It's one of the world's premier art museums, ranking with the Louvre. The Prado is home to some 4,000 masterpieces, many of them acquired by Spanish kings. The wealth of Spanish art is staggering—everything from Goya's *Naked Maja* to the celebrated *Las Meninas* (*The Maids of Honor*) by Velázquez (our favorite). Masterpiece after masterpiece unfolds before your eyes: You can imagine your fate in Hieronymus Bosch's *Garden of Earthly Delights* or recoil from the horror of Goya's *Disasters of War* etchings. When the Spanish artistic soul gets too dark, escape to the Italian salons and view canvases by Caravaggio, Fra Angelico, and Botticelli. Be warned, though, that a quick run-through won't suffice: It would take a lifetime to savor the Prado's wonders. See chapter 6.
- **Feasting on Tapas in the *Tascas.*** Tapas, those bite-size portions washed down with wine, beer, or sherry, are reason enough to go to Madrid! Spanish tapas are so good their once-secret recipes have been broadcast around the world, but they always taste better at home. A *tapeo* is akin to a London pub crawl—you travel from one tapas bar to another. Each has a different specialty. Tapas bars, called *tascas,* are a quintessential Spanish experience, be it in Galicia, Andalusia, Catalonia, or Castile. Originally, tapas were cured ham or *chorizo* (spicy sausage). Today they are likely to include everything—*gambas* (deep-fried shrimp), anchovies marinated in vinegar, stuffed peppers, a cool, spicy gazpacho, or hake salad. To go really native, try lamb's sweetbreads or bulls' testicles. These dazzling spreads will hold you over until the fashionable 10pm dining hour. The best streets for your *tasca* crawl include Ventura de la Vega, the area around Plaza de Santa Ana or Plaza de Santa Bárbara, Cava Baja, or Calle de Cuchilleros. See chapter 6.
- **Lounging in an Outdoor Cafe.** In sultry summertime, Madrileños come alive on their *terrazas.* The drinking and good times can go on until dawn. In glamorous hangouts or on lowly street corners, the cafe scene takes place mainly along an axis shaped by the Paseo de la Castellana, Paseo del Prado, and Paseo de Recoletos. Wander up and down the boulevards and select a spot that appeals to you. For traditional atmosphere, the terrazas at Playa Mayor win out. See chapter 6.
- **Shopping the Rastro.** Madrid's flea market represents a tradition that's 500 years old. Savvy shoppers arrive before 7am every Sunday to beat the rush and claim the best merchandise. The teeming place doesn't really get going until about 9am, and then it's shoulder-to-shoulder stretching down Calle Riberia de Curtidores. Real or fake antiques, secondhand clothing, porno films, Franco-era furniture, paintings (endless copies of Velázquez), bullfight posters, old books, religious relics, and plenty of just plain junk, including motorcycles from World War II, are for sale. These streets also contain some of the finest permanent

antique shops in Madrid. But beware: Pickpockets are out in full force. More than a few mugging victims have later found their purses here for resale—thoroughly emptied, of course. See chapter 6.

- **Sunday Strolling in the Retiro.** Spread across 350 cool acres in sweltering Madrid, Parque de Retiro was originally designed as the gardens of Buen Retiro palace, occupied by Philip IV in the 1630s. In 1767 Charles III opened part of the gardens to the general public. Only after the collapse of Isabella II's monarchy in 1868 did the park become available to all Madrileños. Statues dot the grounds (a towering 1902 monument to Alfonso XII presides over the lake), which also contain some 15,000 trees, a rose garden, and a few art galleries. The best time for a stroll is Sunday morning before lunch, when vendors hawk their wares, magicians perform their acts, and fortune-tellers read tarot cards. You can even rent a boat and laze away the morning on the lake. See chapter 6.
- **Nursing a Drink at Chicote.** The 1930s interior at Madrid's most famous bar looks the same as it did during the Civil War. Shells might have been flying along the Gran Vía, but the international press corps covering the war drank on. After the war, the crowd of regulars included major writers, artists, and actors. By the late 1960s it had degenerated into a pickup bar frequented by prostitutes. But today it has regained the *joie de vivre* of yore and is one of the smart, sophisticated spots to rendezvous in Madrid. See p. 219.
- **Experiencing the *Movida.*** We can't tell you exactly how to go about this. Just go to Madrid—the *movida* will seek you out. Very roughly translated as the "shift" or the "movement," movida characterizes post-Franco life in Madrid, after Madrileños threw off the yoke of dictatorship and repression. In a larger context, the *movida* is a cultural renaissance affecting all aspects of local life, encompassing a wide range of social projects and progressive causes. *Movida* is best experienced around midnight, when the town just starts to wake up; the action centers around hipper-than-thou places with names like Bar Cock. Madrileños hop from club to club as if they're afraid they'll miss out on something if they stay in one place too long. To truly catch a whiff of *movida,* head for the lively nightlife areas of Chueca, Huertas, and Malasaña, and the big clubs around Calle Arenal. See chapter 6.

3 Frommer's Favorite Seville Experiences

- **Getting Caught Up in the Passions of Flamenco.** It's best heard in some old tavern, in a neighborhood like the Barrio de Triana in Seville. From the lowliest *taberna* to the poshest nightclub, you can hear the staccato heel clicking, foot stomping, castanet rattling, hand clapping, and sultry guitar and tambourine sound. Some say its origins lie deep in Asia, but the Spanish gypsy has given the art form, which dramatizes inner conflict and pain, an original style. Performed by a great artist, flamenco can tear your heart out with its soulful and throaty singing. See chapter 8.
- **Celebrating *Semana Santa* (Holy Week).** Since the 16th century, the city's processions and celebrations at Easter have been the

biggest and most elaborate in Spain. Solemn evening processions take place each day of the week before Easter, organized by *codafrías,* or religious brotherhoods. Members of various codafrías dress as penitents in hoods, capes, and masks—a little spooky. Huge platforms, called *pasos,* are carried on their shoulders, and religious statues are paraded through the streets. But it's not all solemn; Sevillanos indulge in almost pagan celebrations of singing, eating, and drinking, too. With hardly enough time for a breather, Semana Santa segues into Feria de Abril, a 6-day festival of bullfights, street dancing, parades, fireworks, and flamenco performances. See chapter 8.

- **Strolling Through Barrio Santa Cruz.** Wandering this area of whitewashed houses, winding streets, and artisans' shops is one of the scenic adventures of a trip to Seville. In the Middle Ages the barrio was the home of Seville's Jewish community. Enter at Calle de Mateus Gago, which intersects with the monumental realm of Plaza de la Virgen de los Reyes, and plunge right in. The neighborhood is filled with restaurants and *tascas,* so you can take a break whenever you choose. Most historic figures of Seville have passed through this barrio, although few traces of its former Jewish heritage remain. All the former synagogues have been turned into churches, including Santa María la Blanca, with Murillo's *Last Supper.* Go during the day—the risk of mugging is high at night. See chapter 8.
- **Discovering the Mysteries of Casa de Pilatos.** This palace for the marqués de Tarifa, completed in 1540, was partially modeled on the House of Pontius Pilate, which the marqués had visited in Jerusalem. It's a riot of Mudéjar design: textured wood ceilings, carved stucco filigree, brightly patterned tiles, a Plateresque portal, a central patio with Moorish arches, a Gothic balustrade, and a bubbling fountain. There's nothing else quite like it in Seville. It's still the home of the duque de Medinaceli, who sequesters himself in a private wing when visitors come to call. See p. 272.
- **Climbing La Giralda.** All that remains of the former Almohad mosque is La Giralda, a 20-story bell tower that you can climb on a clear day to see olive groves in a 360-degree view around Seville. It was once the minaret of a great Moorish mosque; so intrigued were conquering Christians with its ingenious *sebka* rhomboid brick pattern that they spared the tower and incorporated it into the design of the cathedral they built on the site. The "Apples of Yanmur," the golden spheres with which the Almohads crowned the tower in the 1100s, are long gone. Today the 92m (308-ft.) tower is topped by a belfry, a lantern, and a revolving statue dedicated to the Christian religion. It's quite a climb to the top, but the view from this remarkable monument is worth the effort. See p. 270.
- **Shopping Along Calle Sierpes.** A narrow pedestrian street in the heart of Seville, Calle Sierpes is lined with everything from chic boutiques to innumerable pricey fan shops. The bevy of sidewalk cafes on hand allows you to take a break and watch the action. Back in Franco-era Spain, a popular saying of Sevillanos (male, of course) was, "The three finest pleasures a man can know are to be young, to be in Sevilla, and to stand in Sierpes at dusk when the

girls are passing." The saying might still be true, though in today's Spain it could be said by ladies admiring the young men. Cervantes reputedly began work on *Don Quixote* in a royal prison that once stood on this street. All that's left is a plaque commemorating the poet. See chapter 8.

- **Visiting El Arenal and Triana.** El Arenal and Triana were Seville's 17th-century seafaring quarters, immortalized by such writers as Cervantes, Lope de Vega, and Quevedo. As the site of the 12-sided Torre del Oro, a "gold tower" constructed by the Almohads in 1220, El Arenal draws the most visitors. (The tower was once covered in gold tiles.) Stroll along Marqués de Contadero, which stretches from the banks of the Guadalquivir River to the base of the Torre del Oro. From here you can take a tiled boardwalk to the Plaza de Toros, one of the most famous bullrings in Spain, home to the great school of *tauromaquia.* Seville's most important museum, the Museo Provincial de Bellas Artes, is also here, with an impressive collection of works by Seville painters, including Murillo. Across the river, Triana was once Seville's gypsy quarter, home to potters and tile makers; gentrification has now jacked up real-estate values. At Calle Betis, a terraced riverside promenade, enjoy a panoramic view of the city skyline. See chapter 8.
- **Attending the Opera in Seville.** Seville has been the setting for some of the world's best-loved operas—Bizet's *Carmen,* Donizetti's *La Favorita,* Beethoven's *Fidelio,* Verdi's *La Forza del Destino,* Mozart's *The Marriage of Figaro,* and Rossini's *The Barber of Seville.* Ironically, it wasn't until 1991 that Seville got its own opera house—the Teatro de la Maestranza at Núñez de Balboa, which quickly became one of the world's premier venues for operatic performances. Although you may hear *The Barber of Seville* performed everywhere from Milan to New York, it always sounds better in its hometown. See p. 284.

4 Best Barcelona Hotel Bets

- **Best Historic Hotel:** When the great hotelier César Ritz founded the **Hotel Ritz** (© **93-318-52-00**) in 1919, it was immediately considered the grande dame of Barcelona hotels. Although the term may seem dated, the sentiment still holds true in this case. It's Barcelona's traditional and authentic old-world favorite, ranking along with the Ritz in Madrid for prestige. Although there's great competition in Barcelona's luxury hotel market, the rich and famous still show up on the doorstep of the glamorous, thoroughly renovated Hotel Ritz. See p. 71.
- **Best for Business Travelers:** It's not the grandest hotel in town, but the 12-story **Barcelona Hilton** (© **800/445-8667** in the U.S. and Canada, or 93-495-77-77), near the main soccer stadium, has a state-of-the-art business center and four floors of executive rooms, one reserved exclusively for women. Guest rooms have bedside controls and security locks; rapid checkout means you'll get to the airport on time; and the highly professional staff can help connect you with the movers and shakers in Barcelona with whom you'll be doing business. See p. 70.

- **Best for a Romantic Getaway:** Barcelona isn't exactly a summer resort town, but the **Claris** (✆ **800/888-4747** in the U.S., or 93-487-62-62), which some regard as the best hotel in the city, offers such luxury and comfort that it should suffice. This beautifully restored 19th-century palace boasts a Japanese water garden and a rooftop pool. Even its duplex configurations—separating sleeping from living areas—add to the private, romantic ambience. The owners' collection of Egyptian and Indian artifacts creates an exotic flavor. The most romantic (also expensive) public area in the hotel is Caviar Caspa, a pocket of posh set among cozy, intimate surroundings. See p. 70.
- **Best Fashionable Hotel:** The **Hotel Arts** (✆ **800/241-3333** in the U.S., or 93-221-10-00), the only hotel in Europe commanded by the prestigious Ritz-Carlton group, is the place to stay for the fashionable and for those who want to be. The 44-story glass-and-steel tower has a dramatic seafront location, and the view from the open-air pool is simply splendid. It's a glamorous and chic rendezvous. See p. 73.
- **Best Hotel Lobby for Pretending You're Rich:** There's the Ritz, of course (see above), but the **Avenida Palace** (✆ **93-301-96-00**) recaptures some of the city's long-ago glamour. Set in an old stone palace, this longtime favorite has a rich, historic atmosphere. It boasts one of the plushest lobbies in the world, with glittering chandeliers, red carpeting (the only color to use, of course), and a curving marble staircase fancy enough to make you feel like a Morgan, Ford, or Getty of yesteryear. See p. 71.
- **Best for Families:** In the Barri Gòtic opposite the cathedral, the **Hotel Colón** (✆ **800/845-0636** in the U.S., or 93-301-14-04) has long been a favorite thanks to its choice location near many of the major sights of Barcelona. This traditional hotel has a Spanish-style lobby and high-ceilinged rooms in a part of town usually known for accommodations with small, dark bedrooms. Families should try for one of the nine sixth-floor units with spacious terraces. Babysitting can be arranged, and families can avail themselves of the relatively speedy laundry service. See p. 64.
- **Best Moderately Priced Hotel:** Cited for its good value, the **Hotel Regencia Colón** (✆ **93-318-98-58**) is a sibling of the Colón (see above). It enjoys the same remarkable location in the Barri Gòtic near the cathedral, but charges far less for the privilege of staying here. Updated in 1991, it offers good housekeeping and roomy comfort. Antiques are used here and there to create a warm, welcoming atmosphere, and many rooms have such amenities as big closets and private safes. See p. 65.
- **Best Budget Hotel:** One of the oldest continuously functioning hotels in Barcelona, **Sant Agusti** (✆ **93-318-16-58**), still thrives and keeps bettering itself, or at least keeps up with the times. Benefiting from face-lifts, it is still the best candidate for old world charm for nostalgia seekers. See p. 67.
- **Best B&B:** For the price, the **Hostal Levante** (✆ **93-317-95-65**) is a rather good-size B&B with a total of 38 decent and well-kept rooms. Of course, only seven of them contain a private bathroom, but those down the hall are

generally kept immaculate. It's a viable alternative for those hoping to keep costs low in a very high-priced city. You'll also save money on sightseeing; the hotel is only a brief stroll from Plaça de Sant Jaume, which is in the exact center of the Barri Gòtic. See p. 66.

- **Best Service:** Many hotels in its price range are better than the **Princesa Sofía** (© **93-330-71-11**), but the manager at this HUSA chain entry has hired one of the best, most professional, and most polite staffs in town (and nearly everyone speaks English). Even though the hotel is gargantuan, they somehow seem to address personal problems carefully and to fulfill requests quickly and efficiently without ever losing their cool. The Sofía's business service facilities are on par with those of the Barcelona Hilton. For a complete review of the Princesa Sofía, please visit www.frommers.com (enter "Hotel Princesa" in the search engine, then click on the hotel's name).
- **Best Location:** There's the Colón and its sibling, the Regencia Colón (see above), but there's also **Le Meridien Barcelona** (© **800/543-4300** in the U.S., or 93-318-62-00), the only five-star hotel in the old town. Former guests may remember it as the seedy Hotel Manila, but it was completely renovated in 1988 and is now one of the city's leading hotels. Handsomely furnished and decorated, Le Meridien is just steps from the Rambles. You can literally walk out your door and be involved in Barcelona street life within a minute. The Colón is still a better location for those who want to be in the heart of the old quarter, but for the Rambles and its dozens of restaurants and attractions, Le Meridien is the stellar choice. See p. 61.
- **Best Hotel Health Club:** Massive but plush, the **Princesa Sofía** (© **93-330-71-11**) provides an attractive mixture of formal service in a hypermodern format, with a design placing great emphasis on such American-style amenities as the health club. Consequently, what you'll find one level below the lobby manages to incorporate everything you'd find at a well-run California gym, with a Catalán staff that really seems to care about the state of your physical well-being. Views from the exercise bikes and treadmills encompass a verdant garden and a very large outdoor pool measuring about 24m (80 ft.) in length. This Americanized health club is open only to hotel guests. An American-style restaurant serves cool drinks, light meals, and salads in the hotel's garden, midway between the pool and the health club. For a complete review of the Princesa Sofía, please visit www.frommers.com (enter "Hotel Princesa" in the search engine, then click on the hotel's name).
- **Best Hotel Pool:** The 44-story **Hotel Arts** (© **800/241-3333** in the U.S., or 93-221-10-00) soars above a position close to the edge of the sea, adjacent to the harbor used for Olympic sailing events. Part of the hotel's allure derives from its azure-colored outdoor pool, the focal point of the second floor, which excels in both functional and aesthetic capacities. No one will mind if you aggressively swim several laps, but for sitting there's an alfresco restaurant, the Marina, that serves party-colored drinks and flavorful food throughout the day and evening. Water buffs appreciate the pool's proximity to the beach, and as such, can

alternate between fresh and saltwater swimming. See p. 73.

- **Best Views:** The **Rey Juan Carlos I** (✆ **800/448-8355** in the U.S., or 93-364-40-40), which made its debut in 1993, is a 17-story marble-and-glass tower built around the most dramatic atrium in town. The glass-bubble elevators are worth riding for the panoramic view of Barcelona alone. Not only that, but the hotel offers interior balconies as well. Even more vistas unfold from the hotel's big outdoor swimming pool and sundeck, which are set in a large garden. See p. 71.

5 Best Barcelona Restaurant Bets

- **Best Catalán Cuisine:** This hip Gràcia town house, **Jean Luc Figueras** (✆ **93-415-28-77**), offers a sultry *Kama Sutra* dining experience. Traditional and innovative at the same time, the cookery here is a showcase for the talents of the clever chef and owner, Jean Luc Figueras, who stamps every dish—made from the finest raw materials—with his personal touch. See p. 85.
- **Best View:** Part of the fun of going to Barcelona is dining with a view of the water, and **Can Costa** (✆ **93-221-59-03**) not only offers that but also serves up some of the city's most succulent seafood. It has prospered since the eve of World War II, luring patrons who came to sample traditional recipes from the best baby squid in town to a classic Valencian shellfish paella. See p. 89.
- **Best Decor:** Once **Beltxenea** (✆ **93-215-30-24**) was a chic, elegant apartment in the Eixample, but in 1987 it was converted into a restaurant. The dining rooms still retain the atmosphere of exclusivity and elegance, and these days, the restaurant serves some of the best Basque cookery in Catalonia. See p. 83.
- **Best Value:** The most celebrated restaurant in La Boquería, the covered food market of Barcelona, is **Garduña** (✆ **93-302-43-23**). Originally a hotel, it was converted into a restaurant in the 1970s, today serving artists, writers, actors, and others in a blue-collar atmosphere. The food is superfresh; you get hearty seafood medleys here at prices far below what most other restaurants charge. It also offers one of the best fixed-price menus in town. See p. 81.
- **Best Seafood:** On the main thoroughfare of Gràcia is **Botafumeiro** (✆ **93-218-42-30**), where you get the city's best array of seafood. The chief attraction is mariscos Botafumeiro, a myriad selection of the best shellfish in Spain, with one plate arriving right after the other. The fresh fish is flown daily to Barcelona, often from the coast of Galicia, where the restaurant owner comes from. See p. 87.
- **Best Continental Cuisine:** In this chic part of town, chef Josep Bullick of **La Dama** (✆ **93-202-06-86**) turns out a delectable cuisine that rivals many of the top restaurants of Paris. After sampling such dishes as the langoustine salad with orange vinegar, you'll be won over by his bold innovative cuisine. Peerless ingredients and a faultless technique produce such dishes as roast filet of goat, which may not sound appetizing, but in this chef's hands it becomes a dish of wonder. See p. 84.
- **Best French Cuisine: Jaume de Provença** (✆ **93-430-00-29**) boasts modern French cuisine that's often perfumed with the

delicate spices and aromas of Provence. Chef Jaume Bargués enjoys a well-earned reputation as one of Barcelona's finest chefs. Haute cuisine is handled here with deft hands, and imagination and vision go into the constantly changing menus that depend on what's the best and the freshest in any given season. See p. 83.

- **Best for Creative Cuisine:** Red-haired Mey Hoffmann, daughter of a German father and a Catalán mother, lures the most discriminating palates to **Restaurant Hoffmann** (**© 93-319-58-89**), in the Barri Gòtic. Her cuisine is the city's most creative, a perfect medley of dishes inspired by both Catalonia and neighboring France. Everything from her *fine tarte* with deboned sardines to her ragout of crayfish with green risotto tastes superb, each dish inventive and based on market-fresh ingredients. See p. 75.
- **Best Wine List: Neichel** (**© 93-334-06-99**) enjoys a dedicated loyal following, drawn not only to Jean-Louis Neichel's French and Catalán cuisine, but also to the best wine list in the city—a medley of the finest vintages from both France and Catalonia, as well as throughout Spain. The sommelier helpfully guides you to the perfect wine for your meal, which might include filet of sea bass in a sea urchin cream sauce. He doesn't push the most expensive selections, either. See p. 88.
- **Best for Late-Night Dining:** The good food at **Els Quatre Gats** (**© 93-302-41-40**) is prepared in an unpretentious style of Catalán cookery called *cucina de mercat* (based on whatever looks fresh at the market that day).This is the most legendary cafe in Barcelona, patronized by the likes of Picasso when he was wandering around the port at the tender age of 18. In the heart of the Barri Gòtic, it becomes particularly animated late at night, serving food and drink until 2am. See p. 79.
- **Best Local Favorite:** Since 1836, **7 Portes** (**© 93-319-30-33**) has been feeding locals its several variations of paella, including versions with rabbit or with sardines. It offers one of the most extensive menus in Barcelona, and is a classic, mellow place with waiters wearing long white aprons. See p. 90.
- **Best Desserts:** There's no contest. Imagine a restaurant, **Espai Sucre** (Sugar Space) (**© 93-268-16-30**) that does nothing but create spectacular desserts, except for a few savories. Barcelona's most unusual restaurant weaves magic with an array of dessert concoctions that are daringly inventive and great tasting. See p. 79.
- **Best Picnic Fare:** There's no better place for the makings of a picnic than the **Mercat de la Boquería,** in the center of the Rambles. Also known as the Mercat de Sant Josep, it's one of the world's most extensive produce markets, an attraction in its own right. Dating from 1914, it offers aisle upon aisle of attractively displayed produce from both sea and land. Many of the ingredients are already cooked and prepared, and can be packed for you to carry along in your picnic basket. See p. 93.

6 Best Madrid Hotel Bets

- **Best Historic Hotel:** Inaugurated by Alfonso XIII in 1910, the **Ritz** (**© 800/225-5843** in the U.S. and Canada, or 91-701-67-67), the gathering place of Madrid society, is still the capital's leading luxury choice. This Edwardian hotel is mellower than ever before, the old haughtiness of former management gone with the wind—it long ago rescinded its policy of not allowing movie stars as guests. The rich and famous continue to parade through its portals; today in the lobby you're likely to encounter nearly anyone, from the secretary-general of NATO to Paloma Picasso. See p. 158.

- **Best for Business Travelers:** The concierge at the **Park Hyatt Villa Magna** (✆ **800/223-1234** in the U.S. and Canada, or 91-587-12-34) is one of the most skillful in Madrid, well versed in procuring virtually anything a traveler could conceivably need during a trip to the Spanish capital. One floor below lobby level, this five-star hotel's business center is well stocked with access to translators, word processors, fax machines, and photocopiers. There's a branch of Hertz car rental on the premises, and enough stylish conference rooms (staffed with butlers and stocked with caviar if the nature of your business meeting calls for it) to provide a place for any sales or executive meeting. See p. 157.
- **Best for a Romantic Getaway:** The **Santo Mauro Hotel** (✆ **91-319-69-00**) opened in 1991 in a villa built in 1894 for the duke of Santo Mauro. The lavish property has an ageless grace, although it has been brought up to a state-of-the-art condition. In good weather guests retreat to a beautiful garden pavilion and enjoy many facilities such as a gym and indoor pool. It's resort-like in nature, although situated in Madrid. If you can afford it, go for one of the suites with a fireplace. See p. 161.
- **Best Fashionable Hotel:** A former rundown apartment house, the **Hotel Villa Real** (✆ **91-420-37-67**) has blossomed into a fashionable address, opposite the Cortes and next to the Palace Hotel. This is a 19th-century building of classic French architecture. Some of the town's most important movers and shakers can be found in the cocktail bar. A chic rendezvous patronized by the cognoscenti of Spain, it's where you'd invite the duchess of Alba for tea. See p. 150.
- **Best Hotel Lobby for Pretending You're Rich:** The **Westin Palace** (✆ **800/325-3535** in the U.S., 800/325-3589 in Canada, or 91-360-80-00), between the Prado and the Cortes, is a Victorian wedding cake of a place. To sit and people-watch in this lobby—the grandest Belle Epoque lobby in Madrid—is to be at the epicenter of Spanish political life. Head for the dazzling stained-glass cupola of the main rotunda lounge, and take in the fanciful ceiling frescoes and the custom-made carpets along the way. See p. 150.
- **Best for Families:** The family-friendly, chain-run **Novotel Madrid** (✆ **800/221-4542** in the U.S. and Canada, or 91-724-76-00) on the outskirts of town is a good place for the whole clan. Rates are reasonable, and the bedrooms can easily be arranged to sleep children. There's also a pool, and the breakfast buffet is one of the most generous in Madrid. Children 15 and under stay free in their parents' room. See p. 160.
- **Best Moderately Priced Hotel:** Built in 1966 and still going strong, the reasonably priced **Fiesta Gran Hotel Colón** (✆ **91-573-59-00**) is west of Retiro Park in a relatively safe area of Madrid that's easily connected to the center by subway. It's well maintained and kept up-to-date, offering

well-designed bedrooms with comfortably traditional furnishings. See p. 159.

- **Best Budget Hotel:** In the very heart of old Madrid, off the Plaza Mayor, **Hostal la Macarena** (© **91-365-92-21**), has been housing readers comfortably and well—all for an affordable price—for decades. Surrounded by ancient buildings, the little inn is modest itself, but its welcome is warm, its staff accommodating, and its price is right. See p. 155.
- **Best Service:** There are grander hotels in Madrid, but it's hard to find a staff as highly motivated, professional, and efficient as the one at the **Castellana Inter-Continental Hotel** (© **800/327-0200** in the U.S., or 91-310-02-00). Room service is offered around the clock, and the staff is adept at solving your Madrid-related problems. Nothing seems to make them lose their cool, even when there's a long line at the desk. See p. 160.
- **Best Location: Tryp Reina Victoria** (© **91-531-45-00**) is for those who want to be in the heart of Old Madrid, within easy walking distance of all those midtown Hemingway haunts. Dozens of the finest tapas bars are literally at your doorstep, and you can walk among the flower vendors, cigarette peddlers, and lottery-ticket hawkers, enjoying an atmosphere that's missing from the newer and more modern section of Madrid. See p. 155.
- **Best Hotel Health Club:** The **Ritz** (© **800/225-5843** in the U.S. and Canada, or 91-701-67-67) is not only the most historic hotel in Madrid, but it's also got a state-of-the-art fitness center on its top floor. The 533-sq.-m (1,727-sq.-ft.) gym overlooks the Prado Museum, Los Jerónimos Church, and the tree-lined Paseo del Prado. All Ritz guests have complimentary use of most of the center's services and facilities, which include English-speaking professional trainers, the latest exercise equipment, saunas, UVA rays, dressing rooms, showers, lockers, and an outside jogging trail that's open March to October. See p. 158.
- **Best Views:** Often called the Waldorf-Astoria of Spain, the 26-story **Crowne Plaza Madrid City Centre** (© **91-547-12-00**) has been one of Madrid's massive landmarks since 1953. From its bedroom windows you'll have views of the city skyline. Try for one of the units on the eighth floor with a balcony. See p. 152.

7 Best Madrid Restaurant Bets

- **Best for a Romantic Dinner: El Amparo** (© **91-431-64-56**) sits in one of Madrid's most elegant enclaves, with cascading vines on its facade. You can dine grandly, enjoying not only the romantic ambience but also some of the finest food in the city. A sloping skylight bathes the interior with sunlight during the day, and at night lanterns cast soft, flattering glows, making you and your date look luscious. See p. 175.
- **Best for a Business Lunch:** For decades the influential leaders of Madrid have come to **Jockey** (© **91-319-24-35**) to combine power lunches with one of the true gastronomic experiences in Madrid. In spite of increased competition, Jockey is still among the favorite rendezvous sites for heads of state, international celebrities, and diplomats. It's the perfect place to close that business deal with your Spanish partner—he or

she will be impressed with your selection. See p. 178.

- **Best for a Celebration:** At night the whole area around Plaza Mayor becomes one giant Spanish fiesta, with singers, guitar players, and bands of roving students serenading for their sangria and tapas money. Since 1884 it has always been party night at **Los Galayos** (✆ **91-366-30-28**) too, with tables and chairs set out on the sidewalk for people-watching. The food's good as well—everything from suckling pig to roast lamb. See p. 185.
- **Best View:** The cafe tables on the terrace of the **Café de Oriente** (✆ **91-541-39-74**) afford one of the most panoramic views in Madrid—a view that takes in everything from the Palacio Real (Royal Palace) to the Teatro Real. Diplomats, even royalty, have patronized this place, known for its good food and attractive Belle Epoque decor, which includes banquettes and regal paneling. See p. 172.
- **Best Decor: Las Cuatro Estaciones** (✆ **91-553-63-05**) has the most spectacular floral displays in Madrid. These flowers, naturally, change with the seasons, so you never know what you'll see when you arrive to dine. The entrance might be filled with hydrangeas, chrysanthemums, or poinsettias. The food is equally superb, but it's the stunningly modern and inviting decor that makes Las Cuatro Estaciones the perfect place for a lavish dinner on the town. See p. 179.
- **Best for Kids: Foster's Hollywood** (✆ **91-564-63-08**) wins almost hands-down. Since 1971 it has lured kids with Tex-Mex selections, one of the juiciest hamburgers in town, and what a *New York Times* reporter found to be "probably the best onion rings in the world." The atmosphere is fun too, evoking a movie studio with props. See p. 179.
- **Best Basque Cuisine:** Some food critics regard **Zalacaín** (✆ **91-561-48-40**) as the best restaurant in Madrid. Its name comes from Pío Baroja's 1909 novel, *Zalacaín El Aventurero,* but its cuisine comes straight from heaven. When the maitre d' suggests a main dish of cheeks of hake, you might turn away in horror—until you try it. Whatever is served here is sure to be among the finest food you'll taste in Spain—all the foie gras and truffles you desire, but many innovative dishes to tempt the palate as well. See p. 181.
- **Best American Cuisine:** Not everything on the menu at **La Gamella** (✆ **91-532-45-09**) is American, but what there is here is choice, inspired by California. Owner Dick Stephens, a former choreographer, now runs this prestigious restaurant in the house where the Spanish philosopher Ortega y Gasset was born. Even the king and queen of Spain have tasted the savory fare, which includes everything from an all-American cheesecake to a Caesar salad with strips of marinated anchovies. It's also known for serving what one food critic called, "the only edible hamburger in Madrid," and that palate had tasted the hamburger at Foster's Hollywood (see above). See p. 176.
- **Best Continental Cuisine:** Although the chef at **El Mentidero de la Villa** (✆ **91-308-12-85**) roams the world for culinary inspirations, much of the cookery is firmly rooted in French cuisine. Continental favorites are updated here and given new twists

and flavors, sometimes betraying a Japanese influence. From France come the most perfect noisettes of veal (flavored with fresh tarragon) that you're likely to be served in Spain. Even the Spanish dishes have been brought up-to-date and are lighter and subtler in flavor. See p. 169.

- **Best Seafood:** On the northern edges of Madrid, **El Cabo Mayor** (✆ **91-350-87-76**) consistently serves the finest and freshest seafood in the country. Members of the royal family are likely to come here for their favorite seafood treats, which might be a savory kettle of fish soup from Cantabria (a province between the Basque country and Asturias), or stewed sea bream flavored with thyme. Even the atmosphere is nautically inspired. See p. 182.
- **Best Steakhouse:** Spanish steaks at their finest are offered at **Casa Paco** (✆ **91-366-31-66**). Señor Paco was the first in Madrid to sear steaks in boiling oil before serving, so that the almost-raw meat continues to cook on the plate, preserving the natural juices. This Old Town favorite also has plenty of atmosphere, and has long been a celebrity favorite as well. See p. 172.
- **Best Roast Suckling Pig:** Even hard-to-please Hemingway agreed: The roast suckling pig served at **Sobrino de Botín** (✆ **91-366-30-26**) since 1725 is the best and most aromatic dish in the Old Town. You'd have to travel to Segovia (home of the specialty) for better fare than this. Under time-aged beams, you can wash down your meal with Valdepeñas or Aragón wine. See p. 185.
- **Best Wine List:** Although it may no longer be considered the finest restaurant in Madrid, as it once was, **Horcher** (✆ **91-532-35-96**) does have one of the city's most laudable wine lists. The cuisine is also just as good as it ever was, but there's so much competition these days that other shining stars have toppled Horcher from its throne. Nevertheless, its wine cellars have won praise from kings and gourmands throughout Europe. It offers not only Spain's best vintages but also those from the rest of the continent. Trust the sommelier: He's one of the best in the business, and his advice is virtually always spot-on. See p. 175.

8 Best Seville Hotel Bets

- **Best Historic Hotel:** The **Hotel Alfonso XIII** (✆ **800/221-2340** in the U.S. and Canada, or 95-491-70-00), a reproduction of a Spanish palace, opened in 1929 for the Iberoamerican Exposition and was completely remodeled for Expo '92. It has hosted all the leading stars, politicians, and luminaries who have come through Seville over the years—everyone from Jackie Onassis to Grace Kelly to Spain's most famous matadors. It remains the grandest period piece in Andalusia, with an ornate lobby filled with pillars and coffered ceilings. See p. 255.
- **Best for a Romantic Getaway:** On a hillside in the hamlet of Sanlúcar, 19.3km (12 miles) south of Seville, is the **Hacienda Benazuza** (✆ **95-570-33-44**). This manor house on 40 acres boasts one of the most romantic and tranquil settings in all of Andalusia. Operated since 1992 by Basque entrepreneurs, this delightful retreat,

with elegant rooms, reflecting pools, and landscaped gardens, offers welcome relief after hot, dusty Seville. See p. 263.

- **Best for Families:** The **Hotel Doña María** (✆ **95-422-49-90**), just steps from the cathedral, is best for families that want a central location so they can walk to all of Seville's major attractions. The hotel is a winner in its own right, with a swimming pool on the upper floor. Many of the rooms are large enough to accommodate families traveling together. Overall, it's a gracious choice with a helpful staff. See p. 259.
- **Best Moderately Priced Hotel:** The **Residencia y Restaurante Fernando III** (✆ **95-421-77-08**) is in Barrio Santa Cruz, the old Jewish ghetto, reached along a maze of narrow streets. Although the four-story hotel is modern and commercial, its many Andalusian touches convey a cozy atmosphere. The English-speaking staff is helpful and efficient, making this a winning choice. See p. 261.
- **Best Budget Hotel: Hotel Murillo** (✆ **95-421-60-95**), in the heart of the Barrio Santa Cruz, is named after the artist, who used to live in the district. It's close to the gardens of the Alcázar, within walking distance of all of Seville's major attractions. The functional rooms are a good value. This has been the old-quarter favorite of budgeteers for decades. See p. 263.
- **Best Service:** Seville's most efficient staff—each member polite, professional, and helpful—operates in the **Hotel Inglaterra** (✆ **95-422-49-70**), in the heart of town three blocks north of the bullring. Employees welcome guests (most often in English) with friendly smiles; there's 24-hour room service, and every wish (within reason) is fulfilled speedily and efficiently. See p. 258.
- **Best Location:** Close to the Santa Cruz *barrio,* the little inn called **Casa Número 7** (✆ **95-422-15-81**), lies right in the heart of Seville. Evocative of an elegant private home, it is ensconced in a sensitively restored 19th century mansion. You live with style and grace here befitting life in Old Seville. It's the town's best small hotel. See p. 256.
- **Best Hotel Health Club:** Although Seville's hoteliers were late in discovering the world demand for health clubs in hotels, the **Hotel Meliá Sevilla** (✆ **800/336-3542** in the U.S., or 95-442-15-11) responded to the challenge and opened the most professional facility. The staff is very skilled, guiding you through the hotel's array of facilities, ranging from the best sauna and whirlpool in town to a gym and squash courts. There's also a pool. See p. 258.
- **Best Restoration:** In the historic core of the city, **Casa Imperial** (✆ **95-450-03-00**) is a hotel of charm and grace, lovingly restored. In the 15th century, it was the home of the butler to the Marquis of Tarifa, and he lived very well indeed in a setting of sparkling chandeliers and beamed ceilings. See p. 256.
- **Best Secret Address:** Diners know that the **Taverna del Alabardero** (✆ **95-456-06-37**) is one of the city's best restaurants, but those in-the-know also realize it's one of the most charming places to stay in Seville. This restored 19th-century mansion has only seven bedrooms, but they are choice and comfortable, each spaciously and individually decorated in an Andalusian style. See p. 259.

9 Best Seville Restaurant Bets

- **Best Andalusian Cuisine:** A small, cozy restaurant, close to the cathedral, **Enrique Becerra** (**© 95-421-30-49**) is a whitewashed house with wrought-iron window grilles that offers the city's best array of traditional Andalusian home-cooked dishes. Other restaurants are more innovative, but Enrique Becerra sticks fast to Sevillian tradition, both in decor and in menu offerings. Try, for example, *jarrete de ternera a la cazuela* (a regional veal stew). Every time-tested favorite is launched by a soothing bowl of gazpacho, and washed down with sangria. See p. 268.
- **Best Continental Cuisine:** Seville has no finer dining selection than **Egaña Oriza** (**© 95-422-72-11**), located in a restored mansion adjacent to Murillo Park. A chic Basque enclave of nouvelle cuisine, Egaña Oriza features a few Basque specialties, but most of the dishes are rooted in the continental style. The food is innovative and beautifully prepared: Instead of the typical gazpacho with vegetables and olive oil, the preparation here includes succulent Sanlúcar prawns. Steak, for example, comes with foie gras in a grape sauce. See p. 264.
- **Best Italian Cuisine:** In spite of the name, the **Pizzería San Marco** (**© 95-421-43-90**) serves not just pizza, but a wide array of delectable Italian specialties: among them chicken Parmesan, various forms of scaloppine, and some savory pastas. The cookery has both flavor and flair. See p. 269.
- **Best Modern Cuisine: Taverna del Alabardero** (**© 95-456-06-37**) serves an Andalusian cuisine, but it's a nouvelle one, imaginatively updated and creative in presentation. Dishes have flair and flavor, everything from spicy peppers stuffed with the pulverized thigh of a bull to an Andalusian white fish set on a compote of aromatic tomatoes flavored with fresh coriander. It's even hosted the king and queen of Spain. The tavern is also a restaurant *avec chambres,* renting seven beautifully and traditionally furnished bedrooms. See p. 259.
- **Best Pizza:** The **Pizzería San Marco** wins again; see "Best Italian Cuisine," above, and p. 269.
- **Best Seafood: La Isla** (**© 95-421-26-31**), in the Arenal district, is the place to go for the freshest fish. Though Seville is inland, fish is rushed to the restaurant from the Huelva or Cádiz coasts, and more exotic catches are flown in from Galicia, in the northwest. Many of the fish dishes are based on traditional Galician cooking methods. The *parillada de mariscos y pescados,* a fish and seafood grill for two people, is the best dish on the menu. See p. 264
- **Best View:** The **Río Grande** (**© 95-427-39-56**) is a classic Sevillian restaurant with large terraces opening onto the Guadalquivir River. Near Plaza de Cuba in front of the Torre del Oro, it has the most panoramic view in town. Although many diners find the vista absorbing, the restaurant's Andalusian cuisine is also delightful, prepared with old-fashioned care. Here are all the matador favorites—everything from bull tail Andalusian to garlic-chicken Giralda, the latter dish dedicated to the tower adjoining the cathedral. See p. 269.

- **Best Outdoor Dining:** See the **Río Grande** ("Best View," above) and **Hostería del Laurel** ("Best Local Favorite," below). See p. 269.
- **Best Local Favorite:** In the heart of the Barrio Santa Cruz, the **Hostería del Laurel** (✆ **95-422-02-95**) is one of the most enduring restaurants in town, long popular with visitors and locals alike. In summer patrons can dine on an outdoor terrace on the square. The decor is old-fashioned—white walls, leather-backed chairs, and heavy wooden tables. The food is traditional Spanish fare, with many Andalusian specialties. See p. 269.
- **Best Spot to Meet a Matador: El Burladero,** in the Hotel Tryp Colón (✆ **95-422-55-99**), is the local favorite of visiting matadors. The bullring in Seville often draws the country's biggest stars. They like to relax and unwind here in a setting devoted to the memorabilia of their trade. Photographs adorning the walls trace the history of bullfighting. Even the name of the restaurant comes from the wooden barricades in the ring where bullfighters can escape the charge of an enraged bull. See p. 264.

2

Planning Your Trip to Barcelona, Madrid & Seville

This chapter is devoted to the where, when, and how of your trip—the advance planning required to get it together and take it on the road.

1 Visitor Information & Entry Requirements

VISITOR INFORMATION

TOURIST OFFICES You can begin your info search with Spain's tourist offices located in the following places:

In the United States For information before you go, contact the **Tourist Office of Spain,** 666 Fifth Ave., 5th Floor, New York, NY 10103 (© **212/265-8822**). It can provide sightseeing information, events calendars, train and ferry schedules, and more. Elsewhere in the United States, branches of the Tourist Office of Spain are located at: 8383 Wilshire Blvd., Suite 956, Beverly Hills, CA 90211 (© **323/658-7188**); 845 N. Michigan Ave., Suite 915E, Chicago, IL 60611 (© **312/642-1992**); and 1221 Brickell Ave., Suite 1850, Miami, FL 33131 (© **305/358-1992**).

In Canada Contact the **Tourist Office of Spain,** 102 Bloor St. W., Suite 3402, Toronto, Ontario M5S 1M9, Canada (© **416/961-3131**).

In Great Britain Write to the **Spanish National Tourist Office,** 22–23 Manchester Square, London W1M 5AP (© **020/7486-8077**).

WEBSITES On the Net you can find lots of great information at the following sites:

Spain in General **Tourist Office of Spain** (www.okspain.org), **All About Spain** (www.red2000.com), **Cybersp@in** (www.cyberspain.com).

Barcelona **Barcelona: Barcelona Prestige** (www.bcn-guide.com); **Barcelona Guide** (www.bcn.es), and **Turisme de Barcelona** (www. barcelona turisme.com).

Madrid **Madrid by All About Spain** (www.red2000.com), **Madridman** (www.madridman.com), **Time Out: Madrid** (www.timeout.com), **Soft Guide Madrid** (www.softguides.com), **Web Madrid** (www.web madrid.com).

Seville **Seville by All About Spain** (www.red2000.com); **Sevilla On Line** (www.sol.com), **Andalucia.com** (www.andalucia.com), **Andalucía: There's Only One** (www.andalucia.org).

ENTRY REQUIREMENTS

PASSPORTS A valid passport is all that an American, British, Canadian, or New Zealand citizen needs to enter Spain, and one can be secured as follows. (Australians, however, need a visa—see below.)

In the United States You can apply for passports in person at one of 13 regional offices or by mail. To apply, you'll need a passport application form, available at U.S. post offices and federal court offices, and proof of citizenship, such as a birth certificate or naturalization papers; an expired passport is also accepted. First-time applicants for passports pay $60 ($40 if under 18 years of age). Persons 18 or older who have an expired passport that's not more than 12 years old can reapply by mail. The old passport must be submitted along with new photographs and a pink renewal form (DSP-82).

If your expired passport is more than 12 years old, or if it was granted to you before your 16th birthday, you must apply in person. The fee is $40. Call ✆ **202/647-0518** at any time for information. You can also write to Passport Service, Office of Correspondence, Department of State, 1111 19th St., NW, Suite 510, Washington, DC 20522-1075. Information can also be obtained at www.travel.state.gov or by calling the **National Passport Information Center (NPIC)** at ✆ **900/225-5674.** The cost is 35¢ per minute for 24-hour automated service, or $1.05 per minute 9am to 3pm for live operator service.

In Canada Citizens may go to one of 28 regional offices located in major cities. Alternatively, you can mail your application to the Passport Office, External Affairs and International Trade Canada, Ottawa, ON K1A 0G3. Post offices have application forms. Passports cost C$60, and proof of Canadian citizenship is required, along with two signed identical passport-size photographs. Passports are valid for five years. For more information, call ✆ **800/567-6868;** www.dfait-maeci.gc.ca/passport/menu.asp.

In Great Britain British subjects may apply to one of the regional offices in Liverpool, Newport, Glasgow, Peterborough, Belfast, or London. You can also apply in person at a main post office. The fee is £28, and the passport is good for 10 years. Two photos must accompany the application. For more information regarding fees, documentation requirements, and to ask for an emergency passport, telephone the London Passport office at ✆ **0870/521-0410;** www.ukpa.gov.uk.

In Australia Citizens may apply at the nearest post office. Provincial capitals and other major cities have passport offices. Application fees are subject to review every three months. Call ✆ **02/13-12-32** or visit www.passports.gov.au for the latest information. Australians must pay for a departure tax stamp costing A$20 at a post office or airport; children 11 and under are exempt. Australian citizens will also need a visa to enter Spain. Apply at a Spanish consulate well before departure time. Spanish consulates are located at 31 Market St., Sydney, NSW 2000 (✆ **02/9261-2433**), and at 766 Elizabeth St., Melbourne, VIC 3000 (✆ **03/9347-1966**).

In New Zealand Citizens may go to their nearest consulate or passport office to obtain an application, which may be filed in person or by mail. To obtain a 10-year passport, proof of citizenship is required, plus a fee of NZ$80. Passports are processed at the New Zealand Passport Office, Documents of National Identity Division, Department of Internal Affairs, 47 Boulcott House St., Wellington (✆ **0800/22-50-50;** www.passports.govt.nz).

In Ireland Contact the passport office at Setna Centre, Molesworth St., Dublin 2 (✆ **01/671-16-33**). The charge is 58€. Applications are sent by mail. Irish citizens living in North America can contact the Irish Embassy, 2234 Massachusetts Ave., NW, Washington, DC 20008 (✆ **202/462-3939;** www.irelandemb.org). The embassy can issue a new passport or direct you to one of three North American consulates that have jurisdiction over a particular region; the charge is $80.

CUSTOMS You can take into Spain most personal effects and the following items duty-free: two still cameras and 10 rolls of film per camera, tobacco for personal use, 1 liter each of liquor and wine, a portable radio, a tape recorder, a typewriter, a bicycle, sports equipment, fishing gear, and two hunting weapons with 100 cartridges each.

Returning to Your Home Country Returning **U.S. citizens** who have been away for 48 hours or more are allowed to bring back, once every 30 days, $400 worth of merchandise duty-free. You'll be charged a flat rate of 10% duty on the next $1,000 worth of purchases. Be sure to have your receipts handy. On gifts, the duty-free limit is $100. For more specific guidance, write to the **U.S. Customs Service,** 1301 Constitution Ave., Washington, DC 20044 (✆ **202/354-1000**), requesting the free pamphlet *Know Before You Go.* You can also download the pamphlet from the Internet at **www.customs.ustreas.gov**.

Citizens of **Canada** can write for the booklet *I Declare,* issued by **Revenue Canada,** 333 Dunsmuir St., Vancouver, BC, Canada V6B 5R4 (✆ **800/461-9999** or 506/636-5064; www.ccra-adrc.gc.ca). Canada allows its citizens a C$750 exemption, and you are allowed to bring back duty-free 200 cigarettes, 2.2 pounds of tobacco, 40 imperial ounces (1.2 qt.) of liquor, and 50 cigars. In addition, you are allowed to mail gifts to Canada from abroad at the rate of C$60 a day, provided they are unsolicited and aren't alcohol or tobacco (write on the package: "Unsolicited gift, under $60 value"). All valuables should be declared on the Y-38 Form before departure from Canada, including serial numbers of, for example, expensive foreign cameras that you already own. ***Note:*** The C$750 exemption can be used only once a year and only after an absence of at least 7 days.

If you're a citizen of the **United Kingdom,** you can buy wine, spirits, or cigarettes in an ordinary shop in any other European Union country and bring home *almost* as much as you like. (U.K. Customs and Excise does set theoretical limits.) But if you buy your goods in a duty-free shop, then the old rules still apply—you're allowed to bring home 200 cigarettes and 2 liters of table wine, plus 1 liter of spirits or 2 liters of fortified wine. If you're returning home from a non-EU country, the same allowances apply, and you must declare any goods in excess of these allowances. British customs tends to be strict and complicated in its requirements. For details, get in touch with **HM Customs and Excise Office,** Passenger Enquiry Point, Wayfarer House, Great South West Road, Feltham, Middlesex, TW14 8NP (✆ **0845/010-9000;** outside U.K. 44/020-8910-3744; www.hmce.gov.uk).

The duty-free allowance in **Australia** is A$400 or, for those under 18, A$200. Australian citizens are allowed to mail gifts to Australia from abroad duty-free to a limit of A$200 per parcel. There are no other restrictions on unsolicited gifts; however, you could be subject to a customs investigation if you send multiple parcels of the same gift to the same address. Upon returning to Australia, citizens can bring in 250 cigarettes or 250 grams of loose tobacco, and 1,125 milliliters of alcohol. If you're returning with valuable goods you already own, such as foreign-made cameras, you should file form B263. A helpful brochure, available from Australian consulates or customs offices, is *Know Before You Go.* For more information, contact **Australian Customs Services,** GPO Box 8, Sydney NSW 2001 (✆ **02/9213-2000;** www.customs.gov.au).

Destination: Spain—Red Alert Checklist

- Citizens of EU countries can cross into Spain for as long as they wish. Citizens of other countries must have a passport.
- If you purchased traveler's checks, have you recorded the check numbers and stored the documentation separately from the checks?
- Did you pack your camera and an extra set of camera batteries, and purchase enough film? If you packed film in your checked baggage, did you invest in protective pouches to shield film from airport x-rays?
- Do you have a safe, accessible place to store money?
- Did you bring your ID cards that could entitle you to discounts such as AAA and AARP cards, student IDs, etc.?
- Did you bring emergency drug prescriptions and extra glasses and/or contact lenses?
- Do you have your credit card PINs?
- If you have an E-ticket, do you have documentation?
- Did you leave a copy of your itinerary with someone at home?
- Did you check to see if any travel advisories have been issued by the U.S. State Department (http://travel.state.gov/travel_warnings.html) regarding your destination?
- Do you have the address and phone number of your country's embassy with you?

The duty-free allowance for **New Zealand** is NZ$700. New Zealanders are allowed to mail gifts to New Zealand from abroad duty-free to a limit of NZ$70 per parcel. Beware of sending multiple parcels of the same gift to the same address; a customs investigation could await your return home. Citizens over 17 years of age can bring in 200 cigarettes, or 50 cigars, or 250 grams of tobacco (or a mixture of all three if their combined weight doesn't exceed 250g); plus 4.5 liters of wine and beer, or 1.125 liters of liquor. New Zealand currency does not carry import or export restrictions. Fill out a certificate of export, listing the valuables you are taking out of the country; that way, you can bring them back without paying duty. Most questions are answered in a free pamphlet available at New Zealand consulates and Customs offices: *New Zealand Customs Guide for Travellers,* Notice no. 4. For more information, contact **New Zealand Customs,** 17–21 Whitmore St., Box 2218, Wellington, NZ (© **04/473-609;** in New Zealand 800/428-786; www.customs.govt.nz).

2 Money

If there is one thing old Spaniards wax nostalgically over, it's not the police state they experienced under the dictatorship of Franco, but the prices paid back then. How they miss the days when you could go into a restaurant and order a meal with wine for 50 pesetas.

Regrettably, Spain is no longer a budget destination. In such major cities as Barcelona or Madrid, you can often find hotels charging the same prices as in London or Paris.

Taken as a whole, though, Spain remains slightly below the cost-of-living index of such countries as England, Italy, Germany, and France. Unless the current monetary situation is drastically altered, there is a very favorable exchange rate in Spain when you pay in U.S. dollars.

Prices in Spain are generally high, but you get good value for your money. Hotels are usually clean and comfortable, and restaurants generally offer good cuisine and ample portions made with quality ingredients. Trains are fast and on time, and most service personnel treat you with respect.

In Spain, many prices for children—generally defined as ages 6 to 17—are lower than for adults. Fees for children under 6 are generally waived.

CURRENCY

The **euro** (€), the new single European currency, became the official currency of Spain and 11 other participating countries on January 1, 1999.

However, the euro didn't go into general circulation until early in 2002. The old currency, the Spanish peseta, disappeared into history on March 1, 2002, replaced by the euro, whose official abbreviation is "EUR." Exchange rates of participating countries are locked into a common currency fluctuating against the dollar.

For more details on the euro, check out **www.europa.eu.int/euro**.

THE EURO

In January of 2002, the largest money-changing operation in history led to the deliberate obsolescence of many of Europe's individual national currencies, including the Spanish peseta. In its place was substituted the euro, a currency that, at this writing, was based on the fiscal participation of a dozen nations of Europe.

For American Readers: One euro equals approximately 89 U.S. cents, and 1 U.S. dollar equals approximately 1.12€. This was the rate of exchange used to calculate the dollar values, each of which was rounded to the nearest nickel, throughout this book.

The Dollar, the British Pound & the Euro

Euro	US$	UK£	Euro	US$	UK£
1	0.89	0.70	75	66.98	52.5
2	1.79	1.40	100	89.30	70.00
3	2.68	2.10	125	111.63	87.50
4	3.57	2.80	150	133.95	105.00
5	4.47	3.50	175	156.28	122.50
6	5.36	4.20	200	178.60	140.00
7	6.25	4.90	225	200.93	157.50
8	7.14	5.60	250	223.25	175.00
9	8.04	6.30	275	245.58	192.50
10	8.93	7.00	300	267.90	210.00
15	13.40	10.50	350	312.55	245.00
20	17.86	14.00	400	357.20	280.00
25	22.33	17.50	500	446.50	350.00
50	44.65	35.00	1000	893.00	700.00

For British Readers: Great Britain still uses the pound sterling, with 1 euro equaling approximately 70 pence, and £1 equaling approximately 1.43€. This was the rate of exchange used to calculate the pound sterling values laid out in the table below.

Note: The relative value of the euro fluctuates against the U.S. dollar, the pound sterling, and most of the world's other currencies, and its value might not be the same by the time you actually travel to Spain. Consequently, this table should be used only as an indication of approximate values.

Exchange rates are more favorable at the point of arrival. Nevertheless, it's often helpful to exchange at least some money before going abroad (standing in line at the ***cambio*** [exchange bureau] in the Madrid or Barcelona airport could make you miss the next bus leaving for downtown). Check with any of your local American Express or Thomas Cook offices or major banks. Or, order euros in advance from the following: **American Express** (✆ **800/221-7282;** www.americanexpress.com), **Thomas Cook** (✆ **800/223-7373;** www.thomascook.com), or **Capital for Foreign Exchange** (✆ **888/842-0880**).

It's best to exchange currency or traveler's checks at a bank, not a *cambio,* hotel, or shop. Currency and traveler's checks (for which you'll receive a better rate than cash) can be changed at all principal airports and at some travel agencies, such as American Express and Thomas Cook. Note the rates and ask about commission fees; it can sometimes pay to shop around and ask the right questions.

Many hotels in Spain don't accept dollar- or pound-denominated checks; those that do will almost certainly charge for the conversion. In some cases, they'll accept countersigned traveler's checks or a credit card, but if you're prepaying a deposit on hotel reservations, it's cheaper and easier to pay with a check drawn on a Spanish bank.

This can be arranged by a large commercial bank or by a specialist such as **Ruesch International,** 700 11th St. NW, 4th Floor, Washington, DC 20001-4507 (✆ **800/424-2923;** www.ruesch.com), which performs a wide variety of conversion-related tasks, usually for only $5 to $15 per transaction.

If you need a check payable in euros, call Ruesch's toll-free number, describe what you need, and note the transaction number given to you. Mail your dollar-denominated personal check (payable to Ruesch International) to the address above. Upon receiving this, the company will mail a check denominated in euros for the financial equivalent, minus the $2 charge. The company can also help you with many different kinds of wire transfers and conversions of VAT (value-added tax, known as IVA in Spain), refund checks, and also will mail brochures and information packets on request. Brits can contact Ruesch International Ltd., Marble Arch Tower, 14 Floor, 55 Bryanston St., London W14 7AA, England (✆ 0207/563-3300).

ATM NETWORKS

PLUS, Cirrus, and other networks connecting automated-teller machines operate in Spain. If your bank card has been programmed with a PIN (personal identification number), it is likely that you can use your card at ATMs abroad to withdraw money directly from your home bank account. Check with your bank to see if your PIN must be reprogrammed for usage in Spain. Before leaving, always determine the frequency limits for withdrawals and what fees, if any, your bank will assess. For Cirrus locations abroad, call ✆ **800/424-7787;** www.mastercard.com. For PLUS usage abroad, contact your local bank or

Tips Emergency Cash—The Fastest Way

If you need emergency cash over the weekend when all banks and American Express offices are closed, you can have money wired to you from **Western Union** (✆ **800/325-6000**; www.westernunion.com). You must present valid ID to pick up the cash at the Western Union office. However, in most countries, you can pick up a money transfer even if you don't have valid identification, as long as you can answer a test question provided by the sender. Be sure to let the sender know in advance that you don't have ID. If you need to use a test question instead of ID, the sender must take cash to his or her local Western Union office, rather than transferring the money over the phone or online.

check Visa's website at **www.visa.com.**

TRAVELER'S CHECKS

Although ATM usage is becoming increasingly commonplace, many people prefer the security of traveler's checks. Purchase them before leaving home and arrange to carry some ready cash (usually about $250, depending on your needs). In the event of theft, if the checks are properly documented, the value of your checks will be refunded. Most large banks sell traveler's checks, charging fees that average between 1% and 2% of the value of the checks you buy, although some out-of-the-way banks, in rare instances, have charged as much as 7%. If your bank wants more than a 2% commission, call the traveler's check issuers directly for the address of outlets where this commission will cost less.

American Express (✆ **800/221-8472** in the U.S. and Canada) is one of the largest and most immediately recognized issuers of traveler's checks. No commission is charged to members of the AAA and to holders of certain types of American Express credit cards. The company issues checks denominated in U.S. dollars, Canadian dollars, and British pounds, among other currencies. The vast majority of checks sold in North America are denominated in U.S. dollars. For questions or problems that arise outside the United States or Canada, contact any of the company's many regional representatives.

Citicorp (✆ **800/645-6556** in the U.S. and Canada, or 813/623-1709, collect, from other parts of the world) issues checks in U.S. dollars as well as British pounds. **Thomas Cook** (✆ **800/223-7373** in the U.S., or 020/7530-7080; www.thomascook.com, from other parts of the world) issues MasterCard traveler's checks denominated in U.S. dollars, British pounds, euros, and Australian dollars. Depending on individual banking laws in each of the various states, some of these currencies may not be available in every outlet. **Visa Travelers Checks** (✆ **800/221-2426** in the U.S. and Canada, or 212/858-8500 from most other parts of the world) sells Visa checks sponsored by a consortium of member banks and the Thomas Cook organization. Traveler's checks can be denominated in U.S. or Canadian dollars or British pounds.

CREDIT CARDS

American Express, Visa, and **Diners Club** are widely recognized in Spain. If you see the **EuroCard** or **Access** sign on an establishment, it means that it accepts **MasterCard. Discover** cards are accepted only in the United States.

3 When to Go

CLIMATE

Spring and fall are ideal times to visit any of these cities. May and October are the best months, in terms of both weather and crowds. In our view, however, the balmy month of May (with an average temperature of 61°F/16°C) is the most glorious time for making your own discovery of Barcelona, Madrid, or Seville.

In summer, it's hot, hot, and hotter still, with the cities in Castile (Madrid) and Andalusia (Seville and Córdoba) stewing up the most scalding brew. Madrid has dry heat; the temperature can hover around 84°F (29°C) in July, 75°F (24°C) in September. Seville has the dubious reputation of being the hottest part of Spain in July and August, often baking under *average* temperatures as high as 93°F (34°C).

Barcelona, cooler in temperature, is often quite humid. The overcrowded Costa Brava has temperatures around 81°F (27°C) in July and August.

August remains the major vacation month in Europe. The traffic into Spain from France, the Netherlands, and Germany becomes a veritable migration, and low-cost hotels along the coastal areas are virtually impossible to find. To compound the problem, many restaurants and shops also decide that it's time for a vacation, thereby limiting the visitor's selections for both dining and shopping.

Weather Chart for Spain

Barcelona

	Jan	Feb	Mar	Apr	May	Jun	Jul	Aug	Sept	Oct	Nov	Dec
Temp (°F)	48	49	52	55	61	68	73	73	70	63	55	50
Temp (°C)	9	9	11	13	16	20	23	23	21	17	13	10
Rainfall (in.)	1.70	1.40	1.90	2.00	2.20	1.50	90	1.60	3.10	3.70	2.90	2.00

Madrid

	Jan	Feb	Mar	Apr	May	Jun	Jul	Aug	Sept	Oct	Nov	Dec
Temp (°F)	42	45	49	53	60	69	76	75	69	58	48	43
Temp (°C)	6	7	9	12	16	21	24	24	21	14	9	6
Rainfall (in.)	1.60	1.80	1.20	1.80	1.50	1.00	.30	.40	1.10	1.50	2.30	1.70

Seville

	Jan	Feb	Mar	Apr	May	Jun	Jul	Aug	Sept	Oct	Nov	Dec
Temp (°F)	59	63	68	75	81	90	97	97	90	79	68	61
Temp (°C)	15	17	20	24	27	32	36	36	32	26	20	16
Rainfall (in.)	2.60	2.40	3.60	2.30	1.60	.30	0	.20	.80	2.80	2.70	3.20

HOLIDAYS

Holidays include January 1 (New Year's Day), January 6 (Feast of the Epiphany), March 19 (Feast of St. Joseph), Good Friday, Easter Monday, May 1 (May Day), June 10 (Corpus Christi), June 29 (Feast of St. Peter and St. Paul), July 25 (Feast of St. James), August 15 (Feast of the Assumption), October 12 (Spain's National Day), November 1 (All Saints' Day), December 8 (Immaculate Conception), and December 25 (Christmas).

No matter how large or small, every city or town in Spain also celebrates its local saint's day. In Madrid, it's May 15 (St. Isidro). You'll rarely know what the local holidays are in your next destination in Spain. Try to keep money on hand, because you may arrive in town only to find banks and stores closed. In some cases, intercity bus services are suspended on holidays.

CALENDAR OF EVENTS: BARCELONA, MADRID & SEVILLE

The dates given below may not be precise. Sometimes the exact days may not be announced until six weeks before the actual festival. Check with the National Tourist Office of Spain (see "Visitor Information," at the beginning of this chapter) if you're planning to attend a specific event.

January

Three Kings Day (Día de los Reyes), Barcelona. Parades are staged throughout the main arteries of old Barcelona in anticipation of the Feast of the Epiphany (Jan 6). Parades usually take place on January 5 or 6.

February

ARCO (Madrid's International Contemporary Art Fair), Madrid. One of the biggest draws on Spain's cultural calendar, this exhibit showcases the best in contemporary art from Europe and America. At the Crystal Pavilion of the Casa de Campo, the exhibition draws galleries from throughout Europe, the Americas, Australia, and Asia, who bring with them the works of regional and internationally known artists. To buy tickets, you can contact El Corte Ingles at ✆ **91-418-88-00,** or Madrid Rock at ✆ **91-547-24-23.** The cost is between 19€ and 23€. You can get schedules from the tourist office closer to the event. Dates vary, but usually mid-February.

Madrid Carnaval. The carnival kicks off with a big parade along the Paseo de la Castellana, culminating in a masked ball at the Círculo de Bellas Artes on the following night. Fancy-dress competitions last until February 28, when the festivities end with a tear-jerking "burial of a sardine" at the Fuente de los Pajaritos in the Casa de Campo. This is followed that evening by a concert in the Plaza Mayor. Call ✆ **91-429-31-77** for more information. Dates vary.

Salón de Anticuarios en Barcelona. This giant antiques fair is usually held from late February to mid-March in the Feria de Barcelona.

March

Marathon Catalunya, Barcelona. This annual marathon begins in Mataró, winds its way through the city, and ends at the Olympic Stadium in Montjuïc. Usually in mid-March.

Semana Santa (Holy Week), Seville. Although many of the country's smaller towns stage similar celebrations (especially notable in Zamora), the festivities in Seville are by far the most elaborate. From Palm Sunday until Easter Sunday a series of processions with hooded penitents moves to the piercing wail of the *saeta,* a love song to the Virgin or Christ. *Pasos* (heavy floats) bear images of the Virgin or Christ. Again, make hotel reservations way in advance. Call the Seville Office of Tourism for details (✆ **95-422-14-04**). Usually last week of March.

April

Bullfights, all over Spain. Holy week traditionally kicks off the season all over Spain, especially in Madrid and Seville. Although not as popular in Barcelona as in the rest of the country, this national pastime affords the visitor an unparalleled insight into the Spanish temperament.

Feria de Sevilla (Seville Fair). This is the most celebrated week of revelry in the country, with all-night flamenco dancing, merrymaking in *casetas* (entertainment booths), bullfights, horseback riding, flower-decked coaches, and dancing in the streets. You'll need to reserve a hotel early for this one. For general information and exact festival dates, contact the Office of Tourism in Seville (✆ **95-422-14-04**). Second week after Easter.

Festivat de Sant Jordi and **Parades de Libres I Roses,** Barcelona. On the feast day of Catalonia's patron saint, Sant Jordi, citizens of Barcelona shower each other with books and roses. April 23.

May

Fiesta de San Isidro, Madrid. Madrileños run wild with a 10-day celebration honoring their city's patron saint. Food fairs, Castilian folkloric events, street parades, parties, music, dances, bullfights, and other festivities mark the occasion. Make hotel reservations early. Expect crowds and traffic (and beware of pickpockets). For information, write to Oficina Municipal de Información y Turismo, Plaza Mayor 3, 28014 Madrid, or call ✆ **91-588-16-36.** May 13 to 20, 2003.

Fira del Libre de Barcelona. This annual book fair is located primarily on the Passeig de Gràcia in Barcelona. Late May to early June.

June

Corpus Christi, all over Spain. A major holiday on the Spanish calendar, this event is marked by big processions, especially in such cathedral cities as Toledo, Málaga, Seville, and Granada. June 2, 2003.

Verbena de Sant Joan, Barcelona. This traditional festival occupies all Cataláns. Barcelona literally "lights up," with fireworks, bonfires, and dances until dawn. The highlight of the festival is the fireworks show at Montjuïc. Dates vary.

July

Veranos de la Villa, Madrid. Called "the summer binge" of Madrid, this program presents folkloric dancing, pop music, classical music, zarzuelas, and flamenco at various venues throughout the city. Open-air cinema is a feature in the Parque del Retiro. Ask at the various tourist offices for complete details (the program changes every summer). Sometimes admission is charged, but often these events are free. Mid-July until the end of August.

August

Fiestas of Lavapiés and La Paloma, Madrid. These two fiestas begin with the Lavapiés on August 1 and continue through the hectic La Paloma celebration on August 15, the day of the Virgen de la Paloma. Thousands of people race through the narrow streets. Apartment dwellers hurl buckets of cold water onto the crowds below to cool them off. Children's games, floats, music, flamenco, and zarzuelas, along with street fairs, mark the occasion. For more information, call ✆ **91-429-31-77.** August 1 to 15, 2003.

September

Diada, Barcelona. This is the most significant festival in Catalonia. It celebrates the region's autonomy from the rest of Spain, following years of repression under the dictator Franco. Demonstrations and flag-waving events take place. The *senyera,* the flag of Catalonia, is much in evidence. Not your typical tourist fare, but interesting nevertheless. September 11, 2003.

Fiesta de la Mercé, Barcelona. The city abounds with various musical and theatrical performances in honor of one of the city's patron saints, the Virgen de la Mercé. Shows are staged throughout Barcelona. A pageant and fireworks display signal the end of the festival. Week of September 24, 2003.

October

Autumn Festival, Madrid. Both Spanish and international artists participate in this cultural program, with a series of operatic, ballet, dance, music, and theatrical performances. From Strasbourg to Tokyo, this event is a premier attraction, yet ticket prices are reasonable. Make hotel reservations early, and for tickets write to **Festival de Otoño,** Plaza de España 8, 28008 Madrid (✆ **91-580-25-75**). Late October to late November.

Grape Harvest Festival, Jerez de la Frontera. The major wine festival in Andalusia honors the famous sherry of Jerez, with 5 days of processions, flamenco dancing, bullfights, livestock on parade, and, of course, sherry drinking. For information, call ✆ **95-633-11-50.** Mid-October (dates vary).

November

All Saints' Day, Seville. This holy day is celebrated all over Spain, but the citizens of Seville show a certain fervor in lamenting the souls of the dead, as family and friends place wreaths and garlands on their graves. November 1.

Festival Internacional de Jazz de Barcelona. The festival lasts all month, and locations for this jazz festival change yearly. For information, call Turisme de Barcelona ✆ **93-368-97-30.**

December

Día de los Santos Inocentes, Seville. Another countrywide holiday celebrated with particular gusto in sunny Seville. On this day, the Spanish play many practical jokes and in general do *loco* things to one another—it's the Spanish equivalent of April Fools' Day. December 28.

4 Health, Insurance & Safety

TRAVEL INSURANCE AT A GLANCE

Since Spain for most of us is far from home, and a number of things could go wrong—lost luggage, trip cancellation, a medical emergency—consider the following types of insurance.

Check your existing insurance policies before you buy travel insurance to cover trip cancellation, lost luggage, medical expenses, or car rental insurance. You're likely to have partial or complete coverage. But if you need some, ask your travel agent about a comprehensive package. The cost of travel insurance varies widely, depending on the cost and length of your trip, your age and overall health, and the type of trip you're taking. Insurance for extreme sports or adventure travel, for example, will cost more than coverage for a European cruise. Some insurers provide packages for specialty vacations, such as skiing or backpacking. More dangerous activities may be excluded from basic policies.

- **Access America** (✆ **800/284-8300;** www.accessamerica.com)
- **Travel Assistance International** (✆ **800/821-2828;** www.travelassistance.com)
- **Travel Guard International** (✆ **800/826-1300;** www.travelguard.com)

Tips **On Time in Spain**

In Spain, a time change occurs the first weekend of spring. Check your watch. Many unsuspecting visitors have arrived at the airport too late and missed their planes.

- **Travel Insured International** (✆ **800/243-3174;** www.travelinsured.com)
- **Travelex Insurance Services** (✆ **800/228-9792;** www.travelex-insurance.com)

TRIP-CANCELLATION INSURANCE (TCI)

There are three major types of trip-cancellation insurance—one, in the event that you pre-pay a European tour that gets cancelled, and you can't get your money back; a second when you or someone in your family gets sick or dies, and you can't travel (but beware that you may not be covered for a pre-existing condition); and a third, when bad weather makes travel impossible. Some insurers provide coverage for events like jury duty; natural disasters close to home, like floods or fire; even the loss of a job. A few have added provisions for cancellations because of terror activities. Always check the fine print before signing on, and don't buy trip-cancellation insurance from the tour operator that may be responsible for the cancellation; buy it only from a reputable travel insurance agency. Don't overbuy. You won't be reimbursed for more than the cost of your trip.

MEDICAL INSURANCE

Most health insurance policies cover you if you get sick away from home—but check, particularly if you're insured by an HMO. With the exception of certain HMOs and Medicare/Medicaid, your medical insurance should cover medical treatment—even hospital care—overseas. However, most out-of-country hospitals make you pay your bills up front, and send you a refund after you've returned home and filed the necessary paperwork. Members of **Blue Cross/Blue Shield** can now use their cards at select hospitals in most major cities worldwide (✆ **800/810-BLUE** or www.bluecares.com for a list of hospitals).

Some credit cards (American Express and certain gold and platinum Visas and MasterCards, for example) offer automatic flight insurance against death or dismemberment in case of an airplane crash if you charged the cost of your ticket.

- **MEDEX International,** 9515 Deereco Rd., Timonium, MD 21093-5375 (✆ **888/MEDEX-00** or 410/453-6300; fax 410/453-6301; www.medexassist.com)
- **Travel Assistance International** (✆ **800/821-2828;** www.travelassistance.com), 9200 Keystone Crossing, Suite 300, Indianapolis, IN 46240 (for general information on services, call the company's Worldwide Assistance Services, Inc., at ✆ 800/777-8710).

The cost of travel medical insurance varies widely. Check your existing policies before you buy additional coverage. Also, check to see if your medical insurance covers you for emergency medical evacuation. If you have to buy a one-way same-day ticket home and forfeit your nonrefundable round-trip ticket, you may be out big money.

LOST-LUGGAGE INSURANCE

On international flights (including U.S. portions of international trips),

---

Tips Quick ID

Tie a colorful ribbon or piece of yarn around your luggage handle, or slap a distinctive sticker on the side of your bag. This makes it less likely that someone will mistakenly appropriate it. And if your luggage gets lost, it will be easier to find.

A Note on Discrimination

A fierce sense of national pride might lead many Spaniards to bristle at the suggestion that racism is a problem in their country, but recent events and a new report by Amnesty International have brought to the fore concerns over racism and racial profiling in Spain. In January 2002, Rodney Mack, an African American and the principal trumpet player with the Barcelona Symphony Orchestra, was attacked and beaten in Madrid by four police officers who later said they mistook the musician for a car thief. The thief had been described as a black man of roughly Mr. Mack's height, and a police official later admitted that Mack was singled out because of "the color of his skin and his height." In April 2002, Amnesty International cited the Mack case in an exhaustive report accusing Spain of "frequent and widespread" mistreatment of foreigners and ethnic minorities. The report investigated more than 320 cases of abuse from 1995 to 2002, including deaths and rapes while in police custody, as well as beatings, verbal abuse, and the use of racial profiling by police. The report claims that an increase in racist attacks in Spain has coincided with a dramatic growth in the country's immigrant population over the last 20 years. Spanish officials, however, rejected the report, and Congressman Ingacio Gil-Lázaro of Spain's ruling Popular Party said, "The police and Civil Guard confront immigration in a deeply humanitarian way."

While Amnesty's report may rightfully dispel the notion that Spain is exempt from the problems of racism, it does not suggest that the country is Europe's only offender. In recent years, Amnesty has pointed up race-based abuses in numerous European nations, including Austria, Greece, and Italy, as well as the United States. Travelers of color may have a perfectly enjoyable trip in Spain, but visitors to the area should travel with the knowledge that racism and xenophobia may well be as serious a problem in Spain as anywhere in Europe or the United States. If you encounter discrimination or mistreatment while traveling in Spain, please report it to your embassy immediately.

—John Vorwald

baggage is limited to approximately $9.07 per pound, up to approximately $635 per checked bag. If you plan to check items more valuable than the standard liability, you may purchase "excess valuation" coverage from the airline, up to $5,000. Be sure to take any valuables or irreplaceable items with you in your carry-on luggage. If you file a lost luggage claim, be prepared to answer detailed questions about the contents of your baggage, and be sure to file a claim immediately, as most airlines enforce a 21-day deadline. Before you leave home, compile an inventory of all packed items and a rough estimate of the total value to ensure you're properly compensated if your luggage is lost. You will only be reimbursed for what you lost, no more. Once you've filed a complaint, persist in securing your reimbursement; there are no laws governing the length of time it takes for a carrier to reimburse you.

If you arrive at a destination without your bags, ask the airline to forward them to your hotel or to your next destination; they will usually comply. If your bag is delayed or lost, the airline may reimburse you for reasonable expenses, such as a toothbrush or a set of clothes, but the airline is under no legal obligation to do so.

Lost luggage may also be covered by your homeowner's or renter's policy. Many platinum and gold credit cards cover you as well. If you choose to purchase additional lost-luggage insurance, be sure not to buy more than you need. Buy in advance from the insurer or a trusted agent (prices will be much higher at the airport).

CAR-RENTAL INSURANCE (LOSS/DAMAGE WAIVER OR COLLISION DAMAGE WAIVER)

If you hold a private auto insurance policy, you probably are covered in the U.S., but not in Spain, for loss or damage to the car, and liability in case a passenger is injured. The credit card you used to rent the card also may provide some coverage.

Car-rental insurance probably does not cover liability if you caused the accident. Check your own auto insurance policy, the rental company policy, and your credit card coverage for the extent of coverage. Is your destination covered? Are other drivers covered? How much liability is covered if a passenger is injured? (If you rely on your credit card for coverage, you may want to bring a second credit card with you, as damages may be charged to your card, and you may find yourself stranded with no money.)

THE HEALTHY TRAVELER

Spain should not pose any major health hazards. The rich cuisine—garlic, olive oil, and wine—may give some travelers mild diarrhea, so take along some anti-diarrhea medicine, moderate your eating habits, and even though the water is generally safe, drink mineral water only. Fish and shellfish from the horrendously polluted Mediterranean should only be eaten cooked.

If you are traveling around Spain (particularly southern Spain) over the summer, limit your exposure to the sun, especially during the first few days of your trip and, thereafter, from 11am to 2pm. Use a sunscreen with a high protection factor and apply it liberally. Remember that children need more protection than adults do.

The water is safe to drink through Spain; however, do not drink the water in mountain streams, regardless of how clear and pure it looks.

WHAT TO DO IF YOU GET SICK AWAY FROM HOME

Spanish medical facilities are among the best in the world. If a medical emergency arises, your hotel staff can usually put you in touch with a reliable doctor. If not, contact the American embassy or a consulate; each one maintains a list of English-speaking doctors. Medical and hospital services aren't free, so be sure that you have appropriate insurance coverage before you travel.

Pack prescription medications in your carry-on luggage. Carry written prescriptions in generic, not brand name form, and dispense all prescription medications from their original vials. Also bring along copies of your prescriptions in case you lose your pills or run out.

5 Tips for Travelers with Special Needs

FOR TRAVELERS WITH DISABILITIES

Because of Spain's many hills and endless flights of stairs, visitors with disabilities may have difficulty getting around the country. But conditions are slowly improving: Newer hotels are more sensitive to the needs of persons with disabilities, and the more expensive restaurants are generally wheelchair-accessible. However, since most places have very limited, if any, facilities for people with disabilities, consider taking an organized tour specifically designed to accommodate such travelers.

For the names and addresses of such tour operators as well as other related information, contact the **Society for Accessible Travel and Hospitality,** 347 Fifth Ave., New York, NY 10016 (✆ **212/447-7284**). Annual membership dues are $45, or $30 for seniors and students.

You can also obtain a free copy of *Air Transportation of Handicapped Persons,* published by the U.S. Department of Transportation. Write for Free Advisory Circular No. AC12032, Distribution Unit, U.S. Department of Transportation, Publications Division, M-4332, Washington, DC 20590.

For the blind or visually impaired, the best source is the **American Foundation for the Blind,** 15 W. 16th St., New York, NY 10011 (✆ **800/232-5463** to order information kits and supplies, or 212/502-7600). It offers information on travel and various requirements for the transport and border formalities for Seeing Eye dogs. It also issues identification cards to those who are legally blind.

One of the best organizations serving the needs of persons with disabilities (wheelchairs and walkers) is **Flying Wheels Travel,** 143 W. Bridge, P.O. Box 382, Owatonna, MN 55060 (✆ **800/535-6790** or 507/451-5005; www.flyingwheelstravel.com), which offers various escorted tours and cruises internationally.

For a $35 annual fee, consider joining **Mobility International USA,** P.O. Box 10767, Eugene, OR 97440 (✆ **888/241-3366,** 541/343-1284 voice and TDD; www.miusa.org). It answers questions on various destinations and also offers discounts on videos, publications, and programs it sponsors.

If you're flying around Spain, the airline and ground staff will help you on and off planes and reserve seats for you with sufficient legroom, but it is essential to arrange for this assistance *in advance* by contacting your airline.

For British Travelers with Disabilities The annual vacation guide *Holidays and Travel Abroad* costs £5 from **Royal Association for Disability and Rehabilitation** (RADAR), Unit 12, City Forum, 250 City Rd., London EC1V 8AF (✆ **020/7250-3222;** www.radar.org.uk). RADAR also provides a number of information packets on such subjects as sports and outdoor vacations, insurance, financial arrangements for persons with disabilities, and accommodations in nursing care units for groups or for the elderly. Each of these fact sheets is available for £2. Both the fact sheets and the holiday guides can be mailed outside the United Kingdom for a nominal postage fee.

Another good service is the **Holiday Care,** 2nd Floor Imperial Buildings, Victoria Road, Horley, Surrey RH6 7PZ (✆ **01293/774-535;** fax 01293/784-647; www.holidaycare.org.uk), a national charity that advises on accessible accommodations for elderly people or those with disabilities. Annual membership costs £15 (U.K. residents) and £30 (abroad). Once you're a member, you can receive a newsletter and access to a free reservations network for hotels throughout Britain and, to a lesser degree, Europe and the rest of the world.

FOR GAYS & LESBIANS

In 1978, Spain legalized homosexuality among consenting adults. In April 1995, the parliament of Spain banned discrimination based on sexual orientation. Madrid and Barcelona are the major gay centers of the country. The leading gay resort is Sitges, south of Barcelona.

To learn about gay and lesbian travel in Spain, you can secure publications or join data-dispensing organizations before you go. ***Frommer's Gay & Lesbian Europe*** has chapters on Madrid and Barcelona, as well as Sitges and Ibiza. Men can order *Spartacus,* the international gay guide, or *Odysseus 2001: The International Gay Travel Planner,* a guide to international gay accommodations. Both lesbians and gay men might want to pick up a copy of *Gay Travel A to Z,* which provides general information as well as listings for bars, hotels, restaurants, and places of interest for gay travelers throughout the world.

Our World, 1104 N. Nova Rd., Suite 251, Daytona Beach, FL 32117 (✆ **904/441-5367;** www.ourworldmag.com), is a magazine devoted to options and bargains for gay and lesbian travel worldwide. It costs $35 for 10 issues. ***Out and About,*** 995 Market St., 14 Floor, San Francisco, CA (✆ **800/929-2268;** www.outandabout.com), has been hailed for its "straight" reporting about gay travel. It profiles the best gay or gay-friendly hotels, gyms, clubs, and other places, with coverage of destinations throughout the world. It costs $49 a year for 10 information-packed issues. It aims for the most upscale gay male traveler and has been praised by everybody from *Travel & Leisure* to the *New York Times.*

The **International Gay & Lesbian Travel Association (IGLTA),** 4331 N. Federal, Suite 304, Ft. Lauderdale, FL 33308 (✆ **800/448-8550** or 954/776-2626; www.iglta.com), encourages gay and lesbian travel worldwide. With around 1,200 member agencies, it specializes in networking travelers with the appropriate gay-friendly service organization or tour specialist. It offers a quarterly newsletter, marketing mailings, and a membership directory that is updated four times a year. Travel agents who are IGTA members will be tied into this organization's vast information resources.

FOR SENIORS

Many discounts are available for seniors, but often you need to be a member of an association to obtain them.

For information before you go, write for the free booklet, *101 Tips for the Mature Traveler,* available from **Grand Circle Travel,** 347 Congress St., Suite 3A, Boston, MA 02210 (✆ **800/221-2610** or 617/350-7500; www.gct.com).

One of the most dynamic travel organizations for seniors is **Elderhostel,** 75 Federal St., Boston, MA (✆ **877/426-8056;** www.elderhostel.org). Established in 1975, it operates an array of programs throughout Europe, including Spain. Most courses last around three weeks and are a good value, since they include airfare, accommodations in student dormitories or modest inns, all meals, and tuition. Courses involve no homework, are not graded, and are often liberal arts-oriented. These are not luxury vacations, but they are fun and fulfilling. Participants must be at least 60 years old. A companion must be at least 50 years old; spouses may participate regardless of age.

SAGA Holidays, 222 Berkeley St., Boston, MA 02116 (✆ **800/343-0273;** www.sagaholidays.com), runs tours for seniors 50 and older. Many tours are all-inclusive; all cover air transfers and accommodations. Insurance, both baggage and medical, is also included in the net price of the tours.

In the United States, the best organization to join is the **AARP,** 601 E St. NW, Washington, DC 20049 (✆ **800/424-3410** or 202/434-AARP; www.aarp.org). Members are offered discounts on car rentals, hotels, and airfares.

Uniworld, 16000 Ventura Blvd., Encino, CA 91436 (✆ **800/733-7820** or 818/382-7820), specializes in single tours for the mature person. It arranges for you to share an accommodation with another single person or gets you a low-priced single supplement. Uniworld specializes in travel to certain districts of England, France, Spain, Italy, and Scandinavia.

6 Getting There

BY PLANE

Any information about fares or even flights in the highly volatile airline industry is not written in stone; even travel agencies with banks of computers have a hard time keeping abreast of last-minute discounts and schedule changes. For up-to-the-minute information, including a list of the carriers that fly to Barcelona and Madrid, check with a travel agent or the individual airlines.

THE MAJOR AIRLINES

FROM NORTH AMERICA Flights to Barcelona and Madrid from the U.S. East Coast take 6 to 7 hours, depending on the season and prevailing winds.

The national carrier of Spain, **Iberia Airlines** (✆ **800/772-4642;** www.iberia.com), offers more routes to and within Spain than any other airline, with nonstop service to Madrid from both New York and Miami. From Miami, Iberia takes off for at least eight destinations in Mexico and Central America, and in cooperation with its air partner, Ladeco (an airline based in Chile), to dozens of destinations throughout South America as well. Iberia also flies from Los Angeles to Madrid, with a brief stop in Miami. Iberia offers service to Madrid through Montreal two and three times a week, depending on the season. Also available are attractive rates on fly/drive programs within Iberia and Europe.

Iberia's fares are lowest if you reserve an APEX (advance-purchase excursion) ticket at least 21 days in advance, schedule your return 7 to 30 days after your departure, and leave and return between Monday and Thursday. Iberia does not offer direct flights to Barcelona or Seville; all passengers must transfer planes in Madrid. Fares, which are subject to change, are lower during off-season. Most transatlantic flights are on carefully maintained 747s and DC-10s, and in-flight services reflect Spanish traditions, values, and cuisine.

American Airlines (✆ **800/433-7300;** www.aa.com) offers daily nonstop service to Madrid from its massive hub in Miami, with excellent connections from there to the rest of the airline's impressive North and South American network.

Delta (✆ **800/241-4141;** www.delta.com) maintains daily nonstop service from Atlanta (centerpiece of its worldwide network) to Madrid, with continuing service (and no change of equipment) to Barcelona. Delta's Dream Vacation department maintains access to fly/drive programs, land packages, and escorted bus tours through the Iberian Peninsula. Delta also offers daily nonstop service between New York's JFK and Barcelona's El Prat airports.

Since 1991, **United Airlines** (✆ **800/241-6522;** www.ual.com) has flown passengers nonstop every day to Madrid from Washington. United also offers fly/drive programs and escorted motor coach tours.

Continental Airlines (✆ **800/231-0856;** www.continental.com) offers between six and seven nonstop flights per week, depending on the season, to Madrid from Newark, New Jersey, an airport many New York residents prefer.

Tips Europass: A Cost-Cutting Technique

A noteworthy cost-cutting option is Iberia's Europass. Available only to passengers who simultaneously arrange for transatlantic passage on Iberia and a minimum of two additional flights, it allows passage on any flight within Iberia's European or Mediterranean dominion for $250 for the first two flights and $133 for each additional flight. This is especially attractive for passengers wishing to combine trips to Spain with, for example, visits to such far-flung destinations as Cairo, Tel Aviv, Istanbul, Moscow, and Munich. For details, ask Iberia's phone representative. Iberia's main Spain-based competitor is **Air Europa** (✆ **888/238-7672;** www.air-europa.es), which offers nonstop service from New York's JFK Airport to Madrid, with continuing service to major cities within Spain. Fares are competitive.

US Airways (✆ **800/428-4322;** www.usairways.com) offers daily nonstop service between Philadelphia and Madrid. US Airways offers connections to Philadelphia from more than 50 cities throughout the United States, Canada, and the Bahamas.

Most U.S.-based carriers offer service solely to Madrid; once in Madrid, Spain's airline, Iberia, offers low fares to cities throughout the country.

FROM GREAT BRITAIN The two major carriers that fly between the United Kingdom and Spain are **British Airways (BA)** (✆ **0845/773-3377,** or 020/8759-5511 in London; www.british-airways.com) and **Iberia** (✆ **020/7830-0011** in London). In spite of the frequency of their routes, however, we suspect most vacationing Brits fly charter (see below).

More than a dozen daily flights, on either BA or Iberia, depart from both London's Heathrow and Gatwick airports. The Midlands is served by flights from Manchester and Birmingham, two major airports that can also be used by Scots flying to Spain. Approximately seven flights a day go between London and Madrid, with at least six to Barcelona (trip time: 2–2½ hr.). From either the Madrid airport or the Barcelona airport, you can tap into Iberia's domestic network—flying, for example, to Seville or the Costa del Sol (centered at the Málaga airport). The best air deals on scheduled flights from the United Kingdom are those requiring a Saturday night stopover.

NEW AIR TRAVEL SECURITY MEASURES

In the wake of the terrorist attacks of September 11, 2001, the airline industry began implementing sweeping security measures in airports. Expect a lengthy check-in process and extensive delays. Although regulations vary from airline to airline, you can expedite the process by taking the following steps:

- **Arrive early.** Arrive at the airport at least 2 hours before your scheduled flight.
- **Try not to drive your car to the airport.** Parking and curbside access to the terminal may be limited Call ahead and check.
- **Don't count on curbside check-in.** Some airlines and airports have stopped curbside check-in altogether, whereas others offer it on a limited basis. For up-to-date information on specific regulations and implementations, check with the individual airline.
- **Be sure to carry plenty of documentation.** A government-issued photo ID (federal, state, or local)

is now required. You may need to show this at various checkpoints. With an E-ticket, you may be required to have with you printed confirmation of purchase, and perhaps even the credit card with which you bought your ticket (see "All about E-Ticketing," below). This varies from airline to airline, so call ahead to make sure you have the proper documentation. And be sure that your ID is **up-to-date;** an expired driver's license, for example, may keep you from boarding the plane altogether.

- **Know what you can carry on—and what you can't.** Travelers in the United States are now limited to one carry-on bag, plus one personal bag (such as a purse or a briefcase). The FAA has also issued a list of newly restricted carry-on items; see the box "What You Can Carry On—and What You Can't."
- **Prepare to be searched.** Expect spot-checks. Electronic items, such as a laptop or cellphone, should be readied for additional screening. Limit the metal items you wear on your person.
- **It's no joke.** When a check-in agent asks if someone other than you packed your bag, don't decide that this is the time to be funny. The agents will not hesitate to call an alarm.
- **No ticket, no gate access.** Only ticketed passengers will be allowed beyond the screener checkpoints, except for those people with specific medical or parental needs.

FLYING FOR LESS: TIPS FOR GETTING THE BEST AIRFARE

Passengers within the same airplane cabin are rarely paying the same fare. Business travelers who need to purchase tickets at the last minute, change their itinerary at a moment's notice, or get home for the weekend pay the premium rate. Passengers who can book their ticket long in advance, who can stay over Saturday night, or who are willing to travel on a Tuesday, Wednesday, or Thursday after 7pm, will pay a fraction of the full fare. Here are a few other easy ways to save.

- **Take advantage of APEX fares.** Advance-purchase booking, or APEX, fares are often the key to getting the lowest fare. You

Tips All About E-Ticketing

Only yesterday **electronic tickets (E-tickets)** were the fast and easy ticket-free alternative to paper tickets. E-tickets allowed passengers to avoid long lines at airport check-in, all the while saving the airlines money on postage and labor. With the increased security measures in airports, however, an E-ticket no longer guarantees an accelerated check-in. You often can't go straight to the boarding gate, even if you have no bags to check. You'll probably need to show your printed E-ticket receipt or confirmation of purchase, as well as a photo ID, and sometimes even the credit card with which you purchased your E-ticket. That said, buying an E-ticket is still a fast, convenient way to book a flight; instead of having to wait for a paper ticket to come through the mail, you can book your fare by phone or on the computer, and the airline will immediately confirm by fax or e-mail. In addition, airlines often offer frequent-flier miles as incentive for electronic bookings.

generally must be willing to make your plans and buy your tickets as far ahead as possible: The **21-day APEX** is seconded only by the **14-day APEX,** with a stay in Italy of 7 to 30 days. Because the number of seats allocated to APEX fares is sometimes less than 25% of plane capacity, the early bird gets the low-cost seat. There's often a surcharge for flying on a weekend, and cancellation and refund policies can be strict.

- **Watch for sales.** You'll almost never see sales during July and August or the Thanksgiving or Christmas seasons, but at other times you can get great deals. In the last couple of years, there have been amazing prices on winter flights to Rome. If you already hold a ticket when a sale breaks, it might pay to exchange it, even if you incur a $50 to $75 penalty charge. Note, however, that the lowest-priced fares are often nonrefundable, require advance purchase of 1 to 3 weeks and a certain length of stay, and carry penalties for changing dates of travel. Make sure you know exactly what the restrictions are before you commit.
- If your schedule is flexible, ask if you can secure a cheaper fare by **staying an extra day** or by **flying midweek.** (Many airlines won't volunteer this information.)
- **Consolidators,** also known as bucket shops, are a good place to find low fares, often below even the airlines' discounted rates. Basically, they're just big travel agents who get discounts for buying in bulk and pass some of the savings on to you. Before you pay, however, be aware that consolidator tickets are usually nonrefundable or come with stiff cancellation penalties.

We've gotten great deals on many occasions from Cheap Tickets (✆ 800/377-1000; www.cheaptickets.com). Council Travel (✆ 800/2COUNCIL; www.counciltravel.com) and STA Travel (✆ 800/781-4040; www.statravel.com) cater especially to young travelers, but their bargain-basement prices are available to

Tips What You Can Carry On—And What You Can't

The Transportation Security Administration (TSA), the government agency that now handles all aspects of airport security, has devised new restrictions for carry-on baggage, not only to expedite the screening process but to prevent potential weapons from passing through airport security. Passengers are now limited to bringing just one carry-on bag and one personal item onto the aircraft (previous regulations allowed two carry-on bags and one personal item, like a briefcase or a purse). For more information, go to the TSA's website www.tsa.gov. The agency has released an updated list of items passengers are not allowed to carry onto an aircraft:

Not permitted: knives and box cutters, corkscrews, straight razors, metal scissors, golf clubs, baseball bats, pool cues, hockey sticks, ski poles, ice picks.

Permitted: nail clippers, nail files, tweezers, eyelash curlers, safety razors (including disposable razors), syringes (with documented proof of medical need), walking canes and umbrellas (must be inspected first).

The airline you fly may have **additional restrictions** on items you can and cannot carry on board. Call ahead to avoid problems.

Tips Cancelled Plans

If your flight is cancelled, don't book a new fare at the ticket counter. Find the nearest phone and call the airline directly to reschedule. You'll be relaxing while other passengers are still standing in line.

people of all ages. Other reliable consolidators include Lowestfare.com (✆ 888/278-8830; www.lowestfare.com); 1-800/AIRFARE (www.1800airfare.com); Cheap Seats (✆ 800/451-7200; www.cheapseatstravel.com); and 1-800/FLY-CHEAP (www.flycheap.com).

- Join a travel club such as **Moment's Notice** (✆ **718/234-6295;** www.moments-notice.com) or **Sears Discount Travel Club** (✆ **800/433-9383,** or 800/255-1487 to join; www.travelersadvantage.com), which supply unsold tickets at discounted prices. You pay an annual membership fee to get the club's hotline number. Of course, you're limited to what's available, so you have to be flexible.
- Join **frequent-flier clubs.** It's best to accrue miles on one program, so you can rack up free flights and achieve elite status faster. But it makes sense to open as many accounts as possible, no matter how seldom you fly a particular airline. It's free, and you'll get the best choice of seats, faster response to phone inquiries, and prompter service if your luggage is stolen, your flight is canceled or delayed, or if you want to change your seat.
- Search the **Internet** for cheap fares—though it's still best to compare your findings with the research of a dedicated travel agent, if you're lucky enough to have one, especially when you're booking more than just a flight. Among the better-respected virtual travel agents are **Travelocity** (www.travelocity.com), **Expedia** (www.expedia.com), and **Yahoo! Travel** (http://travel.yahoo.com).

TIPS FOR BRITISH TRAVELERS

A regular fare from the United Kingdom to Spain is extremely high, so savvy Brits usually call a travel agent for a deal—either a charter flight or some special air-travel promotion. These so-called deals are almost always available, due to great interest in Spain as a tourist destination. Another way to keep costs down is an APEX (Advance Payment Excursion) ticket. Alternatively, a PEX (public excursion fare) ticket offers a discount without the strict booking restrictions. You might also ask the airlines about a Eurobudget ticket, which has restrictions or length-of-stay requirements.

British periodicals are always full of classified advertisements touting "slashed" fares to Spain. Good sources include the London-based magazine *Time Out,* the daily travel section of London's *Evening Standard,* and the Sunday edition of almost any newspaper.

Most vacationing Brits looking for air-flight bargains go charter. Delays can be frequent (some last 2 whole days and nights), and departures are often at inconvenient hours. Booking conditions can also be severe, and one must read the fine print carefully and deal with only a reputable travel agent. Stays rarely last a month, and booking must sometimes be made at least a month in advance, although a 2-week period is sometimes possible.

Charter flights leave from most British regional airports for various destinations (for example, Málaga), bypassing the congestion at the Madrid airports. Figure on saving approximately 10% to 15% off regularly scheduled flight tickets. Recommended companies include **Trailfinders** (© **020/7937-5400** in London; www.trailfinders.com) and **Avro Tours** (© **020/8715-0000** in London).

In London, many bucket shops around Victoria Station and Earls Court offer low fares. Make sure the company you deal with is a member of the IATA, ABTA, or ATOL. These umbrella organizations will help you out if anything goes wrong.

CEEFAX, a British television information service included on many home and hotel TVs, runs details of package holidays and flights to Europe and beyond. Just switch to your CEEFAX channel to find a menu of listings that includes travel information.

BY TRAIN

If you're already in Europe, you may want to go to Spain by train, especially if you have a Eurailpass. Even if you don't, the cost is moderate. Rail passengers who visit from Britain or France should make *couchette* and sleeper reservations as far in advance as possible, especially during the peak summer season.

Since Spain's rail tracks are of a wider gauge than those used for French trains (except for the TALGO and Trans-Europe-Express trains), you'll probably have to change trains at the border unless you're on an express train (see below). For long journeys on Spanish rails, seat and sleeper reservations are mandatory.

The most comfortable and the fastest trains in Spain are the TER, TALGO, and Electrotren. However, you pay a supplement to ride on these fast trains. Both first- and second-class fares are sold on Spanish trains. Tickets can be purchased in either the United States or Canada at the nearest office of FrenchRail or from any reputable travel agent. Confirmation of your reservation will take about a week.

If you want your car carried, you must travel Auto-Expreso in Spain. This type of auto transport can be booked only through travel agents or rail offices once you arrive in Europe.

To go from London to Spain by rail, you'll need to change not only the train but also the rail terminus in Paris. In Paris it's worth the extra bucks to purchase a TALGO express or a "Puerta del Sol" express—that way, you can avoid having to change trains once again at the Spanish border. Trip time from London to Paris is about 6 hours; from Paris to Madrid, about 15 hours or so, which includes 2 hours spent in Paris changing trains and stations. Many rail passes are available in the United Kingdom for travel in Europe.

BY BUS

Bus travel to Spain is possible but not popular—it's quite slow. But coach services do operate regularly from major capitals of Western Europe to Madrid and Barcelona, from which bus connections can be made to Seville. The busiest routes are from London and are run by **Eurolines Limited,** 52 Grosvenor Gardens, London SW1W 0AU (© **0990/143-219** or 020/7730-8235). The journey from London's Victoria Station to Madrid is provided by two services: Service 180 is an express from Victoria Station to Madrid, departing London daily at 9pm, arriving in Madrid the following day at 9:30pm; and Service 181 leaves London at 9pm on the first day, arriving in Madrid at 12:30am on the third day.

Other bus trips can be arranged from London to Barcelona, Alicante, Benidorm, and Marbella.

Aerolíneas (© **93-490-40-00** in Barcelona or 01582/40-4511 in Britain) operates a coach that departs from London's Victoria Station on Monday, Wednesday, and Saturday. It leaves London at 11am and arrives in Barcelona the following morning at 11am. On Wednesday the bus leaves at 9:30am and gets into Barcelona at 11:45am. An English-speaking staff in Barcelona can make reservations for you and supply more details.

BY CAR

If you're touring the rest of Europe in a rented car, you might, for an added cost, be allowed to drop off your vehicle in a major city such as Madrid or Barcelona.

Motor approaches to Spain are across France via expressways. The most popular border crossing is east of Biarritz. For the best route to Madrid, take the E-70 west of Bilbao; then cut south on the E-804 to the junction with the E-05, which heads southwest to Burgos. Bypass Burgos and continue south on the route to Madrid, which is also known as the N-I.

To get to Barcelona from the north, take the A-7 or the E-9 to A-18; from the Costa Brava, take the A-19 heading southwest; and from the south, enter Barcelona on the A-16.

If you're driving from Madrid to Seville, connect with the E-90 and head southwest toward Mérida; from there, head south on the E-803 to Seville. For an alternative route, head south on the E-5 to Córdoba. After exploring Córdoba, continue southwest on the E-5; this highway will take you to Seville.

If you're driving from Britain, make sure you have a cross-Channel reservation, as traffic tends to be very heavy, especially in summer. The major ferry crossings connect Dover and Folkestone with Dunkirk. Newhaven is connected with Dieppe, and the British city of Portsmouth with Roscoff. One of the fastest crossings is by Hovercraft from Dover to Boulogne or Calais. It costs more than the ferry, but it takes only about half an hour.

You can also take the "Chunnel," the underwater Channel Tunnel linking Britain (Folkestone) and France (Calais) by road and rail—a great engineering feat that was first envisioned by Napoléon way back in 1802. Travel time between the English and French highway systems is about 1 hour.

7 Escorted Tours & Package Deals

Before you start your search for the lowest airfare, you may want to consider booking your flight as part of a travel package such as an escorted tour or a package tour. What you lose in adventure, you'll gain in time and money saved when you book accommodations, and maybe even food and entertainment, along with your flight.

PACKAGE TOURS FOR INDEPENDENT TRAVELERS

Package tours are not the same thing as escorted tours. With a package tour, you travel independently but pay a group rate. Packages usually include airfare, a choice of hotels, and car rentals, and packagers often offers several options at different prices. In many cases, a package that includes airfare, hotel, and transportation to and from the airport will cost you less than just the hotel alone would have, had you booked it yourself. That's because packages are sold in bulk to tour operators—who resell them to the public at a cost that drastically undercuts standard rates.

RECOMMENDED PACKAGE TOUR OPERATORS

One good source of package deals is the airlines themselves. Most major airlines offer air/land packages. See "By Plane," above; most airlines offer packages that may include car rentals and accommodations in addition to your airfare.

The best place to start your search is the travel section of your local Sunday newspaper. Also check the ads in the back of national travel magazines like *Travel & Leisure, National Geographic Traveler,* and *Condé Nast Traveler.* One of the biggest packages in the Northeast, **Liberty Travel** (✆ **888/271-1584;** www.libertytravel.com), usually boasts a full-page ad in Sunday papers. **American Express Travel** (✆ **800/941-2639;** www.travelimpressions.com) is another option.

Among the airline packagers, **Iberia Airlines** (✆ **800/772-4642** or 902/400/500 [Spain]; www.iberia.com) leads the way. Other packages for travel in Spain are offered by **United Airlines** (✆ **800/241-6522;** www.ual.com), **American Airlines Vacations** (✆ **800/321-2121;** www.aavacations.com), and **Delta Vacations** (✆ **800/872-7786;** www.deltavacations.com).

Solar Tours (✆ **800/388-7652;** www.solartours.com) is a wholesaler that offers a number of package tours to Madrid, Barcelona, and Seville, as well as to major beach resorts. Self-drive packages through Andalusia and other areas are also featured. A 9-day "Moorish Escapade" tour of Andalusia is its most popular jaunt. **Spanish Heritage Tours** (✆ **800/456-5050;** www.shtours.com) is known for searching for low-cost airfare deals to Spain—round-trips from the U.S. to Madrid for $429 or to Málaga for $529. The tour agent also features both air and land packages to Barcelona and Madrid. **Discover Spain Vacations** (✆ **800/227-5858;** www.farandwide.com), the marketing arm of Iberia, is the most reliable tour operator and the agency used for air and land packages to some of the highlights of Spain, including Madrid, Córdoba, Seville, Granada, and the Costa del Sol. Naturally, round-trip airfares on Iberia are included in the deal. Several fly/drive packages are also offered.

ESCORTED TOURS (TRIPS WITH GUIDES)

Escorted tours are structured group tours, with a group leader. The price usually includes everything from airfare to hotels, meals, tours, admission costs, and local transportation.

RECOMMENDED ESCORTED TOUR OPERATORS

There are many escorted tour companies to choose from, each offering transportation to and within Spain, prearranged hotel space, and such extras as bilingual tour guides and lectures. Many of these tours to Spain include excursions to Morocco or Portugal.

Some of the most expensive and luxurious tours are run by **Abercrombie & Kent International** (✆ **800/323-7308** or 630/954-2944; www.abercrombiekent.com), including deluxe 13- or 19-day tours of the Iberian Peninsula by train. Guests stay in fine hotels, ranging from a late medieval palace to the exquisite Alfonso XIII in Seville.

Trafalgar Tours (✆ **800/854-0103** or 212/689-8977; www.trafalgartours.com) offers a number of tours of Spain. One of the most popular offerings is a 18-day trip called "The Best of Spain" (this land-only package is $1,735; with land and air, it's $2,155–$2,565).

Insight Vacations "Highlights of Spain" is a 11-day tour that begins in Madrid, sweeps along the southern and eastern coasts, and concludes in Madrid. The company offers the tour for $1,370 to $1,785 including airfare, accommodations, and some meals. For information, contact your travel agent or Insight International (© **800/582-8380;** www.insightvacations.com).

Alternative Travel Group Ltd. (© **01865/310-399**) is a British firm that organizes walking and cycling vacations, plus wine tours in Spain, Italy, and France. Tours explore the scenic countryside and medieval towns of each country. If you'd like a brochure outlining the tours, call © **01865/315-663.**

Petrabax Tours (© **800/634-1188;** www.petrabax.com) attracts those who prefer to see Spain by bus, although fly/drive packages are also offered, featuring stays in paradors. A number of city packages are also available, plus a 10-day trip that tries to capture Spain in a nutshell, with stops in places ranging from Madrid to Granada. **Basque Travel** (© **888/527-0110;** www.basquetravel.com) escorts visitors to the Basque country and the highlights of the northern coast, including stopovers in Bilbao to see the Guggenheim Museum. **Escapade Vacations** (© **800/356-2405;** www.isram.com) sells both escorted and package tours to Spain. It can book you on bus tours as well as land and air packages. Its grandest offering is "Ultimate Spain" with a private driver and guides. Naturally, only Spain's best hotels are used by this upmarket outfitter.

Recently, more and more special-interest tours to Spain are being offered, including tours by **Archetours, Inc.** (© **800/770-3051;** www.archetours.com), which features tours devoted to Spanish architecture. These tours encompass Barcelona's **Modernise,** plus the art and architecture of Bilbao and Barcelona. On the other hand, **Camino Tours** (© **800/938-9311;** www.caminotours.com) will take you across the country on foot or by bike. Walking tours cross the Pyrenees and the Picos de Europa, and biking tours go through the south of Spain or La Rioja wine country. Tours are limited to groups of 6 to 20 people.

8 Planning Your Trip Online

Researching and booking your trip online can save time and money. Then again, it may not. It is simply not true that you always get the best deal online. Most booking engines do not include schedules and prices for budget airlines, and from time to time you'll get a better last-minute price by

Frommers.com: The Complete Travel Resource

For an excellent travel-planning resource, we highly recommend **Frommers.com** (www.frommers.com). We're a little biased, of course, but we guarantee that you'll find the travel tips, reviews, monthly vacation giveaways, and online-booking capabilities thoroughly indispensable. Among the special features are our popular **Message Boards,** where Frommer's readers post queries and share advice (sometimes even our authors show up to answer questions); **Frommers.com Newsletter,** for the latest travel bargains and inside travel secrets; and Frommer's **Destinations Section,** where you'll get expert travel tips, hotel and dining recommendations, and advice on the sights to see for more than 2,500 destinations around the globe. When your research is done, the **Online Reservation System** (www.frommers.com/booktravelnow) takes you to Frommer's favorite sites for booking your vacation at affordable prices.

calling the airline directly, so it's best to call the airline to see if you can do better before booking online.

Some sites, such as Expedia. com, will send you **e-mail notification** when a cheap fare becomes available to your favorite destination. Some will also tell you when fares to a particular destination are lowest.

TRAVEL PLANNING & BOOKING SITES

Keep in mind that because several airlines are no longer willing to pay commissions on tickets sold by online travel agencies, these agencies may either add a $10 surcharge to your bill if you book on that carrier—or neglect to offer those carriers' schedules.

The list of sites below is selective, not comprehensive. Some sites will have evolved or disappeared by the time you read this.

- **Travelocity** (www.travelocity.com or www.frommers.travelocity.com) and **Expedia** (www.expedia.com) are among the most popular sites, each offering an excellent range of options. Travelers search by destination, dates and cost.
- **Orbitz** (www.orbitz.com) is a popular site launched by United, Delta, Northwest, American, and Continental airlines. (Stay tuned: At press time, travel-agency associations were waging an antitrust battle against this site.)
- **Qixo** (www.qixo.com) is another powerful search engine that allows you to search for flights and accommodations from some 20 airline and travel-planning sites (such as Travelocity) at once. Qixo sorts results by price.
- **Priceline** (www.priceline.com) lets you "name your price" for airline tickets, hotel rooms, and rental cars. For airline tickets, you can't say what time you want to fly—you have to accept any flight between 6am and 10pm on the dates you've selected, and you may have to make one or more stopovers. Tickets are nonrefundable, and no frequent-flier miles are awarded.

9 Recommended Books

THE ARTS

The Moors contributed much to Spanish culture, leaving Spain with a distinct legacy that is documented in Titus Burckhardt's *Moorish Culture in Spain* (McGraw-Hill).

Antoni Gaudí is the Barcelona architect who most excites visitors' curiosity. The latest study is *Gaudí,* by Gijs van Hensbergen, published in 2001. The author claims Gaudí was "drunk on form," and that the architect still has not lost his power to astonish with his idiosyncratic and innovative designs.

Spain's most famous artist was Pablo Picasso. The most controversial book about the late painter is *Picasso, Creator and Destroyer* by Arianna Stassinopoulos Huffington (Simon & Schuster).

Spain's other headline-grabbing artist was Salvador Dalí. In *Salvador Dalí: A Biography* (Dutton), author Meryle Secrest asks: Was he a mad genius or a cunning manipulator?

Andrés Segovia: An Autobiography of the Years 1893–1920 (Macmillan), with a translation by W. F. O'Brien, is worth seeking out.

Residents of Catalonia truthfully maintain that their unique language, culture, and history have been overshadowed (and squelched) by the richer and better-publicized accomplishments of Castile. Robert Hughes, a former art critic at *Time* magazine, has written an elegant testament to the glories of the capital of this region: *Barcelona* (Knopf); this book offers a well-versed and often witty articulation of the city's architectural and cultural legacy. According to the *New York Times,* the book is probably destined to become "a classic in the genre of urban history."

FICTION & BIOGRAPHY

Denounced by some as superficial, James A. Michener's *Iberia* (Random House) remains the classic travelog on Spain. The *Houston Post* claimed that this book "will make you fall in love with Spain."

The latest biography on one of the 20th century's most durable dictators is *Franco: A Concise Biography,* which was released in the spring of 2002. Gabrielle Ashford Hodges documents with great flair the Orwellian repression and widespread corruption that marked the notorious regime of this "deeply flawed" politician.

The most famous Spanish novel is *Don Quixote* by Miguel de Cervantes. Readily available everywhere, it deals with the conflict between the ideal and the real in human nature. Despite the unparalleled fame of Miguel de Cervantes within Spanish literature, very little is known about his life. One of the most searching biographies of the literary master is Jean Canavaggio's *Cervantes,* translated from the Spanish by J. R. Jones (Norton).

Although the work of Cervantes has attained an almost mystical significance in the minds of many Spaniards, in the words of Somerset Maugham, "It would be hard to find a work so great that has so many defects." Nicholas Wollaston's *Tilting at Don Quixote* (André Deutsch Publishers) punctures any illusions that the half-crazed Don is only a matter of good and rollicking fun.

Ernest Hemingway completed many works on Spain, none more notable than his novels of 1926 and 1940, respectively: *The Sun Also Rises* (Macmillan) and *For Whom the Bell Tolls* (Macmillan), the latter based on his experiences in the Spanish Civil War. Don Ernesto's *Death in the Afternoon* (various editions) remains the English-language classic on bullfighting.

For a very different, but dated, view of Spain, read W. Somerset Maugham's *Don Fernando* (Ayer), with the famed English author's comments on everything from the Spanish diet to *Don Quixote.*

3 Settling into Barcelona

Blessed with rich and fertile soil, an excellent harbor, and a hardworking population, Barcelona has always prospered. At a time when Madrid was still a dusty and unknown Castilian backwater, Barcelona was a powerful, diverse capital, one influenced more by the Mediterranean empires that conquered it than by the cultures of the arid Iberian plains to the west. Carthage, Rome, and Charlemagne-era France each overran Catalonia, and each left an indelible mark on the region's identity.

The Catalán people have clung fiercely to their unique culture and language—both of which, earlier in this century, Franco systematically tried to eradicate. But Catalonia has endured, becoming a semiautonomous region of Spain (with Catalán as its official language). And Barcelona, the region's lodestar, has truly come into its own. The city's most powerful monuments open a window onto its history: the intricately carved edifices that comprise the medieval Gothic Quarter; the curvilinear modernismo (Catalán Art Nouveau) that inspired Gaudí's Sagrada Família; and the seminal surrealist works of Picasso and Miró, found in museums that peg Barcelona as a crucial incubator for 20th-century art.

As if those attractions weren't enough, Barcelona is on the doorstep of some of the great playgrounds and vacation retreats of Europe: the Balearic Islands to the east, the Costa Brava (Wild Coast) to the north, the Penedés wine country to the west, the Roman city of Tarragona, the monastery at Montserrat, and such Costa Dorada resort towns as Sitges, to the south.

Despite its allure, Barcelona grapples with problems common to many major cities: the increasing polarization of rich and poor, a rising tide of drug abuse, and an escalating crime rate, mostly theft. Pickpockets consider tourists fair game. One New Yorker, claiming an 80-year residence in the city, said that on a 3-day trip to Barcelona someone attempted to pick his pockets three times, twice on the underground.

A revitalized Barcelona eagerly prepared for and welcomed thousands of visitors as part of the 1992 Summer Olympic Games. But the action didn't end when the last medal was handed out. Barcelona turned its multimillion-dollar building projects into permanently expanded facilities for sports and tourism. Its modern 150-million-euro terminal at El Prat de Llobregat Airport can accommodate 12 million passengers a year; and ever-pragmatic Barcelona moved into the 21st century with a restructuring program called "Post Olympic."

1 Orientation

GETTING THERE

BY PLANE During the months before the 1992 Olympics, airlines scrambled to provide nonstop transatlantic service to Barcelona. In the post-Olympic world, however, most passengers must first change aircraft in Madrid. The only exception is **Delta** (✆ **800/241-4141;** www.delta.com). Passengers originating in such European capitals as London, Paris, and Rome can fly nonstop to Barcelona (usually on their national airlines), but most passengers, for whatever reason, opt for transit through Madrid. For more information on flying into Madrid, see "Getting There," in chapter 2.

Within Spain, the most likely carrier is **Iberia** (✆ **800/772-4642;** www.iberia.com), which offers peak-hour shuttle flights at 15-minute intervals between Madrid and Barcelona. Service from Madrid to Barcelona at less congested times of the day averages around one flight every 30 to 40 minutes. Iberia also offers flights between Barcelona and Valencia, Granada, Seville, and Bilbao. Within Barcelona, you can arrange ticketing at **Iberia,** Plaça de Espanya s/n (✆ **93-325-73-58**) or Disputació 258 (✆ **93-401-33-95**). Generally cheaper than Iberia, both **Air Europa** (✆ **93-298-33-28;** www.air-europa.es) and **Spanair** (✆ **93-298-33-62;** www.spanair.com) run shuttles between Madrid and Barcelona. Frequency of shuttle flights depends on demand, with more in the early morning and late afternoon.

El Prat de Llobregat, 08820 Prat de Llobregat (✆ **93-298-38-38;** www.barcelona-airport.com), the Barcelona airport, is 12km (7½ miles) southwest of the city. The route to the center of town is carefully marked. A train runs daily between the airport and Barcelona's Estació Central de Barcelona-Sants from 6:14am (the first airport departure) to 10:44pm (the last city departure). The 21-minute trip costs 1.85€ Monday to Friday and 2.10€ Saturday and Sunday. If your hotel is near Plaça de Catalunya, you might opt instead for an Aerobús that runs daily every 15 minutes between 5:30am and 10pm. The fare is 2.85€. A taxi from the airport into central Barcelona will cost 18€ to 21€.

BY TRAIN A train called the Barcelona-TALGO provides rail service between Paris and Barcelona in 11½ hours. For many other connections from the mainland of Europe, it's necessary to change trains at Port Bou, on the French-Spanish border. Most trains issue seat and sleeper reservations.

Trains departing from the **Estació de França,** Avenida Marqués de l'Argentera (Metro: Barceloneta, L3), cover long distances within Spain as well as international routes, carrying a total of 20,000 passengers daily. Express night trains serve Paris, Zurich, Milan, and Geneva. Every international route served by the state-owned RENFE railway company uses the Estació de França, including some of its most luxurious express trains, such as the *Pau Casals* and the *TALGO Catalán.*

This modernized 1929 station includes a huge screen with updated information on train departures and arrivals, personalized ticket dispatching, a passenger attention center, a tourism information center, showers, internal baggage control, a first-aid center, and kiosks for hotel reservations and car rentals. But it is much more than a departure point: The station has an elegant restaurant, a cafeteria, a book-and-record store, a jazz club, and even a disco. Estació de França is just steps away from Ciutadella Park, the zoo, and the port and is near Vila Olímpica.

From this station you can book tickets to the major cities of Spain: Madrid (5 TALGOS trains per day, 7 hr.; and 3 *rápidos,* 10 hr.), Seville (2 trains daily, 10½ hr.), and Valencia (11 daily, 4 hr.).

RENFE also has a terminal at **Estació Central de Barcelona-Sants,** Plaça de Països Catalanes (Metro: Sants-Estació).

For general RENFE information, call ✆ **90-224-02-02.**

BY BUS Bus travel to Barcelona is possible but not popular—it's pretty slow. **Eurolines Limited,** Grosvenor Gardens, London SW1W 0AU (✆ **0870/514-3219** or 020/7730-8235), can arrange your trip from London to Barcelona. **Enatcar,** Estació del Nord in Barcelona (✆ **93-245-25-28**), can arrange service to southern France and Italy, and **Linebús,** also found at the Estació del Nord (✆ **93-265-07-00**), offers six bus trips a week to Paris. **Julià Via,** Carrer Viriato (✆ **93-490-40-00**), operates four buses a week to Frankfurt, Germany, and another four per week to Marseille, France.

Enatcar, Estació del Nord (✆ **93-245-25-28**), operates 14 buses per day to Madrid (trip time: 8 hr.) and 9 buses per day to Valencia (trip time: 4½ hr.). A one-way ticket to Madrid costs 22€; to Valencia, 20€. For bus travel to one of the beach resorts along the Costa Brava, go to **Sarfa,** Estació del Nord (✆ **93-265-11-58**), which operates buses from Barcelona to such resorts as Tossa de Mar. Trip time is usually 2 hours.

BY CAR **From France** (the usual European road approach to Barcelona), the major access route is at the eastern end of the Pyrenees. You have a choice of the express highway (**E-15**) or the more scenic coastal road. *But be warned:* If you take the scenic coastal road in July and August, you'll often encounter bumper-to-bumper traffic. From France, you can also approach Barcelona via Toulouse. Cross the border into Spain at Puigcerdà (frontier stations are here), near the principality of Andorra. From here, take the **N-152** to Barcelona.

From Madrid, take the **N-2** to Zaragoza, then the **A-2** to El Vendrell, followed by the **A-7** motorway to Barcelona. **From the Costa Blanca** or **Costa del Sol,** follow the **E-15** north from Valencia along the eastern Mediterranean coast.

BY FERRY **Transmediterránea,** Moll Sant Bertran s/n (✆ **90-245-46-45**), operates daily voyages to the Balearic island of Majorca (trip time: 8 hr.) and also to Minorca (trip time: 9 hr.). In summer, it's important to have a reservation as far in advance as possible, due to overcrowding.

VISITOR INFORMATION

Barcelona has two types of tourist offices. The local government office deals with Spain in general and Catalunya in particular, with basic information about Barcelona. This organization has an office at the airport, **El Prat de Llobregat** (✆ **93-478-47-04**), which you'll pass as you clear customs. Summer hours are Monday to Saturday from 9:30am to 8:30pm; off-season hours are Monday to Saturday from 9:30am to 8pm; year-round, it's open Sunday from 9:30 to 3pm. There's another large office in the center of Barcelona at the **Palau de Rubert,** Passeig de Gràcia 107 (✆ **93-238-40-00**), where there are often exhibitions. It's open daily from 10am to 7pm.

The other organization, the **Oficina de Informació de Turisme de Barcelona,** Plaça de Catalunya 17-S (✆ **93-238-40-00,** or 906-30-12-82 from inside Spain), deals exclusively with Barcelona. The staff can help you make hotel reservations in person and by telephone (✆ **93-363-63-63**). This is also where you can obtain detailed information about the city and the Barcelona card for tourist discounts. The office is open daily from 9am to 9pm. The same organization has an office at the **Estació Central de Barcelona-Sants** (Sants railway station), Plaça Països Catalanes (no phone; Metro: Sants-Estació). In summer it's open daily from 8am to 8pm; off-season, Monday to Friday from 8am to 8pm, Saturday and Sunday from 8am to 2pm.

For more information on what's taking place in the city, call ✆ **010** Monday to Friday from 7am to 11pm and Saturday from 9am to 2pm.

CITY LAYOUT

MAIN SQUARES, STREETS & ARTERIES **Plaça de Catalunya** (Plaza de Cataluña in Spanish) is the city's heart; the world-famous **Rambles** (Ramblas) are its arteries. Rambles begin at the Plaça Portal de la Pau, with its 164-foot-high monument to Columbus and a panoramic view of the port, and stretch north to the Plaça de Catalunya, with its fountains and trees. Along this wide promenade you'll find bookshops and newsstands, stalls selling birds and flowers, and benches or cafe tables and chairs, where you can sit and watch the passing parade.

At the end of the Rambles is the **Barri Xinés** (Barrio Chino or Chinese Quarter), which has enjoyed notoriety as a haven of prostitution and drugs, populated in Jean Genet's *The Thief's Journal* by "whores, thieves, pimps, and beggars." Still a dangerous district, it is best viewed during the day, if at all.

Off the Rambles lies **Plaça Reial** (Plaza Real), the most harmoniously proportioned square in Barcelona. Come here on Sunday morning to see the stamp and coin collectors peddle their wares.

The major wide boulevards of Barcelona are the **Avinguda** (Avenida) **Diagonal** and **Passeig** (Paseo) **de Colom,** and an elegant shopping street, the **Passeig de Gràcia.**

A short walk from the Rambles will take you to the **Passeig del Moll de la Fusta,** a waterfront promenade developed in the 1990s, with some of the best (but not the cheapest) restaurants in Barcelona. If you can't afford the high prices, come here at least for a drink in the open air and to take in a view of the harbor.

To the east is the old port of the city, called **La Barceloneta,** which dates from the 18th century. This strip of land between the port and the sea has traditionally been a good place for seafood.

Barri Gòtic (Barrio Gótico, Gothic Quarter in English) lies to the east of the Rambles. This is the site of the city's oldest buildings, including the cathedral.

North of Plaça de Catalunya, the **Eixample** unfolds. An area of wide boulevards, in contrast to the labyrinthine Gothic Quarter, it contains two major roads leading out of Barcelona, the Avinguda Diagonal and Gran Vía de les Corts Catalanes. Another major neighborhood, working-class **Gràcia,** lies north of the Eixample.

Montjuïc, one of the mountains of Barcelona, begins at Plaça d'Espanya, a traffic rotary, just beyond which are Barcelona's famous fountains. Montjuïc was the setting for the principal events of the 1992 Summer Olympic Games. The other mountain is **Tibidabo,** in the northwest, which boasts great views of the city and the Mediterranean. It contains an amusement park.

FINDING AN ADDRESS/MAPS Finding an address in Barcelona can be a problem. The city is characterized by long boulevards and a complicated maze of narrow, twisting streets. Therefore, knowing the street number is all-important. If you see the designation *s/n* it means that the building has no number (*sin número*). Therefore, it's crucial to learn the cross street if you're seeking a specific address.

The rule about street numbers is that there is no rule. On most streets, numbering begins on one side and runs up that side until the end, then runs in the opposite direction on the other side. Therefore, number 40 could be opposite 408. But there are many exceptions. Sometimes street numbers on buildings in the older quarters have been obscured by the patina of time.

Arm yourself with a good map before setting out. Those given away free by tourist offices and hotels aren't adequate, since they don't label the little streets.

The best map for exploring Barcelona, published by **Falk,** is available at most bookstores and newsstands, such as those found along the Rambles. This pocket map includes all the streets, along with an index of how to find them.

NEIGHBORHOODS IN BRIEF

BARRI GÒTIC The Gothic Quarter rises to the north of Passeig de Colom, with its **Columbus Monument,** and is bordered on its east by a major artery, Via Laietana, which begins at La Barceloneta at Plaça d'Antoni López and runs north to Plaça d'Urquinaona. Les Rambles forms the western border of the Gothic Quarter, and on the northern edge is the Ronda de Sant Pere, which intersects with **Plaça de Catalunya** and the **Passeig de Gràcia.** The heart of this medieval quarter is the **Plaça de Sant Jaume,** which was a major crossroads in the old Roman city. Many of the structures in the old section are ancient, including the ruins of a Roman temple dedicated to Augustus. Antique stores, restaurants, cafes, museums, some hotels, and bookstores fill the place today. It's also the headquarters of the **Generalitat,** seat of the Catalán government.

LES RAMBLES The most famous promenade in Spain, ranking with Madrid's Paseo del Prado, was once a drainage channel. These days, street entertainers, flower vendors, news vendors, cafe patrons, and strollers flow along its length. This gradual 1.6km (1-mile) descent toward the sea has often been called "a metaphor for life," because of its bustling scene that is a combination of cosmopolitanism and crude vitality—in all, a rich, dazzling human spectacle. Les Rambles (Las Ramblas) is actually composed of five different sections, each a particular *rambla,* with names like Rambla de Canaletes, Rambla dels Estudis, Rambla de Sant Josep, Rambla dels Caputxins, and Rambla de Santa Mónica. The pedestrian esplanade is shaded as it makes its way from the Plaça de Catalunya to the port—all the way to the Columbus Monument. Along the way you'll pass the **Gran Teatre del Liceu,** on Rambla dels Caputxins, one of the most magnificent opera houses in the world until it caught fire in 1994. Miró created a sidewalk mosaic at the Plaça de la Boquería. During the stagnation of the Franco era, this street grew seedier and seedier. But the opening of the Ramada Renaissance hotel and the restoration of many buildings have brought energy and hope for the street.

BARRI XINES (EL RAVAL) Despite the name, this isn't "Chinatown," as most people assume—in fact, historians are unsure just how the neighborhood got its name. For decades it's had an unsavory reputation, known for its houses of prostitution. Franco outlawed prostitution in 1956, but apparently no one ever told the denizens of this district of narrow, often murky old streets and dark corners. Nighttime can be dangerous, so exercise caution; still, most visitors like to take a quick look to see what all the excitement is about. Just off Les Rambles, the area lies primarily between the waterfront and Carrer de l'Hospital. Although it's got a long way to go, Barri Xinés is undergoing tremendous change that began with the preparation for the 1992 Olympics. Barcelona has launched a program of urban renewal that has led to the destruction of some of the seedier parts of the barrio. The opening of the **Museu d'Art Contemporani** at

Plaça dels Angels—designed by the noted American architect Richard Meier—has led to a revitalization of the area and the opening of a lot more art galleries. The official name that Barcelona has given to the district is **El Raval.**

BARRI DE LA RIBERA Another neighborhood that stagnated for years but is now well into a renaissance, the Barri de la Ribera is adjacent to the Barri Gòtic, going east to Passeig de Picasso, which borders the Parc de la Ciutadella. The centerpiece of this district is the **Museu Picasso,** housed in the 15th-century Palau Agüilar, at Montcada 15. Numerous art galleries have opened around the museum, and the old quarter is fashionable. Many mansions in this area were built at the time of one of the major maritime expansions in Barcelona's history, principally in the 1200s and 1300s. Most of these grand homes still stand along **Carrer de Montcada** and other nearby streets.

LA BARCELONETA & THE HARBOR Although Barcelona was founded on seagoing tradition, its waterfront was in decay for years. Today, it's bursting with activity along the waterfront promenade, **Passeig del Moll de la Fusta.** The best way to get a bird's-eye view of the area is to take an elevator to the top of the Columbus Monument in Plaça Portal de la Pau.

In the vicinity of the monument were the **Reials Drassanes,** or royal shipyards, a booming place of industry during Barcelona's maritime heyday in the Middle Ages. Years before Columbus landed in the New World, ships sailed the world from here, flying the traditional yellow-and-red flag of Catalonia.

To the east lies a mainly artificial peninsula called **La Barceloneta** (Little Barcelona), formerly a fishing district, dating mainly from the 18th century. It's now filled with seafood restaurants. The blocks here are long and surprisingly narrow—architects planned them that way so that each room in every building fronted a street. Many bus lines terminate at the Passeig Nacional here, site of the **Barcelona Aquarium.**

EIXAMPLE To the north of the Plaça de Catalunya lies the Eixample, or Ensanche, the section of Barcelona that grew beyond the old medieval walls. This great period of enlargement (*eixample* in Catalán), came mainly in the 19th century. Avenues form a grid of perpendicular streets, cut across by a majestic boulevard—**Passeig de Gràcia,** a posh shopping street ideal for leisurely promenades. The area's main traffic artery is **Avinguda Diagonal,** which links the expressway and the heart of this congested city.

The Eixample was the center of Barcelona's modernismo movement, and it possesses some of the most original buildings any architect ever designed—not just those by Gaudí, but by others as well. Gaudí's Sagrada Família is one of the major attractions.

MONTJUÏC & TIBIDABO Montjuïc, called Hill of the Jews after a Jewish necropolis there, gained prominence in 1929 as the site of the World's Fair and again in 1992 as the site of the Summer Olympic Games. Its major attractions are the Joan Miró museum, the Olympic installations, and the **Poble Espanyol** (Spanish Village), a 5-acre site constructed for the World's Fair, where examples of Spanish art and architecture are displayed against the backdrop of a traditional Spanish village. Tibidabo (495m/1,650 ft.) is where you should go for your final look at

Tips: Save with The Barcelona Card

An ideal way to appreciate Barcelona better and save money at the same time is with the Barcelona card. It's definitely a bargain if you'll stay in the city for more than an afternoon and do any sightseeing at all. For 24 hours it costs 17 for adults, 14 for children 6 to 15. For 48 hours it is 20 for adults, 17 for children; for 72 hours, 23 and 20 for children.

The card offers visitors many advantages. The 24-hour card covers 10 free journeys on the Metro or bus, and the 48- and 72-hour cards offer unlimited travel on all public transport. Cardholders receive 25% discounts on the Tombbus (which runs along the best shopping route in central Barcelona) and the Tibibus (to the Fun Fair on Mount Tibidabo). On airport and tourist buses, fares are reduced by 15%.

Culture vultures with the card get discounts of 30% to 50% in 28 museums. Eleven theaters and shows grant a 10% to 25% discount, which also applies at 16 leisure and night venues. Barcelona is famous for its designers, whose work ranges from clothes to ceramics. With this card you get a 12% discount at 23 leading stores. Finally, there is an 8% discount in 11 restaurants. The cards specify where they can be used. They're for sale at the tourist offices at the airport, at Sants station, and in the Plaça de Catalunya (see "Visitor Information," above).

Barcelona. On a clear day, you can see the mountains of Majorca (the largest and most famous of the Balearic Islands). Reached by train, tram, and cable car, Tibidabo is the most popular Sunday excursion in Barcelona.

PEDRALBES Pedralbes is where wealthy Barcelonans live, some in stylish blocks of apartment houses, others in 19th-century villas behind ornamental fences, and still others in stunning modernismo structures. Set in a park, the **Palau de Pedralbes** (at Av. Diagonal 686) was constructed in the 1920s as a gift from the city to Alfonxo XIII, the grandfather of today's King Juan Carlos. The king abdicated and fled in 1931, never making much use of the palace. Today, it has a new life, housing a museum of carriages and a group of European paintings called the **Colecció Cambó.**

VILA OLIMPICA This seafront property contains the tallest buildings in the city. The revitalized site, in the post-Olympic Games era, is the setting for numerous showrooms for imported cars, designer clothing stores, restaurants, and business offices. The "village" was where the athletes lived during the 1992 games. A regular city-in-miniature is taking shape, complete with banks, art galleries, nightclubs, bars, even pastry shops.

2 Getting Around

To save money on public transportation, buy one of two transportation cards, each good for 10 trips: **Tarjeta T-1,** costing 5.86€, is good for the Metro and the bus; **Tarjeta T-2,** for 5.86€, is good on everything but the bus.

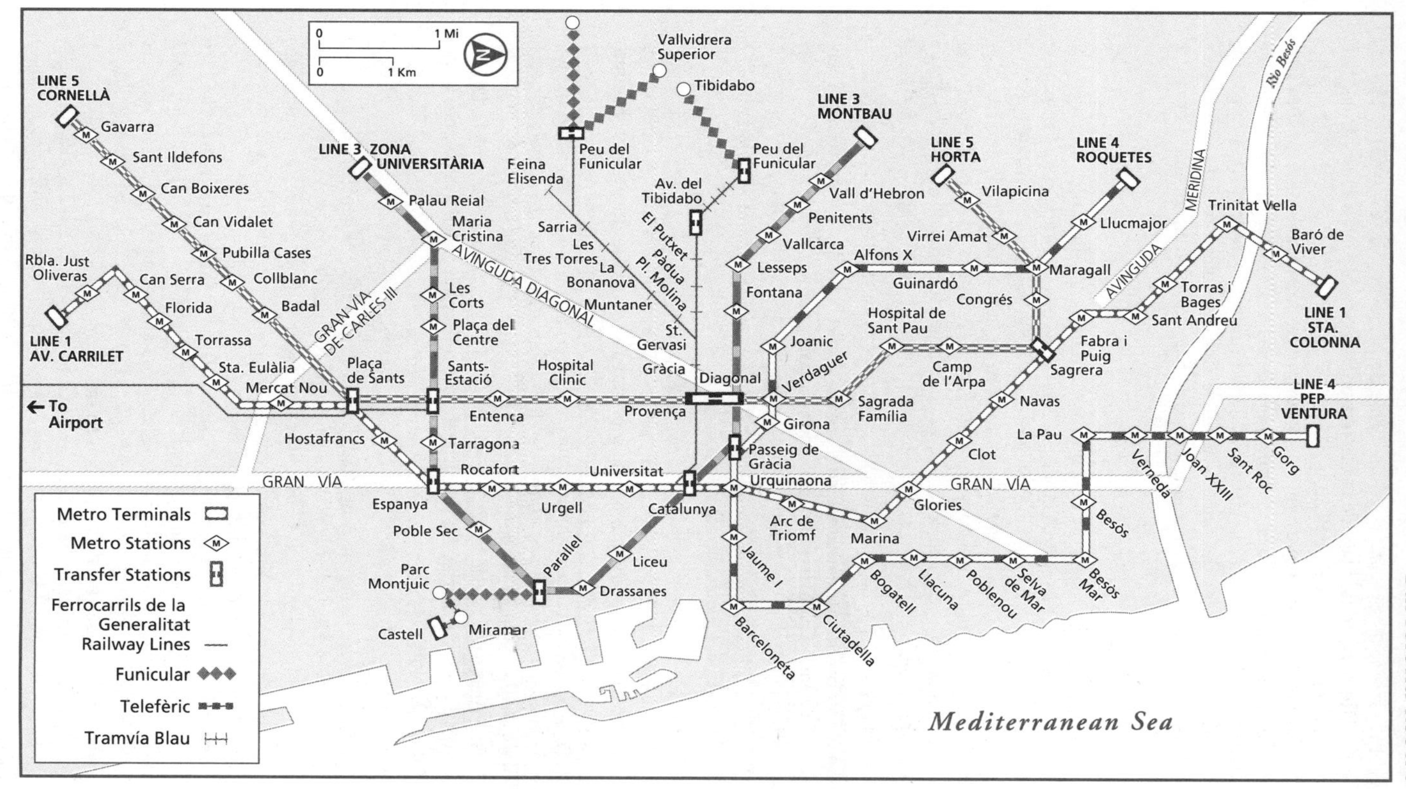

LINE 5 CORNELLÀ
Gavarra
Sant Ildefons
Can Boixeres
Can Vidalet
Pubilla Cases
Collblanc
Badal
Rbla. Just Oliveras
Can Serra
Florida
Torrassa
Sta. Eulàlia
Mercat Nou
LINE 1 AV. CARRILET
To Airport
LINE 3 ZONA UNIVERSITÀRIA
Palau Reial
Maria Cristina
Les Corts
Plaça del Centre
Sants-Estació
Plaça de Sants
Hostafrancs
Espanya
Poble Sec
Parc Montjuic
Castell
Miramar
Paral·lel
Drassanes
Liceu
Catalunya
Universitat
Urgell
Rocafort
Tarragona
Entença
Hospital Clinic
Provença
Diagonal
Feina Elisenda
Sarria
Les Tres Torres
La Bonanova
Muntaner
St. Gervasi
Gràcia
Pl. Molina
Pàdua
El Putxet
Av. del Tibidabo
Peu del Funicular
Vallvidrera Superior
Tibidabo
Peu del Funicular
LINE 3 MONTBAU
Vall d'Hebron
Penitents
Vallcarca
Lesseps
Fontana
Joanic
Verdaguer
Girona
Passeig de Gràcia
Urquinaona
Jaume I
Barceloneta
Ciutadella
Bogatell
Llacuna
Poblenou
Selva de Mar
Besòs Mar
Besòs
La Pau
Verneda
Joan XXIII
Sant Roc
Gorg
LINE 4 PEP VENTURA
LINE 5 HORTA
Vilapicina
Virrei Amat
Maragall
Alfons X
Guinardó
Congrés
Hospital de Sant Pau
Camp de l'Arpa
Sagrada Família
LINE 4 ROQUETES
Llucmajor
Trinitat Vella
Baró de Viver
Torras i Bages
Sant Andreu
LINE 1 STA. COLONNA
Fabra i Puig
Sagrera
Navas
Clot
Glories
Marina
Arc de Triomf
Río Besós
AVINGUDA MERIDIANA
GRAN VÍA
AVINGUDA DIAGONAL
GRAN VÍA DE CARLES III
Mediterranean Sea
0 1 Mi
0 1 Km
N
Metro Terminals
Metro Stations
Transfer Stations
Ferrocarrils de la Generalitat Railway Lines
Funicular
Telefèric
Tramvía Blau

Passes (*abonos temporales*) are available at the office of **Transports Metropolita de Barcelona,** Plaça de la Universitat, open Monday to Friday from 8am to 5pm and Saturday from 8am to 1pm.

To save money on sightseeing tours during summer, take a ride on **Bus Turistic,** which passes by 24 of the most popular sights. You can get on and off the bus as you please and also ride the Tibidabo funicular and the Montjuïc cable car and funicular for the price of a single ticket. Tickets, which may be purchased on the bus or at the tourist office at Plaça de Catalunya, cost 14€ for 1 day or 18€ for 2 days.

BY SUBWAY

Barcelona's Metro system consists of five main lines; it crisscrosses the city more frequently and with greater efficiency than the bus network. Two commuter trains also service the city, fanning out to the suburbs. Service is Monday to Friday from 5am to 11pm, Saturday from 5am to 1am, and Sunday and holidays from 6am to 1am. A one-way fare is .85€. The entrance to each Metro station is marked with a red diamond. The major station for all subway lines is **Plaça de Catalunya.**

BY BUS

Some 50 bus lines traverse the city, and as always, you don't want to ride them at rush hour. The driver issues a ticket as you board at the front. Most buses operate daily from 6:30am to 10pm; some night buses go along the principal arteries 11pm to 4am. Buses are color-coded—red ones cut through the city center during the day, and yellow ones do the job at night. A one-way fare is 1€.

BY TAXI

Each yellow-and-black taxi bears the letters SP (*servicio público*) on both its front and its rear. A lit green light on the roof and a "Libre" sign in the window indicate that the taxi is free to pick up passengers. The basic rate begins at 1.25€. Check to make sure you're not paying the fare of a previously departed passenger; taxi drivers have been known to "forget" to turn back the meter. For each additional kilometer in slow-moving traffic, you are assessed .45€ to .65€. Supplements might also be added—.80€ for a large suitcase that is placed in the trunk, for instance. Rides to the airport carry a supplement of 1.80€. For a taxi, call ✆ **93-330-08-04.**

BY CAR

Driving is frustrating in congested Barcelona, and it's potentially dangerous. Besides, it's unlikely that you'd ever find a place to park. Try other means of getting around. Save your car rentals for 1-day excursions from the Catalonian capital to such places as Sitges and Tarragona to the south, Montserrat to the west, or the resorts of the Costa Brava to the north.

All three of the major U.S.-based car-rental firms are represented in Barcelona, both at the airport and often (except for Budget) at downtown offices. The company with the longest hours and some of the most favorable rates is the airport office of **Budget** (✆ **93-410-25-08**), open Monday to Friday (without a midday break) from 7am to midnight.

Other contenders include **Avis,** Calle Corcega 293 (✆ **93-237-56-80**), open Monday to Friday from 8am to 2pm and 4 to 7pm, and Saturday from 9am to 1pm. **Hertz** maintains its office at Tuset 10 (✆ **93-217-80-76**); it's open Monday to Friday from 8am to 2pm and 4 to 7pm, and Saturday from 9am to 1pm.

Both Hertz and Avis are closed on Sunday, forcing clients of those companies to trek out to the airport to pick up or return their cars; however, after-hours arrangements can be made by request.

Remember that it's usually cheaper and easier to arrange your car rental before leaving North America by calling one of the firms' toll-free numbers.

BY FUNICULAR & RAIL LINK

At some point in your journey, you may want to visit Tibidabo or Montjuïc (or both). A train called **Tramvía Blau** (Blue Streetcar) goes from Plaça Kennedy to the bottom of the funicular to Tibidabo. It operates every 15 to 20 minutes from 9:05am to 9:35pm on weekends only. The fare is 2€ one-way, 3€ round-trip. During the week, buses run from the Plaça Kennedy to the bottom of the funicular from approximately 7am to 9:30pm daily. The bus costs .90€ one-way.

At the end of the run, you can go the rest of the way by funicular to the top, at 503m (1,650 ft.), for a stunning panoramic view of Barcelona. The funicular operates only when the Fun Fair at Tibidabo is open. Opening times vary according to the time of year and the weather conditions. As a rule, the funicular starts operating 20 minutes before the Fun Fair opens, then every half an hour. During peak visiting hours, it runs every 15 minutes. The fare is 2€ one-way, 3€ round-trip.

The **Tibibus** (✆ **93-211-79-42**) goes from the Plaça de Catalunya, in the center of the city, to Tibidabo from June 24 to September 15, Tuesday to Sunday, and on every weekend out of season. It runs every 30 minutes from 10:30am to 6:30pm and sometimes 8:30pm, depending on when the park closes. The one-way fare is 1.60€. To reach Montjuïc, the site of the 1992 Olympics, take the **Montjuïc funicular** (✆ **93-318-70-74**). It links with subway line 3 at Paral.lel. The funicular operates June 13 to September 30 daily from 11am to 10pm. In winter it operates daily from 10:45am to 8pm. The round-trip fare is 3.60€.

A **cable car** linking the upper part of the Montjuïc funicular with Castell de Montjuïc is in service in winter, daily from 11:15am to 6:30pm (until 7:30pm on weekends). The one-way fare is 2.40€; the round-trip fare is 3.60€ for adults, 3€ for children. From June 28 to September 15 and holidays it operates Monday to Friday from 11:15am to 8pm, until 9pm on weekends.

The **Montjuïc telèferic** (cable car) runs from Barceloneta to Montjuïc. Service from June 20 through September 15 is daily from 10:30am to 7pm, and noon to 5pm in winter. The fare is 6€ one-way, 7€ round-trip.

FAST FACTS: Barcelona

American Express For your mail or banking needs, the American Express office in Barcelona is at Passeig de Gràcia 101 (✆ **93-255-00-70;** Metro: Diagonal), near the corner of Carrer del Rosselló. It's open Monday to Friday from 10am to 6pm and Saturday from 9:30am to noon.

Babysitters Most major hotels can arrange for babysitters with adequate notice. You'll have to make a special request for an English-speaking babysitter.

Bookstores The best selection of English-language books, including travel maps and guides, is at LAIE, Pau Claris 85 (✆ **93-318-17-39;** Metro: Plaça de Catalunya or Urquinaona), 1 block from the Gran Vía de les Corts Catalanes. It's open Monday to Friday from 10am to 9pm and Saturday from 10:30am to 9pm. The bookshop has an upstairs cafe with international newspapers and a little terrace, serving breakfast, lunch (salad bar), even dinners. The cafe is open Monday to Saturday from 9am to 1am. The shop also presents cultural events, including art exhibits and literary presentations.

Consulates The **U.S. Consulate,** Reina Elisenda 23 (© **93-280-22-27;** train: Reina Elisenda), is open Monday to Friday from 9am to 12:30pm and 3 to 5pm. The **Canadian Consulate,** Calle Eiisenda de Pinos (© **93-204-27-00;** Metro: Reina Elisenda) is open Monday to Friday from 10am to noon. The **U.K. Consulate,** Av. Diagonal 477 (© **93-366-62-00;** Metro: Hospital Clínic), is open Monday to Friday from 9:30am to 1:30pm and 4 to 5pm. The **Australian Consulate** is at Gran Vía Carlos III 98, 9th floor (© **93-330-94-96;** Metro: María Cristina), and is open Monday to Friday from 10am to noon.

Currency Exchange Most banks will exchange currency Monday to Friday from 8:30am to 2pm and Saturday from 8:30am to 1pm. Saturday hours are not valid in summer. A major *oficina de cambio* (exchange office) is at the Estació Central de Barcelona-Sants, the principal rail station for Barcelona. It's open Monday to Saturday from 8:30am to 10pm, Sunday from 8:30am to 2pm and 4:30 to 10pm. Exchange offices are also available at Barcelona's airport, El Prat de Llobregat, open daily from 7am to 11pm.

Dentists Call Clínica Dental Beonadex, Paseo Bona Nova 69, 3rd Floor (© **93-418-44-33**), for an appointment. It's open Monday from 3 to 9pm and Tuesday to Friday from 8am to 3pm.

Doctors See "Hospitals," below.

Drugstores The most central one is Farmacia Manuel Nadal i Casas, Rambla de Canaletes 121 (© **93-317-49-42;** Metro: Plaça de Catalunya), open daily from 9am to 1:30pm and 4:30 to 10pm. Various pharmacies take turns staying open late at night. Pharmacies that aren't open post the names and addresses of the pharmacies in the area that are open.

Emergencies In case of fire, call © **080;** for the police, © **092;** and for an ambulance, © **061.**

Hospitals Barcelona has many hospitals and clinics, including the Hospital Clínic and the Hospital de la Santa Creu i Sant Pau, at the intersection of Carrer Cartagena and Carrer Sant Antoni María Claret (© **93-291-90-00;** Metro: Hospital de Sant Pau).

Internet Access **Conéctate,** Calle Pau Claris 134 (© **93-467-04-43**), is open 7 days a week, 24 hours a day; the minimum cost for access is 1.20€.

Laundry Ask at your hotel for the one nearest you, or try one of the following: Lavandería Brasilia, Av. Meridiana 322 (© **93-352-72-05;** Metro: Plaça de Catalunya), is open Monday to Friday from 9:30am to 1:30pm and 4 to 8pm. Also centrally located is Lavandería Yolanda, Carrer Carma 114 (© **93-329-43-68;** Metro: Liceu, at Les Rambles); it's open Monday to Friday from 9am to 1:30pm and 4 to 8pm, Saturday from 9am to 1:30pm.

Newspapers & Magazines The *International Herald-Tribune* is sold at major hotels and nearly all the news kiosks along Les Rambles. Sometimes you can also obtain copies of *USA Today* or one of the London newspapers, such as the *Times.* The two leading daily newspapers of Barcelona, which often list cultural events, are *El Periódico* and *La Vanguardia.*

Police In an emergency, dial ✆ **092.**

Post Office The main post office is at Plaça d'Antoni López (✆ **93-318-38-31;** Metro: Jaume I). It's open Monday to Friday from 8am to 10pm and on Saturday from 8am to 8pm.

Radio & TV If your hotel room has a radio or a TV set (unlikely in budget accommodations), you can often get Britain's BBC World Service. Deluxe and some first-class hotels subscribe to CNN. Two national TV channels (1 and 2) transmit broadcasts in Spanish, and two regional channels (3 and 33) broadcast in Catalán; there are also some private TV channels, such as Canal +. If you're listening to radio, tune in to the Spanish music program, "Segundo Programa," with everything from classical music to jazz (nights only).

Restrooms Some public restrooms are available, including those at popular tourist spots, such as Tibidabo and Montjuïc. You'll also find restrooms at the major museums of Barcelona, at all train stations and airports, and at Metro stations. The major department stores, such as El Corte Ingles, also have good restrooms. Otherwise, out on the streets you may be a bit hard-pressed. Sanitation is questionable in some of the public facilities. If you use the facilities of a cafe or tavern, it's customary to make a small purchase at the bar, even if only a glass of mineral water.

Safety Be particularly careful with cameras, purses, and wallets, all favorite targets of thieves and pickpockets in Barcelona; particularly on the world-famous Rambles. The southern part of Les Rambles, near the waterfront, is the most dangerous section, especially at night. Proceed with caution.

Taxes If you're not a European Union (EU) resident and you make purchases in Spain worth more than 90€, you can get a tax refund. (The internal tax, known as VAT [value-added tax] in most of Europe, is called IVA in Spain.) Depending on the goods, the rate usually ranges from 7% to 16% of the total worth of your merchandise. Luxury items are taxed at 33%.

To get this refund, you must complete three copies of a form that the store will give you, detailing the nature of your purchase and its value. Citizens of non-EU countries show the purchase and the form to the Spanish Customs Office. The shop is supposed to refund the amount due you. Inquire at the time of purchase how they will do so and discuss in what currency your refund will arrive.

Telegrams & Telex These can be sent at the main post office (above). You can also send telex and fax messages at all major and many budget hotels.

Telephones If you don't speak Spanish, you may find it easier to telephone from your hotel, but remember that this is often very expensive because hotels impose a surcharge on every operator-assisted call. In some cases this can be as high as 40% or more. On the street, phone booths (known as *cabinas*) have dialing instructions in English; you can make local calls by inserting a .15€ coin for 3 minutes.

In Spain many smaller establishments, especially bars, discos, and a few informal restaurants, don't have phones. Further, many summer-only bars and discos secure a phone for the season only, then get a new number the next season. Many attractions, such as small churches or even minor museums, have no staff to receive inquiries from the public.

In 1998, all telephone numbers in Spain changed to a nine-digit system instead of the six- or seven-digit method used previously. Each number is now preceded by its provincial code for local, national, and international calls. For example, when calling to Barcelona from Barcelona or another province within Spain, telephone customers must dial 93-123-45-67.

To call Spain from another country, first dial the international long-distance code (011) plus the country code (34), followed by the 9-digit number. Hence, when calling Barcelona from the United States, dial (011-34) 93-123-45-67.

To make an international call from Spain, you must dial 07, followed by the country code, the area code, and the telephone number. When in Spain, the access number for an **AT&T** calling card is ✆ **1-800-CALL-ATT.** The access number for **Sprint** is ✆ **800/888-0013.** More information is also available on the Telefónica website at www.telefonica.es.

Tipping Don't overtip. The government requires restaurants and hotels to include their service charges—usually 15% of the bill. However, that doesn't mean you should skip out of a place without dispensing some extra pesetas. The following are some guidelines:

Your hotel porter should get .50€ per bag and never less than .75€, even if you have only one suitcase. Maids should be given 1€ per day, more if you're generous. Tip doormen 1€ for assisting with baggage and .40€ for calling a cab. In top-ranking hotels the concierge will often submit a separate bill, showing charges for newspapers and other services; if he or she has been particularly helpful, tip extra. For cab drivers, add about 10% to the fare as shown on the meter. At airports, such as Barajas in Madrid and major terminals, the porter who handles your luggage will present you with a fixed-charge bill.

In both restaurants and nightclubs, a 15% service charge is added to the bill. To that, add another 3% to 5% tip, depending on the quality of the service. Waiters in deluxe restaurants and nightclubs are accustomed to the extra 5%, which means you'll end up tipping 20%. If that seems excessive, you must remember that the initial service charge reflected in the fixed price is distributed among all the help.

Barbers and hairdressers expect a 10% to 15% tip. Tour guides expect 1.25€, although a tip is not mandatory. Theater and bullfight ushers get from .40€ to .50€.

3 Where to Stay

The hotel offerings in Barcelona have never been better or as plentiful as they are now. In the wake of the 1992 Olympics, old palaces were restored and converted into hotels, and long-seedy and tarnished hotels were renovated in time for the games. Since then, even more hotels have opened. The result is an abundance of good hotels in all price ranges. Along with Madrid, Barcelona still ranks as one of the most expensive cities in Spain, but the tariffs charged by its first-class and deluxe hotels are completely in line with other major cities of continental Europe, and reasonable in price when stacked up against such cities as Paris and London. A favorable exchange rate in relation to the U.S. dollar also makes these prices more affordable.

Safety is an important factor to consider when choosing a hotel in Barcelona. Some of the least expensive hotels are not in good locations. A popular area for the budget-conscious traveler is the **Barri Gòtic** (Gothic Quarter), located in the heart of town. You'll live and eat less expensively here than in any other part of Barcelona—but you should be careful when returning to your hotel late at night.

More modern, but also more expensive, accommodations can be found north of the Barri Gòtic in the **Eixample district,** centered around the Metro stops Plaça de Catalunya and Universitat. Although many buildings are *modernista,* from the first two decades of this century, sometimes the elevators and plumbing tend to be of the same vintage. The Eixample is a desirable and safe neighborhood, especially along its wide boulevards. Noise is the only problem you might encounter.

Farther north still, above the Avinguda Diagonal, you'll enter the **Gràcia area,** where you can enjoy distinctively Catalán neighborhood life. You'll be a bit away from the main attractions, but they can be reached easily by public transportation.

Many of Barcelona's hotels were built before the invention of the automobile, and even those built later rarely found space for a garage. When parking is available at the hotel, the price is indicated; otherwise, the hotel staff will direct you to a garage somewhere in the general vicinity. Expect to pay upwards of 14€ for 24 hours; you might as well park your car, as you can't see traffic-congested Barcelona comfortably by automobile—rely on your trusty feet and public transportation instead.

CIUTAT VELLA

The Ciutat Vella ("Old City" in Catalán) forms the monumental center of Barcelona, taking in Les Rambles, Plaça de Sant Jaume, Via Laietana, Passeig Nacional, and Passeig de Colom. In its older structures it contains some of the city's best hotel bargains. Most of the glamorous and more expensive hotels are in Sur Diagonal (p. 70).

VERY EXPENSIVE

Le Meridien Barcelona ★★★ This is the finest hotel in the old town of Barcelona, a fact to which guests such as Michael Jackson can surely attest. It is superior in both amenities and comfort to its two closest rivals in the area: Colón and Rivoli Ramblas. Built in 1956, in the darkest days of the Franco regime, it was for years called the Hotel Manila and remained a lackluster choice. Then it was completely renovated and opened as the Ramada Renaissance in 1988. Finally, in 1991, the French-owned Meridien chain took over. It's now a medley of artful pastels and tasteful decorating. Guest rooms are spacious and comfortable, with such amenities as extra-large beds, heated bathroom floors, in-house videos, two phones, and double-glazed windows. However, that doesn't prevent noise from Les Rambles from penetrating the rooms.) The Renaissance Club—an executive floor popular with businesspeople—provides extra amenities.

Les Rambles 111, 08002 Barcelona. ✆ **800/543-4300** in the U.S., or 93-318-62-00. Fax 93-301-77-76. www.meridienbarcelona.com. 212 units. 300€–330€ double; from 505€ suite. AE, DC, MC, V. Parking 18€. Metro: Liceu. **Amenities:** Restaurant; bar; health club; room service; babysitting; laundry/dry cleaning. *In room:* A/C, TV, minibar, hair dryer, safe.

Central Barcelona Accommodations

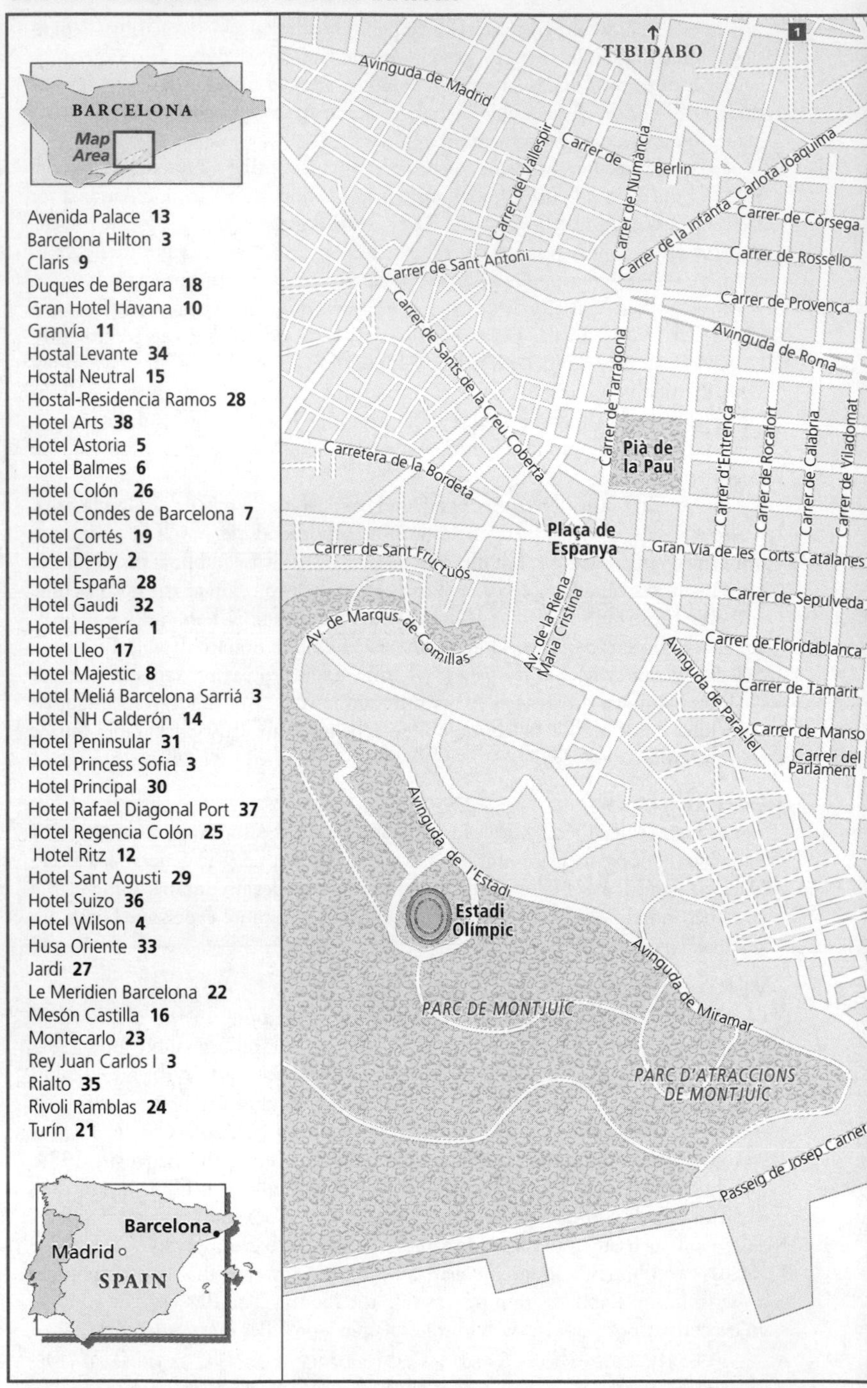

Plaça de Francesc Macia
Travessara de Gràcia
Carrer de Buenos Aires
Carrer de Londres
Carrer de Paris
Avinguda Diagonal
Carrer de Còrsega
EIXAMPLE
Carrer de Provença
Carrer de Rossello
Av. de Sant Antoni Maria Claret
Carrer de la Industria
Carrer de Roger de Flor
Plaça de la Sagrada Família
Carrer de Mallorca
Carrer de Valencia
Carrer d'Aragó
Carrer de Balmes
Rambla de Catalunya
Passeig de Gràcia
Carrer de Pau Claris
Carrer de Comte Borrell
Carrer del Comte d'Urgell
Carrer de Villarroel
Carrer de Casanova
Carrer de Muntaner
Carrer d'Aribau
Carrer del Consell de Cent
Carrer de la Diputació
Gran Vía de les Corts Catalanes
Plaça de la Universitat
Carrer de R. de Llúcia
Carrer del Bruc
Carrer de Girona
Carrer de Bailèn
Passeig de Sant Joan
Carrer de Napols
Carrer de Sicilia
Plaça de Tetuan
Ronda Universitat
Carrer de Pelai
Ronda de Sant Antoni
Plaça Catalunya
Plaça Urquinaona
Carrer de Casp
Carrer d'Ausias Marc
Carrer d'Ali Bei
Ronda de Sant Pere
Carrer de Ribes
Carrer de Sardenya
Passeig de Carles I
RAVAL
Ronda Sant Pau
Carrer de Hospital
Av. Portal de l'Angel
Via Laietana
La Rambla
BARRI GÒTIC
Carrer de Sant Pau
Carrer de Ferran
Carrer de la Princesa
Carrer de Comerc
Passeig de Luis Companys
Passeig de Pujades
Carrer Nou de la Rambla
Avinguda de les Drassanes
LA RIBERA
Passeig de Picasso
PARC DE LA CIUTADELLA
Carrer de Wellington
Carrer Ample
Passeig de Colom
PARC ZOOLOGIC
Villa Olimpic
Plaça Portal de la Pau
Moll de la Fusta
Moll d'Espanya
Avinguda d'Icàvia
BARCELONETA
0 1/4 mi
0 0.25 km
2 3 4 5 6 7 8 9 10 11 12 13 14 15 16 17 18 19 20 21 22 23 24 25 26 27 28 29 30 31 32 33 34 35 36 37 38

EXPENSIVE

Hotel Colón ★★ Kids The Colón is an appropriate choice if you plan to spend a lot of time exploring Barcelona's medieval neighborhoods. Blessed with what might be the most dramatic location in the city, immediately opposite the main entrance to the cathedral, this hotel sits behind a dignified neoclassical facade graced with carved pilasters and ornamental wrought-iron balustrades. Inside, you'll find conservative and slightly old-fashioned public spaces, a helpful staff, and guest rooms filled with comfortable furniture and, despite recent renovations, an appealingly dowdy charm. Although not all rooms have views, all have private bathrooms with shower-tub combinations; the units in back are quieter. Sixth-floor rooms with balconies overlooking the square are the most desirable; some of the lower rooms are rather dark.

Av. de la Catedral 7, 08002 Barcelona. ✆ **800/845-0636** in the U.S., or 93-301-14-04. Fax 93-317-29-15. www.hotelcolon.es. 145 units. 180€–240€ double; from 340€ suite. AE, DC, MC, V. Bus: 16, 17, 19, or 45. **Amenities:** Restaurant; bar; room service; babysitting; laundry/dry cleaning. *In room:* A/C, TV, minibar, hair dryer, safe.

Hotel NH Calderón ★ Efficient, well-maintained, and well-staffed with a multilingual corps of employees, this hotel will deliver exactly what it promises: safe and comfortable accommodations in a well-conceived, standardized format that's akin to many other modern hotels around the world. Originally built in the 1960s in a high-rise, 10-story style that wasn't particularly imaginative, this hotel was greatly improved in the early 1990s after its acquisition by NH, with frequent renovations ever since. Accommodations contain comfortable, contemporary-looking furnishings with hints of high-tech design, good lighting, lots of varnished hardwood, and colorful fabrics. All units also come with well-maintained bathrooms with shower-tub combinations.

Rambla de Catalunya 26, 08007 Barcelona. ✆ **93-301-00-00.** Fax 93-412-41-93. www.nh-hoteles.es. 235 units. Mon–Thurs 213€ double; Fri–Sun 166€ double. AE, DC, MC, V. Parking 14€. Metro: Passeig de Gràcia or Plaça de Catalunya. **Amenities:** Restaurant; bar; pool; health club; sauna; room service; babysitting; laundry/dry cleaning. *In room:* A/C, TV, minibar, hair dryer, safe.

Rivoli Ramblas ★ Behind a dignified, Art Deco town house on the upper section of the Rambles, a block south of the Plaça de Catalunya, this recently renovated hotel incorporates many fine examples of avant-garde Catalán design into its stylish interior. The Colón has more tradition and style, and the Meridien more modern comfort; this is choice number three in the old town. Still, the public rooms glisten with polished marble and a pristinely contrived minimalism. Guest rooms are carpeted, soundproof, and elegant, although rather cramped for the price. Along with well-kept bathrooms equipped with shower-tub combinations, guest rooms boast such electronic extras as VCRs, radios, and TVs with satellite hookups.

Les Rambles 128, 08002 Barcelona. ✆ **93-302-66-43.** Fax 93-317-50-53. www.rivolihotels.com. 87 units. 180€ double; from 300€ suite. Rates include breakfast. AE, DC, MC, V. Metro: Plaça de Catalunya or Liceu. **Amenities:** Restaurant; bar; health spa; sauna; car rental; room service; babysitting; laundry/dry cleaning; solarium. *In room:* A/C, TV, minibar, hair dryer, safe.

MODERATE

Duques de Bergara ★ This upscale hotel occupies what was originally built in 1899 as the private town house of the Duke of Bergara. In 1998, the original five-story structure was more than doubled in size with the addition of a new seven-story tower, where bedrooms are outfitted with the same conservatively

Family-Friendly Hotels

Hotel Colón (p. 64) Opposite the cathedral in the Gothic Quarter, this hotel has been compared to a country home. Families ask for and often get spacious rooms.

Hotel Hespería (p. 73) At the northern edge of the city, this hotel lies in a safe neighborhood setting. The rooms are generous enough in size for an extra bed.

traditional comforts that appear within units in the older wing. All of the units are large in size with good lighting and well-maintained marble bathrooms with shower-tub combinations. Public areas manage to artfully contain most of the paneling, stained glass, and decorative accessories originally installed by the modernista architect who designed the place, Emilio Salas i Cortes, a professor of the movement's greatest luminary, Gaudí. In the hotel's reception area, look for stained-glass panels containing the heraldic coat of arms of the building's original occupant and namesake, the Duke of Bergara.

Bergara 11, 08002 Barcelona. ✆ **93-301-51-51.** Fax 93-317-34-42. 149 units. 180€ double; 228€ triple. AE, DC, MC, V. Public parking nearby 18€. Metro: Plaça de Catalunya. **Amenities:** Restaurant; bar; cafe; pool; room service; babysitting; laundry/dry cleaning. *In room:* A/C, TV, minibar, hair dryer, safe.

Hotel Gaudí This is one of the most centrally located hotels in Barcelona and is named to honor the city's most famous architect. In remembrance, the hotel has a Gaudí-inspired lobby and cafe-bar. The bedrooms, however, don't carry through on this theme, and are furnished in a simple yet comfortable modern, each with a tiled bathroom with shower. We prefer one of the units that open onto views of Gaudí's Palau Güell or else one of the bedrooms with a large terrace (these are booked first, of course). The hotel, an eyesore for a long time, has been totally refurbished. There is a pleasant bar and lounge, plus a fast food cafeteria on site that's open until midnight. The original architecture of this antique building was respected in part, with an authentic old monastery vault at the entrance.

Carrer Nou de la Rambla 12 08001 Barcelona. ✆ **93-317-90-32.** Fax 93-412-26-36. www.hotelgaudi.es. 73 units. 113€ double, 139€ suite. Rates include breakfast. AE, DC, MC, V. Parking: 12€. Metro: Liceu. **Amenities:** Bar; room service; laundry. *In room:* A/C, TV, safe.

Hotel Regencia Colón ★ *Value* This stately stone six-story building stands directly behind the more prestigious, superior, and more expensive Hotel Colón—both lie in the shadow of the cathedral. The Regencia Colón is attractive to tour groups. The formal lobby seems a bit dour, but the well-maintained rooms are comfortable and often spacious, albeit worn. All units are insulated against sound, and 40 of them have full tub baths (the remainder have showers). All have piped-in music. The hotel's location at the edge of the Barri Gòtic is a plus. Considering what you get for the reasonable prices charged, the hotel is a good value for Barcelona.

Sagristans 13–17, 08002 Barcelona. ✆ **93-318-98-58.** Fax 93-317-28-22. www.hotelregenciacolon.com. 55 units. 145€ double; 170€ triple. AE, DC, MC, V. Metro: Plaça de Catalunya or Urquinaona. **Amenities:** Bar; babysitting; laundry/dry cleaning. *In room:* A/C, TV, minibar, hair dryer, safe.

INEXPENSIVE

Granvía A grand hotel on one of the most fashionable boulevards in Barcelona, the Granvía has public rooms that reflect the opulence of the 1860s—chandeliers, gilt mirrors, and French provincial furniture—and a grand balustraded staircase. It's your best choice if you want to feel like royalty. Although the traditional guest rooms contain interesting antique reproductions, they are comfortable rather than luxurious. Expect fancifully shaped headboards and pastel-colored chenille bedspreads along with upholstery that could use refreshing. The courtyard, which has a fountain and palm trees, is set with tables for alfresco drinks; continental breakfast is served in the garden room off the courtyard. Centrally heated in the winter, the hotel has one drawback: street noise, which might disturb the light sleeper.

Gran Vía de les Corts Catalanes 642, 08007 Barcelona. ✆ **93-318-19-00.** Fax 93-318-99-97. www.nnhotels.es. 50 units. 100€ double. AE, DC, MC, V. Parking 20€. Metro: Plaça de Catalunya. **Amenities:** Room service; laundry/dry cleaning. *In room:* A/C, TV, minibar, safe.

Hostal Gat Raval *Value* When euros are running low, this newly created *hostal* will furnish you a decent bed at a very affordable price for the night. The location in the heart of old Barcelona means that much of what you want to see will be within an easy walk of the funky green doors of this establishment, which is especially popular with a young, international crowd. Many of the front rooms overlook the landmark Plaça dels Angels. Accommodations facing Carrer Joaquin Costa get a lot of traffic noise. Bedrooms are simply furnished with functional modern pieces. Many of the units don't have private bathrooms but shared facilities in the hallways are generally adequate.

Carrer Joaquin Costa 44, 08001 Barcelona. ✆ **93-481-66-70.** Fax 93-342-66-97. www.gataccommodation.com. 24 units, 6 with bathroom. 49€ double without bathroom, 67€ double with bathroom. AE, MC, V. Parking: 9€. Metro: Plaça Universidad. **Amenities:** Hair dryer in lobby. *In room:* TV.

Hostal Levante ★★ This is one of the nicest and most reasonably priced places to stay in Barcelona. In a quiet, imposing building more than two centuries old, it stands just a short distance from Plaça de Sant Jaume, in the center of the Barri Gòtic. The units are clean and comfortable, and there's central heating and a well-kept bathroom with a shower unit. The staff speaks English. No meals are served.

Baïxada de Sant Miguel 2, 08002 Barcelona. ✆ **93-317-95-65.** www.hostallevante.com. 38 units. 35€ double without bathroom; 40€ double with bathroom. MC, V. Metro: Liceu or Jaume I. **Amenities:** Lounge; laundry. *In room:* A/C, TV.

Hostal-Residencia Ramos This pension, noted for its comfortable but cheap bedrooms, occupies the second and third floor of an antique building that still has its old-fashioned tile-clad entrance and a charming baroque-like staircase. It's seen a few renovations in past years, but still maintains its quaint charm. It overlooks the classic Plaça Sant Augustí. Rambla attractions are right at your doorstep if you stay here. Rooms are medium in size and come with small bathrooms with shower. The best units are two outside corner rooms with balconies overlooking the bustling square.

Carrer Hospital 36, 08001 Barcelona. ✆ **93-302-07-23.** Fax 93-302-04-30. www.net4.com/barcelona-hotels. 23 units. 62€ double, 105€ suite. DC, MC, V. Parking: 16€. Metro: Liceu. **Amenities:** Room service; laundry. *In room:* A/C, TV, safe.

Hotel Cortés A short walk from the cathedral, the Cortés was originally built around 1910 and, like many of its competitors in Barcelona, was thoroughly renovated in time for the 1992 Olympics. It competes effectively against the Continental. Guest rooms are scattered over five floors, and about half overlook a quiet central courtyard (the other half open onto the street). All units come with private bathrooms, most of which contain shower-tub combinations. The hotel's ground floor contains a simple, unpretentious restaurant and bar, where breakfast is served and where you can enjoy a beer throughout the day and night.

Santa Ana 25, 08002 Barcelona. ✆ **93-317-91-12.** Fax 93-412-66-08. 44 units. 70€–90€ double. Rates include breakfast. AE, DC, MC, V. Metro: Plaça de Catalunya. **Amenities:** Restaurant; bar; room service; laundry/dry cleaning. *In room:* A/C, TV, safe.

Hotel España Although the rooms at this cost-conscious hotel have none of the architectural grandeur of Barcelona's modernist age, they're well-scrubbed, comfortably sized, functional, and outfitted with functional furniture and well-kept bathrooms with shower-tub combinations. The building itself is a relic of the city's turn-of-the-century splendor, constructed in 1902 by fabled architect Domenech I Montaner, designer and architect of the Palau de la Música. There's an elevator that can carry you up the building's four floors; a facade that still evokes the past; and a hard-working staff that's comfortable with foreign, non-Spanish-speaking visitors. The lower Rambla, near which this hotel sits, evokes either cultural fascination or indignation, depending on how urbanized you are, but overall, it's an acceptable and well-managed choice at a relatively reasonable price. There's a restaurant on the premises, the España, open daily for lunch and dinner, and serves food and drink to locals and hotel residents alike.

Carrer Sant Pau 11, 08002 Barcelona. ✆ **93-318-17-58.** Fax 93-317-11-34. 60 units. 59€–83€ double. AE, DC, MC, V. Metro: Liceu or Drassanes. **Amenities:** 2 restaurants; lounge; room service. *In room:* A/C, TV, hair dryer, safe.

Hotel Peninsular *Value* In a converted nunnery just off Les Rambles, this converted hotel in the Art Nouveau style is a welcoming haven for the budget traveler. Constructed within the shell of a former monastery, which had a passageway connecting it to Sant Agusti church, the hotel was thoroughly modernized in the early 1990s. Its use of wicker furnishings still lends somewhat of a colonial aura, and its inner courtyard, lined with plants, is its most attractive grace note. In the typical Modernist style of its era, the Peninsular still has long hallways, high doorways and ceilings. The bedrooms are well maintained but rather simply, though comfortably furnished, each with a bathroom with shower.

Sant Pau 34–36, 08001 Barcelona. ✆ **93-302-31-38.** Fax 93-412-36-99. 59 units. 78€. MC, V. Rates include breakfast. MC, V. Metro: Liceu. **Amenities:** Restaurant; bar. *In room:* A/C, TV, safe.

Hotel Principal Although right off the Rambla, this is a fairly tranquil hotel even though in a busy area. A favorite of the frugal traveler, it was recently renovated, and is furnished quite ornately. All of the bathrooms are modernized, each with bath and shower. The owners of Principal also own the slightly less expensive Joventut Hotel, which is linked to the main building.

Carrer Junta de Comerç 8, 08001 Barcelona. ✆ **93-318-89-74.** Fax 93-412-08-19. www.hotelprincipal.es. 108 units. 80.60€ double, 106.50€ triple, 132€ quad. AE, DC, MC, V. Metro: Liceu. **Amenities:** Restaurant; bar; babysitting. *In room:* A/C, TV, minibar, safe.

Hotel Sant Agusti ★★ *Kids* This is one of the oldest continuously functioning hotels in Barcelona, having seen wars and generations come and go since 1746. After more than a century, the Tura-Monistrol family is still in charge. The old world charm is relatively intact, although the hotel received two facelifts in the '90s. The rooms for romantics are on the top floor with their oak-beamed ceilings and views over the ancient monuments of the Gothic old town. Accommodations range from small to spacious, the largest a trio of very big ones furnished with two bathrooms and sleeping up to six, ideal for families. As in the 19th-century Barcelona, the rooms open onto a spacious interior patio. You'll think you're in Seville. The hotel is convenient to all the attractions of the Rambla sector.

Plaça Sant Augusti 3, 08001 Barcelona. ✆ **93-318-16-58.** Fax 93-317-29-28. www.hotelsa.com. 77 units. 120€–135€ double, 150€ triple. Rates include continental breakfast. AE, DC, MC, V. Parking: 20€. Metro: Liceu. **Amenities:** Restaurant; bar; laundry/dry cleaning; babysitting. *In room:* A/C, TV, hair dryer, safe.

HUSA Oriente Right on the bustling Rambles, this hotel, a government-rated, three-star, was once one of the original "grand hotels" of Barcelona. On the site of a Franciscan monastery, the hotel dates from 1842. It was so prominent in its day that it attracted the likes of Toscanini and Maria Callas. It even became part of Hollywood legend when Errol Flynn checked in. He became so drunk he passed out in the bar. The manager ordered two bartenders to carry him upstairs where they were instructed to strip the swashbuckling star. The manager then sent word to guests down below that they could see the star in the nude. They filed in one by one for the viewing all night. When Flynn woke up with a hangover the next morning, he was none the wiser. Renovations have improved the hotel but it lacks the character of its former glory, today attracting mainly frugal travelers. The arched ballroom of yesterday has been turned into an atmospheric lounge, and the dining room still has a certain grandeur. Each simple but comfortable room has a tiled bathroom with shower.

Les Rambles 45, 08002 Barcelona. ✆ **93-302-25-58.** Fax 93-412-38-19. www.husa.es. 142 units. 115€. AE, MC, V. Metro: Liceu. **Amenities:** Restaurant; bar; room service; babysitting. *In room:* A/C, TV, safe.

Jardí *Value* Sought out for its location, this little hotel opens onto the tree-shaded Plaça Sant Josep Oriols with its many cafes and the severe Gothic architecture of the medieval church of Santa María del Pi. The building in the heart of Barcelona's Gothic quarter rests on ancient Roman foundations. The five-floor hotel has recently been upgraded and improved, with the installation of an elevator. Bar del Pi, on the ground floor, is a favorite of artists and students who live nearby. In the modernization, much of the original architectural charm was maintained, although rooms remain rather basic but are comfortable with newly restored bathrooms with tub and with shower. The quieter rooms are on top, of course. Five of the units have private terraces, and 26 of them open onto private but rather small balconies.

Plaça Sant Josep Orio 1, 08002 Barcelona. ✆ **93-301-59-00.** Fax 93-318-36-64. 42 units. 70€–85€ double; 85€ triple. AE, DC, MC, V. Metro: Liceu. **Amenities:** Bar. *In room:* A/C, TV.

Mesón Castilla This two-star hotel, in a former apartment building, has a Castilian facade, with a wealth of Art Nouveau detailing, and its high-ceilinged lobby is filled with cabriole-legged chairs. Owned and operated by the Spanish hotel chain HUSA, the Castilla is clean, charming, and well maintained. Its nearest rival is the Regencia Colón, to which it is comparable in atmosphere and government ratings. It is far superior to either the Cortés or the Continental. The rooms are comfortable—beds have ornate Catalán-style headboards—and some open onto large terraces. All units have well-kept bathrooms with shower-tub combinations. Breakfast is the only meal served, but it is a fine buffet, with ham, cheese, and eggs. One reader found the location of the hotel "fantastic," right in the center of Barcelona, close to the Rambles.

Fun Fact **Catalàns First Into the Murky Depths**

In one of the little known facts of maritime history, a Catalán inventor, Narcis Monturiol, invented *Ictineo,* the first submarine back in the year 1858—two years before America's own Civil War. Teaming with Josep Missé and Josep Oliu, Monturiol oversaw its construction of this formidable weapon in Barcelona's shipyard. On July 23, 1859, as thousands watched, *Ictineo* with three men aboard plunged to a depth of about 20m (66 ft.), traveling at a speed of 3 knots. The men later resurfaced and the world's first submarine launch was hailed as a success. For mysterious reasons, the government of Spain never followed up on this success. Why? Rumor has it that England, ruler of the world's waves, bribed government officials to suppress development, knowing that the submarine, in the hands of an enemy, could challenge England's domination of the sea.

Valldoncella 5, 08002 Barcelona. ✆ **93-318-21-82.** Fax 93-412-40-20. www.mesoncastilla.com. 56 units. 115€ double. V. Parking 20€. Metro: Plaça de Catalunya or Universitat. **Amenities:** Breakfast room; lounge; babysitting; laundry/dry cleaning. *In room:* A/C, minibar, hair dryer, safe.

Turín This neat and well-run government-rated three-star hotel is in a terracotta grillwork building located in a shopping district. It offers small, streamlined accommodations with balconies and well-kept bathrooms with shower-tub combinations. An elevator will take you to your room. The Turín also has a restaurant specializing in grilled meats and fresh fish. It's a clean, safe choice, comparable to the Lleó, but in its price range inferior in atmosphere to the Mesón Castilla.

Carrer Pintor Fortuny 9–11, 08001 Barcelona. ✆ **93-302-48-12.** Fax 93-302-10-05. www.hotelturin.com. 59 units. 112€ double; 139€ triple. AE, DC, MC, V. Parking 14€. Metro: Plaça de Catalunya. **Amenities:** Restaurant; bar; lounge; laundry/dry cleaning. *In room:* A/C, TV, hair dryer, safe.

BARCELONETA

VERY EXPENSIVE

Eurostars Grand Marina Hotel ★★ This new and deluxe 8-story choice combines a Mediterranean atmosphere with avant-garde art. Barcelona's World Trade Center complex is, of course, is the major international business center in Spain, and visitors are housed here in grand style. The architecture of the hotel was created by the same firm that designed the controversial Pyramid for the Louvre in Paris. Rooms, ranging from midsize to spacious, open onto scenic views of the city including Tibidabo in the distance. Each unit comes with an attractive midsize bathroom with tub and shower combo. Many guests prefer this hotel because of its Mediterranean atmosphere and proximity to the marina. It's one of your best bets if you want a location near the Old Port. The Royal Yacht Club, the Maremagnum, and the Rambles are close at hand. Most of the interior decoration was inspired by the simplicity of Japanese design.

World Trade Center, Moll de Barcelona, 08039 Barcelona. ✆ **93-603-90-00.** Fax 93-603-90-90. www.grandmarinahotel.com. 273 units. 325€ double, 600€–800€ suite. AE, DC, MC, V. Metro: Drassanes. Parking: 21€ ($18.75). **Amenities:** 3 restaurants; bar; room service; laundry/dry cleaning; pool; gym; sauna; babysitting. *In room:* A/C, TV, minibar, hair dryer, safe.

INEXPENSIVE

Marina Folch ★ *Finds* A little family-run hideaway in Barceloneta near the port, this inn is pleasing to both the eye and the purse. An antique building has been renovated, and each midsize room is furnished comfortably with modern, functional pieces. All come with a neatly tiled bathroom with shower and tub. Although in business since 1993, it remains relatively undiscovered. The location is only a five-minute walk from a beach. If you're in the area sightseeing, consider a stopover at its excellent little restaurant on the ground floor.

Calle Mar 16, 08003 Barcelona. ✆ **93-310-37-09.** Fax 93-310-53-27. www.interhotel.com/spain/en/hoteles/1693.html. 10 units. 55€ double. Bus: 15, 57, 59, and 64. **Amenities:** Restaurant; bar. *In room:* A/C, TV.

SUR DIAGONAL

VERY EXPENSIVE

Barcelona Hilton ★★ Opened in 1990 as one of the most publicized hotels in Barcelona, this five-star property lies in a desirable position on one of the most famous and elegant boulevards. Opposite the gates to the fairgrounds of Barcelona (beyond that, to the Olympic Stadium), this is a huge seven-floor corner structure, with a massive tower placed on top of it. It hides behind a rather lackluster white marble facade. The lobby is sleek with lots of marble, and public lounges are furnished with black leather and velvet chairs. Most guest rooms are large and finely equipped, although none are set aside for nonsmokers. Furnishings are standard Hilton, but with suitable extras such as private safes. Bathrooms are also well equipped with such features as large mirrors and shower-tub combinations.

Av. Diagonal 589–591, 08014 Barcelona ✆ **800/445-8667** in the U.S. and Canada, or 93-495-77-77. Fax 93-495-77-00. www.hilton.com. 288 units. 270€–300€ double; 335€–380€ suite. AE, DC, MC, V. Parking 18€. Metro: María Cristina. **Amenities:** Restaurant; cafe; bar; health club; business center; 24-hr. room service; babysitting; laundry/dry cleaning. *In room:* A/C, TV, minibar, hair dryer, safe.

Claris ★★ One of the most unusual hotels built in Barcelona since the 1930s, this postmodern hotel is the only five-star grand luxe lodging in the city center. It incorporates vast quantities of teak, marble, steel, and glass with the historically important facade of a landmark 19th-century building (the Verdruna Palace). Although we prefer the Ritz (see below), many hotel critics hail the Claris as the stellar choice in Barcelona. It opened in 1992 in time for the Barcelona Olympics. Its seven stories include a garden on the roof, a small museum of Egyptian antiquities from the owner's valuable collection on the second floor, and two restaurants, one of which specializes in different brands of caviar. Each of the guest rooms is painted an iconoclastic shade of blue-violet and combines unusual art objects with state-of-the-art electronic accessories and beautifully maintained bathrooms with shower-tub combinations. (Art objects, depending on the inspiration of the decorator, include Turkish kilims, English antiques, Hindu sculptures, Egyptian stone carvings, and engravings inspired by Napoléon's campaigns in Egypt.) Committed to celebrating the many facets of Catalán culture, the hotel's owner and developer, art collector Jordi Clos, named his hotel after the 19th-century Catalán writer Pau Claris.

Even if you're not a guest of the Claris, you might want to visit its new restaurant, East 47, with dim lighting, lithographs from Andy Warhol, and self-described "chill-out music." You'll think you're back in New York, as you enjoy the chef's creations that match colors, flavors, and aromas most harmoniously.

Carrer de Pau Claris 150, 08009 Barcelona. ✆ **800/888-4747** in the U.S., or 93-487-62-62. Fax 93-215-79-70. www.derbyhotels.es. 120 units. Mon–Thurs 257€–281€ double; from 391€ suite. Fri–Sun rates include breakfast. AE, DC, MC, V. Parking 17€ ($15.20). Metro: Passeig de Gràcia. **Amenities:** 2 restaurants; bar; pool; fitness center; sauna; room service; babysitting; laundry/dry cleaning; private museum. *In room:* A/C, TV, minibar, hair dryer, safe.

Hotel Ritz ★★★ Acknowledged by many as the finest, most prestigious, and most architecturally distinguished hotel in Barcelona, the Art Deco Ritz was built in 1919. Richly remodeled during the late 1980s (and suffering a brief name change to HUSA Palace during the '90s), it has welcomed more millionaires, famous people, and aristocrats—with their official and unofficial consorts—than any other hotel in the region. One of the finest features is the cream-and-gilt neoclassical lobby, whose marble floors and potted palms are flooded with sunlight from an overhead glass canopy, and where afternoon tea is served to the strains of a string quartet. Guest rooms are as formal, with high-ceilings, and richly outfitted as you'd expect, some with Regency furniture; bathrooms are accented with mosaics and bathtubs inspired by those in ancient Rome.

Gran Vía de les Corts Catalanes 668, 08010 Barcelona. ✆ **93-318-52-00.** Fax 93-318-01-48. www.rogerdelluria.com. 122 units. 360€ double; from 450€ suite. AE, DC, MC, V. Parking 21€. Metro: Passeig de Gràcia. **Amenities:** Restaurant; bar; fitness center; sauna; car rental; room service; babysitting; laundry/dry cleaning. *In room:* A/C, TV, minibar, hair dryer, safe.

Rey Juan Carlos I ★★★ Named for the Spanish king, who attended its opening and who has visited it several times since, this five-star choice competes effectively against the Ritz, Claris, and Hotel Arts. Opened just before the Olympics, it rises 17 stories from a position at the northern end of the Diagonal, within a prestigious neighborhood known for corporate headquarters, banks, and upscale stores. Note that it's a bit removed, however, from many of Barcelona's top-flight attractions. The design includes a soaring inner atrium, with a bank of glass-sided elevators glide silently up and down at one end. Guest rooms contain many electronic extras, conservatively comfortable furnishings, and in many cases, views out over Barcelona to the sea.

Av. Diagonal 661, 08028 Barcelona. ✆ **800/448-8355** in the U.S., or 93-364-40-40. Fax 93-364-42-64. www.hrjuancarlos.com. 412 units. 350€–420€ double; 490€–665€ suite. Occasional weekend discounts. AE, DC, MC, V. Free parking. Metro: Zona Universitària. **Amenities:** 2 restaurants; 2 bars; 2 pools; fitness center; hairdresser; car rental; room service; laundry/dry cleaning. *In room:* A/C, TV, minibar, hair dryer, safe.

EXPENSIVE

Avenida Palace ★ Set in an enviable 19th-century neighborhood filled with elegant shops and apartment buildings, this hotel lies behind a pair of mock-fortified towers that were built (like the hotel) in 1952. Despite its relative modernity, it evokes an old-world sense of charm, thanks to the attentive staff, the scattering of flowers and antiques, and the 1950s-era accessories that fill its well-upholstered public rooms. Guest rooms, all with private bathrooms equipped with shower-tub combinations, are solidly traditional and quiet, and some are set aside for nonsmokers, a rarity in Spain.

Gran Vía de les Corts Catalanes 605 (at Passeig de Gràcia), 08007 Barcelona. ✆ **93-301-96-00.** Fax 93-318-12-34. 160 units. 255€ double; 297€ suite. AE, DC, MC, V. Parking 16€ ($14.30). Metro: Passeig de Gràcia. **Amenities:** 2 restaurants; bar; hairdresser; room service; babysitting; laundry/dry cleaning; currency exchange. *In room:* A/C, TV, minibar, hair dryer, safe.

Hotel Balmes Set within a seven-story building from the late 1980s, this chain hotel successfully combines a conservative and well-conceived decor with modern accessories and a well-trained staff. Bedrooms are vaguely English in their inspiration, but with a warmly monochromatic color scheme of yellows and browns, marble-trimmed bathrooms with shower-tub combinations, and enough space to allow residents, many of whom are in Barcelona on business trips, to live and work comfortably. If you're looking for a maximum of peace and quiet, rooms overlooking the back of the hotel—site of an outdoor swimming pool and a small garden—are quieter and calmer than those facing the busy street. There's a bar on the premises, but the in-house restaurant follows only a limited schedule, serving breakfast daily, and lunch Monday to Friday. Other than that, no meals are served.

Carrer Mallorca 216, 08008 Barcelona. ✆ **93-451-19-14.** Fax 93-451-00-49. www.derbyhotels.es. 100 units. 157€–175€ double. AE, DC, MC, V. Parking 13€. Metro: Diagonal. **Amenities:** Restaurant; bar; room service; laundry/dry cleaning. *In room:* A/C, TV, minibar, hair dryer.

Hotel Condes de Barcelona ★ Located off the architecturally splendid Passeig de Gràcia, this four-star hotel, originally designed to be a private villa (1895), is one of Barcelona's most glamorous. Business was so good, it opened a 74-room extension, which regrettably lacks the élan of the original core. It boasts a unique neomedieval facade, influenced by Gaudí's modernismo movement. During a recent renovation, just enough hints of high-tech furnishings were added to make the lobby exciting, but everything else has the original opulence. The curved lobby-level bar and its adjacent restaurant add a touch of Art Deco. All the comfortable guest rooms, in salmon, green, or peach color schemes, have marble bathrooms with shower-tub combinations, reproductions of Spanish paintings, and soundproof windows. Some rooms are already beginning to show a post-Olympian wear and tear.

Passeig de Gràcia 73–75, 08008 Barcelona. ✆ **93-467-47-80.** Fax 93-467-47-85. www.condesdebarcelona.com. 183 units. 223€ double; 504€ suite. AE, DC, MC, V. Parking 15€. Metro: Passeig de Gràcia. **Amenities:** Restaurant; bar; cafe; pool; room service; babysitting; laundry/dry cleaning. *In room:* A/C, TV, minibar, hair dryer, safe.

Hotel Majestic ★ The Majestic functioned as one of Barcelona's most visible landmarks beginning in the 1920s, when it was built in a sought-after location within a 10-minute walk from Plaça Catalunya. In the early 1990s, it was radically renovated and upgraded into a four-star format that retained the dignified stateliness of the public areas, but added a sense of color and contemporary drama to each of the bedrooms. Today, these are each outfitted in a different, usually monochromatic color scheme, with carpets, artwork, and upholsteries. Each unit comes with a well-kept bathroom containing a shower-tub combination. The staff is hardworking and conscientious, albeit sometimes swamped with tour buses containing dozens of clients arriving all at once.

Passeig de Gràcia 68, 08007 Barcelona. ✆ **93-488-17-17.** Fax 93-488-18-80. www.hotelmajestic.es. 322 units. 240€–270€ double; 450€–480€ suite. AE, DC, MC, V. Parking 21€. Metro: Passeig de Gràcia. **Amenities:** 2 restaurants; bar; pool; fitness center; sauna; room service; laundry/dry cleaning. *In room:* A/C, TV, minibar, hair dryer.

Hotel Meliá Barcelona Sarrià ★ Located just a block away from the junction of Avinguda Sarrià and Avinguda Diagonal, right in the modern business heart of Barcelona, this five-star hotel opened in 1976. Some of its rooms were renovated as late as 1993, but others are beginning to look a bit worn. It offers comfortably upholstered and carpeted guest rooms in a neutral international modern style. All units have well-kept bathrooms with shower-tub combinations. The hotel, a member of the nationwide Spanish chain Meliá, caters to both the business traveler and the vacationer.

Av. Sarrià 50, 08029 Barcelona. ✆ **800/336-3542** in the U.S., or 93-410-60-60. Fax 93-410-77-44. www.solmelia.com. 314 units. 273€ double; from 435€ suite. AE, DC, MC, V. Parking 18€. Metro: Hospital Clinic. **Amenities:** Restaurant; bar; health club; sauna; room service; babysitting; laundry/dry cleaning. *In room:* A/C, TV, minibar, hair dryer, safe.

INEXPENSIVE

Hotel Astoria ★ *Value* One of our favorite hotels, and an excellent value, the Astoria is located near the upper part of the Rambles, near the Diagonal. It has an Art Deco facade that makes it appear older than it is. The high ceilings, geometric designs, and brass-studded detailing in the public rooms could be Moorish or Andalusian. Each of the comfortable guest rooms is soundproofed; half have been renovated with slick louvered closets and glistening white paint. The more old-fashioned rooms have warm textures of exposed cedar and elegant, pristine modern accessories. All come equipped with private bathrooms containing showers. If you'd like an American-style buffet breakfast, the Astoria is one of the best bets in town. Its buffet offers eggs, bacon, juice, fried potatoes, even pancakes.

París 203, 08036 Barcelona. ✆ **93-209-83-11.** Fax 93-202-30-08. www.derbyhotels.es. 115 units. 173€ double; 210€ suite. AE, DC, MC, V. Parking nearby 15€. Metro: Diagonal. **Amenities:** Bar; lounge; room service; laundry/dry cleaning. *In room:* A/C, TV, minibar, hair dryer, safe.

NORTE DIAGONAL

MODERATE

Hotel Hespería ★ *Kids* This hotel lies on the northern edge of the city, a 10-minute taxi ride from the center, in one of Barcelona's most pleasant residential neighborhoods. Built in the late 1980s, the hotel was renovated before the 1992 Olympics. You'll pass a little Japanese rock garden to reach the stone-floored reception area, with its adjacent bar. Sunlight floods the monochromatic guest rooms—all doubles, although singles can be requested. All rooms have well-maintained bathrooms with shower-tub combinations. The hotel has a long tradition of welcoming the family trade and adjusting beds in its rooms to accommodate them. The uniformed staff offers fine service. A restaurant on the premises serves a regional cuisine.

Los Vergós 20, 08017 Barcelona. ✆ **93-204-55-51.** Fax 93-204-43-92. www.hoteles-hesperia.es. 134 units. 138€–193€ double; 168€–222€ suite. AE, DC, MC, V. Parking 11.50€. Metro: Tres Torres. **Amenities:** Restaurant; bar; room service; babysitting; laundry/dry cleaning. *In room:* A/C, TV, minibar, hair dryer, safe.

AT OR NEAR VILA OLIMPICA

VERY EXPENSIVE

Hotel Arts ★★★ This is the only hotel in Europe managed by the opulent Ritz-Carlton chain, the first of what the company hopes will be a string of hotels across the European continent. It occupies 33 floors of one of the tallest buildings in Spain, and one of Barcelona's only skyscrapers, a 44-floor postmodern tower whose upper floors contain the private condominiums of some of the country's most gossiped-about aristocrats and financiers. Views are straight out over the sea from this location about 2.4km (1½ miles) southwest of Barcelona's historic core, adjacent to the sea and the Olympic Village. Although some rooms were occupied by athletes and Olympic administrators in 1992, the hotel didn't become fully operational until 1994. Its decor is contemporary and elegant, with a large lobby sheathed in slabs of soft gray and yellow marble, and guest rooms outfitted in pastel shades of yellow or blue. The pink marble bathrooms have deluxe luxuries and shower-tub combinations. Rooms have sweeping views over the skyline of Barcelona and the Mediterranean. The staff is youthful, well trained, polite, and hardworking.

Carrer de la Marina 19–21, 08005 Barcelona. ✆ **800/241-3333** in the U.S., or 93-221-10-00. Fax 93-221-10-70. www.ritzcarlton.com. 482 units. 270€–350€ double; 365€–430€ suite. AE, DC, MC, V. Parking 21€. Metro: Ciutadella–Vila Olímpica. **Amenities:** 2 restaurants; bar; cafe; pool; fitness center; room service; laundry/dry cleaning. *In room:* A/C, TV, minibar, hair dryer, safe.

Hotel Rafael Diagonal Port ★★ This was the bright spot of hotel openings in 2001, and it's going stronger than ever. It lies in a section of Barcelona called "Front Marítim," a few yards from Sport's Port, with direct access to the sea and a beach. A favorite among Barcelona's yachting community, it is modern, functional, and yet stylish. King-sized beds are featured in most rooms, and each comes with a marble-clad bathroom with tub and shower combination. Most rooms are midsize and handsomely decorated along clean, crisp, modern lines. Yachties docking nearby have made the hotel bar a fashionable watering hole.

Lope de Vega 4, 08005 Barcelona. ✆ **93-230-20-00.** Fax 93-230-20-10. www.rafaelhoteles.com. 115 units. 155€ double, 218€ suite. AE, DC, MC, V. Parking: 12€. Bus: 41. **Amenities:** Restaurant; bar; room service; laundry/dry cleaning. *In room:* A/C, TV, minibar, hair dryer, safe.

4 Where to Dine

Finding an economical restaurant in Barcelona is easier than finding an inexpensive, safe hotel. There are sometimes as many as eight spots on a block, if you include tapas bars as well as restaurants. Reservations are seldom needed, except in the most expensive and popular places.

Barri Gòtic offers the cheapest meals. There are also many low-cost restaurants in and around the Carrer de Montcada, site of the Picasso museum. Dining rooms in the Eixample tend to be more formal, more expensive, and less adventurous.

However, if you can afford to dine in first-class and deluxe restaurants, you'll find some of the grandest culinary experiences in Europe here. The widely diversified Catalán cuisine reaches its pinnacle in Barcelona, and many of the finest dishes feature fresh seafood. But you don't get just Catalán fare here, as the city is also rich in the cuisines of all the major regions of Spain, including Castile and Andalusia. Because of Barcelona's proximity to France, many of the finer restaurants also serve French or French-inspired dishes, the latter often with a distinctly Catalán flavor.

CIUTAT VELLA

EXPENSIVE

Agut d'Avignon ★ CATALAN Founded in 1962, one of our favorite restaurants in Barcelona is located near the Plaça Reial, in a tiny alleyway (the cross street is Calle d'Avinyó). The restaurant explosion in Barcelona has toppled Agut d'Avignon from its once supreme position, but it's still going strong and has a dedicated following. The restaurant attracts the leading politicians, writers, journalists, financiers, industrialists, and artists of Barcelona—even the king and various ministers of the cabinet, along with the visiting presidents from other countries. Since 1983, the restaurant has been run by Mercedes Giralt Salinas and her son, Javier Falagán Giralt. A small 19th-century vestibule leads into the multilevel dining area, which has two balconies and a main hall; on the whole it evokes a hunting lodge. You might need help translating the Catalán menu. Specialties are prepared according to traditional recipes and are likely to include acorn squash soup served in its shell, fisherman stew with garlic toast, haddock stuffed with shellfish, sole with *nyoca* (a medley of different nuts), large shrimps with aioli (a garlic mayonnaise sauce), duck with figs, and filet of beef steak in a sherry sauce.

Trinitat 3 (at Carrer d'Avinyó). ✆ **93-302-60-34.** Reservations required. Main courses 27€–48€. AE, DC, MC, V. Daily 1–4:30pm and 9pm–12:30am. Metro: Jaume I or Liceu.

Casa Leopoldo ★ *Finds* SEAFOOD An excursion through the somewhat seedy streets of the Barri Xinés is part of the experience of coming to this restaurant, though at night it's safer to come by taxi. This colorful restaurant, founded in 1939, has some of the freshest seafood in town and caters to a loyal clientele. There's a popular stand-up tapas bar in front, then two dining rooms, one slightly more formal than the other. Specialties include eel with shrimp, barnacles, cuttlefish, seafood soup with shellfish, and deep-fried inch-long eels.

Sant Rafael 24. ✆ **93-441-30-14.** Reservations required. Main courses 11€–48€; fixed-price menu 37€. AE, DC, MC, V. Tues–Sun 1:30–4pm; Tues–Sat 9–11pm. Closed Aug and Easter week. Metro: Liceu.

Quo Vadis ★ SPANISH/CONTINENTAL Elegant and impeccable, this is one of the finest restaurants in Barcelona. Within a century-old building near the open stalls of the Boquería food market, it was established in 1967 and has done a discreet but thriving business ever since. Seating is within any of four different dining rooms, each decorated with exposed paneling and a veneer of conservative charm. Personalized culinary creations include a ragout of seasonal mushrooms; fried goose liver with prunes; filet of beef with wine sauce; a wide variety of fish, grilled or, in some cases, flambéed; and a wide choice of desserts made with seasonal fruits imported from all over Spain.

Carme 7. ✆ **93-302-40-72.** Reservations recommended. Main courses 9€–21€. DC, MC, V. Mon–Sat 1:15–4pm and 8:30–11:30pm. Metro: Liceu.

Restaurant Hoffmann ★★ CATALAN/FRENCH/INTERNATIONAL This restaurant in the Barri Gòtic has suddenly become one of the most famous in Barcelona, partly because of its creative cuisine, partly because of its close association with a well-respected training school for future employees of Catalonia's hotel and restaurant industry. The culinary and entrepreneurial force behind it all is Mey Hoffmann, the red-haired offspring of a German father and Catalán mother, whose interior decor reflects her own personality and sense of whimsy. Expect to find masses of verdant plants and fresh flowers, old photographs, dramatic oil paintings, and through the windows, views of the facade of one of Barcelona's most beloved Gothic churches, Santa María del Mar. During clement weather, tables are also set up within a trio of separate courtyards, rich with the detailing of the 18th-century building that surrounds it. Menu items change every two months and are often concocted from French ingredients. Examples include a superb version of *fine tarte* with deboned sardines; foie gras wrapped in puff pastry; baked John Dory with new potatoes and ratatouille; a ragout of crayfish with green risotto; a succulent version of pigs' feet with eggplant; and rack of lamb with grilled baby vegetables. Especially flavorful, if you appreciate beef, is a filet steak cooked in Rioja wine and served with a confit of shallots and a gratin of potatoes. Fondant of chocolate makes a worthy dessert.

Argentaria 74–78. ✆ **93-319-58-89.** Reservations recommended. Main courses 9€–21€; fixed-price lunch (includes wine and coffee) 30€. AE, DC, MC, V. Mon–Fri 1:30–3:30pm and 9–11:30pm. Metro: Jaume I.

MODERATE

Agut ★ *Finds* CATALAN In a historic building in the Barri Xinés, three blocks from the harbor front, Agut epitomizes the bohemian atmosphere surrounding this fairly seedy area. For three quarters of a century, this has been a family-run business, with María Agut García the current reigning empress. Don't confuse Agut with the more famous Agut d'Avignon nearby. The aura is still of the '40s and '50s, with a cozy little bar to the right as you enter. Paintings on the walls are from well-known Catalán artists from the '40s to the '60s.

Central Barcelona Dining

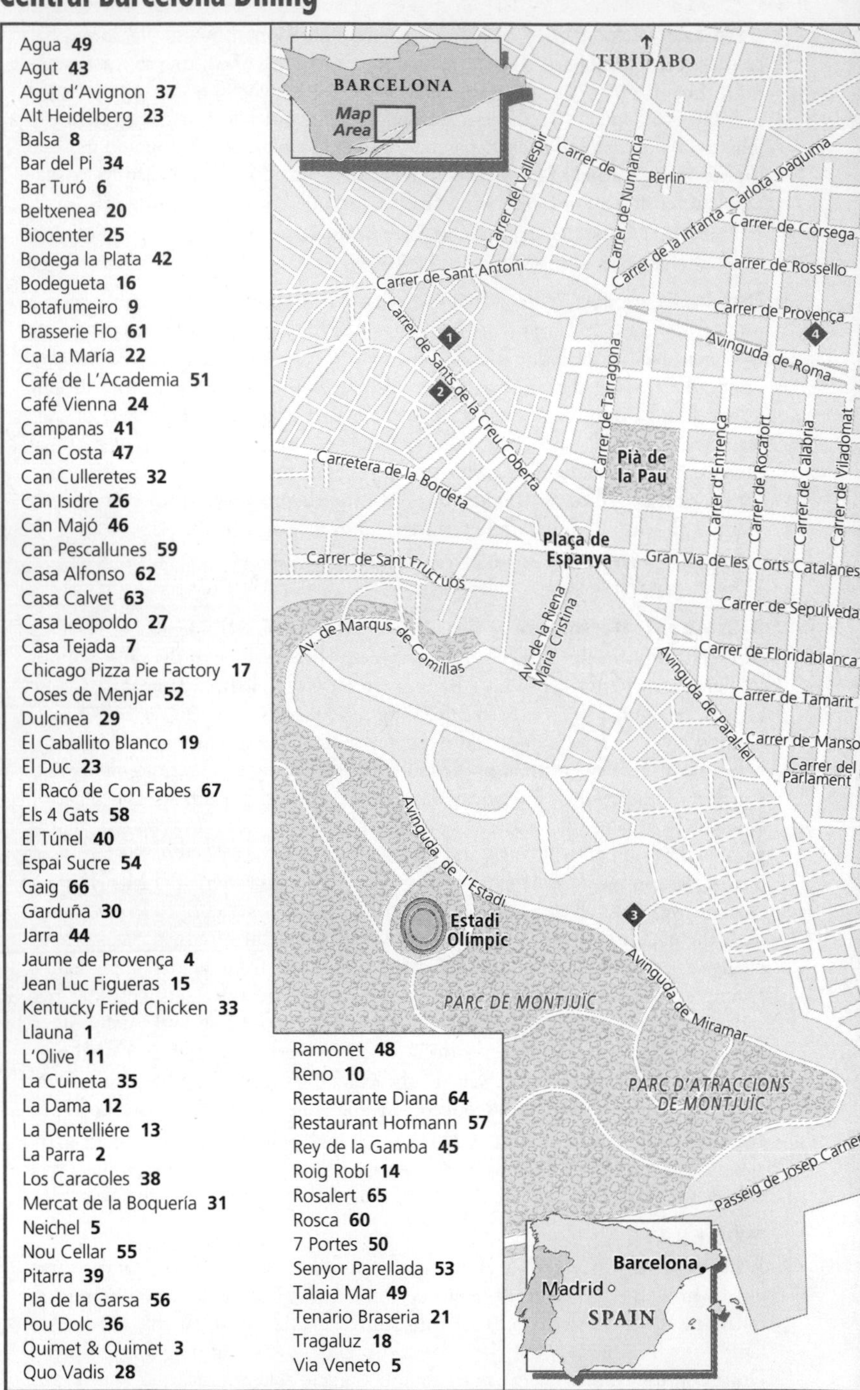

0 1/4 mi
0 0.25 km
Plaça de Francesc Macia
Carrer de Buenos Aires
Carrer de Londres
Carrer de Paris
Travessara de Gràcia
Avinguda Diagonal
Carrer de Còrsega
EIXAMPLE
Carrer de Provença
Carrer de Rossello
Av. de Sant Antoni Maria Claret
Carrer de la Industria
Carrer de Roger de Flor
Plaça de la Sagrada Família
Carrer de Mallorca
Carrer de Valencia
Carrer d'Aragó
Carrer de Comte Borrell
Carrer del Comte d'Urgell
Carrer de Villarroel
Carrer de Casanova
Carrer de Muntaner
Carrer d'Aribau
Carrer de Balmes
Rambla de Catalunya
Passeig de Gracia
Carrer de Pau Claris
Carrer del Consell de Cent
Carrer de la Diputació
Gran Vía de les Corts Catalanes
Plaça de la Universitat
Carrer de R. de Llúcia
Carrer del Bruc
Carrer de Girona
Carrer de Bailen
Passeig de Sant Joan
Carrer de Napols
Carrer de Sicilia
Plaça de Tetuan
Ronda Universitat
Ronda de Sant Antoni
Carrer de Pelai
Plaça Catalunya
Plaça Urquinaona
Carrer de Casp
Carrer d'Ausias Marc
Carrer d'Ali Bei
Ronda de Sant Pere
Carrer de Ribes
Carrer de Sardenya
RAVAL
Ronda Sant Pau
Carrer de Hospital
Av. Portal de l'Angel
La Rambla
BARRI GÒTIC
Via Laietana
Passeig de Lluís Companys
Passeig de Carles I
Carrer de Sant Pau
Carrer de Ferran
Carrer de la Princesa
Carrer de Comerc
Passeig de Pujades
Carrer Nou de la Rambla
LA RIBERA
Passeig de Picasso
PARC DE LA CIUTADELLA
Carrer de Wellington
Avinguda de les Drassanes
Carrer Ample
Passeig de Colom
PARC ZOOLOGIC
Villa Olimpic
Plaça Portal de la Pau
Moll de la Fusta
Moll d'Espanya
Avinguda d'Icàvia
BARCELONETA

The cuisine is solid and time-tested fare; vigorous cookery served at moderate prices. Begin with *mil hojas de butifarra amb zets* or layers of pastry filled with Catalán sausage and mushrooms, or else the *terrine de albergines amb fortmage de cabra* (terrine of eggplant with goat's cheese gratinée). One of our favorite dishes is *soufle de rape amb gambes* (soufflé of monkfish with shrimp). For gastronomes only, try the *pie de cerdo relleno con foie amb truffles* (pork feet stuffed with duck liver and truffles). For dessert, if you order *sortido,* you'll get a combination plate with an assortment of the small homemade cakes of the house.

Gignas 16. ✆ **93-315-17-09.** Reservations required. Main courses 17€–19€; fixed-price lunch 8€. MC, V. Tues–Sun 1:30–4pm and Tues–Sat 9pm–midnight. Closed Aug. Metro: Jaime 1.

Brasserie Flo FRENCH/INTERNATIONAL In a former textiles factory, this handsomely restored warehouse was opened as a restaurant in 1982 by a French group. It is as close as Barcelona gets to an Alsace brasserie. The Art Deco dining room has been compared to one on a transatlantic steamer at the turn of the century—spacious, palm-filled, comfortable, and air-conditioned. Start off with the fresh foie gras. The specialty is a large plate of *choucroute* (sauerkraut) served with a steamed ham hock. Also good are the shrimp in garlic, salmon tartare with vodka, black rice, and stuffed sole with spinach. These dishes, each familiar fare, are nevertheless solid, satisfying, and filling.

Jonqueras 10. ✆ **93-319-31-02.** Reservations recommended. Main courses 11€–34€; fixed-price menu 21€. AE, DC, MC, V. Mon–Thurs 1–4pm and 8:30pm–midnight, Fri–Sun 1–4pm and 8:30pm–1am. Metro: Urquinaona.

Can Culleretes CATALAN Founded in 1786 as a *pastelería* (pastry shop) in the Barri Gòtic, this oldest of Barcelona restaurants still retains many original architectural features. All three dining rooms are decorated in Catalán style, with tile dadoes and wrought-iron chandeliers. The well-prepared food features authentic dishes of northeastern Spain, including sole Roman style, *zarzuela a la marinera* (shellfish medley), cannelloni, and paella. From October to January, special game dishes are available, including *perdiz* (partridge). Signed photographs of celebrities, flamenco artists, and bullfighters who have visited this place decorate the walls.

Quintana 5. ✆ **93-317-64-85.** Reservations recommended. Main courses 8€; *menú del día* 14€. MC, V. Tues–Sun 1:30–4pm, Tues–Sat 9–11pm. Closed 3 weeks in July. Metro: Liceu. Bus: 14 or 59.

Can Pescallunes FRENCH/CATALAN With the look, feel, and menu of a French bistro, this 10-table restaurant is a short walk from the cathedral. It opened in 1980 in this turn-of-the-century building where an elaborate street lantern marks the entrance. Richly flavorful specialties are *rape* (monkfish, pronounced *rah*-peh) with clams and tomatoes, a smooth vichyssoise, chateaubriand with béarnaise sauce, sole cooked in cider, steak tartare, and dessert crepes with Cointreau. The specials change daily, and the prices remain a model of temperance.

Carrer Magdalenas 23. ✆ **93-318-54-83.** Reservations required for lunch. Main courses 19€–27€. AE, DC, MC, V. Mon–Fri 1–3:30pm and 8:30–10:30pm. Closed Aug. Metro: Urquinaona.

Coses de Menjar ★ *Finds* FUSION/MEDITERRANEAN In Catalán, the name of this restaurant translates as "things to eat." That name hardly does justice to the wacky fusion cuisine—first popularized in Madrid—that has spread to Barcelona in all its oddball madness. The Parellada family has launched what's known as a dining dynasty in Barcelona, and daughter Ada is the guiding light

Fun Fact **Picasso & *Les Demoiselles***

Biographers of the 20th century's greatest artist, Spanish-born Pablo Picasso, claim that the artist was inspired to paint one of his masterpieces, *Les Demoiselles d'Avignon,* after a "glorious night" spent in a notorious Bordello on Carrer D'Avinyó.

behind this fun place with its wine glass chandeliers, napkin rings made from bent forks, spoon-shaped lamps, cheese-grater candleholders, and other touches of quirkiness.

A hip hangout for the golden youth of Barcelona's New Age, Coses de Menjar may sound gimmicky—and it is—but its cuisine is superb. If you want beautifully presented and savory Mediterranean cookery, you can get that too, including a meal recently enjoyed of red mullet in almond sauce with a side of fresh figs. The fresh pumpkin salad came with cherries and soft cheese. But the piece de resistance was the grilled foie gras with Parmesan ice cream. Don't knock it until you've tried it. The cheesy ice cream is a taste treat and tour de force of the clever chef. A chestnut ice cream also appears in the most delicious pineapple soup we've sampled this side of Asia. Whatever your final verdict, this place works.

Pla de Palau 5. ✆ **93-310-60-01.** Reservations required. Main courses 12€–22€. MC, V. Open Mon–Thurs 1:30–4pm and 9–11:30pm; Fri–Sat 1:30–4pm and 9pm–midnight. Metro: Jaume I.

Els Quatre Gats ★ CATALAN A Barcelona legend since 1897, the "Four Cats" was a favorite of Picasso, Rusinyol, and other artists who once hung their works on its walls. Located on a narrow cobblestone street near the cathedral, the fin de siècle cafe was the setting for poetry readings by Joan Maragall, piano recitals by Isaac Albéniz and Ernie Granados, and murals by Ramón Casas. It was a base for members of the modernismo movement and played a major role in the intellectual and bohemian life of the city. In Catalán slang, the name of the restaurant translates as "just a few people."

Today, a bar that's become a popular meeting place in the heart of the Barri Gòtic, it was long ago restored but retains its fine old look. The fixed-price menu, offered every day but Sunday, rates as one of the better bargains in town, considering the locale. The good food is prepared in an unpretentious style of Catalán cooking called *cuina de mercat* (based on whatever looks fresh at the market that day). The constantly changing menu reflects the seasons. No hot food is served on Sunday.

Montsió 3. ✆ **93-302-41-40.** Reservations required Sat–Sun. Main courses 8€–18€; fixed-price menu (Mon–Sat) 10€. AE, MC, V. Daily 1–4pm; Mon–Sat 7:30pm–midnight. Cafe daily 8am–2am. Metro: Plaça de Catalunya.

Espai Sucre ★★ *Finds* DESSERTS If you're diabetic, you'll surely go in a coma if you dine here in the Barrio de la Ribera neighborhood. Otherwise, "Sugar Space" (its name in English) is Barcelona's most unusual dining room, with a minimalist decor and seating for 30. For the dessert lover, it is like entering a heaven created by the sugar fairy himself. The place has a gimmick, and it works. The menu is devoted to desserts. There is a short list of savory dishes found almost hidden on the back of the menu, with offerings such as filet of beef but even that comes with green apple sorbet. The grand dessert menu is the attraction. Jordi Butrón is the chef and creator of the menu. Forget all about those tearoom concoctions you'd find in a pastry cafe. The desserts here are original creations. Your "salad" is likely to be small cubes of spicy milk pudding resting on matchsticks of green apple with baby arugula leaves, peppery caramel, dabs of lime kefir and lemon curd, and a straight line of toffee. Smoky tea cream with chocolate, black sesame, and yogurt appears. Even when your platter holds a tiny phyllo pyramid, no bigger than a pencil eraser, you bite in to discover it's filled with lemon and rosemary marmalade. Ever had a soup of litchi, celery, apple, and eucalyptus? If some of the concoctions frighten your palate, you'll find comfort in the more familiar—vanilla cream with coffee sorbet and caramelized banana. Every dessert comes with a recommendation for the appropriate wine to accompany it.

Princesa 53. ✆ **93-268-16-30.** Reservations required. Main courses 8€–11€. 3-dessert platter 21€, 5-dessert platter 32€. DC, MC, V. Tues–Sat 9–11:30pm. Metro: Arc de Triomf.

La Cuineta *Value* CATALAN A well-established restaurant near the center of the Catalán government, this is a culinary highlight of the Barri Gòtic. The restaurant is decorated in typical regional style and favors local cuisine. The fixed-price menu is a good value, or you can order a la carte. The most expensive appetizer is *bellota* (acorn-fed ham), but we suggest that you settle instead for a market-fresh Catalán dish, such as *favas* (broad beans) stewed with *butifarra,* a tasty, spicy local sausage.

Pietat 12. ✆ **93-315-01-11.** Reservations recommended. Main courses 12€–19€; fixed-price menu 25.50€. AE, DC, MC, V. Daily 1–4pm and 8pm–midnight. Metro: Jaume I.

Pou Dolc ★ *Value* CATALAN Born at the dawn of the millennium, this little discovery offers some of the best food for the money in Barcelona. Near the heartbeat Plaça Real in the Gothic old town, it is associated with a cooking school of the same name. The cooks have learned their lessons well. In large rooms with designer furniture, it attracts a wide range of customers from the neighborhood, everybody from bankers to artists. The decor is minimalist but with style. There are 10 tables with a capacity for holding 40 hungry diners, most of whom order the fixed-price menus. The one served at lunch is a steal. As we noted, it's unbeatable for the price. The lunch begins with an *amuse-bouche,* or tiny appetizer. The three-course menu also includes a glass of wine or bottled water. The *carte* changes every day but might begin with a savory whip of scrambled eggs and mushrooms from the forest, cooked with spring garlic. The main dish might be *merluza a la plancha* or grilled hake, perhaps grilled duck liver. Some dishes are accompanied by a deeply flavored onion marmalade. You can also order a la carte, sampling the likes of onion fritters, or a typical Catalán dish of fresh spinach with pine nuts, almonds, raisins, figs, and dried apricots. if featured opt for the ice cream made of fresh oranges and studded with slivers of candied orange peel.

Baixada de Sant Miguel 6. ✆ **93-412-05-79.** Reservations recommended. Main courses 15€–19.50€. Tasting menu 40.50€. Fixed-price lunch 9€. AE, DC, MC, V. Tues–Sat 1:30–4pm and 9–11:30pm. Closed Aug. 13–27. Metro: Liceu.

INEXPENSIVE

Biocenter VEGETARIAN This is the largest and best-known vegetarian restaurant in Barcelona, the creation of Catalonia-born entrepreneur Pep Cañameras, who is likely to be directing the service from his position behind the bar in front. Many clients, vegetarians or not, congregate over drinks in the front room. Some continue on for meals in one of two ground-floor dining rooms, whose walls are decorated with the paintings and artworks of the owner and his colleagues. There's a salad bar, an array of vegetarian casseroles, such soups as gazpacho or lentil, and a changing selection of seasonal vegetables. No meat or fish of any kind are served.

Pintor Fortuny 25. ✆ **93-301-45-83.** Main courses 5€–6€. No credit cards. Bar Mon–Sat 9am–5pm; food Mon–Sat 1–5pm. Metro: Plaça de Catalunya.

Café de L'Academia CATALAN/MEDITERRANEAN In the center of Barri Gòtic, only a short walk from Plaça Sant Jaume, this 28-table restaurant looks expensive but is really one of the best and most affordable in the medieval city. The building dates from the 15th century, although the restaurant was only founded in the mid-1980s. Its owner, Jordí Casteldi, offers an elegant atmosphere in a setting of brown, stone walls and ancient wooden columns. At a small bar you can peruse the menu and study the wines offered. The menu is varied and the dishes always well prepared. Usually dishes of this quality cost three times as much in Barcelona. The chef is proud of his "kitchen of the market," suggesting that only the freshest ingredients from the day's shopping are featured. Try such delights as *lassanye de butifarra i ceps* (lasagna with Catalán sausage and flap mushrooms), *bacalla gratinado i musselina de carofes* (salt cod gratinée with an artichoke mousse), or *terrina d'berengeras amb fortmage de cabra* (terrine of eggplant with goat cheese). A specialty, and a delectable one at that, is *codorniz rellena en cebollitas tiernas y foie de pato* (partridge stuffed with tender onions and duck liver).

Carrer Lledó 1 (Barri Gòtic), Plaça Sant Just. ✆ **93-319-82-53.** Reservations required. Main courses 19€–23€; fixed-price menu (lunch only) 9€. Set dinner 24€. AE, MC, V. Mon–Fri 9am–noon, 1:15–4pm, and 9pm–midnight. Closed last 2 weeks in Aug. Metro: Jaume I.

El Duc ★ CATALAN Set on the lobby level of the previously recommended hotel, within a compound whose oldest section was designed by Emilio Salas i Cortes, an early mentor of Gaudí, this is a well-managed and competent restaurant serving food that's a lot better than what's offered in the dining rooms of many competing hotels. Adjacent to the Plaça de Catalunya, it offers conservative but flavorful dishes that include prawn cocktails, goose-liver paté, margret of duckling in fruit sauce, tenderloin of beef "Café de Paris," grilled entrecôte, and fried fish. Ingredients are very fresh, and the chefs more than competent. They add flavor to every dish without destroying the natural taste. For such an elegant enclave, the prices are extremely reasonable.

In the Duques de Bergara, Bergara 11. ✆ **93-301-51-51.** Reservations recommended. Main courses 7€–13€; fixed-price menu (Mon–Fri only) 15€. AE, DC, MC, V. Daily 1–4pm and 8–11pm. Metro: Plaça de Catalunya.

Garduña ★ *Kids* CATALAN This is the most famous restaurant within Barcelona's covered food market, La Boquería. Originally conceived as a hotel, it eliminated its bedrooms in the 1970s and has concentrated on food ever since. Battered, somewhat ramshackle, and a bit claustrophobic, it nevertheless enjoys a fashionable reputation among actors, sculptors, writers, and painters who appreciate a blue-collar atmosphere that might have been designated as bohemian in an earlier era. Because of its position near the back of the market, you'll pass endless rows of fresh produce, cheeses, and meats before you reach it, a fact that adds to its allure. You can dine downstairs, near a crowded bar, or a bit more formally upstairs. Food is ultra-fresh (the chefs certainly don't have to travel far for the ingredients) and might include "hors d'oeuvres of the sea," cannelloni Rossini, grilled hake with herbs, rape (monkfish) marinara, paella, brochettes of veal, seafood rice, or a zarzuela (stew) of fresh fish with spices.

Jerusalem 18. ✆ **93-302-43-23.** Reservations recommended. Main courses 9€–27€. AE, DC, MC, V. Mon–Sat 1–4pm and 8pm–midnight. Metro: Liceu.

La Rosca CATALAN/SPANISH For more than half a century Don Alberto Vellve, the owner, has welcomed customers into this little Barri Gòtic eatery, close to Plaça de Catalunya. On a short street, the place is easy to miss, except to some of its devotees who have been coming here for decades. Go here if you'd like to see the type of place where people dined inexpensively in the Franco era. A mixture of Catalán and modern Spanish cuisine is served in this small rustic house that has high ceilings and white walls. The decor has nostalgic touches such as old bullfighting posters and pictures of Barcelona in the mid–20th century. There are 60 unadorned tables, which diners fill quickly to take advantage of the cheap three-course luncheon menu. Dig into such hearty fare as veal stew or assorted grilled fish and shellfish. Baby squid is cooked in its own ink, and one of the best and most typical dishes is white beans sautéed with ham and Catalán sausage. For a true treat, ask for the *rape a la planate* or grilled monkfish.

Juliá Portet 6. ✆ **93-302-51-73.** Main courses 5€–12€; fixed-price menu 7€. No credit cards. Sun–Fri 9am–4pm and 8–9:30pm. Closed Aug 20–30. Metro: Urquinaona and Catalunya.

Pitarra CATALAN Founded in 1890, this restaurant in the Barri Gòtic was named after the 19th-century Catalán playwright who lived and wrote his plays and poetry here in the back room. Try the grilled fish chowder or a Catalán salad, followed by grilled salmon or squid Málaga style. Valencian paella is another specialty. The cuisine does not even pretend to be imaginative, but instead adheres strictly to time-tested recipes—"the type of food we ate when growing up," in the words of one diner.

Avinyó 56. ✆ **93-301-16-47.** Reservations required. Main courses 7€–22€; fixed-price lunch 9€. AE, DC, MC, V. Mon–Sat 1–4pm and 8:30–11pm. Closed Aug 3–30. Metro: Liceu.

Pla de la Garsa ★ CATALAN/MEDITERRANEAN In Barrio Ribera, close to the cathedral, this historic building has been fully renovated but still retains some 19th-century fittings such as a cast-iron spiral staircase diners ascend to reach another dining area upstairs. However, the ground floor is more interesting. Here you'll encounter the owner, Ignacio Sulle, an antiques collector who has filled his establishment with an intriguing collection of objets d'art. He boasts one of the city's best wine lists, and features a daily array of traditional Catalán and Mediterranean favorite dishes, and is also known for his variety of French cheese. Every dish has a special something that raises it to a gastronomic height. Begin with one of the patés, especially the goose, or else a confit of duck thighs. You can also order meat and fish patés. One surprise is a terrine with black olives and anchovies. For a main course, try the perfectly seasoned beef bourguignonne or *fabetes fregides amb menta i pernil* (beans with meat and diced Serrano ham). The cheese selection is one of the finest we've found in town, especially bountiful in Catalán goat cheese, including Serrat Gros from the Pyrenees.

Assaonadors 13. ✆ **93-315-24-13.** Reservations recommended for weekends. Main courses 5€–12€. AE, DC, MC, V. Daily 8pm–1am. Metro: Jaume I.

Senyor Parellada CATALAN The glossy, contemporary-looking interior of this place is in distinct contrast to a battered-looking facade of a building that's at least a century old. Inside, within a pair of lemon-yellow and blue dining rooms, you'll be confronted with a choice of menu items that include Italian-style cannelloni, stuffed cabbage, cod "as it was prepared by the monks of the Poblet monastery," baked monkfish with mustard and garlic sauce, roasted duck served with figs, and roasted rack of lamb with red wine sauce. Patrons flock faithfully to this bistro, knowing they'll be served a traditional cuisine of northeast Spain with fine local products. The chefs seem to know how to coax the most flavor out of the premium ingredients.

Argentaria 37. ✆ **93-310-50-94.** Reservations recommended. Main courses 5€–14€. AE, MC, V. Mon–Sat 1–4pm and 8:30pm–midnight. Metro: Jaume I.

SUR DIAGONAL

VERY EXPENSIVE

Beltxenea ★★ BASQUE/FRENCH Set in a structure originally designed in the late 19th century as an Eixample apartment building, this restaurant celebrates the nuances and subtleties of Basque cuisine. Since the Basques are noted as the finest chefs in Spain, this is a grand cuisine indeed—and in this case, it's served in one of the most elegantly and comfortably furnished restaurants in Barcelona. Save a visit here for that special night—it's worth the money. Within a dignified dining room with parquet floors and nautical accessories, you can enjoy a meal that marries the inspiration of the chef and the availability of fresh ingredients. Examples include hake served either fried with garlic or garnished with clams and served with fish broth; well-prepared, succulent roast lamb or grilled rabbit; and excellent desserts. Summer dining is possible outside in the formal garden.

Majorca 275. ✆ **93-215-30-24.** Reservations recommended. Main courses 18€–44€; tasting menu 50€. AE, DC, MC, V. Mon–Fri 1:30–3:30pm, Mon–Sat 8:30–11:30pm. Closed 3 weeks in Aug. Metro: Passeig de Gràcia.

Jaume de Provença ★★★ CATALAN/FRENCH Located a few steps away from the Estació Central de Barcelona-Sants railway station at the western end of the Eixample, this is a small, cozy, and personalized spot with a country-

Kids Family-Friendly Restaurants

Dulcinea (p. 95) This makes a great refueling stop any time of the day—guaranteed to satisfy any chocoholic.

Fast-Food Places (p. 93) Burger King, the Chicago Pizza Pie Factory, and Kentucky Fried Chicken are good bets for familiar fast food that the kids will enjoy.

Garduña (p. 81) This is the best-known restaurant in Barcelona's covered food market, La Boquería. Kids love to go to this battered and ramshackle place, which not only serves good and inexpensive food, but also allows visitors to experience the aura of one of Spain's most bustling food markets. The choice of food items is so wide and varied, there's something here to please everyone.

Poble Espanyol (p. 103) A good introduction to Spanish food. All the restaurants in the "Spanish Village" serve comparable food at comparable prices—let the kids choose what to eat.

rustic decor. It is the only restaurant along the Diagonal that can compare to La Dama (see below). The young-at-heart clientele is served by a polite and hardworking staff. Named after its owner/chef Jaume Bargués, it features modern interpretations of traditional Catalán and southern French cuisine. Examples include a gratin of clams with spinach, a salad of two different species of lobster, foie gras and truffles, pigs' trotters with plums and truffles, crabmeat lasagna, cod with saffron sauce, sole with mushrooms in a port-wine sauce, and a dessert specialty of orange mousse, whose presentation is an artistic statement in its own right. This establishment, incidentally, was launched during the 1940s by Jaume's forebears, who acquiesced to their talented offspring's new and successful culinary theories.

Provença 88. ✆ **93-430-00-29.** Reservations recommended. Main courses 13€–42€. AE, DC, MC, V. Tues–Sun 1–4pm; Tues–Sat 9–11:30pm. Closed Easter week, Aug. Metro: Entença.

La Dama ★★★ CATALAN/INTERNATIONAL This is one of the few restaurants in Barcelona that deserves, and gets, a Michelin star. Located a floor above street level in one of the grandly iconoclastic 19th-century buildings for which Barcelona is famous, this stylish and well-managed restaurant serves a clientele of local residents and civic dignitaries with impeccable taste and confidence. You'll take an Art Nouveau elevator (or the sinuous stairs) up one flight to reach the dining room. The specialties might include salmon steak served with vinegar derived from *cava* (sparkling wine) and onions, cream-of-potato soup flavored with caviar, a salad of crayfish with orange-flavored vinegar, an abundant seasonal platter of autumn mushrooms, and succulent preparations of lamb, fish, shellfish, beef, goat, and veal. The building that contains the restaurant, designed by Manuel Sayrach, is 3 blocks west of the intersection of Avinguda Diagonal and Passeig de Gràcia.

Diagonal 423. ✆ **93-202-06-86.** Reservations required. Main courses 15.50€–30€; fixed-price menus 48€. AE, DC, MC, V. Daily 1:30–3:30pm and 8:30–11:30pm. Metro: Provença.

EXPENSIVE

Can Isidre ★ CATALAN In spite of its seedy location (take a cab at night!), this is perhaps the most sophisticated Catalán bistro in Barcelona, drawing such patrons as King Juan Carlos and Queen Sofía. Opened in 1970, it was also visited by Julio Iglesias and the famous Catalonian bandleader Xavier Cugat. Isidre Gironés and his wife, Montserrat, are known for fresh Catalán cuisine. Flowers and artwork decorate the restaurant, and the array of food is beautifully prepared and served. Try spider crabs and shrimp, a gourmand salad with foie gras, sweetbreads with port and flap mushrooms, or carpaccio of veal in Harry's Bar style. The selection of Spanish and Catalán wines is excellent.

Les Flors 12. ✆ **93-441-11-39.** Reservations required. Main courses 12€–31€. AE, DC, MC, V. Mon–Sat 1:30–4pm and 8:30–11:30pm. Closed Sun June–Aug. Metro: Paral.lel.

Casa Calvet ★ CATALAN/CONTINENTAL This is one of the most visible and popular restaurants of the Eixample district, with a reputation and cachet that has attracted everyone from the Mayor of Barcelona to Queen Sofía and her daughter, the Infanta Cristina. The setting is on the ground floor of one of the great modernist apartment buildings of Barcelona, a stained-glass and wood-trimmed fantasy designed by Antoni Gaudí in 1899. The menu is sophisticated, reflecting influences from both Catalonia and nearby France. Examples include fresh pan-fried duck liver served in a bitter orange sauce, ravioli stuffed with oysters and clams and served in a sparkling cava sauce, and grilled filet of pork with chestnuts and cider sauce.

Carrer Casp 48. ✆ **93-412-40-12.** Reservations recommended. Main courses 20€–29€. AE, MC, V. Mon–Sat 1–3:30pm and 8:30–11pm. Metro: Castro.

Jean Luc Figueras ★★★ CATALAN For a *Kama Sutra*–like dining experience, head for this hip Gràcia town house that was once the studio of Balenciaga. Even if food critics narrowed the list of Barcelona restaurants down to five, the chef and owner, Jean Luc Figueras, would likely appear on the list. The setting is modern and refined, and the cookery is both traditional and innovative, as Figueras stamps every dish with his own personal touch. Highly dedicated to staying on top, Figueras is a seeker of the finest raw materials on the Barcelona market, and his menu is adjusted to take advantage of the best produce in any season. The emphasis is on fresh seafood, although his meat dishes are also sublime. His fried prawn and ginger-flecked pasta in a mango and mustard sauce would make the Gods weep, and his sea bass with cod and blood sausage was no less brilliant. Your tongue will fall in love with you if you're wise enough to select such nouvelle-inspired dishes as shrimp with a velvety smooth and golden pumpkin cream sauce or the pork with a zesty goat cheese enlivened with peach honey. The desserts are homemade and inevitably sumptuous, and we took particular delight in the seven varieties of freshly made bread.

Santa Teresa 10. ✆ **93-415-28-77.** Reservations required. Main courses 15€–25€. Set menus 20€–40€. AE, DC, MC, V. Mon–Sat 1:30–4:30pm and 8:30pm–midnight. Metro: Diagonal.

Restaurante Diana INTERNATIONAL At least part of the allure of dining here involves the chance to visit the most legendary hotel in Barcelona. Located on the lobby level of the Ritz, the restaurant is filled with French furnishings and accessories amid a gilt-and-blue color scheme. The polite and well-trained staff serves such dishes as seafood salad flavored with saffron; filets of sole layered with lobster; filet mignon braised in cognac, cream, and peppercorn sauce; turbot in white-wine sauce; and a wide array of delectable desserts. The cuisine is of a high international standard, although the restaurant doesn't quite reach the sublime culinary experience of La Dama or Jaume de Provença (see above).

In the Hotel Ritz, Gran Vía de les Corts Catalanes 668. ✆ **93-510-11-30.** Reservations recommended. Main courses 17€–25€; fixed-price menus 29€–52€ Sat–Sun. AE, DC, MC, V. Daily 1:30–4pm and 8:30–11pm. Metro: Arc del Triomf.

MODERATE

L'Olive ★ CATALAN/SPANISH You assume that this restaurant is named for the olive that figures so prominently in its cuisine, but actually it's named for the owner, Josep Olive. You can be born with no more apt a name for a Mediterranean restaurateur. In the Eixample, the building is designed in a modern Catalán style with walls adorned with reproductions of famous Spanish paintings by Miró, Dalí, and Picasso. The tables are topped in marble, the floors impeccably polished. There are sections on both floors where it's possible to have some privacy, and overall the feeling is one of elegance with a touch of intimacy. You won't be disappointed by anything on the menu, especially *bacalla cache* (raw salt cod) or *filet de vedella al vi negre al forn* (veal filets cooked in the oven in a red wine sauce), and especially the *salsa magret* of duck with strawberry sauce. One specialty is *amanida de col llombarda amb seitons* (a salad of finely shredded red cabbage that has been parboiled in sherry vinegar and tossed with a purée of olive oil and a small fish similar to white anchovies). Monkfish flavored with roasted garlic is always a palate pleaser, and you can finish with a *crema catalán* (a flan), or one of the delicious Catalán pastries.

Calle Balmes 47 (corner of Concejo de Ciento). ✆ **93-452-19-90.** Reservations recommended. Main courses 9€–16€. *Menú completo* 35€. AE, DC, MC, V. Daily 1–4pm and Mon–Sat 8:30pm–midnight. Metro: Passeig de Gràcia.

Rosalert ★ CATALAN/SEAFOOD At the corner of Carrer Napols, close to La Sagrada Família, this restaurant has been the domain of Jordí Alert for more than four decades. He specializes in *comida de mar a la plancha* (grilled seafood) in a typical setting of hardwood floors and tile-covered walls. The seafood or shellfish are grilled on a heated iron plate without any additives. There is no more awesome glass tank of live crustacea in Barcelona. You choose your meal and the poor victim is extracted with a net and thrown on the grill. Of course, you'll find all the typical offerings: tiny octopus, succulent mussels, fat shrimp, calamares, fresh oysters, and langoustines. If you're daring you can order such unusual seafood as *dátiles* ("dates" in English), a delicious shellfish whose shape resembles that of a date. Begin with one of the freshly made tapas such as salt cod in vinaigrette or broad beans laced with garlic and virgin olive oil. Your best bet might be the *parillada* or assorted fish and shellfish from the grill. One of the best offerings is turbot cooked on the grill with potatoes and fresh mushrooms.

Av. Diagonal 301. ✆ **93-207-10-19.** Main courses 9€–14€. *Menú completo* 36€. AE, DC, MC, V. Tues–Sun 9am–5pm and 8pm–2am. Closed Aug 10–30. Metro: Verdaguer/Sagrada Família.

Tenorio Braseria ★★ MEDITERRANEAN/INTERNATIONAL This is one of the hottest, newest, and sleekest restaurants in town, the creation of Estrella Salieti, darling of the media and a hot interior designer. But it's the cuisine of Chef Jaume Turó who brings in the customers with his imaginative and unique cuisine that's a sort of blend of updated Catalán and fusion fare. The clientele changes from lunch to dinner. Midday brings out the shoppers, with artists, models, and (for some reason) politicians predominating at night. His special paella is reason enough to visit. Often this is a tired old dish in a Spanish restaurant. Turó's concoction is a savory blend of fresh fish aromatically seasoned and cooked with the freshest of vegetables. Meat-lovers are drawn to his Butifarra sausage grill, and we're also fond of his catch of the day cooked in a zesty tomato sauce with virgin olive oil and fresh garlic. Among his offerings, we're fondest of an absolutely delectable artichoke ravioli and aged Spanish ham in a carbonara sauce.

Passeig de Gràcia 37. ✆ **93-272-05-92.** Reservations required. Main courses 6€–20€. AE, DC, MC, V. Daily 7pm–1:30am. Metro: Passeig de Gràcia.

INEXPENSIVE

Ca La María CATALAN This small blue-and-green-tiled bistro (only 18 tables) is on a quiet square opposite a Byzantine-style church near the Plaça de la Universitat. This is not a place for haute cuisine. Look for the constantly changing daily specials. A bit battered in looks, the restaurant serves endearingly homelike food—providing you grew up in a family of Catalán cooks. Despite their simple origins, these dishes are often surprisingly tasty, as exemplified by the baby squid with onions and tomatoes, anglerfish with burnt garlic, and a veal sirloin cooked to taste.

Tallers 76. ✆ **93-318-89-93.** Reservations recommended Sat. Main courses 5€–8€. AE, DC, MC, V. Mon–Sat 1:30–4pm, Tues–Sat 8:30–11pm. Metro: Universitat.

El Caballito Blanco SEAFOOD/INTERNATIONAL This old Barcelona standby famous for its seafood has long been popular among locals. The fluorescent-lit dining area does not offer much atmosphere, but the food is good, varied, and relatively inexpensive unless you order the lobster. The "Little White Horse," in the Passeig de Gràcia area, features a huge selection, including monkfish, mussels marinara, and shrimp with garlic. If you don't want fish, try the grilled lamb cutlets. Several different patés and salads are offered. There's a bar to the left of the dining area.

Mallorca 196. ✆ **93-453-10-33.** Main courses 6€–28€. AE, MC, V. Tues–Sun 1–3:45pm, Tues–Sat 9–10:45pm. Closed Aug. Metro: Hospital Clínic.

La Dentelliére ★ *Finds* FRENCH/MEDITERRANEAN Charming, and steeped in the French aesthetic, this bistro is imbued with a modern, elegant decor. Inside, you'll find a small corner of provincial France, thanks to the dedicated effort of Evelyne Ramelot, the French writer who owns the place. After an aperitif at the sophisticated cocktail bar, you can order from an imaginative menu that includes a lasagna made from strips of salted cod, peppers, and tomato sauce, and a delectable carpaccio of filet of beef with pistachios, lemon juice, vinaigrette, and Parmesan cheese. The wine list is particularly imaginative, with worthy vintages mostly from France and Spain.

Calle Balmes 165, corner Paris. ✆ **93-319-68-21.** Reservations recommended. Main courses 6€–9€; set-price lunch 8€; set-price dinner 15€. MC, V. Tues–Sat 1:30–4pm and 8:30–11:30pm. Closed: Aug. Metro: Diagonal.

Tragaluz ★ MEDITERRANEAN Named after the turn-of-the-century modernist building that contains it, this well-respected restaurant has three very contemporary-looking, mostly beige dining rooms on three separate floors. Menu items are derived from fresh ingredients that vary with the season. Depending on the month of your visit, you might find terrine of duck liver, Santurce-style hake (with garlic and herbs), filet of sole stuffed with red peppers, and beef tenderloin in a Rioja wine sauce. One of the best desserts is a semi-soft slice of deliberately underbaked chocolate cake. Diners seeking low-fat dishes will find solace here, as will vegetarians. The vegetables served are the best and freshest on the market that day. You'll also find a sushi restaurant downstairs. Most dishes are at the lower end of the price scale.

Pasaje Concepción 5, Eixample. ✆ **93-487-01-96.** Reservations recommended. Main courses 9€–21€. AE, MC, V. Daily 1:30–4pm and 8:30pm–midnight. Metro: Diagonale or Provença.

NORTE DIAGONAL

VERY EXPENSIVE

Botafumeiro ★★★ SEAFOOD Although the competition is severe, this classic *marisquería* consistently puts Barcelona's finest seafood on the table. Much of the allure of this place comes from the attention to detail paid by the white-jacketed staff, who will prepare a setting at the establishment's bar for anyone who prefers to dine there. If you do choose to venture to the rear, you'll find a series of attractive dining rooms outfitted with light-grained panels, white napery, polished brass, potted plants, and paintings by Galician artists. These rooms are noted for the ease with which business deals are arranged during the lunch hour, when international business-types make it their rendezvous of choice. The king of Spain is occasionally a patron.

The menu includes the most legendary seafood in Barcelona, prepared ultra-fresh in a glistening, modern kitchen that's visible from parts of the dining room. The restaurant prides itself on its fresh and saltwater fish, clams, mussels, lobster, crayfish, scallops, and several varieties of crustaceans that you may never have seen before. Stored live in holding tanks or in enormous crates near the restaurant's entrance, many of the creatures are flown in daily from Galicia, home of owner Moncho Neira. In contrast to the 100-or-so fish dishes (which might include *zarzuelas,* paellas, and grills), the menu lists only four or five meat dishes, including three kinds of steak, veal, and a traditional version of pork with turnips. The wine list offers a wide array of *cavas* from Catalonia and highly drinkable choices from Galicia.

Gran de Gràcia 81. ✆ **93-218-42-30.** Reservations recommended for dining rooms. Main courses 21€–60€. AE, DC, MC, V. Daily 1pm–1am. Metro: Fontana.

Gaig ★★★ MODERN CATALAN One of the shining culinary showcases of Barcelona, Gaig was founded some 130 years ago by the great-grandmother of the present owner, Carlos Gaig. Back then it was known as a *fonda* or small inn for travelers. Despite the age of the building, the interior design is both modern and luxurious, having recently been restyled by well-known designers. The restaurant is celebrated locally for the quality and freshness of its food, purchased daily at the Boquería market in the heart of the old city. If you order a meal with eggs, they will have been contributed by chickens seen wandering about an outdoor patio where summer dining takes place. The cuisine centers on traditional Catalán recipes transformed to suit more modern palates. Among the best dishes to order are *arroz del delta con pichón y cetas* (delta rice with partridge and mushrooms), *rape asado a la catalana* (grilled monkfish with local herbs), and *els petits filet de vedella amb prunes i pinyons* (small veal filets with prunes and pine nuts). One of the tastiest dishes is marinated roast pork thigh. Desserts include *crema de Sant Joseph* (a warm flan with wild strawberries), homemade chocolates, and a selection of *tartes.*

Passeig de Maragall 402. ✆ **93-429-10-17.** Reservations recommended. Main courses 27€–38€; *menú gastronómico* 56€. AE, DC, MC, V. Tues–Sun 1:30–4pm and 9–11pm, Sun 1:30–4pm. Closed 3 weeks in Aug. Metro: Horta.

EXPENSIVE

Neichel ★★★ FRENCH/MEDITERRANEAN Owned and operated by Alsatian-born Jean Louis Neichel, who has been called "the most brilliant ambassador French cuisine has ever had within Spain," this restaurant serves a clientele best described as stratospheric. Outfitted in cool gray and pastels, with its main decoration derived from a bank of windows opening onto greenery, Neichel is almost obsessively concerned with gastronomy.

Your meal might include a mosaic of foie gras with vegetables, strips of salmon marinated in sesame and served with *escabeche* (vinaigrette) sauce, a prize-winning terrine of sea crab floating on a lavishly decorated bed of cold seafood sauce, escalope of turbot served with *coulis* (purée) of sea urchins, fricassée of Bresse chicken served with spiny lobsters, Spanish milk-fed lamb served with the juice of Boletus mushrooms, rack of lamb gratinéed within an herb-flavored pastry crust, and an array of well-flavored game birds obtained in season from hunters throughout Catalonia and France. Both the European cheeses and the changing array of freshly made desserts are spectacular.

Pedralbes 16. ✆ **93-334-06-99.** Reservations required. Main courses 21€–30€. AE, MC, V. Mon–Fri 1:30–3:30pm; Mon–Sat 8:30–11pm. Closed holidays and Aug. Metro: Palau Reial or María Cristina.

Reno Paradise ★ CATALAN/FRENCH One of the finest and most enduring haute cuisine restaurants in Barcelona, Reno boasts an impeccably mannered staff (formal but not intimidating) and an understated modern decor accented with black leather and oversized mirrors. A discreet row of sidewalk-to-ceiling windows hung with fine-mesh lace shelters diners from prying eyes on the octagonal plaza outside. Specialties, influenced by the seasons and by the traditions of France, might include partridge simmered in wine or port sauce, assorted smoked fish (each painstakingly smoked on the premises), filet of sole either stuffed with foie gras and truffles or grilled with anchovy sauce, Catalán-style civet of lobster, roast duck with a sauce of honey and sherry vinegar, and an appetizing array of pastries wheeled from table to table on a trolley. Dessert might also be one of several kinds of crepes flambéed at your table. The restaurant, incidentally, was established in the 1950s by the present owner's father.

Tuset 27. ✆ **93-200-91-29.** Reservations required. Main courses 9€–24€. AE, DC, MC, V. Sun–Fri 1–4pm; Sun–Sat 8:30–11:30pm. Metro: Diagonal.

Roig Robí ★ CATALAN This restaurant, whose name translated from Catalán means "ruby red" (the color of a perfectly aged Rioja), serves excellent food from an imaginative kitchen. A warm welcome keeps patrons coming back here, although we're not as excited about this restaurant as we once were. It remains, however, one of the city's most dependable choices. Begin by ordering an aperitif from the L-shaped oak bar. Then head down a long corridor to a pair of flower-filled dining rooms. In warm weather, glass doors open onto a walled courtyard, ringed with cascades of ivy and shaded with willows and mimosa. Menu items include fresh beans with pine-nut sauce, hake al Roig Robí, fresh mushroom salad with green beans and fresh tomatoes, shellfish from Costa Brava, ravioli stuffed with spring herbs, chicken stuffed with foie gras, and a cockscomb salad—the latter a dish too adventuresome for many palates.

Séneca 20. ✆ **93-218-92-22.** Reservations required. Main courses 13€–27€; fixed-price menu 42€. AE, DC, MC, V. Mon–Fri 1:30–4pm; Mon–Sat 9–11pm. Metro: Diagonal.

Via Veneto ★★ INTERNATIONAL With a soothing and dignified decor of calming colors and baroque swirls, this restaurant is known for its solid respectability and consistently well prepared cuisine. A short walk from the Plaça de Francesc Macia, it offers such dishes as a tartare of fresh fish with caviar, roasted salt cod with potatoes, veal kidney with truffle sauce, loin of roast suckling pig with baby vegetables of the season, and filet steak served in a brandy, cream, and peppercorn sauce. Innovative and imaginative Catalán recipes are always being created here. The cuisine is finely crafted based on superb local products, and there's a wide array of wines to accompany any meal. Dessert might be a richly textured combination of melted chocolate, cherries, Armagnac, and vanilla ice cream.

Ganduxer 10. ✆ **93-200-72-44.** Reservations required. Main courses 16€–29€. AE, DC, MC, V. Mon–Fri 1:15–4pm, Mon–Sat 8:30–11:30pm. Closed Aug 1–20. Metro: La Bonanova.

MOLL DE LA FUSTA & BARCELONETA

EXPENSIVE

Can Costa ★ SEAFOOD One of the most long-lived seafood restaurants in this seafaring town is Can Costa, an emporium of fish and shellfish whose big windows overlook the water. Originally established in the late 1930s, it has two busy dining rooms, a uniformed, well-seasoned staff, and an outdoor terrace where clients can take advantage of the streaming sunlight and harbor-front breezes. Fresh seafood rules the menu here, prepared according to traditional recipes. They include the best baby squid in town—sautéed in a flash so that it has an almost grilled flavor, and is rarely overcooked or too rubbery. A chef's specialty that has endured through many a season is *fideuá de peix,* which is equivalent to a classic Valencian shellfish paella, except in this case, noodles are used in lieu of rice. All the desserts are homemade by the kitchen staff daily.

Passeig Don Joan de Borbò 70. ✆ **93-221-59-03.** Reservations recommended. Main courses 18€–42€. AE, MC, V. Daily 12:30–4pm; Mon–Sat 8–11:30pm. Metro: Barceloneta.

Can Majó SEAFOOD Located in the old fishing quarter of Barceloneta, Can Majó attracts many people from the fancier quarters, who journey down here for a great seafood dinner. The Suárez-Majó family welcomes you; they're still operating a business where their grandmother first opened a bar. Try a house specialty, *pelada* (Catalán for *paella*), perhaps starting with *entremeses* (hors d'oeuvres), from which you can select barnacles, oysters, prawns, whelks, clams, and crab—whatever was caught that day. The clams with white beans are recommended. The classic all-vegetable gazpacho comes with fresh mussels and shrimp.

Almirante Aixada 23. ✆ **93-221-54-55.** Reservations recommended. Main courses 12€–23€; fixed-price menu 36€. AE, MC, V. Tues–Sun 1–4pm and 8–11:30pm. Metro: Barceloneta.

Ramonet ★ SEAFOOD Located in a Catalán-style villa near the seaport, this rather expensive restaurant serves a large variety of fresh seafood, and has done so since 1763. The front room, with stand-up tables for seafood tapas, beer, and regional wine, is often crowded. In the two dining rooms in back, lined with wooden tables, you can choose from a wide variety of fish—shrimp, hake, and monkfish are almost always available. Other specialties include a portion of pungent anchovies, grilled mushrooms, black rice, braised artichokes, and a tortilla with spinach and beans. Mussels "from the beach" are also sold.

Carrer Maquinista 17. ✆ **93-319-30-64.** Reservations recommended. Main courses 16€–26€; fixed-price menus 29€–44€. AE, DC, MC, V. Daily 10am–4pm and 8pm–midnight. Usually closed Aug 10–Sept 10. Metro: Barceloneta.

MODERATE

Agua ★ CATALAN/SEAFOOD It bustles, it's hip, and it serves well-prepared fish and shellfish in a hypermodern setting that overlooks the beach. A terrace beckons anyone who wants an in-your-face view of the water, but if the wind is blowing with a bit too much chill, you can retreat into the big-windowed blue-and-yellow dining room. Here, amid display cases with the catch of the day, you can order heaping portions of meats and fish that are grilled over an open fire. Excellent examples include grilled versions of chicken, fish, shrimp, crayfish, and an especially succulent version of stuffed squid. Most of these are served with as little culinary fanfare, and as few sauces, as possible, allowing the freshness and flavor of the raw ingredients to shine through the char-grilled coatings. Risottos, some of them studded with fresh clams and herbs, are usually winners, with many versions suitable for vegetarians.

Passeig Marítim de la Barceloneta 30 (Port Marítim). ✆ **93-225-12-72.** Reservations recommended. Main courses 7€–16€. AE, MC, V. Daily 1:30–4:30pm and 8:30pm–midnight (1am on Fri–Sat). Metro: Ciutadella.

7 Portes ★★ SEAFOOD This is a lunchtime favorite for businesspeople (the Stock Exchange is across the way) and an evening favorite for many in-the-know clients who have made it their preferred restaurant in Catalonia. It's been going since 1836. The restaurant's name means "Seven Doors," and it really does have seven doors. These open onto as many rooms, with smaller dining salons on the next landing. A festive and elegant place, it has a high-ceilinged main dining room, numerous gilt-framed mirrors, and a black-and-white marble floor. Waiters wear the long, white aprons of the Belle Epoque era. Regional dishes, served in enormous portions, include fresh herring with onions and potatoes, a different paella daily (sometimes with shellfish, for example, or with rabbit), and a wide array of fresh fish, succulent oysters, and an herb-laden stew of black beans with pork or white beans with sausage.

Passeig d'Isabel II 14. ✆ **93-319-30-33.** Reservations required. Main courses 15€–30€. AE, DC, MC, V. Daily 1pm–1am. Metro: Barceloneta.

NEAR ESTACIÓN DE SANTS

INEXPENSIVE

La Llauna ★ *Finds* CATALAN The name of this restaurant is a reference to the pot in which *calcots* are cooked. Available only in the spring, this rare dish is similar to a spring onion but twice or more the size with an almost meaty taste. It isn't easy to find this delicacy in Barcelona, but this restaurant specializes in them, cooked over an open charcoal grill. In the Sant area, it has two floors for diners, each decorated in a Catalán rustic style with white walls and posters of Mediterranean and local country life. Prices are very reasonable. The menu includes well-prepared regional dishes based on fresh, local products. Locals begin with *pa amb tomaquet* or toasted bread with tomatoes and olive oil, going on to sample such hearty fare as various grilled meats with fried potatoes or *gambas a la Llauna o con conejo* (shrimp or rabbit with *calcots* in wine sauce).

Plaça D'Osca 2. ✆ **93-422-32-25.** Reservations recommended on weekends. Main courses 5€–18€; *menú del día* (at lunch) 10€. MC, V. Thurs–Tues 1–4pm and 8pm–midnight. Metro: Plaça de Sants and Estación de Sants.

La Parra ★ *Finds* CATALAN The local neighborhood near the Barcelona-Santa train station is not so hot, but the food served here is worth the trek. The location is in a converted, two-century-old coach house. Once inside, you'll feel you've landed in the Catalán countryside as you order wine and food in a patio shaded by an ancient grape arbor. There is also a choice of three little rooms as well, each decorated in a rustic style.

We like the way the chef displays the meat or vegetable offerings of the day, everything from wild mushrooms to the best cuts of lamb. Ordered by the half pound here, lamb is the specialty and no one in Barcelona grills it better. It arrives perfectly cooked and aromatic with herbs at your table, accompanied by potatoes freshly baked in the chimney. Begin, perhaps, with pencil-thin asparagus grilled and served in a sauce made of pulverized almonds, hazelnuts, red pepper, and tomato, a delight in every way. Those wild mushrooms such as *pleurottes* or *boletes* are sautéed with aromatic garlic and sweet onions.

Carrer Joanot Martorell 3. ✆ **93-332-51-34.** Reservations required. Main courses 6€–18€. Sat–Sun 12:30–3:30pm, Tues–Sat 7:30–11pm. Closed: Aug. Metro: Hostafrancs.

VILA OLIMPICA

Talaia Mar ★★ CATALAN This is not only the best restaurant at Olympic Port, but has one of the most innovative menus in Catalonia. Marc Sangli, the chef, devises unique menus and turns out food that is both amusing and savory. The presentations are often simple yet always elegant. To discover this chef's talent, sample his crushed almond soup with grapes a la eucalyptus. The man is a culinary genius, turning out such surprises as "bacon ice cream," or corn ice cream with a warm foie gras soup over which vanilla oil is sprinkled. He makes the best potato omelet we've ever sampled, serving it with caramelized onions. Fresh fish from the market is perfectly grilled and served with a potato purée inspired by France's greatest chef, Joel Robuchon, who is celebrated for making the world's greatest mashed potatoes. The menu beat goes on, a tender, aromatically roasted rack of lamb given added flavor by the use of pineapple. Five species of tuna appear in a tartar flavored with trout caviar and soy sauce. We could return here night after night and always find some new dish to tempt the palate. Rising above the port, the restaurant is beside two towers, Hotel Arts and Torée Mapfre.

Marina 16. ✆ **93-221-90-90.** Reservations required. Main courses 10€–25.50€. Set menu 51€. AE, DC, MC, V. Daily 1–4pm and 8pm–midnight. Metro: Ciutadella-Vila Olímpica.

WEST OF TIBIDABO

La Balsa INTERNATIONAL Perched on the uppermost level of a circular tower originally built as a water cistern, La Balsa offers a view over most of the surrounding cityscape. To reach it you must climb up to what was originally the structure's rooftop. Glassed-in walls, awnings, and a verdant mass of potted plants create the decor. You're likely to be greeted by owner and founder Mercedes López before being seated. Menu items emerge from a cramped but well-organized kitchen several floors below. (The waiters here are reputedly the most athletic in Barcelona because they must run up and down the stairs carrying steaming platters.) Often booked several days in advance, the restaurant serves such dishes as a salad of broad beans (*judías verdes*) with strips of salmon in lemon-flavored vinaigrette, stewed veal with wild mushrooms, a salad of warm lentils with anchovies, pickled fresh salmon with chives, undercooked magret (breast) of duck served with fresh and lightly poached foie gras, and baked hake (flown in frequently from faraway Galicia) prepared in squid-ink sauce. The restaurant is 2km (1¼ miles) north of the city's heart, in the Tibidabo district, close to the Science Museum (Museu de la Ciència). The neighborhood is one of the greenbelts of Barcelona.

Infanta Isabel 4. ✆ **93-211-50-48.** Reservations required. Main courses 14€–24€. AE, MC, V. Tues–Sat 2–3:30pm; Mon–Sat 9–11:30pm. Closed Easter week. No buffet in Aug.

ON THE OUTSKIRTS

El Racó de Can Fabes ★★★ MEDITERRANEAN This is one of the greatest restaurants of Spain—maybe the greatest. if you don't mind the 30-minute drive or the 45-minute train ride from Barcelona, a distance of 52km (32 miles), you will be transported to a gourmet citadel, housed in a three-century-old building in the center of the Catalán village of 1,700 people. Santi SantaMaría and Angels Serra, who founded the restaurant in the '80s, seemed rather immune to press acclaim, continuing to show their discipline and craftsmanship in spite of all the raves. They don't let a single platter reach their dining room without getting its keen-eyed sense of approval. This Michelin three-star restaurant (its highest rating) is run with exquisite care and dedication. The restaurant is refined and elegant yet retains a rustic aura. Recent strokes of their inspiration included hot and cold mackerel with cream of caviar and tender pigeon with duck tartare. A heavenly concoction is spicy foie gras with Sauterne and a coulis (essence) of sweet red and green peppers. Two different preparations of crayfish, each one a delight, come both raw and cooked. Roast pigeon is prepared in ways that correspond to the seasons and the "mood of the chef." For dessert, there's nothing finer than their "Festival de chocolate."

Sant Joan 6, Sant Ceoloni. ✆ **93-867-28-51.** Reservations required. Main courses 29€–60€. Set menus 90€–111€. AE, DC, MC, V. Tues–Sun 1:30–3:30pm; Tues–Sat 8:30–10:30pm. Closed Jan 28–Feb 11 and June 24–July 8. Take any RENFE train from the Passeig de Gràcia station, heading for France, disembarking at Sant Ceoloni.

TASCAS

The bars listed below are known for their tapas; for further recommendations, refer to the "Barcelona After Dark" section of chapter 4.

Alt Heidelberg GERMAN/TAPAS Since the 1930s, this has been an institution in Barcelona, offering German beer on tap, a good selection of German sausages, and Spanish tapas. You can also enjoy full meals here—sauerkraut garni is a specialty.

Ronda Universitat 5. ✆ **93-318-10-32.** Tapas 1.55€–10€. MC, V. Mon–Fri 8am–1:30am, Sat–Sun noon–2am. Metro: Universitat.

Bar del Pi TAPAS One of the most famous bars in the Barri Gòtic, this establishment is midway between two medieval squares, opening onto the church of Pi. You can sit inside at one of the cramped bentwood tables or stand at the

Tips Fast Food & Picnic Fare

The Chicago Pizza Pie Factory, Calle de Provença 300 (✆ **93-215-94-15;** Metro: Passeig de Gràcia), offers pizzas for 9 to 27 , the latter big enough for four. It's open daily from 1pm to 1am; happy hour runs 5 to 9pm.

Café Viena, Ramble dels Estudis 115 (✆ **93-317-14-92;** Metro: Plaça de Catalunya), is Barcelona's most elegant fast-food place. Waiters wearing Viennese vests serve croissants with Roquefort for breakfast and, later in the day, toasted ham sandwiches, hamburgers with onions, and pasta with tomato sauce. Meals cost from 6 . Service is Monday to Saturday from 8:30am to 1am, Sunday from 9am to 11pm.

The best place to buy the makings for a picnic is **Mercat de la Boquería** ★, in the center of the Rambles (Metro: Liceu). This is the old marketplace of Barcelona. You'll jostle elbows with butchers and fishmongers in bloodied smocks and see salespeople selling cheeses and sausages. Much of the food is uncooked, but hundreds of items are already prepared, and you can even buy a bottle of wine or mineral water.

Now for where to have your picnic: Right in the heart of Barcelona is the Parc de la Ciutadella (see "Parks & Gardens" in chapter 4), at the southeast section of the district known as the Barri de la Ribera, site of the Picasso Museum. After lunch, take the kids to the park zoo and later go out on the lake in a rented rowboat. It's more scenic to picnic in Montjuïc, site of several events at the 1992 Summer Olympics. After your picnic, you can enjoy the amusement park, take in the Miró museum, or walk through the Poble Espanyol, a re-created Spanish village.

crowded bar. In warm weather, take a table beneath the single plane tree on this landmark square. The selection of tapas is limited; most visitors come to drink coffee, beer, or wine. The plaza, which people spill out onto, usually draws an interesting group of young bohemian sorts and travelers.

Plaça Sant Josep Oriol 1. ✆ **93-302-21-23.** Tapas 1.50€–4.40€. No credit cards. Mon–Fri 9am–11pm, Sat 9:30am–10pm, Sun 10am–10pm. Metro: Liceu.

Bar Turó TAPAS Set in an affluent residential neighborhood north of the old town, Bar Turó serves some of the best tapas in town. In summer you can either sit outside or retreat to the narrow confines of the inside bar. There you can select from about 20 different kinds of tapas, including Russian salad, fried squid, and Serrano ham.

Tenor Viñas 1. ✆ **93-200-69-53.** Tapas 1.80€–9€. MC, V. Mon–Sat 9am–midnight. Metro: María Cristina.

Bodega la Plata TAPAS Established in the 1920s, and part of a trio of famous bodegas on this narrow medieval street, La Plata occupies a corner building whose two open sides allow richly aromatic cooking odors to permeate the neighborhood. This bodega has a marble-topped bar and overcrowded tables. The culinary specialty is *raciones* (small plates) of deep-fried sardines (head and all). You can make a meal with two servings of these, coupled with the house's tomato, onion, and fresh anchovy salad.

Mercè 28. ✆ **93-315-10-09.** Tapas 1.50€–8€. No credit cards. Mon–Sat 9am–11pm. Metro: Barceloneta.

Bodegueta TAPAS Founded in 1940, this old wine tavern specializes in Catalán sausage meats. Everything can be washed down with inexpensive Spanish wines. Beer costs 1.05€ to 1.80€; wine goes for .90€.

Rambla de Catalunya 100. ✆ **93-215-48-94.** Tapas from 1.50€. No credit cards. Mon–Sat 8am–1:45am, Sun 7pm–1:30am. Metro: Diagonal.

Casa Alfonso TAPAS Spaniards love their ham, which comes in a great many forms. The best of the best is *jamón Jabugo,* the only kind sold at this traditional establishment. Entire hams hang from steel braces. They're taken down, carved, and trimmed before you into paper-thin slices. This particular form of cured ham, generically called *jamón Serrano,* comes from pigs fed acorns in Huelva, in deepest Andalusia. Devotees of all things porcine will ascend to piggy-flavored heaven.

Roger de Lluria 6. ✆ **93-301-97-83.** Tapas 4€–12€. No credit cards. Mon–Tues 9am–midnight, Wed–Sat 9am–1am. Metro: Urquinaona.

Casa Tejada TAPAS Covered with rough stucco and decorated with hanging hams, Casa Tejada (established in 1964) offers some of Barcelona's best tapas. Arranged behind a glass display case, they include such dishes as marinated fresh tuna, German-style potato salad, five preparations of squid (including one that's stuffed), and ham salad. For variety, quantity, and quality, this place is hard to beat. There's outdoor dining in summer.

Tenor Viñas 3. ✆ **93-200-73-41.** Tapas 2.10€–15€. MC, V. Daily 10am–2am. Metro: Muntaner.

Las Campanas (Casa Marcos) TAPAS No sign marks the restaurant—from the street Las Campanas looks like a storehouse for cured hams and wine bottles. At a long and narrow stand-up bar, patrons flock here for a chorizo, which is then pinioned between two pieces of bread. Sausages are usually eaten with beer or red wine. The place opened in 1952, and nothing has changed since. A tape recorder plays nostalgic favorites, everything from Edith Piaf to the Andrews Sisters.

Mercè 21. ✆ **93-315-06-09.** Tapas 1.30€–10€. No credit cards. Thurs–Tues 12:30am–4pm and 7pm–2am. Metro: Jaume I.

Quimet & Quimet ★ TAPAS/CHEESE This is a great tapas bar, especially for cheese, of which it offers the finest selection in Barcelona. Built at the turn of the 20th century, the tavern in the Poble Sec sector is still run by the fifth generation of Quimets. Their wine cellar is one of the best stocked of any tapas bar, and their cheese selection is varied. One night we sampled four on the same plate, including *nevat,* a tangy goat cheese; *cabrales,* an intense Spanish blue; *zamorano,* a hardy, nutty sheep's milk cheese, and *torta del Casar,* a soft, creamy farm cheese. Of course, you can also order other delights such as mussels with tomato confit and caviar, razor clams, and even sturgeon.

Poeta Cabanyes 25. ✆ **93-442-31-42.** Tapas 1.50€–9€. V. Metro: Paral.lel.

Rey de la Gamba ★ SHELLFISH The name of this place means "king of prawns," but the restaurant could also be called the House of Mussels since it sells more of that shellfish. In the old fishing village of Barceloneta, dating from the 18th century, this place packs them in, especially on weekends. A wide array of seafood is sold, along with cured ham—the combination is considered a tradition.

Joan de Borbò 48–53. ✆ **93-221-75-98.** Tapas 6€–12€. MC, V. Daily 11am–1am. Metro: Barceloneta.

DESSERT

Dulcinea Kids CHOCOLATE At this, the most famous chocolate shop in Barcelona, established in 1941, the specialty is *melindros* (sugar-topped soft-sided biscuits), which the regulars who flock here love to dunk into the very thick hot chocolate—so thick, in fact, that imbibing it feels like eating a melted chocolate bar. A cup of hot chocolate with cream costs 2.40€, and a *ración* of chocolate-flavored *churros* (a deep-fried pastry) goes for 1.20€.

Via Petrixol 2. ✆ **93-302-68-24.** Cup of chocolate 2.40€–3.60€. AE, MC, V. Daily 9am–1pm and 4:30–9pm. Closed Aug. Metro: Liceu.

4

Exploring Barcelona

Long a Mediterranean center of commerce, Barcelona is also one of the focal points of European tourism, a role sparked by the 1992 Olympic Games. Spain's second-largest city is also its most cosmopolitan and avant-garde.

Because of its rich history, Barcelona is filled with landmark buildings and world-class museums. These include Antoni Gaudí's famed Sagrada Família, the Museu Picasso, the Gothic cathedral, and Les Rambles, the famous tree-lined promenade cutting through the heart of the old quarter.

The capital of Catalonia, Barcelona sits at the northeast end of the Costa Brava, Spain's gateway to the Mediterranean. A half-hour flight east will land you on any of the Balearic Islands—fast-paced Majorca, rowdy Ibiza, or sleepy Minorca. (For more information on the Balearic Islands, consult *Frommer's Spain.*) You can also branch out from Barcelona to one of the sites of interest in its environs, including the beaches of Sitges, the monastery at Montserrat, and the Penedés vineyards (see "Side Trips from Barcelona," later in this chapter).

To begin, however, you'll want to take in the artistic and intellectual aura of this unique seafaring city. Residents take justifiable pride in their Catalán heritage, and they are eager to share it with you. Many of these sights can be covered on foot, and this chapter includes three walking tours.

An array of nightlife (Barcelona is a *big* bar town), shopping possibilities, and sports programs are also covered in this chapter, along with some organized tours, special events, and trips to Catalonia's wine country. It makes for some serious sightseeing; you'll need plenty of time to take it all in.

1 In & Around the Ciutat Vella (Old City)

The **Barri Gòtic** ★★ is the old aristocratic quarter of Barcelona, parts of which have survived from the Middle Ages. Spend at least 2 to 3 hours exploring its narrow streets and squares, which continue to form a vibrant, lively neighborhood today. Start by walking up the Carrer del Carme, east of Les Rambles. A nighttime stroll takes on added drama, but exercise caution.

The buildings, for the most part, are austere and sober, the cathedral being the crowning achievement. Roman ruins and the vestiges of 3rd-century walls add further interest. This area is intricately detailed and filled with many attractions that are easy to miss. For a tour of the Barri Gòtic, see the Walking Tour later in this chapter.

Catedral de Barcelona ★★ Barcelona's cathedral stands as a celebrated example of Catalonian Gothic architecture. Except for the 19th-century west facade, the basilica was begun at the end of the 13th century and completed in the mid–15th century. The three naves, cleaned and illuminated, have splendid Gothic details. With its large bell towers, blending of medieval and Renaissance styles, beautiful cloister, high altar, side chapels, sculptured choir, and Gothic arches, it ranks as one of the most impressive cathedrals in Spain. Vaulted galleries in the cloister surround a garden of magnolias, medlars, and palm trees; the galleries are further enhanced by forged iron grilles. The historian Cirici called this the loveliest oasis in Barcelona. The cloister, illuminated on Saturday and fiesta days, also contains a museum of medieval art. The most notable work displayed is the 15th-century *La Pietat* of Bartolomé Bermejo. At noon on Sunday you can see the *sardana,* a Catalonian folk dance, performed in front of the cathedral.

Plaça de la Seu s/n. ✆ **93-315-15-54.** Free admission to cathedral; museum, 1.20€. Cathedral, daily 8am–1:30pm and 4–7:30pm; cloister museum, daily 10am–1pm. Metro: Jaume I.

Museu d'Art Contemporani de Barcelona ★ A soaring, glistening white edifice in Barcelona's once-shabby but on-the-rebound Raval district, the Museum of Contemporary Art is to Barcelona what the Pompidou Center is to Paris. Designed by the American architect Richard Meier, the building itself is a work of art, manipulating sunlight to offer brilliant, natural interior lighting. On display in the 74,000 square feet of exhibit space are the works of such modern luminaries as Tàpies, Klee, Miró, and many others. The museum has a library, bookstore, and cafeteria.

Plaça dels Angels 1. ✆ **93-412-08-10.** Admission 6€ adults, 4€ students, free for children. Wed–Sat 11am–7:30pm, Sun 10am–3pm. Metro: Plaça de Catalunya.

Museu de l'Erotica In the heart of Barcelona, this offbeat museum offers a series of tantalizing exhibits that range from the tame to the tempestuous. At least it proves that sex wasn't discovered by the hippies of the 1960s. The museum publishes very lofty sounding information about its goal to examine the anthropological and sociological aspect of "humanity's history and culture." But, let's face it: Most visitors come here to see the "dirty stuff." And there's plenty of that, especially those vintage porn flicks from the '20s where such stars as Joan Crawford got her start. Sculptures depict more than Rodin's "The Kiss," and there are sketches revealing acrobatics that might be unfamiliar to you. The most amusing exhibit? We'd vote for the so-called "pleasure chair" dating from the Middle Ages. In all, there are more than 800 pieces of erotic art, spanning various cultures. One section is devoted to contemporary erotic art as well. In this modern section, the subject is still sex: it's just photographed differently.

Rambla 96. ✆ **93-318-98-65.** Admission 7€ adults, 6€ students. June–Sept daily 10am–midnight, Oct–May daily 11am–9pm. Metro: Liceu.

Museu Frederic Marès ★★ One of the biggest repositories of medieval sculpture in the region is the Frederic Marès Museum, located just behind the cathedral. It's housed in an ancient palace whose interior courtyards, chiseled stone, and soaring ceilings are impressive in their own right, an ideal setting for the hundreds of polychrome sculptures. The sculpture section dates from pre-Roman times to the 20th century. Also housed in the same building is the Museu Sentimental, a collection of everyday items that help to illustrate life in Barcelona during the past two centuries. Admission to both museums is included in the ticket price.

Plaça de Sant Iú 5–6. ✆ **93-310-58-00.** Admission 3€ adults, free for children 12 and under. Tues–Sat 10am–7pm; Sun 10am–3pm. Metro: Jaume I. Bus: 17, 19, or 45.

Palau Reial (Royal Palace) ★ The former palace of the counts of Barcelona, this later became the residence of the kings of Aragón. It is believed

Central Barcelona Attractions

Casa Amatller **18**
Casa Batlló **17**
Casa de L'Ardiaca **29**
Casa Lleó Morera **19**
Casa Milá **13**
Casa Museu Gaudí **9**
Castell de la Ciutat/Ayuntamiento **27**
Castell de Montjuic **1**
Castell de Tres Dragons **35**
Catedral de Barcelona **28**
Center of Contemporary Culture of Barcelona **20**
Fundació Antoni Tàpies **16**
Fundación Francisco Godia **14**
Fundació Joan Miró **3**
Galeria Olimpica **2**
Gran Teatre del Liceu **23**
L'Aquarium de Barcelona **26**
Mirador de Colón **25**
Monastir de Pedrables **10**
Monument à Colom **25**
Museu Arqueológic **4**
Museu-Barbier-Mueller Art Precolombí **33**
Museu d'Art Contemporàreo de Barcelona **21**
Museu d'Art Modern **38**
Museu de la Ciència **10**
Museu de les Arts Decoratives **8**
Museu Egipic de Barcelona **15**
Museu de l'Erotica **22**
Museu Frederic Marès **31**
Museu Geològie **36**
Museu d'Historia de la Ciutat **29**
Museu Marítim **25**
Museu Nacional d'Art de Catalunya **5**
Museu Picasso **34**
Museu Tèxtil i d'Indumentària **32**
Palau Güell **24**
Palau Reial (Royal Palace) **30**
Parc de Joan Miró **7**
Parc de la Ciutadella **37**
Parc Guëll **11**
Parc Zoologic **39**
Proble Espanyol **6**
Sagrada Famîla **12**
Torre de Collserola **9**

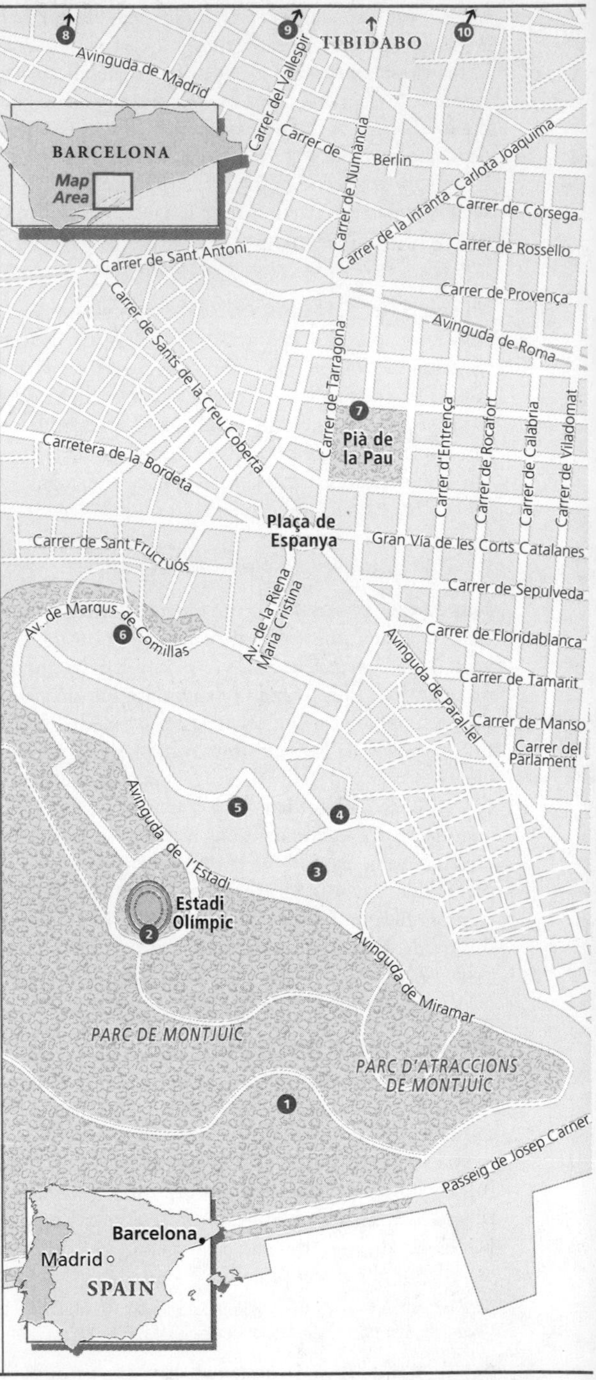

Plaça de Francesc Macia
Travessara de Gràcia
Carrer de Buenos Aires
Carrer de Londres
Carrer de Paris
Avinguda Diagonal
Carrer de Còrsega
EIXAMPLE
Carrer de Provença
Travessara de Gràcia
Av. de Sant Antoni Maria Claret
Carrer de la Industria
Carrer de Rossello
Carrer de Roger de Flor
Plaça de la Sagrada Família
Avinguda Diagonal
Carrer de Mallorca
Carrer de Valencia
Carrer d'Aragó
Passeig de Gracia
Rambla de Catalunya
Carrer de Balmes
Carrer de Pau Claris
Carrer de Comte Borrell
Carrer del Comte d'Urgell
Carrer de Villarroel
Carrer de Casanova
Carrer de Muntaner
Carrer d'Aribau
Carrer del Consell de Cent
Carrer de la Diputació
Plaça de la Universitat
Gran Vía de les Corts Catalanes
Carrer de R. de Llúcia
Carrer del Bruc
Carrer de Girona
Carrer de Bailèn
Passeig de Sant Joan
Carrer de Napols
Carrer de Sicilia
Plaça de Tetuan
Carrer de Pelai
Ronda Universitat
Ronda de Sant Antoni
Plaça Catalunya
Plaça Urquinaona
Carrer de Casp
Carrer d'Ausias Marc
Carrer d'Ali Bei
Carrer de Ribes
Carrer de Sardenya
RAVAL
Ronda de Sant Pere
Av. Portal de l'Angel
Ronda Sant Pau
Carrer de Hospital
La Rambla
BARRI GÒTIC
Via Laietana
Passeig de Lluis Companys
Passeig de Carles I
Carrer de Sant Pau
Carrer de Ferran
Carrer de la Princesa
Carrer de Comerc
Passeig de Pujades
Carrer Nou de la Rambla
Passeig de Picasso
Avinguda de les Drassanes
LA RIBERA
PARC DE LA CIUTADELLA
Carrer de Wellington
La Rambla
Carrer Ample
Passeig de Colom
PARC ZOOLOGIC
Villa Olimpic
Plaça Portal de la Pau
Moll de la Fusta
Avinguda d'Icàvia
Moll d'Espanya
BARCELONETA
0 1/4 mi
0 0.25 km
N
11 12 13 14 15 16 17 18 19 20 21 22 23 24 25 26 27 28 29 30 31 32 33 34 35 36 37 38 39

that Columbus was received here by Isabella and Ferdinand when he returned from his first voyage to the New World. Here, some believe, the monarchs got their first look at a Native American. The Saló del Tinell, a banquet hall with a wood-paneled ceiling held up by half a dozen arches, dates from the 14th century. Rising five stories above the hall is the Torre del Reí Martí, a series of porticoed galleries.

Plaça del Rei. ✆ **93-315-11-11.** Admission 3.50€. Summer, Tues–Sat 10am–8pm; off-season, Tues–Sat 10am–2pm and 4–8pm; year-round Sun 10am–2pm. Bus: 16, 17, 19, 22, or 45.

Museu Barbier-Mueller Art Precolombí ★★ Inaugurated by Queen Sofía in 1997, this is one of the most important collections of pre-Columbian art in the world. In the restored Palacio Nadal, built during the Middle Ages, the collection contains almost 6,000 pieces of tribal and ancient art. Josef Mueller (1887–1977) acquired the first pieces by 1908. Pre-Columbian cultures created religious, funerary, and ornamental objects of great stylistic variety with relatively simple means. Stone sculpture and ceramic objects are especially outstanding. For example, the Olmecs, who settled on the Gulf of Mexico at the beginning of the first millennium B.C., executed notable monumental sculpture in stone and magnificent figures in jade. Many exhibits focus on the Mayan culture, the most homogenous and widespread of its time, dating from 1000 B.C. Mayan artisans mastered painting, ceramics, and sculpture. Note also the work by the pottery makers of the Lower Amazon, particularly those from the island of Marajó.

Carrer de Montcada 12–14. ✆ **93-319-75-03.** Admission 3€ adults, 1.25€ students, free for children under 12. Free to all first Sat of every month. Tues–Sat 10am–8pm, Sun and holidays 10am–3pm. Metro: Jaume I. Bus: 14, 17, 19, 39, 40, 45, or 51.

2 In the Eixample

Fundació Antoni Tàpies ★ When it opened in 1990, this became the third Barcelona museum devoted to the work of a single artist. In 1984 the Catalán artist Antoni Tàpies set up a foundation bearing his name, and the city of Barcelona donated an ideal site: the old Montaner i Simon publishing house near the Passeig de Gràcia in the 19th-century Eixample district. One of the landmark buildings of Barcelona, the brick-and-iron structure was built between 1881 and 1884 by that exponent of Catalán Art Nouveau, architect Lluís Domènech i Montaner. The core of the museum is a collection of works by Tàpies (most contributed by the artist himself), covering the different stages of his career as it evolved into abstract expressionism. Here you can see the entire spectrum of mediums in which he worked: painting, assemblage, sculpture, drawing, and ceramics. His associations with Picasso and Miró are apparent. The largest of all the works by Tàpies is on top of the building itself: a controversial gigantic sculpture made from 2,700m (9,000 ft.) of metal wiring and tubing, entitled *Cloud and Chair.*

Aragó 255. ✆ **93-487-03-15.** Admission 4.20€ adults, 2.10€ students, free for children under 11. Tues–Sun 10am–8pm. Metro: Passeig de Gràcia.

Fundación Francisco Godia *Finds* In the heart of Barcelona, this new museum showcases the famous art collection of Francisco Godia Sales, the Catalán art collector and entrepreneur. He amassed one of the great private collections of art in the country. Godia (1921–90) combined a love of art with a head for business and a passion for motor racing. When he wasn't driving fast ("the most wonderful thing in the world"), he was amassing his art collection. As a collector, he showed exquisite taste and great artistic sensibility.

Moments Taking the Bull by the Horns

Cataláns don't pursue bullfighting with as much fervor as do the Castilians of Madrid. Nevertheless, you may want to attend a *corrida* in Barcelona. Bullfights are held April to September, usually Sunday at 6:30pm at the Plaça de Toros Monumental, Gran Vía de les Corts Catalanes (✆ **93-245-58-04**). Purchase tickets 13€ to 95€ in advance from the office at Muntaner 24 (✆ **93-453-38-21**).

He gathered a splendid array of medieval sculpture and ceramics, but showed a keener instinct for purchasing great paintings, Godia acquired works by some of the most important artists of the 20th century, including Julio González, María Blanchard, Joan Ponç, Antoni Tàpies, and Manolo Hugué, the latter a great friend of Picasso. From its earliest stages, Godia realized the artistic importance of Catalán modernismo and collected works by sculptors like Josep Llimona and painters like Santiago Rusiñol and Ramón Casas. Godia also dipped deeper into the past, acquiring works, for example, of two of the most important artists of the 17th century: Jacob van Ruysdael and Luca Giordano.

Carrer Valencia 284. ✆ **93-272-31-80.** Admission 4.50€ adults, 2.10€ children and students. Free 4 and under. Wed-Mon 10am–8pm. Metro: Passeig de Gràcia.

Museu Egipci de Barcelona Spain's only museum dedicated specifically to Egyptology contains more than 250 pieces from founder Jordí Clos's personal collection. On display are sarcophagi, jewelry, hieroglyphics, and various sculptures and artworks. Exhibits pay close attention to the everyday life of ancient Egyptians, including details regarding education, social customs, religion, and food. The museum possesses its own lab for restorations. A library with more than 3,000 works is open to the public.

Calle València 284. ✆ **93-488-01-88.** Admission 5.50€ adults, 4.50€ students and children. Mon–Sat 10am–2pm and 4–8pm, Sun 10am–2pm. Guided tours Sat. Closed holidays. Metro: Passeig de Gràcia.

La Sagrada Família ★★ Gaudí's incomplete masterpiece is one of the more idiosyncratic creations of Spain—if you have time to see only one Catalán landmark, make it this one. Begun in 1882 and still incomplete at Gaudí's death in 1926, this incredible church—the Church of the Holy Family—is a bizarre wonder. The languid, amorphous structure embodies the essence of Gaudí's style, which some have described as Art Nouveau run rampant. Work continues on the structure, but without any sure idea of what Gaudí intended. Some say that the church will be completed by the mid–21st century. The crypt of the cathedral features a small museum of the architect's scale models. Photographs show the progress (or lack thereof) of construction on the building; there are even photos of Gaudí's funeral.

Majorca 401. ✆ **93-207-30-31.** Admission (includes video) 4.80€. Elevator to the top (about 60m/200 ft.) 1.20€. Daily, Nov–Feb 9am–6pm; Mar and Sept–Oct, 9am–7pm; Apr and Aug, 9am–8pm. Metro: Sagrada Família.

3 In & Around the Parc de la Ciutadella

Museu d'Art Modern This museum shares a wing of the Palau de la Ciutadella with the Catalonian parliament. Constructed in the 1700s, it was once used as an arsenal, forming part of Barcelona's defenses. It later became a royal residence before being turned into a museum early in the last century. Its collection focuses on the early 20th century and features the work of Catalán artists, including Martí Alsina, Vayreda, Casas, Fortuny, and Rusiñol. The collection also encompasses some 19th-century Romantic and neoclassical works, as well as *modernista* furniture (including designs by architect Puig i Cadafalch).

Plaça d'Armes, Parc de la Ciutadella. ✆ **93-319-57-28.** Admission 3€ adults, 2.10€ youths 8–21, free for children under 8. Tues–Sat 10am–7pm, Sun 10am–2:30pm. Closed Jan 1, Dec 25. Metro: Arc de Triomf. Bus: 14, 16, 17, 39, 40, 41, 51, 57, 59, or 64.

Museu Picasso ★★ Two old palaces on a medieval street have been converted into this museum housing works by Pablo Picasso, who donated some 2,500 of his paintings, engravings, and drawings in 1970. Picasso was particularly fond of Barcelona, the city where he spent much of his formative youth. In fact, some of the paintings were done when Picasso was only 9 years old. One portrait, dating from 1896, depicts his stern aunt, Tía Pepa. Another, completed when Picasso was 16, depicts *Science and Charity* (his father was the model for the doctor). Many of the works, especially the early paintings, show the artist's debt to van Gogh, El Greco, and Rembrandt; a famous series, *Las Meninas* (1957), is said to "impersonate" the work of Velázquez. From Picasso's blue period, the *La Vie* drawings are the most interesting. His notebooks contain many sketches of Barcelona scenes. In 1999 the museum acquired two more medieval mansions for its exhibition space, increasing the museum's size by a third. This additional space is used for temporary exhibitions.

Montcada 15–19. ✆ **93-319-63-10.** Admission 4.80€ adults, 2.40€ students and people under 25, free for children under 13. Tues–Sat 10am–8pm, Sun 10am–3pm. Metro: Jaume I.

4 In & Around the Parc de Montjuïc

Fundació Joan Miró ★ Born in 1893, Joan Miró went on to become one of Spain's greatest painters, known for his whimsical abstract forms and brilliant colors. Some 10,000 works by this Catalán surrealist, including paintings, graphics, and sculptures, have been collected here. The foundation building has been greatly expanded in recent years, following the design of Catalán architect Josep Lluís Sert, a close personal friend of Miró. An exhibition in a modern wing charts (in a variety of media) Miró's complete artistic evolution, from his first drawings at the age of 8 to his last works. Temporary exhibitions on contemporary art are also frequently shown.

Plaça de Neptú, Parc de Montjuïc. ✆ **93-443-94-70.** Admission 7.20€ adults, 3.60€ students, free for children under 15. June–Sept, Tues–Wed and Fri–Sat 10am–8pm, Thurs 10am–9:30pm, Sun 10am–2:30pm; Nov–May, Tues–Wed and Fri–Sat 10am–7pm, Thurs 10am–9:30pm, Sun 10am–2:30pm. Bus: 50 at Plaça d'Espanya.

Galería Olímpica An enthusiastic celebration of the 1992 Olympic Games in Barcelona, this is one of the few museums in Europe exclusively devoted to sports and sports statistics. Its exhibits include photos, costumes, and memorabilia, with heavy emphasis on the pageantry, the number of visitors who attended, and the fame the events brought to Barcelona. Of interest to statisticians, civic planners, and sports buffs, the gallery has audiovisual information about the building programs that prepared the city for the onslaught of visitors. There are also conference facilities, an auditorium, video recordings of athletic events, and archives. In the cellar of the Olympic Stadium's southeastern perimeter, the museum is most easily reached by entering the stadium's southern gate (Porta Sud).

Passeig Olímpic s/n, lower level. ✆ **93-426-06-60.** Admission 2.40€. Apr–Sept, Tues–Sat 10am–2pm and 4–7pm, Sun 10am–2pm; Oct–Mar, Tues–Sat 10am–1pm and 4–6pm, Sun 10am–2pm. Metro: Espanya. Bus: 50.

Museu Arqueològic Occupying the former Palace of Graphic Arts, built for the 1929 World's Fair, the Museu Arqueològic reflects the long history of this Mediterranean port city, beginning with prehistoric Iberian artifacts. The collection includes articles from the Greek, Roman (glass, ceramics, mosaics, bronzes), and Carthaginian periods. Some of the more interesting relics were excavated in the ancient Greco-Roman city of Empúries in Catalonia; other parts of the collection came from the Balearic Islands.

Passeig de Santa Madrona 39–41, Parc de Montjuïc. ✆ **93-423-21-49.** Admission 2.40€ adults, 1.80€ students, free for children. Tues–Sat 9:30am–7pm, Sun 10am–2:30pm. Metro: Espanya. Bus: 55.

Museu Nacional d'Art de Catalunya ★★ This museum is the major depository of Catalán art. With massive renovations recently completed, the National Art Museum of Catalonia is perhaps the most important center for Romanesque art in the world. More than 100 pieces, including sculptures, icons, and frescoes, are on display. The highlight of the museum is the collection of murals from various Romanesque churches. The frescoes and murals are displayed in apses, much as in the churches in which they were found. Each is placed in sequential order, providing the viewer with a tour of Romanesque art from its primitive beginnings to the more advanced, late Romanesque and early Gothic era.

Palau Nacional, Parc de Montjuïc. ✆ **93-622-03-60.** Admission 4.80€ adults, 2.40€ youths 7–20, free for children under 7. Tues–Wed and Fri–Sat 10am–7pm, Thurs 10am–9pm, Sun 10am–2:30pm. Metro: Espanya.

Poble Espanyol ★ *Kids* In this re-created Spanish village built for the 1929 World's Fair, various regional architectural styles, from the Levante to Galicia, are reproduced—in all, 115 life-size reproductions of buildings and monuments, ranging from the 10th through the 20th centuries. At the entranceway, for example, stands a facsimile of the gateway to the walled city of Avila. The center of the village has an outdoor cafe where you can sit and have drinks. Numerous shops sell crafts and souvenir items from all of the provinces, and in some of them you can see artists at work, printing fabric and blowing glass. Ever since the 1992 Olympics, the village has offered 14 restaurants of varying styles, one disco, and eight musical bars. In addition, visitors can see an audiovisual presentation about Barcelona and Catalonia in general. Many families delight in the faux Spanish atmosphere here, though more discriminating visitors find it a bit of a tourist trap—overly commercialized and somewhat cheesy. It's a matter of personal taste.

Marqués de Comillas, Parc de Montjuïc. ✆ **93-325-78-66.** Admission 7€ adults, 3.60€ children 7–12, free for children under 7. Audiovisual hall free. Mon 9am–8pm, Tues–Thurs 9am–2am, Fri–Sat 9am–4am, Sun 9am–midnight. Metro: Espanya. Bus: 13 or 50.

5 In La Barceloneta & the Harbor

Mirador de Colón This monument to Christopher Columbus was erected at the Barcelona harbor on the occasion of the Universal Exhibition of 1888. It consists of three parts, the first being a circular structure, raised by four stairways 6m (19½ ft.) wide and eight iron heraldic lions. On the plinth are eight bronze bas-reliefs depicting Columbus's principal feats. (The originals were destroyed; these are copies.) The second part is the base of the column, consisting of an eight-sided polygon, four sides of which act as buttresses; each side contains sculptures. The third part is the 50m (167-ft.) column, which is Corinthian in style. The capital boasts representations of Europe, Asia, Africa, and America—all linked together. Finally, over a princely crown and a hemisphere recalling the newly discovered part of the globe, is an 8m (25-ft.) high bronze statue of Columbus—pointing, ostensibly, to the New World—by Rafael Ataché. Inside the iron column, an elevator ascends to the *mirador.* From here, a panoramic view of Barcelona and its harbor unfolds.

Portal de la Pau. ✆ **93-302-52-24.** Admission 2€ adults, 1.30€ children 4–12, free for children under 4. Sept 25–March, Mon–Fri 10am–2pm and 3:30–6:30pm, Sat–Sun and holidays 10am–6:30pm; Apr–May, Mon–Fri 10am–2pm and 3:30–7:30pm, Sat–Sun 10am–7:30pm. June–Sept 24, daily 9am–8:30pm. Closed Jan 1, Jan 6, Dec 25–26. Metro: Drassanes. Bus: 14, 18, 36, 57, 59, or 64.

L'Aquarium de Barcelona One of the most impressive testimonials to sea life anywhere opened in 1996 in Barcelona's Port Vell, a 10-minute walk from the bottom of the Rambles. The largest aquarium in Europe, it contains 21 glass tanks positioned along either side of a wide curving corridor. Each tank depicts a different marine habitat, with emphasis on everything from multicolored fish and corals to seagoing worms to sharks. The highlight is a huge "oceanarium" representative of the Mediterranean as a self-sustaining ecosystem. You view it from the inside of a glass-roofed, glass-sided tunnel that runs along its entire length, making fish, eels, and sharks appear to swim around you.

Port Vell. ✆ **93-221-74-74.** Admission 9€ adults, 6€ children 4–12 and students, free for children under 4. July and Aug daily 9:30am–11pm; June and Sept daily 9:30am–9:30pm; Oct–May daily 9:30am–9pm. Metro: Drassanes or Barceloneta.

Museu Marítim ★★ Located in the former Royal Shipyards (Drassanes Reials), this 13th-century Gothic complex was used for the construction of ships for the Catalán-Aragonese rulers. The most outstanding exhibition here is a reconstruction of *La Galería Real* of Don Juan of Austria, a lavish royal galley. Another special exhibit features a map by Gabriel de Vallseca that was owned by explorer Amerigo Vespucci.

Av. de las Drassanes s/n. ✆ **93-342-99-20.** Admission 5.40€ adults, 2.70€ children 7–17 and seniors, free for children under 7. Tues–Sat 10am–7pm. Closed holidays. Metro: Drassanes. Bus: 14, 18, 36, 38, 57, 59, 64, or 91.

6 Outside the City Center

Museu de la Ciència (Science Museum) ★ Museu de la Ciència of the La Caixa Foundation is one of the most popular museums in Barcelona, with more than 500,000 people visiting annually. Its modern design and hands-on activities have made it the most important science museum in Spain and a major cultural attraction.

Visitors can touch, listen, watch, and participate in a variety of hands-on exhibits. From the beauty of marine life to the magic of holograms, the museum offers a world of science to discover. Ride on a human gyroscope, hear a friend whisper from 20m (65 ft.) away, feel an earthquake, or use the tools of a scientist to examine intricate life forms with microscopes and video cameras.

More than 300 exhibits explore the wonders of science, from optics to space travel to the life sciences. In the "Optics and Perception" exhibits, visitors can interact with prisms, lenses, and holograms and walk inside a kaleidoscope. In the "Living Planet" area, baby sharks swim, a tornado swirls, and plants magically change their form when touched.

In the "Mechanics" exhibit, visitors can lift a 40kg (88-lb.) weight with little effort. The use of lasers and musical instruments provides a fun way to learn about sound and light waves. Throughout the exhibits, there are computers to help you delve deeper into various topics. Visitors can also walk inside a submarine and make weather measurements in a working weather station. For those who want to explore new worlds, there are planetarium shows where the beauty of the night sky surrounds the audience.

The museum is a bit out of the way: To get here, take a bus (see above) at the Plaça Catalunya and go all the way to Avinguda del Tibidabo. Then follow the signs for two blocks, turning left onto Carrer Teodor Roviralta, where you'll see the museum. It's right at the southern foothills of Tibidabo in a greenbelt district of Barcelona.

Teodor Roviralta 55. ✆ **93-212-60-50.** Admission to museum and planetarium, 3€ Planetarium only 1.50€. Tues–Sun 10am–8pm. Bus: 17, 22, 58, or 73.

Monestir de Pedralbes One of the oldest buildings in Pedralbes (the city's wealthiest residential area) is this monastery, founded in 1326 by Elisenda de Montcada, queen of Jaume II. Still a convent, the establishment is also the mausoleum of the queen, who is buried in its Gothic church. Walk through the cloisters, with nearly 2 dozen arches on each side, rising three stories. A small chapel contains the chief treasure of the monastery, murals by Ferrer Bassa, who was the major artist of Catalonia in the 1300s.

This monastery was a minor attraction of Barcelona until 1993, when 72 paintings and eight sculptures from the famed Thyssen-Bornemisza collection went on permanent display here. Among the more outstanding works of art are Fra Angelico's *The Virgin of Humility* and 20 paintings from the early German Renaissance period. Italian Renaissance paintings range from the end of the 15th century to the middle of the 16th century, as exemplified by works of Dosso Dossi, Lorenzo Lotto, Tintoretto, Veronese, and Titian. The baroque era is also represented, including such old masters as Rubens, Zurbarán, and Velázquez.

Baixada del Monestir 9. ✆ **93-203-92-82.** Admission 4.80€ adults, 3€ students and seniors over 64, free for children under 13. Tues–Sun 10am–2pm. Metro: Reina Elisenda. Bus: 22, 63, 64, 75, or 114.

Museu de les Arts Decoratives Set in a beautiful park, this palace was constructed as a municipal gift to Alfonso XIII. He didn't get to make much use of it, however, as he was forced into exile in 1931. Today it houses a collection of objets d'art, furniture, jewelry, and glassware from the 14th century to the present. More than 200 pieces, all of Spanish origin, are on display.

Palau Reial de Pedralbes, Av. Diagonal 686. ✆ **93-280-50-24.** Admission 3.50€. Free 1st Sun of every month. Tues–Sat 10am–6pm, Sun and holidays 10am–3pm. Metro: Palau Reial. Bus: 7, 63, 67, 68, or 75.

Torre de Collserola Some city planners hailed this as the most ambitious building project of the 1992 Olympics. When it was perceived that Barcelona lacked a state-of-the-art television transmitter, a team of engineers whipped up plans for a space-age needle. Completed within 24 months of its initiation, it rises 282m (940 ft.) above the city's highest mountain ridge, the Collserola, beaming TV signals throughout the rest of Europe. Open now as a tourist attraction, the tower offers panoramic views over Catalonia, as well as insight into some of the most bizarre engineering in town. Trussed with cables radiating outward to massive steel anchors, the tower perches delicately atop an alarmingly narrow vertical post only 4.2m (14 ft.) wide. A high-speed elevator carries visitors from deep inside the mountain (where there's a cafeteria) to an observation platform 546m (1,820 ft.)above the Mediterranean.

Carretera de Vallvidrera, Turó de la Vilana. ✆ **93-406-93-54.** Admission 4.40€. Wed–Fri 11am–2:30pm and 3:30–7pm, Sat–Sun 11am–7pm. A funicular goes to a point near the tower's parking lot; from here, free minivans make frequent runs up the mountain to the tower's base.

7 Parks & Gardens

Barcelona isn't just museums; much of its life takes place outside, in its unique parks and gardens, through which you'll want to stroll. The **Parc Güell** ★★ (✆ **93-424-38-09**) was begun by Gaudí as a real-estate venture for a friend, the wealthy, well-known Catalán industrialist Count Eusebi Güell, but it was never completed. Only two houses were constructed, but it makes for an interesting excursion nonetheless. The city took over the property in 1926 and turned it into a public park. It's open May to September, daily 10am to 9pm; October to April, daily 10am to 6pm. Admission is free. To reach the park, take bus no. 24, 25, 31, or 74.

One of the houses, **Casa-Museu Gaudí,** Carrer del Carmel 28 (✆ **93-219-38-11**), contains models, furniture, drawings, and other memorabilia of the architect. Gaudí, however, did not design the house—Ramón Berenguer claimed that honor. Admission is 3€. The museum can be visited Sunday to Friday from 10am to 8pm.

Gaudí completed several of the public areas of the park, which today look like a surrealist Disneyland, complete with a mosaic pagoda and a lizard fountain spitting water. Originally he planned to make this a model community of 60 dwellings, somewhat like the arrangement of a Greek theater. A central grand plaza with its market below was built, as well as an undulating bench decorated with ceramic fragments. The bizarre Doric columns of the would-be market are hollow, part of Gaudí's drainage system.

Another attraction, **Tibidabo Mountain** ★, offers the finest view of Barcelona. A funicular takes you up 480m (1,600 ft.) to the top. The ideal time to visit this summit (the culmination of the Sierra de Collcerola) north of the port is at sunset, when the city lights are on. An amusement park, with a Ferris wheel swinging over Barcelona, has been opened here. (For more information on this Parc d'Atraccions, see "Especially for Kids," below.) There's also a church, called Temple del Sagrat Cor (Sacred Heart), in this carnival-like setting, plus restaurants and mountaintop hotels. From Plaça de Catalunya, take a bus to Avinguda del Tibidabo, where you can board a special bus that will transport you to the funicular. Hop aboard to scale the mountain. The funicular runs daily 7:15am to 9:45pm and costs 2.70€ each way.

Located in the south of the city, the mountain park of **Montjuïc** (*Montjuch* in Spanish) has splashing fountains, gardens, outdoor restaurants, and museums, making for quite an outing. The re-created Spanish village, the Poble Espanyol, and the Joan Miró Foundation are also in the park. There are many walks and vantage points for viewing the Barcelona skyline.

The park was the site of several events during the 1992 Summer Olympics. An illuminated fountain display, the **Fuentes Luminosas,** at Plaça de la Font Magica, near Plaça d'Espanya, is on view from 8 to 11pm every Saturday and Sunday October to May, and from 9pm to midnight on Thursday, Saturday, and Sunday June to September. See the individual attractions in the park for their various hours of opening. To reach the top, take bus no. 61 from Plaça d'Espanya or the Montjuïc funicular.

Parc de la Ciutadella, Av. Wellington s/n (✆ **93-225-67-80**), gets its name, Park of the Citadel, because it's the site of a former fortress that defended the city. After Philip V won the War of the Spanish Succession (Barcelona was on the losing side), he got his revenge. He ordered that the "traitorous" residential suburb be leveled. In its place rose a citadel. In the mid–19th century it, too, was leveled, though some of the architectural evidence of that past remains in a governor's palace and an arsenal. Today, most of the park is filled with lakes, gardens, and promenades, but it includes a **zoo** (see "Especially for Kids," below) and the **Museu d'Art Modern** (see "In & Around the Parc de la Ciutadella," earlier in this chapter). Gaudí is said to have contributed to the monumental fountain in the park when he was a student. The park is open, without charge, daily 8am to 9pm. To reach the park, take the Metro to Ciutadella.

Parc de Joan Miró, near Plaça de Espanya, is dedicated to one of the most famous artists of Catalonia and occupies an entire city block. One of the parks, added in the 1990s and one of Barcelona's most popular, it's often called Parc de l'Escorxador (slaughterhouse), a reference to what the park used to be. Its main features are an esplanade and a pond from which a sculpture by Miró, *Woman and Bird,* rises up. Palm, pine, and eucalyptus trees, as well as playgrounds and pergolas, complete the picture. To reach the park, take the Metro to Espanya. It's open throughout the day.

8 Especially for Kids

The Catalán people have an obvious affection for children, and although many of the attractions of Barcelona are for adults, there is an entire array of amusements designed for the young and young at heart.

Poble Espanyol, Marqués de Comillas, Parc de Montjuïc (✆ **93-325-78-66**), is described in "In & Around the Parc de Montjuïc," earlier in this chapter. Kids compare a visit here to a Spanish version of Disneyland. Frequent fiestas enliven the place, and it's fun for everybody, young and old.

Parc Zoològic ★ Modern, with barless enclosures, this ranks as Spain's top zoo. One of the most unusual attractions is the famous albino gorilla, Snowflake (*Copito de Nieve*), the only one of its kind in captivity in the world. The main entrances to the Ciutadella Park are via Passeig de Pujades and Passeig de Picasso.

Parc de la Ciutadella. ✆ **93-225-67-80.** Admission 10€ adults, 6.50€ students and children, free for children under 3. Summer, daily 10am–7pm; off-season, daily 10am–5pm. Metro: Ciutadella.

Parc d'Atraccions (Tibidabo) On top of Tibidabo, this park combines the traditional with the modern—rides from the beginning of the century complete with 1990s novelties. In summer the place takes on a carnival-like atmosphere.

Plaça Tibidabo 3–4, Cumbre del Tibidabo. ✆ **93-211-79-42.** Ticket for all rides 17€ adults, 4.20€ adults over 64. May to mid-June, Wed–Sun noon–8pm; mid-June to Sept, Tues–Sun noon–8pm; off-season, Sat–Sun and holidays 11am–8pm. Transit: Bus no. 58 to Av. del Tibidabo to Tramvía Blau, then take funicular.

9 Architectural Standouts

Architecture enthusiasts will find a wealth of fascinating sights in Barcelona. Primary among them, of course, are the fantastical creations of Antoni Gaudí and his *modernista* cohorts.

Centre Cultural Caixa Catalunya Commonly called La Pedrera, Casa Milà is the most famous apartment-house complex in Spain. Antoni Gaudí's imagination went wild when planning its construction; he even included vegetable and fruit shapes in his sculptural designs. Controversial and much criticized upon its completion, today it stands as a classic example of modernismo architecture. The entire building was restored in 1996. The ironwork around the balconies forms an intricate maze, and the main gate has windowpanes shaped like turtle shells. The rooftop, filled with phantasmagorical chimneys known in

Spanish as *espantabrujas* (witch-scarers), affords a view of Gaudí's unfinished cathedral, La Sagrada Família. The Espai Gaudí (Gaudí Space) in the attic has an intriguing multimedia display of the works of this controversial artist.

Passeig de Gràcia 92. ✆ **93-484-59-80.** Tours 6€ adults, 3€ students, free children under 12. In Spanish, daily 10am–8pm; in English, daily at 6pm. Metro: Diagonal.

Casa Amatller Constructed in a cubical design, with a Flemish-Gothic gable, this building was created by Puig i Cadafalch in 1900. It stands in sharp contrast to its neighbor, the Gaudí-designed Casa Batlló. The architecture of the Casa Amatller, actually imposed on an older structure, is a vision of ceramic, wrought iron, and sculptures. The structure combines grace notes of Flemish Gothic—especially on the finish of the facade—with elements of Catalán architecture. The gable outside is in the Flemish style. Inside, visitors may view the original Gothic-Revival interior, now the headquarters of the Institut Amatller d'Art Hispanic.

Passeig de Gràcia 41. ✆ **93-216-01-75.** Free admission, but donations welcome. Thurs 10am, 11am, and noon; you must phone ahead to reserve a time for visitation. Metro: Passeig de Gràcia.

Casa Batlló Next door to the Casa Amatller, Casa Batlló was designed by Gaudí in 1905. Using sensuous curves in iron and stone, the architect gave the facade a lavish baroque exuberance. The balconies have been compared to "sculpted waves." The upper part of the facade evokes animal forms, and delicate tiles are spread across the design—a polychromatic exterior extraordinaire. The downstairs building is the headquarters of an insurance company. Many tourists walk inside for a view of Gaudí's interior, which is basically as he designed it. Since this is a place of business, be discreet.

Passeig de Gràcia 43. ✆ **93-488-06-66.** Daily 9am–2pm. Metro: Passeig de Gràcia.

Casa Lleó Morera Lying between the Carrer del Consell de Cent and the Carrer d' Aragó is one of the most famous buildings of the modernismo movement. It is one of the trio of structures called the Mançana de la Discòrdia (Block of Discord), a play on words and an allusion to the mythical judgment of Paris. Three of the most famous modernismo architects of Barcelona, including Gaudí, competed with their various works along this block. Florid Casa Lleó, designed by Domènech i Montaner in 1905, was revolutionary in its day. That assessment still stands. Today, the building is private; no visits to the interior are possible.

Passeig de Gràcia 35. No phone. Metro: Passeig de Gràcia.

Casa de la Ciutat/Ayuntamiento Originally constructed at the end of the 14th century, the building that houses the municipal government is one of the best examples of Gothic civil architecture in the Catalán-Mediterranean style. Across this landmark square from the Palau de la Generalitat, it has been endlessly renovated and changed since its original construction. Behind a neoclassical facade, the building has a splendid courtyard and staircase. Its major architectural highlights are the 15th-century Salón de Ciento (Room of the 100 Jurors) and the Salón de las Crónicas (Room of the Chronicles), the latter decorated with black marble. The Salón de Ciento, in particular, represents a medley of styles.

Plaça de Sant Jaume. ✆ **93-402-70-00.** Sat–Sun 10am–2pm; other times by special arrangement. Metro: Jaume I.

WALKING TOUR THE GOTHIC QUARTER

Start: Plaça Nova.
Finish: Plaça de la Seu.
Time: 3 hours.
Best Times: Any sunny day.
Worst Times: Rush hours (Mon–Sat 7–9am and 5–7pm), because of traffic.

Begin at the:

❶ Plaça Nova

Set within the shadow of the cathedral, this is the largest open-air space in the Gothic Quarter and the usual site of the Barcelona flea market. Opening onto this square is the Portal del Bisbe, a gate flanked by two round towers that have survived from the ancient Roman wall that once stood here. From Plaça Nova, climb the incline of the narrow asphalt-covered street (Carrer del Bisbe) lying between these massive walls. On your right, notice the depth of the foundation, which indicates how much the city has risen since the wall was constructed.

At the approach of the first street, Carrer de Santa Llúcia, turn left, noticing the elegant simplicity of the corner building with its Romanesque facade, the:

❷ Capilla de Santa Llúcia

The chapel's solidly graceful portal and barrel-vaulted interior were completed in 1268. It's open daily from 9am to 1:15pm and 4 to 6:45pm (✆ **93-315-15-54**),.

Continue down Carrer de Santa Llúcia a few paces, noticing the:

❸ Casa de L'Ardiaca (Archdeacon's House)

Constructed in the 15th century as a residence for Archdeacon Despla, the Gothic building has sculptural reliefs with Renaissance motifs. In its cloister-like courtyard are a fountain and a palm tree. Notice the mail slot, where five swallows and a turtle carved into stone await the arrival of important messages. Since 1919 this building has been home to the **Museu d'Història de la Ciutat (City History Museum).**

As you exit the Archdeacon's House, continue in the same direction several steps until you reach the:

❹ Plaça de la Seu

From this square in front of the main entrance to the **Catedral de Barcelona** (see "In & Around the Ciutat Vella," earlier in this chapter), you can stand and admire the facade of Mediterranean Gothic architecture. On each side of Plaça de la Seu, you can see the remains of Roman walls.

After touring the cathedral, exit from the door you entered and turn right onto Carrer dels Comtes, admiring the gargoyles along the way. After about 100 paces, you'll approach the:

❺ Museu Frederic Marés

On the lower floors are Punic and Roman artifacts, but most of this museum on Plaça de Sant Iú is devoted to the works of this Catalán sculptor.

Exit through the same door you entered and continue your promenade in the same direction. You'll pass the portal of the cathedral's side, where the heads of two rather abstract angels flank the throne of a seated female saint. A few paces farther, notice the stone facade of the:

❻ Arxiu de la Carona d'Aragó

This is the archives building of the crown of Aragón. Formerly called Palacio del Lugarteniente (Deputy's Palace), this Gothic building was the work of Antonio Carbonell. On some maps it also appears as the Palacio de los Virreyes (Palace of the Viceroys). The palace contains medieval and royal documents. Enter its courtyard, admiring the century-old grapevines. Then climb the 11 monumental steps to your left, facing a modern bronze sculpture by a Catalán artist. It represents, with a rather abstract dateline and map, the political history and imperial highlights of Catalonia.

As you exit from the courtyard, you'll find yourself back on Carrer dels Comtes. Continue in the same direction, turning left at the intersection of Baixada de Santa Clara. This street, in 1 short block, will bring you to one of the most famous squares of the Gothic Quarter:

7 Plaça del Rei

The Great Royal Palace, an enlarged building of what was originally the residence of the counts of Barcelona, stands at the bottom of this square. Here at the King's Square you can visit both the **Palau Reial** and the **Museu d'Història de la Ciutat** (see "In & Around the Ciutat Vella," earlier in this chapter). On the right side of the square stands the **Palatine Chapel of Santa Agata,** a 14th-century Gothic temple that is part of the Palau Reial. In this chapel is preserved the altarpiece of the Lord High Constable, a 15th-century work by Jaume Huguet.

Retrace your steps up Baixada de Santa Clara, crossing Carrer dels Comtes, and continue straight to Carrer de la Pietat, which will skirt the semicircular, massively buttressed rear of the cathedral. With the buttresses of the cathedral's rear to your right, pass the 14th-century:

8 Casa del Canonge (House of the Canon)

This building, opening onto Carrer Arzobispo Irurita, was erected in the Gothic style and restored in 1929; escutcheons from the 15th and 16th centuries remain. Notice the heraldic symbols of medieval Barcelona on the building's stone plaques—twin towers supported by winged goats with lion's feet. On the same facade, also notice the depiction of twin angels. The building today is used as a women's training school, the Escola Professional per a la Doña.

Continue walking along Carrer de la Pietat, which makes a sudden sharp left. Notice the carved *Pietà* above the Gothic portal leading into the rear of the cathedral. Continue walking straight. One block later, turn left onto Carrer del Bisbe and continue downhill. Your path will lead you beneath one of the most charming bridges in Spain. Carved into lacy patterns of stonework, it connects the Casa del Canonge with Palau de la Generalitat.

Continue walking until Carrer del Bisbe opens into:

9 Plaça de Sant Jaume

In many ways, this plaza is the political heart of Catalán culture. Across this square, constructed at what was once a major junction for two Roman streets, race politicians and bureaucrats intent on Catalonian government affairs. On Sunday evenings you can witness the *sardana,* the national dance of Catalonia. Many bars and restaurants stand on side streets leading from this square.

Standing in the square, with your back to the street you just left (Carrer del Bisbe), you'll see, immediately on your right, the Doric portico of the **Palau de la Generalitat,** the parliament of Catalonia. Construction of this exquisite work, with its large courtyard and open-air stairway, along with twin arched galleries in the Catalonian Gothic style, began in the era of Jaume I. A special feature of the building is the Chapel of St. George, constructed in flamboyant Gothic style between 1432 and 1435 and enlarged in 1620 with the addition of vaulting and a cupola with hanging capitals. The back of the building encloses an orangery courtyard begun in 1532. In the Salón Dorado, the Proclamation of the Republic was signed. The palace bell tower houses a carillon on which both old and popular music is played each day at noon. Across the square are the Ionic columns of the **Casa de la Ciutat/Ayuntamiento,** the Town Hall of

Walking Tour—The Gothic Quarter

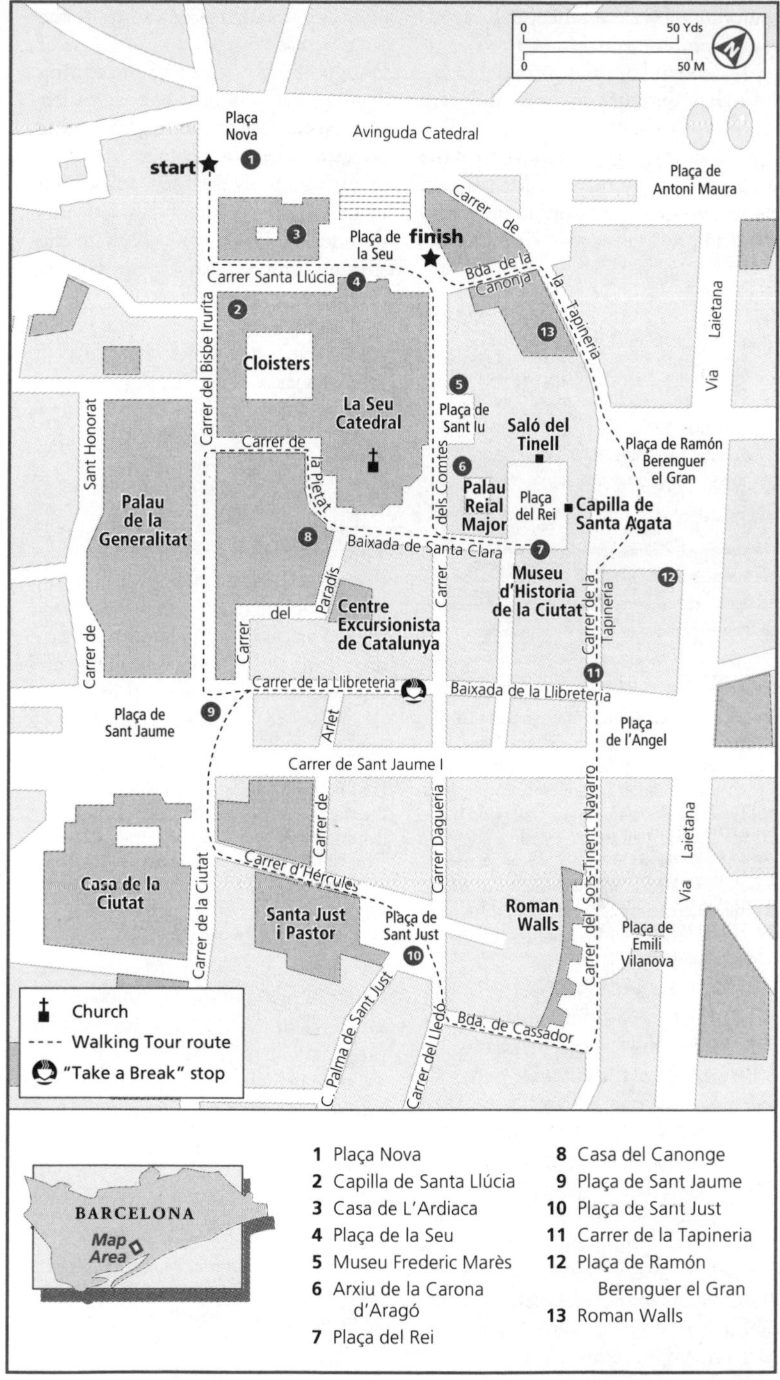

1 Plaça Nova
2 Capilla de Santa Llúcia
3 Casa de L'Ardiaca
4 Plaça de la Seu
5 Museu Frederic Marès
6 Arxiu de la Carona d'Aragó
7 Plaça del Rei
8 Casa del Canonge
9 Plaça de Sant Jaume
10 Plaça de Sant Just
11 Carrer de la Tapineria
12 Plaça de Ramón Berenguer el Gran
13 Roman Walls

Barcelona (see "Architectural Standouts," earlier in this chapter).

With your back to Carrer del Bisbe, turn left onto the narrow and very ancient Carrer de la Llibretería. Two thousand years ago, this was one of the two roads that marked the Roman center of town. Walk uphill on Carrer de la Llibretería for about 1½ blocks.

TAKE A BREAK
Mesón del Café, Llibretería 16 (✆ **93-315-07-54**), founded in 1909, specializes in coffee and cappuccino. It is one of the oldest coffeehouses in the neighborhood, sometimes crowding 50 people into its tiny precincts. Some regulars perch on stools at the bar and order breakfast. Coffee costs .80€, and a cappuccino goes for 1.75€. The cafe is open Monday to Saturday from 7am to 9:30pm.

Retrace your steps along Carrer de la Llibretería and once again enter the Plaça de Sant Jaume. Facing the Town Hall, take the street that parallels its left side, Carrer de la Ciutat. Note the elegant stonework on the building's side, which is carved in a style radically different from the building's neoclassical facade. At the first left, turn onto Carrer d'Hercules, and walk along it for one block until you enter the quiet, somewhat faded beauty of:

⑩ Plaça de Sant Just

The square is dominated by the entrance to the Església dels Sants Just i Pastor. Above the entrance portal, an enthroned Virgin is flanked by a pair of protective angels. The Latin inscription hails her as *Virgo Nigra et Pulchra, Nostra Patrona Pia* (Black and Beautiful Virgin, Our Holy Patroness). This church dates from the 14th century, although work continued into the 16th. Some authorities claim that the church, in an earlier manifestation of the present structure, is the oldest in Barcelona. Visiting hours are erratic (✆ **93-301-73-33**); you'll find that its doors are usually closed except during Sunday mass.

Opposite the facade of the church, at Plaça de Sant Just 4, is an aristocratic town house covered with faded but still elegant frescoes of angels cavorting among garlands, an example of the artistry, taste, and wealth of a bygone era. With your back to the Virgin, turn right onto the narrow, cobblestone street, Carrer del Lledo, which begins at the far end of the square. One short block later, turn left onto Baixada de Cassador. As you descend the steep slope of this narrow street, notice the blue-and-white covering of the House of the Blue Tiles at the bottom of the hill.

Turn left onto Carrer del Sots Tinent Navarro. The massive graystone wall rising on your left is the base of an ancient Roman fort. Note the red bricks of a 13th-century palace on top of the Roman wall. The solitary Corinthian column rising from the base is another reminder of Barcelona's Roman past.

Continue on to Plaça d'Emili Vilanova. Near the top of the Roman wall, note the pair of delicate columns of a Gothic window. Continue another block to the cross street, Carrer Jaume I. Cross it and approach Plaça de l'Angel. Continue walking to the:

⑪ Carrer de la Tapinería

For centuries, Catalonia has been the center of Spain's footwear industry. In medieval times, this was the street of the shoemakers. In fact, the industry is so entrenched that there is even a museum devoted to antique footwear, the **Museu del Calçat Antic,** Plaça Sant Felip Neri 5 (✆ **93-301-45-33**), open Tuesday to Sunday from 11am to 2pm. Admission is 1.80€.

In 1 short block Carrer de la Tapinería leads to:

⑫ Plaça de Ramón Berenguer el Gran

An equestrian statue dedicated to this hero (1096–1131) is ringed with the gravel of a semicircular park, whose backdrop is formed by the walls of the ancient Roman fort and, nearby, a Gothic tower.

Traverse the park, crossing in front of the equestrian statue, until you once again reach the edge of the Roman wall as you head toward the park's distant end. Here Carrer de la Tapinería will lead you on a path paralleling the ancient:

⑬ Roman Walls

These are one of Barcelona's most important treasures from its past. The walls, known as *Las Murallas* in Spanish, were constructed between A.D. 270 and 310. The walls followed a rectangular course, and were built so that their fortified sections would face the sea. By the 11th and 12th centuries, Barcelona had long outgrown their confines. Jaume I ordered the opening of the Roman Walls, and the burgeoning growth that ensued virtually destroyed them, except for the foundations you see today.

Continue your promenade, but turn left at the narrow Baixada de la Canonja. A short walk down this cobblestone alleyway will return you to **Plaça de la Seu,** not far from where you began this tour.

10 Organized Tours

Pullmantur, Gran Vía de les Corts Catalanes 635 (✆ **93-317-12-97;** Metro: Plaça de Catalunya), offers a number of tours and excursions with English-speaking guides. For a preview of the city, you can take a morning tour. They depart from the company's terminal at 9:30am, and take in the cathedral, the Gothic Quarter, Les Rambles, the monument to Columbus, and the Spanish Village and the Olympic Stadium. Tickets cost 32€. An afternoon tour leaves at 3:30pm and visits some of the most outstanding architecture in the Eixample, including Gaudí's Sagrada Família, Parc Güell, and a stop at the Picasso Museum. This tour costs 32€.

Pullmantur also offers several excursions outside Barcelona. The daily tour of the monastery of Montserrat includes a visit to the Royal Basilica to view the famous sculpture of the Black Virgin. This tour, which costs 41€, departs at 9:30am and returns at 2:30pm to the company's terminal. A full-day Girona–Figueres tour includes a visit to Girona's cathedral and its Jewish quarter, plus a trip to the Dalí museum. This excursion, which costs 82€, leaves Barcelona at 9am and returns at approximately 6pm. Call ahead—a minimum number of participants is required or the tour isn't conducted.

Another company that offers tours of Barcelona and the surrounding countryside is **Juliatours,** Ronda Universitat 5 (✆ **93-317-64-54**). Itineraries and prices are similar to Pullmantur's. One tour, the "Visita Ciudad Artística," focuses on the city's artistic significance. The tour also passes Casa Lleó Morera, designed in 1905 by Domènech i Montaner in a floral modernist mode, and takes in many of Gaudí's brilliant buildings, including the Casa Milá (La Pedrera) and La Sagrada Família. Also included is a visit to the Museu Picasso or Museu d'Art Modern, depending on the day of your tour. This tour, which leaves at 3:30pm and returns at 7pm, costs 32€.

11 Active Pursuits

AN OUTSTANDING FITNESS CENTER

The city's main fitness center is adjacent to the Olympic Stadium in an indoor-outdoor complex whose main attractions are its two beautifully designed swimming pools. Built for the 1992 Summer Olympics, the facility contains a health club and gym. It's open to the public for 8€ for a full day's pass. For the address and hours, see the Piscina Bernardo Picornell listing in "Swimming," below.

GOLF

One of the city's best courses, **Club de Golf Vallromanas,** Afueras s/n, Vallromanas, Barcelona (© **93-572-90-64**), is 20 minutes north of the center by car. Nonmembers who reserve tee times in advance are welcome to play. The greens fee is 60€ on weekdays, 102€ on weekends. The club is open Wednesday through Monday from 9am to 9pm. Established in 1972, it is the site of Spain's most important golf tournament.

Reial Club de Golf El Prat, El Prat de Llobregat (© **93-379-02-78**), is a prestigious club that allows nonmembers to play under two conditions: They must have a handicap issued by the governing golf body in their home country; and they must prove membership in a golf club at home. The club has two 18-hole par-72 courses. Greens fees are 85€ on weekdays, 169€ on weekends. From Barcelona, follow Avinguda Once de Septiembre past the airport to Barrio de San Cosme. From there follow the signs along Carrer Prat to the golf course.

SWIMMING

Most city residents head to the beaches near the Vila Olímpica or Sitges when they feel like swimming. If you're looking for an uncrowded pool, you'll find one at the **Esportiu Piscina DeStampa,** Carrer Rosich 12, in the Hospitalet district (© **93-334-56-00**). It's open Monday through Friday from 8am to 10pm, Saturday from 10am to 2pm and 4 to 8pm, Sunday from 10am to 2pm. Weekday admission is 2.30€ Saturday and Sunday, it's 2.70€.

A much better choice, however, allows you to swim where some Olympic events took place, at **Piscina Bernardo Picornell,** Av. de Estadi 30–40, on Montjuïc (© **93-423-40-41**). Adjacent to the Olympic Stadium, it incorporates two of the best swimming pools in Spain (one indoors, one outdoors). Custom-built for the Olympics, they're open to the public Monday through Friday from 7am to midnight, Saturday from 7am to 9pm, Sunday from 7am to 4pm. Admission costs 8€ and allows full use throughout the day of whichever pool is open, plus the gymnasium, the sauna, and the whirlpools. Bus no. 61 makes frequent runs from the Plaça d'Espanya.

12 Shopping

Barcelonans look more to Paris and their own sense of design than to Madrid for their fashions and style. *Moda joven* (young fashion) is all the rage in Barcelona.

If your time and budget are limited, you may want to patronize Barcelona's major department store, **El Corte Inglés,** for an overview of Catalán merchandise at reasonable prices. Barcelona is filled with boutiques, but clothing is an expensive item here, even though the city has been a textile center for centuries.

Markets (see below) are very popular in Barcelona and are suitable places to search for good buys.

THE SHOPPING SCENE

If you're a window shopper, stroll along the **Passeig de Gràcia** from the Avinguda Diagonal to the Plaça de Catalunya. Along the way, you'll see some of the most elegant and expensive shops in Barcelona, plus an assortment of splendid turn-of-the-century buildings and cafes, many with outdoor tables. Another prime spot for shopping is the **Ramble de Catalunya** (upper Rambles).

Another shopping expedition is to the **Mercat de la Boquería,** Rambla 101 (© **93-318-25-84**), near Carrer del Carme. Here you'll see a wide array of straw bags and regional products, along with a handsome display of the food that you are likely to be eating later in a local restaurant: fruits, vegetables (artfully displayed), breads, cheeses, meats, and fish. Vendors sell their wares Monday to Saturday from 7:30am to 9pm.

In the **old quarter,** not far from Plaça de Catalunya, the principal shopping streets are all five Rambles, plus Carrer del Pi, Carrer de la Palla, and Avinguda Portal de l'Angel, to cite some of the major ones. Moving north in the **Eixample** are Passeig de Catalunya, Passeig de Gràcia, and Rambla de Catalunya. Going even farther north, **Avinguda Diagonal** is a major shopping boulevard. Other prominent shopping streets include Bori i Fontesta, via Augusta, Carrer Muntaner, Travessera de Gràcia, and Carrer de Balmes.

In general, shopping hours are Monday to Saturday from 9am to 8pm. Some smaller shops close from 1:30 to 4pm.

The **American Visitors Bureau,** Gran Vía, 59134 (© **93-301-01-50**), between Rambla de Catalunya and Carrer de Balmes, will pack and ship your purchases and gifts and even handle excess luggage and personal effects. The company also operates a travel agency here, booking flights and hotel accommodations for those needing it. It's open Monday to Friday from 9am to 1pm and 4 to 7pm, Saturday from 9am to 1pm.

Watch for sales (*rebajas,* or *rebaixes* in Catalán) in mid-January, late July, and August. Merchandise is often heavily discounted by stores getting rid of their winter and summer stock.

SHOPPING A TO Z

Barcelona, a city known for its design and fashion, offers a wealth of shopping opportunities. In general, prices tend to be slightly lower than in London, Paris, and Rome.

In addition to modern, attractively designed, and stylish **clothing, shoes,** and **decorative objects** are often good buys. In the city of Miró, Tàpies, and Picasso, **art** is a major business, and the reason so many gallery owners from around the world come to visit. You'll find dozens of galleries, especially in the Barri Gòtic and around the Picasso Museum. Barcelona is also noted for its **flea markets,** where good purchases are always available if you search hard enough.

Antiques abound here, but rising prices have put much of them beyond the means of the average shopper. However, the list below includes some shops where you can look, if nothing else. Most shoppers from abroad settle happily for handicrafts, and the city is rich in offerings, ranging from pottery to handmade furniture. Barcelona has been in the business of creating and designing **jewelry** since the 17th century, and its offerings in this field are of the widest possible range—as are the prices.

What follows is only a limited selection of some of the hundreds of shops in Barcelona.

ANTIQUES

El Bulevard des Antiquaris This 70-unit shopping complex, just off one of the town's most aristocratic avenues, has a huge collection of art and antiques assembled in a series of boutiques. There's a cafe/bar on the upper level. In summer, it's open Monday to Friday from 9:30am to 8:30pm; in winter, on Monday from 4:30 to 8:30pm and Tuesday to Saturday from 10:30am to 8:30pm.

Some boutiques keep shorter hours. Passeig de Gràcia 55. No central phone. Metro: Passeig de Gràcia.

Sala d'Art Artur Ramón One of the finest antique and art dealers in Barcelona can be found in this three-level emporium, which boasts high ceilings and a medieval kind of grace. Set on a narrow flagstone-covered street near Plaça del Pi (the center of the antique district), it stands opposite a tiny square, the Placeta al Carrer de la Palla, whose foundations were laid by the Romans. The store, which has been operated by four generations of men named Artur Ramón, also operates branches nearby and is known for its 19th and 20th century painting and sculpture, its 19th and 20th century drawings and engravings, and its 18th and 19th century decorative arts and objets d'art along with rare ceramics, porcelain, and glassware. Prices are high, as you'd expect, for items of quality and lasting value. Open Monday to Saturday from 10am to 1:30pm and 5 to 8pm. Carrer de la Palla 25. © **93-302-59-70.** Metro: Jaume I.

Urbana Urbana sells an array of architectural remnants (usually from torn-down mansions), antique furniture, and reproductions of brass hardware. There are antique and reproduction marble mantelpieces, wrought-iron gates and garden seats, even carved wood fireplaces with the modernismo look. It's an impressive, albeit costly, array of merchandise rescued from the architectural glory of yesteryear. Open Monday to Friday from 10am to 2pm and 5 to 8pm. Còrsega 258. © **93-218-70-36.** Metro: Hospital Sant Pau.

ARCHITECTURAL OBJECTS

Otranto This mammoth warehouse is a temporary burial place for intriguing architectural objects rescued from antique houses or stores about to be demolished. Since this is Barcelona, land of Gaudí, you might be able to purchase—say, a pair of hand-carved Modernist doors, certainly marble columns, elaborate grillwork, and wrought-iron balustrades from some long-vanished staircase. The owner, Rosma Barnils, will ship anywhere in the world. Open Monday to Friday from 10am to 2pm and 4 to 8pm. Paseo de San Juan 142. © **93-207-26-97.** Metro: Jacinto Verdager.

DEPARTMENT STORES

El Corte Inglés Just one of the local representatives of the largest and most glamorous department store chain in Spain, this store sells a wide variety of merchandise, ranging from Spanish handicrafts to high-fashion items, from Spanish or Catalán records to food. Not only that, but you can have shoes re-heeled, hair and beauty treatments, and food and drink in the rooftop cafe. The store also has restaurants and cafes and offers a number of consumer-related services, such as a travel agent. It has a department that will arrange the mailing of your purchases back home. Open Monday to Friday from 10am to 9:30pm. Plaça de Catalunya 14. © **93-306-38-00.** Metro: Plaça de Catalunya. **El Corte Inglés** has two other Barcelona locations at Av. Diagonal 617–619 (© **93-366-71-00,** Metro: María Cristina); and at Av. Diagonal 471 (© **93-493-48-00,** Metro: María Cristina).

DESIGNER HOUSEWARES

Vinçón Fernando Amat's Vinçón is the best in the city, with 10,000 products—everything from household items to the best in Spanish contemporary furnishings. Its mission is to purvey items of good design, period. Housed in the former home of artist Ramón Casas—a contemporary of Picasso during his Barcelona stint—with gilded columns and mosaic-inlaid floors, the showroom is filled with the best Spain has, with each item personally selected because of its quality and craft. The always creative window displays alone are worth the trek there: Expect *anything.* Open Monday to Saturday from 10am to 1:30pm and 5 to 8pm. Passeig de Gràcia 96. ✆ **93-215-60-50.** Metro: Passeig de Gràcia.

FABRICS & WEAVINGS

Coses de Casa Appealing fabrics and weavings are displayed in this 19th-century store, called simply "Household Items." Many are hand-woven in Majorca, their boldly geometric patterns inspired by Arab motifs of centuries ago. The fabric, for the most part, is 50% cotton, 50% linen; much of it would make excellent upholstery material. Open Monday to Friday from 9:45am to 2pm and 4:30 to 8pm, Saturday from 10am to 2pm and 5 to 8:30pm. Plaça de Sant Josep Oriol 5. ✆ **93-302-73-28.** Metro: Jaume I.

FASHION

Adolfo Domínguez This shop, one of many outlets spread across Spain and Europe, displays fashion that has earned for the store the appellation of "The Spanish Armani." There's one big difference. Domínguez's suits for both women and men, unlike Armani, are designed for those with some hips. They cover all ages at their stores including the youth market. As one fashion critic said of their latest offerings, "They are austere but not strict, forgivingly cut in urbane earth tones." Passeig de Gràcia 32. ✆ **93-487-41-70.** Mon-Sat 10am-8:30pm. Metro: Passeig de Gràcia.

Antonio Miró This shop is devoted exclusively to the clothing design of Miró, without the Groc label (see below). Before purchasing anything at Groc, you should also survey the wares of this store, which seems even more stylish. Fashionable clothing for both men and women is sold here. Open Monday to Saturday from 10am to 2pm and 4:30 to 8pm. Consejo de Ciento 349. ✆ **93-487-06-70.** Metro: Passeig de Gràcia.

Groc Designs for both women and men are sold here. One of the most stylish shops in Barcelona, it is expensive but filled with high-quality apparel made from the finest of natural fibers. The men's store is downstairs, the women's store one flight up. Open Monday to Saturday from 10am to 2pm and 4:30 to 8pm. The August hours are Monday through Friday from 11am to 2pm and 5 to 8pm. Ramble de Catalunya 100. ✆ **93-215-74-74.** Metro: Plaça de Catalunya.

Textil i d'Indumentaria Operated as a showcase for Catalonian design and ingenuity by Barcelona's Museum of Textile and Fashion, and set on a medieval street across from the Picasso Museum, this shop proudly displays and sells clothing for men, women, and children, all of which is either designed or at least manufactured within the region. Inventories include shoes, men's and women's sportswear and formal wear, jewelry, teddy bears, suitcases and handbags, umbrellas, and towels, each shaped and cut by up-and-coming Cataláns. Two of the most famous designers include menswear specialist Antonio Miró (no relation to the 1950s and '60s artist Joan Miró) and women's clothing designer Lydia Delgado. Open Tuesday to Saturday from 10am to 8:30pm, and Sunday from 10am to 3pm. 12 Carrer Montcada. ✆ **93-310-74-04.** Metro: Jaume I.

FURNISHINGS

Bd Ediciones de Diseño We know of no more beautiful furniture store in all of Spain. In 1972 six talented Catalán architects opened this retail outlet in a former print shop behind a decorative tile and stone facade. One of the modernista architects, Cristian Cirici, designed the spacious, airy interior. Instead of a furniture store, you'll think you're in a museum. As you wander about, imagine what a modern house would look like if furnished from this place. The furnishings span the 20th century, including reproductions of the works of various European masters such as Charles Mackintosh, Salvador Dalí, and Gaudí. The range goes up until today as evoked by the gleaming aluminum shelving of Oscar Tusquets, one of the co-founders. Even if you don't buy, it's fun to visit. Open Monday to Friday from 10am to 1:30pm and 4:30 to 8pm. 2191 Carrer Mallorca. ✆ **93-458-69-09.** Metro: Verdaguer.

GALLERIES

Art Picasso Here you can get good lithographic reproductions of works by Picasso, Miró, and Dalí, as well as T-shirts emblazoned with the designs of these masters. Tiles sold here often carry their provocatively painted scenes. Open Monday to Saturday from 10am to 8pm and Sunday from 10am to 3pm. Tapinería 10. ✆ **93-310-49-57.** Metro: Jaume I.

Sala Parés Established in 1840 by the Maragall family, this is an institution among art galleries in the city, recognizing and promoting the work of many Spanish and Catalán painters and sculptors who have gone on to acclaim. Paintings are displayed in a two-story amphitheater, whose high-tech steel balconies are supported by a quartet of steel columns evocative of Gaudí. Exhibitions of the most avant-garde art in Barcelona change about every three weeks. Open Monday to Saturday from 10:30am to 2pm and 4:30 to 8:30pm. Petritxol 5. ✆ **93-318-70-20.** Metro: Plaça de Catalunya.

GIFTS

Beardsley Named after the Victorian English illustrator, this store is on the same street where the works of Picasso and Dalí were exhibited before they became world famous. The wide array of gifts, perhaps the finest selection in Barcelona, includes a little bit of everything—dried flowers, writing supplies, silver dishes, unusual bags and purchases, and lots more. Open Monday to Friday from 10am to 2pm and 4:30 to 8pm, Saturday from 10am to 2pm and 5 to 8:30pm. Petritxol 12. ✆ **93-301-05-76.** Metro: Plaça de Catalunya.

Bon Original Shop Found at the tourist offices, this shop sells a variety of articles inspired by Barcelona and designed so that the visitor can take away an appropriate and often worthy souvenir. A representative range of products are sold, including textiles, ceramics, jewelry, stationery, gift items, and travel-related gear. Open Monday to Saturday from 9:30am to 8pm. Plaça de Catalunya 17-S. ✆ **93-304-31-23.** Metro: Plaça de Catalunya.

LEATHER

Loewe The biggest branch in Barcelona of this prestigious Spanish leather-goods chain is in one of the best-known modernismo buildings in the city. Everything is top-notch, from the elegantly spacious showroom to the expensive merchandise to the helpful salespeople. The company exports its goods to branches throughout Asia, Europe, and North America. Open Monday to Saturday from 9:30am to 2pm and 4:30 to 8pm. Passeig de Gràcia 35. ✆ **93-216-04-00.** Metro: Passeig de Gràcia.

MARKETS

El Encants antique market is held every Monday, Wednesday, Friday, and Saturday in Plaça de les Glòries Catalanes (Metro: Glòries). There are no specific times—go anytime during the day to survey the selection.

Coins and postage stamps are traded and sold in **Plaça Reial** on Sunday from 10am to 2pm. The location is off the southern flank of Les Rambles (Metro: Drassanes).

A book-and-coin market is held at the **Ronda Sant Antoni** every Sunday from 10am to 2pm (Metro: Universitat).

MUSIC

Casa Beethoven The most complete collection of sheet music in town can be found here. In a narrow store established in 1920, the collection naturally focuses on the works of Spanish and Catalán composers. Music lovers might make some rare discoveries here. Open Monday to Friday from 9am to 1:30pm and 4 to 8pm, Saturday from 9am to 1:30pm and 5 to 8pm. Rambles 97. ✆ **93-301-48-26.** Metro: Liceu.

PORCELAIN

Kastoria This large store near the cathedral carries many kinds of leather goods, including purses, suitcases, coats, and jackets. But most people come here to look at its famous Lladró porcelain—they are authorized dealers and have a big selection. Open Monday to Saturday from 10am to 7pm and Sunday from 10am to 2pm. Av. Catedra 6–8. ✆ **93-310-04-11.** Metro: Plaça de Catalunya.

POTTERY

Artesana Coses Here you'll find pottery and porcelain from every major region of Spain. Most of the pieces are heavy and thick-sided—designs in use in the country for centuries. Open Monday to Saturday from 10:30am to 8pm, Sunday from 10am to 3pm. Placeta de Montcada 2. ✆ **93-319-54-13.** Metro: Jaume I.

Itaca This shop carries a wide array of handmade pottery, not only from Catalonia and other parts of Spain, but also from Portugal, Mexico, and Morocco. The merchandise has been selected for its basic purity, integrity, and simplicity. Open Monday to Friday from 10am to 2pm and 4:30 to 8pm, Saturday from 10am to 2pm and 5 to 8:30pm. Carrer Ferran 26. ✆ **93-301-30-44.** Metro: Liceu.

SHOPPING CENTERS & MALLS

The landscape of Barcelona has exploded since the mid-1980s with the construction of several American-style shopping malls, some of which are too far from the city's historic core to be convenient to most foreign visitors. Here's a description, however, of some of the city's best.

Centre Comercial Barcelona Glòries Built in 1995, this is the largest shopping center in downtown Barcelona, a three-story emporium of the good life, based on California models but crammed into a distinctly urban neighborhood. More than 100 shops are here: some posh, others much less so. Although there's a typical shopping-mall anonymity to some aspects of this place, you'll still be able to find virtually anything you might have forgotten while packing for your trip. Open Monday to Saturday from 10am to 10pm. Av. Diagonal 208. ✆ **93-486-04-04.** Metro: Glòries.

Diagonal Center Smaller than the above-mentioned Centre Comercial Barcelona Glòries, with about half the number of shops, this two-story mall contains stores devoted to luxury products, as well as a scattering of bars, cafes, and simple but cheerful restaurants favored by office workers and shoppers. Built in the early 1990s, it even has an area devoted to video games, where teenagers can make as much electronic noise as they want while their guardians go shopping. It's open Monday to Saturday from 10am to 9:30pm. Av. Diagonal 557. ✆ **93-444-00-00.** Metro: María Cristina.

Maremagnum The best thing about this place is its position adjacent to the waterfront of Barcelona's historic seacoast; it's also well suited to outdoor promenades. Built in the early 1990s near the Columbus Monument, it contains a handful of shops selling touristy items and lots of cafes, bars, and places to sit. You might get the idea that only a few of the people who come here are really interested in shopping, despite the fact that the place defines itself as a shopping mall. Open Monday through Saturday from 11am to 11pm. Moll d'Espanya s/n. ✆ **93-225-81-00.** Metro: Drassanes.

Poble Espanyol This is not technically a shopping mall but a "village" (see "In & Around the Parc de Montjuïc," earlier in this chapter) with about 35 stores selling typical folk crafts from every part of Spain: glassware, leather goods, pottery, paintings, and carvings—you name it. Stores keep various hours, but you can visit any time during the day. Marqués de Comillas, Parc de Montjuïc. ✆ **93-325-78-66.** Metro: Espanya, then free red double-decker bus to Montjuïc, or Bus 13, which costs .85€.

STRAW PRODUCTS

La Manual Alpargatera In addition to its large inventory of straw products, such as hats and bags, this shop is known mainly for its footwear, called espadrilles (*alpargatas* in Spanish). This basic rope-soled shoe (whose design is said to be 1,000 years old) is made on the premises. Some Cataláns wear only espadrilles when performing the *sardana,* their national dance. Open Monday to Saturday from 9:30am to 1:30pm and 4:30 to 8pm. Avinyó 7. ✆ **93-301-01-72.** Metro: Jaume I or Liceu. Turn off Les Rambles at Carrer Ferran, walk 2 blocks, and make a right.

13 Barcelona After Dark

Barcelona comes alive at night—the funicular ride to Tibidabo or the illuminated fountains of Montjuïc are especially popular. During the Franco era, the center of club life was the cabaret-packed district near the south of Les Rambles, an area, incidentally, known for nighttime muggings—so use caution if you go there. But the most fashionable clubs long ago deserted this seedy area and have opened in nearly every major district of the city.

Your best source of local information is a little magazine called *Guía del Ocio,* which previews "La Semana de Barcelona" (This Week in Barcelona). It's in Spanish, but most of its listings will probably be comprehensible. The magazine is sold at virtually every news kiosk along Les Rambles.

Nightlife begins for many Barcelonans with a promenade (*paseo*) along Les Rambles in the early evening, usually from 5 to 7pm. Then things quiet down a bit, until a second surge of energy brings out Les Rambles crowds again, from 9 to 11pm. After that the esplanade clears out quite a bit, but it's always lively.

If you've been scared off by press reports of Les Rambles between the Plaça de Catalunya and the Columbus Monument—though the area's really been cleaned

up in the past decade—you'll feel safer along the Ramble de Catalunya, in the Eixample, north of the Plaça de Catalunya. This street and its offshoots are lively at night, with many cafes and bars.

The array of nighttime diversions in Barcelona is staggering. There is something to interest almost everyone and to fit most pocketbooks. For families, the amusement parks are the most-frequented venues. Sometimes locals opt for an evening in the *tascas* (taverns) or pubs, perhaps settling for a bottle of wine at a cafe, an easy and inexpensive way to spend an evening of people-watching. Serious drinking in pubs and cafes begins by 10 or 11pm. But for the most fashionable bars and discos, Barcelonans delay their entrances until at least 1am.

Cultural events are big in the Catalonian repertoire, and the old-fashioned dance halls, too, still survive in some places. Although disco has waned in some parts of the world, it is still going strong in Barcelona. Decaying movie houses, abandoned garages, and long-closed vaudeville theaters have been taken over and restored to become nightlife venues for the after-dark movement that sweeps across the city until dawn.

Flamenco isn't the rage here that it is in Seville and Madrid, but it still has its devotees. The city is also filled with jazz aficionados. Best of all, the old tradition of the music hall with vaudeville lives on in Barcelona.

If you're very young, you might want to check out the nightlife scene at **Maremagnum** (see "Shopping Centers & Malls," above).

SPECIAL EVENTS & DISCOUNTS In summer you'll see plenty of free entertainment just by walking the streets—everything from opera to monkey acts. The Rambles is a particularly good place to watch.

There's almost always a **festival** happening in the city, and many of the events can be enjoyed for free. The tourist office can give you details of when and where. Some **theaters** advertise discount or half-price nights. Check in the weekly *Guía del Ocio.*

THE PERFORMING ARTS

Culture is deeply ingrained in the Catalán soul. The performing arts are strong here—some, in fact, taking place on the street, especially along Les Rambles. Crowds will often gather around a singer or mime. A city square will suddenly come alive on Saturday night with a spontaneous festival—"tempestuous, surging, irrepressible life and brio," is how the writer Rose MacCauley described it.

Long a city of the arts, Barcelona experienced a cultural decline during the Franco years, but now it is filled once again with the best opera, symphonic, and choral music.

CLASSICAL MUSIC

La Casa dels Músics Pianist Luís de Arquer has established a small chamber company in his 19th-century Gràcia home. Here in an intimate atmosphere, small-scale productions of *opera buffa* and *bel canto* are presented, usually beginning at 9pm (but you must call to confirm if presentations will go on and to make reservations). For the true music lover, this could be your most charming evening in Barcelona. Carrer Encarnació 25. ✆ **93-284-99-20.** Tickets 18€. Metro: Fontana.

Palau de la Música Catalana In a city chock-full of architectural highlights, this one stands out. In 1908 Lluís Domènech i Montaner, a Catalán architect, designed this structure, including stained glass, ceramics, statuary, and ornate lamps, among other elements. It stands today, restored, as a classic example of modernismo. Concerts and leading recitals are presented here. The box office is open Monday to Friday from 10am to 9pm, Saturday from 3 to 9pm. Sant Francesc de Paula 2. ✆ **93-295-72-00.** Box office Mon–Sat.

THEATER

Theater is presented in the Catalán language and therefore will not be of interest to most visitors. For those who do speak the language, or perhaps are fluent in Spanish (even then, though, you're unlikely to understand much of the goings-on), here are some recommendations.

Gran Teatre del Liceu This monument to Belle Epoque extravagance, a 2,700-seat opera house, is one of the grandest theaters in the world. It was designed by the Catalán architect Josep Oriol Mestves. On January 31, 1994, fire gutted the opera house, shocking Catalonians, many of whom regarded this place as the citadel of their culture. The government immediately vowed to rebuild, and the new Liceu was reopened in 1999, well before the millennium deadline set by the cultural czars. Rambla dels Caputxins. ✆ **93-485-99-00.** Metro: Liceu.

Mercat de Los Flors Housed in a building constructed for the 1929 International Exhibition at Montjuïc is this other major Catalán theater. Peter Brook first used it as a theater for a 1983 presentation of *Carmen.* Innovators in drama, dance, and music are showcased here, as are modern dance companies from Europe, including troupes from Italy and France. The 999-seat house also has a restaurant overlooking the rooftops of the city. Lleida 59. ✆ **93-426-18-75.** Tickets 9€–20€. Metro: Espanya.

Teatre Lliure This self-styled free theater is the leading Catalán-language company in Barcelona. Once a workers' union, since 1976 the building has been the headquarters of a theater cooperative. Its directors are famous in Barcelona for their bold presentations here, including works by Bertolt Brecht, Luigi Pirandello, Jean Genet (who wrote about Barcelona), and even Molière and Shakespeare. New dramas by Catalán playwrights are also presented. The house seats from 200 to 350. Montseny 47. ✆ **93-218-92-51.** Tickets 12€–15€ Tues–Thurs, 15€–18€ Fri–Sun. Metro: Fontana.

Teatre Nacional de Catalunya This leading company is directed by Josep María Flotats, an actor-director who was trained in the tradition of theater repertory, working in such theaters in Paris as the Théâtre de la Villa and the Comédie-Français. He founded his own company in Barcelona, where he presents both classic and contemporary plays. Plaça de les Arts 1. ✆ **93-306-57-06.** Tickets 16€–21€. Closed Aug. Metro: Monumental.

FLAMENCO

El Tablao de Carmen This club provides a highly rated flamenco cabaret in the re-created village. You can go early and explore the village if you wish and even have dinner here. This place has long been a tourist favorite. The club is open Tuesday to Sunday from 8pm to past midnight. During the week, it sometimes closes around 1am, but often stays open until 2 or 3am on weekends, depending on business. The first show is always at 9:30pm; the second show Tuesday to Thursday and Sunday is at 11:30pm, on Friday and Saturday at midnight. Reservations are encouraged. Poble Espanyol de Montjuïc. ✆ **93-325-68-95.** Dinner and show 51€; one drink and show 26€.

Los Tarantos Established in 1963, this is the oldest flamenco club in Barcelona, with a rigid allegiance to the tenets of Andalusian flamenco. Its roster of artists changes regularly, and are often imported from Seville or Córdoba, stamping out their well-rehearsed passions in ways that make the audience appreciate the nuances of Spain's most intensely controlled dance idiom. No food is served here—instead, the place most resembles a cabaret theater, where up to 120 clients at a time can drink, talk quietly, and savor the nuances of a dance that combines elements from medieval Christian and Muslim traditions. Each show lasts around 1¼ hours. Shows are Monday to Saturday at 10pm and again at midnight. Plaça Reial 17. ✆ **93-318-30-67.** Cover (includes one drink) 24€. Metro: Liceu.

Tablao Flamenco Cordobés At the southern end of Les Rambles, a short walk from the harbor front, you'll hear the strum of the guitar, the sound of hands clapping rhythmically, and the haunting sound of the flamenco, a tradition here since 1968. Head upstairs to an Andalusian-style room where performances take place with the traditional *cuadro flamenco*—singers, dancers, and guitarist. Cordobés is said to be the best showcase for flamenco in Barcelona. From November 1 to March 31 (except for one week in Dec), the show with dinner begins at 8:30pm and the show without dinner at 10pm. From April 1 to October 31 and December 25 to December 31, four shows are offered nightly: with dinner at 8pm and 9:45pm, without dinner at 9:30pm and 11:15pm. Reservations are required. It's closed in January. Les Rambles 35. ✆ **93-317-66-53.** Dinner and show 50€; one drink and show 29€. Closed Jan. Metro: Drassanes.

CABARET

Espai Barroc One of Barcelona's most culture-conscious nightspots occupies some of the showplace rooms of the Palau Dalmases, a stately palace within the Barri Gòtic that was built in stages between the 13th and 18th centuries. Within a stately looking room that's painted in tones of terra cotta and lined with grand art objects, you can listen to recorded opera arias and sip glasses of beer or wine. The most appealing night here is Thursday, when, beginning at 11pm, you'll hear a group of 10 singers perform a roster of arias from assorted operas, one of which is invariably *Carmen.* Since its establishment in 1996, the place has thrived, attracting a clientele where it seems that virtually everyone around the bar has at least heard of the world's greatest operas, and some can even discuss them more or less brilliantly. Open Tuesday to Sunday from 8pm to2am. Carrer Montcada 20. ✆ **93-310-06-73.** Cover (includes one drink) 18€. Metro: Jaime I.

Luz de Gas This theater/cabaret has the hottest Latino jazz in this port city on weekends. On weeknights, there's cabaret. The place is an Art Nouveau delight, with colored glass lamps and enough voluptuous nudes to please Rubens himself. This club was once a theater, and now its original multiple seating has been turned into different areas, each with its own bar. The lower two levels open onto the dance floor and stage. If you'd like to talk, head for the top tier with its glass enclosure. You'll have to call to see what the lineup is on any given night: jazz, pop, soul, rhythm and blues, salsa, bolero, whatever. Carrer de Muntaner 246. ✆ **93-209-77-11.** Cover (includes one drink) 15€. Bus: 7, 15, 33, 58, or 64.

DANCE CLUBS & DISCOS

Bikini Set in the basement of a commercial-looking shopping center is this comprehensive and wide-ranging nightlife compound, with at least two venues for dancing in every conceivable genre (including funk, indie, rock-and-roll, and golden-oldie music). There's a separate room for Puerto Rican salsa (the owners refer to it as a "salsoteca") and a large area where fans of emerging musical groups applaud wildly to the music of their favorite band of the minute. The action changes every night of the week, and has even been known to include sophisticated adaptations of conventional tango music. The establishment has provided a showcase for the career ambitions of dozens of youthful singers and rock-and-roll bands. Open Monday to Thursday from 7pm to 4:30am, Friday and Saturday from 7pm to 6am. Deu i Mata 105. ✆ **93-322-00-05.** Cover 9€–24€. Metro: Les Corts.

La Paloma Those feeling nostalgic may want to drop in on Barcelona's most famous dance hall. Remember the fox trot? The mambo? If not, learn about them here, along with the tango, the cha-cha, and the bolero. Live orchestras provide the music. The ornate old hall is open Wednesday through Sunday. Matinees are from 6 to 9:30pm; night dances are from 11:30pm to 5am. Drink prices start at 7€. Tigre 27. ✆ **93-301-68-97.** Cover 6€. Metro: Universitat.

Up and Down The chic atmosphere of this disco attracts the elite of Barcelona, across the generational divide. The more mature patrons, specifically the black-tie, post-opera crowd, head for the upstairs section, leaving the downstairs to the loud music and flaming youth. Up and Down, with a black-and-white decor, is the most cosmopolitan disco in Barcelona, with a carefully planned ambience, impeccable service, and a welcoming atmosphere. Waiters are piquant and sassy. Technically, this is a private club—you can be turned away at the door. The restaurant is open Monday to Saturday from 10pm to 2am, serving meals costing from 33€. The disco is open Tuesday to Saturday from 12:30am to anytime between 5 and 6:30am, depending on business. Drinks in the disco cost 12€ for a beer or from 17€ for a mixed drink. Numancia 179. ✆ **93-205-51-94.** Cover (includes one drink) 12€–17€. Metro: María Cristina.

JAZZ & BLUES

Barcelona Pipa Club If you find the Harlem Jazz Club (see below) small, wait until you get to the "Pipe Club." Long beloved by jazz aficionados, this is for pure devotees. Ring the buzzer and you'll be admitted (at least we hope you will) to a club reached after a climb of two flights up a seedy rundown building. This is hardly a trendy nighttime venue: Instead, it attracts lovers of hot jazz. Five rooms are decorated with displays or photographs of pipes—naturally Sherlock Holmes gets in on the act. Depending on the performer, music ranges from New Orleans jazz to Brazilian rhythms. Jazz is featured Thursday to Sunday from 10pm to 5am, although the club with its comfortable bar is open daily during the same hours. Plaça Reial 3. ✆ **93-302-47-32.** Admission is free. Metro: Liceu.

Harlem Jazz Club On a nice street in the Ciutat Vella, this is one of Barcelona's oldest and finest jazz clubs. Live music begins at 9pm and often lasts until the late set at 3am. No matter how many times you've heard "Black Orpheus" or "The Girl from Ipanema," it always sounds new again here. Music is viewed with a certain reverence; no one talks when the performers are on. Even the decor doesn't distract, consisting of black-and-white photographs of jazz greats hanging on the smoke-colored walls. The place is unbelievably small, with only a handful of tables. Live jazz, blues, tango, Brazilian music—the sounds are always fresh. Hours are Tuesday to Thursday from 8pm to 4am, Saturday and Sunday until 5am. Closed in August. Comtessa de Sobradiel 8. ✆ **93-310-07-55.** One-drink minimum. No cover. Closed Aug. Metro: Jaume.

Jamboree In the heart of the Barri Gòtic, this has long been one of the city's premier venues for good blues and jazz. It varies its musical performances, though, and doesn't feature jazz every night—perhaps a Latin dance band will be scheduled. Sometimes a world-class performer will appear here, but most

Finds A Wine Taster's Secret Address

It doesn't get much better in Barcelona than an afternoon spent on the terrace of **La Vinya del Senyor,** Plaça Santa María 5 (✆ **93-310-33-79**), taking in the glorious Gothic facade of Santa María del Mar. You could even take a wine connoisseur like Mel Brooks (when not counting his take on *The Producers*), and we think even this hard-to-please man would be pleased. The wine list will inspire awe. Imagine, for example, 13 Priorats, 31 Riojas, and more than a dozen vintages of the legendary Vega Sicilia. In all, there are more than 300 wines and selected *cavas,* sherries, and *moscatells,* and the list is constantly rotated so you can always expect some new surprise on the *carte.* If you don't want a bottle, you'll find some two dozen wines offered by the glass, including a sublime '94 Jané Ventura Cabernet Sauvignon. To go with your wine, tantalizing tapas are served, including walnut rolls drizzled in olive oil, cured Iberian ham, and French cheese. Tapas cost from 1.65€ to 5.90€, and hours are Tuesday to Saturday from noon to 1:30am and Sunday from noon to midnight. Metro: Jaume I or Barceloneta. AE, DC, MC, V.

likely it'll be a younger group. The crowd knows its jazz and seems to demand only the best talent for the evening jazz sessions. On our last visit, we were entertained by an evening of Chicago blues. Shows are at midnight, and the club is open daily 9pm to 5am. Plaça Reial 17. ✆ **93-301-75-64.** Cover (includes one drink) 9€–12€. Metro: Liceu.

BARS & PUBS

In addition to the bars listed below, several Barcelona tapas bars are recommended in the "Where to Dine" section of chapter 3.

Café Bar Padam The tapas served here are derived from time-honored Catalán culinary traditions, but the clientele and decor are modern, hip, and often gay. The bar is on a narrow street in the Ciutat Vella, about 3 blocks east of the Ramble dels Caputxins. The only color in the black-and-white rooms comes from fresh flowers and modern paintings. Tapas include fresh anchovies and tuna, plus cheese platters. Jazz is sometimes featured. Open Monday to Saturday from 7pm to 2:30am. Rauric 9. ✆ **93-302-50-62.** Metro: Liceu.

Cocktail Bar Boadas This intimate and conservative bar is usually filled with regulars. Established in 1933, it lies near the top of Les Rambles. Many visitors stop here for a pre-dinner drink and snack before wandering to one of the district's many restaurants. You can choose from among a wide array of Caribbean rums, Russian vodkas, and English gins—the skilled bartenders know how to mix them all. The place is especially well known for its daiquiris. Open daily noon to 2am. Tallers 1. ✆ **93-318-95-92.** Metro: Plaça de Catalunya.

El Born Facing a rustic-looking square, this place, once a fish store, has been cleverly converted. There are a few tables near the front, but our preferred spot is the inner room, decorated with rattan furniture, ceramic jugs, books, and modern paintings. Music here could be anything from Louis Armstrong to classic rock-and-roll. Dinner can also be had at the upstairs buffet. The room is somewhat cramped, but there you'll find a simple but tasty collection of fish, meat, and vegetable dishes, all carefully laid out; a full dinner without wine costs from 16€ to 27€; wine 1.40€. Open Monday to Saturday from 6pm to 3am. Passeig del Born 26. ✆ **93-319-53-33.** Metro: Jaume I.

Otto Zutz Club Boasting a neo-industrial decor, this nightspot is the last word in hip and a magnet for the city's artists and night people. Facetiously named after a German optician and the recipient of thousands of Euros worth of interior drama, it sits behind an angular facade that reminds some visitors of a monument to some mid-20th-century megalomaniac. Built to house a textile factory, the building contains a labyrinth of metal staircases decorated in shades of blue, highlighted with endless spotlights, and warmed with lots of exposed wood. Open Wednesday from 10pm to 6am and Thursday and Saturday from 11pm to 6am. Carrer Lincoln 15. ✆ **93-238-07-22.** Cover 12€. Metro: Passeig de Gràcia or Fontana.

Schilling A young and stylish crowd can be seen crossing Plaça Reial with its Gaudí lampposts, heading for this old cafe to sample its drink, its succulent pastas, savory tapas, and *panini.* Forsaking Barcelona's fabled modernism, Schilling gleefully lingers in another era, with its iron columns, marble tables, and wall of wine bottles. A large gay crowd often dominates the night along with some hip, supposedly straight young things and a few aging pensioners. On a recent visit, we noted three models that would give Jennifer Lopez competition and at least two young Catalán versions of Brad Pitt. A waiter confided to us, "We're famous for our slow service." His appraisal was right on the mark. Carrer Ferran 23. ✆ **93-317-67-87.** Mon-Sat 10am–1:30am, Sun noon–2:30am. Metro: Liceu.

Zig-Zag Bar Favored by actors, models, cinematographers, and photographers, this bar claims to have inaugurated Barcelona's trend toward high-tech minimalism in its watering holes. Owned by the same entrepreneurs who developed the state-of-the-art nightclub Otto Zutz, it offers an unusual chance to see Spain's nightlife in action. Open Monday to Thursday from 10pm to 2:30am, Friday and Saturday from 10pm to 3am. Platón 13. ✆ **93-201-62-07.** Metro: Muntaner.

Moments Piaf, Drag Queens & a Walk on the Wild Side

Do you long to check out the seedy part of Barcelona that writers such as Jean Genet brought so vividly to life in their books? Much of it is gone forever, but *la vida* nostalgically lives on in pockets like the **Bar Pastis.** Valencianos Carme Pericás and Quime Ballester opened this tiny bar just off the southern end of Les Rambles in 1947. They made it a shrine to Edith Piaf, and her songs still play on an old phonograph in back of the bar. The decor consists mostly of paintings by Ballester, who had a dark, rather morbid vision of the world. You can order four kinds of pastis in this dimly lit "corner of Montmartre." Outside the window, check out the view—usually a parade of transvestite hookers. The crowd is likely to include almost anyone, especially people who used to be called bohemians. There's live music Sunday and Tuesday at 11:30pm. Open Monday through Thursday from 7:30pm to 2:30am; Friday, Saturday, and Sunday until 3am. Carrer Santa Mónica 4. ✆ **93-318-79-80.** Metro: Drassanes.

Finds The Night is Yours with Catalán Bubbly

The Cataláns call their own version of sparkling wine *cava.* In Catalán, champagne bars are called *xampanyerías.* The Spanish wines are often excellent, and some consider them better than their French counterparts. With more than 50 Spanish companies producing *cava,* and each bottling up to a dozen grades of wine, the best way to learn about Spanish champagne is to visit the vineyard or to sample the products at a *xampanyería.*

Champagne bars usually open at 7pm and stay open into the wee hours of the morning. They serve tapas, ranging from caviar to smoked fish to frozen chocolate truffles. Most establishments well only a limited array of house *cavas* by the glass, and more esoteric varieties by the bottle. You'll be offered a choice of *brut* (slightly sweeter) or *brut nature.* The most acclaimed brands include Mont-Marçal, Gramona, Mestres, Parxet, Torello, and Recaredo.

The little champagne bar, **El Xampanyet,** Carrer Montcada 22 (✆ **93-319-70-03**), our favorite in Barcelona, has been operated by the same family since the 1930s. When the Picasso Museum opened nearby, its popularity was assured. On this ancient street, the tavern is adorned with colored tiles, antique curios, marble tables, and barrels. With your sparkling wine, you can order fresh anchovies in vinegar or other tapas. If you don't want the *cava,* you can order fresh cider at the old-fashioned zinc bar. Open Tuesday to Saturday from noon to 4pm and 6:30 to 11:30pm and Sunday from noon to 4pm. Closed in August. Metro: Jaume I.

No, Bogie never took Ingrid Bergman here, but **Xampanyería Casablanca,** Bonavista 6 (✆ **93-237-63-99**), likes to imagine that he did as time goes by. Honoring the 1943 Bogart/Bergman classic, the bar serves four kinds of house *cava* by the glass, plus a good selection of tapas, especially patés. We did spot a 21st-century Sydney Greenstreet here one night—in a fez, no less. Open Monday to Saturday from 8am until 3am. Metro: Passeig de Gràcia.

At a corner of Plaça de Tetuan, **Xampú Xampany,** Gran Via de les Corts Catalanes 702 (✆ **93-265-04-83**), offers a variety of hors d'oeuvres in addition to wine. Abstract paintings, touches of high tech, and bouquets of flowers break up the pastel color scheme. Open Monday through Saturday from 6pm to 3:30am. Metro: Girona.

GAY & LESBIAN BARS

Café Dietrich As if you didn't already know by its namesake, this cafe stages the best drag strip shows in town, a combination of local and foreign divas "falling in love again" like the great Marlene herself. It remains Barcelona's most popular gay haunt. The scantily clad bartenders are hot, and the overly posh decor lives to its reputation as a "divinely glam musical bar/disco." Many of the drag queens like to fraternize with the handsomest of the patrons, to whom they offer deep kisses on the mouth. Open Monday to Thursday from 6pm to 2:30am, Friday to Sunday from 6pm to 3am. Consell de Cent 255. ✆ **93-451-77-07.** Metro: Gràcia.

Medusa This minimalist decorated bar draws a trendy young crowd, mainly of cute boys. "The cuter you are, the better your chances of getting in if we get crowded as the night wears on," we were assured by one of the staff. A super trendy place, Medusa draws the *fashionistas.* We prefer its DJs to all other in town. The place gets very cruisy after 1am. Open Sunday to Thursday from 11pm to 3am, Friday to Saturday from 11pm to 3:30am. Casanova 75. ✆ **93-454-53-63.** Metro: Urgell.

Metro Still one of the most popular gay discos in Barcelona, Metro attracts a diverse crowd—from young fashion victims to more rough-and-ready macho types. One dance floor plays contemporary house and dance music, and the other traditional Spanish music mixed with Spanish pop. This is a good opportunity to watch men of all ages dance the *sevillanas* together in pairs with a surprising degree of grace. The gay press in Barcelona quite accurately dubs the backroom here as a "notorious, lascivious labyrinth of lust." One interesting feature appears in the bathrooms, where videos have been installed in quite unexpected places. Open Monday to Thursday from midnight to 5am; Friday to Saturday from midnight to 6am. Sepúlveda 185. ✆ **93-323-52-27.** Cover 8€. Metro: Universitat.

New Chaps Gay Barcelonans refer to this saloon-style watering hole as Catalonia's premier leather and denim bar. In fact, the dress code usually is leather of a different stripe: more boots and jeans than leather and chains. Behind a pair of swinging doors evocative of the old American West, Chaps contains two different bar areas. Some of Barcelona's horniest guys flock to the downstairs darkroom in the wee hours. Open daily from 9pm to 3am. Av. Diagonal 365. ✆ **93-215-53-65.** Metro: Diagonal.

Punto BCN Barcelona's largest gay bar attracts a mixed crowd of young "hotties" and foreigners. Always crowded, it's a good base to start out your evening. There is a very popular happy hour on Wednesday from 6 to 9pm. On Friday and Saturday there are lots of surprises and giveaways. Open Monday to Thursday and Sunday from 6pm to 2am; Friday to Saturday from 6pm to 2:30am. Muntaner 63–65. ✆ **93-453-61-23.** Metro: Eixample.

Salvation This leading gay dance club has been going strong since 1999. It's still the flashiest dive on the see-and-be-seen circuit, and a good place to wear your see-through clothing, especially as the hour grows late. There are two rooms devoted to a different type of music, the first with house music and DJs and the other with more commercial and "soapy" themes. An habitué told us, "I come here because of the sensual waiters," and indeed they are the handsomest and most muscular in town. Look your most gorgeous, buffed self if you want to get past the notoriously selective doorman. On Friday and Saturday nights women need special passes to gain entrance. These can be requested at Dietrich (see above). Open Friday to Saturday from midnight to 5am. Ronda de Sant Pere 19-21. ✆ **93-318-06-86.** Entrance 9€. Metro: Urquinaona.

14 Side Trips from Barcelona

The major day trips include those to the beaches of Sitges, the monastery of Montserrat, the Penedés vineyards, and the canonical church in Cardona. Among other popular stopovers are the resorts north of Barcelona along the Costa Brava, which are covered extensively in *Frommer's Spain.*

SITGES

Sitges, 40km (25 miles) south of Barcelona, is one of the most popular resorts of southern Europe. It's especially crowded in summer, mostly with affluent young northern Europeans, many of them gay. For years the resort largely drew prosperous middle-class industrialists from Barcelona, but those staid days have gone; Sitges is as swinging today as Benidorm and Torremolinos down the coast, but nowhere near as tacky.

Sitges has long been known as a city of culture, thanks in part to resident artist, playwright, and Bohemian mystic Santiago Rusiñol. The 19th-century modernismo movement began largely at Sitges, and the town remained the scene of artistic encounters and demonstrations long after the movement waned. Sitges continued as a resort of artists, attracting such giants as Salvador Dalí and poet Federico García Lorca. The Spanish Civil War (1936–39) erased what has come to be called the "golden age" of Sitges. Although other artists and writers arrived in the decades to follow, none had the name or the impact of those who had gone before.

ESSENTIALS

GETTING THERE **By Train** RENFE runs trains from Barcelona-Sants to Sitges, a 30-minute trip, costing 2€. Call ✆ **90-224-02-02** in Barcelona for information about schedules. Four trains leave Barcelona per hour.

Moments We'll Have a Gay Old Time

Along with Ibiza, Key West, and Mikonos, Sitges has established itself firmly on the "A" list of gay resorts. It's a perfect destination for those who want a ready-made combination of beach and bars, all within a few minutes walk of each other. It also works well as a temporary, calmer alternative to Barcelona, which is about 30 minutes away by train, and so is great for a day trip or a few days out of the city. Off-season, it's pretty quiet on the gay front apart from the carnival in February. Summer, however, is pure hedonism, and the town draws the boys in from all over Europe to the gay beach in the middle of the town in front of the Passeig Marítim. The other beach is nudist and farther out of town between Sitges and Vilanova. The best directions would be to go as far as the L'Atlántida disco and then follow the train track to the farther of the two beaches.

By Car Sitges is a 45-minute drive from Barcelona along the **C-246,** a coastal road. An express highway, the **A-7,** opened in 1991. The coastal road is more scenic, but it can be extremely slow on weekends because of the heavy traffic, as all of Barcelona seemingly heads for the beaches.

VISITOR INFORMATION The **tourist office** is at Carrer Sínis Morera 1 (**© 93-894-42-51**). June to September 15, it's open daily 9am to 9pm; September 16 to May, hours are Monday to Friday from 9am to 2pm and 4 to 6:30pm, and Saturday from 10am to 1pm.

SPECIAL EVENTS The **Carnaval** at Sitges is one of the outstanding events on the Catalán calendar. For more than a century, the town has celebrated the days before the beginning of Lent. Fancy dress, floats, feathered outfits, and sequins all make this an exciting event. The party begins on the Thursday before Lent with the arrival of the king of the Carnestoltes and ends with the Burial of a Sardine on Ash Wednesday. Activities reach their flamboyant best on Sant Bonaventura, where gay people hold their own celebrations.

FUN ON & OFF THE BEACH

The old part of Sitges used to be a fortified medieval enclosure. The castle is now the seat of the town government. The local parish church, called *La Punta* (The Point) and built next to the sea on top of a promontory, presides over an extensive maritime esplanade, where people parade in the early evening. Behind the side of the church are the Museu Cau Ferrat and the Museu Maricel (see below).

Most people are here to hit the beach. The beaches have showers, bathing cabins, and stalls; kiosks rent motorboats and water-sports equipment. Beaches on the eastern end and those inside the town center are the most peaceful—for example, **Aiguadoiç** and **Els Balomins. Playa San Sebastián, Fragata Beach,** and the **"Beach of the Boats"** (below the church and next to the yacht club) are the area's family beaches. A young, happening crowd heads for the **Playa de la Ribera,** to the west.

All along the coast women can and certainly do go topless. Farther west are the most solitary beaches, where the scene grows more racy, especially along the **Playas del Muerto,** where two tiny nude beaches lie between Sitges and Vilanova i la Geltrú. A shuttle bus runs between the cathedral and Golf Terramar. From Golf Terramar, go along the road to the club L'Atlántida, then walk along the railway. The first beach draws nudists of every sexual persuasion, and the second is almost solely gay. Be advised that lots of action takes place in the woods in back of these beaches.

Beaches aside, Sitges has some choice museums, which really shouldn't be missed.

Museu Cau Ferrat The Catalán artist Santiago Rusiñol combined two 16th-century cottages to make this house, where he lived and worked and which upon his death in 1931 he willed to Sitges along with his art collection. More than anyone else, Rusiñol made Sitges a popular resort. The museum collection includes two paintings by El Greco and several small Picassos, including *The Bullfight.* A number of Rusiñol's works are also on display.

Carrer del Fonallar. © **93-894-03-64.** Admission 3€ adults, 1.50€ students, free for children under 16; combination ticket for the 3 museums listed in this section: 5€ adults, 3€ students and children. June 22–Sept 10, Tues–Sat 9:30am–2pm and 4–9pm, Sun 9:30am–2pm; Sept 11–June 21, Tues–Fri 9:30am–2pm and 4–6pm, Sat 9:30am–2pm and 4–8pm, Sun 9:30am–2pm.

Museu Maricel Opened by the king and queen of Spain, Museu Maricel contains art donated by Dr. Jesús Pérez Rosales. The palace, owned by American Charles Deering when it was built right after World War I, is made up of two parts connected by a small bridge. The museum has a good collection of Gothic and Romantic paintings and sculptures, as well as many fine Catalán ceramics. There are also three noteworthy works by Santiago Rebull and an allegorical painting of World War I by José María Sert.

Carrer del Fonallar. © **93-894-03-64.** Admission 3€ adults, 1.50€ students, free for children under 16; admission included in combination ticket (see Museu Cau Ferrat, above). June 21–Sept 11, Tues–Sat 9:30am–2pm and 4–8pm, Sun 9:30am–2pm; Sept 12–June 20, Tues–Fri 9:30am–2pm and 4–6pm, Sat 9:30am–2pm and 4–8pm, Sun 9:30am–2pm.

Museu Romàntic ("Can Llopis") This museum recreates the daily life of a Sitges land-owning family in the 18th and 19th centuries. The family rooms, furniture, and household objects are most interesting. You'll also find wine cellars, and an important collection of antique dolls (upstairs).

Sant Gaudenci 1. © **93-894-29-69.** Admission 3€ adults, 1.50€ students, free for children under 16; admission included in combination ticket (see above). June 21–Sept 11, Tues–Sat 9:30am–2pm and 4–8pm, Sun 9:30am–2pm; Sept 12–June 20, Tues–Fri 9:30am–2pm and 4–6pm, Sat 9:30am–2pm and 4–8pm, Sun 9:30am–2pm.

WHERE TO STAY

Hotel Calípolis ★ This 11-story hotel fits in a gently undulating curve against the resort's beachfront and seaside promenade. The good-size rooms contain expansive balconies, marble bathrooms with shower-tub combinations, and a comfortably conservative decor of contemporary furniture. Most offer sea views; the remainder offer views of the mountains.

Av. Sofía 2–4, 08870 Sitges. © **93-894-15-00.** Fax 93-894-07-64. www.hoteles-hesperia.es. 170 units. 126€–145€ double; from 200€ suite. AE, DC, MC, V. Parking 12€. **Amenities:** Restaurant; bar; pool; car rental; room service; laundry/dry cleaning. *In room:* A/C, TV, minibar, hair dryer, safe.

Hotel Platjador One of the best hotels in town, the Platjador, on the esplanade fronting the beach, has comfortably furnished and recently restored rooms, many with big French doors opening onto balconies and sea views. Each unit has a well-kept bathroom with a shower-tub combination. The dining room, facing the beach, is known for its good cuisine, including gazpacho, paella, fresh fish, and flan for dessert.

Passeig de la Ribera 35, 08870 Sitges. © **93-894-50-54.** Fax 93-811-03-84. 59 units. 65€–112€ double. Rates include breakfast. MC, V. Closed Nov–Apr. **Amenities:** Restaurant; bar; pool. *In room:* A/C, TV, safe.

San Sebastián Playa ★★ The best in Sitges, opposite San Sebastián beach, this four-star hotel with its wedding cake facade has been around since 1990. The functional Art Deco interior is beautiful. A lot of attention has gone into the rooms, which are spacious and comfortable, with such modern conveniences as fully equipped bathrooms containing shower-tub combinations. Each also has a balcony opening onto the sea.

Port Alegre 53, 08070 Sitges. ✆ **93-894-86-76.** Fax 93-894-04-30. www.hotelsansebastian.com. 51 units. 109€–166€ double; 181€–241€ suite. AE, DC, MC, V. Parking 13€. **Amenities:** Restaurant; bar; pool; room service; babysitting; laundry/dry cleaning. *In room:* A/C, TV, minibar, hair dryer, safe.

WHERE TO DINE

Els Quatre Gats ★ CATALAN When it opened in the early 1960s as a bar/cafe a few steps from the beachfront Passeig de la Ribera., it adopted the name of one of Catalonia's most historic cafes, Els Quatre Gats (see "Barcelona After Dark"). By 1968, the newcomer was firmly established as one of the leading restaurants in Sitges, serving a well-received *cocina del mercado,* based on whatever was fresh and available in the local markets. In a setting accented with paintings and varnished paneling, you can enjoy fresh grilled fish, garlic soup, lamb cutlets with local herbs, roast chicken in wine sauce, and veal kidneys in sherry sauce.

Sant Pau 13. ✆ **93-894-19-15.** Reservations recommended. Main courses 11€–17€; *menú del día* 15€. AE, DC, MC, V. Thurs–Tues 1–4pm and 8–11pm. Closed Nov–Mar.

El Velero ★ SEAFOOD This is one of the leading restaurants of Sitges, occupying a position along the beachfront promenade. The most desirable tables are found on the glass greenhouse terrace, opening onto the esplanade, although there is a more glamorous restaurant inside. Try a soup, such as clam and truffle or whitefish, followed by a main dish such as paella marinara (with seafood) or supreme of salmon in pine-nut sauce.

Passeig de la Ribera 38. ✆ **93-894-20-51.** Reservations required. Main courses 17€–35.50€; fixed-price menu 24€. AE, DC, MC, V. Daily 1:30–4pm and 8:30–11:30pm.

SITGES AFTER DARK

One of the best ways to pass an evening in Sitges is to walk the waterfront esplanade, have a leisurely dinner, then retire at about 11pm to one of the open-air cafes for a nightcap and some serious people-watching. Few local dives can compete with the scene taking place on the streets.

If you're straight, you may have to hunt to find a bar that isn't predominantly gay. There are so many gay bars, in fact, that a map is distributed pinpointing their locales. Nine of them are concentrated on **Carrer Sant Bonaventura** in the center of town, a 5-minute walk from the beach (near the Museu Romàntic). If you grow bored with the action in one place, you just have to walk down the street to find another. Drink prices run about the same in all the clubs.

Mediterráneo, Sant Bonaventura 6 (no phone), is the largest gay disco/bar. It sports a formal Iberian garden and sleek modern styling. Upstairs in this restored 1690s house just east of the Plaça d'Espanya, there are pool tables and a covered terrace. On summer nights, the place is filled to overflowing. Other gay bars include **Bourbon's,** Sant Bonaventura 13 (✆ **93-894-33-47**), which appeals to a predominately youngish crowd, and **El Candil,** Carrer de la Carreta 9 (no phone), where the age range is wider and which has a dark room and video shows. **El Horno,** Joan Tarrida 6 (✆ **93-894-09-09**), with slight leather overtones that grow more prominent as the night progresses, opens earlier, at 5:30pm, and also features videos and a dark room.

Another of the town's most popular nightspots, with DJs spinning the latest dance hits, is **Ricky's Disco,** Sant Pau 25 (✆ **93-894-96-81**), which charges a cover of 9€ to 12€. This place caters to an international mix of gays and straights. It's set back from the beach on a narrow street noted for its inexpensive restaurants and folkloric color. **Trailer,** Angel Vidal 36 (no phone), is an extremely popular club and the best place to end the night. It closes at 5:30am, and the entry cost of 9€ includes one drink.

MONTSERRAT

Montserrat is 56km (35 miles) northwest of Barcelona and 592km (368 miles) east of Madrid. The **monastery at Montserrat,** which sits atop a 1.2km (4,000-ft.) mountain 11km (7 miles) long and 5.5km (3½ miles) wide, is one of the most important pilgrimage spots in Spain. It ranks alongside Zaragoza and Santiago de Compostela. Thousands travel here every year to see and touch the medieval statue of *La Moreneta* (The Black Virgin), the patron saint of Catalonia. Many newly married couples flock here for her blessings. Avoid visiting on Sunday, if possible. Thousands of locals pour in, especially if the weather is nice. Remember that the winds blow cold up here; even in summer, visitors should take along warm sweaters, jackets, or coats. In winter, thermal underwear might not be a bad idea.

ESSENTIALS

GETTING THERE **By Train** The best and most exciting way to go is via the Catalán railway—Ferrocarrils de la Generalitat de Catalunya (Manresa line), with five trains a day leaving from the Plaça d'Espanya in Barcelona. The central office is at Plaça de Catalunya 1 (✆ **93-205-15-15**). The train connects with an aerial cableway (*Aeri de Montserrat*), which is included in the rail passage of 11.60€ round-trip.

By Bus The train with its funicular tie-in has taken over as the preferred means of transport. However, a long-distance bus service is provided by **Autocars Julià** in Barcelona. Daily service from Barcelona to Montserrat is generally operated, with departures near Estació Central de Barcelona-Sants, Plaça de Països Catalanes. One bus makes the trip at 9am, returning at 5pm; the round-trip ticket costs 8.70€. Contact the Julià company at Carrer Viriato (✆ **93-490-40-00**).

By Car Take the **N-2** southwest of Barcelona toward Tarragona, turning west at the junction with the **N-11.** The signposts and exit to Montserrat will be on your right. From the main road, it's 14.5km (9 miles) up to the monastery through eerie rock formations and dramatic scenery.

VISITOR INFORMATION The **tourist office** is at Plaça de la Creu (✆ **93-877-77-77**). It's open from 10am to 6pm.

SEEING THE SIGHTS

One of the **monastery**'s noted attractions is the 50-member **Escolanía** ★ (boys' choir), one of the oldest and most renowned in Europe, dating from the 13th century. At 1pm daily you can hear them singing *Salve Regina* and the *Virolai* (hymn of Montserrat) in the basilica. The basilica is open daily 8 to 10:30am and noon to 6:30pm. Admission is free. To view the Black Virgin, a statue from the 12th or 13th century, enter the church through a side door to the right. At the Plaça de Santa María you can also visit the **Museu de Montserrat** (✆ **93-877-77-77**), known for its collection of ecclesiastical paintings, including works by Caravaggio and El Greco. Modern Spanish and Catalán artists are also represented (see Picasso's early *El Viejo Pescador,* dating from 1895), as well as works by Dalí and such French impressionists as Monet, Sisley, and Degas. The collection of ancient artifacts is also interesting. And look for the crocodile mummy, which is at least 2,000 years old. The museum is open Monday to Friday from 10am to 6pm, Saturday and Sunday from 9:30am to 6:30pm; admission is 4.50€ for adults, 3€ for children and students.

The 9-minute **funicular ride** to the 1.2km (4,119-ft.) high peak, Sant Jeroni, makes for a panoramic trip. The funicular operates about every 20 minutes from April to October, daily 10am to 6:40pm. The cost is 6.10€ round-trip. From the top, you'll see not only the whole of Catalonia but also the Pyrenees and the islands of Majorca and Ibiza.

You can also make an excursion to **Santa Cova (Holy Grotto),** the alleged site of the discovery of the Black Virgin. The grotto dates from the 17th century and was built in the shape of a cross. You go halfway by funicular but must complete the trip on foot.

The chapel is open April to October, daily 9am to 6:30pm; off-season hours are daily 10am to 5:30pm. The funicular operates from April to October only, every 15 minutes daily 10am to 7pm, at a cost of 2.50€ round-trip.

WHERE TO STAY & DINE

Abat Cisneros On the main square, this is a well-maintained modern hotel with few pretensions and a history of family management dating from 1958. Guest rooms are simple and clean with bathrooms equipped with shower-tub combinations. The in-house restaurant offers regional dishes of Catalonia.

Plaça de Monestir, 08199 Montserrat. ✆ **93-877-77-01.** Fax 93-877-77-24. 56 units. 40€–76€ double. AE, DC, MC, V. Parking 2.70€. **Amenities:** Restaurant; bar; lounge; laundry/dry cleaning. *In room:* TV, safe.

PENEDES WINERIES: HOME OF *CAVA*

From the Penedés wineries comes the famous *cava,* Catalán champagne, which can be sampled in the champagne bars of Barcelona. You can see where this wine originates by journeying 40km (25 miles) from Barcelona, via highway A-2, to Exit 27. There are also daily trains to Sant Sadurní d'Anoia, home to 66 cava firms. Trains depart from Barcelona Sants.

The firm best equipped to receive visitors is **Codorníu** (✆ **93-818-32-32**), the largest producer of cava (some 40 million bottles a year). Codorníu is ideally visited by car because of unreliable public transportation. However, it's sometimes possible to get a taxi from the station at Sant Sadurní d'Anoia.

Groups are welcomed at Codorníu (there must be at least four people present before a tour is conducted). Advance reservations are not necessary. Tours are presented in English, among other languages, and last 1½ hours; visitors will explore some of the 16km (10 miles) of underground cellars by electric cart. Take a sweater, even on a hot day. A former pressing section has been turned into a museum, exhibiting winemaking instruments through the ages. The museum is housed in a building designed by the great *modernista* architect Puig i Cadafalch—one reason King Juan Carlos has declared the plant a national historic and artistic monument.

The tour ends with a cava tasting. Tours are conducted Monday to Friday from 9am to 5pm. Call the number above for more information. The ideal time for a visit is during the autumn grape harvest. Admission is free Monday to Friday, 1.50€ Saturday and Sunday.

CARDONA: CATALAN CASTLE VILLAGE

Another popular excursion from Barcelona is to Cardona, 97km (60 miles) northwest. Take the N-11 west, then go north on Route 150 to Manresa. Cardona, reached along Route 1410, lies northwest of Manresa, a distance of 32km (20 miles). The home of the dukes of Cardona, the town is known for its canonical church, **Sant Vicenç de Cardona,** placed inside the walls of the castle. The church was consecrated in 1040. The great Catalán architect Josep Puig i Cadafalch wrote, "There are few elements in Catalán architecture of the 12th century that cannot be found in Cardona, and nowhere better harmonized." The church reflects the Lombard style of architecture. The castle (now a parador—see below) was the most important fortress in Catalonia.

Parador Nacional Duques de Cardona Atop a cone-shaped mountain towering 99m (330 ft.) over Cardona, this restored castle opened as a four-star parador in 1976. Once the seat of Ludovici Pio (Louis the Pious) and a stronghold against the Moors, it was later expanded by Guifré el Pilós (Wilfred the Hairy). In the 9th century the palace went to Don Ramón Folch, nephew of Charlemagne. The massive fortress proved impregnable to all but the inroads of time, and several ancient buildings in this complex have been restored and made part of the parador. The spacious units are furnished with hand-carved wood canopied beds and woven bedspreads and curtains. All bathrooms are neatly kept and contain shower-tub combinations. The public rooms boast antique furniture, tapestries, and paintings of various periods. The bar is in a former dungeon, with meals served in the stone-arched medieval dining room. Try the Catalán bouillabaisse, accompanied by wines whose taste would be familiar to the Romans. Service is daily 1 to 4pm and 8 to 10:30pm.

Castillo de Cardona s/n, 08261 Cardona. ✆ **93-869-12-75.** Fax 93-869-16-36. www.parador.es. 54 units. 92€–107€ double; 141€–153€ suite. AE, DC, MC, V. **Amenities:** Restaurant; bar; fitness center; sauna; room service; babysitting; laundry/dry cleaning. *In room:* A/C, TV, minibar, hair dryer, safe.

5

Settling into Madrid

Madrid was conceived, planned, and built when Spain was at the peak of its confidence and power and the city became the solid and dignified seat of a great empire stretching around the world. Monumental Madrid glitters almost as much as Paris, Rome, or London and parties more than any other city. Although it lacks the spectacular Romanesque and Gothic monuments of older Spanish cities, Madrid never fails to convey its own sense of grandeur.

Madrid has the highest altitude of any European capital and its climate can be blisteringly hot in summer but quite cold in winter. Traffic roars down wide boulevards that stretch for miles—from the narrow streets of the city's historic 17th-century core to the ugly concrete suburbs that have spread in recent years.

Don't come to Madrid expecting a city that looks classically Iberian. True, many of the older buildings in the historic core look as Spanish as those you might have encountered in rural towns across the plains of La Mancha. However, a great number of the monuments and palaces mirror the architecture of France—an oddity that reflects the genetic link between the royal families of Spain and France.

Most striking is how the city has blossomed since Franco's demise. Madrid was the epicenter of *la movida* (the movement), a renaissance of the arts after years of dictatorial creative repression. Today, despite stiff competition from such smaller cities as Barcelona and Seville, Madrid still reigns as the country's artistic and creative centerpiece.

More world-class art is on view in the central neighborhood around the stellar Prado than within virtually any other concentrated area in the world: the Caravaggios and Rembrandts at the Thyssen-Bornemisza; the El Grecos and Velázquezes at the Prado itself; and the Dalís and Mirós—not to mention Picasso's wrenching *Guernica*—at the Reina Sofía. Ironically, much of the city's art was collected by 18th-century Spanish monarchs whose artistic sense was frequently more astute than their political savvy.

Regrettably, within the city limits you'll also find sprawling expanses of concrete towers, sometimes paralyzing traffic, a growing incidence of street crime, and entire districts that, as in every other metropolis, bear no historic or cultural interest for the tourist. Many long-time visitors to the city find that its quintessential Spanish feel has subsided somewhat in the face of a Brussels-like "Europeanization" that has occurred since Spain's 1986 induction into the European Union. The city's gems remain the opulence of the **Palacio Real,** the bustle of **El Rastro**'s flea market, and the sultry fever of late-night flamenco. When urban commotion starts to overwhelm, seek respite in the **Parque del Retiro,** a vast, verdant oasis in the heart of the city a stone's throw from the Prado.

1 Orientation

ARRIVING

BY PLANE Madrid's international airport, **Barajas,** lies 14.5km (9 miles) east of the center and has two terminals—one for international traffic, the other for domestic—connected by a moving sidewalk. For Barajas Airport information, call ✆ **91-305-83-43.**

Air-conditioned yellow airport buses can take you from the arrival terminal to a bus depot beneath the central Plaza de Colón. You can get off at stops along the way, provided that your baggage isn't stored in the hold. The fare is 2.40€; buses leave every 15 minutes, either to or from the airport.

By taxi, expect to pay 24€ and up, plus surcharges, for the trip to the airport and for baggage handling. If you take an unmetered limousine, make sure you negotiate the price in advance.

The most convenient way to reach the center of Madrid from the airport is via a new subway link. Fitted with luggage racks, trains make the trip in only 12 minutes with three stops along the way. A one-way ticket costs .90€, and the line operates daily from 6am to 1:30am. Trains from Barajas arrive at the Nuevos Ministerios section of Madrid, north of the center. From here there is access to two other Metro lines, 10 bus routes, and a number of commuter train lines. The facility at Nuevos Ministerios also has 34 check-in counters for departing flights such as those on Iberia. It's possible to check your luggage and receive boarding passes up to 24 hours in advance, except for the popular Madrid/Barcelona air shuttle.

BY TRAIN Madrid has three major railway stations: **Atocha** (Av. Ciudad de Barcelona; Metro: Atocha RENFE), for trains to and from Lisbon, Toledo, Andalusia, and Extremadura; **Chamartín** (in the northern suburbs at Augustín de Foxá; Metro: Chamartín), for trains to and from Barcelona, Asturias, Cantabria, Castilla-León, the Basque country, Aragón, Catalonia, Levante (Valencia), Murcia, and the French frontier; and **Estación Príncipe Pío** or Norte (Paseo del Rey 30; Metro: Norte), for trains to and from northwest Spain (Salamanca and Galicia). For information about connections from any of these stations, call RENFE (Spanish Railways) at ✆ **90-224-02-02,** daily from 7am to 11pm.

For tickets, go to the principal office of **RENFE,** Alcalá 44 (✆ **91-506-63-29;** Metro: Banco de España). The office is open Monday through Friday from 9:30am to 8pm.

BY BUS Madrid has at least eight major bus terminals, including the large **Estación Sur de Autobuses,** Calle Méndez Alvaro (✆ **91-468-42-00;** Metro: Palos de la Frontera). Most buses pass through this station.

Highways to Madrid

Route	From	Distance to Madrid
N-I	Irún	507km (315 miles)
N-II	Barcelona	626km (389 miles)
N-III	Valencia	349km (217 miles)
N-IV	Cádiz	625km (388 miles)
N-V	Badajoz	409km (254 miles)
N-VI	Galicia	602km (374 miles)

BY CAR All highways within Spain radiate outward from Madrid. The following are the major highways into Madrid, with information on driving distances to the city:

VISITOR INFORMATION

The most convenient **tourist office** is near the American Express office, on Duque de Medinaceli 2, Banco de España (✆ **91-429-31-77;** Metro: Plaza de España); it's open Monday through Friday from 9am to 7pm and Saturday from 9:30am to 1pm. Ask for a street map of the next town on your itinerary, especially if you're driving. The staff here can give you a list of hotels and *hostales* (hostels) but cannot recommend any particular lodging.

CITY LAYOUT

All roads lead to Madrid, which has outgrown its previous boundaries and is branching out in all directions.

MAIN ARTERIES & SQUARES Every new arrival must find the **Gran Vía,** which cuts a winding pathway across the city beginning at the **Plaza de España,** where you'll find one of Europe's tallest skyscrapers, the Edificio España. This avenue is home to the largest concentration of shops, hotels, restaurants, and movie houses in the city, with **Calle de Serrano** a close runner-up.

South of the Gran Vía lies the **Puerta del Sol,** the starting point for all road distances within Spain. However, its tourism significance has declined, and today it is a prime hunting ground for pickpockets and purse snatchers. **Calle de Alcalá** begins here at Sol and runs for 4km (2½ miles).

The **Plaza Mayor** lies at the heart of Old Madrid and is an attraction in itself with its mix of French and Georgian architecture. (Again, be wary of thieves here, especially late at night.) Pedestrians pass under the arches of the huge square onto the narrow streets of the old town, where you can find some of the capital's most intriguing restaurants and *tascas,* serving tasty tapas and drinks. The colonnaded ground level of the plaza is filled with shops, many selling souvenir hats of turn-of-the-century Spanish sailors or army officers.

The area south of the Plaza Mayor—known as *barrios bajos*—is made up of narrow cobblestone streets lined with 16th- and 17th-century architecture. From the Plaza, take **Arco de Cuchilleros,** a street packed with markets, restaurants, flamenco clubs, and taverns, to explore this district.

Gran Vía ends at Calle de Alcalá, and at this juncture lies the grand **Plaza de la Cibeles,** with its fountain to Cybele, "the mother of the gods," and the main post office (known as "the cathedral of post offices"). From Cibeles, the wide **Paseo de Recoletos** begins a short run north to Plaza de Colón. From this latter square rolls the serpentine central artery of Madrid: **Paseo de la Castellana,** flanked by expensive shops, apartment buildings, luxury hotels, and foreign embassies.

Heading south from Cibeles is **Paseo del Prado,** where you'll find Spain's major attraction, the Museo del Prado, as well as the *Jardín Botánico* (Botanical Garden). The *paseo* leads to the Atocha Railway Station. To the west of the garden lies **Parque del Retiro,** a magnificent park once reserved for royalty, with restaurants, nightclubs, a rose garden, and two lakes.

STREET MAPS Arm yourself with a good map before setting out. Falk publishes the best, and it's available at most newsstands and kiosks in Madrid. The free maps given away by tourist offices and hotels aren't really adequate for more than general orientation, as they don't list the maze of little streets that is Old Madrid.

Tips **Finding an Address**

Madrid is a city of both grand boulevards and of cramped meandering streets. Finding an address can sometimes be a problem, primarily because of the way buildings are numbered. On most streets, the numbering begins on one side and runs consecutively until the end, resuming on the other side and going in the opposite direction. Thus, number 50 could be opposite number 250. But there are many exceptions to this system. That's why it's important to know the cross street as well as the number of the address you're looking for. To complicate matters, some addresses don't have a number at all. What they have is the designation *s/n,* meaning *sin número* (without number). For example, the address of the *Panteón de Goya* (Goya's Tomb) is Glorieta de San Antonio de la Florida s/n. Note that in Spain, as in many other European countries, the building number comes after the street name.

NEIGHBORHOODS IN BRIEF

Madrid can be divided into three principal districts—Old Madrid, which holds the most tourist interest; Ensanche, the new district, often with the best shops and hotels; and the periphery, which is of little interest to visitors.

PLAZA MAYOR/PUERTA DEL SOL This is the heart of Old Madrid, often called the tourist zone. Filled with taverns and bars, it is bounded by Carrera de San Jerónimo, Calle Mayor, Cava de San Miguel, Cava Baja, and Calle de la Cruz. From Plaza Mayor, the Arco de Cuchilleros is filled with Castilian restaurants and taverns; more of these traditional spots, called *cuevas,* line the Cava de San Miguel, Cava Alta, and Cava Baja. To the west of this old district is the Manzanares River. Also in this area is Muslim Madrid, which is centered on the Palacio de Oriente and Las Vistillas. What is now Plaza de la Paja was actually the heart of the city and its main marketplace during the medieval period. In 1617 the Plaza Mayor became the hub of Madrid, and it remains the nighttime center of tourist activity, more so than the Puerta del Sol.

THE SALAMANCA QUARTER Ever since Madrid's city walls came tumbling down in the 1860s, the district of Salamanca to the north has been the fashionable address. Calle de Serrano cuts through this neighborhood and is lined with stores and boutiques. Calle de Serrano is also home to the U.S. Embassy.

GRAN VIA/PLAZA DE ESPAÑA Gran Vía is the city's main street, lined with cinemas, department stores, and the headquarters of banks and corporations. It begins at the Plaza de España, with its bronze figures of Don Quixote and his faithful squire, Sancho Panza.

ARGÜELLES/MONCLOA The university area is bounded by Pintor Rosales, Cea Bermúdez, Bravo Murillo, San Bernardo, and Conde Duque. Students haunt its famous alehouses.

CHUECA This old and decaying area north of the Gran Vía includes the main streets of Hortaleza, Infantas, Barquillo, and San Lucas. It is the center of gay nightlife, with dozens of clubs and cheap restaurants. It can be dangerous at night, although police presence has increased.

CASTELLANA/RECOLETOS/PASEO DEL PRADO Not a real city district, this is Madrid's north-south axis, its name changing along the way. The Museo del Prado and some of the city's more expensive hotels are found here. Many restaurants and other hotels are located along its side streets. In summer its large medians serve as home to open-air terraces filled with animated crowds. The most famous cafe is the Gran Café de Gijón (see "Where to Dine," later in this chapter).

2 Getting Around

Getting around Madrid is not easy, because everything is spread out. Even many Madrileño taxi drivers, often new arrivals themselves, are unfamiliar with their own city once they're off the main boulevards.

BY SUBWAY

The Metro system is quite easy to learn and use. The fare is .95€ for a one-way trip, and the central converging point is the Puerta del Sol. The Metro operates 6am to 1:30am, and you should try to avoid rush hours. For information, call ✆ **91-429-31-77.** You can save money on public transportation by purchasing a 10-trip ticket known as a *bonos*—it costs 5€.

BY BUS

A bus network also services the city and suburbs, with routes clearly shown at each stop on a schematic diagram. Buses are fast and efficient because they travel along special lanes. Both red and yellow buses charge .95€ per ride. For 5€ you can purchase a 10-trip *bonos* ticket (but without transfers) for Madrid's bus system. It's sold at **Empresa Municipal de Transportes,** Alcántara 24 (✆ **91-406-88-00**), where you can buy a guide to the bus routes. The office is open daily from 8am to 2pm.

BY TAXI

Cab fares are pretty reasonable. When you flag down a taxi, the meter should register 1.35€; for every kilometer thereafter, the fare increases by .65€. A supplement is charged for trips to the railway station or the bullring, as well as on Sunday and holidays. The ride to Barajas Airport carries a 4€ surcharge, and there is a 2€ supplement from railway stations. In addition, there is a 1.35€ supplement on Sunday and holidays, plus a .81€ supplement at night. It's customary to tip at least 10% of the fare.

Instead of a regular taxi, you can take an **AeroCITY** shuttle service (✆ **91-571-50-47**), transporting you in an air-conditioned minivan to your doorstep in Madrid. This service is sometimes less expensive than a regular taxi, depending on the number of people traveling in the vehicle at one time. Service is 24 hours daily.

Warning: Make sure the meter is turned on when you get into a taxi. Otherwise, some drivers assess the cost of the ride, and their assessment, you can be sure, will involve higher mathematics.

Also, there are unmetered taxis that hire out for the day or the afternoon. They are legitimate, but some drivers operate as gypsy cabs. Since they're not metered, they can charge high rates. They are easy to avoid—always take either a black taxi with horizontal red bands or a white one with diagonal red bands.

If you take a taxi outside the city limits, the driver is entitled to charge you twice the rate shown on the meter.

To call a taxi, dial ✆ **91-447-51-80.**

BY CAR

Driving in congested Madrid is a nightmare and potentially dangerous. It always feels like rush hour, although theoretically, these are from 8 to 10am, 1 to 2pm, and 4 to 6pm Monday through Saturday. Parking is next to impossible except in expensive garages. About the only time you can drive around Madrid with a minimum of hassle is in August, when thousands of Madrileños have taken their cars and headed for Spain's vacation oases. Save your car rentals for excursions from the capital. If you drive into Madrid from another city, ask at your hotel for the nearest garage or parking possibility and leave your vehicle there until you're ready to leave.

For more information on renting a car before you leave home, see "Getting Around" in chapter 3. If you decide you want to rent one while in Madrid to explore its environs or to move on, you have several choices. In addition to its office at Barajas Airport (✆ **91-393-72-22**), Avis has a main office in the city center at Gran Vía 60 (✆ **91-547-20-48**). Hertz, too, has an office at Barajas Airport (✆ **91-393-72-28**) and another in the heart of Madrid in the Edificio España, Gran Vía 88 (✆ **91-542-58-03**). Budget Rent-a-Car maintains its headquarters at Barajas Airport (✆ **91-393-72-16**). It's known in Spain as Interrent.

BY BICYCLE

Ever wonder why you see so few people riding bicycles in Madrid? Those who tried were overcome by the traffic pollution. It's better to walk.

FAST FACTS: Madrid

American Express For your mail or banking needs, you can go to the American Express office at the corner of Marqués de Cubas and Plaza de las Cortes 2, across the street from the Palace Hotel (✆ **91-322-55-00** or 91-322-54-45; Metro: Gran Vía). Open Monday through Friday from 9am to 7:30pm and Saturday from 9am to 2pm.

Babysitters Most major hotels can arrange for babysitters, called *canguros* (literally, kangaroos) or *niñeras.* Usually the concierge keeps a list of reliable nursemaids and will contact them for you, provided you give adequate notice. Rates vary considerably but are usually reasonable. Although many babysitters in Madrid speak English, don't count on it.

Car Rentals Should you want to rent a car while in Madrid, you have several choices. In addition to its office at Barajas Airport (✆ 91-393-72-22), **Avis** has a main office in the city center at Gran Vía 60 (✆ 91-547-20-48). **Hertz,** too, has an office at Barajas Airport (✆ 91-393-72-28), and another in the heart of Madrid in the Edificio España, Gran Vía 88 (✆ 91-542-58-05). **Budget** maintains its offices at Barajas Airport (✆ 91-393-72-16). It's known in Spain as Inter-rent.

Currency Exchange The currency exchange at Chamartín railway station (Metro: Chamartín) is open 24 hours and gives the best rates in the capital. If you exchange money at a bank, ask about the minimum commission charged.

Many banks in Spain still charge a 1% to 3% commission with a minimum charge of 3€. However, branches of **Banco Central Hispano** charge no commission. Branches of **El Corte Inglés,** the department store chain,

Madrid Metro

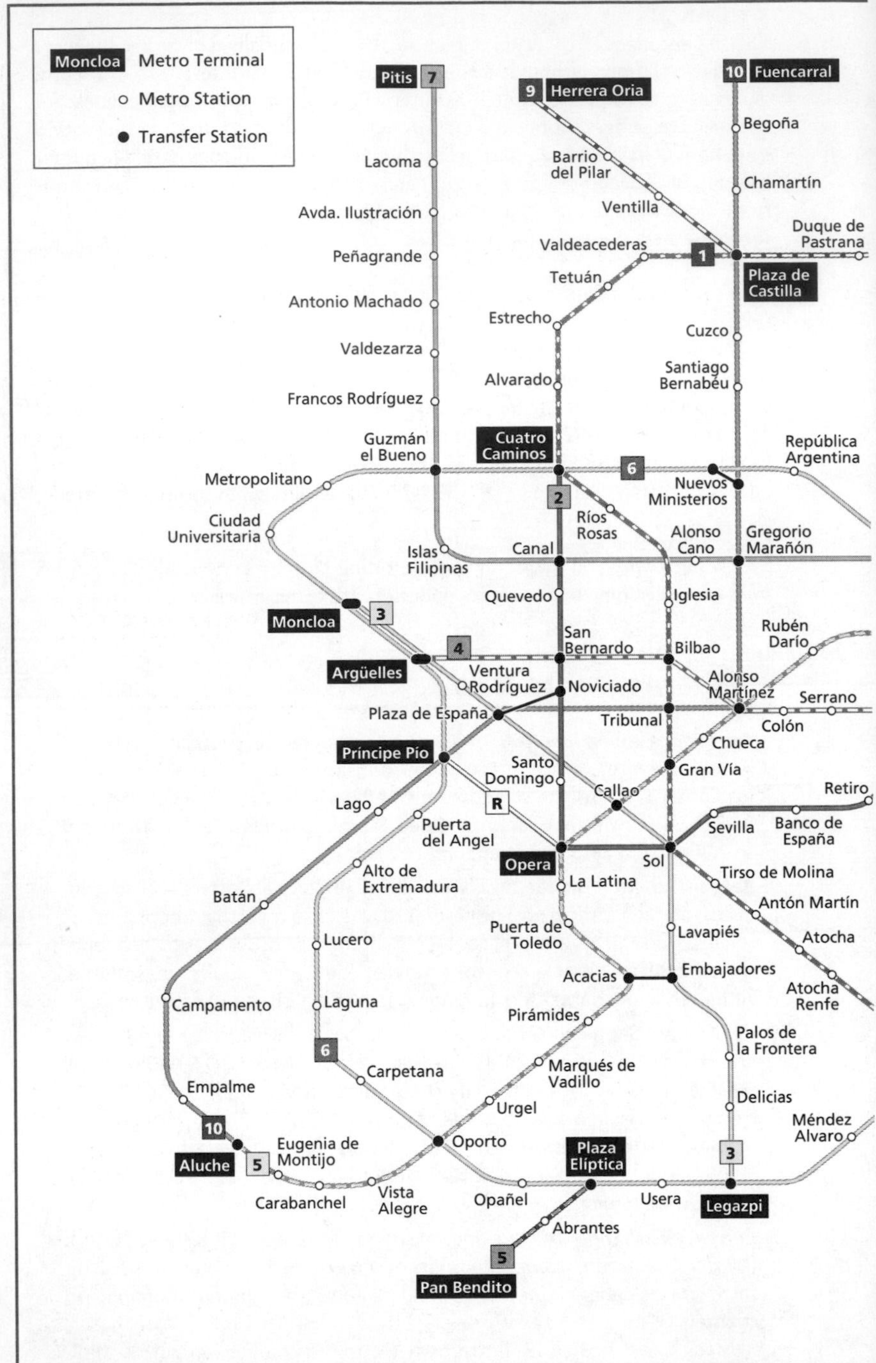

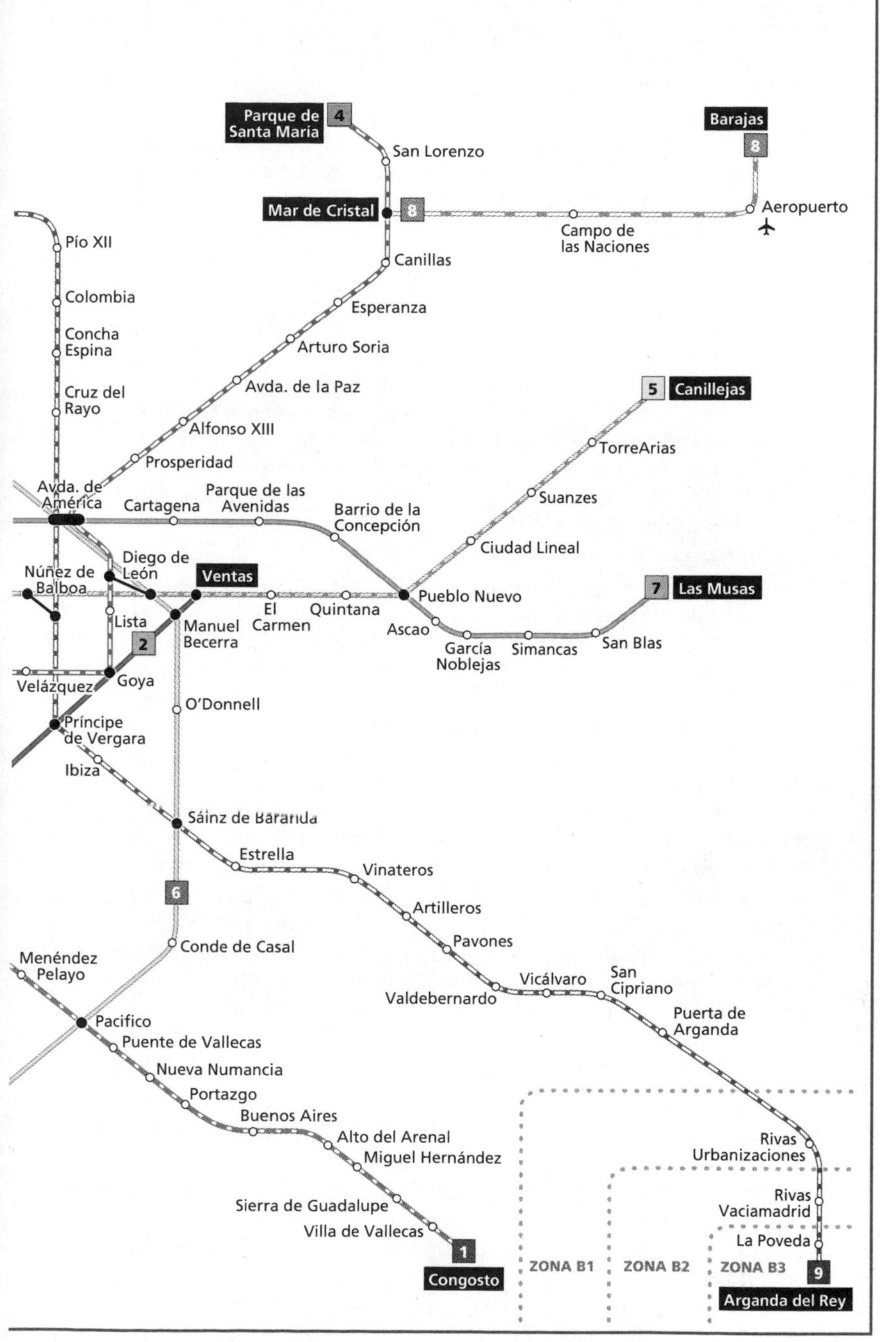
Parque de Santa María
4
San Lorenzo
Barajas
8
Mar de Cristal
8
Aeropuerto
Campo de las Naciones
Pío XII
Canillas
Colombia
Esperanza
Concha Espina
Arturo Soria
Cruz del Rayo
Avda. de la Paz
5
Canillejas
Alfonso XIII
TorreArias
Prosperidad
Avda. de América
Parque de las Avenidas
Suanzes
Cartagena
Barrio de la Concepción
Ciudad Lineal
Diego de León
Núñez de Balboa
Ventas
7
Las Musas
Pueblo Nuevo
El Carmen
Quintana
Lista
Manuel Becerra
Ascao
García Noblejas
Simancas
San Blas
2
Velázquez
Goya
O'Donnell
Príncipe de Vergara
Ibiza
Sáinz de Baranda
Estrella
Vinateros
6
Artilleros
Pavones
Conde de Casal
Menéndez Pelayo
Vicálvaro
San Cipriano
Valdebernardo
Pacifico
Puerta de Arganda
Puente de Vallecas
Nueva Numancia
Portazgo
Buenos Aires
Alto del Arenal
Miguel Hernández
Rivas Urbanizaciones
Rivas Vaciamadrid
Sierra de Guadalupe
Villa de Vallecas
La Poveda
1
Congosto
ZONA B1
ZONA B2
ZONA B3
9
Arganda del Rey

offer currency exchange facilities at various rates. You get the worst rates at street kiosks such as Chequepoint, Exact Change, and Cambios-Uno. Although they're handy and charge no commission, their rates are very low. Naturally, **American Express** offices offer the best rates on their own checks. ATMs are plentiful in Madrid.

Dentist For an English-speaking dentist, contact the **U.S. Embassy,** Serrano 75 (✆ **91-587-22-00**); it maintains a list of dentists who have offered their services to Americans abroad. For dental services, also consult **Unidad Médica Anglo-Americana,** Conde de Arandá 1 (✆ **91-435-18-23**). Office hours are Monday through Friday from 9am to 8pm and Saturday from 10am to 1pm, and there is a 24-hour answering service.

Doctor For an English-speaking doctor, contact the **U.S. Embassy,** Serrano 75 (✆ **91-587-22-00**).

Drugstores For a late-night pharmacy, look in the daily newspaper under *Farmacias de Guardia* to learn which drugstores are open after 8pm. Another way to find one is to go to any pharmacy, which, even if closed, always posts a list of nearby pharmacies that are open late that day. Madrid has hundreds of pharmacies, but one of the most central is **Farmacia Gayoso,** Arenal 2 (✆ **91-521-28-60;** Metro: Puerta del Sol). It is open Monday through Saturday from 9:30am to 9:30pm.

Embassies/Consulates If you lose your passport, fall seriously ill, get into legal trouble, or have some other serious problem, your embassy or consulate can help. These are the Madrid addresses and hours: The **United States Embassy,** Calle Serrano 75 (✆ **91-587-22-00;** Metro: Núñez de Balboa), is open Monday through Friday from 9am to 6pm. The **Canadian Embassy,** Núñez de Balboa 35 (✆ **91-423-32-50;** Metro: Velázquez), is open Monday through Friday from 8:30am to 5:30pm. The **United Kingdom Embassy,** Calle Fernando el Santo 16 (✆ **91-319-02-00;** Metro: Colón), is open Monday through Friday from 9am to 1:30pm and 3 to 6pm. The **Republic of Ireland** has an embassy at Claudio Coello 73 (✆ **91-576-35-00;** Metro: Serrano); it's open Monday through Friday from 9am to 2pm. The **Australian Embassy,** Plaza Diego de Ordas 3, Edificio Santa Engracia 120 (✆ **91-441-93-00;** Metro: Ríos Rosas), is open Monday though Thursday from 8:30am to 5pm and Friday from 8:30am to 2:15pm. Citizens of **New Zealand** have an embassy at Plaza de la Lealtad 2 (✆ **91-523-02-26;** Metro: Banco de España); it's open Monday through Friday from 9am to 1:30pm and 2:30 to 5:30pm.

Emergencies A centralized number for fire, police, or ambulance is ✆ **112.**

Hospitals/Clinics **Unidad Médica Anglo-Americana,** Conde de Arandá 1 (✆ **91-435-18-23;** Metro: Ritero), is not a hospital but a private outpatient clinic offering the services of various specialists. This is not an emergency clinic, although someone on the staff is always available. The daily hours are from 9am to 8pm. For a real medical emergency, call ✆ **112** for an ambulance.

Internet Access Head for **Net Café,** San Bernardo 81 (✆ **91-594-09-99;** http://netcafe.cl), open daily from 11am to 2am, if you just have to check your e-mail (5€ per hr.).

Laundry & Dry Cleaning Try a self-service facility, Lavandería Donoso Cortés, Donoso Cortés 17 (✆ **91-446-96-90;** Metro: Quevedo); it's open Monday to Friday from 9am to 2pm and 3:30 to 8pm, Saturday from 9am to 2pm. A good dry-cleaning service is provided by El Corte Inglés department store at Raimundo Fernández Villaverde 79 (✆ **91-418-88-00;** Metro: Gregorio Marañón), where the staff speaks English.

Luggage Storage & Lockers These can be found at both the Atocha and Chamartín railway terminals, as well as the major bus station at the Estación Sur de Autobuses, Calle Méndez Alvaro (✆ **91-468-42-00;** Metro: Méndez Alvaro). Storage is also provided at the air terminal underneath the Plaza de Colón.

Newspapers & Magazines The Paris-based *International Herald Tribune* is sold at most newsstands in the tourist districts, as is *USA Today,* plus the European editions of *Time* and *Newsweek. Guía del Ocio,* a small magazine sold in newsstands, contains entertainment listings and addresses, though in Spanish only.

Police In an emergency, dial ✆ **112.**

Post Office If you don't want to receive your mail at your hotel or the American Express office, direct it to *Lista de Correos* at the central post office in Madrid. To pick up mail, go to the window marked *Lista,* where you'll be asked to show your passport. Madrid's central office is in Palacio de Comunicaciones at Plaza de la Cibeles (✆ **91-396-20-00**).

Radio & TV On short-wave radio you can hear the Voice of America and the BBC daily. There is also an English-language radio program in Madrid called "Buenos Días" (Good Morning), which airs many useful hints for visitors; it's broadcast Monday to Friday from 6 to 8am on 657 megahertz. Radio 80 broadcasts news in English Monday to Saturday from 7 to 8am on 89 FM. Some TV programs are broadcast in English in the summer months. Many hotels—but regrettably not most of our budget ones—also bring in satellite TV programs in English.

Restrooms Some public restrooms are available, including those in the Parque del Retiro and on Plaza de Oriente across from the Palacio Real. Otherwise, you can always go into a bar or *tasca,* but you should order something. The major department stores, such as Galerías Preciados and El Corte Inglés, have good, clean restrooms.

Safety Because of an increasing crime rate in Madrid, the U.S. Embassy has warned visitors to leave valuables in a hotel safe or other secure place when going out. Your passport may be needed, however, as the police often stop foreigners for identification checks. The embassy advises against carrying purses and suggests that you keep valuables in front pockets and carry only enough cash for the day's needs. Be aware of those around you and keep a separate record of your passport number, traveler's check numbers, and credit-card numbers.

Purse snatching is common, and criminals often work in pairs, grabbing purses from pedestrians, cyclists, and even from cars. A popular scam involves one miscreant's smearing the back of the victim's clothing, perhaps with mustard, ice cream, or something worse. An accomplice then pretends to help clean up the mess, all the while picking the victim's pockets.

Every car can be a target, parked or just stopped at a light, so don't leave anything in sight in your vehicle. If a car is standing still, a thief may open the door or break a window in order to snatch a purse or package, even from under the seat. Place valuables in the trunk when you park and always assume that someone is watching to see whether you're putting something away for safekeeping. Keep the car locked while driving.

Taxes There are no special city taxes for tourists, except for the VAT (value-added tax; known as IVA in Spain) levied nationwide on all goods and services, ranging from 7% to 33%. In Madrid the only city taxes are for home and car owners, which need not concern the casual visitor. For information on how to recover VAT, see "Shopping" in chapter 6.

Telephone See "Fast Facts: Barcelona" in chapter 3, as the same conditions apply in Madrid.

Tipping See "Fast Facts: Barcelona" in chapter 3 as the same rules apply in Madrid.

3 Where to Stay

Though expensive, Madrid's hotels are among the finest in the world. The city's much-maligned reputation, earned in the days of Franco, is but a long, distant, and unpleasant memory: No more rooms last renovated in 1870 or food that tastes of acidic olive oil left over from the Spanish-American War.

More than 50,000 hotel rooms blanket the city—from *grand luxe* bedchambers fit for a prince to bunker-style beds in the hundreds of neighborhood *hostales* and *pensiones* (low-cost boardinghouses). Three-quarters of our recommendations are modern, yet many guests prefer the landmarks of yesteryear, including those grand old establishments, the Ritz and the Palace (ca. 1910–12). *But beware:* Many older hostelries in Madrid haven't kept abreast of the times.

Traditionally, hotels are clustered around the Atocha Railway Station and the Gran Vía. In our search for the most outstanding hotels, we've downplayed these two popular, but noisy, districts. The newer hotels have been built away from the center, especially on residential streets jutting off from Paseo de la Castellana. Bargain seekers, however, will still find great pickings along the Gran Vía and in the Atocha district.

In inexpensive hotels, be warned that you'll have to carry your bags to and from your room. Don't expect bellboys or doormen in cheaper hotels.

An Anglo-American travel company, based in Madrid, **Madrid & Beyond** (**© 91-758-00-63;** www.madridandbeyond.com), is staffed by an enthusiastic, English-speaking team of UK and US ex-pats, who share an in-depth knowledge of Spain. They recommend and reserve quality hotels throughout the country, specializing in Madrid and Barcelona. They aim to match each customer's taste and budget with a particular property. They also arrange many activities as well, including walking and cycling tours.

Note: Mention of private bathrooms is made *only* if all the rooms in the hotel in question do *not* come with a bathroom. Also, breakfast is not included in the quoted rates unless otherwise specified. A 7% government room tax is added to all rates.

Tips If You Have an Early Flight

Unless absolutely necessary, it's worth making the journey into Madrid rather than staying at bleak Barajas, where the airport is located. If you find that you have to stay here, one of the best options is **Tryp Barajas,** Av. de Logroño 35, 28042 Madrid (✆ **91-747-77-00;** fax 91-747-87-17), a government-rated four-star hotel standing in spacious grounds. With a classic modern decor, it is comfortable and inviting, offering midsize to spacious units, costing 135 for a double or 336 for a suite. The 270-unit, 3-floor hotel also has a restaurant, bar, and room service, plus babysitting and a pool. Each air-conditioned room comes with TV, minibar, hair dryer, and safe. AE, DC, MC, V. Metro: Barajas. Bus: 115

Another member of the Tryp chain, the 80-unit **Tryp Alameda,** Av. de Logroño 100, 28042 Madrid (✆ **91-747-48-00;** fax 91-747-89-28), is a case of two peas in a pod. When one hotel overflows, the other fills in the gap. Rooms are fairly bland, but comfortable, each with a tub and shower combo. The only difference is that this hotel has a small gym. On site are a restaurant and bar, and amenities include room service, laundry, babysitting, sauna, and pool. In the room are air conditioning, TV, minibar, hair dryer, and safe. Rates range from 155 to 205 in a double, 326 in a suite. AE, DC, MC, V. Metro: Barajas. Bus: 115. Both chain members have free 24-hour shuttle service to the airport.

A final possibility is **Hotel Villa de Barajas,** Av. de Logroño 331, 28042 Madrid (✆ **91-329-28-18;** fax 91-329-28-04), a government-rated three-star member of the Best Western chain. Simpler than the two Tryp choices above, it charges only 93 for a double room. Each midsize unit comes with a TV and phone as well as air conditioning, and on site are a restaurant and bar. AE, DC, MC, V. Metro: Barajas. Bus: 115. It too offers free shuttle service to the airport.

RESERVATIONS Most hotels require at least a day's deposit before they will reserve a room for you. Preferably, this can be accomplished with an international money order or, if agreed to in advance, with a personal check or credit-card number. You can usually cancel a room reservation one week ahead of time and get a full refund. A few hotel keepers will return your money up to three days before the reservation date, but some will take your deposit and never return it, even if you cancel far in advance. Many budget hotel owners operate on such a narrow margin of profit that they find just buying stamps for airmail replies too expensive by their standards. Therefore, it's important that you enclose a prepaid International Reply Coupon with your payment, especially if you're writing to a budget hotel. Better yet, call and speak directly to the hotel of your choice or send a fax.

If you're booking into a chain hotel, such as a Hyatt or a Forte, you can call toll free in North America and easily make reservations over the phone. Whenever such a service is available, toll-free numbers are indicated in the individual hotel descriptions.

Central Madrid Accommodations

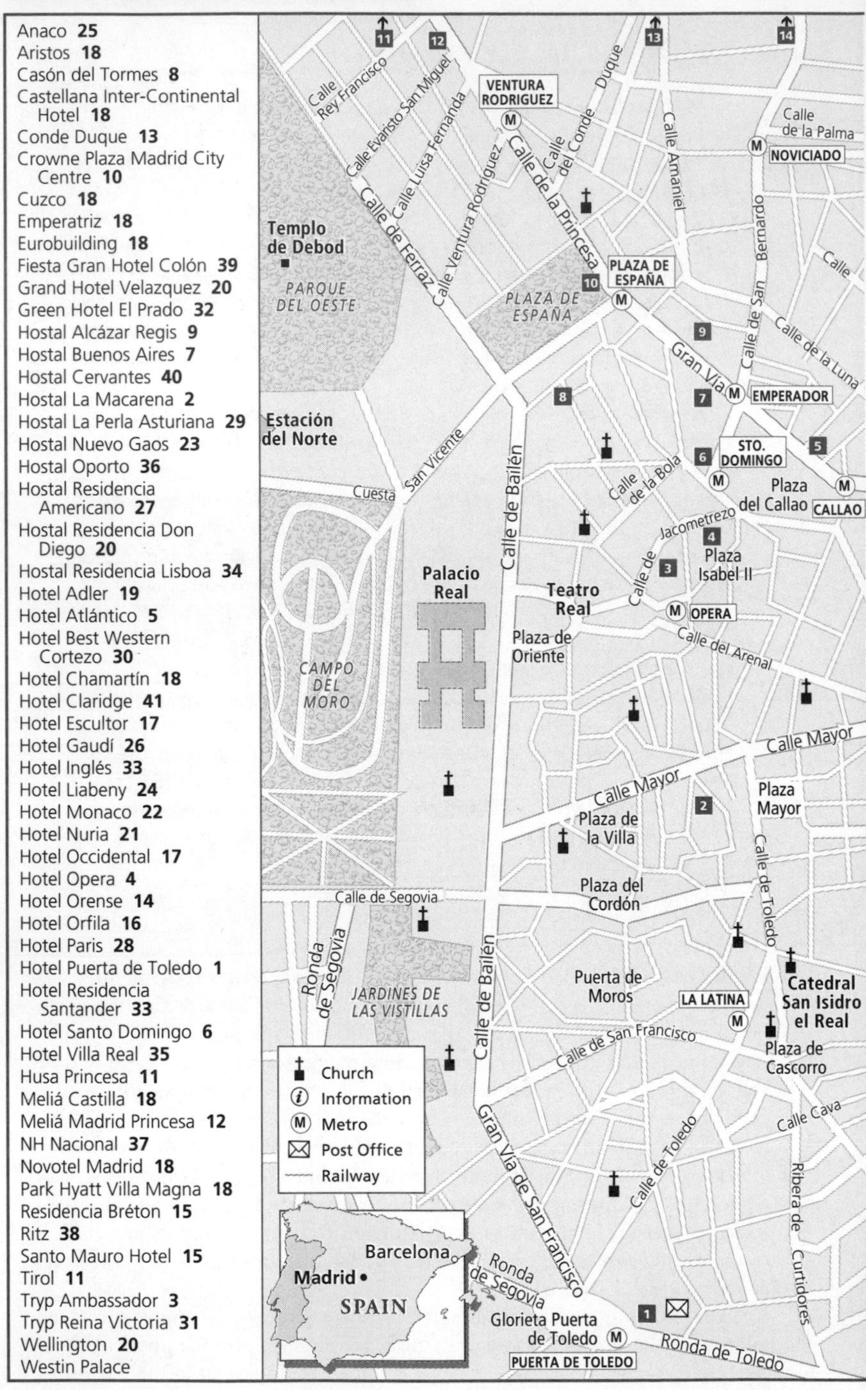

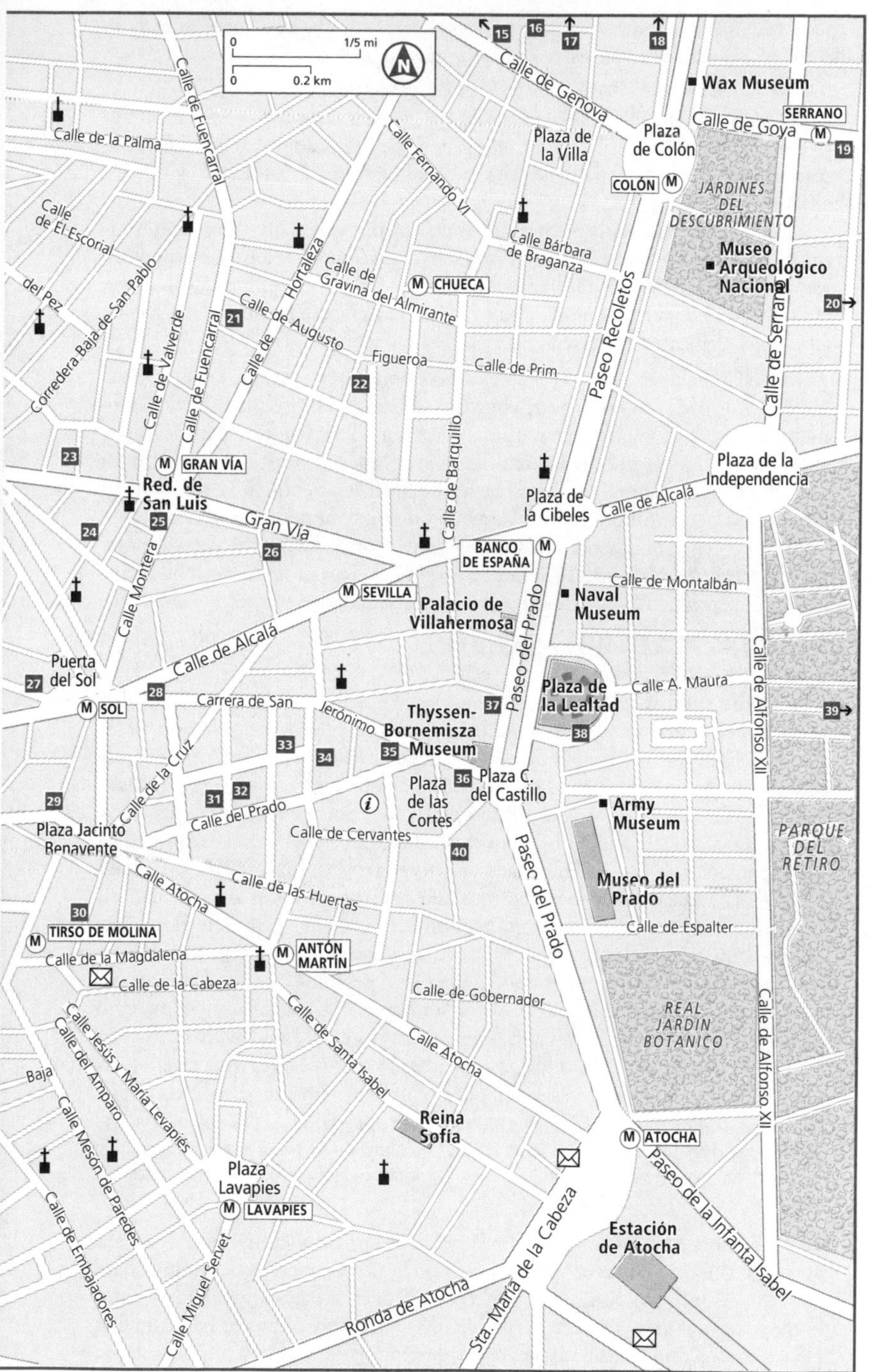
0 1/5 mi
0 0.2 km
N
15
16
17
18
19
20
21
22
23
24
25
26
27
28
29
30
31
32
33
34
35
36
37
38
39
40
Wax Museum
SERRANO
Calle de Genova
Plaza de Colón
Calle de Goya
Plaza de la Villa
COLÓN
JARDINES DEL DESCUBRIMIENTO
Museo Arqueológico Nacional
Calle de Serrano
Calle de Fuencarral
Calle de la Palma
Calle Fernando VI
Calle de El Escorial
Calle Bárbara de Braganza
Calle de Hortaleza
Calle de Gravina del Almirante
CHUECA
del Pez
Calle Baja de San Pablo
Calle de Augusto
Figueroa
Calle de Prim
Paseo Recoletos
Corredera Baja de San Pablo
Calle de Valverde
Calle de Fuencarral
Calle de
Calle de Barquillo
GRAN VÍA
Red. de San Luis
Plaza de la Independencia
Plaza de la Cibeles
Calle de Alcalá
Gran Vía
BANCO DE ESPAÑA
Calle Montera
SEVILLA
Calle de Montalbán
Palacio de Villahermosa
Naval Museum
Paseo del Prado
Calle de Alcalá
Puerta del Sol
Plaza de la Lealtad
Calle A. Maura
Calle de Alfonso XII
SOL
Carrera de San Jerónimo
Thyssen-Bornemisza Museum
Calle de la Cruz
Plaza C. del Castillo
Plaza de las Cortes
Army Museum
Calle del Prado
Plaza Jacinto Benavente
Calle de Cervantes
PARQUE DEL RETIRO
Calle Atocha
Calle de las Huertas
Paseo del Prado
Museo del Prado
TIRSO DE MOLINA
Calle de Espalter
Calle de la Magdalena
ANTÓN MARTÍN
Calle de la Cabeza
Calle de Gobernador
Calle de Santa Isabel
Calle Atocha
Calle Jesús y María Levapiés
Calle del Amparo
REAL JARDIN BOTANICO
Baja
Calle Mesón de Paredes
Reina Sofía
ATOCHA
Plaza Lavapies
LAVAPIES
Paseo de la Infanta Isabel
Calle de Embajadores
Calle Miguel Servet
Sta. María de la Cabeza
Ronda de Atocha
Estación de Atocha

If you arrive without a reservation, begin your search for a room as early in the day as possible. If you arrive late at night, you have to take what you can get, often for a much higher price than you'd like to pay.

RATINGS Spain officially rates its hotels by star designation, from one to five stars. Five stars is the highest rating in Spain, signaling a deluxe establishment complete with all the amenities and the high tariffs associated with such accommodations.

Most of the establishments recommended in this guide are three- and four-star hotels. Hotels granted one and two stars, as well as pensions (guesthouses), are less comfortable, with limited plumbing and other physical facilities, although they may be perfectly clean and decent places. The latter category is strictly for dedicated budgeters.

PARKING This is a serious problem. Few hotels have garages because many buildings turned into hotels were constructed before the invention of the automobile. Street parking is rarely available, and even if it is, you run the risk of having your car broken into. If you're driving into Madrid, most hotels (and most police) will allow you to park in front of the hotel long enough to unload your luggage. Someone on the staff can usually pinpoint the location of the nearest garage in the neighborhood, often giving you a map showing the way—be prepared to walk 2 or 3 blocks to your car. Parking charges given in most hotel listings are the prices these neighborhood garages charge for an average-size vehicle.

NEAR THE PLAZA DE LAS CORTES

VERY EXPENSIVE

Hotel Villa Real ★★★ It's not on the same level as the Ritz, but it is the first major hotel nearby to give the Westin Palace serious competition. Until 1989, the Villa Real was little more than a run-down 19th-century apartment house across a three-sided park from the Spanish parliament (*Congreso de los Diputados*) between Puerta del Sol and Paseo del Prado. Since then, developers have poured lots of *dinero* into renovations to produce this stylish hotel patronized by the cognoscenti of Spain. The facade combines an odd mix of neoclassical and Aztec motifs and is guarded by footmen and doormen. Rooms at the Villa Real are more consistent in quality than those offered by its neighbor, the Palace (see below), but lack the latter's mellow charm and patina. The interior contains a scattering of modern paintings amid neoclassical detailing.

Each of the accommodations offers soundproofing, a sunken salon with leather-upholstered furniture, and built-in furniture accented with burl-wood inlays. Although rooms aren't imaginative, they're mostly large, with separate sitting areas and big, bright, well-equipped bathrooms with tub/shower combos.

Plaza de las Cortes 10, 28014 Madrid. ✆ **91-420-37-67.** Fax 91-420-25-47. www.derbyhotels.es. 115 units. 321€ double; from 418€ suite. AE, DC, MC, V. Parking 18€. Metro: Sevilla, Banco de España. **Amenities:** Restaurant; bar; room service; pool; gym; babysitting; laundry/dry cleaning. *In room:* A/C, TV, minibar, hair dryer, safe.

Westin Palace Hotel ★★★ The Palace is an ornate Victorian wedding cake known as the *gran dueña* of Spanish hotels. It had an auspicious beginning, inaugurated personally by King Alfonso XIII in 1912, and covers an entire city block in the historical and artistic area. It faces the Prado and Neptune Fountain and lies within walking distance of the main shopping center and best antiques shops. Some of the city's most intriguing *tascas* and restaurants are a short stroll away.

Finds Life in a Former Bordello

Time was, Spanish dons didn't go to the present **Hotel Mónaco,** Barbieri 5, 28004 Madrid (✆ **91-522-46-30;** fax 91-521-16-01) just to sleep—at least not alone. Once a closely guarded, "secret" address, the Mónaco wasn't exactly what the French called a *maison de tolerance.* In other words, the prostitutes didn't work on the premises. The Spanish don arrived for his night out with his lady already selected from somewhere else in Madrid. He was then rented a room with his mistress. Even King Alfonso XIII, noted for his eccentricity (including the then revolutionary wearing of pink shirts) came here with his favorite of the moment. He preferred room 20 if you're interested in nostalgia. Today the bedrooms have been restored and are furnished in much of their old style, including lavish bathtubs for that cozy two-in-a-tub session, riotous neo-Rococo moldings, and ceiling mirrors to better observe the action in bed. The location is on one of Madrid's inner city streets with almost more bars and restaurants than any other. A total of 34 units are rented, costing 72 in a double, with parking going for 12 to 15 extra. On site is a bar, and each accommodation is air conditioned with TV, hair dryer, and safe. AE, DC, MC, V. Metro: Gran Via.

Architecturally, the Palace captures the grand pre–World War I style, with an emphasis on space and comfort. Although it doesn't achieve the snob appeal of its nearby siblings, the Ritz and the Villa Real, it's one of the largest hotels in Madrid and offers first-class service. The air-conditioned hotel has conservative, traditional rooms, boasting plenty of space, large bathrooms, and lots of extras. Accommodations vary widely, with the best rooms found on the fourth, fifth, and sixth floors. Rooms on the side are noisy and lack views. Many rooms appear not to have been renovated for some time. All units contain immaculate bathrooms with tub/shower combos.

Plaza de las Cortes 7, 28014 Madrid. ✆ **800/325-3535** in the U.S., 800/325-3589 in Canada, or 91-360-80-00. Fax 91-360-81-00. www.palacemadrid.com. 465 units. 400€ double; from 500€ suite. AE, DC, MC, V. Parking 20€. Metro: Banco de España. **Amenities:** 2 restaurants; bar; lounge; room service; gym; sauna; babysitting; laundry. *In room:* A/C, TV, minibar, hair dryer, safe.

INEXPENSIVE

Hostal Cervantes *Value* One of Madrid's most pleasant family-run hotels, the Cervantes is much appreciated by our readers and has been for years. You'll take a tiny birdcage-style elevator to the immaculately maintained second floor of this stone-and-brick building. Each room contains a comfortable bed, spartan furniture, and a tiny bathroom with a shower-tub combination. No breakfast is served, but the owners, the Alfonsos, will direct you to a nearby cafe. The establishment is convenient to the Prado, Retiro Park, and the older sections of Madrid.

Cervantes 34, 28014 Madrid. ✆ **91-429-83-65.** Fax 91-429-27-45. 14 units. 45€ double. MC, V. Metro: Banco de España. **Amenities:** Lounge. *In room:* TV, safe.

Hostal Oporto ★ *Value* Across from the Thyssen Museum, this clean, immaculately kept *hostal* is a real find for the frugal traveler. You get not only a decent, comfortable bedroom with private bath with shower, but a friendly welcome and an accommodating staff. In summer the small to midsize bedrooms get rather hot, but a ceiling fan keeps the air stirred up. The decor is a bit tacky but you're not paying for style. Some of the larger accommodations are suitable for three or more persons.

Calle Zorrilla 9, 28014 Madrid. ✆ or fax **91-429-78-56.** www.hostaloporto.com. 12 units. 42€ double, 58€ triple. MC, V. Metro: Sevilla. **Amenities:** Laundry. *In room:* TV.

NEAR THE PLAZA ESPAÑA

EXPENSIVE

Crowne Plaza Madrid City Centre ★ *Kids* Built in 1953 atop a city garage, the Crowne Plaza could be called the Waldorf-Astoria of Spain. A massive rose-and-white structure soaring upward to a central tower 26 stories high, it's one of the tallest skyscrapers in Europe. Once one of the best hotels in Spain, the Crowne Plaza has long since ceased to be a market leader. Its accommodations include conventional doubles as well as luxurious suites, each containing a sitting room and abundant extras, such as bedside controls and even in some cases alcoves for sitting. Many families are drawn to this hotel because of its spacious accommodations, great location, and special welcome provided by the staff. Each room, regardless of its size, has a marble bathroom with a tub/shower combo. Furniture is usually of a standardized modern style, in harmonized colors. The upper floor rooms are quieter.

Plaza de España, 28013 Madrid. ✆ **800/465-4329** in the U.S., or 91-547-12-00. Fax 91-548-23-89. http://madrid-citycentre.crownplaza.com. 306 units. 220€–314€ double; from 358€ suite. AE, DC, MC, V. Parking 10.22€. Metro: Plaza de España. **Amenities:** Restaurant; bar; health club; sauna; whirlpool; hairdresser; room service; laundry. *In room:* A/C, TV, minibar, hair dryer, trouser press.

MODERATE

Casón del Tormes This attractive hotel is around the corner from the Royal Palace and Plaza de España. Behind a four-story red-brick facade with stone-trimmed windows, it overlooks a quiet one-way street. A long, narrow lobby contains a marble floor opening into a separate room. Guest rooms are generally roomy and comfortable with color-coordinated fabrics and dark wood, including mahogany headboards. Bathrooms are very small but with adequate shelf space and shower-tub combinations. Motorists appreciate the public parking lot near the hotel.

Calle del Río 7, 28013 Madrid. ✆ **91-541-97-46.** Fax 91-541-18-52. www.bestwestern.com/es/hotelcasondeltormes. 63 units. 99€ double; 123€ triple. AE, DC, MC, V. Parking 14€. Metro: Plaza de España. **Amenities:** Restaurant; bar; room service; babysitting; laundry/dry cleaning. *In room:* A/C, TV, hair dryer, safe.

ON OR NEAR THE GRAN VIA

EXPENSIVE

Hotel A. Gaudí ★ In a turn-of-the-century building in the heart of Madrid, this hotel is located in a beautifully restored landmark Modernist building. It was constructed in 1898 by Emilio Salas y Cortés, one of the teachers of the great Barcelona architect Gaudí, and was overhauled in 1998. Some of the most important attractions of Madrid are within an easy walk, including the Prado, the Thyssen Museum, and the Plaza Mayor with its rustic taverns. The bedrooms come in a number of sizes, but each is comfortably furnished and beautifully maintained with bathrooms containing tub/shower combos.

Gran Vía 9, 28013 Madrid. ✆ **91-531-22-22.** Fax 91-531-54-69. www.hoteles-catalonia.es. 184 units. 172€–186€ double; 300€ suite. AE, DC, MC, V. Metro: Gran Vía. **Amenities:** Restaurant; bar; whirlpool; sauna; room service; laundry. *In room:* A/C, TV, minibar, hair dryer, safe.

Hotel Santo Domingo ★ This stylish, carefully decorated hotel rises from a position adjacent to the Gran Vía, a 2-minute walk from the Plaza de España. It was inaugurated in 1994, after an older building was gutted and reconfigured into the comfortable modern structure you'll see today. Rooms are decorated individually, each in a style a wee bit different from that of its neighbor, in pastel-derived shades. Some contain gold damask wall coverings, faux tortoiseshell desks, and striped satin bedspreads. Bathrooms are generally spacious and outfitted with ceramics, marble slabs, and tub/shower combos. The best units are the fifth-floor doubles, especially those with furnished balconies and views over the tile roofs of Old Madrid. Each is soundproofed to guard against noise from the street and from its neighbors.

Plaza Santo Domingo 13, 28013 Madrid. ✆ **91-547-98-00.** Fax 91-547-59-95. www.hotelsantodomingo.com. 120 units. Mon–Thurs 179€–203€ double; Fri–Sun 148.50€–179€ double. Breakfast free Sat–Mon mornings; otherwise, 10.50€ extra. AE, DC, MC, V. Parking 16€ ($14.30). Metro: Santo Domingo. **Amenities:** Restaurant; bar; room service; babysitting; laundry/dry cleaning. *In room:* A/C, TV, minibar, hair dryer, safe.

MODERATE

Hotel Atlántico Refurbished in stages between the late 1980s and 1994, this hotel occupies five floors of a grand turn-of-the-century building on one of Madrid's most impressive avenues. Established in 1989 as a Best Western affiliate, it offers security boxes in relatively unadorned but well-maintained guest rooms, which have been insulated against noise. Accommodations are rather small. All units contain well-managed bathrooms with shower-tub combinations. The hotel contains an English-inspired bar serving drinks and snacks that's open 24 hours a day.

Gran Vía 38, 28013 Madrid. ✆ **800/528-1234** in the U.S. and Canada, or 91-522-64-80. Fax 91-531-02-10. www.hotel-atlantico.com. 80 units. 151€ double. Rates include breakfast. AE, DC, MC, V. Parking 15€. Metro: Gran Vía. **Amenities:** Restaurant; bar; laundry/dry cleaning. *In room:* A/C, TV, minibar, hair dryer, safe.

MODERATE

Hotel Liabeny The Liabeny, behind an austere stone facade, is in a prime location midway between the Gran Vía and Puerta del Sol. It has seven floors of comfortable, contemporary rooms, which are newly redecorated but a bit pristine. They are of a good size and functionally furnished with comfortable beds and neatly organized bathrooms, mainly with shower stalls.

Calle Salud 3, 28013 Madrid. ✆ **91-531-90-00.** Fax 91-532-74-21. www.liabeny.es. 222 units. 135.50€ double; 157.25€ triple. AE, MC, V. Parking 10.25€. Metro: Puerta del Sol or Gran Vía. **Amenities:** Restaurant; 2 bars; room service; babysitting; laundry/dry cleaning. *In room:* A/C, TV, minibar, hair dryer, safe.

INEXPENSIVE

Anaco Modest yet modern, the Anaco is just off the Gran Vía but opens onto a tree-shaded plaza. It's for those who want a clean resting place for a good price, and don't expect much more. The rooms are compact and contemporary, with built-in headboards, reading lamps, and lounge chairs. Each has a compact tiled bathroom with a shower stall. Ask for one of the five terraced rooms on the top floor, which rent at no extra charge. English is spoken here. There's a municipally operated garage nearby.

Tres Cruces 3, 28013 Madrid. ✆ **91-522-46-04.** Fax 91-531-64-84. www.anacohotel.com. 40 units 65€–86€ double; 110€–115€ triple. AE, DC, MC, V. Parking 12€. Metro: Gran Vía, Callao, or Puerta del Sol. **Amenities:** Restaurant; bar; room service; babysitting; laundry/dry cleaning. *In room:* A/C, TV, hair dryer, safe.

Green Hotel El Prado You might get the feeling this hotel is both overbooked and understaffed. But it has comfortable rooms, relatively reasonable rates, and a well-scrubbed interior less than a decade old. You'll register in a somewhat claustrophobic lobby, then head upstairs to a room that's cozy and sleekly outfitted with contemporary-looking, full-grained walls and partitions. Each unit comes with a small tiled bathroom with shower. Other than breakfast, no meals are served.

Calle Prado 11, 28014 Madrid. ✆ **91-369-02-34.** Fax 91-429-28-29. www.green-hoteles.com. 50 units. 113€–141€ double. AE, MC, V. Metro: Antón Martín. **Amenities:** Restaurant; bar, cafe; room service; babysitting; laundry/dry cleaning. *In room:* A/C, TV, minibar, hair dryer.

Hostal Alcázar Regis Conveniently located in the midst of Madrid's best shops is this post–World War II building, complete with a circular Greek-style temple as its crown. On the building's fifth floor, you'll find long and pleasant public rooms, wood paneling, lead glass windows, parquet floors, crystal chandeliers, and high-ceilinged guest rooms, each with a new bathroom with a shower-tub combination.

Gran Vía 61, 28013 Madrid. ✆ **91-547-93-17.** 10 units. 44€ double. No credit cards. Metro: Plaza de España or Santo Domingo. **Amenities:** Lounge; laundry/dry cleaning. *In room:* A/C, TV, safe.

Hostal Nuevo Gaos On three floors of a 1930s building just off the Gran Vía, this *residencia* offers the chance to enjoy simple comfort at bargain prices. Rooms are humble and small with plain, livable furnishings. Bathrooms are adequate, with stall showers. The place lies directly north of Puerta del Sol, across the street from the popular flamenco club Torre Bermejas. Breakfast can be taken at a nearby cafe.

Calle Mesonero Romanos 14, 28013 Madrid. ✆ **91-532-71-07.** 23 units. 57€ double; 64€ suite. AE, DC, MC, V. Parking 11€. Metro: Callao or Gran Vía. **Amenities:** Lounge; babysitting; laundry/dry cleaning. *In room:* A/C, TV, hair dryer, safe.

NEAR THE PUERTA DEL SOL

EXPENSIVE

Hotel Preciados ★ *Kids* One of Madrid's newest hotels has been created from a historic 1861 structure. The original facade, entryway, grand staircase, and other architectural details have been retained, but everything else has been reconstructed from scratch for modern comfort. The five-floor hotel, which opened in 2001, is close to such landmarks as the royal palace, the opera house, and the Puerta del Sol (the very center of Madrid). Children are especially welcome here, and there are special facilities for them such as extra beds that can be added to the standard rooms and even a special kiddies menu in the restaurant. Bedrooms are midsize to spacious, and the bathrooms have all new plumbing, including large sinks and tub-and-shower combinations. The on-site restaurant, serving a savory Mediterranean cuisine, used to be the famous Café Varela, a favorite of Madrid's *literati.*

Preciados 37, 28013 Madrid. ✆ **91-454-44-00.** Fax 91-454-44-01. www.allrez.com/static/spain/madrid/HOTEL-PRECIADOS.asp. 73 UNITS. 120€–250€. MC, V. Parking: 18€. Metro: Puerta del Sol. Santo Domingo/Callao. **Amenities:** Restaurant; bar; room service; babysitting; laundry/dry cleaning; dance club. *In room:* A/C, TV, minibar, hair dryer, safe.

Tryp Ambassador ★ In the 19th century the dukes of Granada made their town house home in Madrid, but from the early 1990s on it's been the property of the Tryp hotel chain. The result is a lavishly restored, four-story historic hotel with grand public areas that's interconnected via a sunny lobby to a six-story annex containing about 60% of the establishment's rooms. All rooms are conservatively modern, and outfitted in white and salmon accented with mahogany. Most are large and soundproofed and come with twin beds. Bathrooms contain marble tub/shower combos, robes, and deluxe toiletries.

Cuesta Santo Domingo 5 and 7, 28013 Madrid. ✆ **91-541-67-00.** Fax 91-559-10-40. www.solmelia.es. 183 units. 238€ double; from 321€ suite. AE, DC, MC, V. Metro: Opera or Santo Domingo. **Amenities:** Restaurant; bar; room service; babysitting; laundry/dry cleaning. *In room:* A/C, TV, minibar, hair dryer, safe.

Tryp Reina Victoria ★ This hotel is as legendary as the famous bullfighter Manolete who used to stay here, giving lavish parties and attracting mobs in the square below. Since the recent renovation and upgrading of this property by Spain's Tryp Hotel Group, it's less staid and more impressive than ever.

Built in 1923, the hotel sits behind an ornate stone facade, which the Spanish government protects as a historic monument. Although it's located in a congested and noisy neighborhood in the center of town, the Reina Victoria opens onto one of Madrid's landmark plazas. Activity on this square begins about 8:30 in the morning and goes on until well past midnight, so this is not the place for the "noise-sensitive."

The accommodations are midsize and fairly standard, with tidily organized bathrooms with shower-tub combinations and marble vanities.

Plaza Santa Ana 14, 28012 Madrid. ✆ **91-531-45-00.** Fax 91-522-03-07. www.solmelia.es. 201 units. 172€–215€ double; from 287€ suite. AE, DC, MC, V. Metro: Tirso de Molina or Puerta del Sol. **Amenities:** Restaurant; bar; room service; babysitting; laundry/dry cleaning. *In room:* A/C, TV, minibar, hair dryer, safe.

MODERATE

Hotel Opera ★★ *Finds* Don't judge this little discovery by its dreary facade or its narrow windows; it livens up considerably once you enter. Set close to the royal palace and the opera house, this hotel isn't regal but offers first-rate comfort and a warm welcome from its English-speaking staff. Guest rooms range from medium to surprisingly spacious, each with first-rate furnishings. Bathrooms are excellent, clad in marble with dual basins and tub/shower combos. It's adorned with fabric-covered walls and horsey art. The Opera remains one of Madrid's relatively undiscovered boutique hotels.

Cuesta de Santo Domingo 2, 28013 Madrid. ✆ **91-541-28-00.** Fax 91-541-69-23. 79 units. 105€ double. AE, DC, MC, V. Parking 12€. Metro: Opera. **Amenities:** Restaurant; bar; laundry/dry cleaning. *In room:* A/C, TV, minibar, hair dryer, safe.

INEXPENSIVE

Hostal la Macarena ★ *Value* Known for its reasonable prices and praised by readers for its warm hospitality, this unpretentious *hostal* is run by the Ricardo González family. A 19th-century facade with Belle Epoque patterns stands in ornate contrast to the chiseled simplicity of the ancient buildings facing it. The location is one of the *hostal*'s assets: it's on a street (a noisy one) immediately behind Plaza Mayor near one of the best clusters of *tascas* in Madrid. Rooms range from small to medium and are all well kept, with modest furnishings and comfortable beds. Windows facing the street have double panes. Bathrooms are tiny and contain stall showers.

Cava de San Miguel 8, 28005 Madrid. ✆ **91-365-92-21.** Fax 91-364-27-57. 25 units. 63€ double; 84€ triple; 96€ quad. MC, V. Metro: Puerta del Sol, Opera, or La Latina. **Amenities:** Bar; lounge. *In room:* TV, hair dryer.

Hostal la Perla Asturiana Ideal for those who want to stay in the heart of old Madrid (1 block off Plaza Mayor and 2 blocks from Puerta del Sol), this small family-run place welcomes you with a courteous staff at the desk 24 hours a day for security and convenience. You can socialize in the small, comfortable lobby adjacent to the reception area but stay here for the cheap prices and location, not grand comfort. Each of the small rooms comes with a comfortable bed plus a simple and adequate bathroom with a shower unit. Many inexpensive restaurants and tapas bars are nearby. No breakfast is served.

Plaza Santa Cruz 3, 28012 Madrid. ✆ **91-366-46-00.** Fax 91-366-46-08. www.perlaasturiana.com. 33 units. 40€–42€ double; 54€ triple. MC, V. Metro: Puerta del Sol. **Amenities:** Lounge; laundry/dry cleaning. *In room:* TV.

Hostal Residencia Americano Americano, on the third floor of a five-floor building, is suitable for those who want to be in the thick of Puerta del Sol. Most of the guest rooms are outside chambers with balconies facing the street and all have been refurbished. The rooms are small, especially when three or four guests are crowded in. Bathrooms are bleak, clean cubicles with showers. No breakfast is served.

Puerta del Sol 11, 28013 Madrid. ✆ **91-522-28-22.** Fax 91-522-11-92. 44 units. 43€ double; 57€ triple; 64€ quad. AE, MC, V. Metro: Puerta del Sol. **Amenities:** Lounge. *In room:* TV.

Hostal Residencia Lisboa Our only complaint about the Lisboa, on Madrid's most famous restaurant street, is that it can be a bit noisy. The hotel is a neat, modernized town house with compact rooms and a staff that speaks five languages. Most of the rooms, on four floors of this old building, are small but a few are comfortably larger. Most come equipped with a double bed, some with twins. Bathrooms are small, mainly with shower stalls. The Lisboa does not serve breakfast, but budget dining rooms, cafes, and *tascas* surround the neighborhood.

Ventura de la Vega 17, 28014 Madrid. ✆ **91-429-98-94.** Fax 91-429-46-76. hostallisboa@inves.es. 26 units. 51€ double. AE, DC, MC, V. Parking 13€. Metro: Puerta del Sol. **Amenities:** Lounge; babysitting; laundry/dry cleaning. *In room:* A/C, TV, hair dryer, safe.

Hotel Inglés ★ You'll find this little hotel (where Virginia Woolf used to stay) on a central street lined with *tascas.* Behind the red-brick facade is a modern, impersonal hotel with contemporary, well-maintained rooms. The lobby is air-conditioned, but guest rooms are not; guests who open their windows at night are likely to hear noise from the enclosed courtyard, so light sleepers beware. Rooms come in a variety of shapes, most of them small, and some in the back are quite dark. Tiled bathrooms are cramped but tidily maintained, with shower stalls.

Calle Echegaray 8, 28014 Madrid. ✆ **91-429-65-51.** Fax 91-420-24-23. 58 units. 85€ double; 108€ suite. AE, DC, MC, V. Parking 10€. Metro: Puerta del Sol or Sevilla. **Amenities:** Cafeteria; bar; exercise room; room service; babysitting; laundry/dry cleaning. *In room:* TV, hair dryer, safe.

Hotel París Originally built in grandiose style in the 1870s when it was undoubtedly more chic than it is today, this hotel occupies a prime location adjacent to the hysterical traffic of the Puerta del Sol. It contains five floors of simple but clean and comfortable rooms, each with parquet floors, white walls, and views that extend either over the surrounding neighborhood or over a quiet courtyard. Rooms are generally small. Bathrooms are also small, with shower stalls. Something about the dark-paneled lobby might remind you of the old-fashioned, hot, and somnolent Spain of long ago. This hotel is a good bargain if your tastes aren't too demanding, if you're not a budding decorator, or if you just want a central location.

Alcalá 2, 28014 Madrid. ✆ **91-521-64-96.** Fax 91-531-01-88. 121 units. 84€ double. Rates include breakfast. AE, DC, MC, V. Metro: Puerta del Sol. **Amenities:** Bar; laundry/dry cleaning. *In room:* A/C, TV, safe.

NEAR ATOCHA STATION

EXPENSIVE

NH Nacional ★ This stately hotel was built around 1900 to house the hundreds of passengers flooding into Madrid through the nearby Atocha railway station. In 1997, a well-respected nationwide chain, NH Hotels, ripped out much of the building's dowdy interior, reconstructing the public areas and bedrooms into a smooth, seamless decor that takes maximum advantage of the building's tall ceilings and large spaces. In the bedrooms the Belle-Epoque trappings of another day have been replaced with modern designer decor, even avant-garde art, giving the units a welcoming ambience. Rooms also come equipped with immaculately kept bathrooms containing tub/shower combos. Today the Nacional is a destination for dozens of corporate conventions.

Paseo del Prado 48, 28014 Madrid. ✆ **91-429-66-29.** Fax 91-369-15-64. www.nh-hoteles.es. 214 units. 192€–210€ double; 425€ suite. AE, DC, MC, V. Metro: Atocha. **Amenities:** Restaurant; bar; room service; babysitting; laundry/dry cleaning. *In room:* A/C, TV, minibar, hair dryer, safe.

NEAR RETIRO/SALAMANCA

INEXPENSIVE

Hotel Best Western Cortezo Just off Calle de Atocha, which leads to the railroad station of the same name, the Cortezo is a short walk from Plaza Mayor and Puerta del Sol. The accommodations are comfortable but simply furnished, with contemporary bathrooms containing tub/shower combos. Beds are springy and the furniture is pleasantly modern; many rooms have sitting areas with a desk and armchair. The public rooms match the guest rooms in freshness. The hotel was built in 1959 and last renovated in 1997.

Doctor Cortezo 3, 28012 Madrid. ✆ **91-369-01-01.** Fax 91-369-37-74. 88 units. 75€–115€ double; 150€ suite. AE, DC, MC, V. Parking 15€. Metro: Tirso de Molina. **Amenities:** Restaurant; bar; room service; babysitting; laundry/dry cleaning. *In room:* A/C, TV, minibar, hair dryer, safe.

Hotel Husa Mercátor Only a 3-minute walk from the Prado, Centro de Arte Reina Sofía, and the Thyssen-Bornemisza Museum, the Mercátor is orderly, well run, and clean, with enough comforts to please the weary traveler. Its public rooms are simple, outfitted in modern minimalism. Some of the guest rooms are more inviting than others, especially those with desks and armchairs. Twenty-one units are air-conditioned. Bathrooms are usually cramped although they are equipped with good showerheads. The Mercátor is a *residencia*—that is, it offers breakfast only and does not have a formal restaurant for lunch and dinner. The hotel has a garage and is within walking distance of American Express.

Calle Atocha 123, 28012 Madrid. ✆ **91-429-05-00.** Fax 91-369-12-52. 87 units. 84€ double; 98€ suite. AE, DC, MC, V. Parking 10€. Metro: Atocha or Antón Martín. **Amenities:** Restaurant; bar; room service; babysitting; laundry/dry cleaning. *In room:* A/C, TV, minibar, hair dryer.

NEAR RETIRO/SALAMANCA

VERY EXPENSIVE

Park Hyatt Villa Magna ★★★ One of the finest hotels in Europe, the nine-story Park Hyatt is faced with slabs of rose-colored granite set behind a bank of pines and laurels on the city's most fashionable boulevard. It's an even finer choice than the Palace or Villa Real and is matched in luxury, ambience, and service only by the Ritz, which has a greater patina since it's much older.

Separated from the busy boulevard by a park-like garden, the hotel has contemporary lines. In contrast, its interior recaptures the style of Carlos IV, with paneled walls, marble floors, and bouquets of fresh flowers. Almost every film star shooting on location in Spain stays here. This luxury palace has plush but dignified rooms decorated in Louis XVI, English Regency, or Italian provincial style. Each comes with a neatly kept bathroom with a tub/shower combo.

Paseo de la Castellana 22, 28046 Madrid. ✆ **800/223-1234** in North America, or 91-587-12-34. Fax 91-431-22-86. www.madrid.hyatt.com. 182 units. 500€ double; from 750€ suite. AE, DC, MC, V. Parking 19€. Metro: Rubén Darío. **Amenities:** 2 restaurants; 2 bars; car rental; hairdresser; room service; babysitting; laundry/dry cleaning. *In room:* A/C, TV, minibar, hair dryer, safe.

The Ritz ★★★ The Ritz is the most legendary hotel in Spain. With soaring ceilings and graceful columns, it offers all the luxury and pampering you'd expect of a grand hotel. Although the building has been thoroughly modernized, great effort was expended to retain its Belle Epoque character and architectural details.

No other Madrid hotel, except the Palace, has a more varied history. One of *Les Grands Hôtels Européens,* the Ritz was built in 1908 by King Alfonso XIII with the aid of César Ritz. It looks out onto the circular Plaza de la Lealtad in the center of town, near 300-acre Retiro Park, facing the Prado, the Palacio de Villahermosa, and the Stock Exchange. The Ritz was constructed when costs were relatively low and when spaciousness and luxury were the standard. Its facade has even been designated a historic monument. The glory days of 1910 live on in the rooms with their spacious closets, antique furnishings, and handwoven carpets. Bathrooms are spacious, with robes, dual basins, deluxe toiletries, and tub/shower combos. The hotel requests that male guests wear a jacket and tie after 11am in the public areas. Nonetheless, casual wear, even blue jeans, is seen at the hotel, but such guests are conspicuous by their lack of what the Spanish call *gracia.*

Plaza de la Lealtad 5, 28014 Madrid. ✆ **800/225-5843** in the U.S. and Canada, or 91-701-67-67. Fax 91-701-67-76. www.ritz.es. 167 units. 625€–695€ double; from 1,150€ suite. AE, DC, MC, V. Parking 24€. Metro: Banco de España. **Amenities:** Restaurant; bar; fitness center; sauna; car rental; room service; laundry/dry cleaning. *In room:* A/C, TV, minibar, hair dryer, safe.

EXPENSIVE

Hotel Adler ★★ At the intersection of Velázquez and Goya streets, this is one of the newest and most elegant places to stay in Madrid. You're housed in grand comfort at a location nicknamed "the golden triangle of art" (near El Prado, Reina Sofía, and the Thyssen-Bornemisza collection). The exclusive shops of Serrano are also near at hand. The classic building has been carefully restored and offers gracious comfort in a setting that retains the evocation of the 1880s but with decidedly modern touches. The bedrooms are user friendly: you live and sleep in ultimate comfort with *luxe* furnishings and totally modernized bathrooms with tub and shower combination. The on-site restaurant is one of the better hotel dining rooms in this upmarket section of Market.

Calle Velázquez 33, 28001 Madrid. ✆ **91-426-32-30.** Fax 91-548-78-85. www.travel-in-madrid.com/hotel/adler/english.htm. 45 units. 322€–378€ double, 440€ suite. AE, DC, MC, V. Metro: Velázquez. **Amenities:** Restaurant; bar; laundry/dry cleaning; room service; babysitting. *In room:* A/C, TV, minibar, hair dryer, safe.

Hotel Emperatriz ★ This hotel lies just off the wide Paseo de la Castellana. Built in the 1970s, it has been recently renovated in a combination of Laura Ashley and Spanish contemporary styles by Madrid's trendiest firm, Casa & Jardín. Rooms are comfortable and classically styled in cheery yellows and salmons, and

Kids Family-Friendly Hotels

Crowne Plaza Madrid City Centre (p. 152) Safe and reliable, and located at the very heart of Madrid, this 26-story hotel offers roomy accommodations and good beds and attracts a large family trade to its precincts. It's got location, reasonable prices, and all the services, including laundry, that most family travelers need.

Meliá Castilla Children can spend hours and all their extra energy in the hotel's swimming pool and gymnasium. On the grounds is a showroom exhibiting the latest European automobiles. Hotel services include babysitting, providing fun for kids and parents too. ✆ **91-567-50-00.**

The Tirol This centrally located government-rated three-star hotel is a favorite of families seeking good comfort at moderate price. It has a cafeteria. ✆ **91-548-19-00.**

come with neatly kept bathrooms containing tub/shower combos. Ask for a room on the seventh floor, where you get a private terrace at no extra charge.

López de Hoyos 4, 28006 Madrid. ✆ **91-563-80-88.** Fax 91-563-98-04. www.emperatrizhotel.com. 158 units. 250€ double; 438€ suite. AE, DC, MC, V. Metro: Rubén Darío. **Amenities:** Restaurant; bar; hairdresser; room service; babysitting; laundry/dry cleaning. *In room:* A/C, TV, minibar, hair dryer, safe.

MODERATE

Fiesta Gran Hotel Colón ★ East of Retiro Park, Gran Hotel Colón is just a few minutes from the city center by subway. Built in 1966, it offers comfortable yet reasonably priced accommodations in a modern setting. More than half of the accommodations have private balconies, and all contain traditional furniture, much of it built-in. Rooms vary in size but most offer roomy comfort, dark wood beds and adequate closet space. Bathrooms are small, with stall showers, but with suitable shelf space. Other perks include two dining rooms, a covered garage, and bingo games. One of the Colón's founders was an interior designer, which accounts for the unusual stained-glass windows and murals in the public rooms and the paintings by Spanish artists in the lounge.

Pez Volador 1–11, 28007 Madrid. ✆ **91-573-59-00.** Fax 91-573-08-09. www.fiesta-hotels.com. 359 units. 111€–148€ double. AE, DC, MC, V. Parking 13€. Metro: Sainz de Baranda. **Amenities:** Restaurant; bar; health club; sauna; babysitting; hairdresser; room service; laundry/dry cleaning. *In room:* A/C, TV, minibar, hair dryer, safe.

Gran Hotel Velázquez ★ This is one of the most attractive medium-size hotels in Madrid, with plenty of comfort and convenience. Opened in 1947 on an affluent residential street near the center of town, it has a 1930s-style Art Deco facade and a 1940s interior filled with well-upholstered furniture and richly grained paneling. Several public rooms lead off a central oval area. As in many hotels of its era, the rooms vary. Some are large enough for entertaining, with a small separate sitting area. All contain piped-in music and walk-in closets. Bathrooms are decorated in marble or tiles, with either stall showers or tubs.

Calle de Velázquez 62, 28001 Madrid. ✆ **91-575-28-00.** Fax 91-575-28-09. www.chh.es. 146 units. 237€ double; from 338€ suite. AE, DC, MC, V. Parking 13€. Metro: Velázquez. **Amenities:** 2 restaurants; bar; salon; room service; babysitting; laundry/dry cleaning. *In room:* A/C, TV, minibar, hair dryer, safe.

MODERATE

Novotel Madrid Novotel was originally intended to serve the hotel needs of a cluster of multinational corporations with headquarters 2.4km (1½ miles) east of the center of Madrid, but its guest rooms are so comfortable and its prices so reasonable that tourists have begun using it as well. Opened in 1986, it is located on the highway, away from the maze of sometimes confusing inner-city streets, which makes it attractive to motorists.

Bedrooms are laid out in a standardized format whose popularity in Europe has made it one of the hotel industry's most notable success stories. Each contains a well-designed bathroom equipped with a shower-tub combination, in-house movies, and soundproofing. The sofas, once their bolster pillows are removed, can be transformed into comfortable beds for children. The English-speaking staff is well versed in both sightseeing attractions and solutions to most business-related problems.

Calle Albacete 1 (at Av. Badajos), 28027 Madrid. ✆ **800/221-4542** in the U.S. and Canada, or 91-724-76-00. Fax 91-724-76-10. www.novotel.com. 240 units. 160€ double. Children 15 and under stay free in parents' room. AE, DC, MC, V. Parking 15€. Metro: Concepción. Exit from M-30 at Barrio de la Concepción/Parque de las Avenidas, just before reaching the city limits of central Madrid, then look for the chain's trademark electric-blue signs. **Amenities:** Restaurant; bar; room service; pool; fitness center; sauna; babysitting; laundry/dry cleaning. *In room:* A/C, TV, minibar, hair dryer, safe.

INEXPENSIVE

Hotel Claridge This contemporary building, last renovated in 1994, is beyond Retiro Park, about 5 minutes from the Prado by taxi or subway. The rooms are well organized and pleasantly styled, though small and compact. They include small, well-organized bathrooms containing tub/shower combos. You can take your meals in the hotel's cafeteria and relax in the modern lounge.

Plaza Conde de Casal 6, 28007 Madrid. ✆ **91-551-94-00.** Fax 91-501-03-85. 150 units. Mon–Thurs 86€–107€ double; Fri–Sun 70€–74€ double; 150€ suite. AE, DC, MC, V. Metro: Conde de Casal. **Amenities:** Restaurant; bar; laundry/dry cleaning. *In room:* A/C, TV, hair dryer, safe.

CHAMBERI

VERY EXPENSIVE

Castellana Inter-Continental Hotel ★★ Solid, spacious, and conservatively modern, this is one of Madrid's most reliable hotels. Originally built in 1963, the Castellana Inter-Continental lies behind a barrier of trees in a neighborhood of apartment houses and luxury hotels. Its high-ceilinged public rooms are gorgeous, with terrazzo floors and giant abstract murals pieced together from multicolored stones and tiles. Most of the accommodations have private balconies and traditional furniture. Most rooms have generous living space with safes and very large beds, often king size. Bathrooms are tiled and well equipped with robes, phones, and tub/shower combos.

Paseo de la Castellana 49, 28046 Madrid. ✆ **800/327-0200** in the U.S., or 91-310-02-00. Fax 91-319-58-53. 310 units. 350€–430€ double; from 900€ suite. AE, DC, MC, V. Parking 18€. Metro: Gregorio Marañón. **Amenities:** 3 restaurants; bar; health club; sauna; solarium; hairdresser; room service; babysitting; laundry. *In room:* A/C, TV, minibar, hair dryer, safe.

Hotel Orfila ★★ *Finds* Though not as spectacular as Santo Mauro, this small 19th-century palace in a residential area is a gem and a classic example of elegant, tasteful decoration. Many visitors are deserting such old favorites as Villa Magna or the Westin Palace to stay here. In 1886 it was a family home but in the 1990s was converted to a luxury hotel that still pays homage to its Belle Epoque past. The midsize to spacious bedrooms are decorated in a rich 19th-century style that would make one of the old *gran señores* feel at home. Each comes with a well-kept bathroom containing a shower-tub combination. The public lounges also evoke its former aristocratic associations, and the lobby is installed in what used to be the courtyard of the town house, where horse-drawn carriages pulled in. The hotel also offers an elegant restaurant serving an international cuisine. Diners usually savor an aperitif first in the palace garden.

Orfila 6, 28010 Madrid. ✆ **91-702-77-70.** Fax 91-702-77-72. www.hotelorfila.com. 32 units. 282€–361€ double; from 565€ suite. AE, DC, MC, V. Metro: Alonso Martinez. **Amenities:** Restaurant; bar; room service; babysitting; laundry/dry cleaning. *In room:* A/C, TV, minibar, hair dryer, safe.

Santo Mauro Hotel ★★★ This hotel offers even more style and elegance than the Inter-Continental (see above). It opened in 1991 in what was once a neoclassical villa built in 1894 for the duke of Santo Mauro. Set within a garden and done in a French style, it's decorated with rich fabrics and Art Deco accents and furnishings. Staff members outnumber rooms by two to one. Each of the rooms contains an audio system with a wide choice of tapes and CDs as well as many lovely details, like raw silk curtains, Persian carpets, antique prints, and parquet floors. Rooms are large and come in combinations ranging from studios to duplex suites, all containing bathrooms with tub/shower combos.

Calle Zurbano 36, 28010 Madrid. ✆ **91-319-69-00.** Fax 91-308-54-77. www.ac-hoteles.com/ac_stomauro.htm. 54 units. 298€–361€ double; from 397€ suite. AE, DC, MC, V. Parking 15€. Metro: Rubén Darío or Alonso Martínez. **Amenities:** Restaurant; bar; pool; health club; sauna; room service; massage; babysitting; laundry/dry cleaning. *In room:* A/C, TV, minibar, hair dryer.

EXPENSIVE

Hotel Occidental Miguel Angel ★ Just off Paseo de la Castellana, this hotel is sleek and modern. It opened its doors in 1975 and has been renovated periodically ever since. It has a lot going for it: ideal location, contemporary styling, good furnishings, an efficient staff, and plenty of comfort. There's an expansive sun terrace on several levels, with clusters of garden furniture surrounded by paintings of semitropical scenes. The soundproof rooms are done in color-coordinated fabrics and carpets, and in many cases reproductions of classic Iberian furniture, each with a superbly comfortable bed and bathroom containing a tub/shower combo.

Miguel Angel 29–31, 28010 Madrid. ✆ **91-442-00-22.** Fax 91-442-53-20. 263 units. 240€–299€ double. AE, DC, MC, V. Parking 15.30€. Metro: Gregorio Marañón. **Amenities:** 2 restaurants; bar; pool; fitness center; sauna; hairdresser; room service; babysitting; laundry/dry cleaning. *In room:* A/C, TV, minibar, hair dryer, safe.

MODERATE

Hotel Escultor This comfortably furnished hotel built in 1975 provides fewer services and facilities than others within its category, but it compensates with larger rooms, each with its own charm. All units contain neatly kept bathrooms with tubs, and the hotel has a very knowledgeable staff.

Miguel Angel 3, 28010 Madrid. ✆ **91-310-42-03.** Fax 91-319-25-84. 57 units. From 120€ double; from 200€ suite. AE, DC, MC, V. Parking 15€ nearby. Metro: Rubén Darío. **Amenities:** Bar; room service; babysitting; laundry/dry cleaning. *In room:* A/C, TV, minibar, hair dryer, safe.

Hotel Orense ★ At first glance, you might mistake this silver-and-glass tower for one of many upscale condominium complexes surrounding it on all sides. Stylish and streamlined, with a design inaugurated in the late 1980s and renovated in 1996, it offers reproduction Oriental carpets and conservatively contemporary furniture that's comfortable, tasteful, and upscale. Accommodations are appropriate for a stay of up to several weeks, equipped along the lines of a private apartment. (In fact, management rents some of them to international corporations for long-term lodging and office space.) All rooms contain private bathrooms with tubs.

Pedro Teixeira 5, 28020 Madrid. ✆ **91-597-15-68.** Fax 91-597-12-95. www.hotelorense.com. 140 units. Mon–Thurs 140€–218€ double; Fri–Sun 86€ double. AE, DC, MC, V. Metro: Santiago Bernabeu. **Amenities:** Restaurant; bar; room service; laundry/dry cleaning. *In room:* A/C, TV, minibar, hair dryer, safe.

INEXPENSIVE

Hostal Residencia Don Diego ★ On the fifth floor of an elevator building, Don Diego is in a combination residential/commercial neighborhood that's relatively convenient to many of the city monuments. The vestibule contains an elegant winding staircase with iron griffin heads supporting its balustrade. The hotel is warm and inviting, filled with leather couches and comfortably angular but attractive furniture. Rooms are a bit small but comfortable for the price. Bathrooms are cramped but adequate, with shower stalls. The staff is very service oriented and keeps the place humming along efficiently.

Calle de Velázquez 45, 28001 Madrid. ✆ **91-435-07-60.** Fax 91-431-42-63. 58 units. 78€ double; 105€ triple. MC, V. Metro: Velázquez. **Amenities:** Cafeteria; laundry/dry cleaning. *In room:* A/C, TV, safe.

CHAMARTIN

EXPENSIVE

The Cuzco ★ Popular with businesspeople and tour groups, the Cuzco lies in a commercial neighborhood of big buildings, government ministries, and the main Congress Hall. The Chamartín railway station is only a 10-minute walk north, so this is a popular and convenient place to stay. The 15-floor structure, set back from Madrid's longest boulevard, has been redecorated and modernized many times since it was completed in 1967. The rooms are spacious, with separate sitting areas, video movies, and modern furnishings. Bathrooms come equipped with tub/shower combos.

Paseo de la Castellana 133, 28046 Madrid. ✆ **91-556-06-00.** Fax 91-556-03-72. 330 units. 190€ double; from 223€ suite. AE, DC, MC, V. Parking 16€. Metro: Cuzco. **Amenities:** Restaurant; bar; health club; sauna; salon; room service; massage; babysitting; laundry/dry cleaning. *In room:* A/C, TV, minibar, hair dryer, safe.

Eurobuilding ★ Even while the Eurobuilding was on the drawing boards, the rumor was that this government-rated five-star sensation of white marble would provide "a new concept in deluxe hotels." It is actually two hotels linked by a courtyard, away from the city center, but right in the midst of apartment houses, boutiques, nightclubs, first-class restaurants, and the modern Madrid business world.

The more glamorous of the twin buildings is the main one, named Las Estancias de Eurobuilding. It contains only suites, all recently renovated in pastel shades. Ornately carved gold-and-white beds, large terraces for breakfast and cocktail entertaining—all are tastefully coordinated. Across the courtyard the neighbor Eurobuilding contains less-impressive, but still very comfortable, double rooms, many with views from private balconies of the formal garden below. All accommodations have private bathrooms with tub/shower combos.

Calle Padre Damián 23, 28036 Madrid. ✆ **91-353-73-00.** Fax 91-345-45-76. 490 units. 231€–259€ double; from 471€ suite. AE, DC, MC, V. Parking 20€. Metro: Cuzco. **Amenities:** Restaurant; bar; pool; health club; sauna; room service; babysitting; laundry/dry cleaning. *In room:* A/C, TV, minibar, hair dryer, safe.

MODERATE

Hotel Chamartín This brick-sided hotel soars nine stories above the northern periphery of Madrid. It's part of the massive modern shopping complex attached to the Chamartín railway station, although once you're inside your soundproofed room, the noise of the railway station will seem far away. The owner of the building is RENFE, Spain's government railway system, but the nationwide chain that administers it is HUSA Hotels. The hotel lies 15 minutes by taxi from both the airport and the historic core of Madrid and sits atop one of the capital's busiest Metro stops. The well-appointed rooms are good size, with cushiony furnishings, along with orderly bathrooms with stall showers. Especially oriented to the business traveler, the hotel offers a video screen that posts the arrival and departure of all of Chamartín station's trains.

Augustín de Foxá, 28036 Madrid. ✆ **91-334-49-00.** Fax 91-733-02-14. www.husa.es. 378 units. 158€ double; from 252€ suite. AE, DC, MC, V. Metro: Chamartín. Bus: 5. **Amenities:** Restaurant; lounge; car rental; room service; laundry/dry cleaning. *In room:* A/C, TV, minibar, hair dryer, safe.

4 Where to Dine

Even more than Barcelona, Madrid boasts the most varied cuisine and the widest choice of dining opportunities in Spain. At the fancy tourist restaurants, prices are comparable to those in New York, London, or Paris, but there are many low-cost taverns and family restaurants as well.

It's the custom in Madrid to consume the big meal of the day from 2 to 4pm. After a recuperative siesta, Madrileños then enjoy tapas—and indeed, no culinary experience would be complete without a tour of the city's many tapas bars (see "An Early-Evening *Tapeo,*" below, and "The Best of the *Tascas,*" at the end of this chapter).

All this nibbling is followed by a light supper in a restaurant, usually from 9:30pm to as late as midnight. Many restaurants, however, start serving dinner at 8pm to accommodate visitors from other countries who don't like to dine so late.

Many of Spain's greatest chefs have opened restaurants in Madrid, energizing the city's culinary scene. Gone are the days when mainly Madrileño food was featured, which meant Castilian specialties such as *cocido* (a chickpea-and-sausage stew) or roasts of suckling pig or lamb. Now, you can take a culinary tour of the country without ever leaving Madrid—from Andalusia with its gazpacho and braised bull's tails to Asturias with its *fabada* (a rich pork stew) and *sidra* (cider) to the Basque country, which has the most sophisticated cuisine in Spain. There is also a host of Galician and Mediterranean restaurants in Madrid. Amazingly, although Madrid is a landlocked city surrounded by a vast arid plain, you can order some of the freshest seafood in the country here.

Meals include service and tax (7%–12%, depending on the restaurant) but not drinks, which add to the tab considerably.

In most cases service can seem perfunctory by U.S. standards. Waiters are matter-of-fact, do not fawn over you, nor do they return to the table to ask how things are. This can seem off-putting at first, but if you observe closely you'll see that Spanish waiters typically handle more tables than American waiters and that they generally work quickly and more efficiently.

Central Madrid Dining

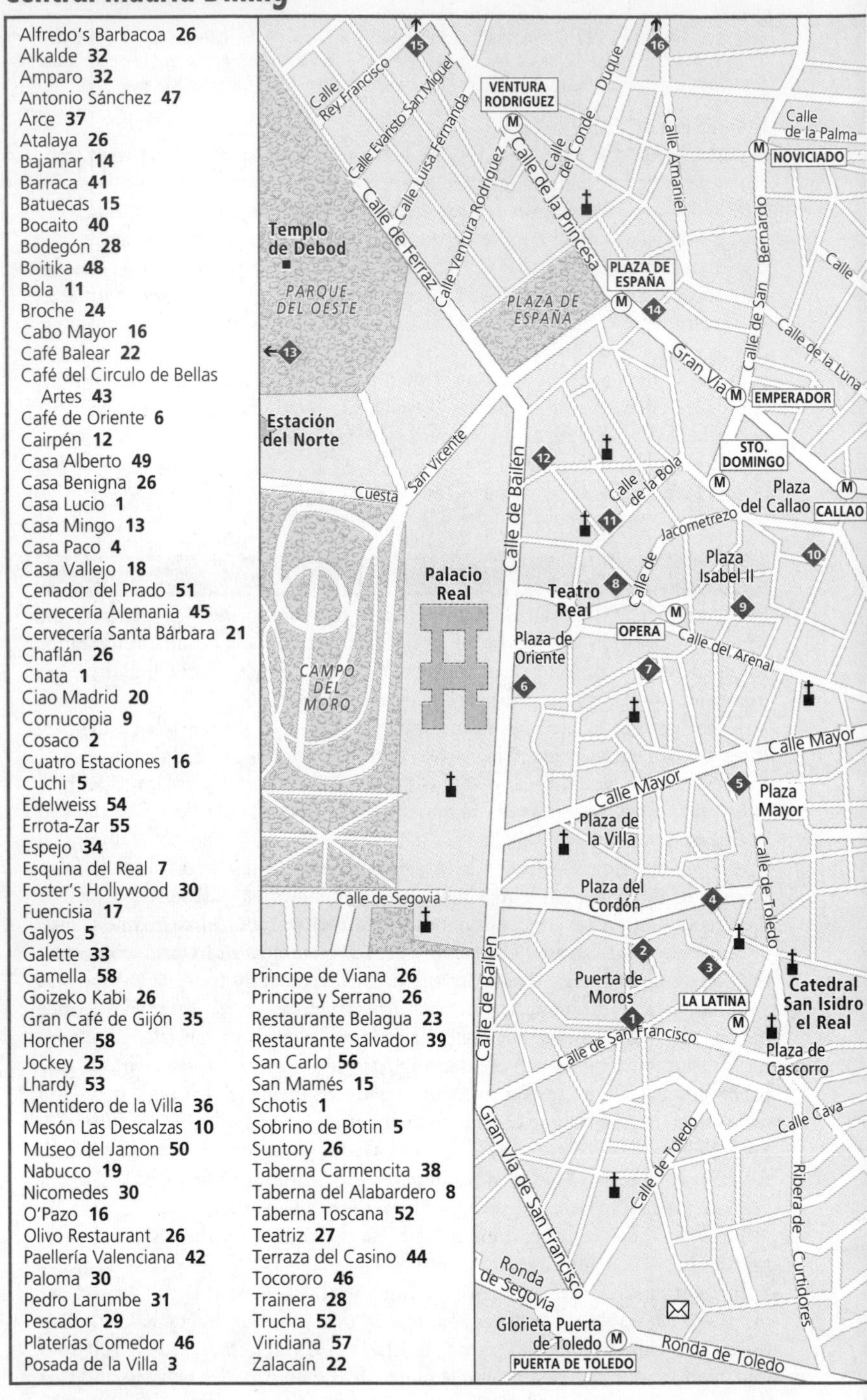

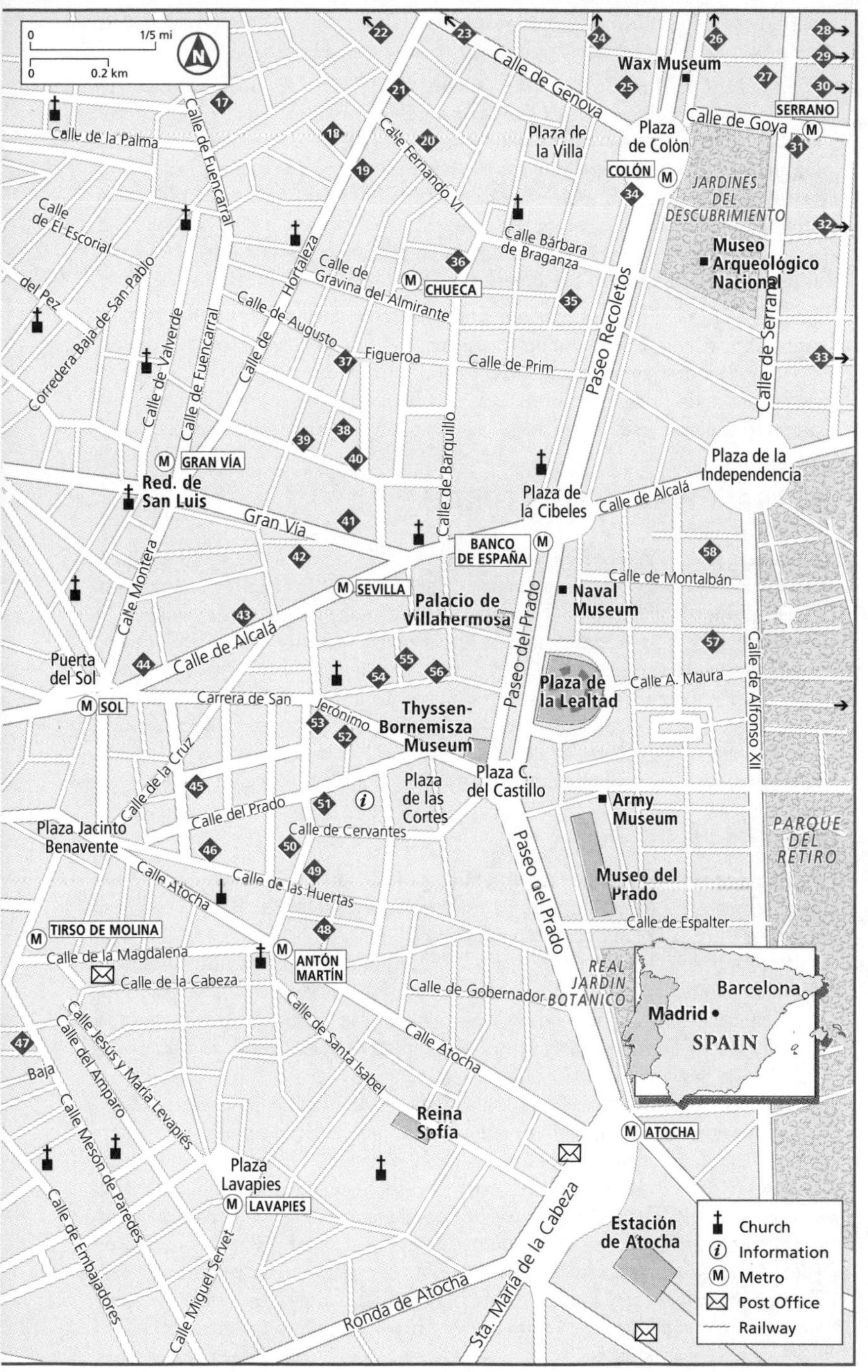

0 1/5 mi
0 0.2 km
N
Calle de Genova
Wax Museum
Plaza de Colón
Calle de Goya
SERRANO
COLÓN
JARDINES DEL DESCUBRIMIENTO
Museo Arqueológico Nacional
Plaza de la Villa
Calle Fernando VI
Calle Bárbara de Braganza
Calle de la Palma
Calle de Fuencarral
Calle de El Escorial
del Pez
Corredera Baja de San Pablo
Calle de Valverde
Calle de Hortaleza
Calle de Gravina del Almirante
CHUECA
Calle de Augusto Figueroa
Calle de Prim
Paseo Recoletos
Calle de Serrano
Plaza de la Independencia
GRAN VÍA
Red. de San Luis
Gran Vía
Calle de Barquillo
Plaza de la Cibeles
Calle de Alcalá
BANCO DE ESPAÑA
Calle Montera
SEVILLA
Palacio de Villahermosa
Paseo del Prado
Naval Museum
Calle de Montalbán
Puerta del Sol
SOL
Carrera de San Jerónimo
Thyssen-Bornemisza Museum
Plaza de la Lealtad
Calle A. Maura
Calle de Alfonso XII
Calle de la Cruz
Plaza de las Cortes
Plaza C. del Castillo
Army Museum
Calle del Prado
Calle de Cervantes
Plaza Jacinto Benavente
Calle Atocha
Calle de las Huertas
Museo del Prado
PARQUE DEL RETIRO
Calle de Espalter
TIRSO DE MOLINA
Calle de la Magdalena
ANTÓN MARTÍN
Calle de la Cabeza
Calle de Santa Isabel
Calle de Gobernador
REAL JARDIN BOTANICO
Barcelona
Madrid
SPAIN
Baja
Calle Jesús y María Levapiés
Calle del Amparo
Calle Mesón de Paredes
Reina Sofía
ATOCHA
Plaza Lavapies
LAVAPIES
Calle de Embajadores
Calle Miguel Servet
Ronda de Atocha
Sta. María de la Cabeza
Estación de Atocha
Church
Information
Metro
Post Office
Railway

Follow the local custom and don't overtip. Theoretically, service is included in the price of the meal, but it's customary to leave an additional 10%.

MENU DEL DIA* & *CUBIERTO Order the *menú del día* (menu of the day) or *cubierto* (fixed price)—both fixed-price menus based on what is fresh at the market that day. They are the dining bargains in Madrid, although often lacking the quality of more expensive a la carte dining. Usually each will include a first course, such as fish soup or hors d'oeuvres, followed by a main dish, plus bread, dessert, and the wine of the house. You won't have a large choice. The *menú turístico* is a similar fixed-price menu, but for many it's too large, especially at lunch. Only those with big appetites will find it the best bargain.

CAFETERIAS These usually are not self-service establishments but restaurants serving light, often American, cuisine. Go for breakfast instead of dining at your hotel, unless it's included in the room price. Some cafeterias offer no hot meals, but many feature combined plates of fried eggs, french fries, veal, and lettuce-and-tomato salad, which make adequate fare, or snacks like hot dogs and hamburgers.

NEAR THE PLAZA DE LAS CORTES

MODERATE

El Espejo ★ INTERNATIONAL Here you'll find good food and one of the most perfectly crafted Art Nouveau decors in Madrid. If the weather is good, you can sit at one of the outdoor tables and be served by uniformed waiters who carry food across the busy street to a green area flanked with trees. We prefer a table inside, within view of the tile maidens with vines and flowers entwined in their hair. Upon entering, you'll find yourself in a charming cafe/bar, where many visitors linger before heading toward the spacious dining room. Dishes include grouper ragout with clams, steak tartare, guinea fowl with Armagnac, and duck with pineapple. Try profiteroles with cream and chocolate sauce for dessert.

Paseo de Recoletos 31. ✆ **91-308-23-47.** Reservations required. *Menú del día* 21€. AE, MC, V. Daily 1–4pm and 9pm–midnight. Metro: Colón. Bus: 27 or 45.

Errota-Zar BASQUE Next to the House of Deputies and the Zarzuela Theater, Errota-Zar means "old mill," a nostalgic reference to the Basque country, home of the Olano family, owners of the restaurant.

A small bar at the entrance displays a collection of fine cigars and wines, and the blue-painted walls are adorned with paintings of Basque landscapes. The restaurant has only about 2 dozen tables, which can easily fill up. The Basque country is long known as the gastronomic capital of Spain, and Errota-Zar provides a fine showcase for its cuisine.

Try such appetizers as the rare tolosa kidney bean or fried anchovies. Many Basques begin their meal with a *tortilla de bacalao* (salt cod omelet). For main dishes, sample the delights of *chuletón de buey* (oxtail), along with grilled vegetables, or *kokotxas de merluza en aceite* (the cheeks of the hake fish cooked in virgin olive oil). Hake cheeks may not sound appetizing, but Spaniards and many foreigners praise this dish. You might opt instead for *foie al Pedro Jiménez* (duck liver grilled and served with a sweet wine sauce). The best homemade desserts are *cuajada de la casa,* a thick yogurt made from sheep's milk, or *tarta de limón,* a lemon cake. You might also try rice ice cream in prune sauce.

Jovellanos 3, 1st floor. ✆ **91-531-25-64.** Reservations recommended. Main courses 17€–19€; *menú completo* 28€. AE, DC, MC, V. Mon–Sat 1–4pm and 9pm–midnight. Closed Aug 15–30. Metro: Banco España and Sevilla.

La Trucha SPANISH/SEAFOOD With its Andalusian tavern ambience, La Trucha boasts a street-level bar and small dining room with arched ceiling and whitewashed walls. The decor is made festive with hanging braids of garlic, dried peppers, and onions. On the lower level the walls of a second bustling area are covered with eye-catching antiques, bullfight notices, and other bric-a-brac. There's a complete a la carte menu including *trucha* (trout), *verbenas de ahumados* (a selection of smoked delicacies), a glorious stew called *fabada* (made with beans, Galician ham, black sausage, and smoked bacon), and a *comida casera rabo de toro* (home-style oxtail). No one should miss nibbling on the *tapas variadas* in the bar.

If this branch turns out to be too crowded, there's another **Trucha** at Núñez de Arce 6 (✆ **91-532-08-82**).

Manuel Fernández González 3. ✆ **91-429-58-33.** Reservations recommended. Main courses 15€–30€. AE, MC, V. Daily 12:30–4pm and 7:30pm–midnight. Metro: Sevilla.

INEXPENSIVE

Edelweiss GERMAN This German standby has provided good-quality food and service at moderate prices since World War II. Here you will be served hearty portions of food, mugs of draft beer, and fluffy pastries; that's why there's always a wait.

Start with Bismarck herring, then dive into goulash with spaetzle or *Eisbein* (pigs' knuckles) with sauerkraut and mashed potatoes, the most popular dish at the restaurant. Finish with the homemade apple tart. The decor is vaguely German, with travel posters and wood-paneled walls. Edelweiss is air-conditioned in summer.

Jovellanos 7. ✆ **91-521-03-26.** Reservations recommended. Main courses 11€–21€; fixed-price lunch 16€. AE, DC, MC, V. Daily 1–4pm and Mon–Sat 8pm–midnight. Metro: Cibeles. Bus: 5.

NEAR PLAZA DE LA CIBELES

MODERATE

Bocaito SPANISH/TAPAS Inside this 150-year-old house, four original columns of wood encircle the high ceiling, and bullfighting posters adorn the white-tile walls. Behind a bar shaped into two horseshoes, the staff cooks and prepares some of the most appreciated tapas in Madrid. The selection ranges from simple delights such as *ajos tiernos en aceite* (tender garlic in olive oil), cured Serrano ham, *gambas fritas* (fried shrimp), and green asparagus in scrambled eggs to some very sophisticated delicacies, such as *bacalao con caviar* (salt cod paté with caviar). The famous *mejimecha* (marinated mussels with ham and onions in béchamel sauce) is sublime, as are the anchovies of the house and tasty croquettes. The prices for the tapas range from 5.40€ to 7.20€. Don Miguel Benavente, the chef and owner for more than 3 decades, recommends the *plato combinado* (a combination platter of all tapas), which, together with a glass of their very palatable Rioja house wine, is available at a cost of 9€. A selection of the culinary treats on offer includes lentils with *chorizo* (Spanish sausage), *merluza* (hake), *osso buco al horno* (braised veal shank), and typical Andalusian and Castilian dishes.

Calle Libertad 4–6 (2 blocks north of *Las Cibeles*). ✆ **91-532-12-19.** Reservations recommended. Main courses 12€–18€. MC, V. Mon–Fri 1–4pm and 8:30pm–midnight; Sat 8:30pm–midnight. Closed last 2 weeks Aug. Metro: Banco de España.

Tocororo CUBAN This is Madrid's finest Cuban restaurant. The nostalgia is evident in the pictures of Old Havana, and in the paintings of famous artists such as Lam y Mattos that adorn the walls. The wait staff is as lively as the pop Cuban music playing on the stereo. The dishes are typical Caribbean dishes, such as *ceviche* (marinated fish), *ropa vieja* (shredded meat served with black beans and rice), or lobster enchilada. If you prefer a simpler repast, try a selection of *empanadas y tamales* (fried potato pastries and plantain dough filled with onions and ground meat). Special cocktails of the house include *mojito* (rum, mint, and a hint of sugar) and daiquiris. In winter there is live Cuban music. With a discreet but pleasant ambience, this restaurant is located in the zone of *La Marcha* (most of the bars and discos are in this area).

Calle del Prado 3 (at the corner of Echegaray). ✆ **91-369-40-00.** Reservations required Thurs–Sat. Main courses 13€–16€; fixed-price menu 9€. AE, DC, MC, V. Tues–Wed 1:30–4pm and 8:30pm–midnight; Thurs–Sun 1:30–4pm and 8:30pm–1:30am. Closed last 2 weeks Feb. and last week Sept. Metro: Sevilla.

Moments An Early-Evening *Tapeo*

What's more fun than a pub-crawl in London or Dublin? In Madrid, it's a *tapeo,* and you can drink just as much or more than in those far northern climes. One of the unique pleasures of Madrid, a *tapeo* is the act of strolling from one bar to another to keep yourself amused and fed before the fashionable Madrileño dining hour of 10pm.

Most of the world knows that tapas are Spain's delectable appetizers, and restaurants around the world now serve them. In Madrid they're served almost everywhere, in *tabernas, tascas,* bars, and cafes.

Although Madrid took to tapas with a passion, they may have originated in Andalusia, especially around Jerez de la Frontera, where they were traditionally served to accompany the sherry produced there. The first tapa (which means a cover or lid) was probably *chorizo* (a spicy sausage) or a slice of cured ham perched over the mouth of a glass to keep the flies out. Later, the government mandated bars to serve a "little something" in the way of food with each drink to dissipate the effects of the alcohol. This was important when drinking a fortified wine like sherry, as its alcohol content is more than 15% higher than that of normal table wines. Eating a selection of tapas as you drink will help preserve your sobriety.

Tapas can be relatively simple: toasted almonds; slices of ham, cheese, or sausage; potato omelets; or the ubiquitous olives. They can be more elaborate too: a succulent veal roll; herb-flavored snails; *gambas* (shrimp); a saucer of peppery *pulpo* (octopus); stuffed peppers; *anguila* (eel); *cangrejo* (crabmeat salad); *merluza* (hake) salad; and even bull testicles.

Each bar in Madrid gains a reputation for its rendition of certain favorite foods. One bar, for example, specializes in very garlicky grilled mushrooms, usually accompanied by pitchers of sangria. Another will specialize in *gambas.* Most chefs are men in Madrid, but at tapas bars or *tascas,* the cooks are most often women—often the owner's wife.

For a selection of our favorite bars, see "Our Favorite *Tascas,*" later in this chapter. There are literally hundreds of others, many of which you'll discover on your own during your strolls around Madrid.

NEAR THE PLAZA DE ESPAÑA

EXPENSIVE

Bajamar SEAFOOD Bajamar, one of the best fish houses in Spain, is right in the heart of the city. Both fish and shellfish are flown in fresh daily, the prices depending on what the market charges. Lobster, king crab, prawns, and soft-shell crabs are all priced according to weight. There is a large array of reasonably priced dishes as well. The service is smooth and professional and the menu is in English. For an appetizer order the half-dozen giant oysters or rover crayfish. The special seafood soup is a most satisfying meal in itself; the lobster bisque is also worth trying. Some of the noteworthy main courses include turbot Gallego style, seafood paella, and baby squid cooked in its ink. The simple desserts include the chef's custard.

Gran Vía 78. ✆ **91-559-59-03.** Reservations recommended. Main courses 22€–60€. AE, DC, MC, V. Daily 1–4pm and 8pm–midnight. Metro: Plaza de España.

MODERATE

La Bola MADRILEÑA This is *the taberna* in which to savor the 19th century. Just north of the Teatro Real, it's one of the few restaurants (if not the only one) left in Madrid with a blood-red facade; at one time, nearly all fashionable restaurants were so coated. Time stands still inside this restaurant with its traditional atmosphere, gently polite waiters, Venetian crystal, and aging velvet. Ava Gardner, with her entourage of bullfighters, used to patronize this establishment. Grilled sole, filet of veal, and roast veal are regularly featured. Basque-style hake and grilled salmon are well recommended. Refreshing dishes to begin your meal include grilled shrimp, red-pepper salad, and lobster cocktail.

Calle de la Bola 5. ✆ **91-547-69-30.** Reservations required. Main courses 14€–19€. No credit cards. Mon–Sat 1–4pm; daily 8:30–11pm. Metro: Opera. Bus: 1 or 2.

ON OR NEAR THE GRAN VIA

EXPENSIVE

Arce ★ BASQUE Arce has brought some of the best modern interpretations of Basque cuisine to Madrid, thanks to the enthusiasm of owner/chef Iñaki Camba and his wife, Theresa. Within a comfortably decorated dining room, you can enjoy dishes made of the finest ingredients using flavors designed to dominate your taste buds. Examples include a salad of fresh scallops and an oven-baked casserole of fresh boletus mushrooms, seasoned lightly so the woodsy vegetable taste comes through. Look for unusual preparations of hake and seasonal variations of such game dishes as pheasant and woodcock.

Augusto Figueroa 32. ✆ **91-522-59-13.** Reservations recommended. Main courses 17€–35€. AE, DC, MC, V. Mon–Fri 1:30–4pm; Mon–Sat 9pm–midnight. Closed the week before Easter and Aug 15–31. Metro: Chueca.

El Mentidero de la Villa ★ MEDITERRANEAN The Mentidero ("Gossip Shop" in English) is a truly multicultural experience. The owner describes the cuisine as "modern Spanish with Japanese influence and a French cooking technique." That may sound confusing, but the result is an achievement; each ingredient manages to retain its distinct flavor. The kitchen plays with such adventuresome combinations as veal liver in sage sauce; a spring roll filled with fresh shrimp and leeks; noisettes of veal with tarragon; filet steak with a sauce of mustard and brown sugar; and medallions of venison with purée of chestnut and celery. One notable dessert is the sherry trifle. The postmodern decor includes trompe l'oeil ceilings, exposed wine racks, ornate columns with unusual lighting, and a handful of antique carved merry-go-round horses.

Santo Tomé 6. ✆ **91-308-12-85.** Reservations required. Main courses 25€–33€. AE, DC, MC, V. Mon–Fri 1:30–4:30pm; Mon–Sat 9pm–midnight. Closed Aug. Metro: Alonso Martínez, Colón. Bus: 37.

La Barraca VALENCIAN La Barraca is like a country inn right off the Gran Vía, and it's a longtime local favorite. The food, frankly, used to be better, but perhaps our tastes have changed since our student days. This Valencian-style restaurant is a well-managed establishment recommended for its tasty Levante cooking. There are four different dining rooms, three of which lie one flight above street level; they're colorfully cluttered with ceramics, paintings, photographs, Spanish lanterns, flowers, and local artifacts. The house specialty, paella a la Barraca, is made with pork and chicken. Specialties in the appetizer category include *desgarrat* (a salad of cod and red peppers), mussels in a white-wine sauce, and shrimp sautéed with garlic. In addition to the recommended paella, you can select at least 16 rice dishes, including black rice and queen paella. Main-dish specialties include brochette of angler and prawns and rabbit with fines herbes. Lemon-and-vodka sorbet brings the meal to a fitting finish.

Reina 29–31. ✆ **91-532-71-54.** Reservations recommended. Main courses 12€–20€. AE, DC, MC, V. Daily 1–4pm and 8:30pm–midnight. Metro: Gran Vía or Sevilla. Bus: 1, 2, or 74.

INEXPENSIVE

Paellería Valenciana SPANISH This lunch-only restaurant ranks as one of the best values in the city. The specialty is paella, which you must order by phone in advance. Once you arrive, you might begin with a homemade soup or the house salad, then follow with the rib-sticking paella, served in an iron skillet for two or more only. Among the desserts, the chef's special pride is razor-thin orange slices flavored with rum, coconut, sugar, honey, and raspberry sauce. A carafe of house wine comes with the set menu, and after lunch the owner comes around dispensing free cognac.

Caballero de Gracia 12. ✆ **91-531-17-85.** Reservations recommended. Main courses 8€–18€. AE, MC, V. Mon–Sat 1:30–4:30pm. Metro: Gran Vía.

NEAR THE PUERTA DEL SOL

VERY EXPENSIVE

Lhardy ★★ SPANISH/INTERNATIONAL This is Madrid's longest running culinary act. Lhardy has been a Madrileño legend since opening in 1839 as a gathering place for the city's literati and political leaders. At street level is what may be the most elegant snack bar in Spain. Within a dignified antique setting of marble and hardwood, cups of steaming consommé are dispensed from silver samovars into delicate porcelain cups, and rows of croquettes, tapas, and sandwiches are served to stand-up clients who pay for their food at a cashier's kiosk near the entrance. The ground-floor deli and takeout service is open daily from 9am to 3pm and 5 to 9:30pm.

The real culinary skill of the place, however, is on Lhardy's second floor, where you'll find a formal restaurant decorated in the ornate Belle-Epoque style of Isabel Segunda. Specialties of the house include fish, pork, veal, tripe in a garlicky tomato and onion wine sauce, and *cocido,* the celebrated chickpea stew of Madrid. *Soufflé sorpresa* (baked Alaska) is the dessert specialty.

Carrera de San Jerónimo 8. ✆ **91-521-33-85.** Reservations recommended in the upstairs dining room. Main dishes 13€–21€. AE, DC, MC, V. Mon–Sat 1–3:30pm and 8:30–11pm. Closed Aug. Metro: Puerta del Sol.

La Terraza del Casino ★★★ SPANISH/INTERNATIONAL The city's most imaginative chef, Ferran Adrià, isn't in Madrid. He's still tending those pots and pans in the little town of Roses near Girona in Catalonia. But the innovative master of cuisine created all the dishes on the menu here and flies in regularly to see that his cooks are following his orders. His *luxe* restaurant in Madrid lies on the top floor of the Casino in Madrid, a historical building and a former gentlemen's club with a history going back to 1910. Even the grand dons of those days surely didn't dine as well as you can today.

His dishes are exquisite, and food critics (and we concur) are always writing about taste "explosions" in your mouth. His Catalán restaurant is El Bulli, meaning "innovative" in Spanish. The same name could apply to this Madrid dining hot spot that provides a panoramic view of the heart of Madrid and can be reached by an elevator or by a sweeping 19th-century staircase designed to impress. The decor is classically restrained with high ceilings and crystal chandeliers. The exquisite food uses fresh seasonal ingredients and reinterprets Spanish dishes. An example is *raya* in oil and saffron with parsley purée and nuts on a bed of finely diced fries. More traditional dishes include the succulent *merluza a la gallega* (Galician hake), *crema de la fabada asturiana* (creamed Asturian bean soup), and the steeply priced *jamón Jabugo* (cured ham from acorn-fed pigs) served with a *menestra* (mixed vegetables) al dente. Only French champagne and Spanish wines are listed, and one of the best is the rounded woody red, the Ribeira de Duero from the province of Valladolid.

Alcalá 15. ✆ **91-521-87-00.** Main courses 25€–33€; fixed-price menu 66€. AE, DC, MC, V. Mon–Fri 1–3:30pm and 9–11:30pm; Sat 9–11:30pm. Closed Aug. Metro: Sevilla.

EXPENSIVE

Caripén ★ ITALIAN/FRENCH This restaurant stands in a historic district near the Royal Opera House and the Spanish Senate. It was once El Tablao, the flamenco club of Lola Flores, one of the most famous of all Spanish dancers. Its Art Deco decor has been restored, and instead of flamenco, you get the inspired French bistro cookery of Daniel Boute. The restaurant is especially popular with the Madrid locals, or *gatos* (cats) because it serves until 3am when most other quality establishments are shuttered. (Local residents are called *gatos* because they like to roam about at night.) Go for the *mejillones de roca* (mussels in white

Kids Family-Friendly Restaurants

Children visiting Spain will delight in patronizing any of the restaurants at the Parque de Atracciones in the **Casa de Campo** (see "Especially for Kids" in chapter 6). Another good idea is to go on a picnic (see "Picnics, Madrid Style," later in this chapter).

For a taste of home, there are always the fast-food chains: McDonald's, Burger King, and Kentucky Fried Chicken are everywhere. Remember, however, that the burgers and chicken will have a slightly different taste from those served back home.

A place with juicy hamburgers, plus lots of fare familiar to American kids, is **Foster's Hollywood** (p. 179). Or try taking the family to a local *tasca,* where children are bound to find something they like from the wide selection of tapas.

wine and cream sauce), a perfectly prepared steak tartare, *foie* with *setas* (duck liver and mushrooms), or skate in black butter. You can finish off with such desserts as tiramisu, freshly made fruit tarts, or crepes.

Plaza de la Marina Española 4. ✆ **91-541-11-77.** Reservations recommended on weekends. Main courses 12€–16€. MC, V. Mon–Sat 9pm–3am. Closed Aug. Metro: Opera/Santo Domingo.

Platerías Comedor SPANISH One of the most charming dining rooms in Madrid, Platerías Comedor has richly brocaded walls evocative of 19th-century Spain. Busy socializing may take place on the plaza outside, but this serene oasis makes few concessions to the new generation in its food, decor, or formally attired waiters. Specialties include beans with clams, stuffed partridge with cabbage and sausage, duck liver with white grapes, tripe *a la Madrid,* veal stew with snails and mushrooms, and guinea hen with figs and plums. Follow up any of these with the passion fruit sorbet. Many restaurants have sprouted up in recent years that serve better food, but Platerías Comedor continues to thrive as a culinary tradition; its old-fashioned atmosphere is hard to come by.

Plaza de Santa Ana 11. ✆ **91-429-70-48.** Reservations recommended. Main courses 12€–17€. AE, DC, MC, V. Tues-Sat 1:30–4pm and 8:30pm–midnight; Sat 9pm–midnight. Metro: Puerta del Sol.

MODERATE

Café de Oriente FRENCH/SPANISH The Oriente is a cafe-and-restaurant complex, the former being one of the most popular in Madrid. From the cafe tables on its terrace, there's a spectacular view of the Palacio Real (Royal Palace) and the Teatro Real. The dining rooms—Castilian upstairs, French Basque downstairs—are frequented by royalty and diplomats. Typical of the refined cuisine are vichyssoise, fresh vegetable flan, and many savory meat and fresh-fish offerings. Service is excellent. Most visitors, however, patronize the cafe, trying if possible to get an outdoor table. The cafe is decorated in turn-of-the-century style, with banquettes and regal paneling, as befits its location. Pizza, tapas, and drinks (including Irish, Viennese, Russian, and Jamaican coffees) are served.

Plaza de Oriente 2. ✆ **91-541-39-74.** Reservations recommended in restaurant only. Restaurant, main courses 15€–21€. Cafe, tapas 3.60€–7.25€; coffee 4€. AE, DC, MC, V. Daily 1–4pm and 9pm–midnight. Metro: Opera.

MODERATE

Casa Paco ★★ STEAK Madrileños defiantly name Casa Paco, just beside the Plaza Mayor, when someone dares to denigrate Spanish steaks. They know that here you can get the thickest, juiciest, tastiest steaks in Spain, priced according to weight. Señor Paco sears his steaks in boiling oil before serving them on plates so hot that the almost-raw meat continues to cook, preserving the natural juices. Located in the Old Town, this two-story restaurant has three dining rooms but reservations are imperative. If you face a long wait, sample the tapas at the bar in front. Around the walls are autographed photographs of notables.

Casa Paco isn't just a steakhouse; you can start with fish soup and proceed to grilled sole or baby lamb, or try *Casa Paco cocido,* the house version of Madrid's famous chickpea and pork soup. As tempting as the fresh shellfish looks, it is sold at no set price but "at market rates," which change from day to day. The bill for your appetizers might equal the national budget for Nepal. You might top it off with one of the luscious desserts, but Paco no longer serves coffee. It made customers linger, keeping tables occupied while potential patrons had to be turned away.

Plaza Puerta Cerrada 11. ✆ **91-366-31-66.** Reservations required. Main courses 11€–18€. Fixed-price menu 27€. DC, MC, V. Mon–Sat 1–4pm and 8:30pm–midnight. Closed Aug. Metro: Puerta del Sol, Opera, or La Latina. Bus: 3, 21, or 65.

El Cenador del Prado ★ INTERNATIONAL In this elegant restaurant's anteroom, an attendant will check your coat into an elaborately carved armoire before the maitre d' ushers you into one of a trio of rooms. Two of the rooms have cove moldings, English furniture, and floor-to-ceiling gilded mirrors. A third room is ringed with lattices and flooded with sun from a skylight.

The imaginative food reflects a French influence with an occasional Asian flourish. You might enjoy such specialties as crepes with salmon and Iranian caviar; a salad of red peppers and salted anchovies; a casserole of snails and oysters with mushrooms; a ceviche of salmon and shellfish; potato-leek soup studded with tidbits of hake and clams; sea bass with candied lemons; veal scaloppini stuffed with asparagus and garlic sprouts; or medallions of venison served with pepper-and-fig chutney.

Calle del Prado 4. ✆ **91-429-15-61.** Reservations recommended. Main courses 12.50€–24€; fixed-price menu 24€; vegetarian menu 19€. AE, DC, MC, V. Mon–Fri 1:45–4pm; Mon–Sat 9pm–midnight. Closed Aug 12–19. Metro: Antón Martín.

La Esquina del Real FRENCH Next to the Teatro Real you'll find this restaurant in an impressive 17th-century building with an ancient stone facade, thick granite walls, and the original wooden beams supporting old ceilings. This place has a sophisticated atmosphere, yet prices are very reasonable. One Madrid food critic recently called this place one of the city's "best kept" culinary secrets. The hospitable owner and chef, Marcel Magossian, extends a hearty welcome to patrons and feeds them well. Fresh ingredients are transformed into tasty concoctions, like large prawns with a delicate flavoring of raspberry vinaigrette or roast oxtail with mashed potatoes and fresh mushrooms. A rather common dish, veal fricassee in mushroom sauce, is transformed into something sublime here. To end your repast, you might opt for a combination platter of warm cheese, or try tart tatin, ice cream with a crunchy caramel sauce flambéed at your table.

Calle de la Unión 8. ✆ **91-559-43-09.** Reservations recommended on weekends. Main courses 24€–30€. AE, MC, V. Mon–Fri 2–4pm and 9pm–midnight; Sat 9pm–midnight. Closed last 2 weeks of Aug. Metro: Opera/Sol.

INEXPENSIVE

Café del Círculo de Bellas Artes ★ *Finds* This former members-only club is now open to the general public. If you eat and drink here, you still get the feeling you're crashing a private party. (Incidentally, this is a time-honored tradition in Madrid.) With its 1920s style ceilings, chandeliers, artistic statues, and soaring pillars, this cafe lies in an arts center. It's the best place to take a refueling stop when you're so tired you confused van Gogh with the Goyas at the Thyssen or the Real Academia de Bellas Artes.

Locals don't even know the place by its formal name, having nicknamed it *la pecera,* or aquarium. The food and drink are served in a palatial hall. At lunchtime join politicians and bankers from the nearby parliament or the Banco d'España to enjoy a variety of pork, beef, fresh fish, and chicken dishes. The menu is rotated daily. Hopefully, you'll be here on the day the chef decided to prepare his robust *cocido,* the "granddaddy of Spanish stews." It will put hair on your chest even if you're a woman. At night a more artsy crowd flocks to the place, devouring the succulent tapas such as shrimp and fresh anchovies and the rum cocktails that make you think you're back in Barbados. Only tapas are served at night but if you order three or four they become meals unto themselves.

Calle Alcalá 42. ✆ **91-521-69-42.** Lunch main courses 10.50€ each. Evening tapas 2.55€–5.80€. MC, V. Sun–Thurs 9:30am–1am; Fri–Sat 9:30am–3am. Metro: Banco de España.

Casa Alberto CASTILIAN One of the oldest *tascas* in the neighborhood, Casa Alberto is from 1827 and has thrived ever since. On the street level of a house where Miguel de Cervantes lived briefly in 1614, it contains an appealing mixture of bullfighting memorabilia, engravings, and reproductions of Old Master paintings. Many visitors opt only for the tapas, continually replenished from platters on the bar, but there's a sit-down dining area for more substantial meals. Specialties include fried squid, shellfish in vinaigrette sauce, *chorizo* (sausage) in cider sauce, and several versions of baked or roasted lamb.

Huertas 18. ✆ **91-429-93-56.** Reservations recommended. Main courses 11€–21€. AE, DC, MC, V. Tues–Sat 1–4pm; Tues–Sun 8:30pm–midnight. Metro: Antón Martín.

La Boitika *Finds* VEGETARIAN Vegetarian cuisine doesn't get a lot of attention in most Madrid restaurants, but this discovery is a rare exception. Opening east of the landmark Plaza Santa Ana, it is intimate and charming. It serves the capital's best macrobiotic vegetarian cuisine, and does so exceedingly well. We always begin with one of the homemade soups, which are made fresh daily, then have one of the large, fresh salads. The bread is also made fresh daily. One specialty is a "meatball without meat" (made with vegetables but shaped like a meatball). Tofu with zucchini and many other offerings appear daily.

Amor de Dios 3. ✆ **91-429-07-80.** Main courses 5€–9€. *Menú del día* 7€–8€. No credit cards. Daily 1–4pm and 8–11pm. Metro: Antón Martín.

Mesón las Descalzas SPANISH Las Descalzas, a recommended tavern-style restaurant, has a massive tapas bar that's often crowded at night. Behind a glass-and-wood screen is the restaurant section, its specialties including kidneys with sherry, *sopa castellana* (seafood soup), Basque-style hake, crayfish, shrimp, oysters, clams, and paella with shellfish. There is folk music for entertainment.

Postigo San Martín 3. ✆ **91-522-72-17.** Reservations recommended. Main courses 11€–15€; fixed-price menu 9€. AE, DC, MC, V. Daily 1–4pm and 8pm–midnight. Metro: Callao.

Museo del Jamón SPANISH/TAPAS The displays on the walls of this unique establishment explain the bewildering name: "The Museum of Ham." As in an art exhibition, large amounts of different kinds of hams—cured by a variety of methods—hang from the ceilings. The popular *chorizos* are hooked in rows reminiscent of one of those scenes in Golden Age paintings. This is indeed a real museum of the most celebrated fast food in Spain. On certain nights, the tavern offers live entertainment in the dining area upstairs, often a guitarist. The *paella* for two is reasonably priced. The aged *jamón Serrano* is a great delicacy now highly prized at tapas bars throughout Spain, Europe, and North America. You might try it in small sandwiches known as *bocattas* or as an always-available tapa. The daily menu is varied and served in generous portions. Service is efficient, though not too friendly, but customers don't seem to mind.

Carrera de San Jerónimo 6 (1 block east of Puerta del Sol). ✆ **91-521-03-46.** *Menú del día* 7€–11€; *platos combinados* 3€–4.50€. MC, V. Daily 9am–12:30am. Metro: Puerta del Sol.

Taberna del Alabardero BASQUE/SPANISH In close proximity to the Royal Palace, this little Spanish classic is known for its selection of tasty tapas, ranging from squid cooked in wine to fried potatoes dipped in hot sauce. Photographs of famous former patrons, including Nelson Rockefeller and the racecar driver Jackie Stewart, line the walls. The restaurant in the rear is said to be one of the city's best-kept secrets. Decorated in typical tavern style, it serves a savory Spanish and Basque cuisine with market-fresh ingredients.

Felipe V 6. ✆ **91-547-25-77.** Reservations required for restaurant only. Bar: tapas 2.70€–9€; glass of house wine 1.80€. Restaurant: main courses 13€–18€. AE, DC, MC, V. Daily 8am–1am. Metro: Opera.

RETIRO/SALAMANCA

EXPENSIVE

Alkalde ★ BASQUE For decades Alkalde has been known for serving top-quality Spanish food in an old tavern setting, and it continues to do so exceedingly well. Decorated like a Basque inn, it has beamed ceilings with hams hanging from the rafters. Upstairs is a large *típico* tavern; downstairs is a maze of stone-sided cellars that are pleasantly cool in summer (although the whole place is air-conditioned).

Basque cookery is the best in Spain, and Alkalde honors that noble tradition. Begin with the cream of crabmeat soup, followed by *gambas a la plancha* (grilled shrimp) or *cigalas* (crayfish). Other recommended dishes include *mero salsa verde* (brill in green sauce), trout Alkalde, stuffed peppers, and chicken steak. The dessert specialty is *copa Cardinal* (ice cream topped with fruit).

Jorge Juan 10. ✆ **91-576-33-59.** Reservations required. Main courses 27€–39€; fixed-price menu from 36€. AE, DC, MC, V. Daily 1:15–midnight. Closed Sat–Sun in July–Aug. Metro: Retiro or Serrano. Bus: 8, 20, 21, or 53.

El Amparo ★★ BASQUE Behind the cascading vines on El Amparo's facade is one of Madrid's most elegant gastronomic enclaves. Inside this converted carriage house, three tiers of rough-hewn wooden beams surround tables set with pink linens and glistening silver. A sloping skylight floods the interior with sun by day; at night, pinpoints of light from the high-tech hanging lanterns create intimate shadows. Polite, uniformed waiters serve well-prepared nouvelle cuisine versions of cold marinated salmon with a tomato sorbet, cold cream of vegetable and shrimp soup, bisque of shellfish with Armagnac, ravioli with crayfish dressed with balsamic vinegar and vanilla-scented oil, roast lamb chops with garlic purée, breast of duck, ragout of sole, steamed fish of the day, roulades of lobster with soy sauce, and steamed hake with pepper sauce.

Callejón de Puigcerdà 8 (at corner of Jorge Juan). ✆ **91-431-64-56.** Reservations required. Main courses 15€–30€. AE, MC, V. Mon–Fri 1:30–3:30pm; Mon–Sat 9–11:30pm. Closed week before Easter. Metro: Serrano. Bus: 21 or 53.

El Pescador ★ SEAFOOD El Pescador is a popular spot, packing in crowds with more than 30 kinds of fish served, all prominently displayed in a glass case. Many of them are unknown in North America, and some originate off the coast of Galicia. The management airfreights them in and prefers to serve them *a la plancha* (grilled). You might start off with spicy fish soup and accompany it with one of the many good wines from northeastern Spain. If you're not sure what to order, try one of the many varieties and sizes of shrimp. They go under the names *langostinos, cigalas, santiaguinos,* and *carabineros.* Many of them are expensive and priced by weight, so be careful when you order.

Calle José Ortega y Gasset 75. ✆ **91-402-12-90.** Reservations required. Main courses 18€–36€. MC, V. Mon–Sat noon–4pm and 8pm–midnight. Closed Aug. Metro: Lista or Diego de León.

Horcher ★ GERMAN/INTERNATIONAL Horcher originated in Berlin in 1904. In 1943, prompted by a tip from a high-ranking German officer that Germany was losing the war, Herr Horcher moved his restaurant to Madrid. For years it was known as the best dining room in the city, but fierce competition has lately stolen that crown. Nevertheless, the restaurant is still going strong, continuing its grand European traditions, including excellent service.

You might try the skate or shrimp tartare or the distinctive warm hake salad. Both the venison stew with green pepper and orange peel and the crayfish with parsley and cucumber are typical of the elegant fare served with style. Spanish aristocrats often come here in autumn to sample game dishes, including venison, wild boar, and roast wild duck. Other main courses include veal scaloppini in tarragon and sea bass with saffron. For dessert, the house specialty is crepes Sir Holden, prepared at your table with fresh raspberries, cream, and nuts.

Alfonso XII 6. ✆ **91-532-35-96.** Reservations required. Jackets and ties for men. Main courses 36€–60€. AE, DC, MC, V. Mon–Fri 1:30–4pm; Mon–Sat 8:30pm–midnight. Metro: Retiro.

La Gamella ★★ CALIFORNIAN/CASTILIAN La Gamella established its gastronomic reputation shortly after it opened several years ago in another part of town. In 1988, its Illinois-born owner Dick Stephens moved his restaurant into the 19th-century building where the Spanish philosopher Ortega y Gasset was born. The prestigious Horcher, one of the capital's legendary restaurants (see above), is just across the street, but the food at La Gamella is better. The russet-colored, high-ceilinged design invites customers to relax. Mr. Stephens has prepared his delicate and light-textured specialties for the king and queen of Spain, as well as for Madrid's most talked-about artists and merchants, many of whom he knows and greets personally between sessions in his kitchen.

Typical menu items include a ceviche of Mediterranean fish, sliced duck liver in truffle sauce, a dollop of goat cheese served over caramelized endive, duck breast with peppers, and an array of well-prepared desserts, including an all-American cheesecake. Traditional Spanish dishes such as chicken with garlic have been added to the menu, plus what has been called "the only edible hamburger in Madrid."

Alfonso XII 4. ✆ **91-532-45-09.** Reservations required. Main courses 30€–45€. AE, DC, MC, V. Daily 1:30–4pm and 9pm–midnight. Closed 4 days around Easter. Metro: Retiro. Bus: 19.

La Trainera ★ SEAFOOD This restaurant is more expensive, and more chic, than its sprawling, paneled interior might imply. Capable of seating up to 300 diners at a time, it occupies a quartet of dining rooms within a turn-of-the-century building in the glamorous shopping neighborhood of Serrano. Look for vaguely Basque-inspired platters of very fresh seafood, which arrive steaming hot and drizzled with subtle combinations of herbs, wines, and olive oils. No meat of any kind is served here. Instead, you'll find spicy and garlic-enriched versions of fish soup, filet of sole prepared in any of several different versions, Cantabrian crayfish, and well-conceived versions of a *salpicón de mariscos* (a platter of shellfish). Other fish include red mullet, swordfish with capers, monkfish, and virtually anything else that swims. Any of them can be preceded with a heaping platter of shellfish set atop a bed of artfully arranged seaweed. Succulent shellfish, including lobster, shrimp, crab, and mussels, plus an array of other items, is market-priced by weight.

Calle Lagasca 60. ✆ **91-576-80-35.** Reservations recommended. Main courses 18€–40€. AE, DC, MC, V. Mon–Sat 1–4pm and 8pm–midnight. Metro: Serrano.

Pedro Larumbe ★ BASQUE/FRENCH You dine in style here in an opulent section of La Castellana close to the Plaza de Colón. This century-old building was once the headquarters of the famous newspaper *ABC*. Today, it is the elegant restaurant of National Gastronomic Award winner Pedro Larumbe. There are three dining areas, each as elegant as the others: the classic Salón Pompeyano, the Art Deco Salón Fundador, and the beautifully tiled Patio Andalús. This Navarrese chef not only likes a fin-de-siècle decor, he prefers turn-of-the-century cookery as well. His specialties are often from the tried-and-true recipes of yesterday, as evoked by his *solomillo a la mostaza,* or steak with mustard sauce. He also specializes in hake in green sauce with mussels, a favorite dish of the Basque country. One of his specialties is *ensalada de bocavante con salsa de almendras* (lobster salad with almond dressing), a true delight. The service is impeccable, the wine list well chosen, and the desserts something to write home about: tiramisu with a sweet wine and caramel sauce or "tear drops" of chocolate—that is dark and rich tear-shaped chocolate pieces.

Serrano 61. ✆ **91-575-11-12.** Reservations required. Main course 17€–30€; *menú completo* 45€. AE, DC, MC, V. Mon–Fri 1:30–4pm and 9pm–midnight; Sat 9pm–midnight. Closed Aug 15–30 and Easter week. Metro: Rubén Darío and Núñez de Balboa.

Suntory ★ JAPANESE This is Madrid's leading Japanese restaurant. Already acclaimed for its chain restaurants around the world, Suntory has invaded an attractive section of La Castellana and is winning converts to its impeccably prepared cuisine. Decorated in a minimalist style evocative of other Japanese restaurants around the world, this is the domain of Ken Sato, acclaimed as the finest Japanese chef in Spain. There are three dining areas, including the Teppan Yaki, the Shabu-Shabu, and a sushi bar. The finest and freshest of fish and shellfish is served here. Visiting Japanese praise the quality of fish found in Spanish waters. Try some of the exquisite sushi or the Mediterranean prawn tempura. The red tuna sashimi is our favorite. Finish these delicacies with a tempura helado or cake with vanilla icing.

Paseo Castellana 36. ✆ **91-577-37-34.** Reservations recommended. *Menú completo* 39€–72€. AE, DC, MC, V. Mon–Sat 1:30–3:30pm and 8:30–11:30pm. Metro: Rubén Darío.

Viridiana INTERNATIONAL Viridiana—named after the 1961 Luis Buñuel film classic—is praised as one of the up-and-coming restaurants of Madrid, known for the creative imagination of its chef and part-owner, Abraham García, who has lined the walls with stills from Buñuel films. (He is also a film historian, not just a self-taught chef.) Menu specialties are contemporary adaptations of traditional recipes, and they change frequently according to availability. Examples of the individualistic cooking include a salad of exotic lettuces served with smoked salmon, a chicken pastilla laced with cinnamon, baby squid with curry served on a bed of lentils, roasted lamb served in puff pastry with fresh basil, and the choicest langostinos from Cádiz. The food is sublime, and the inviting ambience makes you relax as you sit back to enjoy dishes that dazzle the eye, notably venison and rabbit arranged on a plate with fresh greens to evoke an autumnal scene in a forest.

Juan de Mena 14. ✆ **91-531-52-22.** Reservations recommended. Main courses 28€–48€. V. Mon–Sat 1:30–4pm and 9pm–midnight. Closed 1 week at Easter. Metro: Banco.

MODERATE

Gran Café de Gijón SPANISH If you want food and atmosphere like it was in Franco's heyday, drop in here. Each of the old European capitals has a coffeehouse that traditionally attracts the literati—in Madrid it's the Gijón, which opened in 1888 in the heyday of the Belle Epoque. Artists and writers still patronize this venerated old cafe, many of them spending hours over one cup of coffee. Open windows look out onto the wide paseo and a large terrace is perfect for sun worshippers and bird-watchers. Along one side of the cafe is a stand-up bar; on the lower level is a restaurant. In summer, sit in the garden to enjoy a *blanco y negro* (black coffee with ice cream) or a mixed drink.

Paseo de Recoletos 21. ✆ **91-521-54-25.** Reservations required for restaurant. Main courses 14€–21€; fixed-price menu 9.60€–22€. AE, DC, MC, V. Sun–Fri 7am–1:30am; Sat 7am–2am. Metro: Banco de España, Colón, or Recoletos.

CHAMBERI

VERY EXPENSIVE

Jockey ★★★ INTERNATIONAL This is a deluxe culinary citadel. For decades, this was the premier restaurant of Spain. A favorite of international celebrities, diplomats, and heads of state, it was once known as the Jockey Club, although "Club" was eventually dropped because it suggested exclusivity. The restaurant, with tables on two levels, isn't large. Wood-paneled walls and colored linen provide a cozy ambience. Against the paneling are a dozen prints of jockeys mounted on horses—hence the name.

Since Jockey's establishment shortly after World War II, each chef who has come along has prided himself on coming up with new and creative dishes. You can still order Beluga caviar from Iran, but might settle happily for the goose-liver terrine or slices of Jabugo ham. Cold melon soup with shrimp is soothing on a hot day, especially when followed by grill-roasted young pigeon from Talavera or sole filets with figs in chardonnay. Stuffed small chicken Jockey style is a specialty, as is *tripa madrileña,* a local dish. Desserts are sumptuous.

Amador de los Ríos 6. ✆ **91-319-24-35.** Reservations required. Main courses 21€–35€. AE, DC, MC, V. Daily 1–4pm and 9pm–midnight. Closed Aug. Metro: Colón.

EXPENSIVE

La Fuencisla ★ SPANISH Near El Museo Romántico is this small but comfortable restaurant that for nearly half a century has been serving meals in the traditional Spanish style. A family business, La Fuencisla (named as an offering to the Virgin of Segovia) is run by Señor and Señora de Frutos. Señor de Frutos greets the visitors in the front while the Señora creates tasty homemade meals in the kitchen. The dishes are typical of the Segovian kitchen, and ingredients are prepared according to time-tested recipes. No dish is more typical than the grilled chops of milk-fed lamb, praised by gastronomes. Begin with fresh asparagus in country butter and aromatic garlic or savory mussels in a marinara sauce. Filet of tuna freshly baked in the oven is another pleaser. For desserts, the cooks always prepare homemade tarts, which are especially good when the fresh fruit comes in. Otherwise, you might opt for the rice pudding or *flan de coco* (coconut pudding).

San Mateo 4. ✆ **91-521-61-86.** Reservations recommended. Main courses 15€–20€; *menú completo* 36€. AE, DC, MC, V. Mon–Sat 2–4pm and 9pm–1am. Closed Aug. Metro: Tribunal.

La Paloma ★ BASQUE/FRENCH In the exclusive Barrio Salamanca, this small but comfortable restaurant is the showcase for the culinary talents of chef-owner Segundo Alonso, who made a stellar reputation at the more exclusive El Amparo. Many of his fans followed him here and have since become regulars. His restaurant is in a nostalgic old restored house with high ceilings and wooden beams. His French and Basque dishes are some of the finest of their kind in

Madrid. His food is robust, and he's known for what is called "variety meats," especially pigs' trotters. Even if you have never sampled this dish before, dare to here. You might be glad you did. You could settle instead for his equally celebrated wood pigeon stuffed with foie gras. He also does an excellent lasagna with crabmeat, spinach, and leeks, and a fine *rabo de toro* (bull's tail) stewed in red-wine sauce. The best fish dish is grilled turbot with tomato paste and thyme or sea urchin gratinéed and served with quail eggs. For dessert, try fresh dates with Chantilly cream or a velvety almond mousse with cinnamon ice cream.

Jorge Juan 39. ✆ **91-576-86-92.** Reservations recommended. Main courses 17€–26€; *menú completo* 51€. AE, DC, MC, V. Mon–Sat 1:30–4pm and 9pm–midnight. Metro: Vergara and Velázquez.

Las Cuatro Estaciones ★★★ MEDITERRANEAN Las Cuatro Estaciones is placed by gastronomes and horticulturists alike among their favorite Madrid dining spots, and is neck-and-neck with the prestigious Jockey. In addition to superb food, the establishment prides itself on decorating with masses of flowers that change with the season. Depending on the time of year, the mirrors surrounding the multilevel bar near the entrance reflect thousands of hydrangeas, chrysanthemums, or poinsettias. Each person involved in food preparation spends a prolonged apprenticeship at restaurants in France before returning home to try their talents on the taste buds of aristocratic Madrid.

Representative specialties include crab bisque; a petite marmite of fish and shellfish; and a nouvelle cuisine version of blanquette of monkfish so tender it melts in your mouth. The desserts include daily specials brought temptingly to your table.

General Ibáñez Ibero 5. ✆ **91-553-63-05.** Reservations required. Main courses 42€–54€; fixed-price dinner 45€. AE, DC, MC, V. Mon–Fri 1:30–4pm; Mon–Sat 9pm–midnight. Closed Easter and Aug. Metro: Guzmán el Bueno.

Restaurante Belagua BASQUE This glamorous restaurant was originally built in 1894 as a small palace in the French neoclassical style. In 1991 Catalán designer Josep Joanpere helped transform the building into a carefully detailed hotel (the Santo Mauro), which we've recommended separately (see earlier in this chapter). On the hotel premises is this highly appealing postmodern restaurant, today one of the capital's finest.

Assisted by the well-mannered staff, you'll select from a menu whose inspiration and ingredients change with the seasons. Examples include watermelon-and-prawn salad, light cream of cold ginger soup, haddock baked in a crust of potatoes tinted with squid ink, filet of monkfish with prawn-and-zucchini sauce, and duck with honey and black cherries. Depending on the selection that day, dessert might include miniature portions of flan with strawberry sauce plus an array of the day's pastries. The restaurant's name, incidentally, derives from a village in Navarre known for its natural beauty.

In the Hotel Palacio Santo Mauro, Calle Zurbano 36. ✆ **91-319-69-00.** Reservations recommended. Main courses 15€–25€. AE, DC, MC, V. Daily 1:30–3:30pm and 8:30–11:30pm. Metro: Rubén Darío or Alonso Martínez.

MODERATE

Teatriz ★ ITALIAN Decorated by the famed French architect and designer Philippe Starck, this old theater is now transformed into a top-notch Italian restaurant. Theater seats have long given way to dining tables, but Starck kept many of the elements of the old theater. As you head for the restrooms, you encounter a stunning fountain of marble, silver, and gold, everything bathed in a bluish light, making you think you're in a nightclub. The kitchen closes at midnight, but the bar remains open until 3am. The dishes are genuine and cleverly crafted. Launch yourself with fresh mozzarella with tomatoes in virgin olive oil or raw salmon and turbot flavored with fresh dill. One of the best pastas is a tortellini filled with Parmesan-flavored ground meat. The desserts are worth saving room for, including cannelloni stuffed with dark chocolate or a fresh cheese mousse with mango ice cream. There is also a velvety smooth tiramisu.

Calle Hermosilla 15. ✆ **91-577-53-79.** Reservations recommended. Main courses 11€–17€; *menú completo* 20€. AE, DC, MC, V. Daily 1:30–4pm and 8:30pm–12:30am. Closed Aug. Metro: Serrano.

INEXPENSIVE

Foster's Hollywood *Kids* AMERICAN When your addiction to Stateside food becomes overwhelming, head here. When Foster's opened its doors in 1971, it was not only the first American-style restaurant in Spain, but one of the first in Europe. Since those early days, it has grown to 15 restaurants in Madrid and has even opened branches in Florida. A popular hangout for both locals and visiting Yanks, it offers a choice of dining rooms, ranging from classical club to a faux film studio with props. The varied menu includes Tex-Mex selections, ribs, steaks, sandwiches, freshly made salads, and, as its signature product, hamburgers grilled over natural charcoal. The *New York Times* once claimed that it had "probably the best onion rings in the world."

Paseo de la Castellana 116–118 ✆ **91-564-63-08.** Main courses 6€–17€. AE, DC, MC, V. Sun–Thurs 1pm–midnight; Fri–Sat 1pm–2am. Metro: Nuevo Ministerio.

NEAR ALONSO MARTINEZ

MODERATE

Café Balear PAELLA/SEAFOOD Only a handful of other restaurants in Madrid focus as aggressively as this one on the national dish of Spain, paella, which here comes in 14 different versions with permutations that might surprise even the most jaded aficionado. Within a yellow-and-white dining room loaded with potted plants, you can order any of several paellas here, including versions with shellfish, with chicken and shellfish, with pork, with crabs, with lobster, and an all-black version that's tinted with squid ink for extra flavor. There's even a vegetarian version if you absolutely, positively hate fish. Lots of journalists, writers, poets, and artists seem to have adopted this place.

Calle Sagunto 18. ✆ **91-447-91-15.** Reservations recommended. Main courses 10€–14€. AE, MC, V. Daily 1:30–4pm; Tues–Sat 8:30–11:30pm. Metro: Iglesia.

Casa Vallejo SPANISH This hardworking bistro with a not terribly subtle staff offers less exposure to international clients than some of its competitors. Despite that, you'll find a sense of culinary integrity that's based on a devotion to fresh ingredients and a rigid allegiance to time-tested Spanish recipes. Occupying a turn-of-the-century building, it contains room for only 42 diners at a time. Menu items include garlic soup; tartlets layered with tomatoes, zucchini, and cheese; a ragout of clams and artichokes; croquettes of chicken; breast of chicken garnished with a fricassee of fresh wild mushrooms; pork filet; duck breast in orange or prune sauce; and creamy desserts. Budget gourmands in Madrid praise the hearty flavors here, the robust cookery, and the prices.

Calle San Lorenzo 9. ✆ **91-308-61-58.** Reservations recommended. Main courses 7€–17€; fixed-price menu (available Mon–Fri only) 11.12€–17.43€. MC, V. Mon–Sat 2–4pm; Tues–Sat 9:30pm–midnight. Metro: Tribunal or Alonso Martínez.

Ciao Madrid ITALIAN These two highly successful Italian restaurants are run by members of the extended Laguna family. The older of the two is the branch on Calle Apodaca, established about a dozen years ago; its cohort entered the scene in the early 1990s. Both maintain the same hours, prices, menu, and a decor inspired by the tenets of minimalist Milanese decor, with good-tasting food items that include risottos and pastas, such as ravioli or tagliatelle with wild mushrooms. No one will mind if you order pasta as a main course (lots of clients here do, accompanying it with a green salad). If you're in the mood for a more substantial main course, consider osso buco, veal scaloppini, chicken or veal parmigiana, and any of several kinds of fish.

Calle Apodaca 20 (✆ **91-447-00-36;** Metro: Tribunal) and Calle Argensola 7 (✆ **91-308-25-19;** Metro: Alonso Martínez). Reservations recommended. Pastas 7€–11€; main courses 10€–16€. AE, DC, MC, V. Mon–Fri 1:30–3:45pm; Mon–Sat 9:30pm–midnight. The branch at Calle Apodaca is closed in Sept; branch at Calle Argensola is closed in Aug.

CHAMARTIN

VERY EXPENSIVE

El Chaflán ★ SPANISH One of Madrid's hot new chefs, Juan Pablo Felipe Pablado, is a master in the kitchen. He can take almost any dish, including the classics, and give it a new flavor and texture. For example, he virtually deconstructs the most famous soup of Spain, gazpacho, and reassembles it into *glaces* and mousses. There's a firm hand in control here, and the chef personally selects the best produce, fish, and local meats to concoct his dishes. A recent mushroom risotto was perfectly prepared and full of flavor, as was the main course, a roast suckling pig that would rival any in Segovia, where they say this dish is prepared better than anywhere else in the world.

Av. Pío XII 34. ✆ **91-350-61-93.** Reservations required. Main courses 22€–30€; fixed-price menus 45€–89€. AE, DC, MC, V. Mon–Fri 1:30–4pm; Mon–Sat 9–11:30pm. Metro: Pío XII.

Zalacaín ★★★ INTERNATIONAL Outstanding in both food and decor, Zalacaín is credited with bringing nouvelle cuisine to Spain when it opened its doors back in 1973. It is reached by an illuminated walk from Paseo de la Castellana and housed at the garden end of a modern apartment complex. It's within an easy walk of such deluxe hotels as the Castellana and the Miguel Angel. The name of the restaurant comes from the intrepid hero of Basque author Pío Baroja's 1909 novel, *Zalacaín El Aventurero.* Zalacaín is small, exclusive, and expensive. It has the atmosphere of an elegant old mansion: The walls are covered with textiles, and some are decorated with Audubon-type paintings. Men should wear jackets and ties.

The menu features many Basque and French specialties, often with nouvelle cuisine touches. It might offer a superb sole in a green sauce, but it also knows the glory of grilled pigs' feet. Among the best dishes are oysters with caviar and sherry jelly; crepes stuffed with smoked fish; ravioli stuffed with mushrooms, foie gras, and truffles; bouillabaisse; and veal escalopes in orange sauce. For dessert, we'd suggest one of the custards, perhaps raspberry or chocolate.

Alvarez de Baena 4. ✆ **91-561-48-40.** Reservations required. Main courses 25€–40€; fixed-price menu 82€. AE, DC, MC, V. Mon–Fri 1:15–4pm; Mon–Sat 9pm–midnight. Closed week before Easter and in Aug. Metro: Rubén Darío.

EXPENSIVE

El Bodegón INTERNATIONAL/BASQUE/SPANISH El Bodegón is imbued with the atmosphere of a gentleman's club for hunting enthusiasts. International globetrotters are attracted here, especially in the evening, as the restaurant is near such deluxe hotels as the Castellana and the Miguel Angel. King Juan Carlos and Queen Sofía have dined here.

Waiters in black and white, with gold braid and buttons, bring dignity to the food service. Even bottled water is served champagne-style, chilled in a silver floor stand. There are two main dining rooms, both conservative and oak-beamed in the country-inn style. We recommend starting with cream of crayfish bisque or velvety vichyssoise. Main-course selections include grilled filet mignon with classic béarnaise sauce and venison bourguignonne. Other choices include shellfish au gratin Escoffier, quails Fernand Point, tartare of raw fish marinated in parsley-enriched vinaigrette, and smoked salmon.

Pinar 15. ✆ **91-562-88-44.** Reservations required. Main courses 20€–30€. AE, DC, MC, V. Mon–Fri 1:30–4pm, Mon–Sat 9pm–midnight. Closed holidays and Aug. Metro: Rubén Darío.

El Olivo Restaurant ★★ MEDITERRANEAN Locals praise the success of a non-Spaniard (in this case, French-born Jean Pierre Vandelle) in recognizing the international appeal of two of Spain's most valuable culinary resources: olive oil and sherry. Designed in tones of green and amber, this is the only restaurant in Spain that wheels a cart stocked with 40 regional olive oils from table to table. From the cart, diners select a variety to soak up with chunks of rough-textured bread seasoned with a dash of salt.

Menu specialties include grilled filet of monkfish marinated in herbs and olive oil, then served with black-olive sauce over compote of fresh tomatoes, and four preparations of cod arranged on a single platter and served with a *pil-pil* sauce (cod gelatin and herbs whipped into a mayonnaise-like consistency with olive oil). Dessert might be one of several different chocolate pastries.

Note: Many clients deliberately arrive early as an excuse to linger within El Olivo's one-of-a-kind sherry bar. Although other drinks are offered, the bar features more than 100 brands of *vino de Jerez,* more than practically any other establishment in Madrid. Priced at 1.50€ to 4.50€ per glass, they make the perfect aperitif. Also note that most main courses fall at the lower end of the price listing below.

General Gallegos 1. ✆ **91-359-15-35.** Reservations recommended. Main courses 18.50€–26.50€; fixed-price meals 42€. AE, DC, MC, V. Tues–Sat 1–4pm and 9pm–midnight. Closed Aug 15–31 and 4 days around Easter. Metro: Plaza de Castilla.

La Broche ★★ CATALAN The Catalán chef, Sergi Arola, is generating culinary excitement in Madrid, a Castilian city that in the past never paid a lot of respect to the cuisine of Barcelona. Arola trained under Catalonia's greatest chef, El Ferran Adrià of El Bulli, Arola learned from the master, but in Madrid he is creating his own magic with imaginative dishes. Forget the dull lobby of the Hotel Miguel Angel, a holdover from the 1970s, and enter this elegant dining enclave. Deluxe ingredients, personally selected by the chef and changed to take advantage of the best in any season, are fashioned into some of the capital's most flavor-filled dishes. Launch yourself into your repast with raw seafood and sea-water gelée and then proceed across the heavenly menu, perhaps selecting a salmon risotto or a carpaccio of wild mushrooms. Even the bread placed on your table is freshly made and a delight, as are the creative desserts.

Calle Miguel Angel 29. ✆ **91-399-34-37.** Reservations required. Main courses 24€–26€. AE, DC, MC, V. Mon–Fri 2–3:15pm and 9–11:30pm. Closed Aug. Metro: Rubén Darío or Gregorio Marañón.

Príncipe de Viana ★ BASQUE This place has gotten rave reviews. Fish is of course the most important staple of Basque cuisine, and there is a wide selection from which to choose. You might go the traditional route, with *bacalao ajoarriera* (cod with red peppers and tomatoes) and *merluza en salsa verde* (hake in parsley, garlic, and olive oil sauce). There are more adventurous modern concoctions, such as a salad with *chipirones* (baby squid) and *mollejas* (sweet meats) in a soya vinaigrette. Those with a sweet tooth will be more than satisfied with the dessert of cream cheese and mango sorbet. From the many Spanish and occasional foreign wines to choose from, the Albirino from Galicia is particularly recommended.

Calle Manuel de Falla 5. ✆ **91-457-15-49.** Reservations required. Main courses 12€–18€. AE, DC, MC, V. Mon–Fri 1–4pm and 9–11:30pm; Sat 9–11:30pm. Closed in Aug. Metro: Lima or Cuzco.

MODERATE

El Cabo Mayor ★★ SPANISH Near Chamartín train station, this is one of the best, most popular, and most stylish restaurants in Madrid, attracting on occasion the king and queen of Spain. An open-air staircase leading to the entranceway descends from a manicured garden on a quiet side street where a battalion of uniformed doormen stands ready to greet arriving taxis. The restaurant's decor is nautically inspired, with hardwood panels, brass trim, pulleys and ropes, a tile floor custom-painted with sea-green and blue replicas of waves, and hand-carved models of fishing boats. Some dozen bronze statues honoring fishers and their craft are displayed in brass portholes in illuminated positions of honor.

Menu choices include paprika-laden peppers stuffed with fish, a salad composed of Jabugo ham and foie gras of duckling, Cantabrian fish soup, stewed sea bream with thyme, asparagus mousse, salmon in sherry sauce, and loin of veal in cassis sauce. Desserts include a rice mousse with pine-nut sauce.

Juan Ramón Jiménez 37. ✆ **91-350-87-76.** Reservations recommended. Main courses 14€–30.65€. AE, DC, MC, V. Mon–Sat 1:30–4pm and 8:45–11:45pm. Closed 1 week at Easter. Metro: Cuzco.

Goizeko Kabi ★ BASQUE This restaurant serves some of the best Basque dishes in Madrid in an intimate, understated interior. Particularly delicious is the starter of *boquerones,* almost sweet anchovies marinated in garlic and olive oil. We loved the *bacalao pil-pil vizcaina* (cod in a Basque garlic sauce) and the wonderfully juicy king prawns. Dessert lovers will revel in the orange mousse with a coating of bitter chocolate or the more experimental black bread ice cream with coffee sauce.

Comandante Zorita 37. ✆ **91-533-01-85.** Reservations recommended. Main courses 11€–30€. AE, DC, MC, V. Mon–Sat 1–4pm and 8:30pm–midnight. Metro: Alvarado.

O'Pazo ★ GALICIAN/SEAFOOD This deluxe Galician restaurant is viewed by local cognoscenti as one of the top seafood places in the country. The fish is flown in daily from Galicia and mostly priced by weight at market rates. In front is a cocktail lounge and bar, all polished brass, with low sofas and paintings. Carpeted floors, cushioned Castilian furniture, soft lighting, and colored-glass windows complete the picture.

The fish and shellfish soup is delectable, although others gravitate to the seaman's broth as a beginning course. Natural clams are succulent, as are *cigalas* (a kind of crayfish), spider crabs, and Jabugo ham. Main dishes range from baby eels to sea snails, from Galician style scallops to *zarzuela* (a seafood casserole).

Calle Reina Mercedes 20. ✆ **91-553-23-33.** Reservations required. Main courses 13€–25€. MC, V. Mon–Sat 1–4pm and 8:30pm–midnight. Closed Aug. Metro: Nuevos Ministerios or Alvarado. Bus: 3 or 5.

INEXPENSIVE

Alfredo's Barbacoa AMERICAN Alfredo's is a popular rendezvous for Americans longing for home-style food. Al himself arrives at his bar/restaurant wearing boots, blue jeans, and a 10-gallon hat; his friendly welcome has made the place a center for both his friends and newcomers to Madrid. You *can* have hamburgers here, but they are of the barbecued variety, and you might prefer the barbecued spareribs or chicken. The salad bar is an attraction. And it's a rare treat to be able to have corn on the cob in Spain.

The original **Alfredo's Barbacoa,** Lagasca 5 (✆ **91-576-62-71;** Metro: Retiro), is still in business, and also under Al's auspices.

Juan Hurtado de Mendoza 11. ✆ **91-345-16-39.** Reservations recommended. Main courses 6.75€–15€. AE, DC, MC, V. Mon–Sat 1–4:30pm and 8:30pm–midnight (Fri and Sat until 1am). Metro: Cuzco.

CHUECA

INEXPENSIVE

Nabucco ITALIAN In a neighborhood of Spanish restaurants, the Italian trattoria format here comes as a welcome change. The decor resembles a postmodern update of an Italian ruin, complete with trompe l'oeil walls painted like marble. Roman portrait busts and a prominent bar lend a dignified air. Menu choices include cannelloni, a good selection of veal dishes, and such main courses as osso buco. You might begin your meal with a selection of antipasti.

Calle Hortaleza 108. ✆ **91-310-06-11.** Reservations recommended. Pizza 4.55€–6€; main courses 6€–10€. AE, DC, MC, V. Daily 1:30–4pm; Sun–Thurs 8:45pm–midnight; Fri–Sat 8:45pm–1am. Metro: Alonso Martínez. Bus: 7 or 36.

Restaurante Salvador SPANISH/BASQUE This is a robust, macho enclave of Madrid. The owner of this bustling restaurant, José Blasquez García, configured it as a mini-museum to his hobby and passion, the Spanish art of bullfighting. Inside, near a bar that stocks an impressive collection of sherries and whiskies, you'll find the memorabilia of years of bull-watching, including photographs of great matadors beginning in the 1920s, and agrarian artifacts used in the raising and development of fighting bulls. The menu is as robust and two-fisted as the decor, featuring macho-sized platters of oxtail in red-wine sauce; different preparations of hake, one of which is baked delectably in a salt crust; stuffed peppers, fried calamari, and shrimp; and for dessert, the local version of *arroz con leche.*

Calle Barbieri 12. ✆ **91-521-45-24.** Reservations recommended. Main courses 10€–21€. AE, MC, V. Mon–Sat 1:30–4pm and 9–11:30pm. Closed Aug. Metro: Chueca.

Taberna Carmencita *Finds* SPANISH/BASQUE Carmencita, founded in 1840 and exquisitely restored, is a street-corner enclave of old Spanish charm filled with 19th-century detailing and tile work. It was a favorite hangout for the poet Federico García Lorca, as well as a meeting place for intelligentsia in the pre–Civil War days. Meals might include entrecôte with green pepper sauce, escalope of veal, braised mollusks with port, filet of pork, cod with garlic, and Bilbao-style hake. Every Thursday the special dish is a complicated version of Madrid's famous *cocido,* which patrons wax lyrical over.

Libertad 16. ✆ **91-531-66-12.** Reservations recommended. Main courses 6€–17€; fixed-price menu 9€ available only at lunch. AE, DC, MC, V. Mon–Fri 1–4pm; Mon–Sat 9pm–midnight. Metro: Chueca or Banco de España.

Tienda de Vinos SPANISH Officially this restaurant is known as Tienda de Vinos (the Wine Store), but ever since the 1930s Madrileños have called it "El Comunista" (The Communist). Its now-deceased owner was a fervent Communist, and many locals who shared his political beliefs patronized the establishment. This rickety old wine shop with a few tables in the back is quite fashionable with actors and journalists looking for Spanish fare without frills. There is a menu, but no one ever looks at it—just ask what's available. Nor do you get a bill; you're just told how much to pay. Guests sit at simple wooden tables with wooden chairs and benches; walls are decorated with old posters, calendars, pennants, and clocks. Start with garlic or vegetable soup or lentils, followed by lamb chops, tripe in a spicy sauce, or meatballs and soft-set eggs with asparagus.

Augusto Figueroa 35. ✆ **91-521-70-12.** Main courses 2.50€–7.50€. No credit cards. Mon–Sat 1–4pm and 9pm–midnight. Metro: Chueca.

OFF THE PLAZA MAYOR

MODERATE

Casa Lucio CASTILIAN Set on a historic street whose edges once marked the perimeter of Old Madrid, this is a venerable *tasca* with all the requisite antique accessories. Dozens of cured hams hang from hand-hewn beams above the well-oiled bar. Among the clientele is a stable of sometimes surprisingly well-known public figures—perhaps even the king of Spain. The two dining rooms, each on a different floor, have whitewashed walls, tile floors, and exposed brick. A well-trained staff offers classic Castilian food, which might include Jabugo ham with broad beans, shrimp in garlic sauce, hake with green sauce, several types of roasted lamb, and a thick steak served sizzling hot on a heated platter, called *churrasco de la casa.*

Cava Baja 35. ✆ **91-365-32-52.** Reservations recommended. Main courses 15€–22€. AE, DC, MC, V. Sun–Fri 1–4pm; daily 9pm–midnight. Closed Aug. Metro: La Latina.

El Schotis ★ SPANISH El Schotis was established in 1962 on one of Madrid's oldest and most historic streets. A series of large and pleasingly old-fashioned dining rooms is the setting for an animated crowd of Madrileños and foreign visitors, who receive ample portions of conservative, well-prepared vegetables, salads, soups, fish, and above all, meat. Specialties of the house include roast baby lamb, grilled steaks and veal chops, shrimp with garlic, fried hake in green sauce, and traditional desserts. Although one reader found everything but the gazpacho ho-hum, this local favorite pleases thousands of diners annually. There's a bar near the entrance for tapas and before- or after-dinner drinks.

Cava Baja 11. ✆ **91-365-32-30.** Reservations recommended. Main courses 10.50€–16.50€; fixed-price menu 21€. AE, DC, MC, V. Mon–Sat 1–4pm and 8:30pm–midnight; Sun 1–4pm. Metro: Puerta del Sol or La Latina.

La Posada de la Villa SPANISH/GRILLED MEATS This historic inn founded in 1642 offers a modern, more sanitized version of the earthy, grilled cuisine that fed the stonemasons who built the building's thick walls. Within a trio of dining rooms whose textured plaster and old stonework absolutely reeks of Old Castile, you'll find a hardworking staff and a menu that focuses on a time-honored specialty—roasted baby lamb—that's ordered more often than anything else on the menu. Other excellent choices include different versions of hake, Madrid-style tripe, and the rich, savory stew (*cocido madrileño*) that many local residents remember fondly from the days of their childhood. Notice that many of the chairs have brass plaques bearing the names of famous patrons—we saw one labeled "Janet Jackson" last time!

Cava Baja 9. ✆ **91-366-18-60.** Reservations recommended. Main courses 11€–18€. DC, MC, V. Daily 1–4pm; Mon–Sat 8pm–midnight. Closed Aug. Metro: La Latina.

Los Galayos ★★ SPANISH Its location is among the most desirable in the city, on a narrow side street about three steps from the arcades of Plaza Mayor. Within two separate houses, the restaurant has flourished on this site since 1894.

In summer, cascades of vines accent a series of tables and chairs on the cobblestones outside, perfect for tapas sampling and people-watching. Some visitors consider an evening here among the highlights of their trip to Spain.

The ambience inside evokes Old Castile, with vaulted or beamed ceilings in several dining rooms. The Grande family, your multilingual hosts, prepares traditional versions of fish, shellfish, pork, veal, and beef in time-tested ways. Suckling pig, baby goat, and roasted lamb are almost always featured.

Calle Botoneras 5. ✆ **91-366-30-28.** Reservations recommended. Main courses 10€–24€. AE, DC, MC, V. Daily 8:30am–1am. Metro: Puerta del Sol.

Sobrino de Botín ★★ SPANISH Ernest Hemingway made this restaurant famous. In the final two pages of his novel, *The Sun Also Rises,* Jake invites Brett to Botín for the Segovian specialty of roast suckling pig, washed down with Rioja Alta.

As you enter, you step back to 1725, the year the restaurant was founded. You'll see an open kitchen with a charcoal hearth, hanging copper pots, an 18th-century tile oven for roasting the suckling pig, and a big pot of soup whose aroma wafts across the tables. Painter Francisco Goya was once a dishwasher here. Your host, Antonio, never loses his cool—even when he has 18 guests standing in line waiting for tables.

The two house specialties are roast suckling pig and roast Segovian lamb. From the a la carte menu, you might try the fish-based "quarter-of-an-hour" soup. Good main dishes include baked Cantabrian hake and filet mignon with potatoes. The dessert list features strawberries (in season) with whipped cream. You can accompany your meal with Valdepeñas or Aragón wine, although most guests order sangria.

Calle de Cuchilleros 17. ✆ **91-366-30-26.** Reservations required. Main courses 16€–46€; fixed-price menu 27.55€. AE, DC, MC, V. Daily 1–4pm and 8pm–midnight. Metro: La Latina or Opera.

INEXPENSIVE

El Cosaco RUSSIAN One of the few Russian restaurants in Madrid sits adjacent to one of the most charming and evocative squares in town. Inside, you'll find a trio of dining rooms outfitted with paintings and artifacts from the former Soviet Union. Menu items seem to taste best when preceded with something from a long list of vodkas, many of them from small-scale distilleries you might not immediately recognize. Items include rich and savory cold-weather

---

Moments Picnic, Anyone?

On a hot day, do as the Madrileños do: Secure the makings of a picnic lunch and head for Casa de Campo (Metro: El Batón), those once-royal hunting grounds in the west of Madrid across the Manzanares River. Children delight in this adventure, as they can also visit a boating lake, the Parque de Atracciones, and the Madrid zoo.

Your best choice for picnic fare is **Rodilla,** Preciados 25 (✆ **91-522-54-67;** Metro: Callao), where you can find sandwiches, pastries, and take-out tapas. Sandwiches, including vegetarian, meat, and fish, begin at .75 . It's open Monday and Tuesday from 8:30am to 10:30pm; Wednesday, Thursday, and Sunday from 9am to 11pm; Friday and Saturday from 9am to 11:30pm.

---

dishes that seem a bit disjointed from the sweltering heat of Madrid, but which you might find as satisfying alternatives from the all-Spanish restaurants in the same neighborhood. Examples include beef Stroganoff; quenelles of pike-perch with fresh dill; and thin-sliced smoked salmon or smoked sturgeon that's artfully arranged with capers, chopped onions, and chopped hard-boiled eggs. Red or white versions of borscht make a worthy starter, and blinis, stuffed with caviar or paprika-laced beef, are always excellent.

Plaza de la Paja 2. ✆ **91-365-35-48.** Reservations recommended. Main courses 6€–14€. AE, DC, MC, V. Daily 9pm–midnight; Sat–Sun 1:30–3:30pm. Metro: La Latina.

IN THE ARTURO SORIA DISTRICT

MODERATE

Nicómedes ★ *Finds* EXTREMADURAN This is a real discovery. This colonial-style building has been completely refurbished by the charming Suárez sisters into a modern-looking château of five floors with beautiful, tall bay windows covering the full height of this impressive edifice. The immensity of the windows allows copious amounts of natural light to flood into the dining areas. The pervading atmosphere is one of openness combined with friendly hospitality. Customers often dine out in fine weather on a summer terrace. The modernity of the building is reflected in the style of the cuisine as well. The dishes from the western province of Extremadura are given a Madrid showcase here. Goat cheese with glazed onions is a tasty opener, as are *bolsitas rellenas de gamba y queso fresco* (crispy pasta balls stuffed with shrimp and freshly made cheese). *Rapa al horno con habitas y ajetes* (baked monkfish with beans and tender garlic) is a savory offering, although *solomillo de buey* (fondue of ox steak) is more typical of the region. For dessert, try the homemade cake of the day or a special sweet "biscuit" made with prunes and served with a caramel sauce.

Moscatelar 18. ✆ **91-388-78-28.** Reservations recommended. Main courses 12€–16€. AE, DC, V. Tues–Sat 1:30–3:30pm and 9:30–midnight; Sun 1:30–3:30pm. Closed Aug. Metro: Esperanza and Arturo Soria.

NEAR PLAZA REPUBLICA ARGENTINA

MODERATE

Principe y Serrano ★ CASTILIAN In an exclusive area of the Serrano district, this classic restaurant exudes distinction. Its sophisticated dining areas on both floors offer a warm and cozy atmosphere, and the outside lawns and flowered patios (one of them resembling a miniature golf course with small swimming pools) make you forget you are in the center of a big city. There is the big *salón central,* two small dining areas for more private dinners, plus a bar downstairs. The cooking is simple, yet cosmopolitan, and always done to perfection. One especially good dish is roast potatoes with mussels. Based on the sea's bounty, try the *manitas de ibérico rellenas de morcilla* (pork filled with chorizo sausage). We take delight in the freshly made apple tart with prune sauce or the crepes filled with mango and served in a fancy caramel cream sauce.

Serrano 240. ✆ **91-458-62-31.** Reservations recommended. Main courses 12€–22€. AE, DC, MC, V. Daily 1:30–4pm; Mon–Sat 9pm–midnight. Closed Aug. Metro: Colombia and Concha Espino.

INEXPENSIVE

La Atalaya *Value* CANTABRIAN The owner of this pleasant restaurant, Gena Sánchez, hails from Santander in Northern Spain and, in the typical style of her hometown, has decorated the yellow walls of her establishment with a plethora of modern paintings. The food is also typical of Spain's green northern coast, with an emphasis on fresh fish. Every Thursday and Saturday the chefs prepare the most typical dish of Santander, a hearty cabbage soup. Called *cocido montanés,* it is also made with sausage, green beans, and black pudding. *Caracoles marucas,* or clams Santander style, prepared in a spicy sauce, is another good offering, as is *sopa de pescado,* or fish soup, one of the finest of its kind in Madrid. You might opt for a *torta de queso caliente,* a warm cheese soufflé. For dessert, traditional regional puddings are served.

Joaquín Costa 31. ✆ **91-562-87-45.** Reservations recommended. Main courses 10€–16€; fixed-price menu 12.20€. AE, DC, MC, V. Tues–Sat 1:30–4pm and 9pm–midnight. Metro: República de Argentina.

NEAR CIUDAD UNIVERSITARIA

EXPENSIVE

San Mamés ★ BASQUE/MADRILEÑA Situated in the north of the city in a historic building, this restaurant has been in the hands of the García family more than 50 years. The *tasca* (tavern) is decorated with colorful ceramic tiles and photographs of the celebrities who have dined here over the years. It is considered something of a secret address. With only two rooms, it has a homelike atmosphere of intimacy and good cheer. The cuisine offered is some of the best from both the Madrid and Basque kitchens. The owners shop carefully for the ingredients to prepare a repertoire of very tasty and well-flavored dishes. Their most typical dish is *callos a la madrileña,* a tripe stew with meat and chickpeas, beloved by their habitués. Otherwise, you might opt for *bacalao ajoarriero* (salt cod prepared with green peppers, tomatoes, and onions). Another dish favored in the Basque country is *cocochas de merluza,* which are the cheeks of the hake fish served with a bread sauce. For dessert, the owners recommend their *requesón con pasas* (cheesecake with raisins), or a hearty pudding called *tocino de cielo.*

Bravo Murillo 88. ✆ **91-534-50-65.** Reservations recommended. Main courses 17€–22€; fixed-price menus 30€–36€. AE, DC, MC, V. Mon–Fri 1:30–4pm and 8:30–11:30pm; Sat 1:30–4pm. Closed Aug. Metro: Cuatro Caminos.

INEXPENSIVE

Las Batuecas *Value* SPANISH This restaurant unpretentiously calls itself a *casa de comidas,* or "meal house." Since 1954, the little restaurant of José Pascual and his family has been located near the *ciudad universitaria.* Many of their customers originally came here as students, and over the years have become devotees of the homemade Spanish food, which is wholesome and good without being pretentious. The decoration is plain, with old paintings and newspaper articles intermixed with cartoons and reviews by travel and food magazines in different languages. It has two floors with tables, all in the rustic style. But no one comes here for decor; the food is the attraction. Come here with a big appetite and launch yourself into a fine meal with such dishes as *tortilla de callos* (omelet with tripe), or perhaps squid cooked in its ink. You can try their fresh artichokes cooked with white wine and ham or *berenjenas rebosadas* (sliced eggplant batter-fried). One of the tastiest main dishes is shoulder flank of lamb roast, perfectly done. Desserts include almond, vanilla, or chocolate cakes, or a fine selection of puddings. Note that dinner is served only two nights a week.

Av. Reina Victoria 17. ✆ **91-554-04-52.** Reservations required. Main courses 16€–24€; *menú completo* 18€. No credit cards. Mon–Sat 1–4pm; Thurs–Fri 9–11pm. Closed Aug. Metro: Guzmán El Bueno and Cuatro Caminos.

NEAR RECOLETOS

La Galette VEGETARIAN/INTERNATIONAL La Galette was one of Madrid's first vegetarian restaurants, and it remains one of the best. Small and charming, it lies in a residential and shopping area in the exclusive Salamanca district, near Plaza de la Independencia and the northern edge of Retiro Park. There is a limited selection of meat dishes, but the true allure lies in this establishment's imaginative preparation of vegetables. Examples include baked stuffed peppers, omelets, eggplant croquettes, and even vegetarian hamburgers. Some of the dishes are macrobiotic. The place is also noted for its mouth-watering pastries. The same owners also operate La Galette II, in the same complex.

Conde de Aranda 11. ✆ **91-576-06-41.** Reservations recommended. Main courses 6€–18€; fixed-price lunch 7€. AE, DC, MC, V. Mon–Sat 2–4pm and 9pm–midnight. Metro: Retiro.

THE BEST OF THE *TASCAS*

Don't starve waiting around for Madrid's fashionable 9:30 or 10pm dinner hour. Throughout the city you'll find *tascas,* bars that serve wine and platters of tempting hot and cold hors d'oeuvres known as tapas: mushrooms, salads, baby eels, shrimp, lobster, mussels, sausage, ham, and, in one establishment at least, bull testicles. Below we've listed our favorite tapas bars. Keep in mind that you can often save euros by ordering at the bar rather than occupying a table.

Antonio Sánchez TAPAS Named in 1850 after the founder's son, who was killed in the bullring, Antonio Sánchez is full of bullfighting memorabilia, including the stuffed head of the animal that gored young Sánchez. Also featured on the dark paneled walls are three works by the Spanish artist Zuloaga, who had his last public exhibition in this restaurant near Plaza Tirso de Molina. A limited array of tapas, including garlic soup, are served with Valdepeñas wine drawn from a barrel—though many guests ignore the edibles in favor of smoking cigarettes and arguing the merits of this or that bullfighter. A restaurant in the back serves Spanish food with a vaguely French influence.

Mesón de Parades 13. ✆ **91-539-78-26.** Tapas (in the bar) 1.50€–2.10€; main courses 7€–11€; fixed-price lunch (Mon–Fri only) 6.60€. MC, V. Daily 1–4pm; Mon–Sat 8pm–midnight. Metro: Tirso de Molina.

Casa Mingo SPANISH Casa Mingo has been known for decades for its cider, both still and bubbly. The perfect accompanying tidbit is a piece of the local Asturian *cabrales* (goat cheese), but the roast chicken is the specialty of the house, with a large number of helpings served daily. There's no formality here; customers share big tables under the vaulted ceiling in the dining room. In summer, the staff sets up tables and wooden chairs out on the sidewalk. This is not so much a restaurant as a *bodega/taverna* that serves food.

Paseo de la Florida 34. ✆ **91-547-79-18.** Main courses 3.30€–7€. No credit cards. Daily 11am–midnight. Metro: Príncipe Pío, then 15-min. walk.

Cervecería Alemania TAPAS This place earned its name because of its long-ago German clients. Opening directly onto one of the liveliest little plazas in Madrid, it clings to its turn-of-the-century traditions. Young Madrileños are fond of stopping in for a mug of draft beer. You can sit at one of the tables leisurely sipping beer or wine since the waiters make no attempt to hurry you along. To accompany your beverage, try the fried sardines or a Spanish omelet. Many of the *tascas* on this popular square are crowded and noisy—often with blaring loud music—but this one is quiet and a good place to have a conversation.

Plaza de Santa Ana 6. ✆ **91-429-70-33.** Beer 1.20€–2.40€; tapas 1.80€–12€. No credit cards. Sun–Thurs 11am–12:30am; Fri–Sat 11am–2am. Metro: Tirso de Molina.

6

Exploring Madrid

In recent years, Madrid has changed drastically. No longer is it fair to say that one should only go there for the Prado and as a base for exploring Toledo or El Escorial. Those are still important draws, of course. But as you'll discover, Madrid has something to amuse and delight everyone.

1 The Major Museums

Museo del Prado ★★★ With more than 7,000 paintings, the Prado is one of the most important repositories of art in the world. It began as a royal collection and was enlarged by the Hapsburgs, especially Charles V, and later the Bourbons. In paintings of the Spanish school the Prado has no equal; on your first visit, concentrate on the Spanish masters (Velázquez, Goya, El Greco, and Murillo).

Major Italian works are exhibited on the ground floor. You'll see art by Italian masters—Raphael, Botticelli, Mantegna, Andrea del Sarto, Fra Angelico, and Correggio. The most celebrated Italian painting here is Titian's voluptuous Venus being watched by a musician who can't keep his eyes on his work.

The Prado is a trove of the work of El Greco (ca. 1541–1614), the Crete-born artist who lived much of his life in Toledo. You can see a parade of "The Greek's" saints, Madonnas, and Holy Families—even a ghostly *John the Baptist.*

You'll find a splendid array of works by the incomparable Diego Velázquez (1599–1660). The museum's most famous painting, in fact, is his *Las Meninas,* a triumph in the use of light effects. The faces of the queen and king are reflected in the mirror in the painting itself. The artist in the foreground is Velázquez, of course.

The Flemish painter Peter Paul Rubens (1577–1640), who met Velázquez while in Spain, is represented by the peacock-blue *Garden of Love* and by the *Three Graces.* Also noteworthy is the work of José Ribera (1591–1652), a Valencia-born artist and contemporary of Velázquez whose best painting is the *Martyrdom of St. Philip.* The Seville-born Bartolomé Murillo (1617–82)—often referred to as the "painter of Madonnas"—has three *Immaculate Conceptions* on display.

The Prado has an outstanding collection of the work of Hieronymus Bosch (1450?–1516), the Flemish genius. *The Garden of Earthly Delights,* the best-known work of "El Bosco," is here. You'll also see his *Seven Deadly Sins* and his triptych *The Hay Wagon.* See also *The Triumph of Death,* by another Flemish painter, Pieter Breughel the Elder (1525?–69), who carried on Bosch's ghoulish vision.

Francisco de Goya (1746–1828) ranks along with Velázquez and El Greco in the trio of great Spanish artists. Hanging here are his unflattering portraits of his patron, Charles IV, and his family, as well as the *Clothed Maja* and the *Naked Maja.* You can also see the much-reproduced *Third of May* (1808), plus a series of Goya sketches (some of which, depicting the decay of 18th-century Spain, brought the Inquisition down on the artist) and his expressionistic "black paintings."

Paseo del Prado. ✆ **91-330-28-00.** Admission 3€ adults, 1.50€ students and seniors. Tues–Sat 9am–7pm, Sun and holidays 9am–2pm. Closed Jan 1, Good Fri, May 1, and Dec 25. Metro: Banco de España or Atocha. Bus: 10, 14, 27, 34, 37, or 45.

Thyssen-Bornemisza Museum ★★★ Until around 1985, the contents of this museum virtually overflowed the premises of a legendary villa near Lugano, Switzerland. One of the most frequently visited sites of Switzerland, the collection had been laboriously amassed over a period of about 60 years by the Thyssen-Bornemisza family, scions of a century-old shipping, banking, mining, and chemical fortune with roots in Holland, Germany, and Hungary. Experts had proclaimed it as one of the world's most extensive and valuable privately owned collections of paintings, rivaled only by the legendary holdings of Queen Elizabeth II.

For tax and insurance reasons, and because the collection had outgrown the boundaries of the lakeside villa that contained it, the works were discreetly marketed in the early 1980s to the world's major museums. Amid endless intrigue, a litany of glamorous supplicants from eight different nations came calling. Among them were Margaret Thatcher and Prince Charles; trustees of the Getty Museum in Malibu, California; the president of West Germany; the duke of Badajoz, brother-in-law of King Carlos II; even emissaries from Walt Disney World in Orlando, Florida, all hoping to acquire the collection for their respective countries or entities.

Eventually, thanks partly to the lobbying by Baron Hans Heinrich Thyssen-Bornemisza's fifth wife, a Spanish-born beauty (and former Miss Spain) named Tita, the collection was awarded to Spain for US$350 million. Controversies over the public cost of the acquisition raged for months. Despite the brouhaha, various estimates have placed the value of this collection between US$1 billion and US$3 billion.

To house the collection, an 18th-century building adjacent to the Prado, the Villahermosa Palace, was retrofitted with the appropriate lighting and security devices, and renovated at a cost of US$45 million. Rooms are arranged numerically so that by following the order of the various rooms (nos. 1–48, spread out over three floors), a logical sequence of European painting can be traced from the 13th through the 20th centuries. The nucleus of the collection consists of 700 world-class paintings. They include works by, among others, El Greco, Velázquez, Dürer, Rembrandt, Watteau, Canaletto, Caravaggio, Hals, Memling, and Goya.

Goya or No Goya, *The Milkmaid* and *The Colossus* are Still Great Art

Spain's most fabled museum, the Prado, shocked the art world—and visitors, too—when it recently announced that two of its most famous paintings, *The Milkmaid of Bordeaux* and *The Colossus,* attributed to Francisco de Goya, are not in fact the work of this Spanish master. Goya specialists agree. The paintings still hang in the Prado, although their attribution has been changed to "attributed" to Goya instead of "by" Goya. Want to see some real Goyas? The Prado has some 150 actual paintings by the artist. At least we think that they do. Some Goya experts are questioning the authorship of some other "supposed" Goyas, especially several portraits. There was such a market for Goyas at the turn of the 19th century that many art dealers—surprise—kept turning up with "long lost" Goyas.

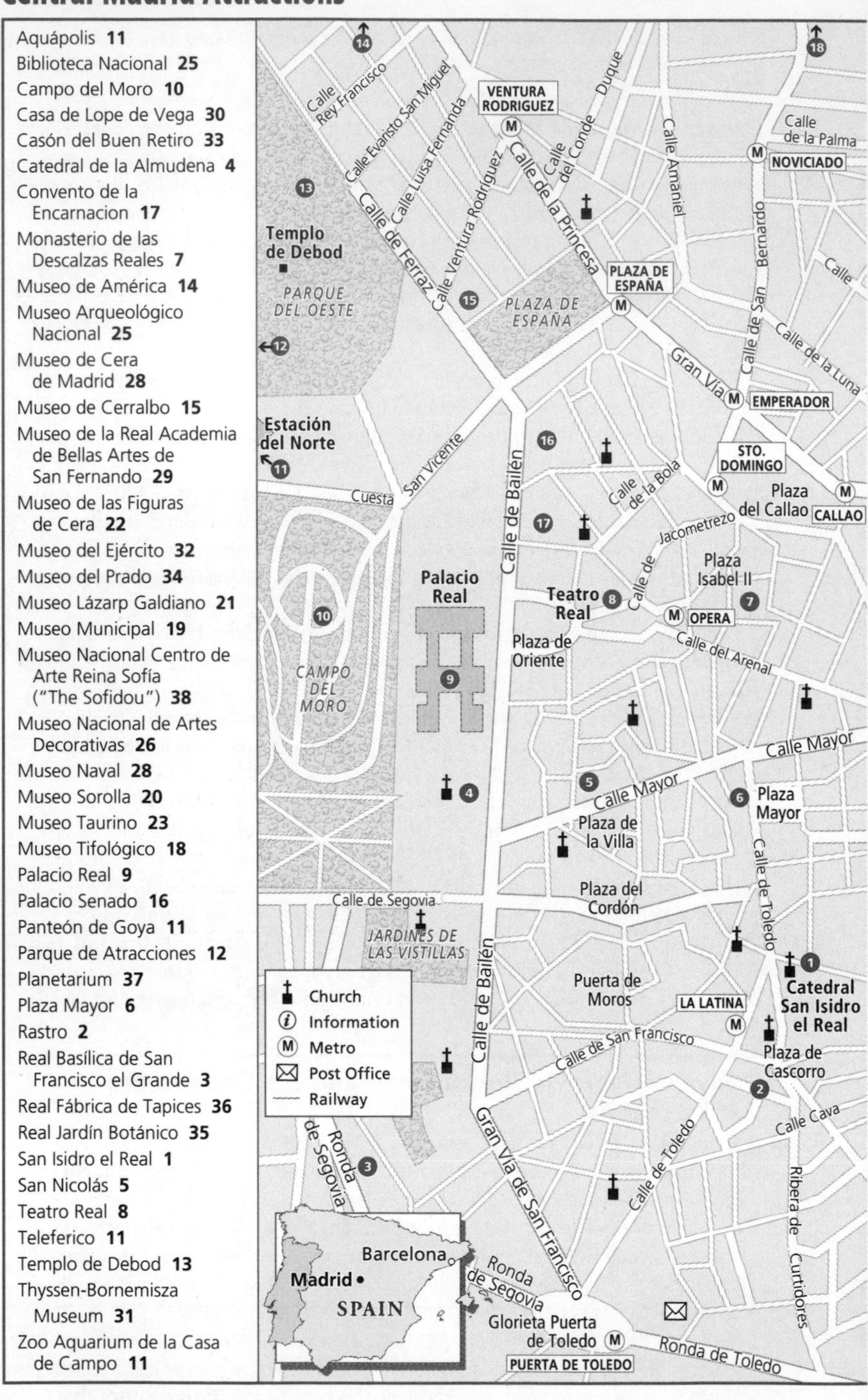
Central Madrid Attractions
Aquápolis 11
Biblioteca Nacional 25
Campo del Moro 10
Casa de Lope de Vega 30
Casón del Buen Retiro 33
Catedral de la Almudena 4
Convento de la Encarnacion 17
Monasterio de las Descalzas Reales 7
Museo de América 14
Museo Arqueológico Nacional 25
Museo de Cera de Madrid 28
Museo de Cerralbo 15
Museo de la Real Academia de Bellas Artes de San Fernando 29
Museo de las Figuras de Cera 22
Museo del Ejército 32
Museo del Prado 34
Museo Lázarp Galdiano 21
Museo Municipal 19
Museo Nacional Centro de Arte Reina Sofía ("The Sofidou") 38
Museo Nacional de Artes Decorativas 26
Museo Naval 28
Museo Sorolla 20
Museo Taurino 23
Museo Tifológico 18
Palacio Real 9
Palacio Senado 16
Panteón de Goya 11
Parque de Atracciones 12
Planetarium 37
Plaza Mayor 6
Rastro 2
Real Basílica de San Francisco el Grande 3
Real Fábrica de Tapices 36
Real Jardín Botánico 35
San Isidro el Real 1
San Nicolás 5
Teatro Real 8
Teleferico 11
Templo de Debod 13
Thyssen-Bornemisza Museum 31
Zoo Aquarium de la Casa de Campo 11
Calle Rey Francisco
Calle Evaristo San Miguel
Calle Luisa Fernanda
Calle Ventura Rodriguez
Calle de Ferraz
Calle de la Princesa
Calle del Conde Duque
Calle Amaniel
Calle de San Bernardo
Calle de la Palma
Calle de la Luna
Gran Vía
VENTURA RODRIGUEZ
NOVICIADO
PLAZA DE ESPAÑA
EMPERADOR
STO. DOMINGO
CALLAO
OPERA
LA LATINA
PUERTA DE TOLEDO
Templo de Debod
PARQUE DEL OESTE
PLAZA DE ESPAÑA
Estación del Norte
Cuesta San Vicente
Calle de Bailén
Calle de la Bola
Calle de Jacometrezo
Plaza del Callao
Plaza Isabel II
Palacio Real
Teatro Real
Plaza de Oriente
Calle del Arenal
CAMPO DEL MORO
Calle Mayor
Plaza Mayor
Plaza de la Villa
Calle de Toledo
Plaza del Cordón
Calle de Segovia
JARDINES DE LAS VISTILLAS
Puerta de Moros
Catedral San Isidro el Real
Calle de San Francisco
Plaza de Cascorro
Calle Cava
Ronda de Segovia
Gran Vía de San Francisco
Ribera de Curtidores
Glorieta Puerta de Toledo
Ronda de Toledo
Church
Information
Metro
Post Office
Railway
Barcelona
Madrid
SPAIN

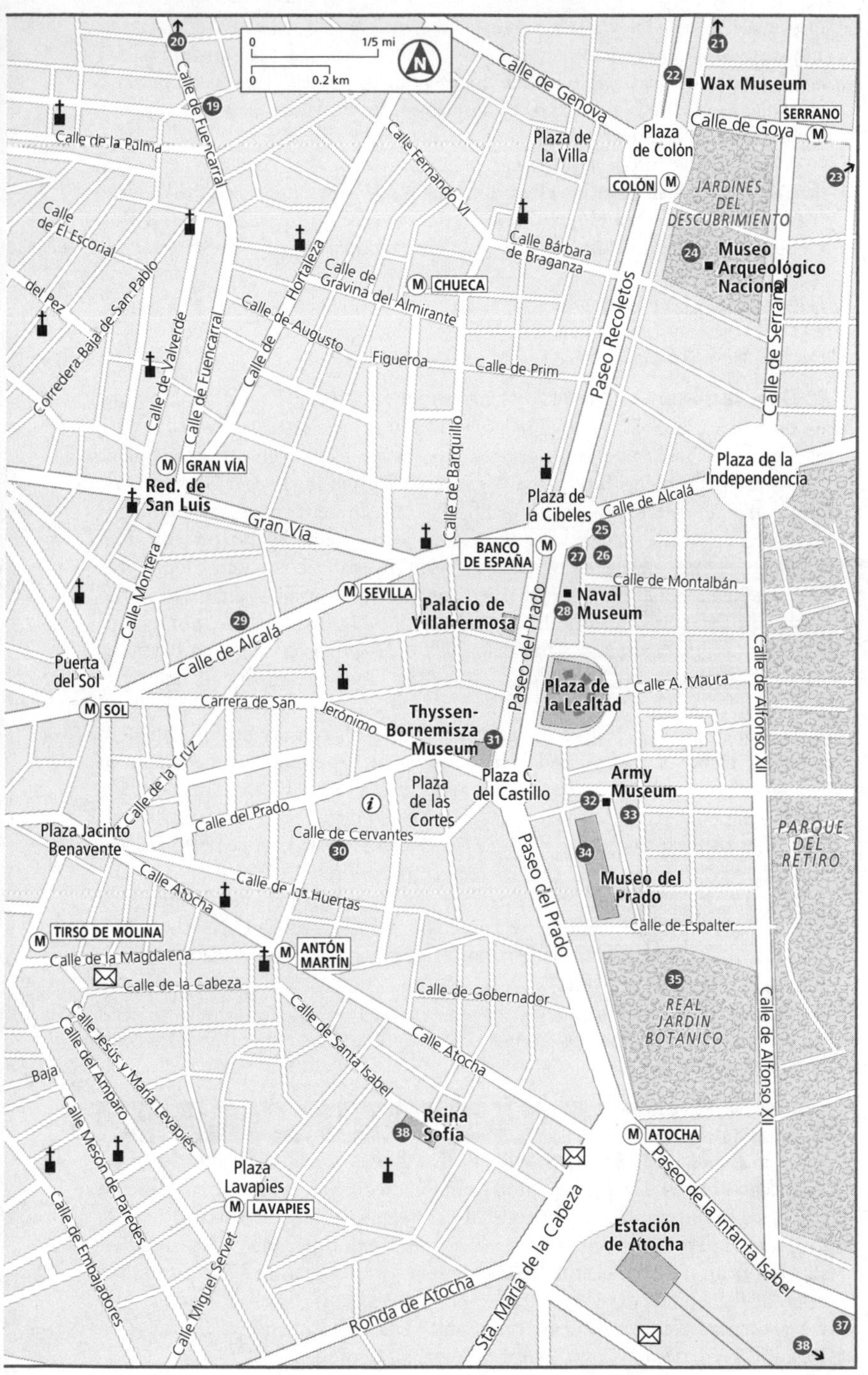
0 1/5 mi
0 0.2 km
N
Wax Museum
Calle de Genova
Plaza de Colón
Calle de Goya
SERRANO
Plaza de la Villa
COLÓN
JARDINES DEL DESCUBRIMIENTO
Museo Arqueológico Nacional
Calle de Fuencarral
Calle de la Palma
Calle Fernando VI
Calle de El Escorial
Calle Bárbara de Braganza
Calle de Hortaleza
Calle de Gravina del Almirante
CHUECA
del Pez
Corredera Baja de San Pablo
Calle de Augusto
Figueroa
Calle de Prim
Paseo Recoletos
Calle de Serrano
Calle de Valverde
Calle de Fuencarral
Calle de Barquillo
GRAN VÍA
Red. de San Luis
Gran Vía
Plaza de la Independencia
Plaza de la Cibeles
Calle de Alcalá
BANCO DE ESPAÑA
Calle Montera
Calle de Montalbán
SEVILLA
Palacio de Villahermosa
Naval Museum
Paseo del Prado
Calle de Alcalá
Puerta del Sol
Plaza de la Lealtad
Calle A. Maura
Calle de Alfonso XII
SOL
Carrera de San Jerónimo
Thyssen-Bornemisza Museum
Calle de la Cruz
Plaza C. del Castillo
Plaza de las Cortes
Army Museum
Calle del Prado
Plaza Jacinto Benavente
Calle de Cervantes
PARQUE DEL RETIRO
Paseo del Prado
Calle Atocha
Calle de las Huertas
Museo del Prado
TIRSO DE MOLINA
Calle de Espalter
ANTÓN MARTÍN
Calle de la Magdalena
Calle de la Cabeza
Calle de Gobernador
REAL JARDIN BOTANICO
Calle de Santa Isabel
Calle Atocha
Calle de Alfonso XII
Calle Jesús y María Levapiés
Calle del Amparo
Baja
Calle Mesón de Paredes
Reina Sofía
ATOCHA
Paseo de la Infanta Isabel
Plaza Lavapies
LAVAPIES
Calle de Embajadores
Calle Miguel Servet
Ronda de Atocha
Sta. María de la Cabeza
Paseo del Prado
Estación de Atocha
19
20
21
22
23
24
25
26
27
28
29
30
31
32
33
34
35
37
38

Unusual among the world's great art collections because of its eclecticism, the Thyssen group also contains goodly numbers of 19th- and 20th-century paintings by many of the notable French impressionists, as well as works by Picasso, Sargent, Kirchner, Nolde, and Kandinsky—artists whose previous absence within Spanish museums had become increasingly obvious.

In addition to European paintings, major American works can also be viewed here, including paintings by Thomas Cole, Winslow Homer, Jackson Pollock, Mark Rothko, Edward Hopper, Robert Rauschenberg, Stuart Davis, and Roy Lichtenstein. There is also an agreeable and moderately priced cafeteria and restaurant on site.

Palacio de Villahermosa, Paseo del Prado 8. ✆ **91-369-01-51.** Admission 4.80€ adults, 3€ students and seniors, free for children 11 and under. Tues–Sun 10am–7pm. Metro: Banco de España. Bus: 1, 2, 5, 9, 10, 14, 15, 20, 27, 34, 45, 51, 52, 53, 74, 146, or 150.

Museo Nacional Centro de Arte Reina Sofía ★★★ Filling for the world of modern art the role that the Prado has filled for traditional art, the "MOMA" of Madrid (its nickname) is the greatest repository of 20th-century art in Spain. Set within the echoing, futuristically renovated walls of the former General Hospital, originally built between 1776 and 1781, the museum is a sprawling, high-ceilinged showplace named after the Greek-born wife of Spain's present king. Once designated "the ugliest building in Spain" by Catalán architect Oriol Bohigas, the Reina Sofía has a design that hangs in limbo somewhere between the 18th and the 21st centuries. It incorporates a 50,000-volume art library and database, a cafe, a theater, a bookstore, Plexiglas-sided elevators, and systems that calibrate security, temperature, humidity, and the quality of light surrounding the exhibits.

Special emphasis is paid to the great artists of 20th-century Spain: Juan Gris, Salvador Dalí, Joan Miró, and Pablo Picasso (the museum has been able to acquire a handful of his works). What many critics feel is Picasso's masterpiece, *Guernica,* now rests at this museum after a long and troubling history of traveling. Banned in Spain during Franco's era (Picasso refused to have it displayed here anyway), it hung until 1980 at New York's Museum of Modern Art. The fiercely antiwar painting immortalizes the town's shameful blanket bombing by the German Luftwaffe, fighting for Franco during the Spanish Civil War. Guernica was the cradle of the Basque nation, and Picasso's canvas made it a household name around the world.

Santa Isabel 52. ✆ **91-467-50-62.** Admission 3€ adults, 1.50€ students; free after 2:30pm on Sat and all day Sun. Mon and Wed–Sat 10am–9pm, Sun 10am–2:30pm. Free guided tours Mon and Wed at 5pm, Sat at 11am. Metro: Atocha.

2 Near the Plaza Mayor & Puerta del Sol

Museo de la Real Academia de Bellas Artes de San Fernando (Fine Arts Museum) ★★ An easy stroll from Puerta del Sol, the Fine Arts Museum is located in the restored and remodeled 17th-century baroque palace of Juan de Goyeneche. The collection—more than 1,500 paintings and 570 sculptures, ranging from the 16th century to the present—was started in 1752 during the reign of Fernando VI (1746–59). It emphasizes works by Spanish, Flemish, and Italian artists. You can see masterpieces by El Greco, Rubens, Velázquez, Zurbarán, Ribera, Cano, Coello, Murillo, Goya, and Sorolla.

Alcalá 13. ✆ **91-524-08-64.** Tues–Sat admission 3€ adults, 1.50€ students. Free for children under 18 Tues–Fri 9am–7pm, Sat–Mon 9am–2pm. Metro: Puerta del Sol or Sevilla. Bus: 3, 15, 20, 51, 52, 53, or 150.

Palacio Real (Royal Palace) ★★ This huge palace was begun in 1738 on the site of the Madrid Alcázar, which burned to the ground in 1734. Some of its 2,000 rooms—which that "enlightened despot" Charles III called home—are open to the public; others are still used for state business. The palace was last used as a royal residence in 1931, before King Alfonso XIII and his wife, Victoria Eugénie, fled Spain.

Highlights of a visit include the Reception Room, the State Apartments, the Armory, and the Royal Pharmacy. To get an English-speaking guide, say "*inglés*" to the person who takes your ticket.

The Reception Room and State Apartments should get priority here if you're rushed. They include a rococo room with a diamond clock; a porcelain salon; the Royal Chapel; the Banquet Room, where receptions for heads of state are still held; and the Throne Room.

The rooms are literally stuffed with art treasures and antiques—salon after salon of monumental grandeur, with no apologies for the damask, mosaics, stucco, Tiepolo ceilings, gilt and bronze, chandeliers, and paintings.

If your visit falls on the first Wednesday of the month, look for the changing of the guard ceremony, which occurs at noon and is free to the public.

In the Armory, you'll see the finest collection of weaponry in Spain. Many of the items—powder flasks, shields, lances, helmets, and saddles—are from the collection of Carlos V (Charles of Spain). From here, the comprehensive tour takes you into the Pharmacy.

Plaza de Oriente, Calle de Bailén 2. ✆ **91-454-87-00.** Admission 6€ adults, 3€ students and children. Mon–Sat 9am–6pm, Sun 9am–3pm. Metro: Opera or Plaza de España.

Real Basílica de San Francisco el Grande Ironically, Madrid, the capital of cathedral-rich Spain, does not itself possess a famous cathedral—but it does have an important church, with a dome larger than that of St. Paul's in London. This 18th-century church is filled with a number of ecclesiastical works, notably a Goya painting of St. Bernardinus of Siena. A guide will show you through.

Plaza de San Francisco el Grande, San Buenaventura 1. ✆ **91-365-38-00.** Admission .70€. Tues–Sat 11am–1pm and 4–6:30pm. Metro: La Latina or Puerta del Toledo. Bus: 3, 60, C, or M4.

3 Along Paseo del Prado

Museo Arqueológico Nacional This stately mansion is a storehouse of artifacts from the prehistoric to the baroque. One of the prime exhibits here is the Iberian statue ***The Lady of Elche*** ★★★, a piece of primitive carving (from the 4th c. B.C.), discovered on the southeastern coast of Spain. Finds from Ibiza, Paestum, and Rome are on display, including statues of Tiberius and his mother, Livia. The Islamic collection from Spain is outstanding. There are also collections of Spanish Renaissance lusterware, Talavera pottery, Retiro porcelain, and some rare 16th- and 17th-century Andalusian glassware.

Many of the exhibits are treasures that were removed from churches and monasteries. A much-photographed choir stall from the palace of Palencia dates from the 14th century. Also worth a look are the reproductions of the Altamira cave paintings (chiefly of bison, horses, and boars), discovered near Santander in northern Spain in 1868.

Serrano 13. ✆ **91-577-79-12.** Admission 3€, free for children and adults over 65. Free for everyone Sat 2:30–8:30pm and Sun. Tues–Sat 9:30am–8:30pm, Sun 9:30am–2:30pm. Metro: Serrano or Retiro. Bus: 1, 9, 19, 51, or 74.

Museo del Ejército (Army Museum) This museum, in the Buen Retiro Palace, houses outstanding exhibits from military history, including El Cid's original sword. In addition, you can see the tent used by Carlos V in Tunisia, relics of Pizarro and Cortés, and an exceptional collection of armor. Look for the piece of the cross that Columbus carried when he landed in the New World. The museum had a notorious founder: Manuel Godoy, who rose from relative poverty to become the lover of María Luisa of Parma, wife of Carlos IV.

Méndez Núñez 1. ✆ **91-522-89-77.** Admission .60€ adults, free for children 18 and under and adults over 65. Tues–Sun 10am–2pm. Metro: Banco de España, or Retiro. Bus: 10, 19, 27, or 34.

Museo Nacional de Artes Decorativas In 62 rooms spread over several floors, this museum, near the Plaza de la Cibeles, displays a rich collection of furniture, ceramics, and decorative pieces. Emphasizing the 16th and 17th centuries, the eclectic collection includes Gothic carvings, alabaster figurines, festival crosses, elaborate dollhouses, elegant baroque four-poster beds, a chapel covered with leather tapestries, and even kitchens from the 18th century. Two new floors focusing on the 18th and 19th centuries have recently been added.

Calle de Montalbán 12. ✆ **91-532-64-99.** Admission 2.40€ adults; 1.20€ students, children, and seniors. Tues–Fri 9:30am–3pm, Sat–Sun 10am–2pm. Metro: Banco de España. Bus: 14, 27, 34, 37, or 45.

Moments Taking the Bull by the Horns

Madrid draws the finest matadors in Spain. If a matador hasn't proven his worth in the **Plaza Monumental de Toros de las Ventas,** Alcalá 237 (✆ **91-356-22-00;** Metro: Ventas), he hasn't been recognized as a top-flight artist. The major season begins during the Fiestas de San Isidro, patron saint of Madrid, on May 15. This is the occasion for a series of fights, during which talent scouts are in the audience. Matadors who distinguish themselves in the ring are signed up for Majorca, Málaga, and other places.

The best way to get tickets to the bullfights is to go to the stadium's box office (open Fri–Sun 10am–2pm and 5–8pm). Concierges for virtually every upper-bracket hotel can also acquire tickets. Alternatively, you can contact one of Madrid's best ticket agents, **Localidades Galicia,** Plaza del Carmen 1 (✆ **91-531-27-32;** Metro: Puerto del Sol), open Tuesday to Saturday from 9:30am to 1:30pm and 4:30 to 7pm, Sunday from 9:30am to 1:30pm. Tickets to bullfights are 12 to 126 , depending on the event and the position of your seat. Front-row seats are *barreras. Delanteras*—third-row seats—are available in both the *alta* (high) and the *baja* (low) sections. The cheapest seats, *filas,* afford the worst view and are in the sun (*sol*) the whole time. The best seats are in the shade (*sombra*). Bullfights are held on Sunday and holidays throughout most of the year, and every day during certain festivals, which tend to last around three weeks, usually in the late spring. Starting times are adjusted according to the anticipated hour of sundown on the day of a performance, usually 7pm from March to October and 5pm during late autumn and early spring. Late-night fights by neophyte matadors are sometimes staged under spotlights on Saturday around 11pm.

Museo Naval The history of nautical science and the Spanish navy, from the time of Isabella and Ferdinand until today, comes alive at the Museo Naval. The most fascinating exhibit is the map made by the first mate of the *Santa María* to show the Spanish monarchs the new discoveries. There are also souvenirs of the Battle of Trafalgar.

Paseo del Prado 5. ✆ **91-379-52-99.** Free admission. Tues–Sun 10am–2pm. Closed Aug. Metro: Banco de España. Bus: 2, 14, 27, 40, 51, 52, or M6.

4 Near the Gran Vía & Plaza de España

Monasterio de las Descalzas Reales ★★ In the mid–16th century, aristocratic women—either disappointed in love or "wanting to be the bride of Christ"—stole away to this convent to take the veil. Each brought a dowry, making this one of the richest convents in the land. By the mid–20th century it sheltered mostly poor women. True, it still contained a priceless collection of art treasures, but the sisters were forbidden to auction anything; in fact, they were literally starving. The state intervened, and the pope granted special dispensation to open the convent as a museum. Today the public can look behind the walls of what had been a mysterious presence on one of the most beautiful squares in Old Madrid.

In the Reliquary are the noblewomen's dowries, one of which is said to contain bits of wood from Christ's Cross; another, some of the bones of St. Sebastian. The most valuable painting is Titian's *Caesar's Money.* The Flemish Hall shelters other fine works, including paintings by Hans de Beken and Breughel the Elder. All of the tapestries were based on Rubens's cartoons, displaying his chubby matrons. Tours are in Spanish.

Plaza de las Descalzas Reales s/n. ✆ **91-542-00-59.** Admission 4.80€ adults, 2.40€ children. Sat and Tues–Thurs 10:30am–12:30pm and 3–5:45pm, Fri 10:30am–12:30pm, Sun 11am–1:15pm. Bus: 1, 2, 5, 20, 46, 52, 53, 74, M1, M2, M3, or M5. From Plaza del Callao, off the Gran Vía, walk down Postigo de San Martín to Plaza de las Descalzas Reales; the convent is on the left.

Templo de Debod This Egyptian temple near Plaza de España once stood in the Valley of the Nile, 31km (19 miles) from Aswan. When the new dam threatened the temple, the Egyptian government dismantled and presented it to Spain. Taken down stone by stone in 1969 and 1970, it was shipped to Valencia and taken by rail to Madrid, where it was reconstructed and opened to the public in 1971. Photos upstairs depict the temple's long history.

Paseo de Rosales. ✆ **91-366-74-15.** Admission 1.80€ adults, .90€ children under 16; free on Wed and Sun. Apr 1–Sept 30, Tues–Fri 10am–2pm and 6–8pm; Oct 1–Mar 31, Tues–Fri 10am–2pm and 4–6pm; Sat and Sun 10am–1pm year-round. Metro: Plaza de España or Ventura Rodríguez. Bus: 25, 33, 39, 46, or 74.

5 In Chamartín, Chueca & Salamanca

Museo Lázaro Galdiano ★★ Imagine 37 rooms in a well-preserved 19th-century mansion bulging with artworks—including many by the most famous old masters of Europe. Visitors usually take the elevator to the top floor and work down, lingering over such artifacts as 15th-century hand-woven vestments, swords and daggers, royal seals, 16th-century crystal from Limoges, Byzantine jewelry, Italian bronzes from ancient times to the Renaissance, and medieval armor.

One painting by Bosch evokes his own peculiar brand of horror, the canvas peopled with creepy fiends devouring human flesh. The Spanish masters are the best represented—among them El Greco, Velázquez, Zurbarán, Ribera, Murillo, and Valdés-Leal.

One section is devoted to works by the English portrait and landscape artists Reynolds, Gainsborough, and Constable. Italian artists exhibited include Tiepolo and Guardi. Salon 30—for many, the most interesting—is devoted to Goya and includes paintings from his "black period."

This off-the-beaten track museum is a gem and usually enjoyably underpopulated, a nice contrast to the overcrowded Prado, Thyssen, and Reina Sofía museums.

Serrano 122. ✆ **91-561-60-84.** Admission 3€. Tues–Sun 10am–2pm. Closed holidays and Aug. Metro: Rubén Darío, Núñez de Balboa. Bus: 9, 16, 19, 27, 45, 51, 61, 89, or 114.

Museo Sorolla From 1912, painter Joaquín Sorolla and his family occupied this elegant Madrileño town house off Paseo de la Castellana. His widow turned it over to the government, and it is now maintained as a memorial. Much of the house remains as Sorolla left it, right down to his stained paintbrushes and pipes. The museum wing displays a representative collection of his works.

Although Sorolla painted portraits of Spanish aristocrats, he was essentially interested in the common people, often depicting them in their native dress. On view are the artist's self-portrait and the paintings of his wife and their son. Sorolla was especially fond of painting beach scenes of the Costa Blanca.

General Martínez Campos 37. ✆ **91-310-15-84.** Admission 2.40€. Tues–Sat 10am–3pm, Sun 10am–2pm. Metro: Iglesia or Rubén Darío. Bus: 5, 16, 61, 40, or M3.

Frommer's Favorite Madrid Experiences

***Tasca* Hopping.** This is the quintessential Madrid experience and the fastest way for a visitor to tap into the local scene. *Tascas* are Spanish pubs serving tapas, those tantalizing appetizers. You can go from one to the other, sampling each tavern's special dishes and wines.

Eating Around Spain. The variety of gastronomic experiences is staggering: You can literally restaurant-hop from province to province without ever leaving Madrid.

Viewing the Works of Your Favorite Artist. Spend an afternoon at the Prado, savoring the works of your favorite Spanish artist.

Bargain Hunting at El Rastro. Madrid has one of the greatest flea markets in Europe, if not the world. Wander through its many offerings to discover that hidden treasure you've been searching for.

Enjoying a Night of Flamenco. Flamenco folk songs (*cante*) and dances (*baile*) are an integral part of the Spanish experience. Spend at least one night in a flamenco tavern listening to the heart-rending laments of gypsy sorrows and dreams.

Outdoor-Cafe Sitting. This is a famous experience for the summertime, when Madrileños come alive again on their *terrazas.* The drinking and good times can go on until dawn. From glamorous hangouts to lowly street corners, the cafe scene takes place mainly along the axis formed by the Paseo de la Castellana, Paseo del Prado, and Paseo de Recoletos (all of which make up one continuous street).

6 Outside the City Center

Museo de América (Museum of the Americas) This museum near the university campus houses an outstanding collection of pre-Columbian, Spanish-American, and Native American art and artifacts. Various exhibits chronicle the progress of the inhabitants of the New World, from the Paleolithic period to the present day. One exhibit, "Groups, Tribes, Chiefdoms, and States," focuses on the social structure of the various peoples of the Americas. Another display outlines the various religions and deities associated with them. Also included is an entire exhibit dedicated to communication, highlighting written as well as nonverbal expressions of art.

Av. de los Reyes Católicos 6. ✆ **91-549-2641.** Admission 3.10€ adults, 1.50€ students, free for children 18 and under and seniors over 65. Tues–Sat 10am–3pm, Sun 10am–2:30pm. Metro: Moncloa.

Museo Taurino (Bullfighting Museum) This museum might serve as a good introduction to bullfighting for those who want to see the real event. Here you'll see the death costume of Manolete, the *traje de luces* (suit of lights) that he wore when he was gored to death at age 30 in Linares's bullring.

Other memorabilia evoke the heyday of Juan Belmonte, the Andalusian who revolutionized bullfighting in 1914 by performing close to the horns. Other exhibits include a Goya painting of a matador, as well as photographs and relics that trace the history of bullfighting in Spain from its ancient origins to the present day.

Plaza de Toros de las Ventas, Alcalá 237. ✆ **91-725-18-57.** Free admission. Mar–Oct, Tues–Fri and Sun 9:30am–2:30pm; Nov–Feb, Mon–Fri 9:30am–2:30pm. Metro: Ventas. Bus: 12, 21, 38, 53, 146, M1, or M8.

Museo Tiflológico This museum is designed for sightless and sight-impaired visitors. Maintained by Spain's National Organization for the Blind, it's one of the few museums in the world that emphasizes tactile appeal. All the exhibits are meant to be touched and felt; to that end, the museum provides audiotapes, in English and Spanish, to guide visitors as they move their hands over the object on display. It also offers pamphlets in large type and Braille.

One section of the museum features small-scale replicas of such architectural wonders as the Mayan and Aztec pyramids of Central America, the Eiffel Tower, and the Statue of Liberty. Another section contains paintings and sculptures created by blind artists, such as Miguel Detrel and José Antonio Braña. A third section outlines the status of blind people throughout history, with a focus on the sociology and technology that led to the development of Braille during the 19th century.

La Coruña 18. ✆ **91-589-42-00.** Free admission. Tues–Fri 10am–2pm and 5–8pm, Sat 10am–2pm. Metro: Estrecho. Bus: 3, 42, 43, 64, or 124.

Panteón de Goya (Goya's Tomb) ★ In a remote part of town beyond the North Station lies Goya's tomb, containing one of his masterpieces—an elaborately beautiful fresco depicting the miracles of St. Anthony on the dome and cupola of the little hermitage of San Antonio de la Florida. This has been called Goya's Sistine Chapel. Already deaf when he began the painting, Goya labored dawn to dusk for 16 weeks, painting with sponges rather than brushes. By depicting common street life—stonemasons, prostitutes, and beggars—Goya raised the ire of the nobility who held judgment until the patron, Carlos IV, viewed it. When the monarch approved, the formerly outrageous painting was deemed acceptable.

The tomb and fresco are in one of the twin chapels (visit the one on the right) that were built in the latter part of the 18th century. Discreetly placed mirrors will help you see the ceiling better.

Glorieta de San Antonio de la Florida s/n. ✆ **91-542-07-22.** Admission 2€. Free on Wed and Sun. Tues–Fri 10am–2pm and 4–8pm, Sat–Sun 10am–2pm (in summer daily 10am–2pm only). Metro: Norte. Bus: 41, 46, 75, or C.

Real Fábrica de Tapices (Royal Tapestry Factory) At this factory, the age-old process of making exquisite (and very expensive) tapestries is still carried on with consummate skill. Nearly every tapestry is based on a cartoon of Goya, who was the factory's most famous employee. Many of these patterns, such as *The Pottery Salesman,* are still in production today. (Goya's original drawings are in the Prado.) Many of the other designs are based on cartoons by Francisco Bayeu, Goya's brother-in-law.

Fuenterrabía 2. ✆ **91-434-05-51.** Admission 2€. Mon–Fri 10am–2pm. Closed Aug and holidays. Metro: Menéndez Pelayo. Bus: 10, 14, 26, 32, 37, C, or M9.

7 Parks & Gardens

For a touch of green in Madrid's sprawling gray urban expanse, visit one of the following:

Casa de Campo ★ (Metro: Lago or Batán) is the former royal hunting grounds—miles of parkland lying south of the Royal Palace across the Manzanares River. You can see the gate through which the kings rode out of the palace grounds, either on horseback or in carriages, on their way to the tree-lined park. A lake in the park is usually filled with rowers. You can have drinks and light refreshments around the water or go swimming in a municipally operated pool. Children will love both the zoo and the Parque de Atracciones (see "Especially for Kids," below). The Casa de Campo can be visited daily from 8am to 9pm.

Parque de Retiro ★ (Metro: Retiro), originally a playground for the Spanish monarchs and their guests, extends over 350 acres. The huge palaces that once stood here were destroyed in the early 19th century; only the former dance hall, the Cáson del Buen Retiro (housing the modern works of the Prado), and the building containing the Army Museum remain. The park boasts numerous fountains and statues, plus a large lake. There are also two exposition centers, the Velásquez and Crystal palaces (built to honor the Philippines in 1887), and a lakeside monument, erected in 1922 in honor of King Alfonso XII. In summer, the rose gardens are worth a visit, and you'll find several places for inexpensive snacks and drinks. The park is open daily 24 hours, but it is safest from 7am to about 8:30pm.

Across Calle de Alfonso XII, at the southwest corner of Parque de Retiro, is the **Real Jardín Botánico (Botanical Garden)** (✆ **91-420-30-17;** Metro: Atocha; bus: 10, 14, 19, 32, or 45). Founded in the 18th century, the garden contains more than 104 species of trees and 3,000 types of plants. Also on the premises are an exhibition hall and a library specializing in botany. The park is open daily from 10am to 9pm except in August; admission is 1.50€.

8 Especially for Kids

Museo de Cera de Madrid (Wax Museum) The kids will enjoy seeing a lifelike wax Columbus calling on Ferdinand and Isabella, as well as Marlene

Tips An Area You May Want to Avoid

The zone by the *teleférico* in the Casa de Campo is a pick-up area for prostitutes, with cars stopping and negotiating deals. It's also a drug zone, so you may want to avoid the area entirely.

Dietrich checking out Bill and Hillary Clinton. The 450 wax figures also include heroes and villains of World War II. Two galleries display Romans and Arabs from the ancient days of the Iberian Peninsula; a show in multivision gives a 30-minute recap of Spanish history from the Phoenicians to the present.

Paseo de Recoletos 41. ✆ **91-319-26-49.** Admission 7.20€ adults, 4.20€ children, children 3 and under free. Daily 10am–2pm and 4–8pm. Metro: Colón. Bus: 27, 45, or 53.

Parque de Atracciones The park was created in 1969 to amuse the young at heart with an array of rides and concessions. The former include a toboggan slide, a carousel, pony rides, an adventure into outer space, a walk through a transparent maze, a visit to a jungle, a motor-propelled series of cars disguised as a tail-wagging dachshund puppy, and a gyrating whirligig clutched in the tentacles of an octopus named El Pulpo. The most popular rides are a pair of roller coasters named "7 Picos" and "Jet Star." The park also has many diversions for adults. See "Madrid After Dark," later in this chapter, for details.

Casa de Campo. ✆ **91-463-29-00.** Admission 4.50€. Apr–May Tues–Fri noon–8pm, Sat–Sun noon–10pm; June–Aug Tues–Fri 6pm–1am, Sat 6pm–2am, Sun noon–1am; Sept Tues–Sun (variable hours; call to check before going); Oct–Mar Sat noon–8pm (sometimes 9pm), Sun 11am–8pm (sometimes 9pm). Take the Teleférico cable car (see below); at the end of this ride, microbuses take you the rest of the way. Alternatively, take the suburban train from Plaza de España and stop near the entrance to the park (Entrada de Batán).

Teleférico Strung high above several of Madrid's verdant parks, this cable car was originally built in 1969 as part of a public fairgrounds (Parque de Atracciones) modeled vaguely along the lines of Disneyland. Today, even for visitors not interested in visiting the park, the *teleférico* retains an allure of its own as a high-altitude method of admiring the cityscape of Madrid. The cable car departs from Paseo Pintor Rosales at the eastern edge of Parque del Oeste (at the corner of Calle Marqués de Urquijo) and carries you high above two parks, railway tracks, and over the Manzanares River to a spot near a picnic ground and restaurant in Casa de Campo. Weather permitting, there are good views of the Royal Palace along the way. The ride takes 11 minutes.

Paseo del Pintor Rosales s/n. ✆ **91-541-74-50.** Fare 2.80€ one way, 4€ round-trip. Apr–Sept, daily 11am–9pm; Oct–Mar, Sat–Sun noon–8:30pm. Metro: Plaza de España or Argüelles. Bus: 21.

Zoo Aquarium de la Casa de Campo This modern well-organized facility allows you to see about 3,000 animals from five continents. Most are in simulated natural habitats, with moats separating them from the public. There's a petting zoo for the kids and a show presented by the Chu-Lin band. The zoo/aquarium complex includes a 520,000-gallon tropical marine aquarium, a dolphinarium, and a parrot club.

Casa de Campo. ✆ **91-512-37-70.** Admission 12.15€ adults, 9.80€ seniors and children 3–8, free for children 2 and under. Daily 10:30am–sunset. Metro: Batán. Bus: 33.

9 Special-Interest Sightseeing

ARCHITECTURAL STANDOUTS

Plaza Mayor ★★ In the heart of Madrid, this famous square was known as the Plaza de Arrabal during medieval times, when it stood outside the city wall. The original architect of Plaza Mayor itself was Juan Gómez de Mora, who worked during the reign of Philip III. Under the Hapsburgs, the square rose in importance as the site of public spectacles, including the abominable *autos de fe,* in which heretics were burned. Bullfights, knightly tournaments, and festivals were also staged here.

Three times the buildings on the square burned—in 1631, 1672, and 1790—but each time the plaza bounced back. After the last big fire, it was completely redesigned by Juan de Villanueva.

Nowadays a Christmas fair is held around the equestrian statue of Philip III (dating from 1616) in the center of the square. On summer nights the Plaza Mayor becomes the virtual living room of Madrid, as tourists sip sangria at the numerous cafes and listen to the music performances, many of which are spontaneous.

Metro: Puerta del Sol.

WALKING TOUR HAPSBURG MADRID

Start: Southeastern corner of the Palacio Real.
Finish: Calle del Arenal.
Time: 3 hours.
Best Times: Saturday or Sunday, when you can also visit the flea market of El Rastro.
Worst Times: Monday to Saturday from 7:30 to 9:30am and 5 to 7:30pm—because of heavy traffic.

This tour encompasses 16th- and 17th-century Madrid, including the grand plazas and traffic arteries that the Hapsburg families built to transform a quiet town into a world-class capital.

The tour begins at the:

1 Palacio Real (Royal Palace)

This palace is at the corner of Calle de Bailén and Calle Mayor. The latter was built by Philip II in the 1560s to provide easy access from the palace to his preferred church, San Jerónimo el Real.

Walk east to:

2 Calle Mayor

Walk on the south side of the street. Within a block, you'll reach a black bronze statue of a kneeling angel, erected in 1906 to commemorate the aborted assassination of King Alfonso XIII (grandfather of the present king, Juan Carlos).

Across the street from the kneeling angel is the:

3 Palacio de Abrantes

Today, this palace, at Calle Mayor 86, is occupied by the Italian Institute of Culture.

On the same side of the street as the kneeling angel, to the statue's left, is the:

4 Palacio de Uceda

This palace, at Calle Mayor 79, is now the headquarters of the Spanish military (their version of the U.S. Pentagon). Both of these palaces are among the best examples of 17th-century civil architecture in Madrid.

Walking Tour—Hapsburg Madrid

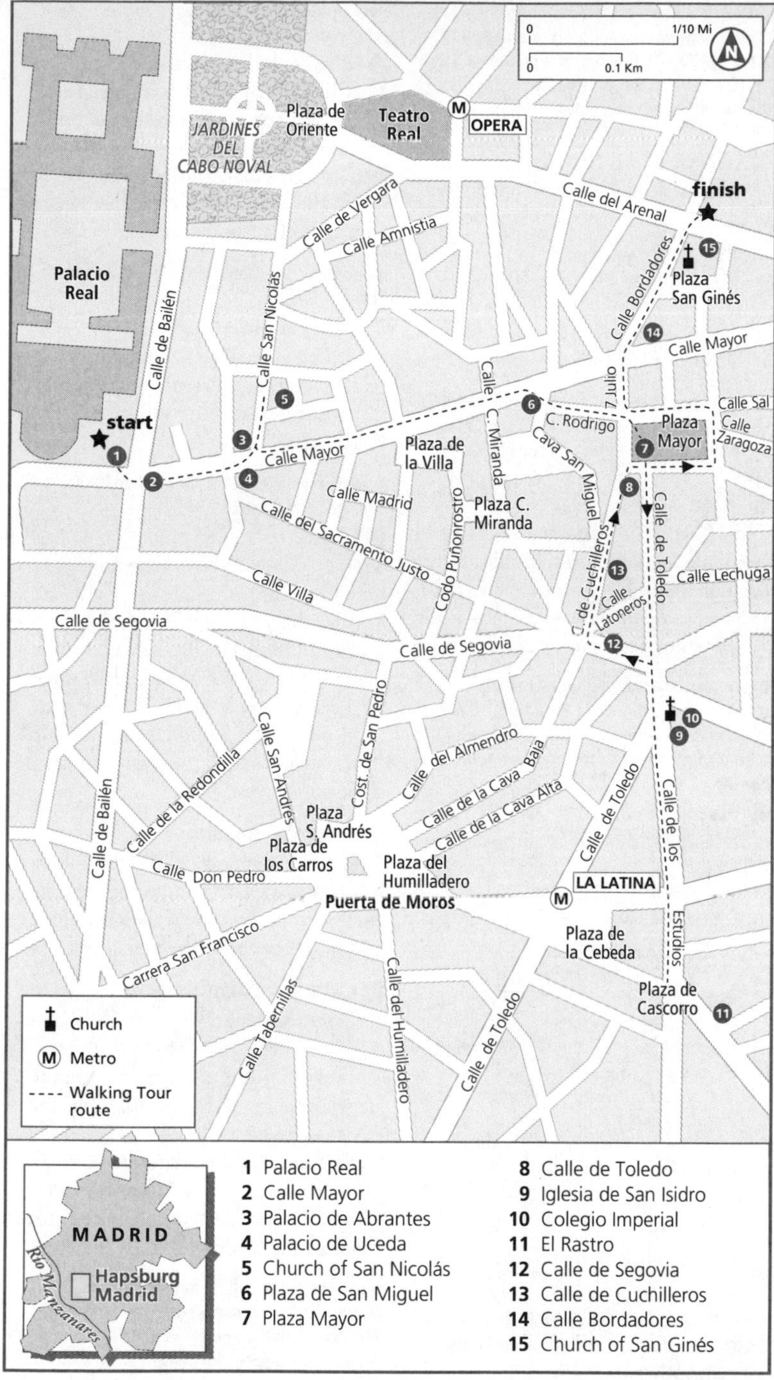

Walk half a block east, crossing to the north side of Calle Mayor and detouring about 20 yards to the left, down narrow Calle de San Nicolás. You'll come to the somber facade of the oldest church in Madrid, the 12th-century:

❺ Church of St. Nicolás

Only a brick tower remains from the original building at the Plaza de San Nicolás. It is one of the few examples of the Mudéjar style in the capital. The reredos at the high altar is the work of Juan de Herrera, also the architect of El Escorial.

Retrace your steps to Calle Mayor. Turn left and continue to walk east. You'll pass Plaza de la Villa on your right, and, one block later:

❻ Plaza de San Miguel

This is an iron-canopied meat-and-vegetable market. You might stock up on ingredients for a picnic here. (The market is open Mon–Fri 9am–2pm and 5–8pm, Sat 9am–2pm.)

Leave Plaza de San Miguel by Ciudad Rodrigo (there might not be a sign), which leads under a soaring granite archway and up a sloping street to the northwestern corner of:

❼ Plaza Mayor

This landmark square is at the heart of Old Madrid.

TAKE A BREAK
Café Bar Los Galayos, Plaza Mayor 1 (✆ **91-366-30-28**), has long been one of the best places for tapas along this square. If you're taking the walking tour during the day, you may want to return to this cafe/bar at night, when it is most lively. In summer you can select one of the outdoor tables for your drinks and tapas. The cafe is open daily from noon to 1am.

Stroll through Plaza Mayor, crossing it diagonally and exiting at the closer of its two southern exits. A dingy steep flight of stone stairs leads down to the beginning of the:

❽ Calle de Toledo

Note in the distance the twin domes of the yellow-stucco and granite:

❾ Iglesia de San Isidro

This is the legendary burial place of Madrid's patron saint and his wife, Santa María de la Cadeza. The church lost its status as a cathedral in 1992, when the honor went to the larger Church of La Almudena.

Adjacent to San Isidro is the baroque facade of the:

❿ Colegio Imperial

This Lope de Vega, Calderón, and many other famous men studied at this institute, which was also run by the Jesuits.

If your tour takes place on a Saturday or Sunday before 3pm, visit:

⓫ El Rastro

This is Madrid's world-famous flea market. Continue along Calle de Toledo, then fork left onto Calle Estudios and proceed to Plaza de Cascorro, named after a hero of the Cuban wars. El Rastro begins here. If your tour takes place Monday to Friday, skip the Rastro neighborhood. Instead, turn right onto:

⓬ Calle de Segovia

This street intersects Calle de Toledo just before it passes in front of the Catedral de San Isidro. Walk one block and turn right onto the first street:

⓭ Calle de Cuchilleros

Follow this street north past 16th- and 17th-century stone-fronted houses. Within a block, a flight of granite steps forks to the right. Climb the steps (a sign identifies the new street as Calle Arco de Cuchilleros) and you'll pass one of the most famous *mesones* (typical Castilian restaurants) of Madrid, the Cueva de Luis Candelas.

Once again you will have entered Plaza Mayor, this time on the southwestern corner. Walk beneath the southernmost arcade and promenade counterclockwise beneath the arcades, walking north underneath the square's eastern arcade. Then walk west

beneath its northern arcade. At the northwest corner, exit through the archway onto Calle 7 de Julio. Fifteen meters (50 ft.) later, cross Calle Mayor and take the right-hand narrow street before you. This is:

⓮ Calle Bordadores

During the 17th century, this street housed Madrid's embroidery workshops, staffed exclusively by men.

As you proceed, notice the 17th-century brick walls and towers of the:

⓯ Church of San Ginés

This church at Arenal 15 is one of Madrid's oldest parishes owes its present look to the architects who reconstructed it after a devastating fire in 1872.

At the end of this tour, you'll find yourself on traffic-congested Calle del Arenal, at the doorstep of many interesting old streets.

10 Organized Tours

A large number of agencies in Madrid book organized tours and excursions to sights and attractions both within and outside the city limits. Although your mobility and freedom might be somewhat hampered, some visitors appreciate the ease and convenience of being able to visit so many sights in a single efficiently organized day.

Many of the city's hotel concierges, and all of the city's travel agents, will book anyone who asks for a guided tour of Madrid or its environs with one of Spain's largest tour operators, **Pullmantours,** Plaza de Oriente 8 (✆ **91-541-18-07**). Regardless of their destination and duration, virtually every tour departs from the Pullmantours terminal, at that address. Half-day tours of Madrid include an artistic tour priced at 34€ per person, which includes entrance to a selection of the city's museums, and a panoramic half-day tour for 18.50€.

Toledo is the most popular full-day excursion outside the city limits. Trips cost 59€. These tours (including lunch) depart daily at 9:45am from the abovementioned departure point, last all day, and include ample opportunities for wandering at will through the city's narrow streets. You can, if you wish, take an abbreviated morning tour of Toledo, without stopping for lunch, for 39€.

Another popular tour stops briefly in Toledo and continues on to visit both the monastery at El Escorial and the Valley of the Fallen (*Valle de los Caídos*) before returning the same day to Madrid. With lunch included, this all-day excursion costs 83€.

The third major destination of bus tours from Madrid's center to the city's surrounding attractions is Pullmantours' full-day guided excursion to Avila and Segovia, which takes in a heady dose of medieval and ancient Roman monuments that are really very interesting. With lunch included, the price per person is 63.50€.

The hop-off, hop-on **Madrid Vision Bus** lets you set your own pace and itinerary. A scheduled panoramic tour lasts a half-hour, provided that you don't get off the bus. Otherwise, you can opt for an unlimited number of stops, exploring at your leisure. The Madrid Vision makes four complete tours daily, two in the morning and two in the afternoon; on Sunday and Monday buses depart only in the morning. Check with **Trapsa Tours** (✆ **91-767-17-43**) for departure times, which are variable. The full-day tour, with unlimited stops, costs 10.90€. You can board the bus at the Madrid tourist office.

11 Shopping

Seventeenth-century playwright Tirso de Molina called Madrid "a shop stocked with every kind of merchandise," and it's true—an estimated 50,000 stores sell everything from high-fashion clothing to flamenco guitars to art and ceramics.

If your time is limited, go to one of the big department stores (see below). They all carry a bit of everything.

THE SHOPPING SCENE

SHOPPING AREAS The Center The sheer diversity of shops in Madrid's center is staggering. Their densest concentration lies immediately north of the Puerta del Sol, radiating out from Calle del Carmen, Calle Montera, and Calle Preciados.

Calle Mayor & Calle del Arenal Unlike their more stylish neighbors to the north of Puerta del Sol, shops in this district to the west tend toward the small, slightly dusty enclaves of coin and stamp dealers, family-owned souvenir shops, clock makers, sellers of military paraphernalia, and an abundance of stores selling musical scores.

Gran Vía Conceived, designed, and built in the 1910s and 1920s as a showcase for the city's best shops, hotels, and restaurants, the Gran Vía has since been eclipsed by other shopping districts. Its Art Nouveau–Art Deco glamour still survives in the hearts of most Madrileños, however. The bookstores here are among the best in the city, as are outlets for fashion, shoes, jewelry, furs, and handcrafted accessories from all regions of Spain.

El Rastro It's the biggest flea market in Spain, drawing collectors, dealers, buyers, and hopefuls from throughout Madrid and its suburbs. The makeshift stalls are at their most frenetic on Sunday morning. For more information, refer to the "Flea Markets" section under "Shopping A to Z," below.

Plaza Mayor Under the arcades of the square itself are exhibitions of lithographs and oil paintings, and every weekend there's a loosely organized market for stamp and coin collectors. Within three or four blocks in every direction you'll find more than the average number of souvenir shops.

On Calle Marqués Viudo de Pontejos, which runs east from Plaza Mayor, is one of the city's headquarters for the sale of cloth, thread, and buttons. Also running east, on Calle de Zaragoza, are silversmiths and jewelers. On Calle Postas you'll find housewares, underwear, soap powders, and other household items.

Near the Carrera de San Jerónimo Several blocks east of Puerta del Sol is Madrid's densest concentration of gift shops, crafts shops, and antiques dealers—a decorator's delight. Its most interesting streets include Calle del Prado, Calle de las Huertas, and Plaza de las Cortés. The neighborhood is pricey, so don't expect bargains here.

Northwest Madrid A few blocks east of Parque del Oeste is an upscale neighborhood that's well stocked with luxury goods and household staples. Calle de la Princesa, its main thoroughfare, has shops selling shoes, handbags, fashion, gifts, and children's clothing. Thanks to the presence of the university nearby, there's also a dense concentration of bookstores, especially on Calle Isaac Peral and Calle Fernando el Católico, several blocks north and northwest, respectively, from the subway stop of Argüelles.

Salamanca District It's known throughout Spain as the quintessential upper-bourgeois neighborhood, uniformly prosperous, and its shops are correspondingly exclusive. They include outlets run by interior decorators, furniture shops, fur and jewelry shops, several department stores, and design headquarters whose output ranges from the solidly conservative to the high-tech. The main streets of this district are Calle de Serrano and Calle de Velázquez. The district lies northeast of the center of Madrid, a few blocks north of Retiro Park. Its most central Metro stops are Serrano and Velázquez.

HOURS Major stores are open (in most cases) Monday to Saturday from 9:30am to 8pm. Many small stores take a siesta between 1:30 and 4:30pm. Of course, there is never any set formula, and hours can vary greatly from store to store, depending on the idiosyncrasies and schedules of the owner.

SHIPPING Many art and antiques dealers will crate and ship bulky objects for an additional fee. Whereas it usually pays to have heavy objects shipped by sea, in some cases it's almost the same price to ship crated goods by airplane. Of course, it depends on the distance your crate will have to travel overland to the nearest international port, which, in many cases for the purposes of relatively small-scale shipments by individual clients, is Barcelona. Consequently, it might pay to call two branches of **Emery Worldwide** from within Spain to explain your particular situation, and receive comparable rates. For information about sea transit for your valuables, call **Emery Worldwide Ocean Services** at their only Spanish branch, in Barcelona (✆ **93-479-30-50**). For information about **Emery Worldwide Air Freight,** call their main Spanish office in Madrid (✆ **91-747-56-66**) for advice on any of the dozen air-freight pickup stations they maintain throughout Spain. These include, among many others, Barcelona, Alicante, Málaga, Bilbao, and Valencia. For more advice on this, and the formalities that you'll go through in clearing U.S. customs after the arrival of your shipment in the United States, call **Emery Worldwide** in the United States at ✆ **800/488-9451.**

For most small- and medium-sized shipments, air freight isn't much more expensive than ocean shipping. **Iberia's Air Cargo Division** (✆ **800/221-6002** in the U.S.) offers air-freight service from Spain to New York, Chicago, Miami, or Los Angeles. What will you pay for this transport of your treasured art objects or freight? Here's a rule of thumb: For a shipment under 100 kilograms (220 lb.), from either Barcelona or Madrid to New York, the cost is approximately 4.40€ per pound. The per-pound price goes down as the weight of the shipment increases, declining to, for example, 1.50€ per pound for shipments of more than 1,000 kilograms (2,200 lb.). Regardless of what you ship, there's a minimum charge enforced.

For an additional fee, Iberia or one of its representatives will also pick up your package. For a truly precious cargo, ask the seller to build a crate for it. For information within Spain about air-cargo shipments, call Iberia's cargo division at Madrid's Barajas Airport (✆ **91-587-33-07**) or at Barcelona's airport (✆ **93-401-34-26**).

Remember that your air-cargo shipment will need to clear Customs after it's brought into the United States. This involves some additional paperwork, costly delays, and in some cases a trip to the airport where the shipment first entered the United States. It's usually easier (and in some cases, much easier) to hire a commercial customs broker to do the work for you. **Emery Worldwide,** a division of CF Freightways, can clear most shipments of goods for around US$138, which you'll pay in addition to any applicable duty you owe your home government. For information, you can call ✆ **800/443-6379** within the United States.

Tips **When the Weather & the Sales Are Hot!**

The best sales are usually in summer. Called *rebajas,* they start in July and go through August. As a general rule, merchandise is marked down even more in August to make way for the new fall wares in most stores.

TAX & HOW TO RECOVER IT If you are not a European Union resident and you make purchases in Spain worth more than 90€, you can get a tax refund. (The internal tax, known as VAT in most of Europe, is called IVA in Spain.) Depending on the goods, the rate usually ranges from 7% to 16% of the total worth of your merchandise. Luxury items are taxed at 33%.

To get this refund, you must complete three copies of a form that the store will give you, detailing the nature of your purchase and its value. Citizens of non-EU countries show the purchase and the form to the Spanish Customs Office. The shop is supposed to refund the amount due you. Inquire at the time of purchase how they will do so and discuss in what currency your refund will arrive.

DUTY-FREE—WORTH IT OR NOT? Before you leave home, check the regular retail price of items that you're most likely to buy. Duty-free prices vary from one country to another and from item to item. Sometimes you're better off purchasing an item in a discount store at home. If you don't remember prices back home, you can't tell when you're getting a good deal.

BARGAINING The days of bargaining are, for the most part, long gone. Most stores have what is called *precio de venta al público* (PVP), a firm retail price not subject to negotiation. With street vendors and flea markets, it's a different story because haggling *a la española* is expected. However, you'll have to be very skilled to get the price reduced a lot, as most of these street-smart vendors know exactly what their merchandise is worth and are old hands at getting that price.

SHOPPING A TO Z

Spain has always been known for its craftspeople, many still working in the time-honored and labor-intensive traditions of their grandparents. It's hard to go wrong if you stick to the beautiful handcrafted Spanish objects—hand-painted tiles, ceramics, and porcelain; hand-woven rugs; handmade sweaters; and intricate embroideries. And, of course, Spain produces some of the world's finest leather. Jewelry, especially gold set with Majorca pearls, represents good value and unquestioned luxury.

Some of Madrid's art galleries are known throughout Europe for discovering and encouraging new talent. Antiques are sold in highly sophisticated retail outlets. Better suited to the budgets of many travelers are the weekly flea markets.

Spain continues to make inroads into the fashion world. Its young designers are regularly featured in the fashion magazines of Europe. Excellent shoes are available, some highly fashionable. But be advised that prices for shoes and quality clothing are generally higher in Madrid than in the United States.

ANTIQUES

In addition to the following shops, you might want to visit the flea market (see El Rastro, below).

Centro de Anticuarios Lagasca You'll find about a dozen antiques shops here, clustered into one covered arcade. They operate as individual businesses, although by browsing through each you'll find an impressive assemblage of antique furniture, porcelain, and whatnots. Open Monday to Saturday from 10am to 1:30pm and 5 to 8pm. Lagasca 36. ✆ **91-577-37-52.** Metro: Serrano or Velázquez.

Galería de Arte del Lubre Housed in a mid-19th-century building are several unusual antiques dealers (and a large carpet emporium as well) many of whom specialize in antique, sometimes monumental paintings. Each establishment maintains its own schedule, although the center itself has overall hours. Open Monday to Saturday from 10am to 2pm and 5 to 8:15pm. Serrano 5. ✆ **91-576-96-82.** Metro: Retiro. Bus: 9 or 15.

ART GALLERIES

Galería Kreisler One successful entrepreneur on Madrid's art scene is Ohio-born Edward Kreisler, whose gallery, now run by his son Juan, specializes in figurative and contemporary paintings, sculptures, and graphics. The gallery prides itself on occasionally displaying and selling the works of artists who are critically acclaimed and displayed in museums in Spain. Open Monday to Saturday from 10:30am to 2pm and 5 to 9pm. Closed in August and on Saturday afternoon from July 15 to September 15. Hermosilla 8. ✆ **91-431-42-64.** Metro: Serrano. Bus: 27, 45, or 150.

CERAMICS

Antigua Casa Talavera "The first house of Spanish ceramics" has wares that include a sampling of regional styles from every major area of Spain, including Talavera, Toledo, Manises, Valencia, Puente del Arzobispo, Alcora, Granada, and Seville. Sangria pitchers, dinnerware, tea sets, plates, and vases are all handmade. Inside one of the showrooms is an interesting selection of tiles, painted with reproductions of scenes from bullfights, dances, and folklore. There's also a series of tiles depicting famous paintings in the Prado. At its present location since 1904, the shop is only a short walk from Plaza de Santo Domingo. Open Monday to Friday from 10am to 1:30pm and 5 to 8pm, Saturday from 10am to 1:30pm. Isabel la Católica 2. ✆ **91-547-34-17.** Metro: Santo Domingo. Bus: 1, 2, 46, 70, 75, or 148.

CRAFTS

El Arco de los Cuchilleros Artesanía de Hoy Set within one of the 17th-century vaulted cellars of Plaza Mayor, this shop is entirely devoted to unusual craft items from throughout Spain. The merchandise is one of a kind and in most cases contemporary; it includes a changing array of pottery, leather, textiles, wood carvings, glassware, wickerwork, papier-mâché, and silver jewelry. The hardworking owners deal directly with the artisans who produce each item, ensuring a wide inventory of handicrafts. The staff is familiar with the rituals of applying for tax-free status of purchases here, and speaks several different languages. Open January to September, Monday to Saturday from 11am to 8pm; October to December, Monday to Saturday from 11am to 9pm. Plaza Mayor 9 (basement level). ✆ **91-365-26-80.** Metro: Puerta del Sol or Opera.

DEPARTMENT STORES

El Corte Inglés This flagship of the largest department-store chain in Madrid sells hundreds of souvenirs and Spanish handicrafts, such as damascene steelwork from Toledo, flamenco dolls, and embroidered shawls. Some astute buyers report that it also sells glamorous fashion articles, such as Pierre Balmain designs, for about a third less than equivalent items in most European capitals. Services include interpreters, currency-exchange windows, and parcel delivery either to a local hotel or overseas. Open Monday to Saturday from 10am to 9pm. Preciados 3. ✆ **91-379-80-00.** Metro: Puerta del Sol.

EMBROIDERIES

Casa Bonet The intricately detailed embroideries produced in Spain's Balearic Islands (especially Majorca) are avidly sought for bridal chests and elegant dinner settings. A few examples of the store's extensive inventory are displayed on the walls. Open Monday to Friday from 10:45am to 2pm and 5 to 8pm, Saturday from 10:15am to 2pm. Núñez de Balboa 76. © **91-575-09-12.** Metro: Núñez de Balboa.

ESPADRILLES

Casa Hernanz A brisk walk south of Plaza Mayor delivers you to this store, in business since the 1840s. In addition to espadrilles, they sell shoes in other styles, as well as hats. Open Monday to Friday from 9am to 1:30pm and 4:30 to 8pm, Saturday from 10am to 2pm. Toledo 18. © **91-366-54-50.** Metro: Puerta del Sol, Opera, or La Latina.

FANS & UMBRELLAS

Casa de Diego Here you'll find a wide inventory of fans, ranging from plain to fancy, from plastic to exotic hardwood, from cost-conscious to lavish. Some fans tend to be a bit overpriced; shopping around may increase your chances of finding a real bargain. Now open year-round, Monday to Saturday from 9:45am to 8pm. Puerta del Sol 12. © **91-522-66-43.** Metro: Puerta del Sol.

FASHIONS FOR MEN

For the man on a budget who wants to dress reasonably well, the best outlet for off-the-rack men's clothing is one of the branches of the Corte Inglés department-store chain (see above). Most men's boutiques in Madrid are very expensive and may not be worth the investment.

FASHIONS FOR WOMEN

Herrero The sheer size and buying power of this popular retail outlet for women's clothing make it a reasonably priced emporium for all kinds of feminine garb as well as various articles for gentlemen. An additional outlet lies on the same street at no. 16 (© **91-521-15-24**). Both are open Monday to Saturday from 10:30am to 8pm; some Sundays from noon to 8pm. Preciados 7. © **91-521-29-90.** Metro: Puerta del Sol or Callao.

Modas Gonzalo This boutique's baroque, gilded atmosphere evokes the 1940s, but its fashions are strictly up-to-date, well made, and intended for stylish adult women. Open Monday to Saturday from 10am to 1:30pm and 4:30 to 8pm. Gran Vía 43. © **91-547-12-39.** Metro: Callao or Puerta del Sol.

Sybilla The *fashionistas* of Madrid are buzzing with excitement over the clothes displayed in the tiny atelier here. Fashion critics have hailed Sybilla's clothing as "wearable, whimsical, and inevitably original." Everything is stylish. The outlet also sells articles for the home like sheets, towels, and dishes. Open Monday through Friday from 10am to 2pm and 4 to 8:30pm, and Saturday from 11am to 3pm and 5 to 8:30pm. Jorge Juan 12. © **91-578-13-22.** Metro: Serrano or Banco España.

FLEA MARKETS

El Rastro Foremost among markets is the Sunday morning El Rastro (translated as either flea market or thieves' market), occupying a roughly triangular district of streets and plazas a few minutes' walk south of Plaza Mayor. Its center is Plaza Cascorro and Ribera de Curtidores. This market will delight anyone attracted to a mishmash of fascinating junk interspersed with bric-a-brac and paintings. ***Note:*** Thieves are rampant here (hustling more than just antiques), so secure your wallet carefully, be alert, and proceed with caution. Insofar as scheduling your visit to El Rastro, bear in mind that this is a flea market involving hundreds of merchants who basically pull up their display tables and depart whenever their goods are sold or they get fed up with the crowds. Plaza Cascorro and Ribera de Curtidores. Metro: La Latina. Bus: 3 or 17.

FOOD & WINE

Mallorca Madrid's best-established gourmet shop opened in 1931 as an outlet selling a pastry called *ensaimada,* and this is still one of the store's most famous products. Tempting arrays of cheeses, canapés, roasted and marinated meats, sausages, and about a dozen kinds of paté accompany a spread of tiny pastries, tarts, and chocolates. Don't overlook the displays of Spanish wines and brandies. A stand-up tapas bar is always clogged with clients three deep, sampling the wares before they buy larger portions to take home. Tapas cost from .90€ to 2.40€ per *ración* (portion). Open daily from 9:30am to 9:30pm. Velázquez 59. ✆ **91-431-99-09.** Metro: Velázquez.

LEATHER

Loewe Since 1846 this has been the most elegant leather store in Spain. Its gold medal–winning designers have always kept abreast of changing tastes and styles, but the inventory still retains a timeless chic. The store sells luggage, handbags, and jackets for men and women (in leather or suede). Open Monday to Saturday from 9:30am to 8:30pm. There's another branch with the same hours, and much of the same merchandise, at Serrano 26 (✆ **91-577-60-56**). Gran Vía 8. ✆ **91-522-68-15.** Metro: Banco de España or Gran Vía.

PERFUMES

Alvarez Gómez This is a marvelously old-fashioned *perfumería.* It's been around so long it's newly fashionable again. The shop markets its own fragrances, many based on almost long-forgotten formulas. Even if you're not specifically looking for perfume, you'll find an array of unusual merchandise here, including tortoise shell accessories, custom jewelry, and even women's handbags and belts. Open Monday through Friday from 10am to 8 pm, Saturday from 10am to 2pm. Castellana 111. ✆ **91-555-59-61.** Metro: Cuzco.

Oriental Perfumeries Located at the western edge of the Puerta del Sol, this shop carries one of the most complete stocks of perfume in Madrid—both national and international brands. It also sells gifts, souvenirs, and costume jewelry. Open Monday through Friday from 10am to 9pm, and Saturday from 10am to 12:30pm and 5 to 9pm. Mayor 1. ✆ **91-521-59-05.** Metro: Puerta del Sol.

PORCELAIN

Lasarte This imposing outlet is devoted almost exclusively to Lladró porcelain; the staff can usually tell you about new designs and releases the Lladró company is planning for the near future. Open Monday to Friday from 9:30 to 8pm, Saturday from 10am to 8pm. Gran Vía 44. ✆ **91-521-49-22.** Metro: Callao.

SHOPPING MALLS

ABC Serrano Set within what used to be the working premises of a well-known Madrileño newspaper (*ABC*), this is a complex of about 85 upscale boutiques that emphasize fashion, housewares, cosmetics, and art objects. Although each of the outfitters inside are independently owned and managed, most of them maintain hours of Monday to Saturday from 10am to midnight. On the premises, you'll find cafes and restaurants to keep you fed between bouts of shopping, lots of potted and flowering shrubbery, and acres and acres of Spanish marble and tile. Serrano, 61 or Castellana 34. Metro: Serrano.

12 Madrid After Dark

Madrid abounds in dance halls, *tascas,* cafes, theaters, movie houses, music halls, and nightclubs. You'll have to proceed carefully through this maze, as many of these offerings are strictly for residents or for Spanish-speakers.

Because dinner is served late in Spain, nightlife doesn't really get under way until after 11pm, and it generally lasts until around 3am—Madrileños are so fond of prowling around at night that they are known around Spain as *gatos* (cats). If you arrive at 9:30pm at a club, you'll have the place all to yourself, if it's even open.

In most clubs a one-drink minimum is the rule: Feel free to nurse one drink through the entire evening's entertainment.

In summer, Madrid becomes a virtual free festival because the city sponsors a series of plays, concerts, and films. Pick up a copy of the *Guía del Ocio* (available at most newsstands) for listings of these events. This guide also provides information about occasional discounts for commercial events, such as the concerts that are given in Madrid's parks. Also check the program of *Fundación Juan March,* Calle Castello 77 (© **91-435-42-40;** Metro: Núñez de Balboa). Tapping into funds that were bequeathed to it by a generous financier (Sr. Juan March), it stages free concerts of Spanish and international classical music within a concert hall at its headquarters at Calle Castello 77. In most cases, these are 90-minute events that are presented every Monday and Saturday at noon, and every Wednesday at 7:30pm.

Like flamenco clubs, discos tend to be expensive, but they often open for what is erroneously called afternoon sessions (7–10pm). Although discos charge entry fees, at an afternoon session the cost might be as low as 3€, rising to 15€ and beyond for a night session—that is, beginning at 11:30pm and lasting until the early morning hours. Therefore, go early, dance until 10pm, then proceed to dinner (you'll be eating at the fashionable hour).

Nightlife is so plentiful in Madrid that the city can be roughly divided into the following "night zones."

Plaza Mayor/Puerta del Sol The most popular areas from the standpoint of both tradition and tourist interest, they can also be dangerous, so explore them with caution, especially late at night. They are filled with tapas bars and *cuevas* (drinking caves). Here it is customary to begin a *tasca* crawl, going to tavern after tavern, sampling the wine in each, along with a selection of tapas. The major

---

Tips Champagne Entertainment on a Beer Budget

Flamenco in Madrid is geared mainly to prosperous tourists with fat wallets, and nightclubs are expensive. But since Madrid is preeminently a city of song and dance, you can often be entertained at very little cost—in fact, for the price of a glass of wine or beer, if you sit at a bar with live entertainment.

---

streets for such a crawl are Cava de San Miguel, Cava Alta, and Cava Baja. You can order *pinchos y raciones* (tasty snacks and tidbits).

Gran Vía This area contains mainly cinemas and theaters. Most of the after-dark action takes place on little streets branching off the Gran Vía.

Plaza de Isabel II/Plaza de Oriente Another area much frequented by tourists, many restaurants and cafes flourish here, including the famous Café de Oriente.

Chueca Along such streets as Hortaleza, Infantas, Barquillo, and San Lucas, this is the gay nightlife district, with dozens of clubs. Cheap restaurants, along with a few female striptease joints, are also found here. This area can also be dangerous at night, so watch for pickpockets and muggers. As of late, there has been greater police presence at night.

Argüelles/Moncloa For university students, this part of town sees most of the action. Many dance clubs are found here, along with ale houses and fast-food joints. The area is bounded by Pintor Rosales, Cea Bermúdez, Bravo Murillo, San Bernardo, and Conde Duque.

THE PERFORMING ARTS

Madrid has a number of theaters, opera companies, and dance companies. To discover where and when specific cultural events are being performed, pick up a copy of *Guía del Ocio* at any city newsstand. The sheer volume of cultural offerings can be staggering; for a concise summary of the highlights, see below.

Tickets to dramatic and musical events usually range in price from 4.20€ to 40€, with discounts of up to 50% granted on certain days of the week (usually Wed and matinees on Sun).

The concierges at most major hotels can usually get you tickets to specific concerts, if you are clear about your wishes and needs. They charge a considerable markup, part of which is passed along to whichever agency originally booked the tickets. You'll save money if you go directly to the box office to buy tickets. In the event your choice is sold out, you may be able to get tickets (with a reasonable markup) at **Localidades Galicia** at Plaza del Carmen 1 (© **91-531-27-32;** Metro: Puerta del Sol). This agency also markets tickets to bullfights and sporting events. It is open Tuesday to Saturday from 9:30am to 1:30pm and 4:30 to 7:30pm, Sunday from 9:30am to 1:30pm.

Here follows a grab bag of nighttime diversions that might amuse and entertain you. First, the cultural offerings:

MAJOR PERFORMING-ARTS COMPANIES

For those who speak Spanish, the **Compañía Nacional de Nuevas Tendencias Escénicas** is an avant-garde troupe that performs new and often controversial works by undiscovered writers. On the other hand, the **Compañía Nacional de Teatro Clásico,** as its name suggests, is devoted to the Spanish classics, including works by the ever-popular Lope de Vega and Tirso de Molina.

Among dance companies, the national ballet of Spain—devoted exclusively to Spanish dance—is the **Ballet Nacional de España.** Their performances are always well attended. The national lyrical ballet company is the **Ballet Lírico Nacional.**

World-renowned flamenco sensation Antonio Canales and his troupe, **Ballet Flamenco Antonio Canales,** offer spirited high-energy performances. Productions are centered on Canales's impassioned *Torero,* his interpretation of a bullfighter and the physical and emotional struggles within the man. For tickets and information, you can call Madrid's most comprehensive ticket agency, the previously recommended **Localidades Galicia,** Plaza del Carmen 1 (✆ **91-531-27-32**), for tickets to cultural events and virtually any other event in Castile. Other agencies include **Casa de Catalunya** (✆ **91-538-33-00**) and **Corte Inglés** (✆ **91-432-93-00**). Both Casa de Catalunya and Corte Inglés have satellite offices located throughout Madrid.

Madrid's opera company is the **Teatro de la Opera,** and its symphony orchestra is the outstanding **Orquesta Sinfónica de Madrid.** The national orchestra of Spain—widely acclaimed on the continent—is the **Orquesta Nacional de España,** which pays particular homage to Spanish composers.

CLASSICAL MUSIC

Auditorio del Parque de Atracciones The schedule of this 3,500-seat facility might include everything from punk-rock musical groups to the more high-brow warm-weather performances of visiting symphony orchestras. Check with Localidades Galicia to see what's on at the time of your visit (see above). Casa de Campo. Metro: Lago or Batán.

Auditorio Nacional de Música Sheathed in slabs of Spanish granite, marble, and limestone and capped with Iberian tiles, this hall is the ultramodern home of both the National Orchestra of Spain and the National Chorus of Spain. Standing just north of Madrid's Salamanca district, it ranks as a major addition to the competitive circles of classical music in Europe. Inaugurated in 1988, it is devoted exclusively to the performances of symphonic, choral, and chamber music. In addition to the Auditorio Principal (Hall A), whose capacity is almost 2,300, there's a hall for chamber music (Hall B), as well as a small auditorium (seating 250) for intimate concerts. Príncipe de Vergara 146. ✆ **91-337-01-39.** Tickets 4.20€-40€. Metro: Cruz del Rayo.

Fundación Juan March This foundation sometimes holds free concerts at lunchtime. The advance schedule is difficult to predict, so call for information. Castello 77. ✆ **91-435-42-40.** Metro: Núñez de Balboa.

La Fidula Serving as a bastion of civility in a sea of rock-and-roll and disco chaos, this club was converted from an 1800s grocer. Today it presents chamber music concerts nightly at 11:30pm with an additional show at 1am on weekends. The club offers the prospect of a tranquil, cultural evening on the town, at a moderate price. They take performances here seriously—late arrivals may not be seated for concerts. It is open Monday to Thursday and Sunday from 7pm to 3am, Friday and Saturday from 7pm to 4am. Calle Huerta 57. ✆ **91-429-29-47.** Cover 2.15€. Metro: Antón Martín.

Teatro Cultural de la Villa Spanish-style ballet along with *zarzuelas* (musical reviews), orchestral works, and theater pieces, are presented at this cultural center. Tickets go on sale 5 days before the event of your choice, and performances are usually presented at 2 evening shows (8 and 10:30pm). Plaza de Colón. ✆ **91-575-60-80.** Tickets, depending on event, 8€-27€. Metro: Serrano or Colón.

Teatro Real Reopened in 1997 after a massive US$157 million renovation, this theater is one of the world's finest stage and acoustic settings for opera. Its extensive state-of-the-art equipment affords elaborate stage designs and special effects. Today, the building is the home of the Compañía del Teatro Real, a company specializing in opera, and often working with leading Spanish lyric talents, including Plácido Domingo. The theater is also a major venue for classical music. On November 19, 1850, under the reign of Queen Isabel II, the Royal Opera House opened its doors with Donizetti's *La Favorita.* Plaza Isabel II. ✆ **91-516-06-60.** Tickets 24€–192€. Metro: Opera.

THEATER

Madrid offers many different theater performances, useful to you only if you are very fluent in Spanish. If you aren't, check the *Guía del Ocio* for performances by English-speaking companies on tour from Britain or select a concert or subtitled movie instead.

In addition to the major ones listed below, there are at least 30 other theaters, including one devoted almost entirely to children's plays, the **Sala la Bicicleta,** in the Ciudad de los Niños at Casa de Campo. Nonprofessional groups stage dozens of other plays in such places as churches.

Teatro Calderón This is the largest theater in Madrid, with a seating capacity of 2,000. Although in the past this venue included everything from dramatic theater to flamenco, in recent years it has moved to a more serious approach that focuses mostly on opera, with performances beginning most evenings at 8pm. A long-running favorite is Bizet's *Carmen,* whose setting within Spain partly justified its enduring popularity among Madrileños. Atocha 18. ✆ **91-429-58-90.** Tickets 18€–48€. Metro: Tirso de Molina.

Teatro de la Comedia This is the home of the Compañía Nacional de Teatro Clásico. Here, more than anywhere else in Madrid, you're likely to see performances from the classic repertoire of such great Spanish dramatists as Lope de Vega and Calderón de la Barca. There are no performances on Wednesday, and the theater is closed during July and August. The box office is open daily from 11:30am to 1:30pm and 5 to 6pm, and for about an hour before the performances. Príncipe 14. ✆ **91-521-49-31.** Tickets 8€–16€; 50% discount on Thurs. Metro: Sevilla. Bus: 15, 20, or 150.

Teatro Español This company is funded by Madrid's municipal government, its repertoire a time-tested assortment of great and/or favorite Spanish plays. The box office is open daily from 11:30am to 1:30pm and 5 to 6pm. Príncipe 25. ✆ **91-429-62-97.** Tickets 1.20€–16€; 50% discount on Wed. Metro: Sevilla.

Teatro Lírico Nacional de la Zarzuela Near Plaza de la Cibeles, this theater of potent nostalgia produces ballet and an occasional opera in addition to zarzuela. Show times vary. The box office is open daily from noon to 5pm. Jovellanos 4. ✆ **91-524-54-00.** Tickets 7€–27€. Metro: Sevilla.

Teatro Nuevo Apolo Nuevo Apolo is the permanent home of the renowned Antología de la Zarzuela company. It is on the restored site of the old Teatro Apolo, where these musical variety shows have been performed since the 1930s. Prices and times depend on the show. The box office is open daily from 11:30am to 1:30pm and 5 to 6pm. Plaza de Tirso de Molina 1. ✆ **91-369-06-37.** Cover usually 12€–24€. Metro: Tirso de Molina.

CABARET

Madrid's nightlife is no longer steeped in prudishness, as it was (at least officially) during the Franco era. You can now see glossy cabaret acts and shows with lots of nudity.

Café del Foro This old-time favorite in the Malasaña district has suddenly in the 1990s become one of the most fashionable places in Madrid to hang out after dark. Patronizing the club are members of the literati along with a large

The Sultry Sound of Flamenco

The lights dim and the flamenco stars clatter rhythmically across the dance floor. Their lean bodies and hips shake and sway to the music. The word *flamenco* has various translations, meaning everything from "gypsified Andalusian" to "knife," and from "blowhard" to "tough guy."

Accompanied by stylized guitar music, castanets, and the fervent clapping of the crowd, dancers are filled with tension and emotion. Flamenco dancing, with its flash, color, and ritual, is evocative of Spanish culture, although its origins remain mysterious.

Experts disagree as to where it came from, but most claim Andalusia as its seat of origin. Although its influences were both Jewish and Islamic, it was the gypsy artist who perfected both the song and the dance. Gypsies took to flamenco like "rice to paella," in the words of the historian Fernando Quiñones.

The deep song of flamenco represents a fatalistic attitude toward life. Marxists used to say it was a deeply felt protest of the lower classes against their oppressors, but this seems unfounded. Protest or not, over the centuries, rich patrons, often brash young men, liked the sound of flamenco and booked artists to stage *juergas* or fiestas where dancer-

student clientele. You never know exactly what the show for the evening will be, although live music of some sort generally starts at 11:30pm. Cabaret is often featured, along with live merengue, bolero, and salsa. There's a faux starry sky above the stage area, plus Roman colonnades that justify the name Café del Foro. Open daily from 7pm to 3am. Calle San Andrés 38. ✆ **91-445-37-52.** No cover (but may be imposed for a specially booked act). Metro: Bilbao. Bus: 40, 147, 149, or N-19.

Scala Meliá Castilla Madrid's most famous dinner show is a major Las Vegas–style spectacle, with music, water, light, and color. The program is varied, including international or Spanish ballet, magic acts, ice skaters, whatever. Most definitely a live orchestra will entertain you. It is open Tuesday to Saturday from 8:30pm to 3am. Dinner is served beginning at 9pm; the show is presented at 10:45pm. The show with dinner costs 70€, and if you partake you don't have to pay the cover charge above, as it's included in the show/dinner price. Reservations are essential. Calle Capitán Haya 43 (entrance at Rosario Pino, 7). ✆ **91-571-44-11.** Cover 36€, including first drink. Metro: Cuzco.

FLAMENCO

Café de Chinitas One of the best flamenco clubs in town, Café de Chinitas is set one floor above street level in a 19th-century building midway between the Opera and the Gran Vía. It features an array of (usually) gypsy-born flamenco artists from Madrid, Barcelona, and Andalusia, with acts and performers changing about once a month. You can arrange for dinner before the show, although many Madrileños opt for dinner somewhere else and then arrive just for drinks and the flamenco. Open Monday to Saturday, with dinner served from 9 to 11pm and the show lasting from 10:30pm to 2am. Reservations are recommended. Torija 7. ✆ **91-559-51-35.** Dinner and show 66€; show without dinner (but includes one drink) 30€. Metro: Santo Domingo. Bus: 1 or 2.

prostitutes became the erotic extras. By the early 17th century, flamenco was linked with pimping, prostitution, and lots and lots of drinking, both by the audience and the artists.

By the mid–19th century, flamenco had gone legitimate and was heard in theaters and *café cantantes.* By the 1920s, even the pre-Franco Spanish dictator, Primo de Rivera, was singing the flamenco tunes of his native Cádiz. The poet Federico García Lorca and the composer Manuel de Falla preferred a purer form, attacking what they viewed as the degenerate and "ridiculous" burlesque of *flamenquismo,* the jazzed-up, audience-pleasing form of flamenco. The two artists launched a Flamenco Festival in Grenada in 1922. Of course, in the decades since, their voices have been drowned out, and flamenco is more *flamenquismo* than ever.

In his 1995 book *Flamenco Deep Song,* Thomas Mitchell draws a parallel to flamenco's "lowlife roots" and the "orgiastic origins" of jazz. He notes that early jazz, like flamenco, was "associated with despised ethnic groups, gangsters, brothels, free-spending bluebloods, and whoopee hedonism." By disguising their origins, Mitchell notes, both jazz and flamenco have entered the musical mainstream.

Casa Patas This club is now one of the best places to see "true" flamenco as opposed to the more tourist-oriented version presented at Corral de la Morería (see below). It is also a bar and restaurant, with space reserved in the rear for flamenco. Shows are presented midnight on Thursday, Friday, and Saturday and during Madrid's major fiesta month of May. The best flamenco in Madrid is presented here: Proof of the pudding is that flamenco singers and dancers often hang out here after hours. Tapas are priced at 2.70€ to 15€ and are available at the bar. The club is open daily from 8pm to 2:30am. Calle Cañizares 10. ✆ **91-369-04-96.** Admission 20€. Metro: Tirso de Molina.

Corral de la Morería In the old town, the Morería (meaning where the Moors reside) sizzles with flamenco. Colorfully costumed strolling performers warm up the audience around 11pm; a flamenco show follows, with at least 10 dancers. It's much cheaper to eat somewhere else first, then pay only the one-drink minimum. Open daily from 9pm to 3am. Morería 17. ✆ **91-365-84-46.** Dinner and show 70€; show without dinner (includes one drink) 29€. Metro: La Latina or Puerta del Sol.

DANCE CLUBS

The Spanish dance club takes its inspiration from those of other Western capitals. In Madrid most clubs are open from around 6pm to 9pm, later reopening around 11pm. They generally start rocking at midnight or thereabouts.

Joy Eslava Near the Puerta del Sol, this place has survived the passing fashions of Madrileño nightlife with more style than many of its (now-defunct) competitors. Virtually everyone in Madrid is likely to show up here, ranging from traveling sales reps in town from Düsseldorf to the youthful members of the Madrileño *movida.* Open nightly 10pm to 6:30am. Drinks are 9€ each. Arenal 11. ✆ **91-366-37-33.** Cover 15€, including first drink. Metro: Puerta del Sol.

Kapital This is the most sprawling, labyrinthine, and multicultural disco in Madrid at the moment. Set within what was originally a theater, it has seven different levels, each sporting at least one bar and an ambience that's often radically different from the one you just left on a previous floor. Voyeurs of any age can take heart—there's a lot to see at the Kapital, with a mixed crowd that pursues whatever form of sexuality seems appropriate at the moment. Open Thursday to Sunday from 11:30pm to 5:30am. Second drinks cost from 9€ each. Atocha 125. ✆ **91-420-29-06.** Cover 12€–15€, including first drink. Metro: Antón Martín.

Kathmandu This is Madrid's club of the moment, where cutting-edge music echoes through the night—reggae, jungle, hip-hop, jazzy funk. At this alternative disco, be prepared for a dizzy psychedelic experience. The club would feel right at home among the dives in New York's SoHo. Decidedly androgynous, it's an Oriental-inspired, ultramodern scoff at normalcy. The bar on the top floor is a curious retreat with Tibetan textiles draped from the ceiling. Nepalese art decorates part of the downstairs. At times the floor becomes so overcrowded you think the club will sink, but it carries on with wild abandon. Open Thursday from 11am to 5am, Friday and Saturday from 10am until 6am. Señores de Luzón 3. No phone. Cover 8€, including first drink. Metro: Puerta del Sol.

Pachá The carefully contrived setting is pseudo-opulent, and the drinks sometimes hard to get because of the milling crowds. Despite that, Pachá thrives as one of the late-night staples in Madrid for the mid-20s to late-40s clientele (a crowd that often segregates itself by age into distinctly different areas of the place). More than other nightclubs in Madrid, this has been the subject of complaints from neighbors about late-night noise. Open Tuesday to Sunday from 11pm to 5am. Calle Barcelo 11. ✆ **91-446-01-37.** Cover 12€–15€, including first drink. Metro: Tribunal.

JAZZ

Café Central Off the Plaza de Santa Ana, beside the famed Gran Hotel Victoria, the Café Central has a vaguely turn-of-the-century Art Deco interior, with an unusual series of stained-glass windows. Many of the customers read newspapers and talk at the marble-top tables during the day, but the ambience is far more animated during the nightly jazz sessions, which are ranked among the best in Spain and often draw top artists. Open Sunday to Thursday from 1:30pm to 2:30am, Friday and Saturday from 1:30pm to 3:30am; live jazz is offered daily from 10pm to midnight. Beer costs 2.40€. Plaza del Angel 10. ✆ **91-369-41-43.** Cover 7€–9€; prices can vary depending on the show. Metro: Antón Martín.

Café Populart This club is known for its exciting jazz groups, which encourage the audience to dance. It specializes in Brazilian, Afro-bass, reggae, and new wave African music. When the music starts, usually around 11pm, the prices of drinks are nearly doubled. Open daily from 6pm to 2 or 3am. After the music begins, beer costs 4€, whisky with soda 6€. Calle Huertas 22. ✆ **91-429-84-07.** Metro: Antón Martín or Sevilla. Bus: 6 or 60.

Clamores With dozens of small tables and a huge bar in its dark and smoky interior, Clamores, which means noises in Spanish, is the largest and one of the most popular jazz clubs in Madrid. Established in the early 1980s, it has thrived because of the diverse roster of American and Spanish jazz bands that have appeared here. The place is open daily from 6pm to around 3am, but jazz is presented only Tuesday to Saturday. Tuesday to Thursday, performances are at 11pm and again at 1am; Saturday, performances begin at 11:30pm, with an additional show at 1:30am. There are no live performances on Sunday or Monday nights, when the format is recorded disco music. Regardless of the night of the week you consume them, drinks begin at around 4.20€ each. Albuquerque 14. ✆ **91-445-79-38.** Cover Tues–Sat usually 4.80€–24€, but varies with act; Sun–Mon no cover. Metro: Bilbao.

CUBAN SALSA

Café La Palma Live Cuban groups playing salsa dominate the agenda here. As in Paris, anything Cuban is suddenly chic in Madrid. This is a convivial club and one of the most happening clubs in the capital. It's open daily from 4pm to 3am, but go after 10pm for the most action. A group made up of people mainly in their 20s and 30s is attracted here by the live music. La Palma 62. ✆ **91-522-50-31.** Cover 5€–6€. Metro: Noviciado.

BARS & PUBS

Balmoral Its exposed wood and comfortable chairs evoke a London club. The clientele tends toward journalists, politicians, army brass, owners of large estates, bankers, diplomats, and the occasional literary star. *Newsweek* magazine dubbed it one of the "best bars in the world." No food other than tapas is served. Open Monday to Saturday from noon to midnight or 1am. Beer is 3€; drinks are from 6€. Hermosilla 10. ✆ **91-431-41-33.** Metro: Serrano.

Balneario Clients enjoy potent drinks in a setting with fresh flowers, white marble, and a stone bathtub that might have been used by Josephine Bonaparte. Near Chamartín Station on the northern edge of Madrid, Balneario is one of the most stylish and upscale bars in the city. It is adjacent to and managed by one of Madrid's most elegant and prestigious restaurants, El Cabo Mayor, and often attracts that dining room's clients for aperitifs or after-dinner drinks. Tapas include endive with smoked salmon, asparagus mousse, and anchovies with avocado. Open Monday to Saturday from noon to 2:30am. Drinks are 3.90€–8€; tapas cost 3€–11€. Juan Ramón Jiménez 37. ✆ **91-350-87-76.** Metro: Cuzco.

Bar Taurino This bar remains the top gathering spot for bullfight aficionados. A multitiered place, it is still a shrine to Manolete, the greatest matador of the 1950s who was praised by Hemingway. This is no rough-and-tumble bar, but a cultured space often attracting Madrid society. It reaches the peak of its excitement during the San Isidro bullfighting festival, when Spain's top bullfighters often make appearances here in their full death-in-the-afternoon suits of light. Hours are daily from 11am to midnight. In the Hotel Tryp Reina Victoria, Plaza Santa Ana. ✆ **91-531-45-00.** Metro: Antón Martín.

Bar Cock This bar on two floors attracts some of the most visible artists, actors, models, and filmmakers in Madrid. The name comes from the word *cocktail*, or so they say. The decor is elaborate and unique, in contrast to the hip clientele; the martinis are Madrid's best. Open daily from 7pm to 3am; closed December 24 to 31. Drinks are 7€. De la Reina 16. ✆ **91-532-28-26.** Metro: Gran Vía.

Chicote This is Madrid's most famous cocktail bar. It's classic retro chic, with the same 1930s interior design it had when the foreign press came to sit out the Spanish Civil War, although the sound of artillery shells along the Gran Vía could be heard at the time. Long a favorite of artists and writers, the bar became a haven for prostitutes in the late Franco era. No more. It's back in the limelight again, a sophisticated and much-frequented rendezvous. Open daily from 8am to 3am. Drink prices can be high—from 6€—but the waiters serve them with such grace you don't mind. Gran Vía 12. ✆ **91-532-67-37.** Metro: Gran Vía.

Hispano Bar/Buffet This establishment does a respectable lunch trade every day for members of the local business community, who crowd in to enjoy the amply portioned *platos del día.* These might include a platter of roast duck with figs or orange sauce, or a supreme of hake. After around 5pm, however, the ambience becomes that of a busy after-office bar, patronized by stylishly dressed women and many local entrepreneurs. The hubbub continues on into the night. Open daily from 1:30pm to 1:30am. Full meals at lunchtime cost from around 33€ to 36€, while beer costs from 1.80€. Paseo de la Castellana 78. ✆ **91-411-48-76.** Metro: Nuevos Ministerios.

La Venencia On one of the traditional *tasca* streets in Old Madrid, this tavern has a distinct personality. It is dedicated to the art of serving Spain's finest sherry—and that's it. Don't come in here asking for an extra-dry martini. Our favorite remains Manzanilla, a delicate fino with just a little chill on it. If Luis Buñuel were to need extras in a film, surely the patrons here would be ideal. To go with all that sherry, the waiters (a little rough around the edges) will serve tapas, especially those garlicky marinated olives, *majoama* (cured tuna), and blue-cheese canapés. Barrels form the decor, along with antique posters long turned tobacco-gold from the cigarette smoke. Open daily from 7pm to 1:30am. Echegaray 7. ✆ **91-429-73-13.** Metro: Sevilla.

Los Gabrieles Located in the heart of one of Madrid's most visible warrens of narrow streets, in a district that pulsates with after-dark nightlife options, this historic bar served throughout most of the 19th century as the sales outlet for a Spanish wine merchant. Its cellar was once a fabled gypsy bordello. In the 1980s its two rooms were transformed into a bar and cafe, where you can admire lavishly tiled walls with detailed scenes of courtiers, dancers, and Andalusian maidens peering from behind mantillas and fans. Open daily from 1pm to 3am. Beer costs 1.50€ to 3€. Echegaray 17. ✆ **91-429-62-61.** Metro: Tirso de Molina.

Palacio Gaviria Its construction in 1847 was heralded as the architectural triumph of one of the era's most flamboyant aristocrats, the Marqués de Gaviria. Famous as one of the paramours of Queen Isabella II, he outfitted his palace with the ornate jumble of neoclassical and baroque styles that later became known as *Isabelino.* In 1993, after extensive renovations, the building was opened to the public as a concert hall for the occasional presentation of classical music and as a late-night cocktail bar. Ten high-ceilinged rooms now function as richly decorated, multipurpose areas for guests to wander in, drinks in hand, reacting to whatever, or whomever, happens to be there at the time. (One room is discreetly referred to as having been the bedroom-away-from-home of the queen herself.) No food is served, but the libations include a stylish list of cocktails and wines. The often-dull music doesn't match the elegance of the decor. Dance nights are usually Thursday through Saturday, everything from the tango to the waltz. Cabaret is usually featured on most other nights. Open Monday to Friday from 9pm to 3am, Saturday and Sunday from 9pm to 5am. Second drinks start at 7.20€. Arenal 9. ✆ **91-526-60-69.** Cover 7€-15€, including first drink. Metro: Puerta del Sol or Opera.

Teatriz Part of its function is as a restaurant where soft lighting and a decor by world-class decorator Philippe Starck create one of the most stylish environments in Madrid. A meal averages around 20€ at lunch and 24€ in the evening, but if it's just a drink you're looking for, consider an extended session at any of the site's three bars. Here, within a setting not quite like a disco, but with a sound system almost as good, you'll find a music bar environment where stylish folk of all persuasions enjoy drinks and the gossip that often seems to originate at places like this. The restaurant is open daily from 1:30 to 4pm and 9am to 1pm. The bars are best appreciated every night from 9pm to 3am. Hermosilla 15. ✆ **91-577-53-79.** Metro: Serrano.

Viva Madrid A congenial and sudsy mix of students, artists, and foreign tourists cram into the turn-of-the-century interior here, where antique tile murals and blatant Belle Epoque nostalgia contribute to an undeniable charm. In the good old days (the 1950s, that is) the fabled beautiful people showed up here, notably Ava Gardner with the bullfighter Manolete when they couldn't take their hands off each other. But Orson Welles or even Louis Armstrong used to pop in as well. Crowded and noisy, it's a place where lots of beer is swilled and spilled. It's set within a neighborhood of antique houses and narrow streets near the Plaza de Santa Ana. Open Friday from noon to 1am, Saturday from noon to 2am. Beer costs 3€; whisky begins at 6€. Manuel Fernández y González 7. ✆ **91-429-36-40.** Metro: Antón Martín.

CAVE CRAWLING

To capture a peculiar Madrid joie de vivre of the 18th century, visit some mesones and *cuevas,* many found in the barrios bajos. From Plaza Mayor, walk down the Arco de Cuchilleros until you find a gypsy-like cave that fits your fancy. Young people love to meet in the taverns and caves of Old Madrid for communal drinking and songfests. The sangria flows freely, the atmosphere is charged, and the room is usually packed; the sounds of guitars waft into the night air. Sometimes you'll see a strolling band of singing students going from bar to bar, colorfully attired, with ribbons fluttering from their outfits.

Mesón de la Guitarra Our favorite *cueva* in the area, Mesón de la Guitarra is loud and exciting on any night of the week, and it's as warmly earthy as anything you'll find in Madrid. The decor combines terra-cotta floors, antique brick walls, hundreds of sangria pitchers clustered above the bar, murals of gluttons, old rifles, and faded bullfighting posters. Like most things in Madrid, the place doesn't get rolling until around 10:30pm, although you can stop in for a drink and tapas earlier. Don't be afraid to start singing an American song if it has a fast rhythm—60 people will join in, even if they don't know the words. Open daily from 7pm to 1:30am. Beer is 1.80€; wine is from .75€; tapas are 5.40€–9€. Cava de San Miguel 13. ✆ **91-559-95-31.** Metro: Puerta del Sol or Opera.

Mesón del Champiñón In English the name of this place means "mushroom," and that is exactly what you'll see depicted in various sizes along sections of the vaulted ceilings. The bartenders keep a brimming bucket of sangria behind the long stand-up bar as a thirst quencher for the crowd. A more appetizing way to experience a *champiñón* is to order a *ración* of grilled, stuffed, and salted mushrooms, served with toothpicks. Two tiny, slightly dark rooms in the back are where Spanish families go to hear organ music performed. Unless you want to be exiled to the very back, don't expect to get a seat. Practically everybody prefers to stand. Open daily from 6pm to 2am. Cava de San Miguel 17. No phone. Metro: Puerta del Sol or Opera.

Sesamo In a class by itself, this *cueva,* dating from the early 1950s, draws a clientele of young painters and writers with its bohemian ambience. Hemingway was one of those early visitors (a plaque commemorates him). At first you'll think you're walking into a tiny snack bar—and you are. But proceed down the flight of steps to the cellar. Here, the walls are covered with contemporary paintings and

Moments Summer *Terrazas*

At the first blush of spring weather, Madrileños rush outdoors to drink, talk, and sit at a string of open-air cafes, called *terrazas,* throughout the city. The best and most expensive ones are along Paseo de la Castellana between the Plaza de la Cibeles and the Plaza Emilio Castelar, but there are dozens more throughout the city.

You can wander up and down the boulevard, selecting one that appeals to you; if you get bored, you can go on later to another one. Sometimes these *terrazas* are called *chirinquitos.* You'll find them along other paseos, the Recoletos and the Prado, both fashionable areas but not as hip as the Castellana. For old traditional atmosphere, the terraces at the Plaza Mayor win out. The Plaza Santa Ana has several atmospheric choices within the old city. Friday and Saturday are the most popular nights for drinking; many locals sit here all night.

quotations. At squatty stools and tables, an international assortment of young people listens to piano music and sometimes piano or guitar playing. Open daily from 6:30pm to 2am. A pitcher of sangria (for four) is 8.50€; beer costs 2€. Príncipe 7. ✆ **91-429-65-24.** Metro: Sevilla or Puerta del Sol.

GAY & LESBIAN BARS

Black and White This is the major gay bar of Madrid, in the center of the Chueca district. A guard will open the door to a large room—painted, as you might expect, black and white. There's a disco in the basement, but the street-level bar is the premier gathering spot, featuring drag shows beginning at 3am Thursday to Sunday, male striptease, and videos. Old movies are shown against one wall. Open Monday to Friday from 8pm to 5am, Saturday and Sunday from 8pm to 6am. Beer is 4€; whisky costs 6€. Gravina (at the corner of Libertad). ✆ **91-531-11-41.** Metro: Chueca.

Café Figueroa This turn-of-the-century cafe attracts a diverse clientele, including a large number of gay men and lesbians. It's one of the city's most popular gathering spots for drinks and conversation. Open Sunday through Thursday from 4pm to midnight, Friday and Saturday from 4pm to 2:30am. Beer from 2.50€; whisky costs from 4.20€. Augusto Figueroa 17 (at corner of Hortaleza). ✆ **91-521-16-73.** Metro: Chueca.

Cruising One of the predominant gay bars of Madrid, a center for gay consciousness-raising and gay cruising (though they say the name refers to automobile driving), this place has probably been visited at least once by every gay male in Castile. There are practically no women inside, but always a hustler looking for a tourist john. It doesn't get crowded or lively until late at night. Open Monday to Friday from 8pm to 3:30am, Saturday and Sunday from 8pm to 4:30am. Beer costs from 2.40€ to 3€. Pérez Galdos 5. ✆ **91-521-51-43.** Metro: Chueca.

Leather Bar This is another of the premier bars for gay men in Madrid, but despite its supposed emphasis on leather and uniforms, only about 25% of the men who show up actually wear them. You'll find two bars on the establishment's street level and a disco in the basement where same-sex couples can dance. Beer costs 3€. It's open Sunday through Thursday from 7pm to 3am, Friday and Saturday from 8pm to 3:30am. Calle Pelayo 42. ✆ **91-308-14-62.** Admission 3€. Metro: Chueca.

Rick's Rick's takes its name from "Everybody Comes to Rick's," the original title of the Bogie classic *Casablanca.* Many gay bars in the Chueca barrio are sleazy, but this is a classy joint—just like the fictional Rick's in Morocco. It's decorated with Bogie paraphernalia, including marble floors and gilt columns. The only thing missing is a piano player singing "As Time Goes By"—and Bergman, of course. Gay men patronize the place, with the occasional woman showing up, too. Incongruously it has a foosball table in the bar but lavender walls. Open daily from 11:30pm "until some time in the early morning." Calle Clavel 8. ✆ **91-531-91-86.** Cover 7€. Metro: Chueca.

A CASINO

Casino Gran Madrid is at Km 29 along the Carretera La Coruña (the A-6 highway running between Madrid and La Coruña), Apartado 62 (✆ **91-856-11-00**). The largest place for gambling in Madrid, it appeals to nongamblers with a well-choreographed roster of dining and entertainment facilities, including two restaurants, four bars, and a nightclub. And if you happen to enjoy gambling, there are facilities for French and American roulette, blackjack, *punto y banco,* baccarat, and chemin de fer. Presentation of a passport at the door is essential—without it, you won't be admitted. Entrance costs 3€, although that fee is often waived for residents of some of Madrid's larger hotels who arrive with a ticket that's sometimes provided gratis by the hotel's management. The casino and all of its facilities are open daily from 4pm to 5am.

An a la carte restaurant in the French Gaming Room offers international cuisine, with dinners costing from 38€ to 50€. A buffet in the American Gaming Room will cost around 20€. The restaurants are open 9:15pm to 2am.

The casino is about 29km (18 miles) northwest of Madrid. If you don't feel like driving, the casino has buses that depart from Plaza de España 6 every afternoon and evening at 4:30, 6, 7:30, 11pm, and 1am. Note that between October and June, men must wear jackets and ties; T-shirts and tennis shoes are forbidden in any season.

7

Side Trips from Madrid

Madrid makes an ideal base for excursions because it's surrounded by some of Spain's major attractions. The day trips listed below to both New Castile and Old Castile range from 14 to 91km (9–54 miles) outside Madrid, allowing you to leave in the morning and be back by nightfall. In case you choose to stay overnight, however, we've included a selection of hotels in each town.

The satellite cities and towns around Madrid include Toledo, with its El Greco masterpieces; the wondrous El Escorial monastery; Segovia's castles that float in the clouds; and the Bourbon palaces at La Granja.

1 Toledo ★

68km (42 miles) SW of Madrid, 137km (85 miles) SE of Avila

If you have only one day for an excursion outside Madrid, go to Toledo—a place made special by its Arab, Jewish, Christian, and even Roman and Visigothic elements. A national landmark, the city that so inspired El Greco in the 16th century has remained relatively unchanged. You can still stroll through streets barely wide enough for a man and his donkey—much less for an automobile.

Surrounded on three sides by a bend in the Tagus River, Toledo stands atop a hill overlooking the arid plains of New Castile—a natural fortress in the center of the Iberian Peninsula. It was a logical choice for the capital of Spain, though it lost its political status to Madrid in the 1500s. Toledo has remained the country's religious center, as the seat of the Primate of Spain.

If you're driving, the much-painted skyline of Toledo will come into view about 6km (3½ miles) from the city. When you cross the Tagus River on the 14th-century Puente San Martín, the scene is reminiscent of El Greco's moody, storm-threatened *View of Toledo,* which hangs in New York's Metropolitan Museum of Art. The artist reputedly painted that view from a hillside that is now the site of Parador Nacional de Conde Orgaz. If you arrive at the right time, you can enjoy an aperitif on the parador's terrace and watch one of the famous violet sunsets of Toledo (see "Where to Stay," later in this chapter).

Moments A Great Scenic Drive

Another Toledan highlight is the **Carretera de Circunvalación,** the route that threads through the city and runs along the Tagus. Clinging to the hillsides are rustic dwellings, the cigarrales of the Imperial City, immortalized by 17th-century dramatist Tirso de Molina, who named his trilogy *Los Cigarrales de Toledo.*

Madrid Environs

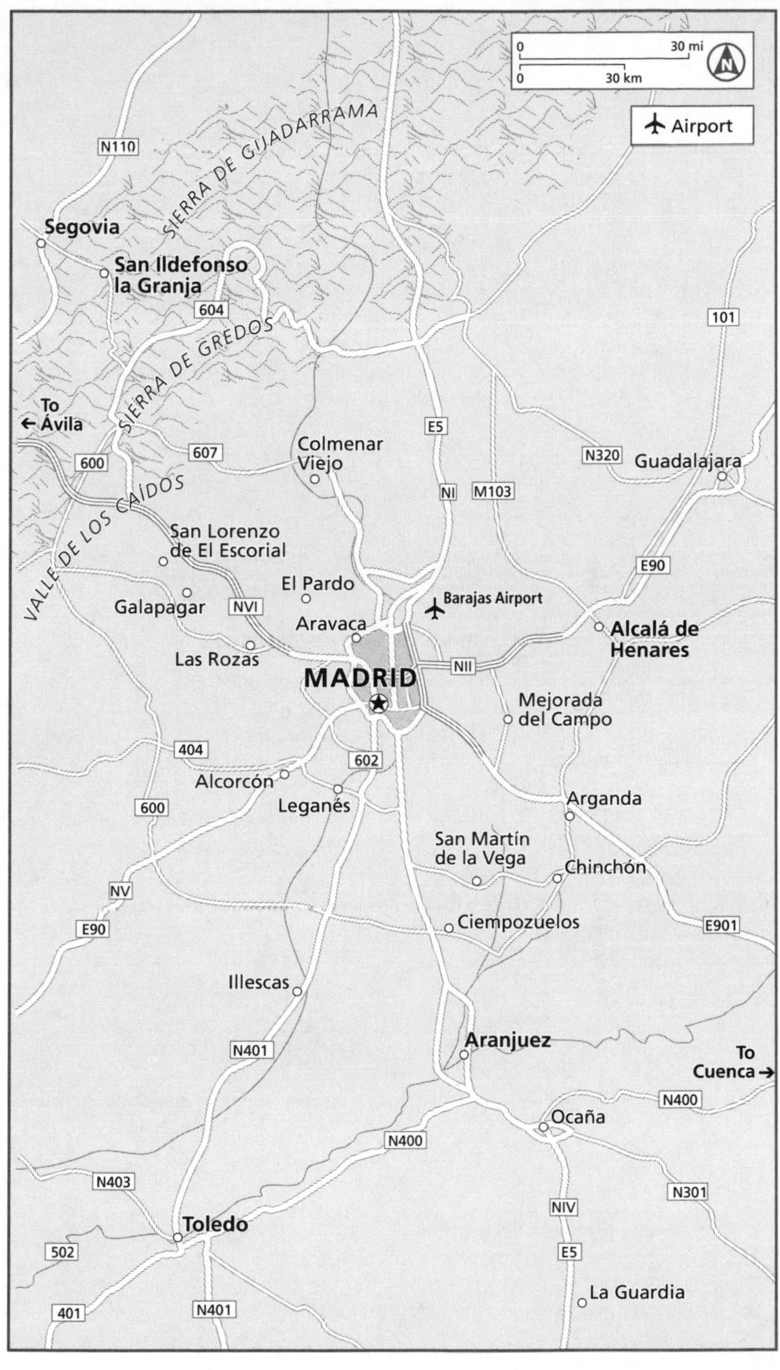

Toledo

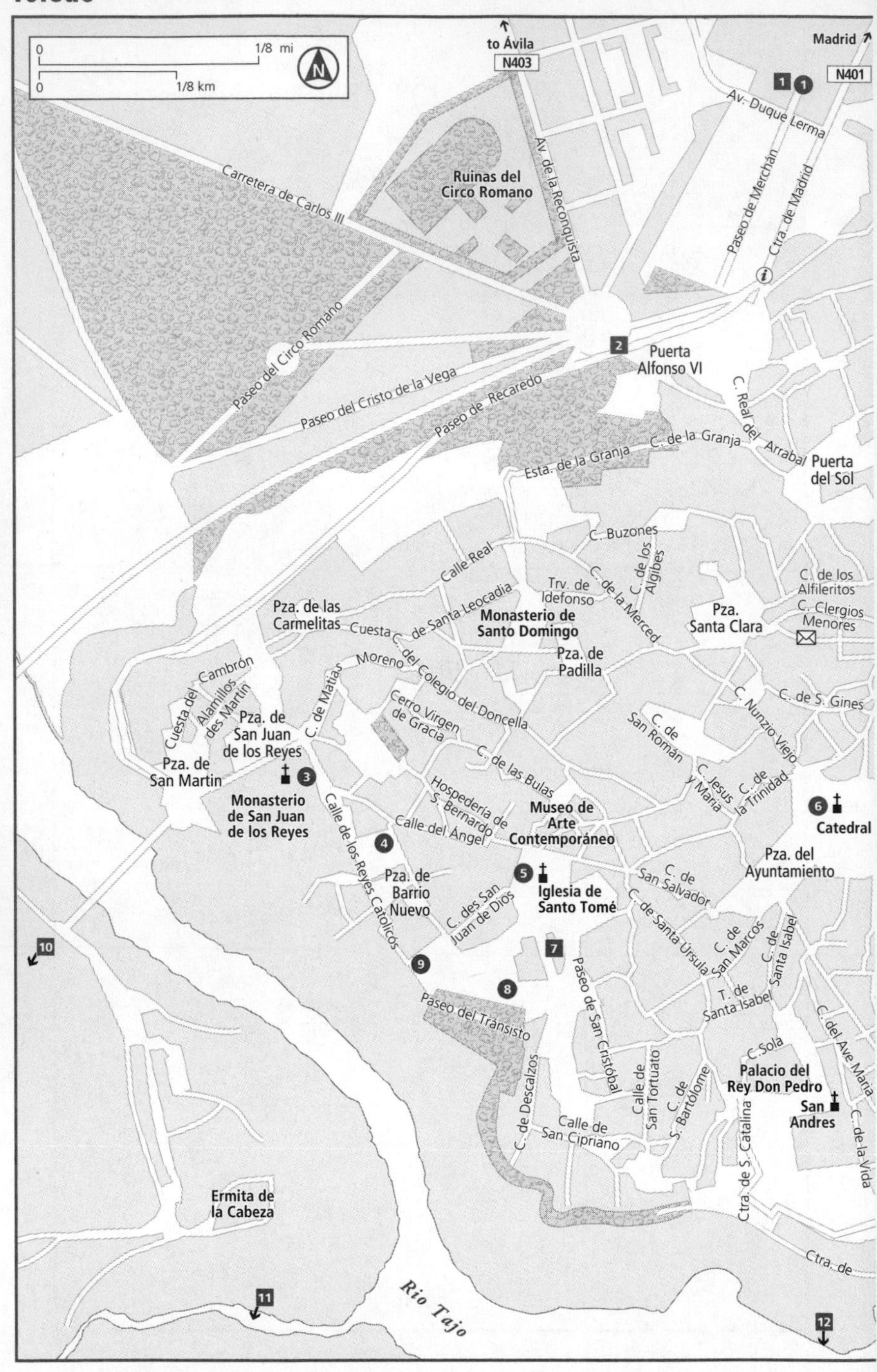

0
1/8 mi
0
1/8 km
N
to Ávila
N403
Madrid
N401
Av. Duque Lerma
Paseo de Merchán
Ctra. de Madrid
Ruinas del Circo Romano
Av. de la Reconquista
Carretera de Carlos III
Paseo del Circo Romano
Paseo del Cristo de la Vega
Paseo de Recaredo
Puerta Alfonso VI
C. Real del Arrabal
Puerta del Sol
C. de la Granja
Esta. de la Granja
C. Buzones
C. de los Algibes
Calle Real
Trv. de Idefonso
C. de la Merced
C. de los Alfileritos
C. Clergios Menores
Pza. Santa Clara
Pza. de las Carmelitas
Cuesta
C. de Santa Leocadia
Monasterio de Santo Domingo
Pza. de Padilla
Moreno
C. del Colegio del Doncella
C. de Matías
Cambrón
Cuesta del
Alamillos des Martin
Pza. de San Juan de los Reyes
Pza. de San Martin
Cerro Virgen de Gracia
C. de las Bulas
C. Nunzio Viejo
C. de S. Gines
C. de San Román
C. Jesus y María
C. de la Trinidad
Catedral
Monasterio de San Juan de los Reyes
Calle de los Reyes Catolicós
Hospedería de S. Bernardo
Calle del Ángel
Museo de Arte Contemporáneo
Pza. del Ayuntamiento
Pza. de Barrio Nuevo
C. des San Juan de Dios
Iglesia de Santo Tomé
C. de San Salvador
C. de Santa Úrsula
C. de San Marcos
C. de Santa Isabel
T. de Santa Isabel
Paseo de San Cristóbal
Paseo del Tránsito
C. del Ave María
C. Sola
Palacio del Rey Don Pedro
San Andres
C. de Descalzos
Calle de San Tortuato
C. de S. Bartólome
Calle de San Cipriano
Ctra. de S. Catalina
C. de la Vida
Ctra. de
Ermita de la Cabeza
Rio Tajo
1
2
3
4
5
6
7
8
9
10
11
12

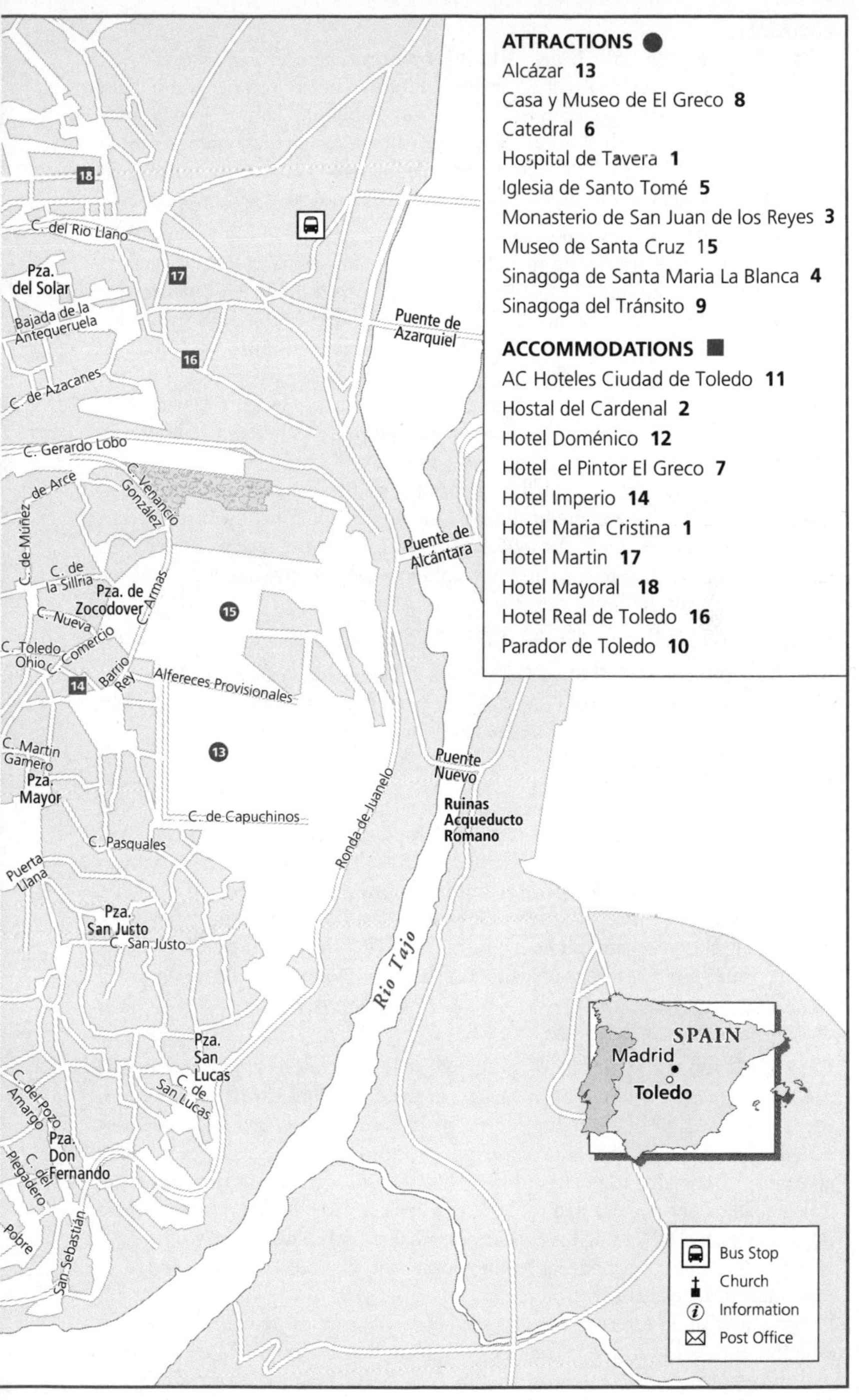
ATTRACTIONS
Alcázar 13
Casa y Museo de El Greco 8
Catedral 6
Hospital de Tavera 1
Iglesia de Santo Tomé 5
Monasterio de San Juan de los Reyes 3
Museo de Santa Cruz 15
Sinagoga de Santa Maria La Blanca 4
Sinagoga del Tránsito 9
ACCOMMODATIONS
AC Hoteles Ciudad de Toledo 11
Hostal del Cardenal 2
Hotel Doménico 12
Hotel el Pintor El Greco 7
Hotel Imperio 14
Hotel Maria Cristina 1
Hotel Martin 17
Hotel Mayoral 18
Hotel Real de Toledo 16
Parador de Toledo 10
C. del Rio Llano
Pza. del Solar
Bajada de la Antequeruela
C. de Azacanes
C. Gerardo Lobo
Puente de Azarquiel
C. de Muñez de Arce
C. Venancio González
Puente de Alcántara
C. de la Sillria
Pza. de Zocodover
C. Armas
C. Nueva
C. Comercio
C. Toledo Ohio
Barrio Rey
Alfereces Provisionales
C. Martin Gamero
Pza. Mayor
Puente Nuevo
Ruinas Acqueducto Romano
C. de Capuchinos
Ronda de Juanelo
C. Pasquales
Puerta Llana
Pza. San Justo
C. San Justo
Rio Tajo
Pza. San Lucas
C. de San Lucas
C. del Pozo Amargo
Pza. Don Fernando
C. del Plegadero
Pobre
San Sebastián
SPAIN
Madrid
Toledo
Bus Stop
Church
Information
Post Office

ESSENTIALS

GETTING THERE **By Train** RENFE trains run here frequently every day. Those departing Madrid's Atocha Railway Station for Toledo run daily from 7am to 9:50pm; those leaving Toledo for Madrid run daily from 7am to 9pm. Traveling time is approximately 2 hours. RENFE also runs two express trains a day to and from Toledo, taking only 1 hour and making a stop at Aranjuez. For train information in Madrid call © **90-224-02-02;** in Toledo call © **92-522-30-99.**

By Bus Bus transit between Madrid and Toledo is faster and more convenient than travel by train. Buses are maintained by several companies, the largest of which include Continental or Galiano. They depart from Madrid's Estación Sur de Autobuses (South Bus Station), Calle Méndez Alvaro (© **91-468-42-00** for information), every day between 6:30am and 10pm at 30-minute intervals. The fastest leave Monday to Friday on the hour. Those that depart weekdays on the half hour, and those that run on weekends, take a bit longer. Travel time, depending on whether the bus stops at villages en route, is between 1 hour and 1 hour 20 minutes. One-way transit costs 3.60€.

Once you reach Toledo, you'll be deposited at the Estación de Autobuses, which lies beside the river, about three-quarters of a mile from the historic center. Although many visitors opt to walk, be advised that the ascent is steep. Bus numbers 5 and 6 run from the station uphill to the center, charging .78€ for the brief ride. Pay the driver directly.

By Car Exit Madrid via Cibeles (Paseo del Prado) and take the N-401 south.

VISITOR INFORMATION The **tourist information office** is at Puerta de Bisagra (© **925-22-08-43**). It's open Monday to Friday from 9am to 6pm, Saturday from 9am to 7pm, and Sunday from 9am to 3pm.

EXPLORING THE TOWN

Alcázar The Alcázar, located at the eastern edge of the old city, dominates the Toledo skyline. It became world famous at the beginning of the Spanish Civil War, when it underwent a 70-day siege that almost destroyed it. Today it has been rebuilt and turned into an army museum, housing such exhibits as a plastic model of what the fortress looked like after the Civil War, electronic equipment used during the siege, and photographs taken during the height of the battle. A walking tour gives a realistic simulation of the siege. Allow an hour for a visit.

Calle General Moscardó 4, near the Plaza de Zocodover. © **92-522-16-73.** Admission 2€ adults, free for children under 10. Tues–Sun 9:30am–2pm. Bus: 5 or 6.

Casa y Museo de El Greco ★ Located in Toledo's *antiguo barrio judío* (the old Jewish quarter, a labyrinth of narrow streets on the old town's southwestern edge), the House of El Greco honors the great master painter, although he didn't actually live here. In 1585 the artist moved into one of the run-down palace apartments belonging to the Marquís of Villena. Although he was to live at other Toledan addresses, he returned to the Villena palace in 1604 and remained there until his death. Only a small part of the original residence was saved from decay. In time, this and a neighboring house became the El Greco museum; today it's furnished with authentic period pieces.

You can visit El Greco's so-called studio, where one of his paintings hangs. The museum contains several more works, including a copy of *A View of Toledo* and three portraits, plus many pictures by various 16th- and 17th-century Spanish artists. The garden and especially the kitchen also merit attention, as does a sitting room decorated in the Moorish style.

Calle Samuel Leví 3. ✆ **92-522-40-46.** Admission 1.20€ adults, free for children under 10. Tues–Sat 10am–2pm and 4–6pm, Sun 10am–2pm. Bus: 5 or 6.

Catedral ★★★ Ranked among the greatest Gothic structures, the cathedral actually reflects several styles, since more than 2½ centuries elapsed during its construction (1226–1493). Many historic events transpired here, including the proclamation of Joanna the Mad and her husband, Philip the Handsome, as heirs to the throne of Spain.

Among its art treasures, the *transparente* stands out—a wall of marble and florid baroque alabaster sculpture overlooked for years because the cathedral was too poorly lit. Sculptor Narcisco Tomé cut a hole in the ceiling, much to the consternation of Toledans, and now light touches the high-rising angels, a *Last Supper* in alabaster, and a Virgin in ascension.

The 16th-century Capilla Mozárabe, containing works by Juan de Borgona, is another curiosity of the cathedral. Mass is still held here using Mozarabic liturgy.

The Treasure Room has a 500-pound 15th-century gilded monstrance—allegedly made with gold brought back from the New World by Columbus—that is still carried through the streets of Toledo during the feast of Corpus Christi.

Other highlights of the cathedral include El Greco's *Twelve Apostles and Spoliation of Christ* and Goya's *Arrest of Christ on the Mount of Olives.* The cathedral shop, where you buy tickets to enter, is well organized and stocks a variety of quality souvenirs, including ceramics and damascene.

Cardenal Cisneros 1. ✆ **92-522-22-41.** Free admission to cathedral; Treasure Room 4.80€. Mon–Sat 10:30am–6:30pm; Sun 2–6:30pm.

Hospital de Tavera This 16th-century Greco-Roman palace north of the medieval ramparts of Toledo was originally built by Cardinal Tavera; it now houses a private art collection. Titian's portrait of Charles V hangs in the banqueting hall. The museum owns five paintings by El Greco: *The Holy Family, The Baptism of Christ,* and portraits of St. Francis, St. Peter, and Cardinal Tavera. Ribera's *The Bearded Woman* also attracts many viewers. The collection of books in the library is priceless. In the nearby church is the mausoleum of Cardinal Tavera, designed by Alonso Berruguete.

Hospital de Tavera 2. ✆ **92-522-04-51.** Admission 3€. Daily 10:30am–1:30pm and 3:30–6pm.

Iglesia de Santo Tomé This modest little 14th-century chapel, situated on a narrow street in the old Jewish quarter, might have been overlooked had it not possessed El Greco's masterpiece ***The Burial of the Count of Orgaz*** ★★★, created in 1586. To avoid the hordes, go when the chapel first opens.

Plaza del Conde 4, Vía Santo Tomé. ✆ **92-525-60-98.** Admission 1.20€. Daily 10am–6:45pm (closes at 5:45pm in winter). Closed Dec 25 and Jan 1.

Monasterio de San Juan de los Reyes ★ Founded by King Ferdinand and Queen Isabella to commemorate their triumph over the Portuguese at Toro in 1476, the church was started in 1477 according to the plans of architect Juan Guas. It was finished, together with the splendid cloisters, in 1504, dedicated to St. John the Evangelist, and used from the beginning by the Franciscan friars. An example of Gothic-Spanish-Flemish style, San Juan de los Reyes was restored after the damage caused during Napoléon's invasion and after its abandonment in 1835; since 1954 it has been entrusted again to the Franciscans. The church is located at the extreme western edge of the old town, midway between the Puente (bridge) of San Martín and the Puerta (gate) of Cambron.

Calle Reyes Católicos 17. ✆ **92-522-38-02.** Admission 1.20€ adults, free for children 8 and under. Winter, daily 10am–1:45pm and 3:30–6pm; summer, daily 10am–1:45pm and 3:30–7pm. Bus: 2.

Museo de Santa Cruz ★★ Today a museum of art and sculpture, this was originally a 16th-century Spanish Renaissance hospice, founded by Cardinal Mendoza—"the third king of Spain"—who helped Ferdinand and Isabella gain the throne. The facade is almost more spectacular than any of the exhibits inside. It's a stunning architectural achievement in the classical Plateresque style. The major artistic treasure inside is El Greco's *The Assumption of the Virgin,* his last known work. Paintings by Goya and Ribera are also on display along with gold items, opulent antique furnishings, Flemish tapestries, and even Visigoth artifacts. In the patio of the museum, you'll stumble across various fragments of carved stone and sarcophagi lids. One of the major exhibits is of a large Astrolablio tapestry of the zodiac from the 1400s. In the basement, you can see artifacts, including elephant tusks, from various archaeological digs throughout the province.

Calle Miguel de Cervantes 3. ✆ **92-522-10-36.** Free admission. Mon–Sat 10am–6pm, Sun 10am–2pm. Bus: 5 or 6. Pass beneath the granite archway on the eastern edge of the Plaza de Zocodover and walk about 1 block.

Sinagoga de Santa María La Blanca ★ In the late 12th century, the Jews of Toledo erected an important synagogue in the *almohada* style, which employs graceful horseshoe arches and ornamental horizontal moldings. Although by the early 15th century it had been converted into a Christian church, much of the original remains, including the five naves and elaborate Mudéjar decorations, mosquelike in their effect. The synagogue lies on the western edge of the city, midway between the El Greco museum and San Juan de los Reyes.

Calle Reyes Católicos 2. ✆ **92-522-72-57.** Admission 1.20€. Apr–Sept, daily 10am–2pm and 3:30–7pm; Oct–Mar, daily 10am–2pm and 3:30–6pm. Bus: 2.

Sinagoga del Tránsito ★ One block west of the El Greco home and museum stands this once-important house of worship for Toledo's large Jewish population. A 14th-century building, it is noted for its superb stucco Hebrew inscriptions, including psalms inscribed along the top of the walls and a poetic description of the Temple on the east wall. The synagogue is the most important part of the **Museo Sefardí** (Sephardic Museum), which opened in 1971 and contains art objects as well as tombstones with Hebrew epigraphy, some of which are dated before 1492.

Calle Samuel Leví. ✆ **92-522-36-65.** Admission 2.40€. Tues–Sat 10am–1:45pm and 4–5:45pm, Sun 10am–1:45pm. Closed Jan 1, May 1, Dec 24–25, and Dec 31. Bus: 2.

SHOPPING

In swashbuckling days, the swordsmiths of Toledo were world renowned. They're still here and still turning out swords today. Toledo is equally renowned for its *damasquinado,* or damascene work, the Moorish art of inlaying gold, even copper or silver threads, against a matte black steel backdrop. Today Toledo is filled with souvenir shops hawking damascene. The price depends on whether the item is handcrafted or machine made. Sometimes machine-made damascene is passed off as the more expensive handcrafted item, so you have to shop carefully. Bargaining is perfectly acceptable in Toledo, but if you get the price down, you can't pay with a credit card—only cash.

Marzipan (called *mazapán* locally) is often prepared by nuns and is a local specialty. Many shops in town specialize in this treat made of sweet almond paste.

Finds The Pottery Towns of Old Castile

The best deals on pottery won't be found in Toledo. If you're interested in buying a number of items, consider a trip to Talavera la Reina, 76km (47 miles) west of Toledo, where most of the pottery is made. Since Talavera is the largest city in the province, it is hardly a picture-postcard little potter's village. Most of the shops lie along the main street of town, where you'll find store after store selling this distinctive pottery in multicolored designs.

Pottery hunters also flock to Puente del Arzobispo, another ceramic center, known for its green-hued pottery. From Talavera drive west on the N-V to Oropesa, then south for 14km (9 miles) to a fortified bridge across the Tagus. In general, ceramics here are cheaper than those sold in Toledo.

Just past Oropesa at the turnoff to Lagartera is the village where the highly sought-after embroidery of La Mancha originates. Virtually every cottage displays samples of this free-form floral stitching, shaped into everything from skirts to tablecloths. Of course, shops in Toledo are also filled with samples of this unique embroidery.

The province of Toledo is also renowned for its pottery, which is sold in so many shops at competitive prices that it's almost unnecessary to recommend specific branches hawking these wares. However, over the years we've found that the prices at the large roadside emporiums on the outskirts of town on the main road to Madrid often have better bargains than the shops within the city walls, where rents are higher.

Casa Bermejo Established in 1910, this factory and store employs almost 50 artisans, whom you can observe at work as part of a visit to its premises. The outlet carries a wide array of damascene objects fashioned into Toledo's traditional Mudéjar designs. These include swords, platters, pitchers, and other gift items. Don't think, however, that everything this place manufactures follows the inspiration of the medieval Arabs. The outfit engraves many of the ornamental swords that are awarded to graduates of West Point in the United States, as well as the decorative, full-dress military accessories used by the armies of various countries of Europe, including France. Open Monday to Friday from 9am to 1pm and 3 to 6pm, Saturday from 8am to 1pm. Closing times are later in July and August, determined solely by business traffic. Calle Airosas 5. ✆ **92-528-53-67.**

Casa Telesforo Many long-time residents of Toledo remember this place as the supplier of the marzipan consumed at their childhood birthday parties and celebrations. A specialist in the almond-and-sugar confection whose origins go back to the year 1806, it sells the best marzipan in town, cunningly made into such whimsical shapes as hearts, diamonds, flowers, and fish. Open daily from 9am to 10pm, later in summer, depending on the crowds. Plaza de Zocodover 13. ✆ **92-522-33-79.**

Felipe Suárez Established in the 1920s, this outfit has manufactured damascene work in various forms ranging from unpretentious souvenir items to art objects of rare museum-quality beauty that sell for as much as 12,000€. You'll find swords, straight-edged razors, pendants, fans, and an array of pearls. The shop maintains extended hours throughout the year, daily from 9:30am to 7pm. Paseo de los Canónigos 19. ✆ **92-522-56-15.**

Santiago Sánchez Martín This is one of the most painstaking and prestigious manufacturers of damascene work in Toledo. It specializes in the elaborately detailed arabesques whose techniques are as old as the Arab conquest of Iberia. Look for everything from decorative tableware (platters, pitchers), to mirror frames, jewelry, letter openers, and ornamental swords. Open Monday to Friday from 9am to 2pm and 5 to 7pm. Calle Río Llano 15. ✆ **92-522-77-57.**

WHERE TO STAY

EXPENSIVE

AC Hoteles Ciudad de Toledo ★★ Opened in 1998, this is the first hotel in years that has emerged as a superior choice to the government-run parador. If El Greco were painting his *A View of Toledo* today, he would surely have come to this site instead of the parador location. On a beltway south of the city—follow the directions to the Parador Nacional de Conde Orgaz—this deluxe property is a member of a chain that also includes the swanky **Santo Mauro** in Madrid. The epitome of luxury living and contemporary lines, this hotel across the river from Toledo is entered at the third floor. You move down through the spiraling architectural design to reach the rest of the hotel. Bedrooms are spacious and luxuriously furnished, all in contemporary styling, each with tiled bathrooms containing shower-tub combinations. The suites have oversize bathtubs and hydromassage.

Carretera de Circunvalación 15, 41005 Toledo. ✆ **92-528-51-25.** Fax 92-528-47-00. www.ac-hoteles.com. 49 units. 117€–151€ double; 179€–231€ suite. AE, MC, V. Free parking. Bus: 5. **Amenities:** Restaurant; bar; room service; babysitting; laundry/dry cleaning. *In room:* A/C, TV, minibar, hair dryer.

Parador de Toledo ★★★ You'll have to make reservations well in advance to stay at this parador, which is built on the ridge of a rugged hill where El Greco is said to have painted his *A View of Toledo.* That view is still here, and it is without a doubt one of the grandest in the world. The main living room/lounge has fine furniture—old chests, brown leather chairs, and heavy tables—and leads to a sunny terrace overlooking the city. On chilly nights, you can sit by the public fireplace. The guest rooms are the most luxurious in all of Toledo, far superior to those at María Cristina (see below). Spacious and beautifully furnished, they contain private bathrooms with shower-tub combinations and reproductions of regional antique pieces.

Cerro del Emperador, 45002 Toledo. ✆ **92-522-18-50.** Fax 92-522-51-66. www.parador.es. 76 units. 129€ double; 160€ suite. AE, DC, MC, V. Free parking. Drive across Puente San Martín and head south for 4km (2½ miles). **Amenities:** Restaurant; bar; room service; pool; babysitting; laundry/dry cleaning. *In room:* A/C, TV, minibar, hair dryer, safe.

MODERATE

Hostal del Cardenal ★★ Although long acclaimed as the best restaurant in Toledo (see below), the fact that this establishment has rooms available is still a well-kept secret. They're not as grand as those at the Parador, but they are choice nevertheless, sought by those wanting to capture an old Toledan atmosphere. The entrance to this unusual hotel is set into the stone fortifications of the ancient city walls, a few steps from the Bisagra Gate. To enter the hotel, you must climb a series of terraces to the top of the crenellated walls of the ancient fortress. Here, grandly symmetrical and very imposing, is the *hostal* (hostel), the former residence of the 18th-century cardinal of Toledo, Señor Lorenzana. Just beyond the entrance, still atop the city wall, you'll find flagstone walkways, Moorish fountains, rose gardens, and cascading vines. The establishment has tiled walls; long, narrow salons; dignified Spanish furniture; and a smattering of antiques. Each room has a private bathroom equipped with a shower-tub combination. The only parking is what's available free on the street. A member of the hotel staff will call you a taxi if you don't want to walk the steep ascent (on narrow to nonexistent sidewalks) into the historic district.

Paseo de Recaredo 24, 45003 Toledo. ✆ **92-522-49-00.** Fax 92-522-29-91. www.cardenal.asernet.es. 27 units. 72€–90€ double; 98€–122€ suite. AE, DC, MC, V. Parking 11.20€. Bus: 2 from rail station. **Amenities:** Restaurant; bar; babysitting; laundry/dry cleaning. *In room:* A/C, TV, hair dryer.

Hotel Doménico ★ A government-rated four-star hotel, one of the finest in Toledo, Doménico is located among Los Cigarrales, the typical country houses lying south of the city and offering panoramic views. The building, though modern, is constructed in a classic and traditional style. Launched in 1993, the hotel is only a 5-minute drive to the historic core of Toledo. Bedrooms are medium in size and comfortably furnished. Some of the rooms have windows in the roof for greater light. All units contain well-kept bathrooms with shower-tub combinations. The second- and third-floor rooms have terraces opening onto the swimming pool or views of the city. A terrace restaurant offers a fine national and international cuisine.

Cerro del Emperador, 45002 Toledo. ✆ **92-528-01-01.** Fax 92-528-02-03. www.hoteldomenico.com. 50 units. 75€–109€ double; 173€ suite. AE, MC, V. Free parking. Bus: 7. **Amenities:** Restaurant; bar; room service; pool; babysitting; laundry/dry cleaning. *In room:* A/C, TV, minibar, hair dryer, safe.

Hotel El Pintor El Greco ★ In the old Jewish quarter, one of the most traditional and historic districts of Toledo, this hotel was converted from a typical *casa toledana* (house in Toledo), which had once been used as a bakery. With careful restoration, especially of its ancient facade, it was transformed into one of Toledo's best and most atmospheric small hotels—the only one to match the antique charm of Hostal del Cardenal (see above), although, it too, seems relatively unknown. Decoration in both the public rooms and bedrooms is in a traditional Castilian style. Bedrooms come in a variety of shapes and sizes, as befits a building of this age, but all are equipped with small bathrooms with shower-tub combinations and adequate shelf space. At the doorstep of the hotel are such landmarks as the Monasterio de San Juan de los Reyes, Sinagoga de Santa María la Blanca, Sinagoga del Tránsito, Casa y Museo de El Greco, and Iglesia de Santo Tomé. Public parking is available for 5€ per day.

Alamillos del Tránsito 13, 45002 Toledo. ✆ **92-528-51-91.** Fax 92-521-58-19. www.hotelpintorelgreco.com. 33 units. 91€–112€ double. AE, DC, MC, V. Parking 5€ ($4.45). **Amenities:** Lounge; babysitting; laundry/dry cleaning. *In room:* A/C, TV, minibar, hair dryer, safe.

Hotel María Cristina Adjacent to the historic Hospital de Tavera and near the northern perimeter of the old town, this stone-sided, awning-fronted hotel resembles a palatial country home. If you're willing to forgo the view from the Parador and the charm of Hostal del Cardenal, this hotel is generally cited as *número segundo* in Toledo. Originally built as a convent in 1560 and later used as a hospital, it was transformed into this comfortable hostelry in the late 1980s. Sprawling, historic, and generously proportioned, it contains clean, amply sized, attractively furnished guest rooms, each with a private bathroom, which are mostly equipped with shower-tub combinations. On site is the very large and well-recommended restaurant, El Abside.

Marqués de Mendigorría 1, 45003 Toledo. ✆ **92-521-32-02.** Fax 92-521-26-50. www.hotelesmayoral.com. 73 units. 87€ double; 143€ suite. AE, DC, MC, V. Parking 7.20€ ($6.45). **Amenities:** Restaurant; bar; room service; laundry/dry cleaning. *In room:* A/C, TV, minibar.

INEXPENSIVE

Hotel Imperio *Value* Long a budget favorite, this modest hotel is a few yards from the Alcazar and Cathedral. Built in the '80s, the hotel was recently renovated (and just in time), adding more comfort to the small rooms. The furnishings are in a rather severe style, but the beds are comfortable and the bathrooms have shower-tub combinations. However, for the price this is one of the city's best choices. Rooms on the second floor have balconies overlooking the street. A snack bar is on site, but some fine restaurants lie just outside the door. The only parking available is on the street.

Cadena 5, 45001 Toledo. ✆ **92-522-76-50.** Fax 92-525-3183. www.hotelimperio.com.ar. 21 units. 38€ double. AE, DC, MC, V. **Amenities:** Bar; lounge; babysitting; laundry. *In room:* A/C, TV.

Hotel Martín A good, serviceable choice, the two-story Martín opened in 1992 in the vicinity of the Bisagra Gate, the main medieval doorway to the city of Toledo. It's only a 10-minute walk to the historic center. The hotel possesses a homelike atmosphere you feel as soon as you enter its precincts behind a red-brick facade with old streetlights and vertical windows. The interior is decorated in wood and soft, pastel colors. The rooms are medium in size and furnished comfortably and unpretentiously. Bathrooms are impeccably maintained with showers.

Calle Espino 10, 45003 Toledo. ✆ and fax **92-522-17-33.** 29 units. 45€ double. MC, V. Parking 7.20€. **Amenities:** Bar; laundry. *In room:* A/C, TV.

Hotel Mayoral In front of the walls of Toledo, next to the bus station, this hotel was inaugurated in 1989 and met with instant approval. A rather formal entrance followed by a severe hallway leads to comfortable, well-furnished, and medium-size bedrooms that offer good beds with well-maintained bathrooms equipped with shower-tub combinations. Most of the accommodations open onto balconies with views of interior patios, although a few have a panoramic view of Toledo. Mayoral maintains an excellent restaurant serving both a Spanish and international cuisine, plus a cozy bar. A buffet breakfast is served daily.

Av. de Castilla-La Mancha 3, 45003 Toledo. ✆ **92-521-60-00.** Fax 92-521-69-54. 110 units. 86.50€ double. AE, DC, MC, V. Parking 7.20€. Bus: 5 or 6. **Amenities:** Restaurant; bar; room service; babysitting; laundry/dry cleaning. *In room:* A/C, TV, minibar, hair dryer, safe.

Hotel Real de Toledo This 19th-century building, located within the ancient city walls between Bisagra and the Sun Gates, has been a hotel since 1991. The facade is made from Castilian brick and is dotted with old large-framed windows. Despite the age of the building, the interior is modern and comfortable. The walls are decorated in beige and finished with pinewood. Many of the rooms open onto a view. Although each is comfortable and well equipped, some don't get enough light. Bathrooms are small and well maintained with shower-tub combinations. The hotel does have a small on-site cafeteria.

Calle Real del Arrabal 4, 45003 Toledo. ✆ **92-522-93-00.** Fax 92-522-87-67. www.socranet.com/hotelreal. 54 units. 63€–81€ double. AE, DC, MC, V. Parking 9€. Bus: 5 or 6. **Amenities:** Bar; room service; laundry/dry cleaning. *In room:* A/C, TV.

WHERE TO DINE

MODERATE

Asador Adolfo ★ SPANISH Less than a minute's walk north of the cathedral, at the corner of Calle Hombre de Palo behind an understated sign, Asador Adolfo is one of the finest restaurants in town (though we prefer the Hostal del Cardenal). Sections of the building were first constructed during the 1400s, although the thoroughly modern kitchen has recently been renovated. Massive beams support the dining room ceilings, and here and there the rooms contain faded frescoes dating from the original building.

Game dishes are a house specialty; such choices as partridge with white beans and venison consistently rate among the best anywhere. Other offerings include hake flavored with local saffron as well as a wide array of beef, veal, or lamb dishes. To start, try the *pimientos rellenos* (red peppers stuffed with pulverized shellfish). The house dessert is marzipan, prepared in a wood-fired oven and noted for its lightness.

La Granada 6. ✆ **92-522-73-21.** Reservations recommended. Main courses 15€–21€. AE, DC, MC, V. Daily 1–4pm, Mon–Sat 8pm–midnight. Bus: 5 or 6.

Casón de los López ★★ CASTILIAN A short walk from the heartbeat Plaza de Zocodover, this charmer of a restaurant serves the lightest and most sophisticated cuisine in Toledo. Its setting alone would make it an enticing choice. In an antique building, it's a virtual museum, furnished with antiques, some from as far back as the 16th century. Castilian iron bars, Mudéjar style wooden ceilings, Arab stucco decorations, a patio ringed with marble statues, a splashing fountain, and caged birds create this mellow atmosphere. And get this: much of the furniture is for sale. Hopefully, some other diner won't buy the table out from under you when your main course is being served.

In such a mellow ambience, you can plunge into a cuisine that sees us returning again and again to sample the bounty of the countryside, especially such game as hare, rabbit, partridge, and pigeon. A recent specialty we enjoyed, loin of venison with fresh, garlic-flecked spinach in a velvety smooth mushroom cream sauce, was irresistibly juicy and a combination of blissful contrasts. Launch yourself with the garlic-ravioli soup, a first for many diners, and top the meal with an extravagant cheese and fresh plum mousse.

Sillería 3. ✆ **92-525-47-74.** Reservations required. Main courses 15€–20€. Set-price menus 33€–45€. Daily 1:30–4pm; Mon–Sat 9–11pm. AE, DC, MC, V.

Hostal del Cardenal ★★ SPANISH Treat yourself to Toledo's best-known restaurant, owned by the same people who run Madrid's Sobrino de Botín (see chapter 5). The chef prepares regional dishes with flair and originality. Choosing from a menu very similar to that of the fabled Madrid eatery, begin with "quarter of an hour" (fish) soup or white asparagus, then move on to curried prawns, baked hake, filet mignon, or smoked salmon. Roast suckling pig is a specialty, as is partridge in casserole. Arrive early to enjoy a sherry in the bar or in the courtyard.

Paseo de Recaredo 24. ✆ **92-522-08-62.** Reservations required. Main courses 7€–17€; fixed-price menu 18€. AE, DC, MC, V. Daily 1–4pm and 8:30–11:30pm. Bus: 2 from rail station.

La Abadía ★ *Finds* CASTILIAN The "Abbey" (its English name) started life as a cervecería or alehouse before it was turned into a convivial restaurant and tapas bar. Next to San Nicolás church, it stands at the intersection of Núñez de Arce and Calle de Alfileteros. It is ideal for a huge Castilian meal or else for wine drinking and tapas eating. The decor is a tasteful combination of modern and rustic styles, and the interior is separated into two sections—both a restaurant and a bar area. In honor of its old function as a cervecería, a wide variety of international beers is offered. The menu is composed of fresh ingredients deftly handled by the kitchen staff. One of the best dishes—and beloved by Toledans—is a partridge casserole with white-wine, bay leaves, and onions.

Filet of venison in a mushroom sauce is another worthy choice, as is *ensalada de verdura a la parilla* (a salad of freshly grilled vegetables). Some of the most delightful tapas include croquettes, roasted red peppers, a selection of cheese, and such meats as venison and Serrano ham. The most unusual dessert is an ice cream made of Manchego cheese.

Plaza de San Nicolás 3. ✆ **92-525-07-46.** Reservations recommended. Main courses 9€-15€; set menu 20€. DC, MC, V. Mon–Fri 8am–11pm; Sat–Sun noon–2:30am.

Mesón Aurelio CASTILIAN Established in the late 1940s, Mesón Aurelio occupies two separate but neighboring dining rooms, with two separate entrances, near the northern edge of the cathedral. It's one of the restaurant staples of Toledo, with its generous portions, Castilian ambience, and efficient service. Traditional versions of *sopa castellana* (a hearty soup of meat and beans), grilled hake, *lubina a la sal* (whitefish cooked in salt), fresh salmon, and roast lamb are on the menu. Note that whereas the main outlet of this restaurant (Calle Sinagoga 6) is usually closed every Wednesday, the smaller of the restaurant's two branches (Calle Sinagoga 1) remains open, opting instead to close every Monday. Despite their different closing days, the food items and prices within the two branches are identical.

Calle Sinagoga 6. ✆ **92-522-20-97.** Reservations recommended. Main courses 7€–25€; fixed-price menu 30€. AE, DC, MC, V. Thurs–Tues 1–4:30pm and 8–11:30pm. Bus: 5 or 6.

Parador Nacional de Conde Orgaz CASTILIAN Sturdy Castilian cuisine is enhanced by one of the most panoramic views from any restaurant in Europe. Located in a fine parador (recommended above), this restaurant is on the crest of a hill—said to be the spot that El Greco chose for his *A View of Toledo.* The place is tourist-trodden, and the food doesn't quite match the view, but it's a worthy choice, nonetheless. The fixed-price meal might include tasty Spanish tapas, hake, then perhaps either veal or beef grilled on an open fire, and dessert. If you're dining lightly, try a local specialty, *tortilla española con magra* (potato omelet with ham or bacon). There is a bar on the upper level.

Cerro del Emperador. ✆ **92-522-18-50.** Reservations not accepted. Main courses 8.50€–18€; fixed-price menu 24€. AE, DC, MC, V. Daily 1–4pm and 8:30–11pm. Drive across Puente San Martín and head south for 4km (2½ miles).

INEXPENSIVE

El Catavinos ★ *Finds* SPANISH/CASTILIAN El Catavinos means wine taster in Spanish, and indeed this charming restaurant started its life as a wine cellar. On the periphery of the center, a 10-minute walk from the Puerta de Bisagra, the restaurant has a convivial bar downstairs and a restaurant upstairs, decorated with old photographs of Peru. In fair weather, guests often eat on the terrace. The menu is filled with exciting and reasonably priced dishes, including such delicacies as partridge salad, bell peppers with a stuffing of hare, and grilled venison and veal meatballs in a savory tomato sauce. The *menú de degustación* is a cornucopia of seven different platters, each accompanied by one of seven different wines. The desserts offered include a cheesecake made from goat milk with a sweet white wine.

Av. Reconquista 10. ✆ **92-522-22-56.** Reservations recommended. Main courses 8€–18€; *menú de degustación* 24€. AE, DC, MC, V. Tues–Sat noon–midnight, Sun noon–4pm.

La Parilla SPANISH Go here for some real Franco-era dishes. This classic Spanish restaurant, within a thick-walled medieval building, stands on a cobbled street near the Hotel Alfonso VI, just east of the cathedral. The menu offers no surprises, but it's reliable. Likely inclusions on the bill of fare are roast suckling pig, spider crabs, Castilian baked trout, stewed quail, baked kidneys, and La Mancha rabbit. This is the type of heavy fare so beloved by Castilians, who still frequent the place in great numbers.

Horno de los Bizcochos 8. ✆ **92-521-22-45.** Main courses 6.50€–13.50€; fixed-price menu 13.25€. AE, DC, MC, V. Daily 1–4pm and 8–10:30pm. Bus: 5 or 6.

La Perdiz ★ *Finds* CASTILIAN La Perdiz is named from the favorite dish of Toledans—partridge. That bird is best showcased here in a dish called *perdiz estofada a la toledana,* partridge stew with white-wine, bay leaf, and onions. Another excellent choice is venison in a mushroom sauce. The menu also has some imaginative offerings such as a fresh fried cheese tossed in an orange dressing.

The best dessert is that local favorite, marzipan, here served as a tart with almond biscuits. On occasion a roast suckling pig is featured. The location is in the center of the old Jewish ghetto, about midpoint between two synagogues, Santa María la Blanca and Tránsito. The restaurant has two floors with views of the historic district, and walls are of wood and brick. Locals, and with good reason, cite the place for its good quality cuisine at affordable prices. The same people who run **La Perdiz** also operate **Asador Adolfo,** Toledo's premier restaurant. But prices at **La Perdiz** are far more reasonable.

Calle Reyes Católicos 7. ✆ **92-521-46-58.** Reservations recommended. Main courses 12€–15€; set menu 19€. AE, MC, V. Tues–Sat noon–11pm, Sun noon–4pm.

La Tarasca CASTILIAN This restaurant, the domain of the Martin brothers, serves good food but it's mainly recommended for its convenience, as it lies only a couple of blocks north of the cathedral. With two dining rooms and a cafeteria, it is also open throughout the day, even serving breakfast. The decor, although plain, still evokes a 19th-century aura. Walls are painted in green with wood paneling resting under beams, and the rooms are joined by archways. The cuisine consists of the hearty, robust fare that Toledans feast on, including the traditional opener, *sopa castellana,* a hearty soup made with various meats and beans. You can opt for such standard dishes as grilled steak and potatoes, but braised game hen would be more traditional, as would trout caught in local waters. One of our favorite dishes is *pimientos rellenos,* stuffed peppers, or else *cordoniz a la toledana,* roasted quail with savory brown sauce. All desserts, including the puddings, are homemade.

Calle Hombre de Palo 6. ✆ **92-522-43-42.** Reservations not required. Main courses 9€–16€; set menu 14.50€. MC, V. Daily 7:30am–11pm.

TOLEDO AFTER DARK

Begin your nighttime crawl through Toledo with a stop at **Bar Ludeña,** Plaza de la Magdalena 13, Corral de Don Diego 10 (✆ **92-522-33-84**), where a loyal clientele comes for delectable tapas. Fixed-price menus range from 9€ to 15€. Glasses of wine are sometimes passed through a small window to clients standing outside enjoying the view of the square. The bar is little more than a narrow corridor, serving *raciones* of tapas that are so generous they make little meals, especially when served with bread. The roasted red peppers in olive oil are quite tasty, along with the stuffed crabs and *calamares* (squid). Huge dishes of pickled cucumbers, onions, and olives are available. They also have a tiny dining room behind a curtain at the end of the bar serving inexpensive fare.

Despite the many tourists that throng its streets during the day, Toledo is quiet at night, with fewer dance clubs than you'd expect from a town of its size.

If you want to hear some recorded music, head for **Bar La Abadía,** Plaza San Nicolás 3 (✆ **92-525-11-40**), where crowds of local residents, many of them involved in the tourism industry, crowd elbow to elbow for pints of beer, glasses of wine, and access to the music of New York, Los Angeles, or wherever. Other spots to hit include **O'Brien's Irish Pub,** Calle Armas 12 (✆ **92-521-26-65**), which seems more appropriate for the streets of Dublin than old Toledo. A crowd in their 20s flocks here, and there's live music every Thursday at 10:30pm. Drop in to **Trébol,** Calle Santa Fe 1 (✆ **92-521-37-02**) to sample their wine, their excellent tapas, and their *bombas* (stuffed potato bombs). Another wine bar hangout is **Enebro,** on the postage stamp-sized Plaza Santiago Balleros, off Calle Cervantes (✆ **92-522-21-11**).

2 Aranjuez

47km (29 miles) S of Madrid, 48km (30 miles) NE of Toledo

This Castilian town, at a confluence of the Tagus and Jarama Rivers, was once home to Bourbon kings in the spring and fall. With the manicured shrubbery, stately elms, fountains, and statues of the Palacio Real and surrounding compounds, Aranjuez remains a regal garden oasis in what is otherwise an unimpressive agricultural flatland known primarily for its strawberries and asparagus.

ESSENTIALS

GETTING THERE **By Train** Trains depart about every 20 minutes from Madrid's Atocha Railway Station to make the 50-minute trip to Aranjuez, a one-way fare costing 3€. Twice a day you can take an express train from Madrid to Toledo, which makes a brief stopover at Aranjuez. This trip takes only 30 minutes. Trains run less often along the east-west route to and from Toledo (a 40-min. ride). The Aranjuez station lies about 1.6km (1 mile) outside town. For information and schedules, call ✆ **90-224-02-02.** You can walk it in about 15 minutes, but taxis and buses line up on Calle Stuart (2 blocks from the city tourist office). The bus that makes the run from the center of Aranjuez to the railway station is marked N-Z.

By Bus Buses for Aranjuez depart every 30 minutes from 7:30am to 10pm from Madrid's Estación Sur de Autobuses, Calle Méndez Alvaro. In Madrid, call ✆ **91-530-46-05** for information. Buses arrive in Aranjuez at the City Bus Terminal, Calle Infantas 8 (✆ **91-891-01-83**).

By Car Driving is easy; it takes about 30 minutes once you reach the southern city limits of Madrid. To reach Aranjuez, follow the signs to Aranjuez and Granada, taking highway N-IV.

VISITOR INFORMATION The **tourist information office** is at Plaza de San Antonio 9 (✆ **91-891-04-27**), open Monday to Friday from 10am to 2pm and 4 to 6pm.

SEEING THE SIGHTS

Casa del Labrador "The House of the Worker," modeled after the Petit Trianon at Versailles, was built in 1803 by Charles IV, who later abdicated in Aranjuez. The queen came here with her youthful lover, Godoy (whom she had elevated to the position of prime minister), and the feeble-minded Charles didn't seem to mind a bit. Surrounded by beautiful gardens, the "bedless" palace is lavishly furnished in the grand style of the 18th and 19th centuries. The marble floors represent some of the finest workmanship of that day; the brocaded walls emphasize the luxurious lifestyle; and the royal toilet is a sight to behold (in those days, royalty preferred an audience). The clock here is one of the treasures of the house. The casita lies .8km (½ mile) east of the Royal Palace; those with a car can drive directly to it through the tranquil Jardín del Príncipe.

Calle Reina, Jardín del Príncipe. ✆ **91-891-03-05.** Admission 5€ adults, 2€ students and children. Apr–Sept, Tues–Sun 10am–6:30pm; Oct–Mar, Tues–Sun 10am–5:30pm.

Jardín de la Isla ★ After the tour of the Royal Palace, wander through the Garden of the Island. Spanish impressionist Santiago Rusiñol captured its evasive quality on canvas, and one Spanish writer said that you walk here "as if softly lulled by a sweet 18th-century sonata." A number of fountains are remarkable: the "Ne Plus Ultra" fountain, the black-jasper fountain of Bacchus, the fountain of Apollo, and the ones honoring Neptune (god of the sea) and Cybele (goddess of agriculture).

You may also stroll through the Jardín del Parterre, located in front of the palace. It's much better kept than the Garden of the Island, but not as romantic.

Directly northwest of the Palacio Real. No phone. Free admission. Apr–Sept, daily 8am–8:30pm; Oct–Mar, daily 8am–6:30pm.

Palacio Real ★★ Since the beginning of a united Spain, the climate and natural beauty of Aranjuez have attracted Spanish monarchs: Ferdinand and Isabella; Philip II, when he managed to tear himself away from El Escorial; Philip V; and Charles III.

The structure you see today dates from 1778 (the previous buildings were destroyed by fire). The palace is lavishly and elegantly decorated: Salons show the opulence of a bygone era, with room after room of royal extravagance. Especially notable are the dancing salon, the throne room, the ceremonial dining hall, the bedrooms of the king and queen, and a remarkable Salon de Porcelana (Porcelain Room). Paintings include works by Lucas Jordan and José Ribera. A guide conducts you through the huge complex (a tip is expected).

Plaza Palacio. ✆ **91-891-13-44.** Admission 4.80€ adults, 2.40€ students and children. Tues–Sun 10am–6:15pm. Bus: Routes from the rail station converge at the square and gardens at the westernmost edge of the palace.

WHERE TO STAY

Hostal Castilla *Value* On one of the town's main streets north of the Royal Palace and gardens, the Castilla consists of the ground floor and part of the first floor of a well-preserved early 18th-century house. Most of the accommodations overlook a courtyard with a fountain and flowers. All units contain well-kept bathrooms with shower-tub combinations. Owner Martín Soria, who speaks English fluently, suggests that reservations be made at least a month in advance. There are excellent restaurants nearby, and the *hostal* has an arrangement with a neighboring bar to provide guests with an inexpensive lunch. This is a good location from which to explore either Madrid or Toledo on a day trip. Parking is available along the street.

Carretera Andalucía 98, 28300 Aranjuez. ✆ **91-891-26-27.** 22 units. 45€ double. AE, DC, MC, V. Rates include breakfast. **Amenities:** Lounge; laundry/dry cleaning. *In room:* A/C, TV.

WHERE TO DINE

Casa José ★★ SPANISH/INTERNATIONAL Set near Town Hall and the Church of Antonio, this well-managed restaurant occupies two ground-floor rooms of a 300-year-old house in the heart of town; it's the premier restaurant of the entire area, and local gastronomes drive for miles around to dine here. The regionally based repertoire of food is prepared with an intelligent association of flavors. Any of the daily offerings is well worth ordering. Menu items focus on fresh ingredients that the staff buys every morning at the town markets. Look for a menu that changes at least four times a year, with an emphasis on pork, veal, fish, chicken, and shellfish. Of special note are braised lamb chops in a fresh tomato and cilantro sauce; Jabugo ham with broad beans; shrimp in garlic sauce; hake with green sauce; and thick juicy steaks.

Calle Abastos 32. ✆ **91-891-14-88.** Reservations recommended. Main courses 16€–18€. AE, DC, MC, V. Tues–Sun 1–4pm and Tues–Sat 9pm–midnight.

Casa Pablo SPANISH An unpretentious and well-managed restaurant near the bus station in the town center, Casa Pablo was established in 1941. At tables set outside beneath a canopy, you can dine while enjoying red and pink geraniums along the tree-lined street; in cooler weather you can eat either upstairs or in the cozy rear dining room. The fixed-price menu includes four courses, a carafe of wine, bread, and gratuity. If it's hot out and you don't feel like having a heavy dinner, try a shrimp omelet or half a roast chicken; once we ordered just a plate of asparagus in season, accompanied by white-wine. If you want a superb dish, try a fish called *mero* (Mediterranean pollack of delicate flavor), grilled over an open fire.

Almibar 42. ✆ **91-891-14-51.** Reservations recommended. Main courses 15€–30€. AE, MC, V. Daily 1–4:30pm and 8pm–midnight. Closed Aug.

La Rana Verde ★ SPANISH "The Green Frog," just east of the Royal Palace and next to a small bridge spanning the Tagus, is still the traditional choice for many. Opened in 1905 by Tomás Díaz Heredero, it is owned and run by a third-generation member of his family, who has decorated it in a 1920s style. The restaurant looks like a summerhouse, with its high-beamed ceiling and soft ferns drooping from hanging baskets. The preferred tables are in the nooks overlooking the river. As in all the restaurants of Aranjuez, asparagus is a special feature. Game, particularly partridge, quail, and pigeon, can be recommended in season; fish, too, including fried hake and fried sole, makes a good choice. Strawberries are served with sugar, orange juice, or ice cream.

Reina 1. ✆ **91-891-32-38.** Reservations recommended. Main courses 7€–14€; fixed-price menu 13€–20€. MC, V. Daily 9pm–midnight.

3 San Lorenzo de El Escorial ★

48km (30 miles) W of Madrid, 52km (32 miles) SE of Segovia

Aside from Toledo, the most important excursion from Madrid is to the austere royal monastery of San Lorenzo de El Escorial. Philip II ordered the construction of this granite-and-slate behemoth in 1563, two years after he moved his capital to Madrid. Once the haunt of aristocratic Spaniards, El Escorial is now a resort where hotels and restaurants flourish in summer, as hundreds come to escape the heat of the capital. Aside from the appeal of its climate, the town of San Lorenzo itself is not very noteworthy. But because of the monastery's size, you might decide to spend a night or two at San Lorenzo—or more if you have the time.

Tips **A More Convenient Base than Madrid**

San Lorenzo makes a good base for visiting nearby Segovia, the royal palace at La Granja, and the Valley of the Fallen.

ESSENTIALS

GETTING THERE **By Train** More than two dozen trains depart daily from Madrid's Atocha, Nuevos Ministerios, and Chamartín train stations. Trip time is little more than an hour. During the summer extra coaches are added. For schedules and information, call ✆ **90-224-02-02.** A one-way fare costs 2.60€.

The railway station for San Lorenzo de El Escorial is located about 1.6km (1 mile) outside of town along Carretera Estación (✆ **91-890-07-14**). The Herranz bus company meets all arriving trains with a shuttle bus that ferries arriving passengers to and from the Plaza Virgen de Gracia, about a block east of the entrance to the monastery.

By Bus The Office of Empresa Herranz, Calle Reina Victoria 3, in El Escorial (✆ **91-890-41-22** or 91-890-41-25), runs some 40 buses per day back and forth between Madrid and El Escorial. On Sunday, service is curtailed to 10 buses. Trip time is an hour, and a round-trip fare costs 5.50€. The same company also runs one bus a day to El Valle de los Caídos. It leaves El Escorial at 3:15pm with a return at 5:30pm. The ride takes only 15 minutes, and a round-trip fare is 8€, El Valle only.

By Car Follow the N-VI highway (marked on some maps as A-6) from the northwest perimeter of Madrid toward Lugo, La Coruña, and San Lorenzo de El Escorial. After about a half hour, fork left onto the C-505 toward San Lorenzo de El Escorial. Driving time from Madrid is about an hour.

VISITOR INFORMATION The **tourist information office** is at Calle Grimaldi 2 (✆ **91-890-53-13**). It is open Monday to Thursday from 11am to 6pm, Friday to Sunday from 10am to 7pm.

SEEING THE SIGHTS

Casa de Príncipe (Prince's Cottage) ★ This small but elaborately decorated 18th-century palace near the railway station was originally a hunting lodge built for Charles III by Juan de Villanueva. Most visitors stay in El Escorial for lunch, visiting the cottage in the afternoon.

Calle Reina s/n. ✆ **91-890-59-03.** Admission included in comprehensive ticket to El Escorial, see above. Sat–Sun and holidays 10am–6:45pm.

El Valle de los Caídos (Valley of the Fallen) ★ This is Franco's El Escorial, an architectural marvel that took two decades to complete, dedicated to those who died in the Spanish Civil War. Its detractors say that it represents the worst of neofascist design; its admirers say they have found renewed inspiration by coming here.

A gargantuan cross nearly 150m (500 ft.) high dominates the Rock of Nava, a peak of the Guadarrama Mountains. Directly under the cross is a basilica with a vault in mosaic, completed in 1959. Here José Antonio Primo de Rivera, the founder of the Falange party, is buried. When this Nationalist hero was buried at El Escorial, many, especially influential monarchists, protested that he was not a royal. Infuriated, Franco decided to erect another monument. Originally it was slated to honor the dead on the Nationalist side only, but the intervention of several parties led to a decision to include all the *caídos* (fallen). In time the mausoleum claimed Franco as well; his body was interred behind the high altar.

A funicular extends from near the entrance to the basilica to the base of the gigantic cross erected on the mountaintop above (where there's a superb view). The fare is 2€, and the funicular runs daily from 10:30am to 1:15pm and 4 to 6pm.

On the other side of the mountain is a Benedictine monastery that has sometimes been dubbed "the Hilton of monasteries" because of its seeming luxury.

✆ **91-890-56-11.** Admission 4.80€ adults, 2.90€ students and children. Apr–Sept, Tues–Sun 9:30am–6pm; Oct–Mar, Tues–Sun 10am–7pm. Bus: Tour buses from Madrid usually include an excursion to the Valley of the Fallen on their 1-day trips to El Escorial (see "By Bus," above). By Car: Drive to the valley entrance, about 8km (5 miles) north of El Escorial in the heart of the Guadarrama Mountains. Once here, drive 6km (3½ miles) west along a wooded road to the underground basilica.

Real Monasterio de San Lorenzo de El Escorial ★★★ This huge granite fortress houses a wealth of paintings and tapestries and also serves as a burial place for Spanish kings. Foreboding both inside and out because of its sheer size and institutional look, El Escorial took 21 years to complete, a remarkably short time considering the bulk of the building and the primitive construction methods of the day. After his death, the original architect, Juan Bautista de Toledo, was replaced by Juan de Herrera, the greatest architect of Renaissance Spain, who completed the structure.

Philip II, who collected many of the paintings exhibited here in the New Museums, did not appreciate El Greco and favored Titian instead. But you'll still find El Greco's *The Martyrdom of St. Maurice,* rescued from storage, and his *St. Peter.* Other superb works include Titian's *Last Supper* and Velázquez's *The Tunic of Joseph.*

The Royal Library houses a priceless collection of 60,000 volumes—one of the most significant in the world. The displays range from the handwriting of St. Teresa to medieval instructions on playing chess. See, in particular, the Muslim codices and a Gothic *Cantigas* from the 13th-century reign of Alfonso X ("The Wise").

You can also visit the Philip II Apartments; these are strictly monastic, and Philip called them the "cell for my humble self" in this "palace for God." Philip became a religious fanatic and requested that his bedroom be erected overlooking the altar of the 90m (300-ft.) high basilica, which has four organs and whose dome is based on Michelangelo's drawings for St. Peter's. The choir contains a crucifix by Cellini. By comparison, the Throne Room is simple. On the walls are many ancient maps. The Apartments of the Bourbon Kings are lavishly decorated, in contrast to Philip's preference for the ascetic.

Under the altar of the church you'll find one of the most regal mausoleums in the world, the Royal Pantheon, where most of Spain's monarchs—from Charles I to Alfonso XII, including Philip II—are buried. In 1993 Don Juan de Borbón, the count of Barcelona and the father of King Juan Carlos (Franco passed over the count and never allowed him to ascend to the throne) was interred nearby. On a lower floor is the "Wedding Cake" tomb for children.

Allow at least three hours for a visit. The guided tour doesn't take you to all the sites, but you are free to explore on your own afterward.

Calle San Lorenzo de El Escorial 1. ✆ **91-890-59-03.** Comprehensive ticket 6€ adults, 3€ children. Guided tour 7€. Apr–Sept, Tues–Sun 10am–7pm; Oct–Mar, Tues–Sun 10am–6pm.

WHERE TO STAY

MODERATE

Hotel Botánico ★★ True to its name, the hotel stands in a lovely manicured garden consisting of both indigenous and exotic shrubbery. Although the building is traditionally Castilian, the decor seems vaguely alpine, with wood paneling and beams in the reception rooms. The clean, well-lit rooms are large and comfortable, with well-kept bathrooms containing shower-tub combinations. There is a restaurant inside the hotel.

Calle Timoteo Padros 16, 28200 San Lorenzo de El Escorial. ✆ **91-890-78-79.** Fax 91-890-81-58. 20 units. 99€–129€ double; 154€–192€ suite. AE, V. Free parking. **Amenities:** Restaurant; bar; room service; babysitting; laundry/dry cleaning. *In room:* A/C, TV, minibar, hair dryer.

Hotel Victoria Palace ★ The Victoria Palace, with its view of El Escorial, is the finest hotel in town, a traditional establishment that has been modernized without losing its special aura of style and comfort. The rooms (some with private terraces) are well furnished and maintained. All units contain neatly kept bathrooms, mostly with shower-tub combinations. The rates are reasonable enough, and a bargain for a government-rated four-star hotel. The dining room serves some of the best food in town.

Calle Juan de Toledo 4, 28200 San Lorenzo de El Escorial. ✆ **91-896-98-90.** Fax 91-896-98-96. 87 units. 97€–137€ double. AE, MC, V. Parking 11.27€. **Amenities:** Restaurant; bar; room service; pool; babysitting; laundry/dry cleaning. *In room:* TV, hair dryer, safe.

INEXPENSIVE

Hostal Cristina ★ *Value* An excellent budget choice, this hotel is run by the Delgado family, who opened it in the mid-1980s. It doesn't pretend to compete with the comfort and amenities of the Victoria Palace or even the Miranda & Suizo (see below), but it has its devotees nonetheless. About 50 yards from the monastery, it stands in the center of town, offering clean and comfortable but simply furnished rooms. Every room has a well-kept bathroom with a shower-tub combination. The helpful staff will direct you to the small garden. Since the food served in the restaurant is both good and plentiful, many Spanish visitors prefer to book here for a summer holiday. Parking is available along the street.

Juan de Toledo 6, 28200 San Lorenzo de El Escorial. ✆ **91-890-19-61.** Fax 91-890-12-04. 16 units. 39€–43€ double. MC, V. **Amenities:** Lounge. *In room:* TV.

Miranda & Suizo ★ On a tree-lined street in the heart of town, within easy walking distance of the monastery, this excellent middle-bracket establishment ranks as a leading government-rated two-star hotel. It is the second choice in town, with rooms not quite as comfortable as those at the Victoria Palace. The Victorian-style building, nevertheless, has good guest rooms, some with terraces. The furnishings are comfortable, the beds often made of brass; sometimes you'll find fresh flowers on the tables. All units have bathrooms with shower-tub combinations. In summer, there is outside dining. Parking is available nearby for 6€ per day.

Calle Floridablanca 20, 28200 San Lorenzo de El Escorial. ✆ **91-890-47-11.** Fax 91-890-43-58. www.mirandasuizo.com. 52 units. 79€–128€ suite. AE, DC, MC, V. **Amenities:** Restaurant; bar; laundry/dry cleaning. *In room:* A/C, TV, minibar.

WHERE TO DINE

MODERATE

Charolés SPANISH/INTERNATIONAL The thick and solid walls of this establishment date, according to its managers, "from the monastic age"—and probably predate the town's larger and better-known monastery of El Escorial. The restaurant contained within was established around 1980, and has been known ever since as the best dining room in town. It has a flower-ringed outdoor terrace for use during clement weather. The cuisine doesn't quite rate a star, but chances are you'll be satisfied. The wide choice of menu items based entirely on fresh fish and meats includes such dishes as grilled hake with green or hollandaise sauce, shellfish soup, pepper steak, a *pastel* (pie) of fresh vegetables with crayfish, and herb-flavored baby lamb chops. Strawberry or kiwi tart is a good dessert choice.

Calle Floridablanca 24. ✆ **91-890-59-75.** Reservations required. Main courses 17€–23€. AE, DC, MC, V. Daily 1–4pm and 9pm–midnight.

Mesón la Cueva ★ CASTILIAN Founded in 1768, this restaurant captures the world of Old Castile, and it is only a short walk from the monastery. A *mesón típico* (typical Spanish bar) built around an enclosed courtyard, "the Cave" boasts such nostalgic accents as stained-glass windows, antique chests, a 19th-century bullfighting collage, faded engravings, paneled doors, and iron balconies. The cooking is on target, and the portions are generous. Regional specialties include Valencian paella and *fabada asturiana* (pork sausage and beans), but the fresh trout broiled in butter is the best of all. The menu's most expensive items are Segovian roast suckling pig and roast lamb (tender inside, crisp outside). Off the courtyard through a separate doorway is La Cueva's *tasca* (tapas bar), filled with Castilians quaffing their favorite before-dinner drinks.

San Antón 4. ✆ **91-890-15-16.** Reservations recommended. Main courses 8.25€–15.50€; *menú del día* 12€; *menú especial* (chef's special menu of the day) 22€. AE, MC, V. Tues–Sun 1–4pm and 8:30–11:30pm.

NEAR THE VALLEY OF THE FALLEN

Hostelería Valle de los Caídos SPANISH There aren't a lot of dining options around the Valley of the Fallen, and of the few that exist, this is about as good a bet as you'll get. Built in 1956, it's set amid a dry but dramatic landscape halfway along the inclined access road leading to Franco's monuments, reachable only by car or bus. It's a mammoth modern structure with wide terraces and floor-to-ceiling windows. The *menú del día* usually includes such dishes as cannelloni Rossini, pork chops with potatoes, a dessert choice of flan or fruit, and wine. The typical fare of roast chicken, roast lamb, shellfish, and paella is somewhat cafeteria-style in nature.

Valle de los Caídos. ✆ **91-890-55-11.** Reservations not accepted. Fixed-price menu 8€. No credit cards. Tues–Sun 9–10am, 2–3:30pm, and 9–10pm. Closed Dec 15–Jan 15.

EL ESCORIAL AFTER DARK

No longer the dead place it was during the long Franco era, the town comes alive at night, fueled mainly by the throngs of young people who pack into the bars and taverns, especially those along Calle Rey and Calle Floridablanca. Some of our favorite bars, offering vats of wine or kegs of beer, include the **Piano Bar Regina,** Floridablanca (✆ **91-890-68-43**); **Gurriato,** Leindro Rubio 3 (✆ **91-890-47-10**); and **Don Felipe II,** Floridablanca (✆ **91-896-07-65**). The hottest disco is **Move it,** Plaza de Santiago 11 (✆ **91-890-54-91**), which rarely imposes a cover unless some special group is featured.

4 Segovia ★★★

91km (54 miles) NW of Madrid, 68km (42 miles) NE of Avila

Less commercial than Toledo, Segovia, more than anywhere else, typifies the glory of Old Castile. Wherever you look, you'll see reminders of a golden era—whether it's the most spectacular Alcázar on the Iberian Peninsula or the well-preserved, still-functioning Roman aqueduct.

Segovia lies on the slope of the Guadarrama Mountains, where the Eresma and Clamores Rivers converge. This ancient city stands in the center of the most castle-rich part of Castile. Isabella herself was proclaimed queen of Castile here in 1474.

The narrow, winding streets of this hill city must be covered on foot to fully view the Romanesque churches and 15th-century palaces along the way.

ESSENTIALS

GETTING THERE **By Train** Fifteen trains leave Madrid's Chamartín Railway Station every day and arrive two hours later in Segovia, where you can board bus no. 3, which departs every quarter-hour for the Plaza Mayor. The trains that leave from Chamartín first travel through Atocha Station, making it closer to some travelers' hotels. The station at Segovia lies on the Paseo Obispo Quesada s/n (✆ **921-42-07-74**), a 20-minute walk southeast of the town center.

By Bus Buses arrive and depart from the Estacionamiento Municipal de Autobuses, Paseo de Ezequiel González 10 (✆ **92-142-77-07**), near the corner of the Avenida Fernández Ladreda and the steeply sloping Paseo Conde de Sepúlveda. There are 10 to 15 buses a day to and from Madrid (which depart from Paseo de la Florida 11; Metro: Norte), and about four a day traveling between Avila, Segovia, and Valladolid. One-way tickets from Madrid cost around 5.33€.

By Car Take the N VI (on some maps it's known as the A-6) or the Autopista del Nordeste northwest from Madrid, toward León and Lugo. At the junction with Route 110 (signposted SEGOVIA), turn northeast.

VISITOR INFORMATION The **tourist information office** is at Plaza Mayor 10 (✆ **92-146-03-34**). It is open daily from 9am to 3pm and 5 to 7pm.

SEEING THE SIGHTS

El Alcázar ★★ If you've ever dreamed of castles in the air, then all the fairytale romance of childhood will return when you view the Alcázar. Many have waxed poetic about it, comparing it to a giant boat sailing through the clouds. View the Alcázar first from below, at the junction of the Clamores and Eresma Rivers. It's on the west side of Segovia, and you may not spot it when you first enter the city—but that's part of the surprise.

The castle dates from the 12th century, but a large segment, which contained its Moorish ceilings, was destroyed by fire in 1862. Restoration has continued over the years.

Royal romance is associated with the Alcázar. Isabella first met Ferdinand here, and today you can see a facsimile of her dank bedroom. Once married, she wasn't foolish enough to surrender her royal rights, as replicas of the thrones attest—both are equally proportioned. Philip II married his fourth wife, Anne of Austria, here as well.

Walk the battlements of this once-impregnable castle, from which its occupants hurled boiling oil onto the enemy below. Or ascend the hazardous stairs of the tower, originally built by Isabella's father as a prison, for a panoramic view of Segovia.

Plaza de La Reina Victoria Eugenia. ✆ **92-146-07-59.** Admission 3.10€ adults, 2.20€ children 8–14, free for children 7 and under. Apr–Sept, daily 10am–7pm; Oct–Mar, daily 10am–6pm. Bus: 3. Take either Calle Vallejo, Calle de Velarde, Calle de Daoiz, or Paseo de Ronda.

Cabildo Catedral de Segovia ★ Constructed between 1515 and 1558, this is the last Gothic cathedral built in Spain. Fronting the historic Plaza Mayor, it stands on the spot where Isabella I was proclaimed queen of Castile. Affectionately called *la dama de las catedrales,* it contains numerous treasures, such as the Blessed Sacrament Chapel (created by the flamboyant Churriguera), stained-glass windows, elaborately carved choir stalls, and 16th- and 17th-century paintings, including a reredos portraying the deposition of Christ from the cross by Juan de Juni. The cloisters are older than the cathedral, dating from an earlier church that was destroyed in the so-called War of the Comuneros. Inside the cathedral museum you'll find jewelry, paintings, and a collection of rare antique manuscripts.

Plaza Catedral, Marqués del Arco. ✆ **92-146-22-05.** Free admission to cathedral; cloisters, museum, and chapel room 1.80€ adults, children 11 and under are free. Spring and summer, daily 9am–7pm; off-season, daily 9:30am–6pm.

Esteban Vicente Contemporary Art Museum ★ *Finds* In the heart of the city, in a newly renovated 15th-century palace, a permanent collection of some 142 works by the Abstract Expressionist artist, Esteban Vicente, has opened. The Spanish-born artist, now in his late '90s, has described himself as "an American painter, with very deep and loving Spanish roots." Born in a small town outside Segovia in 1903, he remained in Spain until 1927, eventually (since 1936) residing in New York, where he played a pivotal role in the development of American abstract art. Today, he is one of the last surviving members of the New York School, whose members include Rothko, de Kooning, and Pollock. Vicente's paintings and collages convey his sense of structure and feelings of luminous serenity with colors of astonishing vibrancy, brilliance, and range. His paintings are shown at the Metropolitan Museum of Art, the Museum of Modern Art, and the Whitney, all in New York—and now Segovia.

Plazuela de las Bellas. ✆ **92-146-20-10.** Admission 2.40€ adults, 1.20€ seniors and students, free for children under 12. Mon–Sat 11am–2pm and 4–7pm, Sun 11am–2pm.

Iglesia de la Vera Cruz Built in either the 11th or the 12th century by the Knights Templar, this is the most fascinating Romanesque church in Segovia. It stands in isolation outside the walls of the old town, overlooking the Alcázar. Its unusual 12-sided design is believed to have been copied from the Church of the Holy Sepulchre in Jerusalem. Inside you'll find an inner temple, rising two floors, where the knights conducted nightlong vigils as part of their initiation rites.

Carretera de Zamarramala. ✆ **92-143-14-75.** Admission 1.50€. Apr–Sept, Tues–Sun 10:30am–1:30pm and 3:30–7pm; Oct–Mar, Tues–Sun 10:30am–1:30pm and 3:30–6pm.

Monasterio del Parral ★ *Finds* The restored "Monastery of the Grape" was established for the Hieronymites by Henry IV (1425–74), a Castilian king known as "The Impotent." The monastery lies across the Eresma River about .8km (½ mile) north of the city. The church is a medley of styles and decoration—mainly Gothic, Renaissance, and Plateresque. The facade was never completed, and the monastery itself was abandoned when religious orders were suppressed in 1835. Today it's been restored and is once again the domain of the *jerónimos,* Hieronymus priests and brothers. Inside, a robed monk will show you the various treasures of the order, including a polychrome altarpiece and the alabaster tombs of the Marquis of Villena and his wife—all the work of Juan Rodríguez.

Subida del Parral 2 (across the Eresma River). ✆ **92-143-12-98.** Free admission. Mon–Sat 10am–2:30pm and 4–6:30pm; Sun 10–11:30am, 4–6:30pm. Take Ronda de Sant Lucía and cross the Eresma River.

Roman Aqueduct (Acueducto Romano) ★★★ This architectural marvel was built by the Romans nearly 2,000 years ago. Constructed of mortarless granite, it consists of 118 arches, and in one two-tiered section it soars 29m (95 ft.) to its highest point. The Spanish call it El Puente. It spans the Plaza del Azoguejo, the old market square, stretching nearly 800 yards. When the Moors took Segovia in 1072, they destroyed 36 arches, which were later rebuilt under Ferdinand and Isabella in 1484.

Plaza del Azoguejo.

WHERE TO STAY

EXPENSIVE

Parador de Segovia ★★★ This 20th-century tile-roofed parador sits on a hill 3km (2 miles) northeast of Segovia (take the N-601). It stands on an estate called El Terminillo, which used to be famous for its vines and almond trees, a few of which still survive. If you have a car and can get a reservation, book here; the comfort level dwarfs that found at either Los Arcos or Los Linajes. The guest rooms are deluxe, containing bathrooms with shower-tub combinations. Furnishings are tasteful (often in blond pieces), and large windows open onto panoramic views of the countryside. Some of the older rooms here are a bit dated, however, with a lackluster decor. The in-house restaurant is one of the best places to enjoy a meal in Segovia.

Carretera Valladolid s/n (N-601), 40003 Segovia. ✆ **92-144-37-37.** Fax 92-143-73-62. www.parador.es. 113 units. 114€ double; from 181€ suite. AE, DC, MC, V. Covered parking 5.50€, free outside. **Amenities:** Restaurant; bar; room service; 2 pools; tennis courts; fitness center; sauna; babysitting; laundry/dry cleaning. *In room:* A/C, TV, minibar, hair dryer, safe.

MODERATE

Hotel Infanta Isabel ★ Named after Queen Isabel, the great-grandmother of the present-day king, the hotel stands overlooking the charming central square and is within a stone's throw of the majestic cathedral. This is where she would stay when on her way to the nearby summer palace of La Granja. The present owners have modernized the interior considerably but a good deal of the building's 19th-century grandeur, such as the staircase, remain. Each room is decorated in its own style, and each is furnished with an eye to comfort. Despite its style, the hotel has every convenience; bathrooms with shower-tub combinations strike a reassuring 20th-century note.

Plaza Mayor, 40001 Segovia. ✆ **92-146-13-00.** Fax 92-146-22-17. 37 units. 63€–93€ double. AC, DC, MC, V. Parking 8.40€ ($7.50). **Amenities:** Bar; lounge; room service; babysitting; laundry/dry cleaning. *In room:* A/C, TV, minibar, hair dryer, safe.

Hotel Los Arcos This concrete-and-glass five-story structure opened in 1987 and is generally cited as the best in town, although you may prefer Los Linajes instead (see below). Well run and modern, it attracts the business traveler, although tourists frequent the place in droves as well. Rooms are generally spacious but furnished in a standard international bland way, except for the beautiful rug-dotted parquet floors. Built-in furnishings and tiny bathrooms with shower-tub combinations are part of the offering. Rooms are well kept, although some furnishings look worn.

Even if you don't stay here, consider dining at the hotel's La Cocina de Segovia, which is the only hotel dining room that competes successfully with Mesón de Cándido (see below). As at the nearby competitors, roast suckling pig and roast Segovia lamb—perfectly cooked in specially made ovens—are the specialties. There's also a tavernlike cafe and bar. In all, it's a smart, efficiently run, and pleasant choice, if not a terribly exciting one.

Paseo de Ezequiel González 26, 40002 Segovia. ✆ **92-143-74-62.** Fax 92-142-81-61. 59 units. 101.50€ double. AE, DC, MC, V. Parking 6€. **Amenities:** Restaurant; bar; lounge; room service; health club; babysitting; laundry/dry cleaning. *In room:* A/C, TV, minibar, hair dryer, safe.

Hotel Los Linajes ★ In the historical district of St. Stephen at the northern edge of the old town stands this hotel, the former home of a Segovian noble family. While the facade dates from the 11th century, the interior is modern, except for some Castilian decorations. Following a 1996 renovation, the hotel looks a bit brighter and fresher than Los Arcos (see below). All units have well-kept bathrooms with shower units. One of the best choices in town, Los Linajes offers gardens and patios where guests can enjoy a panoramic view over the city.

Dr. Velasco 9, 40003 Segovia. ✆ **92-146-04-75.** Fax 92-146-04-79. 53 units. 70€–83.50€ double; 96€–108€ suite. AE, DC, V. Parking 9€. Bus: 1. **Amenities:** Bar; cafe; lounge; room service; laundry/dry cleaning. *In room:* A/C, TV.

INEXPENSIVE

Las Sirenas Standing on the most charming old plaza in Segovia, opposite the Church of St. Martín, this hotel was built around 1950, and has been renovated several times. However, it has long since lost its Franco-era supremacy to Los Arcos (see above). It is modest and well maintained, and decorated in a conservative style. Each bedroom is filled with functional, simple furniture, and well-kept bathrooms with shower units. Breakfast is the only meal served, but the staff at the reception desk can direct clients to cafes and *tascas* nearby.

Juan Bravo 30, 40001 Segovia. ✆ **92-146-26-63.** Fax 92-146-26-57. 39 units. 50€–60€ double. AE, DC, MC, V. **Amenities:** Breakfast salon. *In room:* A/C, TV.

WHERE TO DINE

El Bernardino CASTILIAN El Bernardino, a 3-minute walk west of the Roman aqueduct, is built like an old tavern. Lanterns hang from beamed ceilings, and the view over the red-tile rooftops of the city is delightful. The *menú del día* might include a huge paella, roast veal with potatoes, flan or ice cream, plus bread and wine. You might begin your meal with *sopa castellana* (made with ham, sausage, bread, egg, and garlic). The roast dishes are exceptional here, including roast suckling pig, from a special oven, and roast baby lamb. You can also order grilled rib steak or stewed partridge.

Cervantes 2. ✆ **92-146-24-74.** Reservations recommended. Main courses 6€–5€; fixed-price menu 21€. AE, DC, MC, V. Daily 1–4pm and 8:30–11pm.

Mesón de Cándido ★★ CASTILIAN For years this beautiful old Spanish inn, standing on the eastern edge of the old town, has maintained a monopoly on the tourist trade. Apart from the hotel restaurants—specifically La Cocina de Segovia at the Los Arcos—it is the town's finest dining choice. The Cándido family took it over in 1905, and fourth- and fifth-generation family members still run the place, having fed, over the years, everybody from Hemingway to Nixon. The oldest part of the restaurant dates from 1822, and the place has gradually been enlarged since then. The proprietor of the House of Cándido is known as *mesonero mayor de Castilla* (the major innkeeper of Castile). He's been decorated with more medals and honors than paella has grains of rice. The restaurant's popularity can be judged by the crowds of hungry diners who fill every seat in the six dining rooms. The a la carte menu includes those two regional staples: *cordero asado* (roast baby lamb) and *cochinillo asado* (roast suckling pig). Some of the seating areas are cramped and confining. Opt for a table on the second floor, facing the Aqueduct, or else one of the outdoor cafe tables in front.

Plaza del Azoguejo 5. ✆ **92-142-59-11.** Reservations recommended. Main courses 9€–15€. AE, DC, MC, V. Daily 12:30–4:30pm and 8–midnight.

Mesón de José María SEGOVIAN This centrally located bar and restaurant, 1 block east of the Plaza Mayor, serves quality regional cuisine in a rustic stucco-and-brick dining room. Before dinner, locals crowd in for tapas at the bar, then move into the dining room for such Castilian specialties as roast suckling pig, rural-style conger eel, and freshly caught sea bream. Try the cream of crabmeat soup, roasted peppers, salmon with scrambled eggs, house-style hake, or grilled veal steak. For dessert, a specialty is ice cream tart with a whisky sauce.

Cronista Lecea 11. ✆ **92-146-11-11.** Reservations recommended. Main courses 5.50€–19€; fixed-price menu 24€–36€. AE, DC, MC, V. Daily 1–4pm and 8–11:30pm.

Restaurante Duque ★ CASTILIAN Set on the street that links Segovia's ancient Roman aqueduct with the city's medieval core, this restaurant was established in 1895, and has fed many successive generations of local residents ever since. The severely dignified interior looks almost unchanged since it was built. The decor includes heavy ceiling beams, exposed stone, rough-textured plaster, and battered 19th-century artifacts from long-ago farms. Come here for the kind of cuisine that was in vogue when the restaurant was built, with very few concessions to modern cuisine. There's an excellent version of cream of crabmeat soup; roasted suckling pig slow-cooked on a spit; savory roasted lamb with aromatic rosemary, thyme, and garlic; and different preparations of grilled chicken, veal, beef, and pork. An excellent accompaniment for any of these might include kidney beans cooked with chunks of salted cod, fresh spinach, and mounds of mashed potatoes or rice.

Calle Cervantes 12. ✆ **92-146-24-87.** Reservations recommended. Main courses 12€–21€. AE, DC, MC, V. Daily 12:30–5pm and 8–11:30pm.

AN EASY EXCURSION TO LA GRANJA

To reach La Granja, 11km (7 miles) southeast of Segovia, you can take a 20-minute bus ride from the center of the city. Six to ten buses a day leave from Paseo Conde de Sepulveda at Avenida Fernández Ladreda. A one-way fare costs 9€. For information, call ✆ **92-142-77-07.**

Palacio Real de La Granja San Ildefonso de la Granja was the summer palace of the Bourbon kings of Spain, who replicated the grandeur of Versailles in the province of Segovia. Set against the snowcapped Sierra de Guadarrama, the slate-roofed palace dominates the village that grew up around it (which, these days, is a summer resort).

The founder of La Granja was Philip V, grandson of Louis XIV and the first Bourbon king of Spain (his body, along with that of his second queen, Isabel de Fernesio, is interred in a mausoleum in the Collegiate Church). Philip V was born at Versailles on December 19, 1683, which may explain why he wanted to re-create that atmosphere at Segovia.

Before the palace was built in the early 18th century, a farm stood here—hence the totally incongruous name *la granja,* meaning "the farm" in Spanish. Inside you'll find valuable antiques (many in the Empire style), paintings, and a remarkable collection of tapestries based on Goya cartoons from the Royal Factory in Madrid.

Most visitors, however, seem to find a stroll through the gardens more pleasing, so allow adequate time for that. The fountain statuary is a riot of cavorting gods and nymphs, hiding indiscretions behind jets of water. The gardens are studded with chestnuts and elms. A spectacular display takes place when the water jets are turned on.

Plaza de España 17, San Ildefonso (Segovia). ✆ **92-147-00-19.** Admission 4.81€ adults, 2.25€ children 5–14, free for children 4 and under. Apr–Sept Tues–Sun 10am–6pm; Oct–Mar, Tues–Sat 10am–1:30pm and 3–5pm, Sun 10am–2pm.

SEGOVIA AFTER DARK

Some of the most spontaneous good times can be created around the Plaza Mayor, Plaza Azagejo, and the busy Calle del Carmen that runs into the Plaza Azagejo. Each of those sites contains a scattering of simple bars and cafes that grow more crowded at night as the days grow hotter. If you want to go dancing, two of the most popular discos are **Mansión,** Calle de Juan Bravo (no phone), which is open nightly from 11pm till dawn for dancing, drinking, and flirting with the 20- to 30-year-old crowd; and its somewhat more stylish competitor, **Bar Ginasio,** Paseo del Salon (no phone), which is open nightly from 8pm till dawn, a bit more atmospheric and frequented by persons from ages 25 to around 50.

8

Seville

Sometimes a city becomes famous simply for its beauty and romance. Seville (called Sevilla in Spain), the capital of Andalusia, is such a place. In spite of its sultry heat in summer and its many problems, such as rising unemployment and street crime, it remains one of the most charming Spanish cities.

Don Juan and Carmen—aided by Mozart and Bizet—have given Seville a romantic reputation. Because of the acclaim of *Don Giovanni* and *Carmen,* not to mention *The Barber of Seville,* debunkers have risen to challenge this reputation. But if a visitor can see only two Spanish cities in a lifetime, they should be Seville and Toledo.

All the images associated with Andalusia—orange trees, mantillas, lovesick toreros, flower-filled patios, and castanet-rattling gypsies—come to life in Seville. But it's not just a tourist city; it's a substantial river port, and it contains some of the most important artistic works and architectural monuments in Spain.

Unlike most Spanish cities, Seville has fared rather well under most of its conquerors—the Romans, Arabs, and Christians. Pedro the Cruel and Ferdinand and Isabella held court here. When Spain entered its 16th-century golden age, Seville funneled gold from the New World into the rest of the country and Columbus docked here after his journey to America.

1 Orientation

GETTING THERE

BY PLANE **Iberia** (✆ **800/772-4642** in the U.S. or 90-240-05-00 toll free in Spain) flies several times a day between Madrid (and elsewhere via Madrid) and Seville's Aeropuerto San Pablo, Calle Almirante Lobo (✆ **95-444-90-23**). It also flies several times a week to and from Alicante, Grand Canary Island, Lisbon, Barcelona, Palma de Majorca, Tenerife, Santiago de Compostela, and (once a week) Zaragoza. The airport lies about 9.6km (6 miles) from the center of the city, along the highway leading to Carmona.

BY TRAIN Train service into Seville is now centralized into the Estación Santa Justa, Av. Kansas City s/n (✆ **95-240-02-02** for information and reservations, or 95-454-03-03 for information). Buses C1 and C2 take you from this train station to the bus station at Prado de San Sebastián, and bus EA runs to and from the airport. The high-speed AVE train has reduced travel time from Madrid to Seville to 2½ hours. The train makes 17 trips daily, with a stop in Córdoba. Sixteen trains a day connect Seville and Córdoba; the AVE train takes 45 minutes and a TALGO takes 1½ hours. Three trains a day run to Málaga, taking 3 hours; there are also three trains per day to Granada (4 hr.).

BY BUS Although Seville confusingly has several satellite bus stations servicing small towns and nearby villages of Andalusia, most buses arrive and depart from the city's largest bus terminal, on the southeast edge of the old city, at

Prado de San Sebastián, Calle José María Osborne 11 (✆ **95-441-71-11**). Several different companies make frequent runs to and from Córdoba (2½ hr.), Málaga (3½ hr.), Granada (4 hr.), and Madrid (8 hr.). For information and ticket prices, call Alsina Graells at ✆ **95-441-88-11.** A newer bus station is at Plaza de Armas (✆ **95-490-80-40**), but it usually services destinations beyond Andalusia, including Portugal.

BY CAR Seville lies 540km (341 miles) southwest of Madrid and 217km (135 miles) northwest of Málaga. Several major highways converge on Seville, connecting it with the rest of Spain and Portugal. During periods of heavy holiday traffic, the N-V (E-90) from Madrid through Extremadura—which, at Mérida, connects with the southbound N-630 (E-803)—is usually less congested than the N-IV (E-5) through eastern Andalusia.

VISITOR INFORMATION

The tourist office, **Oficina de Información del Turismo,** at Av. de la Constitución 21B (✆ **95-422-14-04**), is open Monday to Saturday from 9am to 7pm, Sunday and holidays from 10am to 2pm.

CITY LAYOUT

The heart of Seville lies along the east bank of the Guadalquivir River. This **old town,** or *centro histórico,* is a fairly compact area and can be explored on foot—the only real way to see it. Once this part of Seville was enclosed by walls. Today nearly all the sights lie between two of the major bridges of Seville: the Puente de San Telmo, to the south, and the Puente de Isabel II (also known as the Puente de Triana), an Eiffel Tower-like structure from the mid-1800s. Near Puente de San Telmo are such sights as the Torre del Oro, the University of Seville, and the Parque de María Luisa. Near the Puente de Isabel II are the Maestranza bullring, the major shopping streets, and the Museo de Bellas Artes. In the middle of the centro histórico rises the cathedral and its adjoining Giralda tower, the Alcázar, and the colorful streets of the old Jewish quarter, the Barrio Santa Cruz.

MAIN STREETS, SQUARES & ARTERIES The old **Paseo de Colón** is that part of Seville's historic core that opens onto the Guadalquivir River. Any number of streets, including Santander, lead to **Avenida de la Constitución,** where you'll find the major attractions of Seville, including the Alcázar and the cathedral. To the east of both the Alcázar and the cathedral lies the Barrio Santa Cruz. Major historic squares include Plaza Nueva, Plaza de El Salvador, Plaza de Jerez, and Plaza de Triunfo. From Plaza del Duque, the Museo de Bellas Artes is reached by heading west toward the river along Calle Alfonso XII. The best place to start your exploration of Seville is Plaza Virgen de los Reyes. From here many of the major attractions, including the Giralda, the Patio de los Naranjos, and the Archivo de Indias, are all close at hand. Directly south of the plaza is the Alcázar—the whole area, in fact, is historic Seville in a nutshell.

FINDING AN ADDRESS Most of Seville's streets run one way, usually toward the Guadalquivir River. Individual buildings are numbered with odd addresses on one side of the street and even numbers on the opposite side, so no. 14 would likely fall opposite no. 13 and 15. Many addresses are marked *s/n,* which means the building has no number (*sin número*). When this occurs, be sure to obtain the name of a cross street as a reference point.

MAPS Arm yourself with a detailed street map, not the general overview often handed out free at tourist offices. Even if you're in Seville for only a day or two, you'll still need a detailed street map to find such attractions as the Museo de Bellas Artes. The best street maps of Seville are those published by **Euro City,** available at local newsstands and in bookstores. These maps contain not only a detailed street index, but also provide tourist information, places of interest, and even locations of vital SOS services (such as the police station) on the map. Regrettably, no one seems to have come up with an adequate map to get you through the intricate maze of the Barrio Santa Cruz, so you can more or less count on getting lost there. There is, however, a sketch map provided by the tourist office to help get you around the area.

NEIGHBORHOODS IN BRIEF

CENTRO HISTORICO This is the heart of historic Seville, with its most imposing sights, of which the massive cathedral is the dominant attraction. This is the area where you'll want to spend the most time, and it's also where you'll find the finest hotels and restaurants.

BARRIO SANTA CRUZ This is an area of wrought-iron *cancelas* (gates), courtyards with Andalusian tiled fountains, art galleries, restaurants, cafes, *tabernas,* flowerpots of geraniums, and winding narrow alleyways. The former ghetto of Seville's Jews, it's today named after a Christian saint, and is the single most colorful part of the city for exploring, which is best done during the day (at night, muggings might be a danger). Filled with interesting sights, such as Casa Murillo and some fascinating churches, it's one of the architectural highlights of Andalusia.

LA MACARENA Thought to be named for a Roman, Macarios, and the site of his former estate, this is a famous quarter of Seville that seems sadly neglected by visitors, who spend most of their time in the two quarters discussed above. The name also describes a popular rumba. It's filled with interesting attractions such as the Convento de Santa Inés (reached along Calle María Coronel). According to legend, King Pedro the Cruel was so taken with Inés's beauty that he pursued her constantly—until she poured boiling oil over her face to disfigure herself.

TRIANA & EL ARENAL These two districts were immortalized by Cervantes, Quevedo, and Lope de Vega, the fabled writers of Spain's golden age. They were the rough-and-tough seafaring quarters when Seville was a thriving port in the 1600s. In El Arenal, the 12-sided Torre del Oro, or "gold tower," built by the Almohads in 1220, overlooks the river on Paseo Cristóbal Colón. You can take the riverside esplanade, Marqués de Contadero, which stretches along the banks of the river from the tower. The Museo Provincial de Bellas Artes is also found here, containing Spain's best collection of Seville's painters, notably Murillo. Across the river, Triana was once the gypsy quarter but has now been gentrified.

2 Getting Around

BY BUS

You can actually walk most everywhere in Seville, although there are buses, used mainly for visiting the environs, which have little interest for tourists. If you use a bus for getting around the city, you'll find that most lines converge at Plaza de

Tips **Seville: A Driver-Unfriendly City**

Be warned, however, that driving here is a nightmare: Seville was planned for the horse and buggy rather than for the car, and nearly all the streets run one way toward the Guadalquivir River. Locating a hard-to-find restaurant or a hidden little square will require patience and luck.

la Encarnación, Plaza Nueva, or in front of the cathedral on Avenida de la Constitución. Bus service is daily from 6am to 11:15pm. The city tourist office will provide a booklet outlining bus routes. You can purchase a 10-trip bonobús to save money. The best buses for circling through the center of town include C1 and C2 (*circulares interiores*).

BY TAXI

This is quite a viable means of getting around, especially at night, when streets are dangerous because of frequent muggings. Call **Tele Taxi** (✆ **95-462-22-22**) or **Radio Taxi** (✆ **95-458-00-00**). Cabs are metered and charge about .50€ per kilometer.

BY CAR

Chances are you arranged to rent a car before you got to Seville (rates are lower that way). However, if you didn't, you'll find offices of Avis and Hertz at the airport as well as in the city: **Avis** maintains offices at the airport (✆ **95-444-91-21**), and at the train station (✆ **95-453-78-61**). **Hertz** has three Seville offices: at the airport (✆ **95-451-47-20**), at Vía Santa Justa near the train station (✆ **95-442-61-56**), and in the city at Luis Montato 63 (✆ **95-457-00-55**).

BY BICYCLE

Although Seville is intensely hot in summer, bike rentals are possible, even though spring and autumn are better times—at least cooler—for cycling around. Rentals are available at **El Ciclismo,** Paseo Catalina de Ribera 2 (✆ **95-441-19-59**), in Puerta de la Carne, at the northern end of the Jardines de Murillo. It's open Monday to Friday from 10am to 1:30pm and 5 to 8pm, Saturday from 10am to 1:30pm.

FAST FACTS: Seville

American Express The American Express office in Seville is in the Hotel Inglaterra, Plaza Nueva 7 (✆ **95-421-16-17**). Hours are Monday to Friday from 9:30am to 1:30pm and 4:30 to 7:30pm, Saturday from 10am to 1pm.

Business Hours Most banks in Seville are open Monday to Friday 9am to 2pm and on Saturday 9am to noon. (Always conceal your money before walking out of a bank in Seville.) Shops are generally open Monday to Saturday from 9:30am to 1:30pm and 4:30 to 8pm. Most department stores are open Monday to Saturday from 10am to 8pm.

Bus Information The Central Bus Station, Prado de San Sebastián, Calle José María Osborne 11 (✆ **95-441-71-11**), is the place to go for bus information, or you can call daily from 7am to 9pm.

Consulates The **U.S. Consulate** is at Paseo de las Delicias 7 (✆ **95-423-18-85**), open Monday to Friday from 10am to 1pm and 2 to 4:30pm.

Hospital For medical emergencies, go to the Hospital Universitario y Provincial, Av. Doctor Fedriani s/n (✆ **95-455-74-00**).

Internet Access Try the **Cibercenter** at Calle Julio Cesar 8 (✆ **95-422-88-99**), off Calle Reyes Católicos. It is open daily from 9am to 9pm.

Laundry Lavandería Roma, Calle Castelar 2 (✆ **95-421-05-35**), is open Monday to Friday from 9:30am to 2pm and 5 to 8:30pm, Saturday from 9:30am to 1:30pm.

Police The police station is located on Paseo de las Delicias (✆ **95-461-54-50**).

Post Office The post office is at Av. de la Constitución 32 (✆ **95-421-64-76**). It's open Monday to Friday from 8:30am to 7pm, Saturday from 9:30am to 2pm.

Safety With massive unemployment, the city has been hit by a crime wave in recent years. María Luisa Park is especially dangerous, as is the highway leading to Jerez de la Frontera and Cádiz. Dangling cameras and purses are especially vulnerable. Don't leave cars unguarded with your luggage inside. Regrettably, some daring attacks are made—as they are in U.S. cities—when passengers stop for traffic signals.

Taxis See "Getting Around," earlier in this section.

Telephone & Telex The telephone office is at Calle Sierpes 11 (for telephone service information, call ✆ **003**). To send wires by phone, call ✆ **95-422-20-00.**

3 Where to Stay

During Holy Week and the Seville Fair, hotels often double, even triple, their rates. Price increases are often not announced until the last minute. If you're going to be in Seville at these times, arrive with an ironclad reservation and an agreement about the price before checking in.

VERY EXPENSIVE

Hotel Alfonso XIII ★★★ At the southwestern corner of the gardens fronting the Alcázar, this rococo building is one of Spain's three or four most legendary hotels and Seville's premier address. Built in the Mudéjar/Andalusian revival style as a shelter for patrons of the Ibero-American Exposition of 1929 and named after the then-king of Spain, it reigns as a super-ornate and super-expensive bastion of glamour. Its rooms and hallways glitter with hand-painted tiles, acres of marble and mahogany, antique furniture embellished with intricately embossed leather, and a spaciousness nothing short of majestic. All rooms are beautifully kept, with bathrooms containing tub/shower combos.

San Fernando 2, 41004 Sevilla. ✆ **800/221-2340** in the U.S. and Canada, or 95-491-70-00. Fax 95-491-70-99. 146 units. 350€–421€ double; 821€–870€ suite. AE, DC, MC, V. Parking 17€. **Amenities:** 2 restaurants; 2 bars; pool; tennis courts; car rental; room service; babysitting; laundry/dry cleaning. *In room:* A/C, TV, minibar, hair dryer, safe.

Hotel Tryp Colón ★ Set about a quarter mile northwest of the Giralda and about 2 blocks southeast of the Fine Arts Museum (*Museo Provincial de Bellas*

Artes), this hotel is Seville's closest rival in prestige and architectural allure to the legendary Alfonso XIII. Originally built around the turn of the century and overhauled in 1988, it retains such features as a massive stained-glass dome stretching over the lobby, baronial staircases, formal service, and all the niceties of an expensive hotel. The guest rooms, all with private bathrooms containing shower-tub combinations, are conservative and traditional, although some are in need of an overhaul.

Canalejas 1, 41001 Sevilla. ✆ **800/387-8842** in the U.S., or 95-450-55-99. Fax 95-422-09-38. www.tryp.es. 218 units. 260€ double; 400€ suite. Rates include breakfast. AE, DC, MC, V. Parking 15.50€. **Amenities:** 2 restaurants; 2 bars; room service; babysitting; laundry/dry cleaning. *In room:* A/C, TV, minibar, hair dryer, safe.

EXPENSIVE

Al-Andalús Palace ★★ No hotel in Seville has a more avant-garde design than this palace just 5 minutes from the center in the Heliópolis district, an upmarket residential area. The front public rooms are suspended by cable, and the glass facade reflects both the blue skies of Seville and the marble floors. The large guest rooms are elegantly appointed, with large windows; some have balconies. The decor and furnishings are minimalist—functional but modern. Many accommodations have small living rooms and suites with their own breakfast bars. The bathrooms have showers, large tubs, and mirrors; the suites contain hydromassage.

Av. Palmera s/n, 43012 Sevilla. ✆ **95-423-06-00.** Fax 95-423-02-00. www.sol-1.com/hotel/al-andalus. 632 units. 231€ double; 410€ suite. AE, DC, MC, V. Parking 9€. Bus: 34. **Amenities:** Restaurant; bar; pool; health spa; room service; babysitting; laundry/dry cleaning. *In room:* A/C, TV, minibar, hair dryer, safe.

Casa Imperial ★★★ In the historic center, this hotel was launched in the mid-1990s near Casa Pilatos and dates from the 15th century, when it was the home of the butler to the Marquis of Tarifa. The interior is refined, and there are four Andalusian patios adorned with exotic plants. The beamed ceilings are original, and sparkling chandeliers hang from the ceilings. The rooms are large—many have small kitchens and ample terraces. The bathrooms are tastefully decorated with showers and luxurious tubs, some of which are antiques.

Calle Imperial 29, 41003 Sevilla. ✆ **95-450-03-00.** Fax 95-450-03-30. www.casaimperial.com. 24 units. 155€–330€ double; 215€–395€ suite. AE, DC, MC, V. Rates include breakfast buffet. Free parking. **Amenities:** Restaurant; bar; room service; babysitting; laundry/dry cleaning. *In room:* A/C, TV, minibar, hair dryer, safe.

Casa Número 7 ★★ *Finds* This is as close as you can get to staying in an elegant private home in Seville. Next to the Santa Cruz *barrio,* the little inn is in a beautiful, sensitively restored 19th-century mansion where you live in style, as evoked by the butler who serves you breakfast. Small in dimension, Casa No. 7 is big on style and grace notes, recapturing the aura of Old Seville. It thinks of itself, with justification, as a civilized oasis in the midst of a bustling city. In 2001 it won the prestigious Tatler Travel Award as the world's "best small hotel." Rooms are individually decorated in old Sevillano style, with impeccable taste and an eye to comfort. Called more "Chelsea (London) town house than Seville hacienda," the building envelops an old atrium, and is filled with such touches as family photographs, Oriental area rugs, a marble fireplace, and floral print loveseats. All come with good-size bathrooms with tub and shower. We prefer the spacious Yellow Room, with its "Juliet balcony" overlooking the street.

Vírgenes 7, 41004 Sevilla. ✆ **95-422-15-81.** Fax 95-421-45-27. www.casanumero7.com. 6 units. 170€ double. **Amenities:** "Honesty" bar; laundry. *In room:* A/C.

Seville Accommodations

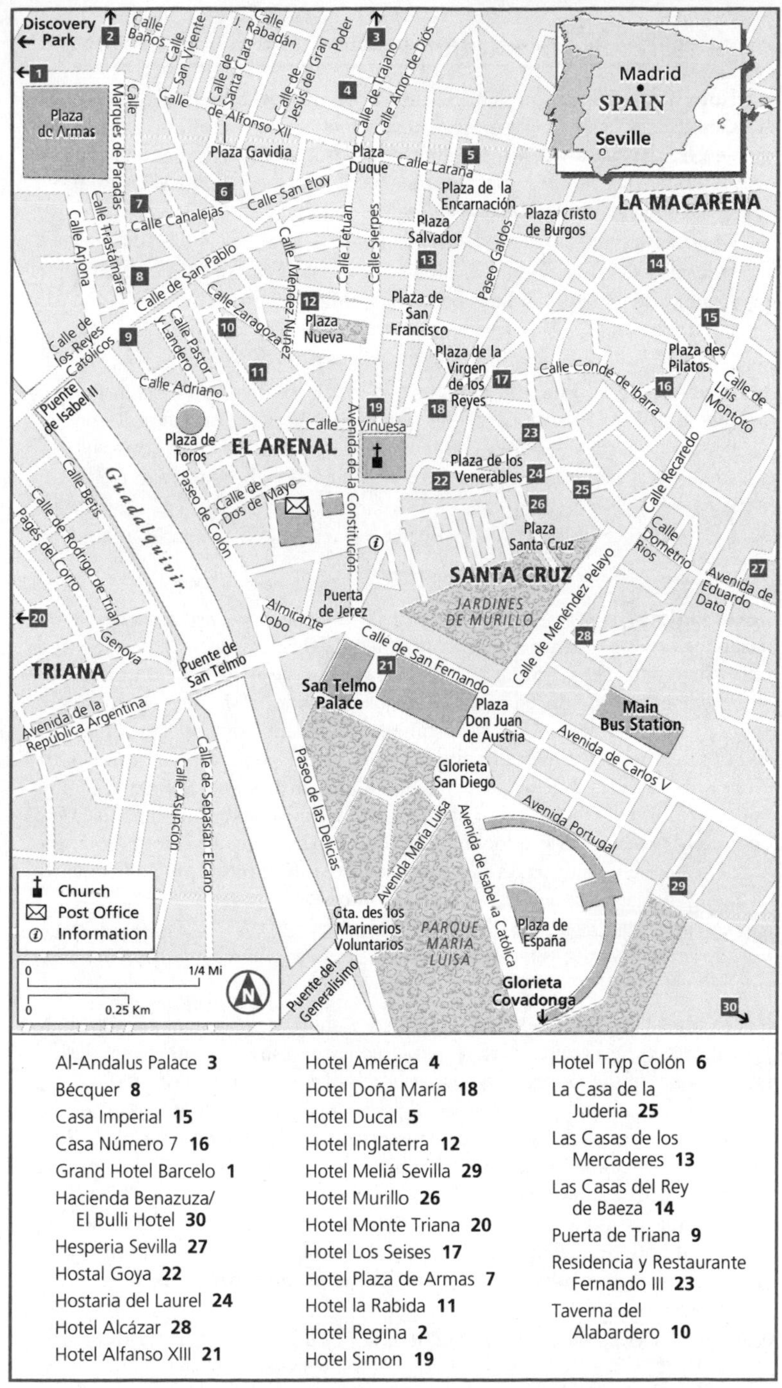

Kids Family-Friendly Hotels

Hotel Doña María (p. 259) Located behind the cathedral and the Giralda, this is one of the most gracious hotels in the old quarter of Seville. The garden courtyard and the rooftop pool delight adults and children alike. Rooms contain wide beds and bathrooms with dual sinks, and some rooms are large enough for the entire family.

Hotel Meliá Sevilla (see below) On the outskirts of town, this 11-story structure offers many facilities appreciated by families, including a pool, fitness center, squash court, and parking garage. Families enjoy dining on a terrace alfresco, and there's also a snack bar on the grounds. Housekeeping in the guest rooms is good.

Residencia y Restaurante Fernando III (p. 261) This hotel lies in the medieval Barrio Santa Cruz, the old Jewish quarter. The helpful and polite staff speaks English and is welcoming to families, offering some guest rooms large enough to accommodate those traveling with children.

Hotel Inglaterra ★★ Established in 1857 and since modernized into a comfortably glossy seven-story contemporary design, this eminently respectable and rather staid hotel lies a 5-minute walk southwest of the cathedral, occupying one entire side of a palm-fringed plaza. Much of its interior is sheathed with acres of white or gray marble, and the furnishings include ample use of Spanish leather and floral-patterned fabrics. Despite their modernity, the bedrooms nonetheless evoke old-fashioned touches of Iberian gentility. The best rooms are on the fifth floor. All units contain well-kept bathroom with shower-tub combinations. One floor above street level, overlooking the mosaic pavements of Plaza Nueva, the hotel's sunny restaurant serves well-prepared fixed-price meals from a frequently changing international menu.

Plaza Nueva 7, 41001 Sevilla. ✆ **95-422-49-70.** Fax 95-456-13-36. 109 units. 111€–162€ double. AE, DC, MC, V. Parking 9€. **Amenities:** Restaurant; bar; room service; babysitting; laundry/dry cleaning. *In room:* A/C, TV, minibar, hair dryer, safe.

Hotel Meliá Sevilla ★★ Kids Located a short walk east of the Plaza de España, near the Parque María Luisa, this is the most elegant, tasteful, and international of the modern skyscraper hotels of Seville. It opened in 1987, rising 11 floors. It incorporates acres of white marble as well as several dozen shopping boutiques and private apartments into its L-shaped floor plan. Bedroom decor is contemporary and comfortable, and each unit offers a private bathroom with a shower and tub, though rooms in the back lack a view. The Meliá was a favorite of the planners of the massive Expo, which transformed the face of both Seville and Andalusia. The hotel lacks the personal touch provided by the staff at Alfonso XIII, but its rooms are superior to those at the Inglaterra.

Doctor Pedro de Castro 1, 41004 Sevilla. ✆ **800/336-3542** in the U.S., or 95-442-15-11. Fax 95-442-16-08. www.solmelia.com. 364 units. 185€ double; from 312.50€ suite. AE, DC, MC, V. Parking 12.70€. **Amenities:** 2 restaurants; bar; room service; pool; fitness center; sauna; Jacuzzi; massage; babysitting; laundry/dry cleaning. *In room:* A/C, TV, minibar, hair dryer, safe.

Las Casas del Rey de Baeza ★ Less luxurious than its sibling, La Casa de la Judería (see below), this antique hotel close to the Casa de Pilatos is still a winning choice with its stone floors and 19th-century Andalusian architecture. A hotel since 1998, it has an interior patio surrounded by a cozy coterie of rooms and a long Andalusian balcony. Some of the beautifully furnished rooms have living rooms, and the decor is finely honed in marble and wood with comfortable furnishings. The bathrooms contain tub/shower combos.

Calle Santiago, Plaza Jesús de la Redención 2, 41003 Seville. ✆ **95-456-14-96.** Fax 95-456-14-41. baeza@zoom.es. 41 units. 118€–151€ double; 167€–205€ suite. AE, DC, MC, V. Parking 12€. **Amenities:** Bar; lounge; pool; babysitting; laundry/dry cleaning. *In room:* A/C, TV, minibar, hair dryer, safe.

Taverna del Alabardero ★★ *Finds* This tavern now houses one of the single most charming places to stay in the city. Close to the bullring and a 5-minute walk from the cathedral, this is a restored 19th-century mansion with a spectacular central patio and a romantic atmosphere. The units on the third floor have balconies overlooking street scenes as well as whirlpool tubs. All the rooms are spacious and comfortable, each individually decorated in a specific regional style. The bathrooms contain tub/shower combos.

Zaragoza 20, 41001 Sevilla. ✆ **95-456-06-37.** Fax 95-456-36-66. 7 units. 135€–224€ double; 165€–260€ suite. Rates include continental breakfast. AE, DC, MC, V. Parking 12€. **Amenities:** Restaurant; bar; lounge; room service; babysitting; laundry/dry cleaning. *In room:* A/C, TV, minibar, hair dryer, safe.

MODERATE

Bécquer A short walk from the action of the Seville bullring and only 2 blocks from the river, Bécquer is on a street full of cafes where you can order tapas and drink Andalusian wine. The Museo Provincial de Bellas Artes is also nearby. Built in the 1970s, the hotel was enlarged and much renovated in the late 1980s. It occupies the site of a former mansion and retains many objets d'art rescued before that building was demolished. You register in a wood-paneled lobby before being shown to one of the functionally furnished rooms—a good value in a pricey city. All have bathrooms with tub/shower combos.

Calle Reyes Católicos 4, 41001 Sevilla. ✆ **95-422-89-00.** Fax 95-421-44-00. www.hotelbecquer.com. 139 units. 124€–158€ double. AE, DC, MC, V. Parking 10.50€. Bus: 21, 24, 30, or 31. **Amenities:** Restaurant; bar; lounge; room service; babysitting; laundry/dry cleaning. *In room.* A/C, TV, minibar, hair dryer, safe.

Hotel Alcázar On the wide and busy Boulevard Menéndez y Pelayo, across from the Jardines de Alcázon, this pleasantly contemporary hotel is sheltered behind a facade of brown brick. Built in 1964, the hotel was last renovated in 1991. Slabs of striated gray marble cool the reception area in the lobby, next to which you'll find a Spanish restaurant and bar. Above, three latticed structures resemble a trio of *miradores.* The medium-size guest rooms have functional modern furniture and private bathrooms with shower-tub combinations.

Menéndez y Pelayo 10, 41004 Sevilla. ✆ **95-441-20-11.** Fax 95-442-16-59. 93 units. 112€–142€ double. Rates include breakfast. AE, DC, MC, V. Parking 12€. **Amenities:** Bar; babysitting; laundry/dry cleaning. *In room:* A/C, TV, hair dryer.

Hotel Doña María ★ *Kids* Staying at this hotel is a worthwhile investment, partly because of the Iberian antiques in the stone lobby and upper hallways. And the location a few steps from the cathedral creates a dramatic view from the Doña María's rooftop terrace. An ornate neoclassical entryway is offset with a pure white facade and iron balconies, which hint at the building's origin in the 1840s as a private villa. Amid the flowering plants on the upper floor you'll find garden-style lattices and antique wrought-iron railings. Each of the one-of-a-kind rooms has a bathroom with a tub/shower combo and is well furnished and comfortable, though some are rather small. A few have four-poster beds, others a handful of antique reproductions. Light sleepers might find the noise of the church bells jarring. Breakfast is the only meal served.

Don Remondo 19, 41004 Sevilla. ✆ **95-422-49-90.** Fax 95-421-95-46. www.hdmaria.com. 64 units. 93€–108€ double. AE, DC, MC, V. Parking 12€. **Amenities:** Breakfast room; bar; pool; room service; babysitting; laundry/dry cleaning. *In room:* A/C, TV, minibar, hair dryer, safe.

Hotel Los Seises Once the 16th-century palace of the archbishop of Seville, this hotel is behind the cathedral in the old Jewish Quarter of Santa Cruz. Renovations have added modern amenities but many of the Andalusian touches have been retained. In this category of antique hotels, we still prefer the Casa Imperial, but what you get here isn't bad. At least it was the pope's choice when he visited Seville. Traditional stucco walls are adorned with modern paintings in contrast to the antique tiles. The rooms range from small to spacious, each with a good bed and a restored bathroom with a tub/shower combo. Be sure to check out the stunning vista of La Giralda you can enjoy while sunbathing on the rooftop.

Calle Segovias 6, 41004 Sevilla. ✆ **95-422-94-95.** Fax 95-422-43-34. www.hotellosseises.com 42 units. 128€–180.30€ double. AE, DC, MC, V. Parking 15.03€. **Amenities:** Restaurant; bar; pool; room service; babysitting; laundry/dry cleaning. *In room:* A/C, TV, minibar, hair dryer, safe.

Hotel Monte Triana In the Triana district, this three-star hotel lies a 15-minute walk from the commercial center and the historic monuments. A hotel since 1991, the building rises four floors behind a dull facade with large windows. Business travelers are more attracted to the hotel than tourists, although it is perfectly acceptable for both. Most of the rooms are on the interior, away from street noises, and connected to a pleasant patio. The decor is not inspired but rather functional, although there is comfort here. The housekeeping is first rate and the bathrooms are well equipped, including shower-tub combinations and complimentary toiletries. A cafeteria serves breakfast and assorted dishes throughout the day.

Clara de Jesús Montero 24, 41010 Sevilla. ✆ **95-434-18-32.** Fax 95-434-33-28. 116 units. 100€. AE, DC, MC, V. Parking 7€. Bus: 43. **Amenities:** Bar; room service; babysitting; laundry/dry cleaning. *In room:* A/C, TV, minibar, hair dryer, safe.

Hotel Plaza de Armas This glass-and-steel hotel is in direct contrast to the antique *casas* of Seville converted into hotels. It was built in 1992 and is the city's most modern-looking structure, lying in the center close to the Plaza de Armas and the cathedral. The interior design consists of architectural lines of almost Japanese simplicity intermixed with steel and wood. The rooms are airy and colorful in severe contemporary style, with roomy bathrooms containing tub/shower combos.

Av. Marqués de Paradas s/n, 41001 Sevilla. ✆ **95-490-19-92.** Fax 95-490-18-32. www.nh-hoteles.es. 262 units. 122€–212€ double; 167€–257€ suite. AE, DC, MC, V. **Amenities:** Restaurant; bar; pool; room service; babysitting; laundry/dry cleaning. *In room:* A/C, TV, minibar, hair dryer, safe.

Hotel Regina Right in the historic center, facing the Parque de la Cartuja and close to the Museo de Bellas Artes, this inviting hotel was constructed in 1992 in anticipation of the Seville Exposition. Its spacious pastel rooms are filled with light woods. The bathrooms are immaculate and come with tub/shower combos. The hotel staff can arrange guided tours of the city.

Calle San Vicente 97, 41002 Sevilla. ✆ **95-490-75-75.** Fax 95-490-75-62. 72 units. 204€ double; 246€ duplex. AE, DC, MC, V. Parking 7.20€. **Amenities:** Breakfast room; laundry/dry cleaning. *In room:* A/C, TV, minibar, hair dryer, safe.

Hotel Simón *Value* This 18th-century mansion next to the cathedral in the Arenal district is a bargain hunter's delight. Within is a beautifully ornate staircase and a patio of tropical plants. The social areas are chic and comfortable, and the lounge displays bric-a-brac belonging to the original mansion. Reservations are recommended as far in advance as possible because the word is out that this is a stylish establishment charging low prices. The rooms are medium to large, each individually decorated in keeping with the history of this place, even with antiques. All units contain bathrooms with tub/shower combos.

Calle García de Vinuesa 190, 41001 Sevilla. ✆ **95-422-66-60.** Fax 95-456-22-41. 31 units. www.hotelsimon sevilla.com. 63€–78€ double; 78€–120€ suite. AE, DC, MC, V. **Amenities:** Lounge; laundry/dry cleaning. *In room:* A/C, hair dryer.

La Casa de la Judería ★★ *Value* In the Santa Cruz district, this hotel is installed in a palace from the 1600s once owned by the duke of Beja, a great character in the history of Spain's aristocracy and known as the patron of Cervantes. Within easy walking distance of the cathedral and other sights, the building has been a hotel since 1991. It's now one of the best places to stay in Seville, offering an excellent bang for your peseta. All the rooms, medium in size, are individually decorated and furnished in an antique style, sometimes with four-poster beds; all have balconies, some facing street scenes and others opening onto one of the four interior patios in the classic Andalusian style. Many units have living rooms, and all the suites contain whirlpool tubs. The bathrooms are beautifully maintained, with tub/shower combos.

Plaza Santa María la Blanca, Callejón de Dos Hermanas 7, 41004 Sevilla. ✆ **95-441-51-50.** Fax 95-442-21-70. 108 units. 102€–123€ double; 175€–199€ suite. AE, DC, MC, V. Parking 12.50€. **Amenities:** Dining room; bar; room service; babysitting; laundry/dry cleaning. *In room:* A/C, TV, minibar, hair dryer, safe.

Las Casas de los Mercaderes ★ In the business center of Seville, this restored mansion lies close to the cathedral between the squares of San Francisco and Salvador. Its name reflects the history of the area, which was once home to many immigrant merchants. The 19th-century original has been fully renovated—at the time, an 18th-century patio was discovered. Much of the original style and grace notes were retained. Most of the medium-size rooms have balconies and classic Spanish furnishings. The modern bathrooms come with tub/shower combos.

Calle Alvarez Quintero 9–13, 41004 Sevilla. ✆ **95-422-58-58.** Fax 95-422-98-84. 46 units. 96€–117€ double. AE, DC, MC, V. Parking 12.50€. **Amenities:** Bar; lounge; room service; babysitting; laundry/dry cleaning. *In room:* A/C, TV, minibar, hair dryer, safe.

Puerta de Triana *Value* This budgeteer's dream is a 5-minute walk from the cathedral in the Paseo Colón district. Last renovated in 1992, it was constructed in the early 1970s in neoclassic style. Antique styles are mixed with modern features, and the interior is surprisingly elegant for a place charging such low prices. The hotel offers simply but comfortably furnished rooms, each with a bath containing a tub/shower combo. If you're driving to this location near the Plaza de Toros, you can ask the staff to direct you to one of the nearby garages where discounts for hotel guests are available.

Reyes Católicos 5, 41001 Sevilla. ✆ **95-421-54-04.** Fax 95-421-54-01. www.hotelpuertadetriana.com. 62 units. 72€–119€ double. AE, DC, MC, V. **Amenities:** Laundry/dry cleaning. *In room:* A/C, TV, hair dryer.

Residencia y Restaurante Fernando III *Kids* You'll find the Fernando III on a narrow, quiet street at the edge of the Barrio Santa Cruz, near the northern periphery of the Murillo Gardens. Its vast lobby and baronial dining hall are reminiscent of a luxurious South American hacienda. The building is modern, constructed around 1970 with marble and hardwood detailing, and is sparsely furnished with leather chairs, plants, and wrought-iron accents. Many of the accommodations—medium in size, comfortably furnished, and well maintained—offer balconies filled with cascading plants; all have private bathrooms with shower-tub combinations. The hotel's restaurant features regional Andalusian cuisine.

San José 21, 41001 Sevilla. ✆ **95-421-77-08.** Fax 95-422-02-46. 157 units. 133€ double. AE, DC, MC, V. Parking 12€. **Amenities:** Restaurant; bar; room service; pool; laundry/dry cleaning. *In room:* A/C, TV, minibar, hair dryer, safe.

INEXPENSIVE

Hostal Goya Its location in a narrow-fronted town house in the oldest part of the barrio is one of the Goya's strongest virtues. The building's gold-and-white facade, ornate iron railings, and picture-postcard demeanor are all noteworthy. The rooms are cozy and simple. Guests congregate in the marble-floored ground-level salon, where a skylight floods the couches and comfortable chairs with sunlight. No meals are served. Reserve well in advance. Parking is often available along the street.

Mateus Gago 31, 41004 Sevilla. ✆ **95-421-11-70.** Fax 95-456-29-88. 20 units (15 with bathroom). 55€–66€ double without bathroom, 60€–70€ double with bathroom. MC, V. *In room:* No phone.

Hostería del Laurel ★ *Finds* Long one of our favorite dining taverns in Santa Cruz, this traditional inn, whose downstairs is hung with cured Andalusian hams and strings of fresh garlic, also offers bargain rooms. During his stay here at in 1844, Don José Zorrilla, Spain's most romantic writer of the time, was so inspired by the atmosphere of the inn that he created his famous character, Don Juan Tenorio. Bedrooms are simply furnished and immaculately kept, opening onto one of the barrio's most delightful and time-mellowed squares. All units come with a small bathroom equipped with tub and shower. The rooms are spread across several floors of restored old houses with their tiny patios and bubbling fountains. When you're hungry, just follow the wafting aromas of well-flavored food to the restaurant downstairs (see "Where to Dine," below).

Plaza de los Venerables 5, 41004 Sevilla. ✆ **95-422-02-95.** Fax 95-421-04-50. www.hosteriadellaurel.com. 21 units. 57€–84€ double. AE, DC, MC, V. **Amenities:** Restaurant; bar. *In room:* A/C, TV.

Hotel América Built in 1976 and partially renovated in 1994, this hotel contains rather small bedrooms but the maids keep the place spick-and-span. Superior features include wall-to-wall carpeting and, in winter, individual heat control that works. All units have well-kept bathrooms with shower-tub combinations. Near the hotel is a parking garage for 600 cars. There isn't a major restaurant, but the América does offer a tearoom, and cafeteria that serves regional and international cuisine. The hotel is set on the northern side of the Plaza del Duque. One of Spain's major department stores, El Corte Inglés, opens onto the same square.

Jesús del Gran Poder 2, 41002 Sevilla. ✆ **95-422-09-51.** Fax 95-421-06-26. 100 units. 114€ double. AE, DC, MC, V. Parking 8€ nearby. **Amenities:** Lounge; laundry/dry cleaning. *In room:* A/C, TV, minibar.

Hotel La Rábida This is a former 19th-century mansion that once belonged to one of Seville's most aristocratic families. It's in the Arenal district, a 5-minute walk from the cathedral. Modestly renovated in 1998, the hotel offers small but clean modern rooms and bathrooms containing tub/shower combos. The hotel's most attractive feature is a lobby patio crowned by a stained-glass skylight.

Calle Castelar 24, 41001 Sevilla. ✆ **95-422-09-60.** Fax 95-422-73-45. 105 units. 65€–100€ double. AE, DC, MC, V. **Amenities:** Restaurant; bar; room service; laundry/dry cleaning. *In room:* A/C, TV, hair dryer.

Hotel Murillo Tucked away on a narrow street in the heart of Santa Cruz, the Residencia Murillo (named after the artist who used to live in this district) is almost next to the gardens of the Alcázar. Inside, the lounges harbor some fine architectural characteristics and antique reproductions; behind a grilled screen is a retreat for drinks. Many of the rooms we inspected were cheerless and gloomy, so have a look before checking in. All units do contain bathrooms with tub/shower combos. You can reach this *residencia* from the Menéndez y Pelayo, a wide avenue west of the Parque María Luisa, where a sign leads you through the **Murillo Gardens** on the left. Motorists should try to park in the Plaza de Santa Cruz. Then walk 2 blocks to the hotel, which will send a bellhop back to the car to pick up your suitcases. If there are two in your party, station a guard at the car, and if you're going out at night, call for an inexpensive taxi to take you instead of strolling through the streets of the old quarter—it's less romantic but a lot safer.

Calle Lope de Rueda 7–9, 41004 Sevilla. ✆ **95-421-60-95.** Fax 95-421-96-16. www.hotelmurillo.com. 57 units. 60€ double; 75€ triple. AE, DC, MC, V. Parking 12€ nearby. **Amenities:** Room service; laundry/dry cleaning. *In room:* A/C, hair dryer.

WHERE TO STAY NEARBY

Hacienda Benazuza/El Bulli Hotel ★★★ On a hillside above the agrarian hamlet of Sanlúcar la Mayor, 19km (12 miles) south of Seville, this legendary manor house is surrounded by 40 acres of olive groves and farmland. Its ownership has been a cross section of every major cultural influence that has swept through Andalusia since the Moors laid its foundations in the 10th century. After the Catholic conquest of southern Spain, the site became a stronghold of the fanatically religious Caballeros de Santiago. In 1992, Basque-born entrepreneur Rafael Elejabeitia bought the property and spent millions of pesetas to transform it into one of Andalusia's most charming hotels. Careful attention was paid to preserving the ancient Moorish irrigation system, whose many reflecting pools nourish the gardens. All but a few of the rooms are in the estate's main building, each individually furnished with Andalusian antiques and Moorish trappings. All units contain neatly kept bathrooms with tub/shower combos. The kitchen is now under the culinary influence of Ferran Adria, the famous chef of Catalonia who is hailed as one of the top two or three best chefs in the country. He's rarely on the premises but his recipes and style of cookery are used. Even if you're not staying here, you might want to call for a dinner reservation. Chances are it'll be one of your finest meals in Seville.

Calle Virgen de las Nieves s/n, 41800 Sanlúcar la Major, Sevilla. ✆ **95-570-33-44.** Fax 95-570-3410. www.hbenazuza.com. 44 units. 310€–410€ double; 420€–1,130€ suite. AE, DC, MC, V. Free parking. Closed Jan. From Seville, follow the signs for Huelva and head south on the A-49 highway, taking exit no. 16. **Amenities:** 2 restaurants; bar; pool; tennis courts; room service; babysitting; laundry/dry cleaning. *In room:* A/C, TV, minibar, hair dryer, safe.

Palacio San Benito ★★★ Motorists who don't mind the hour drive north of Seville to this whitewashed hill town will find themselves ensconced in comfort in one of Andalusia's most alluring B&Bs. Driven from his ancestral home by distant cousins who took over the property, Manuel Morales de Jódar, the leading decorator of Seville, took a stone-built church from the 1300s, lying in ruins, and restored it to more glory than it had in its original incarnation. Into this new place, he hung his Goyas and placed his antiques and other objets d'art.

Bedrooms are beautifully designed, immaculately comfortable, and accompanied by tiled bathrooms with tub and shower. Without resorting to anything of the "Carmen clichés" of Seville, like castanets and frilly shirts, Señor Jódar brings his lucky guests into intimate contact with the essence of Andalusia by hiring the village gypsies to perform flamenco, by having the family cook prepare tapas according to time-tested old recipes, and by hitching up thoroughbred Andalusian horses to take his guests on carriage rides. When you meet the señor, and he hands you the village's trademark cherry aperitif, you'll think you're being welcome to a private house party.

Cazalla de la Sierra, 41370 Sevilla. ✆ **95-488-33-36.** Fax 95-488-31-62. www.palaciodesanbenito.com/historia.htm. 9 units. 120€ double, 210€ suite. Rates include breakfast. AE, DC, MC, V. **Amenities:** Restaurant; bar; room service; laundry; pool; gym. *In room:* A/C, TV, minibar, hair dryer, safe.

4 Where to Dine

VERY EXPENSIVE

Egaña Oriza ★★★ BASQUE/INTERNATIONAL Seville's most stylish restaurant is set within the conservatory of a restored mansion adjacent to the Murillo Gardens. Much of its reputation stems from its role as one of the few game specialists in Andalusia—a province otherwise devoted to seafood. The restaurant was opened by Basque-born owner/chef José Mari Egaña, who manages to combine his passion for hunting with his flair for cooking. Many of the ingredients have been trapped or shot within Andalusia, a region whose potential for sports shooting is underutilized, according to Sr. Egaña. The view from the dining room encompasses a garden and a wall that formed part of the fortifications of Muslim Seville. Specialties depend on the season but might include ostrich carpaccio, gazpacho with prawns, steak with foie gras in grape sauce, casserole of wild boar with cherries and raisins, duck *quenelles* in a potato nest with apple purée, and woodcock flamed in Spanish brandy. The wine list provides an ample supply of hearty Spanish reds to accompany these dishes. Dessert might feature a chocolate tart slathered with freshly whipped cream. Sr. Egaña's wife, Mercedes, runs the dining room.

San Fernando 41. ✆ **95-422-72-11.** Reservations required. Main courses 17€–36€. AE, DC, MC, V. Restaurant, Mon–Fri 1:30–3:30pm, Mon–Sat 9–11:30pm; bar, daily 9am–midnight. Closed Aug.

La Isla ★ SPANISH/ANDALUSIAN This choice is in two large Andalusian dining rooms (thick plaster walls, tile floors, and taurine memorabilia). Its seafood is trucked or flown in from either Galicia or Huelva, one of Andalusia's major ports, and is always fresh. Menu items include *merluza a la primavera* (hake with young vegetables), *solomillo a la castellana* (grilled beefsteak with strips of Serrano ham), chicken croquettes, and shellfish soup. The restaurant is a short walk from the cathedral within a very old building erected, the owners say, on foundations laid by the ancient Romans.

Arfe 25. ✆ **95-421-26-31.** Reservations recommended. Main courses 27€–39€. AE, DC, MC, V. Daily 1–5pm and 8pm–midnight. Closed Aug.

EXPENSIVE

El Burladero ★ CONTINENTAL This restaurant in one of Seville's most prominent hotels is awash with the memorabilia and paraphernalia of bullfighting. The wall tiles were removed from one of the pavilions at the 1929 Seville world's fair, and the photographs adorning the walls are a veritable history of bullfighting. (The restaurant is named after the wooden barricade behind which

Seville Dining

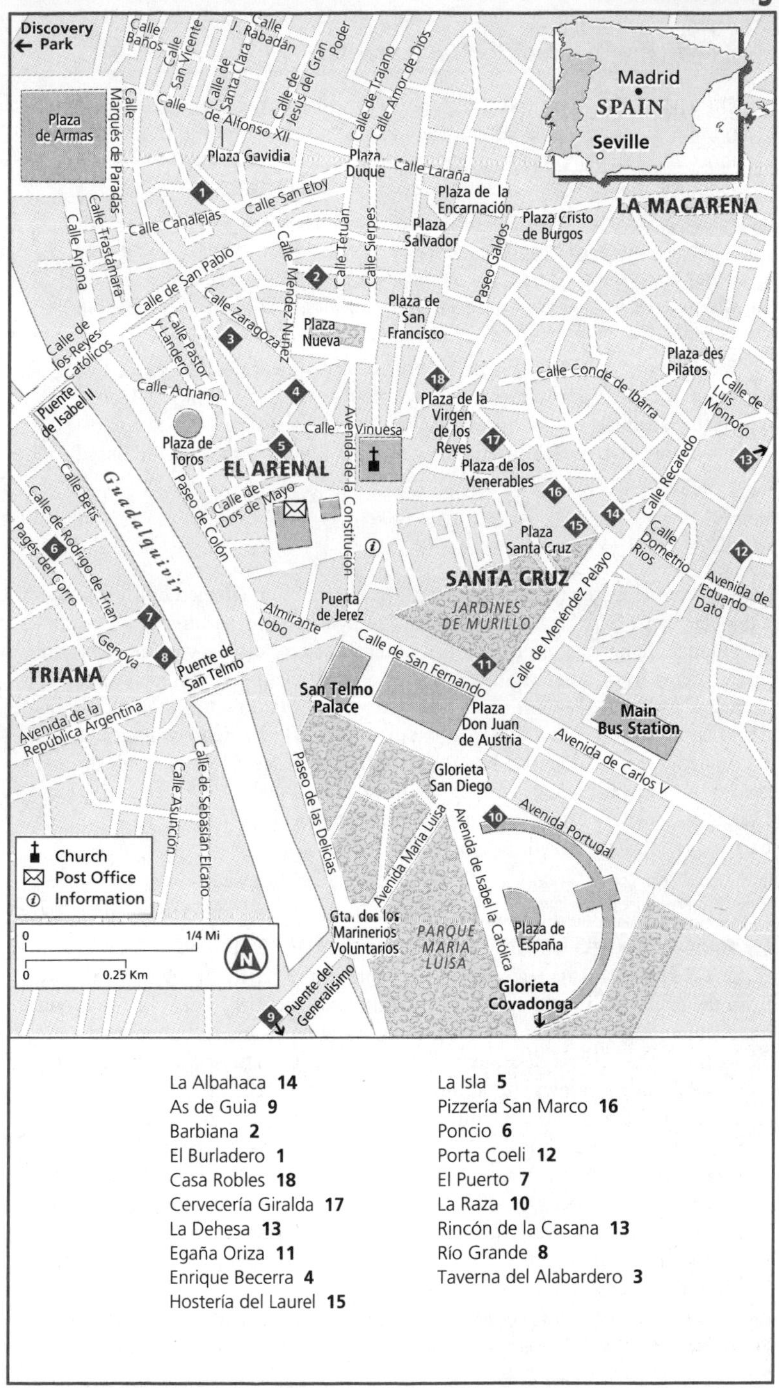

Kids Family-Friendly Restaurants

El Puerto Down by the river, onto which its terraces open, this is a good and inexpensive family seafood restaurant, offering one of the most reasonably priced cubiertos (fixed-price menus) in Seville. It's ideal for the family on a tight budget. ✆ **95-427-17-25.**

Pizzería El Artesano Near the cathedral, this is an ideal place for lunch if you're touring the heart of Seville, viewing the Alcázar and other attractions. The pizzas are good here, and the staff starts serving them at 12:30pm—so you don't have to wait around with hungry children until many restaurants open at 1:30pm. ✆ **95-421-38-58.**

Río Grande (p. 269) This is the best place to go for a classic Sevillian meal. It can turn into a real family affair if you order a big platter of paella, studded with chicken and shellfish. The restaurant sits against the bank of the Guadalquivir River, and there's also a snack bar if you're lunching light.

bullfighters in an arena can escape from the charge of an enraged bull.) It boasts a popular bar, where Sevillanos meet and mingle before their meals. Menu specialties include upscale interpretations of local country dishes, with an attractive mix of items from other regions of Spain as well. Examples include *bacalao al horno con patatas* (baked salt cod with potatoes and saffron sauce), roasted shoulder of lamb stuffed with a deboned oxtail and served in a richly aromatic sauce, clams with white kidney beans, *cocido* (a boiled amalgam of sausages, meats, chickpeas, and vegetables), and a stew of eel meat laced with garlic and spices. Dishes from other parts of Europe include duck liver, truffled filet steak in puff pastry, and salmon cooked in lemon-flavored dill sauce.

In the Hotel Tryp Colón, Canalejas 1. ✆ **95-450-55-99.** Reservations recommended. Main courses 13€–19€; fixed-price menus from 35€. AE, DC, MC, V. Daily 1:30–4:30pm and 9pm–midnight. Closed Aug.

La Dehesa ANDALUSIAN One of the leading restaurants of Seville, La Dehesa is known for its regional decor. It lies in the center of town, 5 minutes from the train station and a 20-minute walk from the cathedral. The restaurant has been serving gastronomes in Seville since the early '90s and is owned by the Meliá hotel chain. It is decorated like an elegant bodega or wine tavern with stucco walls and windows containing potted plants. Each corner is a shrine to a particular bullfighter, all of whom have donated memorabilia. The menu specializes in grilled meats but does all dishes exceedingly well. Try the flavor-filled *ensaladita de la Dehesa* (shrimp, avocado, and a green leaf salad) or else tender grilled lamb cutlets or fresh hake, also perfectly grilled. You might begin in the classic local style with an Andalusian gazpacho. Desserts are all homemade, including tarts and an especially delightful platter of crepes stuffed with nuts and banana ice cream.

Calle Luis de Morales 2. ✆ **95-457-62-04.** Reservations required. Main courses 14.50–17.40€; set menu 31.90€. AE, DC, MC, V. Daily 1:30–4pm and 8:30pm–midnight.

Poncio ★★ Finds ANDALUSIAN Even though your cabbie may tell you that this relatively new dining room in the Triana district doesn't exist, press on to discover some of the finest food in Seville. Eat in style with the Spanish dons who know of this place, even the sherry-makers from Jerez de la Frontera who journey to Seville on business. Chef Willy Moya might have studied with some of the grand cooks of Paris, but when he got back home, he invented his own dishes. Yes, there's still a Parisian influence, but as one faithful diner said, "Moya's roots lay buried deep in the soil of Andalusia." We concur. We always like to start with a platter of the tender, flavorful Jabugo ham, preceded, as always, with a glass of sherry. On our last visit our party ordered an array of tapas so all of us got to share in such delights as baby broad beans with quail eggs and ham; fresh, salted anchovies, and steamed peppers stuffed with prawns and orange cream. Only the croquettes were disappointing, a bit heavy. That "thick tomato soup" on the English menu turns out to be one of Seville's most delightful gazpachos. Ask the waiter to describe the dish of the day (often the best choice on the menu) or stick to such favorites as tender lamb, aromatically roasted in the oven in a wood-burning stove or else salt-encrusted sea bass in a delicate prawn oil served with olive caviar (not caviar, but minced olives that resemble caviar in look, not texture). None of the desserts sampled have ever disappointed. Would you believe hot apple pie with ice cream? The wine list is short but refined and tastefully selected.

Calle Victoria 8. ✆ **95-434-00-10.** Reservations required. Main courses 14€–20€. AE, DC, MC, V. Mon–Sat 2–4:30pm and 9:30pm–1am.

Porta Coeli ★★ MEDITERRANEAN With one of Seville's most sophisticated decors, this is the finest hotel dining in the city. Even if you're not a hotel guest, consider reserving one of the 15 beautifully laid tables set against a backdrop of tapestry-hung walls. The flavor combinations are contemporary, and you'll relish the freshest ingredients. The menu boasts a wide variety of dishes featuring duck, including a delectable duck with fried white beans laced with ham. Another savory offering is *ensalada de bacalao con tomate* (salt cod salad with tomatoes) and *arroz marinero con bogavante* (rice with crayfish). The locals rave about the *corazón de solomillo al foie con zetas al vino* (beef heart with liver and mushroom in red-wine sauce), though this might be an acquired taste. For dessert, nothing is more luscious than the napoleon with fresh fruit.

In the Hotel Hesperia Sevilla, Eduardo Dato 49. ✆ **95-453-35-00.** Reservations recommended. Main courses 11€–29€. AE, DC, MC, V. Daily 1:30–3:30pm and 9pm–midnight. Closed Aug. Bus: 23.

MODERATE

Barbiana ★★ ANDALUSIAN/SEAFOOD Close to the Plaza Nueva in the heart of Seville, this is one of the city's best fish restaurants. Chefs work hard to secure the freshest of the catches, even though Seville is inland. In the classic Andalusian architectural tradition, a tapas bar is up front. In the rear is a cluster of rustically decorated dining rooms. The trick here is not to consume so much wine and tapas in the front that you are too stuffed to partake of the savory viands. If you visit for lunch, the chef's specialty is seafood with rice (not available in the evening). We've sampled many items on the menu, often in the company of friends, but no two ever met more approval from us than *ortiguilla,* a sea anemone, which is fast fried in oil, or the *tortillitas de camarones,* latke-shaped chick pea fritters with bits of chopped shrimp and fresh scallions. Shellfish is the specialty, and the preferred way to order here is *a la plancha* or fresh from the grill. A kettle of fresh fish is also deep fried, and you can order it grilled with a zesty sauce. When available, we order *sargo* or rockfish, which is grilled and flavored with garlic juice and served with sweet roasted red peppers.

Calle Albaredo 11. ✆ **95-421-12-39.** Reservations recommended. Main courses 7.50€–15€. AE, DC, MC, V. Mon–Sat noon–4:30pm and daily 8pm–midnight.

Casa Robles ANDALUSIAN This restaurant is praised by locals and visitors alike. It began life as an unpretentious bar and *bodega* in 1954. Over the years, thanks to a staff directed by owner/chef Juan Robles and his children, it developed into a bustling restaurant on two floors of a building a short walk from the cathedral. Amid an all-Andalusian decor, you can enjoy such dishes as fish soup in the Andalusian style, *lubina con naranjas* (whitefish with Sevillana oranges), hake baked with strips of Serrano ham, and many kinds of fresh fish. The dessert list is long and very tempting.

Calle Alvarez Quintero 58. ✆ **95-421-31-50.** Reservations recommended. Main courses 10€–20€; fixed-price menus 33€–60€. AE, DC, MC, V. Daily 1–5pm and 8:30pm–1:30am.

Enrique Becerra ★ ANDALUSIAN Near the cathedral, this is a cozy retreat in a whitewashed house with wrought-iron window grilles, and its home-cooked dishes are prepared with flair. This popular tapas bar and dining spot has an intimate setting that welcomes you with the feeling that your business is really appreciated. While perusing the menu, you can sip dry Tío Pepe and nibble herb-cured olives with lemon peel. The gazpacho is among the city's best, and the sangria is served ice cold. Specialties include hake *real,* sea bream Bilbao style, and a wide range of well-prepared meat and fish dishes. The wine list is one of the best in Seville.

Gamazo 2. ✆ **95-421-30-49.** Reservations recommended. Main courses 12€–18€; fixed-price menus 42€–4€. AE, DC, MC, V. Mon–Sat 1–5pm and 8pm–midnight.

Rincón de la Casana ★ *Finds* ARGENTINEAN/ANDALUSIAN Close to the old town, this landmark wins new converts every year. Converted from an old building, it has a main door of intricate carving and craftsmanship, and its roof is red tiled in the traditional style. The two-story interior has one of the most interesting decors in the city, with antique tiles and typical Andalusian artifacts. At the entrance is the mounted head of the last bull killed by the famous matador José Luis Vasquez. The chefs know their ingredients right down to the last olive. On our last visit we savored *chuletón de buey* (ox steak) and *carne con chimichurri* (steak with chopped parsley and garlic dressing in virgin olive oil). Desserts are freshly made every day, including traditional puddings and tasty tarts, most often with fresh fruit.

Santo Domingo de la Calzada 13. ✆ **95-453-17-10.** Reservations required. Main courses 11€–17€; set menu 12€. AE, DC, MC, V. Mon–Sat 1–4:30pm and 8:30pm–12:30am.

Taverna del Alabardero ★★ ANDALUSIAN One of Seville's most prestigious restaurants occupies a 19th-century town house 3 blocks from the cathedral. Famous as the dining choice of nearly every politician and diplomat who visits Seville, it has recently hosted the king and queen of Spain, the king's mother, the Spanish president and members of his cabinet, and dozens of well-connected but merely affluent visitors. Amid a collection of European antiques and oil paintings, you'll dine in any of two main rooms or three private ones, and perhaps precede your meal with a drink or tapas on the flowering patio. There's a garden in back with additional tables. Menu items include spicy peppers stuffed with pulverized thigh of bull, Andalusian fish (*urta*) on a compote of aromatic tomatoes with coriander, cod filet with essence of red peppers, and Iberian beefsteak with foie gras and green peppers.

Calle Zaragoza 20, 41001 Seville. ✆ **95-456-06-37.** Fax 95-456-36-66. Reservations recommended. Main courses 7€–21€. AE, DC, MC, V. Daily 1–3:30pm and 8pm–midnight. Closed Aug. Bus: 13, 25,or 26.

INEXPENSIVE

As de Guía ★ ANDALUSIAN In the Heliópolis district, this new restaurant lures with its lobster tank and one of the finest tapas bars in Seville. Meals are inventive and classic at the same time, a favorite with many of the residents who live in the surrounding high-rises. There's nothing fancy here except the food. Begin, perhaps, with a tantalizing amusement such as thin slices of cured, dried tuna, a local delicacy. As in most Andalusian restaurants, scrambled eggs, mixed with various foodstuffs, is a feature. Here the chef whips the eggs with bits of tiny fresh asparagus tips and throws in bits of shrimp and ham for added flavor. We've never sampled anything here better than arroz con Bogavante, rice with lobster, although the fresh crab is a savory second choice. If featured, we'd also cast our votes for the velvety paté of duck. Of course, on any night the grilled fish is an always reliable choice, cooked aromatically with fresh herbs. Finish off with perhaps one of the most luscious of the chef's desserts: a homemade walnut and raisin ice cream.

Av. Ramón Carande 19. ✆ **95-462-81-72.** Reservations recommended. Main courses 6€–16€. AE, DC, MC, V. Mon–Sat noon–5pm, daily 8pm–midnight.

Hostería del Laurel ★ *Finds* ANDALUSIAN In one of the most charming buildings on tiny, difficult-to-find Plaza de los Venerables in the labyrinthine Barrio Santa Cruz, this is a hideaway. It has iron-barred windows stuffed with plants. Inside, amid Andalusian tiles, beamed ceilings, and more plants, you'll enjoy good regional cooking. Many diners stop for a drink and tapas at the ground-floor bar before going into one of the dining rooms. The *hostería* is attached to a well-recommended hotel.

Plaza de los Venerables 5. ✆ **95-422-02-95.** Reservations recommended. Main courses 7€–21€. AE, DC, MC, V. Daily noon–4pm and 7:30pm–midnight.

Pizzería San Marco ★ ITALIAN Although the name may make it sound like a fast-food joint, this is actually a Santa Cruz restaurant with sit-down service and bilingual waiters. Pizza is only one of the many items featured on the menu; most people opt for pasta, salmon salad, duck in orange sauce, osso buco, chicken Parmesan, or scallopini. There's a congenial corner for drinking, named Harry's Bar in honor of grander role models in Venice and elsewhere. Despite the allure of the food, the real interest of the place is its setting: The restaurant is within what was more than 1,000 years ago an Arab bathhouse, and its interior reminds some visitors of a secularized mosque, despite the presence of a modern wing.

Calle Mesón de Moro 6. ✆ **95-421-43-90.** Reservations recommended. Main courses 5.60€–9.75€. AE, DC, MC, V. Daily 1:30–4:30pm and 8:30pm–12:30am.

Río Grande *Kids* ANDALUSIAN This classic Sevillian restaurant is named for the Guadalquivir River, which its panoramic windows overlook. It sits against the bank of the river near the Plaza de Cuba in front of the Torre del Oro. Some diners come here just for a view of the city monuments. Most dishes are priced at the lower end of the scale. A meal might include stuffed sweet pepper *flamenca,* fish-and-seafood soup seaman's style, salmon, chicken-and-shellfish paella, bull tail Andalusian-style, or garlic chicken. A selection of fresh shellfish is brought in daily. Large terraces contain a snack bar, the Río Grande Pub, and a bingo room.

You can often watch sports events on the river in this pleasant (and English-speaking) spot.

Calle Betis s/n. ✆ **95-427-39-56.** Reservations required. Main courses 11€–18€. AE, DC, MC, V. Daily 1–4pm and 8pm–midnight. Bus: 41 or 42.

5 Exploring Seville

Seville has a wide range of palaces, churches, cathedrals, towers, and historic hospitals. Since it would take a week or two to visit all of them, we have narrowed the sights down to the very top attractions. The only way to explore Seville is on foot, with a good map in hand—but remember to be alert to muggers.

THE TOP ATTRACTIONS

Catedral ★★★ The largest Gothic building in the world, and the third-largest church in Europe after St. Peter's in Rome and St. Paul's in London, this church was designed by builders with a stated goal—that "those who come after us will take us for madmen." Construction began in the late 1400s and took centuries to complete.

Built on the site of an ancient mosque, the cathedral claims to contain the remains of Columbus, with his tomb mounted on four statues.

Works of art abound, many of them architectural, such as the 15th-century stained-glass windows, the iron screens (*rejas*) closing off the chapels, the elaborate 15th-century choir stalls, and the Gothic reredos above the main altar. During Corpus Christi and Immaculate Conception observances, altar boys with castanets dance in front of the high altar. In the Treasury are works by Goya, Murillo, and Zurbarán as well as a touch of the macabre in a display of skulls. After touring the dark interior, emerge into the sunlight of the Patio of Orange Trees, with its fresh citrus scents and chirping birds.

Plaza del Triunfo, Av. de la Constitución. ✆ **95-421-49-71.** Admission (including visit to Giralda Tower) 6€ adults, 1.50€ children and students. Daily 11am–5pm.

Giralda Tower ★★★ Just as Big Ben symbolizes London, La Giralda conjures up Seville. This Moorish tower, next to the cathedral, is the city's most famous monument. Erected as a minaret in the 12th century, it has seen later additions, such as 16th-century bells. To climb it is to take the walk of a lifetime. There are no steps—you ascend an endless ramp. If you can make it to the top, you'll have a dazzling view of Seville. Entrance is through the cathedral.

Plaza del Triunfo. Admission included in admission to cathedral (above). Same hours as cathedral (above).

Alcázar ★★★ Pedro the Cruel built this magnificent 14th-century Mudéjar palace, north of the cathedral. It is the oldest royal residence in Europe still in use: On visits to Seville, King Juan Carlos stays here. From the Dolls' Court to the Maidens' Court through the domed Ambassadors' Room, it contains some of the finest work of Sevillian artisans. In many ways, it evokes the Alhambra at Granada. Ferdinand and Isabella, who at one time lived in the Alcázar and influenced its architectural evolution, welcomed Columbus here on his return from America. On the top floor, the Oratory of the Catholic Monarchs has a fine altar

---

Tips Cathedral Alert

Shorts and T-shirts are not allowed in the cathedral. Remember to dress appropriately before you set out so you're not turned away.

Seville Attractions

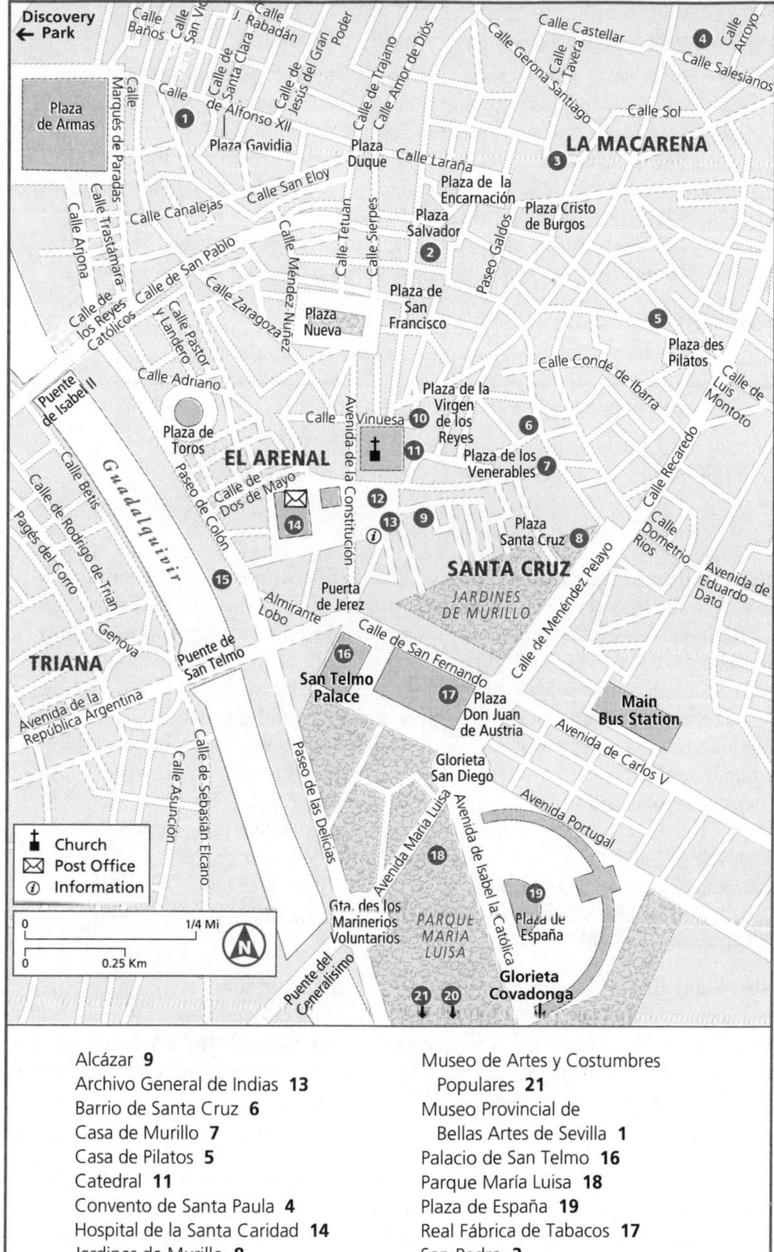

Alcázar **9**
Archivo General de Indias **13**
Barrio de Santa Cruz **6**
Casa de Murillo **7**
Casa de Pilatos **5**
Catedral **11**
Convento de Santa Paula **4**
Hospital de la Santa Caridad **14**
Jardines de Murillo **8**
Giralda Tower **10**
Museo Arqueológico Provincial **20**
Museo de Arte Contemporáneo **12**
Museo de Artes y Costumbres Populares **21**
Museo Provincial de Bellas Artes de Sevilla **1**
Palacio de San Telmo **16**
Parque María Luisa **18**
Plaza de España **19**
Real Fábrica de Tabacos **17**
San Pedro **3**
San Salvador **2**
Torre del Oro **15**

Moments *Olé:* Taking the Bull by the Horns

From Easter until late October, some of the best bullfighters in Spain appear at the **Maestranza bullring,** on Paseo de Colón (✆ **95-422-35-06**). One of the leading bullrings in Spain, the stadium attracts matadors whose fights often receive TV and newspaper coverage throughout Iberia. Unless there's a special festival going on, bullfights (*corridas*) occur on Sunday. The best bullfights are staged during April Fair celebrations. Tickets tend to be pricey and should be purchased in advance at the ticket office (*despacho de entradas*) on Calle Adriano, beside the stadium. You'll also find many unofficial kiosks selling tickets placed strategically along the main shopping street, Calle Sierpes. However, they charge a 20% commission for their tickets—a lot more if they think they can get it.

in polychrome tiles made by Pisano in 1504. The well-kept gardens, filled with beautiful flowers, shrubbery, and fruit trees, are alone worth the visit.

Plaza del Triunfo s/n. ✆ **95-450-23-23.** Admission 5€. Oct–Mar, Tues–Sat 9:30am–5pm, Sun 9:30am–1:30pm; Apr–Sept, Tues–Sat 9:30am–7pm, Sun 9:30am–5pm.

Hospital de la Santa Caridad ★ This 17th-century hospital is intricately linked to the legend of Miguel Manara, portrayed by Dumas and Mérimée as a scandalous Don Juan. It was once thought that he built this institution to atone for his sins, but this has been disproved. The death of Manara's beautiful young wife in 1661 caused such grief that he retired from society and entered the "Charity Brotherhood," burying corpses of the sick and diseased as well as condemned and executed criminals. Today the members of this brotherhood continue to look after the poor, the old, and invalids who have no one else to help them. Nuns will show you through the festive orange-and-sienna courtyard. The baroque chapel contains works by the 17th-century Spanish painters Murillo and Valdés-Leal. As you're leaving the chapel, look over the exit door for the macabre picture of an archbishop being devoured by maggots.

Calle Temprado 3. ✆ **95-422-32-32.** Admission 3€. Mon–Sat 9:30am–1:30pm and 3:30–6pm, Sun 9am–1pm.

Torre del Oro The 12-sided Tower of Gold, dating from the 13th century, overlooks the Guadalquivir River. Originally it was covered with gold tiles, but someone long ago made off with them. Recently restored, the tower has been turned into a maritime museum, Museo Náutico, displaying drawings and engravings of the port of Seville in its golden heyday.

Paseo de Cristóbal Colón. ✆ **95-422-24-19.** Admission 1€. Tues–Fri 10am–2pm, Sat–Sun 11am–2pm.

Casa de Pilatos ★★ This 16th-century Andalusian palace of the dukes of Medinaceli recaptures the splendor of the past, combining Gothic, Mudéjar, and Plateresque styles in its courtyards, fountains, and salons. According to tradition, this is a reproduction of Pilate's House in Jerusalem. Don't miss the two old carriages or the rooms filled with Greek and Roman statues. The collection of paintings includes works by Carreño, Pantoja de la Cruz, Sebastiano del Piombo, Lucas Jordán, Batalloli, Pacheco, and Goya. The museum's first floor is seen by guided tour only, but the ground floor, patios, and gardens are self-guided. The palace is about a 7-minute walk northeast of the cathedral on the northern edge of Barrio Santa Cruz, in a warren of labyrinthine streets whose traffic is funneled through the nearby Calle de Aguilas.

Plaza Pilatos 1. ✆ **95-422-50-55.** Museum, 8€; patio and gardens, 5€. Museum, daily 9am–7pm. Patio and gardens, daily 9am–7pm.

Archivo General de Indias The great architect of Philip II's El Escorial, Juan de Herrera, was also the architect of this building next to the cathedral, originally the *Lonja* (Stock Exchange). Construction on the Archivo General de Indias lasted from 1584 to 1646. In the 17th century it was headquarters for the Academy of Seville, which was founded in part by the great Spanish artist Murillo.

In 1785, during the reign of Charles III, the building was turned over for use as a general records office for the Indies. That led to today's Archivo General de Indias, said to contain some four million antique documents, even letters exchanged between patron Queen Isabella and explorer Columbus (he detailing his discoveries and impressions). These very rare documents are locked in air-conditioned storage to keep them from disintegrating. Special permission has to be acquired before examining some of them. On display in glass cases are fascinating documents in which the dreams of the early explorers come alive again.

Av. de la Constitución 3. ✆ **95-421-12-34.** Free admission. Mon–Fri 10am–1pm.

Museo Provincial de Bellas Artes de Sevilla ★★ This lovely old convent off Calle de Alfonso XII houses one of the most important Spanish art collections. A whole gallery is devoted to two paintings by El Greco, and works by Zurbarán are exhibited; however, the devoutly religious paintings of the Seville-born Murillo are the highlight. An entire wing is given over to macabre paintings by the 17th-century artist Valdés-Leal. His painting of John the Baptist's head on a platter includes the knife—lest you miss the point. The top floor, which displays modern paintings, is less interesting.

Plaza del Museo 9. ✆ **95-422-18-29.** Admission 1.50€, free for students. Tues 3–8pm, Wed–Sat 9am–8pm, Sun 9am–3pm. Bus: C3, C4, 13, or 14.

MORE ATTRACTIONS

Barrio Santa Cruz ★★★ What was once a ghetto for Spanish Jews, who were forced out of Spain in the late 15th century in the wake of the Inquisition, is today the most colorful district of Seville. Near the old walls of the Alcázar, winding medieval streets with names like *Vida* (Life) and *Muerte* (Death) open onto pocket-sized plazas. Flower-filled balconies with draping bougainvillea and potted geraniums jut out over this labyrinth, shading you from the hot Andalusian summer sun. Feel free to look through numerous wrought-iron gates into patios filled with fountains and plants. In the evening it's common to see Sevillians sitting outside drinking icy sangria under the glow of lanterns.

To enter the Barrio Santa Cruz, turn right after leaving the Patio de Banderas exit of the Alcázar. Turn right again at Plaza de la Alianza, going down Calle Rodrigo Caro to Plaza de Doña Elvira.

Fun Fact **Go with the Gold**

Many treasure-hunters come to the Archivo General de Indias hoping to learn where Spanish galleons laden with gold went down off the coasts of the Americas.

Tips **A Romantic Stroll Except for a Mugging**

The most romantic time to stroll around Barrio Santa Cruz is at night. It's also the most dangerous. Use caution in the evening as you parade along. Muggings commonly occur.

Parque María Luisa ★★ This park, dedicated to María Luisa, sister of Isabella II, was once the grounds of the Palacio de San Telmo. The palace, whose baroque facade is visible behind the deluxe Alfonso XIII Hotel, today houses a seminary. The former private royal park is now open to the public.

Running south along the Guadalquivir River, the park attracts those who want to take boat rides, walk along paths bordered by flowers, jog, or go bicycling. The most romantic way to traverse it is by rented horse and carriage, but this can be expensive, depending on your negotiation with the driver.

In 1929 Seville was to host the Spanish American Exhibition, and many pavilions from other countries were erected here. The worldwide depression put a damper on the exhibition, but the pavilions still stand.

Exercise caution while walking through this park, as many muggings have been reported.

Plaza de América Another landmark Sevillian square, Plaza de América represents city planning at its best: Here you can walk through gardens planted with roses, enjoying the lily ponds and the fountains and feeling the protective shade of the palms. And here you'll find a trio of elaborate buildings left over from the world exhibition that never materialized—in the center, the home of the government headquarters of Andalusia; on either side, two minor museums worth visiting only if you have time to spare.

Museo Arqueológico Provincial, Plaza de América s/n (✆ **95-423-24-01**), contains many artifacts from prehistoric times and the days of the Romans, Visigoths, and Moors. It's open Tuesday to Sunday from 10am to 2:30pm. Admission is 1.50€ for adults and free for students and children. Buses 30, 31, and 34 go there.

Nearby is the **Museo de Artes y Costumbres Populares,** Plaza de América s/n (✆ **95-423-25-76**), displaying folkloric costumes, musical instruments, Cordoban saddles, weaponry, and farm implements that document the life of the Andalusian people. It's open Tuesday to Saturday from 9am to 8pm, but closed on holidays. Admission is 1.50€ for adults and free for children and students.

Plaza de España The major building left from the exhibition at the Parque María Luisa (see above) is a half-moon-shaped structure in Renaissance style, set on this landmark square of Seville. The architect, Aníbal González, not only designed but also supervised the construction of this immense structure; today it is a government office building. At a canal here you can rent rowboats for excursions into the park, or you can walk across bridges spanning the canal. Set into a curved wall are alcoves, each focusing on characteristics of one of Spain's 50 provinces, as depicted in tile murals.

Real Fábrica de Tabacos When Carmen waltzed out of the tobacco factory in the first act of Bizet's opera, she made its 18th-century original in Seville world famous. This old tobacco factory was constructed between 1750 and 1766, and 100 years later it employed 10,000 *cigarreras,* of which Carmen was one in the opera. (She rolled cigars on her thighs.) In the 19th century, these tobacco women made up the largest female workforce in Spain. Many visitors arriving today, in fact, ask guides to take them to "Carmen's tobacco factory." The building, the second largest in Spain and located on Calle San Fernando near the city's landmark luxury hotel, the Alfonso XIII, is still here. But the Real Fábrica de Tabacos is now part of the Universidad de Sevilla. Look for signs of its former role, however, in the bas-reliefs of tobacco plants and Indians over the main entrances. You'll also see bas-reliefs of Columbus and Cortés. Then you can wander through the grounds for a look at student life, Sevillian style. The factory is directly south of the Alcázar gardens.

6 Especially for Kids

The greatest thrill for kids in Seville is climbing **La Giralda,** the former minaret of the Great Mosque that once stood here. The view from this 20-story bell tower is certainly worth the climb, but most kids delight in the climb itself. With some inclined ramps and some steps, the climb was originally designed to be ridden up on horseback. Little gargoyle-framed windows along the way allow you to preview the skyline of Seville.

With your family in tow, head for **Plaza de España;** you'll find rowboats as well as *pedaloes* (pedal boats) to rent. A collection of Andalusian donkey carts here adds to the fun, and there are ducks to feed on the Isla de los Patos. If your children take to that, they'll enjoy feeding the pigeons as well.

The tourist office (see "Orientation," earlier in this chapter) will give advice on how to rent *pedaloes* or canoes for trips along the Guadalquivir River. Or you can go to the riverbanks near the Torre del Oro and make your own rental arrangements with **Cruceros Turísticos Torre del Oro,** Paseo Marqués de Contadero (✆ **95-421-13-96**).

Finally, to cap your family trip to Seville, take one of the **horse-and-buggy rides** that leave from Plaza Virgen de los Reyes on Adolfo Rodríguez Jurado, or from the Parque de María Luisa at Plaza de España. Rates are government controlled at 24€, but prices rise during April Fair and Holy Week.

WALKING TOUR THE OLD CITY

Start: At the Giralda by the cathedral.
Finish: At the Hospital de los Venerables in the Barrio Santa Cruz.
Time: 4 hours, including rapid visits to the interiors.
Best Times: Early morning (7–11am) and late afternoon (3–7pm).
Worst Times: After dark or during the heat of midday.

Seville is so loaded with architectural and artistic treasures that this brisk overview of the central zone doesn't begin to do justice to its cultural wealth. Although this walking tour includes the city's most obvious (and spectacular) monuments, such as the Giralda and the cathedral, it also includes lesser-known churches and convents—whose elaborate decorations were paid for by gold imported from the New World during Spain's Age of Exploration. It also features promenades through the city's most desirable shopping district, and meanders through the labyrinthine alleyways of the Barrio Santa Cruz.

Begin with a visit to the:

❶ Cathedral

This Gothic structure is so enormous that even its builders recognized the folly and fanaticism of their dreams. Its crowning summit, the Giralda, one of Europe's most famous towers, was begun in the late 1100s by the Moors and raised even higher by the Catholic monarchs in 1568. Because of the position of these connected monuments near the summit of a hill overlooking the Guadalquivir, some scholars nostalgically refer to the historic neighborhood around them as the Acropolis.

After your visit, walk to the cathedral compound's northeastern corner for a visit to the:

❷ Palacio Arzobispal (Archbishop's Palace)

This 16th-century building rests on 13th-century foundations, with a 17th-century baroque facade of great beauty. Although conceived to house the overseer of the nearby cathedral, it was sometimes pressed into service to house secular visitors. One of these was Napoléon's representative, Maréchal Soult, after he conquered Seville in the name of the Bonaparte family and France early in the 19th century.

From here, walk across the street, heading south, to Plaza Virgen de los Reyes, for a visit to the:

❸ Convento de la Encarnación (Convent of the Incarnation)

Its origins date from the 1300s, shortly after the Catholic reconquest of Seville. Part of its architectural curiosity includes the widespread use of the lobed, horseshoe-shaped arches and windows traditionally used in mosques.

Exit from the church, then walk eastward across Plaza del Triunfo into the entrance of one of the most exotic palaces in Europe, the:

❹ Reales Alcázar (Royal Alcázar)

The oldest royal seat in Spain, it was begun for the Moorish caliphs in A.D. 712 as a fortress, then enlarged and embellished over the next thousand years by successive generations of Moorish and, beginning in 1248, Christian rulers. Its superimposed combination of Arab and Christian Gothic architecture creates one of the most interesting monuments in Iberia. Lavish gardens, as exotic as what you'd expect in the Old Testament, sprawl in an easterly direction in back. More than any other monument on this tour, with the exception of the cathedral, the Alcázar deserves a second visit after the end of this walking tour.

Exit from the Alcázar back onto Plaza del Triunfo. At the plaza's southwestern edge rises the imposing bulk of the:

❺ Archivo General de Indias (Archive of the Indies)

It was designed in the 1580s by Juan de Herrera, whose rectilinear austerity at El Escorial appealed to the religious fanaticism of Philip II. Built as a commodities exchange, it was abandoned for a site in Cádiz when that port replaced Seville as the most convenient debarkation point for ships coming from the New World. In 1758 it was reconfigured as the repository for the financial records and political and cultural archives of anything concerning the development of the Western Hemisphere. Its closets and storerooms contain more than four million dossiers—many bureaucratic and tedious, but some of passionate interest to scholars and academics.

From here, walk half a block west to the roaring traffic of Avenida de la Constitución, then turn north, bypassing the facade of the already-visited cathedral. The avenida will end within 2 blocks at the ornate bulk of Seville's:

❻ Ayuntamiento (Town Hall)

Begun in 1527, and enlarged during the 19th century, it's the city's political showcase. For a view of its most interesting (Plateresque) facade, turn right (east) when you reach it, then flank

Walking Tour—The Old City

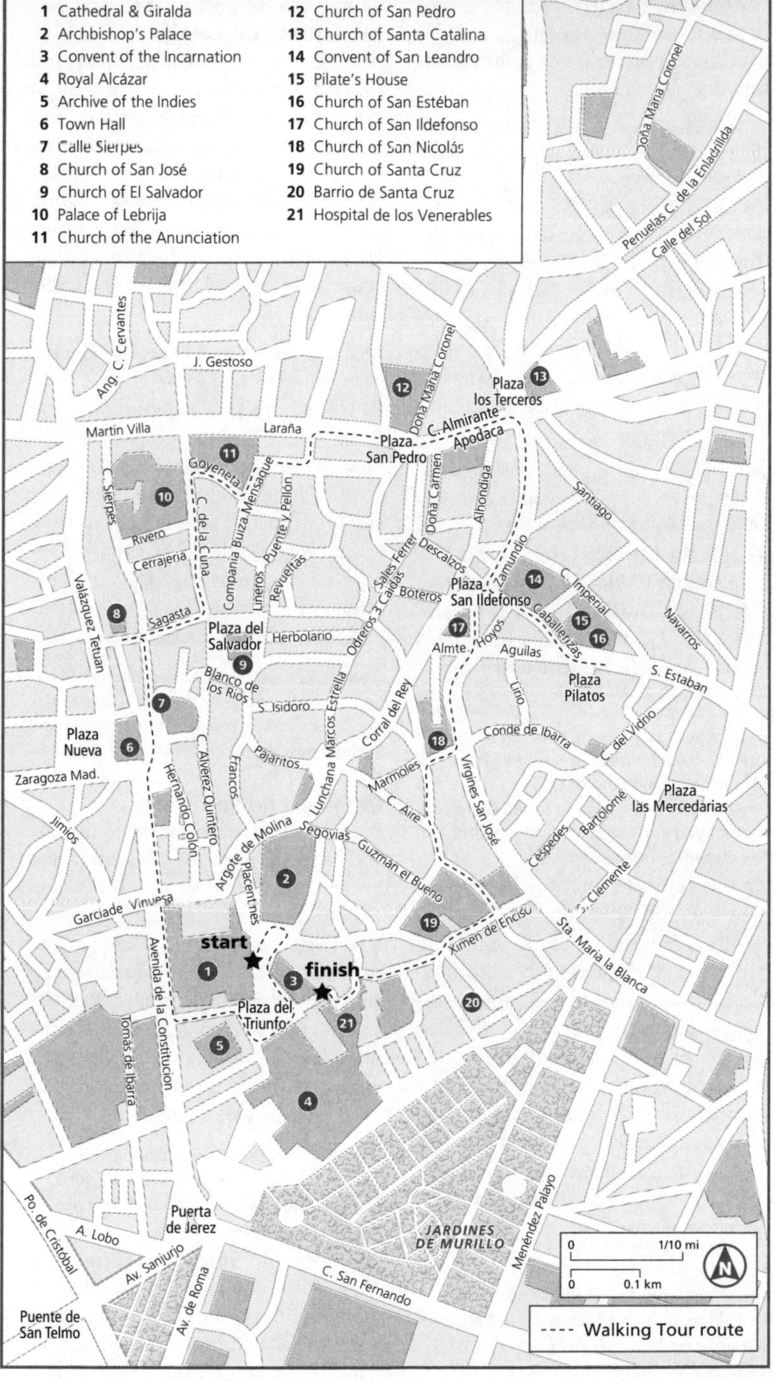

the building's eastern edge for a view of the medallions and allegorical figures that kept teams of stonemasons busy for generations.

The Town Hall's northeastern facade marks the beginning of Seville's most famous and desirable shopping street:

7 Calle Sierpes

This street stretches north from the Town Hall. Its southern terminus, where you're standing, was once the site of a since-demolished debtor's prison where Miguel de Cervantes languished for several years, laying out the plot and characters of his innovative masterpiece *Don Quixote.*

Walk along the western edge of this famous street, turning left (west) after 2 blocks onto Calle Jovellanos for a view of the:

8 Iglesia (Church) de San José

Named in honor of a famous carpenter (St. Joseph, husband of the Virgin), this lavish baroque chapel functioned as the seat of the carpenter's guild after its completion in 1747.

Retrace your steps along Calle Jovellanos to Calle Sierpes, traverse its busy traffic, and continue walking due east along Calle Sagasta. Within a block, Calle Sagasta will deposit you in Plaza del Salvador, in front of the elaborate facade of the:

9 Iglesia del Salvador (Savior)

One of the grandest churches of Seville, preferred by many visitors to the rather chilly pomposity of the previously visited cathedral, this enormous building was begun in 1674 on the site of one of the Muslim world's holiest sites, the mosque of Ibn Addabas. Beneath the Catholic iconography you can still make out the base of the Moorish minaret (converted long ago into a Christian belfry) and the Moorish layout of the building's courtyard.

After your visit, walk 3 blocks north along Calle Cuna (a wide boulevard that Sevillanos usually refer to simply as "Cuna") for an exterior view of one of the most-envied private homes in town, at Calle Cuna 18:

10 Palacio de Lebrija or Casa de la Condesa de Lebrija

Austere on the outside, lavish and Mudéjar on the inside, it was built in the 1400s and managed to incorporate a series of ancient mosaics, dug up from the excavations in the nearby town of Itálica, for incorporation into its floors. Although it's closed to casual visits, it's the most visible vestige of an aristocratic way of life that's rapidly fading.

From here, walk 2 short blocks east along Calle de Goyeneta for a view of the:

11 Iglesia de la Anunciación

Built in 1565 with profits from the New World, and associated for many centuries with both the Jesuits and the city's university, it contains a cold, rather macabre-looking crypt (Panteón de Sevillanos Ilustres) where the bodies of many of the city's governors and their families are buried.

From here, head east, passing through Plaza de la Anunciación onto Calle del Laraña Imagen for a short 2 blocks. Rising ahead of you from its position beside Plaza de San Pedro is the:

12 Iglesia de San Pedro

Built in the Mudéjar style in the 1300s, with some of its portals and towers added during the 1600s and 1700s, it's famous as the site where Spain's greatest painter, Velázquez, was baptized in 1599. Coffered ceilings rise above the building's main sanctuary and its eight shadowy chapels. The site is available for visits only during mass, during which visitors should remain as quiet and discreet as possible.

From Plaza de San Pedro, adjacent to the church's eastern entrance, walk east for 2 blocks along Calle del Almirante Apodaca until you reach the:

13 Iglesia de Santa Catalina

This 14th century Gothic-Mudéjar monument has endured many alterations and additions during its life span. Most significant of these is a simple Gothic portal that was moved into its present position in 1930 from another church. Make it a point to walk around this medieval hybrid for views of horseshoe (lobed) arches that attest to the strong influence of Moorish design on its past.

After your visit, walk south for a block along Calle Carrión, whose name will change after a block to Calle Francisco Mejiás. The massive and severe-looking building that rises in about a block is the:

⓮ Convento de San Leandro

Although the building you see today was begun around 1580, it replaced a much older 13th-century church that was the first to be constructed in Seville after the Christian reconquest in 1248. Severe and simple, with a single barrel vault covering its single aisle, it's open only during early morning (7am) mass and on some holy festival days.

Immediately to the southeast, opening off Plaza de Pilatos, is the grandest and most ornate palace that's open to view in Seville, the:

⓯ Casa de Pilatos (Pilate's House)

One of the city's most frequently visited museums, it was built in 1521 by the marquis de Tarifa after his trip to the Holy Land where, according to legend, he was inspired by the ruined house in Jerusalem from which Pontius Pilate is said to have governed. The main entrance, modeled after an ancient Roman triumphal arch, is fashioned from bronze, jasper, and Carrara marble, and the overall effect is one of imperial Roman grandeur.

After your visit, walk less than a block southeast for a view of the:

⓰ Iglesia de San Estéban

It's one of the finest examples of Mudéjar-Gothic architecture in Andalusia. Constructed during the late 1300s and early 1400s, it combines Moorish-style coffered ceilings with Gothic ribbed vaulting in ways beloved by students of the history of Spanish architecture.

From here, retrace your steps back to Plaza de Pilatos, then fork right onto Calle Caballerizas for a block until you reach Plaza de San Ildefonso. Flanking its edge rises the:

⓱ Iglesia de San Ildefonso

It's one of the most charming baroque churches in Seville, a colorful and graceful small-scale structure filled with artistic treasures partly paid for with profits from the New World. Regrettably, it's open only during the hours of mass, during which discreet visitors can admire the interior.

From here, walk west for 2 short blocks south along Calle Vírgenes until you reach the:

⓲ Iglesia de San Nicolás de Bari

Although the church was built in the 1700s, long after the departure of the Moors, the forest of red-marble columns that support the five aisles of its interior evoke some aspects of a mosque. The eclectic, and somewhat cluttered, aspect of its baroque interior is particularly charming.

From here, walk south for a block along Calle de Federico Rubio until you reach the soaring walls of a building usually described as the gateway to one of Seville's most colorful antique neighborhoods, the:

⓳ Iglesia de Santa Cruz (Holy Cross)

Originally built between 1665 and 1728, and conceived as the parish church of the Barrio Santa Cruz, which you'll visit shortly, it's prefaced with a relatively new facade that was added in 1929. This is a particularly active church, servicing the spiritual needs of a congested neighborhood, and is normally open only during the hours of mass.

At this point your tour will become less rigidly structured, and will allow you to wander through the narrow and labyrinthine alleyways of the:

⓴ Barrio Santa Cruz

Before 1492, when the Jews were driven from Spain by the repressive edicts of Ferdinand and Isabella, this was the Jewish ghetto of Seville. Today it's highly desirable real estate—thick-walled houses, window boxes studded with flowers, severe exteriors opening onto private patios that ooze Andalusian charm. Wander at will through the neighborhood, and don't be surprised if you quickly get lost in the maze of twisting streets. Know that your final destination lies uphill (to the southwest) at a point near the cathedral (discreet signs indicate its direction).

We recommend that you walk southwest along the relatively wide Calle Ximenes de Enriso, ducking into side alleyways at your whim for views of the streets that radiate out from there. At the barrio's southwestern edge, beside Plaza de los Venerables, you'll want to visit one of the barrio's greatest monuments, the:

21 Hospital de los Venerables (Hospice of the Venerable Ones)

It was founded in 1675 as a retirement home for aged priests, was completed 12 years later, and is maintained today as a museum.

TAKE A BREAK

One of the best places in this barrio to have a drink and take tapas is **Casa Román,** on Plaza de los Venerables (✆ **95-421-64-08**). This bygone-era bar has some of the finest tapas in the old quarter, and you can make your selection at a deli counter. It's also a good place to stop for a pick-me-up glass of regional wine.

From here, you're only a very short walk from the point near the cathedral where you initiated this walking tour several hot and dusty, but artistically rewarding, hours ago.

7 Organized Tours

CITY TOURS

One of the best ways to navigate your way around the labyrinth of a complicated, traffic-clogged city like Seville is to take a city tour that offers a historical and geographical overview. A local outfit that handles only the briefest of bus tours is **Transvías de Sevilla,** Plaza de Colón (✆ **95-450-20-99**). Tours of Seville depart every hour, on the hour, year-round, beginning at 10am, with the last departure scheduled for 6pm. The commentary is jaded and a bit blasé, and the overview is fairly superficial, but the cost of 11€ per person is reasonable. Know that during the hour-long tour, you'll never emerge from the bus. Reservations aren't necessary. Departures are from in front of the Transvías office, opposite the Bullring (Maestranza) on Plaza de Colón.

More appealing are the 4-hour city tours conducted twice-daily by **Visitour,** Av. de los Descubrimientos s/n, Isla de la Cartuja (✆ **95-446-36-29**). Morning and afternoon tours are conducted daily at 9, 9:30am, 3:45, 4, 4:30, 8, and 8:30pm, costing about 35€ each. Morning tours include a visit to the cathedral, two museums, and the Santa Cruz district, whereas the afternoon tour is a boat trip around the city and a visit to one museum. The morning tour is the more expensive of the two.

ANDALUSIAN EXCURSIONS

In addition to being loaded with monuments of consuming historic and cultural interest, Seville makes a worthy base for explorations of Andalusia. The best of the tours are offered by **Visitour,** Américo Vespucio 61, Isla de la Cartuja (✆ **95-446-09-85**). A company formed in 1995 from a corps of experienced travel professionals, they are well versed in the charm and lore of the region. Their buses, holding between 8 and 48 passengers, offer some of the best guided tours in Andalusia, always with the option of retrieving and redepositing clients at their hotels. Reservations a day in advance are strongly recommended. Two of the company's most popular tours depart daily. A tour of Granada leaves Seville at 7am, explores all that city's major monuments and neighborhoods, and returns to Seville around 7pm. The price is 87€. A tour of Córdoba departs from Seville at 8:30am and 9am, returning around 6pm and 6:30pm, costing 69€ per person.

Two other worthy tours depart 3 or 4 days a week, depending on the season. A visit to Jerez de la Frontera and Cádiz includes a visit to the riding school at Jerez, a tour of one of the city's most interesting wine bodegas, lunch in an Andalusian village (Puerto de Santa María), and a boat ride that begins on the Guadalete River and ends in Cádiz's Atlantic harbor. The tour, departing at 9am and 9:30am and returning at 6pm and 6:30pm, costs 75€ per person. If at all possible, try to schedule your participation for a Thursday (or, during June and July, for Thurs or Sat), as participants attend a riding exhibition in Jerez that's conducted only on those days. A visit to the historic hamlet of Ronda, conducted several times a week, departing at 9am and 9:30am, returning at 6pm and 6:30pm, costs 75€ per person.

8 Shopping

SHOPPING A TO Z

ART GALLERIES

Rafael Ortíz This is one of the most respected art galleries in Seville, specializing in contemporary paintings, usually from Iberian artists. Exhibitions change frequently, and because of canniness of this emporium's judgments, inventories sell out quickly. It's open Monday to Saturday from 10am to 1:30pm and 4:30 to 8pm. Marmolles 12. ✆ **95-421-48-74.**

BOOKS

The English Bookshop Smaller than many of the other book emporiums in Seville, this is the kind of place where you can find tomes on gardening, political discourse, philosophy, and pop fiction, all gathered into one cozy place. Open Monday to Saturday from 10am to 1:45pm and 5 to 8:30pm, Saturday from 10am to 1:30pm. Eduardo Dato 36. ✆ **95-465-57-54.**

Librería Vértice Set conveniently close to Seville's university, this store stocks books in a polyglot of languages. Inventory ranges from the esoteric and professorial to Spanish romances of the soap-opera genre. Open Monday to Saturday from 10am to 1:30pm and 4:30 to 8:30pm. San Fernando 33. ✆ **95-421-16-54.**

CERAMICS

El Postigo Set in the town center near the cathedral, this shop contains one of the biggest selections in town of Andalusian ceramics. Some of the pieces are much, much too big to fit into your suitcase; others, especially the hand-painted tiles, make charming souvenirs that can easily be transported. Open Monday to Saturday from 10am to 2pm, Monday to Friday from 5 to 8:30pm. Arfe s/n. ✆ **95-456-00-13.**

Martian Set close to Seville's Town Hall, this outfit sells a wide array of painted tiles and ceramics, the kind that invariably look better when transported away from the store and displayed within your home. The inventory includes vases, plates, cups, serving dishes, and statues, all made in or near Seville. Many of the pieces exhibit ancient geometric patterns of Andalusia. Other floral motifs are rooted in Spanish traditions of the 18th century. Open Monday to Saturday from 10am to 2pm and 5 to 8:30pm. Calle Sierpes 74. ✆ **95-421-34-13.**

DEPARTMENT STORES

El Corte Inglés This is the best of the several department stores clustered in Seville's commercial center. A well-accessorized branch of a nationwide chain, it features multilingual translators and rack after rack of every conceivable kind of merchandise for the well-stocked home, kitchen, and closet. If you're in the market for the brightly colored *feria* costumes worn by young girls during Seville's holidays, there's an impressive selection of the folkloric accessories that make Andalusia memorable. Open Monday to Saturday from 10am to 9pm. Plaza Duque 10. ✆ **95-422-09-31.**

FASHION

Iconos This is an excellent example of a small, idiosyncratic boutique loaded with fashion accessories that can be used by everyone from teenage girls to mature women. Silk scarves, costume jewelry, and an assortment of T-shirts with logos lettered in varying degrees of tastelessness—it's all here. Much of the merchandise represents the new, youthful perceptions of post-*movida* Spain. Open Monday to Saturday from 10am to 9pm, Sunday from noon to 5pm. Avenida de la Constitución. ✆ **95-422-14-08.**

Lina If you want to look like Carmen at the Sevilla Fair, head for Lina which celebrates "fiesta de color," with the widest assortment of flamenco dresses (those with the polka dots and ruffled skirts), and a wide variety of dangling earrings, *mantoncillos* (flamenco scarves), and elegant shawls. Open Monday to Friday from 10am to 1:30pm and 5 to 8:30pm, Saturday from 10:30am to 2pm. Calle Lineros 17. ✆ **95-421-24-23.**

Perdales One of the most prestigious purveyors of flamenco dresses and feria costumes in Seville, this shop outfits many professional performers. Much of its merchandise is akin to couture; other items are less expensive and sold off the rack. Open Monday to Saturday from 10am to 2pm, Monday to Friday from 5 to 8pm. Cuna 23. ✆ **95-421-37-09.**

Victorio & Lucchino This outfit has gained a reputation as a purveyor of stylish clothing, often based on Italian models, to well-heeled women of Andalusia. If you've already exhausted the inventories of the boutiques within El Corte Inglés and not found the alluring garment you're looking for, this place will probably have it. Open Monday to Saturday from 10am to 2pm, Monday to Friday from 5 to 8pm. Sierpes 87. ✆ **95-422-79-51.**

GIFTS

Artesanía Textil This shop specializes in the nubby and rough textiles that reflect the earthiness of contemporary Spanish art. Weavings—some using linen, others the rough fibers of Spanish sheep—are the specialty here. Examples include place mats, tablecloths, blankets, shawls, and wall hangings. Open Monday to Saturday from 10am to 2pm, Monday to Friday from 5 to 8pm. Sierpes 70. ✆ **95-456-28-40.**

Matador Souvenirs of the city, T-shirts, hammered wrought-iron whatnots, and ceramics—this store carries these and about a dozen other types of unpretentious gift items you might want to display in your private space back home. Open Monday to Saturday from 10am to 2pm, Monday to Friday from 5 to 8:30pm. Av. de la Constitución 28. ✆ **95-422-62-47.**

Snobismo This shop manages to artfully crowd a wide array of merchandise into its precincts, everything from *sombreros* to *zapatos* (shoes). Tasteful scarves are sold as is a good selection of leather bags and travel luggage. Top brand-name designers range from Armani to Alcocer. There is also a collection of splendid handcrafted jewelry from such places as Florence or Israel. Hours are Monday to Friday from 10am to 1:30pm and 5 to 8:30pm, Saturday from 10:30am to 2pm. Calle Jovellanos 11. ✆ **95-421-82-06.**

Venecia The venue here is upscale, and the inventory includes lots of items you can certainly do without—but might not want to. Crystal, art objects, and fanciful accoutrements to the good life as envisioned by bourgeois Spain can all be found here. Open Monday to Saturday from 10am to 2pm, Monday to Friday from 5 to 8:30pm. Cuna 51. ✆ **95-422-99-94.**

HEAD GEAR

El Sombrero de 3 Picos The best hat shop (for those who still wear head gear) is opposite the Tower of Gold next to the banks of the Guadalquivir River. Smart Andalusian styling doesn't get any better here in its collection of the traditional wide-brimmed hat (worn by both men and women) as well as hunting caps and wedding headdresses. Open Monday to Friday from 10am to 1:30pm and 5 to 8:30pm, Saturday from 10:30am to 1:30pm. Plaza de Cuba 8. ✆ **95-428-34-58.**

JEWELRY

Agatha This is the leading outlet for dramatic costume jewelry in Andalusia. From Seville, Agatha has branched out with outlets from Tokyo to Paris. The firm presents two major collections a year. Its owners claim that their costume jewelry "flaunts itself as such." Open Monday to Friday from 10am to 2:30pm and 5 to 8:30pm, Saturday from 10:30am to 2:30pm. Calle Tetuán 27. ✆ **95-456-39-45.**

Joyero Abrines This is the kind of place where grooms have bought engagement and wedding rings for their brides for generations, and where generations of girlfriends have selected watches and cigarette lighters for the *hombre* of their dreams. There's another branch of this well-known store at Calle de la Asunción 28 (✆ **95-427-42-44**). Both are open Monday to Saturday from 10am to 1:30pm, Monday to Friday from 5 to 8:30pm. Sierpes 47. ✆ **95-427-84-55.**

Tous This outlet celebrates "jewelry full of life" (in the owner's words), and displays some of the most innovative gems in Andalusia. Many of the designs are the creation of some of southern Spain's best artisans. Although there may be slight seasonal variations, regular hours are Monday to Friday from 10am to 2pm and 5 to 8:30pm, Saturday from 10am to 8pm. Calle Sierpes 8. ✆ **95-456-35-63.**

TOBACCO

La Cava de Betis One of the best outlets for the smoker in Andalusia is this well-stocked "fumador," with its collection of handmade cigars. The coveted Cuban cigar that Castro smokes is to be consumed while abroad by Americans, as they're not allowed to be brought back to the United States. However, cigars from the Canary Islands and the Dominican Republic are also sold here. The shop lies in the heart of Triana on the shores of the Guadalquivir River. Open July and August Monday to Friday from 10am to 2pm, Thursday also from 5 to 9pm. From September to May, hours are Monday to Friday from 10am to 2pm and 5 to 9pm, Saturday from 10am to 2pm. La Calle Betis 36. ✆ **95-427-81-85.**

9 Seville After Dark

Everyone from Lord Byron to Jacqueline Onassis has appreciated the unique blend of heat, rhythm, and sensuality that interconnect into nightlife in Seville. If you're looking for a theme to define your nightlife wanderings, three of the most obvious possibilities might involve a bacchanalian pursuit of sherry, wine, and well-seasoned tapas. After several drinks, you might venture to a club whose focus revolves around an appreciation of flamenco as a voyeuristic insight into another era and the melding of the Arab and Christian aesthetic. And when you've finished with that, and if you're not wilted from the heat and the crowds, there's always the possibility of learning the intricate steps of one of southern Spain's most addictive dances, La Sevillana.

To keep abreast of what's happening in the arts and after dark in Seville, pick up a copy of the free monthly leaflet *El Giraldillo,* or consult listings in the local press, *Correo de Andalucía, Sudoeste, Nueva Andalucía,* or *ABC Sevilla.* Everything is listed here from jazz venues to classical music concerts and from art exhibits to dance events. You can also call the cultural hot line at © **010** to find out what's happening. Most of the staff at the other end speak English.

Keep an eye out for classical concerts that are sometimes presented in the cathedral of Seville, the church of San Salvador, and the Conservatorio Superior de Música at Jesús del Gran Poder. Variety productions, including some plays for the kids, are presented at **Teatro Alameda,** Crédito (© **95-438-83-12**). The venerable **Teatro Lope de Vega,** Avenida María Luisa (© **95-459-08-53**), is the setting for ballet performances and classical concerts, among other events. Near Parque María Luisa, this is the leading stage of Seville, but knowledge of Spanish is necessary.

OPERA

Teatro de la Maestranza It wasn't until the 1990s that Seville got its own opera house, but it quickly became one of the world's premier venues for operatic performances. Naturally, the focus is on works inspired by Seville itself, including Verdi's *La Forza del Destino* or Mozart's *Marriage of Figaro.* Jazz, classical music, and even the quintessentially Spanish *zarzuelas* (operettas) are also performed here. The opera house can't be visited except during performances. Tickets (which vary in price, depending on the event staged) can be purchased daily from 10am to 2pm and 5 to 8pm at the box office in front of the theater. Paseo de Colón 22. © **95-422-65-73.**

FLAMENCO

When the moon is high in Seville and the scent of orange blossoms is in the air, it's time to wander the alleyways of Santa Cruz in search of the sound of castanets. Or take a taxi, to be on the safe side.

El Arenal The singers clap, the guitars strum, the tension builds, and the room here feels the ancient and mysterious magic of the flamenco. It's performed at two shows nightly, every evening at 9:30 and 11:30pm. No food is served, but drinks are brought to the minuscule tables in a sweltering back room that's endlessly evocative of Old Andalusia. Calle Rodo 7. © **95-421-64-92.** Cover 27€, including first drink.

El Patio Sevillano In central Seville on the riverbank between two historic bridges, El Patio Sevillano is a showcase for Spanish folk song and dance, performed by exotically costumed dancers. The presentation includes a wide variety of Andalusian flamenco and songs, as well as classical pieces by such composers as de Falla, Albéniz, Granados, and Chueca. From March to October, there are three shows nightly, at 7:30, 10, and 11:45pm. From November to February, there are two shows nightly, at 7:30 and 10pm. Paseo de Cristóbal Colón 11. ✆ **95-421-41-20.** Cover 27€, including first drink.

Los Gallos Negotiating through the labyrinth of narrow streets of the Barrio Santa Cruz seems to contribute to the authenticity of reaching this intimate and high-energy flamenco club, devoted to the preservation of the venerable art form. No food is served during the shows, which begin every night at 9 and 11:30pm. Plaza de Santa Cruz 11. ✆ **95-421-69-81.** Cover 27€, including first drink.

DANCE CLUBS

Disco Antigüedades If you're interested in a more universal kind of dance step (disco fever), this is Seville's most popular dance emporium. Set about 2 blocks north of the cathedral, within an antique, much-renovated building, it opens nightly at 11pm; its closing hour varies, depending on business. Expect lots of salsa and merengue in addition to more international tunes that derive from such cities as Los Angeles, London, and Madrid. Calle Argote de Molina. No phone. Cover 5€, including first drink.

DRINKS & TAPAS

Casa Román Tapas are said to have originated in Andalusia, and this old-fashioned bar, incongruously named Román, looks as if it has been dishing them up since day one (actually since 1934). Definitely include this place on your *tasca*-hopping through the old quarter of the Barrio Santa Cruz. At the deli counter in front you can make your selection; you might even pick up the fixings for a picnic in the Parque María Luisa. Open Monday to Friday from 9am to 3pm and 5:30pm to 12:30am, Saturday and Sunday from 10am to 3pm and 6:30pm to 12:30am. Tapas are priced from 3.50€. Plaza des los Venerables. ✆ **95-421-64-08.**

El Rinconcillo El Rinconcillo has a 1930s ambience, partly because of its real age and partly because of its owners' refusal to change one iota of the decor—this has always been one of the most famous bars in Seville. Actually, it may be the oldest bar in Seville, with a history that dates from 1670. Amid dim lighting, heavy ceiling beams, and iron-based, marble-topped tables, you can enjoy a beer or a full meal along with the rest of the easygoing clientele. The bartender will mark your tab in chalk on a well-worn wooden countertop. El Rinconcillo is especially known for its salads, omelets, hams, and selection of cheeses. Look for the art-nouveau tile murals. El Rinconcillo is at the northern edge of the Barrio Santa Cruz, near the Santa Catalina Church. It's open Thursday to Tuesday

---

Moments Dancing the *Sevillanas*

Flamenco is danced in solitary grandeur, but everyone joins in with the communal but complicated dance steps of the *sevillanas*. The best place to check it out is **El Simpecao,** Calle Bertis s/n (no phone). Beginning at 11pm every night of the year, recorded music presents four distinctly different facets of the complicated and old-fashioned dance steps in which dozens of everyday folk strut their Andalusian style in a way you'll rarely see outside of Spain. The setting is modern and just a wee bit battered. Entrance is free; bottled beer costs from around 2 each.

---

from 1pm to 2am. A complete meal will cost around 20€. Gerona, 40. ✆ **95-422-31-83.**

La Alicantina What is reported to be the best seafood tapas in town are served against a typically Sevillian, glazed-tile decor. Both the bar and the sidewalk tables are always filled to overflowing. The owner serves generous portions of clams marinara, fried squid, grilled shrimp, fried cod, and clams in béchamel sauce. Located about 5 blocks north of the cathedral, La Alicantina is open daily from 11:30am to 3:30pm and 7:30 to 11:30pm. Tapas range upward from 1.80€. Plaza de El Salvador 2. ✆ **95-422-61-22.**

Modesto At the northern end of Murillo Gardens, opening onto a quiet square with flower boxes and an ornate iron railing, Modesto serves fabulous seafood tapas. The bar is air-conditioned, and you can choose your appetizers just by pointing. Upstairs there's a good-value restaurant, offering a meal for 20€, including such dishes as fried squid, baby sole, grilled sea bass, and shrimp in garlic sauce. Modesto is open daily from 8pm to 2am. Tapas are priced from 3€. Cano y Cueto 5. ✆ **95-441-68-11.**

A SPECIAL BAR

Abades A converted mansion in the Barrio Santa Cruz has been turned into a rendezvous that's been compared to "a living room in a luxurious movie set." One member of the Spanish press labeled it "wonderfully decadent, similar to the ambience created in a Visconti film." In the heart of the Jewish ghetto, it evokes the style of the Spanish Romantic era. The house dates from the 19th century, when it was constructed around a central courtyard with a fountain. It became notorious as a love den in Franco's era. Drinks and low-key conversations are the style here, and since its opening in 1980 all the visiting literati and glitterati have put in an appearance. Young men and women in jeans also patronize the place, enjoying the comfort of the sofas and wicker armchairs.

The ingredients of a special drink called *aqua de Sevilla* are a secret, but we suspect sparkling white-wine, pineapple juice, and eggs (the whites and yolks mixed in separately, of course). Classical music is played in the background. Take a taxi to get here at night, as it might not be safe to wander late along the narrow streets of the barrio. In summer, it's open daily from 4pm to 4am; in winter, daily from 4pm to 2:30am. Abades 1. ✆ **95-422-56-22.**

ON THE GAY SIDE

Seville has a large gay and lesbian population, much of it composed of foreigners and of Andalusians who fled here for a better life, escaping smaller, less tolerant towns and villages. Gay life thrives in such bars as **Isbiliyya Café-Bar,** Paseo de Colón (✆ **95-421-04-60**), which is usually open daily from 4pm to 4am. The bar is found across the street from the Puente Isabel II bridge. Outdoor tables are a magnet in summer.

10 Side Trips from Seville

CARMONA ★

34km (21 miles) E of Seville

An easy hour-long bus trip from the main terminal in Seville, Carmona is an ancient city dating from Neolithic times. It grew in power and prestige under the Moors, establishing ties with Castile in 1252.

Surrounded by fortified walls, Carmona has three Moorish fortresses—one a parador, the other two the **Alcázar de la Puerta de Córdoba** and **Alcázar de la**

Seville Environs

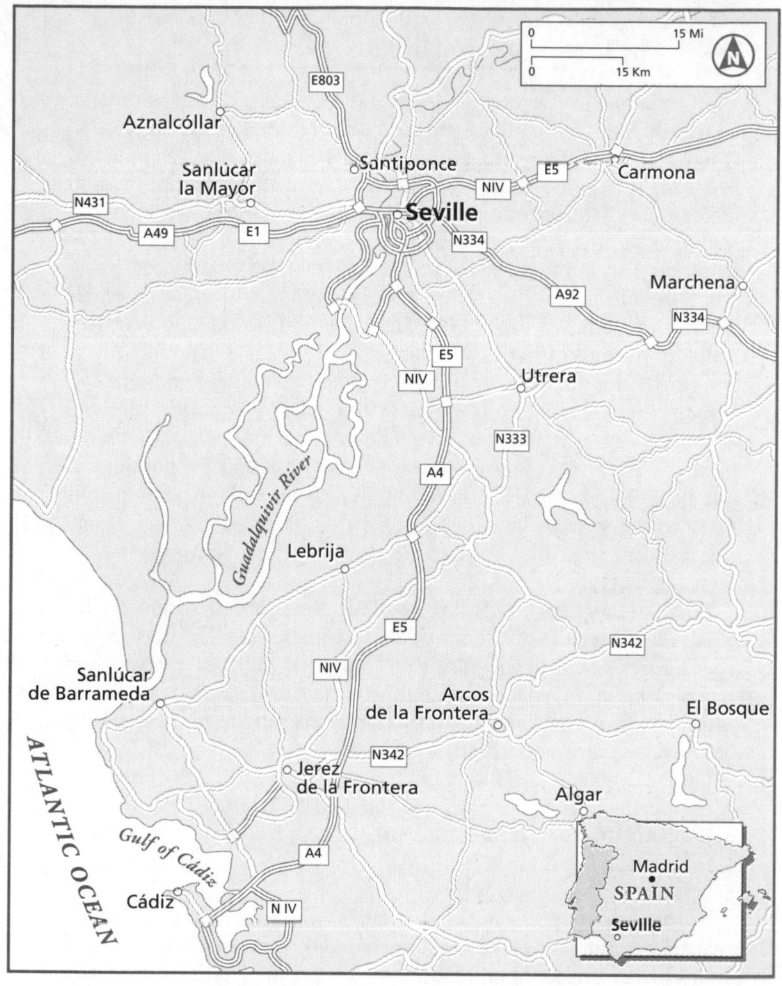

Puerta de Sevilla. The top attraction is **Seville Gate,** with its double Moorish arch, opposite St. Peter's Church. Note too, **Córdoba Gate** on Calle Santa María de Gracia, which was attached to the ancient Roman walls in the 17th century.

The town itself is a virtual national landmark, filled with narrow streets, whitewashed walls, and Renaissance mansions. **Plaza San Fernando** is the most important square, with many elegant 17th-century houses. The most important church is dedicated to **Santa María** and stands on the Calle Martín López. You enter a Moorish patio before exploring the interior with its 15th-century white vaulting.

At Jorge Bonsor there's a **Roman amphitheater** as well as a **Roman necropolis** containing the remains of 1,000 families that lived in and around Carmona 2,000 years ago. Of the two important tombs, the Elephant Vault consists of three dining rooms and a kitchen. The other, the Servilia Tomb, was the size of a nobleman's villa. On site is a **Museo Arqueológico** (© **95-423-24-01**),

The Legacy of al-Andalús

The Moors who once occupied Andalusia—notably Seville, Granada, and Córdoba—left more than such architectural treasures as the Giralda Tower in Seville, the great mosque in Córdoba, and the Alhambra in Granada. Their intellectual and cultural legacies still influence modern life, not only in Spain, but also in the rest of the Western world.

The celebrated Arab princesses and sultans with their harems are long gone, encountered today only in the tales of Washington Irving and others. Yet from A.D. 711, the Moors (Muslims who were an ethnic mixture of Berbers, Hispano-Romans, and Arabs) occupied southern Spain for nearly 8 centuries and turned it into a seat of learning. It was a time of soaring achievements in philosophy, medicine, and music.

Moorish rule brought the importation of the eggplant and the almond, as well as the Arabian steed—not to mention such breakthroughs in academia as astronomy (including charting the positions of the planets) and a new and different view of Aristotle. Arab numerals replaced the more awkward Roman system, and from the Arabs came the gift of algebra. Ibn Muadh of Jaén wrote the first European treatise on trigonometry.

Such intellectual giants emerged as the Córdoba-born Jewish philosopher Maimónides. It is said that Columbus evolved his theories about a new route to the East after hours and hours of studying the charts of Idrisi, an Arabian geographer who drew up a world map as early as 1154. Arabs relied upon the compass as a navigational aid long before its use among Portuguese explorers.

Córdoba desired to shine brighter than Baghdad as a center of science and the arts. In time it attracted Abd ar-Rahman II, who introduced the fifth string to the Arab lute, leading to the development of

displaying artifacts found at the site. From April to October, hours are Tuesday to Saturday from 9am to 5pm; off-season, Tuesday to Saturday from 10am to 2pm. Admission is 1.50€.

If you're driving to Carmona, exit from Seville's eastern periphery onto the N-V superhighway, following the signs to the airport, then to Carmona on the road to Madrid. The Carmona turnoff is clearly marked.

WHERE TO STAY & DINE

Casa de Carmona ★★ One of the most elegant and intimate hotels in Andalusia, this plushly furnished hideaway was originally built as the home of the Lasso family during the 1500s. Several years ago, a team of entrepreneurs added the many features required for a luxury hotel, all the while retaining the marble columns, massive masonry, and graceful proportions of the building's original construction. The most visible public room still maintains vestiges of its original function as a library. Each bedroom is a cozy enclave of opulent furnishings, with distinct decor inspired by ancient Rome, medieval Andalusia, or Renaissance Spain. All units have bathrooms with shower-tub combinations.

On the premises is an outdoor restaurant whose culinary inspiration derives from modern interpretations of Andalusian and international cuisine. Set at the

the six-string guitar. He also ordained the way food should be eaten at mealtimes, a legacy that lives to this day. Before, everybody just helped him- or herself randomly to whatever had been prepared; but he devised a method where courses were served in a regimented order, ending with dessert, fruit, and nuts. Today, Andalusian chefs are reviving many of the old recipes from the Arab cupboard, such as lamb cooked with honey.

Of course, on the entertainment scene, the art form of flamenco can claim significant Middle Eastern influences as well. In his book *In Search of the Firedance,* James Woodall writes, "The music, the literature, the folklore, even religion, but above all the people themselves, speak of it [the epoch of al-Andalús]. It is a matter of attitude, or mentality, and it will be encountered again and again in flamenco."

Arab poetry may have inspired the first ballads sung by European troubadours, which had an enormous impact on later Western literature. Also, many Spanish words today have their origins in the Arabic language, including *alcázar* for fortress, *arroz* for rice, *naranja* for orange, and *limón* for lemon.

The Moors brought an irrigation system to Andalusia, which increased crop production; many of today's systems follow those 1,000-year-old channels. And paper first arrived in Europe through Córdoba.

Although the fanatical Isabella la Católica may have thrown a fit at the heretical idea, it was really a trio of peoples that shaped modern Spain as a nation: the Jews, the Christians, and most definitely the Arabs. The Arabs and the Jews may have been ousted by Isabella and Ferdinand at the close of the 15th century, but their influence still lingers.

edge of the village, the hotel also has a flowery terrace and an inner courtyard covered against the midsummer heat with canvas awning.

Plaza de Lasso 1, 41410 Carmona (Sevilla). ✆ **95-419-10-00,** or 212/686-9213 for reservations within North America. Fax 95-419-01-89. www.casadecarmona.com. 32 units. 190€–300€ double; from 750€ suite. Add about 30% for Feria de Sevilla and Easter (Semana Santa). AE, DC, MC, V. Free parking. **Amenities:** Restaurant; bar; room service; pool; babysitting; laundry/dry cleaning. *In room:* A/C, TV, minibar, hair dryer, safe.

ITALICA

9km (5½ miles) NW of Seville

Lovers of Roman history will flock to Itálica (✆ **95-599-73-76**), the ruins of an ancient city northwest of Seville on the major road to Lisbon, near the small town of Santiponce.

After the battle of Ilipa, Publius Cornelius Scipio Africanus founded Itálica in 206 B.C. Two of the most famous of Roman emperors, Trajan and Hadrian, were born here. Indeed, master builder Hadrian was to have a major influence on his hometown. During his reign, the **amphitheater,** the ruins of which can be seen today, was among the largest in the Roman Empire. Lead pipes that carried water from the Guadalquivir River still remain. A small **museum** displays some of the Roman statuary found here, although the finest pieces have been shipped to Seville. Many mosaics, depicting beasts, gods, and birds, are on exhibit, and others are constantly being discovered. The ruins, including a Roman theater, can be explored for 1.50€. The site is open April through September, Tuesday to Saturday from 9am to 8:30pm and Sunday from 9am to 3pm. From October through March, it's open Tuesday to Saturday from 9am to 5:30pm and Sunday from 10am to 4pm.

If you're driving, exit from the northwest periphery of Seville, following the signs for highway E-803 in the direction of Zafra and Lisbon. If you don't have a car, take the bus marked "Calle de Santiponce" leaving from Calle Marqués de Parada near the railway station in Seville. Buses depart every hour for the 30-minute trip.

JEREZ DE LA FRONTERA ★

87km (54 miles) S of Seville

The charming little Andalusian town of Jerez made a name for itself in England for the thousands of casks of golden sherry it shipped there over the centuries. More than 3,000 years old, Jerez is nonetheless a modern, progressive town with wide boulevards, although it does have an interesting old quarter. Busloads of visitors pour in every year to get free drinks at one of the bodegas where wine is aged and bottled.

The name of the town is pronounced "Her-*ez*" or Her-*eth*," in Andalusian or Castilian, respectively. The French and the Moors called it various names, including Heres and Scheris, which the English corrupted to Sherry.

ESSENTIALS

GETTING THERE **By Plane** Iberia and Avianco offer flights to Jerez every Monday to Friday from Barcelona and Zaragoza; daily flights from Madrid; and several flights a week to and from Valencia, Tenerife, Palma de Majorca, and Grand Canary Island. No international flights land at Jerez. The airport at Carretera Jerez-Sevilla lies about 11km (7 miles) northeast of the city center (follow the signs to Seville). Call ✆ **95-615-00-00** for information.

By Train Trains from Madrid arrive daily. The trip from Madrid to Jerez on the TALGO costs 58€ to 86€ and lasts 4½ hours. The railway station in Jerez is at Plaza de la Estación (✆ **90-224-02-02**), at the eastern end of Calle Medina.

Moments **The Dancing Horses of Jerez**

A rival of sorts to Vienna's famous Spanish Riding School is the **Escuela Andaluza del Arte Ecuestre (Andalusian School of Equestrian Art),** Av. Duque de Abrantes 11 (✆ **95-631-96-35**). In fact, the long, hard schooling that brings horse and rider into perfect harmony originated in this province. The Viennese school was started with Hispano-Arab horses sent from this region, the same breeds you can see today. Every Thursday at noon, crowds come to admire the **Dancing Horses of Jerez** ★★ as they perform in a show that includes local folklore. Numbered seats sell for 18 , with unnumbered seats going for 12 . When performances aren't scheduled, you can visit the stables and tack room, observing as the elegant horses are being trained. Hours are Monday to Wednesday and Friday from 11am to 1pm; admission is 2.70 . Bus 18 goes here.

By Bus Bus connections are more frequent than train connections, and the location of the bus terminal is also more convenient. You'll find it on Calle Cartuja, at the corner of the Calle Madre de Dios, a 12-minute walk east of the Alcázar. About 17 buses arrive daily from Cádiz (1 hr. away) and 3 per day travel from Ronda (2¾ hr.). Seven buses a day arrive from Seville (1½ hr.). Phone ✆ **95-634-52-07** for more information.

By Car Jerez lies on the highway connecting Seville with Cádiz, Algeciras, Gibraltar, and the ferryboat landing for Tangier, Morocco. There's also an overland road connecting Jerez with Granada and Málaga.

VISITOR INFORMATION The **tourist information office** is at Alameda de Cristina s/n (✆ **95-633-11-50**). To reach it from the bus terminals, take Calle Medina to Calle Honda and continue along as the road turns to the right. The English-speaking staff can provide directions, transportation suggestions, open hours, and so on, for any bodega you might want to visit. You will also be given a map pinpointing the location of various bodegas. Open Monday to Friday from 9:30am to 2:30pm and 4:30 to 6:30pm, Saturday and Sunday from 9:30am to 3:30pm.

EXPLORING THE AREA

TOURING THE BODEGAS ★★ Jerez is not surrounded by vineyards, as you might expect. The vineyards lie to the north and west of Jerez, within the "Sherry Triangle" marked by Jerez, Sanlúcar de Barrameda, and El Puerto de Santa María (the latter two towns on the coast). This is where top-quality *albariza* soil is to be found, the highest quality containing an average of 60% chalk—ideal for the cultivation of grapes used in sherry production, principally the white *Palomino de Jerez.* The ideal time to visit is September. However, visitors can count on the finest in hospitality year-round, since Jerez is widely known for the warm welcome it bestows.

There must be more than a hundred bodegas in and around Jerez where you not only can see how sherries are made, bottled, and aged, but also can get free samples. Among the most famous producers are Sandeman, Pedro Domecq, and González Byass, the maker of Tío Pepe.

On a typical visit to a bodega, you'll be shown through several buildings in which sherry and brandy are manufactured. In one building, you'll see grapes being pressed and sorted; in another, the bottling process; in a third, thousands of large oak casks. Then it's on to an attractive bar where various sherries—amber, dark gold, cream, red, sweet, and velvety—can be sampled. If either is offered, try the very dry La Ina sherry or the Fundador brandy, one of the most popular in the world.

Warning: These drinks are more potent than you might expect.

Most bodegas are open Monday to Friday only, from 10:30am to 1:30pm. Regrettably, many of them are closed in August, but many do reopen by the third week of August to prepare for the wine festival in early September.

Of the dozens of bodegas you can visit, the most popular are listed below. Some of them charge an admission fee and require a reservation.

A favorite among British visitors is **Harveys of Bristol,** Calle Arcos 57 (✆ **95-634-60-04**), which doesn't require a reservation. An English-speaking guide leads a 2-hour tour year-round, except during the first 3 weeks of August. Visit Monday to Friday for tours at noon, costing 2.70€.

You'll definitely want to visit **Williams & Humbert Limited,** which offers tours at noon and 1:30pm Monday to Friday, charging 4€. Their premium

Tips Plan B: A Visit to Lebrija

Since many people go to Jerez specifically to visit a bodega, August or weekend closings can be very disappointing. If this happens to you, head to the nearby village of Lebrija, about halfway between Jerez and Seville, 14km (8½ miles) west of the main highway. This local winemaking center, where some very fine sherries originate, offers a good glimpse of rural Spain. At one small bodega, that of Juan García, you're courteously escorted around by the owner. Local citizens will gladly point out the several other area bodegas as well. It's all very casual, lacking the rigidity and formality attached to the bodegas of Jerez.

brands include the world-famous Dry Sack Medium Sherry, Canasta Cream, Fino Pando, and Manzanilla Alegría, in addition to Gran Duque de Alba Gran Reserva Brandy. It is wise to reserve in advance.

Another famous name is **González Byass,** Manuel María González 12 (✆ **95-635-70-16**); admission is 7€, and reservations are required. Tours depart at 10am, 11am, noon, and 1pm Monday to Friday. Equally famous is **Domecq,** Calle San Ildefonso 3 (✆ **95-615-15-00**), requiring a reservation but charging no admission. Reservations are required, and admission is 4€. Tours depart at 10am, 1am, and noon Monday to Friday.

WHERE TO STAY

Expensive

Hotel Avenida Jerez ★ Close to the commercial heart of Jerez, this hotel occupies a modern balconied structure of seven stories and is the best hotel within Jerez itself, although Montecastillo (see below) on the outskirts is a serious challenger. Inside, cool floors of polished stone, leather armchairs, and a variety of potted plants create a restful haven. The good-size rooms are discreetly contemporary and decorated in neutral colors, with big windows, comfortable beds, and private bathrooms equipped with shower-tub combinations.

Av. Alcalde Alvaro Domecq 10, 11405 Jerez de la Frontera. ✆ **95-634-74-11.** Fax 95-633-72-96. www.nh-hoteles.es. 95 units. 96€–191€. AE, DC, MC, V. Parking 9€. **Amenities:** Restaurant; bar; room service; babysitting; laundry/dry cleaning. *In room:* A/C, TV, minibar, hair dryer.

Hotel Royal Sherry Park ★★ Especially noted for its setting in a palm-fringed garden and for its large pool, this is one of the best modern hotels in Jerez. Located on a wide and verdant boulevard north of the historic center of town, it contains a marble-floored lobby, efficiently modern public rooms, and fairly standard but comfortable bedrooms, each with a private tiled bathroom containing a shower-tub combination. The uniformed staff lays out a copious breakfast buffet and serves drinks at several hideaways, both indoors and in the garden.

Av. Alcalde Alvaro Domecq 11 Bis, 11405 Jerez de la Frontera. ✆ **95-631-76-14.** Fax 95-631-13-00. www.sherryparkhotel.com. 172 units. 114€ double; 206€–300€ suite. AE, DC, MC, V. Free parking. **Amenities:** Restaurant; bar; room service; 2 pools; health club; babysitting; laundry/dry cleaning. *In room:* A/C, TV, minibar, hair dryer, safe.

Montecastillo ★★ Giving Hotel Avenida Jerez serious competition is this deluxe country club in the rolling hills of the sherry wine country. The most tranquil retreat in the area, it has rooms with scenic-view balconies overlooking a Jack Nicklaus–designed 18-hole golf course. Just a 10-minute ride from the center of Jerez, the hotel is elegantly furnished and professionally run. The spacious guest rooms are decorated in a provincial French style with elegant fabrics, beautiful linens, and large beds. The marble baths boast plush towels, toiletries, and shower-tub combinations.

Carretera N-342, 11406 Jerez de la Frontera. ✆ **95-615-12-00.** Fax 95-615-12-09. 121 units. 146€–275€ double; 275€–551€ suite. AE, DC, MC, V. Free parking. **Amenities:** Restaurant; bar; room service; 2 pools; 18-hole golf course; health spa; sauna; babysitting; laundry/dry cleaning. *In room:* A/C, TV, minibar, hair dryer.

Moderate

La Cueva Park This charming hotel in a century-old building lies 4 miles from the center of town, attracting motorists, though it's also half a mile from the bus station. The architecture is typical of Andalusia, with a tiled roof overhanging thick brick walls. Gardens surround the hotel. All the medium-size units have a classical decor and are comfortably furnished. There are also nine white-walled bungalow-style apartments, classified as suites, each with its own cooking area, living room, and terrace. All units have well-kept bathrooms with shower-tub combinations. The hotel restaurant, Mesón la Cueva, serves high-quality Andalusian and international dishes.

Carretera de Arcos Km 6.5, Apartado 536, 11406 Jerez de la Frontera. ✆ **95-618-91-20.** Fax 95-618-91-21. www.hotellacueva.com. 58 units. 93€–120€ double; 168€–210€ suite. AE, DC, MC, V. Parking 6€. **Amenities:** Restaurant; bar; room service; babysitting; laundry/dry cleaning. *In room:* A/C, TV, minibar, hair dryer, safe.

Inexpensive

El Coloso *Value* A few steps from the Plaza de la Angustias in the historic center, this is one of the best bargains in town, modest but recommendable in its unpretentious way. The decor is in the conventional local style, with whitewashed walls and a trio of Andalusian-style patios with balconies opening onto street scenes of Jerez. The hotel opened in 1969, and was last renovated in 1998. Bedrooms are a bit cramped but beautifully maintained with good beds and bathrooms equipped with shower-tub combinations. Breakfast is the only meal served. Even though low budget, it does not sacrifice comfort and cleanliness.

Pedro Alonso 13, 11402 Jerez de la Frontera. ✆ or fax **95-634-90-08.** 25 units. 41€–58€ double. Rates include breakfast buffet. MC, V. Parking 5€. *In room:* A/C, TV, hair dryer.

Hotel Serit The modern three-star Hotel Serit, near Plaza de la Angustias, offers rooms that are functionally furnished and comfortable at a good price. Ranging in size from small to medium, rooms are equipped with good Spanish beds, and small but well-maintained private bathrooms, each with a shower-tub combination. There's a pleasant bar downstairs.

Higueras 7, 11402 Jerez de la Frontera. ✆ **95-634-07-00.** Fax 95-634-07-16. 35 units. 66€–100€ double. AE, DC, MC, V. Parking 7€. **Amenities:** Bar; room service; laundry/dry cleaning. *In room:* A/C, TV, hair dryer, safe.

WHERE TO DINE

El Bosque ★ SPANISH/INTERNATIONAL Less than a mile northeast of the city center, the city's most elegant restaurant was established just after World War II. A favorite of the sherry-producing aristocracy, it retains a strong emphasis on bullfighting memorabilia, which makes up most of the decor.

Order the excellent *rabo de toro* (bull's-tail stew) if you want to be a true native. You might begin with a soothing Andalusian gazpacho, then try one of the fried fish dishes, such as hake Seville style. Rice with king prawns and baby shrimp omelets are deservedly popular dishes. Occasionally, Laguna duck in honey with chestnuts and pears is featured. Desserts, including pistachio ice cream, are usually good.

Alcalde Alvaro Domecq 26. ✆ **95-630-33-33.** Reservations required. Main courses 15€–25€. AE, DC, MC, V. Mon–Sat 1:30–5pm and 8:30pm–midnight.

Gaitán ANDALUSIAN Juan Hurtado, who has won acclaim for the food served here, owns this small restaurant near Puerta Santa María. Surrounded by walls displaying celebrity photographs, you can enjoy such Andalusian dishes as garlic soup, various stews, duck *a la sevillana,* and fried seafood. One special dish is lamb cooked with honey, based on a recipe so ancient it goes back to the Muslim occupation of Spain. For dessert, the almond tart is a favorite.

Calle Gaitán 3. ✆ **95-634-58-59.** Reservations recommended. Main courses 12€–15€; fixed-price menu 14€. AE, DC, MC, V. Daily 1–4:30pm, Mon–Sat 8:30–11:30pm.

Mesa Redonda ★★ *Finds* TRADITIONAL SPANISH This restaurant is a rare treat. For the last 15 or so years, the owner and chef, José Antonio Romero and his wife, Margarita, have sought out the traditional recipes that were once served in the private homes of the aristocratic sherry dons of Jerez. They present these to you in winning and tasty combinations in a setting that is like visiting someone's private residence, complete with a library. In the library are many old recipe books and literature about food and wine. Only 10 tables are offered nightly, and these are easily filled. The menu is ever changing, as is the culinary repertoire of this couple. The cookery has wise simplicity and a superb technique. Try *albondiguillas marineras* or fish balls in a shellfish sauce and most definitely *hojaldre de rape y gambas* (a pastry filled with monkfish and prawns). Most recommendable are the *filetes de lenguado con zetas* (filet of sole with mushrooms) and *cordero asado* (grilled lamb). For dessert, there is nothing finer than the lemon and almond cake.

Manuel de la Quintana 3. ✆ **95-634-00-69.** Reservations required. Main courses 11€–13.50€. AE, DC, MC, V. Mon–Sat 1:30–4pm and 9–11pm. Closed last week in July and first 3 weeks in Aug.

Appendix: Barcelona, Madrid & Seville in Depth

Before you arrive in Barcelona, Madrid, or Seville, a little background information goes far to enrich the experience. Each completely different, each a fascination unto itself, these three cities are the most intriguing that Spain has to offer.

1 Ancient Times

Ancestors of the Basques may have been the first settlers in Spain 10,000 to 30,000 years ago, followed, it is believed, by Iberians from North Africa. They, in turn, were followed by Celts, who crossed the Pyrenees around 600 B.C. These groups evolved into a Celtic-Iberian people who inhabited central Spain.

Others coming to the Iberian Peninsula in ancient times were the Phoenicians, who took over coastal areas on the Atlantic beginning in the 11th century B.C. Cádiz, originally the Phoenician settlement of Gades, is perhaps the oldest town in Spain. The Greeks came roughly 500 years after the Phoenicians, lured by the peninsula's wealth of gold and silver. The Greeks established colonies that were later conquered by Carthaginians from North Africa.

Around 200 B.C. the Romans vanquished the Carthaginians and laid the foundations of the present Latin culture. Traces of Roman civilization can still be seen today. By the time of Julius Caesar, Spain (Hispania) was under Roman law and began a long period of peace and prosperity.

Dateline

- **11th century B.C.** Phoenicians settle Spain's coasts.
- **650 B.C.** Greeks colonize the east.
- **600 B.C.** Celts cross the Pyrenees and settle in Spain.
- **6th–3rd century B.C.** Carthaginians make Cartagena their colonial capital, driving out the Greeks.
- **2nd century B.C.–A.D. 2nd century** Rome controls most of Iberia. Christianity spreads.
- **218–201 B.C.** Second Punic War: Rome defeats Carthage.
- **5th century A.D.** Vandals, then Visigoths, invade Spain.
- **8th century** Moors conquer most of Spain.
- **1214** More than half of Iberia is regained by Catholics.
- **1469** Ferdinand of Aragón marries Isabella of Castile.
- **1492** Catholic monarchs seize Granada, the last Moorish stronghold. Columbus lands in the New World.
- **1519** Cortés conquers Mexico. Charles I is crowned Holy Roman Emperor, as Charles V.
- **1556** Philip II inherits throne and launches the Counter-Reformation.
- **1588** England defeats Spanish Armada.

continues

BARBARIAN INVASIONS, THE MOORISH KINGDOM & THE RECONQUEST

When Rome fell in the 5th century, Spain was overrun, first by the Vandals and then by the Visigoths from eastern Europe. The chaotic rule of the Visigothic kings lasted about 300 years, but the barbarian invaders did adopt the language of their new country and tolerated Christianity as well.

In A.D. 711 Moorish warriors led by Tarik crossed over into Spain and conquered the disunited country. By 714, they controlled most of it, except for a few mountain regions around Asturias. For 8 centuries the Moors occupied their new land, which they called *al-Andalús,* or Andalusia, with Córdoba as the capital. A great intellectual center, Córdoba became the scientific capital of Europe; notable advances were made in agriculture, industry, literature, philosophy, and medicine. The Jews were welcomed by the Moors, often serving as administrators, ambassadors, and financial officers. But the Moors quarreled with one another, and soon the few Christian strongholds in the north began to advance south.

The Reconquest, the name given to the Christian efforts to rid the peninsula of the Moors, slowly reduced the size of the Muslim holdings, with Catholic monarchies forming in northern areas. The three powerful kingdoms of Aragón, Castile, and León were joined in 1469, when Ferdinand of Aragón married Isabella of Castile. Catholic kings, as they were called, launched the final attack on the Moors and completed the Reconquest in 1492 by capturing Granada.

That same year, Columbus, the Genoese sailor, landed on the West Indies, laying the foundations for a far-flung empire that brought wealth and power to Spain during the 16th and 17th centuries.

- **1700** Philip V becomes king. War of Spanish Succession follows.
- **1713** Treaty of Utrecht ends war. Spain's colonies reduced.
- **1759** Charles III ascends throne.
- **1808** Napoléon places brother Joseph on the Spanish throne.
- **1813** Wellington drives French out of Spain; the monarchy is restored.
- **1876** Spain becomes a constitutional monarchy.
- **1898** Spanish-American War leads to Spain's loss of Puerto Rico, Cuba, and the Philippines.
- **1923** Primo de Rivera forms military directorate.
- **1930** Right-wing dictatorship ends; Primo de Rivera exiled.
- **1931** King Alfonso XIII abdicates; Second Republic is born.
- **1933–35** Falange party formed.
- **1936–39** Civil War between the governing Popular Front and the Nationalists led by General Francisco Franco.
- **1939** Franco establishes dictatorship, which will last 36 years.
- **1941** Spain technically stays neutral in World War II, but Franco favors Germany.
- **1955** Spain joins the United Nations.
- **1969** Franco names Juan Carlos as his successor.
- **1975** Juan Carlos becomes king. Franco dies.
- **1978** New, democratic constitution initiates reforms.
- **1981** Coup attempt by right-wing officers fails.
- **1982** Socialists gain power after 43 years of right-wing rule.
- **1986** Spain joins the European Community (now the European Union).
- **1992** Barcelona hosts the Summer Olympics; Seville hosts 1992 Expo.
- **1996** A conservative party defeats Socialist party, ending 13-year rule. José María Aznar chosen prime minister.
- **1998** Two cultural milestones for Spain: the inauguration of the controversial Guggenheim Museum at Bilbao and the reopening of Madrid's opera house, Teatro Real.
- **2000** Economy goes on an upswing as the siesta begins to become obsolete.
- **2002** Spain abandons the peseta and falls under the Euro umbrella.

The Spanish Inquisition, begun under Ferdinand and Isabella, sought to eradicate all heresy and secure the primacy of Catholicism. Non-Catholics, Jews, and Moors were mercilessly persecuted, and many were driven out of the country.

2 The Golden Age

Columbus's voyage to America and the conquistadors' subsequent exploration of that land ushered Spain into its golden age.

In the first half of the 16th century, Balboa discovered the Pacific Ocean, Cortés seized Mexico for Spain, Pizarro took Peru, and a Spanish ship (initially commanded by the Portuguese Magellan, who was killed during the voyage) circumnavigated the globe. The conquistadors took Catholicism to the New World and shipped cargoes of gold back to Spain. The Spanish Empire extended all the way to the Philippines. Charles V, grandson of Ferdinand and Isabella, was the most powerful prince in Europe—King of Spain and Naples, Holy Roman Emperor and Lord of Germany, Duke of Burgundy and the Netherlands, and ruler of the New World territories.

But much of Spain's wealth and human resources was wasted in religious and secular conflicts. First Jews, then Muslims, and finally Catholicized Moors were driven out—and with them much of the country's prosperity. When Philip II ascended the throne in 1556, Spain could indeed boast vast possessions: the New World colonies; Naples, Milan, Genoa, Sicily, and other portions of Italy; the Spanish Netherlands (modern Belgium and the Netherlands); and portions of Austria and Germany. But the seeds of decline had already been planted.

Philip, a fanatic Catholic, devoted his energies to subduing the Protestant revolt in the Netherlands and to becoming the standard-bearer for the Counter-Reformation. He tried to return England to Catholicism, first by marrying Mary I ("Bloody Mary") and later by wooing her half sister, Elizabeth I, who rebuffed him. When, in 1588, he resorted to sending the Armada, it was ignominiously defeated; and that defeat symbolized the decline of Spanish power.

In 1700 a Bourbon prince, Philip V, became king, and the country fell under the influence of France. Philip V's right to the throne was challenged by a Hapsburg archduke of Austria, thus giving rise to the War of the Spanish Succession. When it ended, Spain had lost Flanders, its Italian possessions, and Gibraltar (still held by the British today).

During the 18th century, Spain's direction changed with each sovereign. Charles III (1759–88) developed the country economically and culturally. Charles IV became embroiled in wars with France, and the weakness of the Spanish monarchy allowed Napoléon to place his brother Joseph Bonaparte on the throne in 1808.

3 The 19th Century to the Present

Although Britain and France had joined forces to restore the Spanish monarchy, the European conflicts encouraged Spanish colonists to rebel. Ultimately, this led the United States to free the Philippines, Puerto Rico, and Cuba from Spain in 1898.

In 1876, Spain became a constitutional monarchy. But labor unrest, disputes with the Catholic Church, and war in Morocco combined to create political chaos. Conditions eventually became so bad that the Cortés, or parliament, was dissolved in 1923, and General Miguel Primo de Rivera formed a military directorate. Early in 1930, Primo de Rivera resigned, but unrest continued.

On April 14, 1931, a revolution occurred, a republic was proclaimed, and King Alfonso XIII and his family were forced to flee. Initially, the liberal constitutionalists ruled, but soon they were pushed aside by the socialists and anarchists, who adopted a constitution separating church and state, secularizing education, and containing several other radical provisions (for example, agrarian reform and the expulsion of the Jesuits).

The extreme nature of these reforms fostered the growth of the conservative Falange party (*Falange española,* or Spanish Phalanx), modeled after Italy's and Germany's fascist parties. By the 1936 elections, the country was divided equally between left and right, and political violence was common. On July 18, 1936, the army, supported by Mussolini and Hitler, tried to seize power, igniting the Spanish Civil War. General Francisco Franco, coming from Morocco to Spain, led the Nationalist (rightist) forces in the three years of fighting that ravaged the country. Towns were bombed and atrocities were committed in abundance. Early in 1939, Franco entered Barcelona and went on to Madrid; thousands of republicans were executed. Franco became chief of state, remaining so until his death in 1975.

Although Franco adopted a neutral position during World War II, his sympathies obviously lay with Germany and Italy, and Spain, as a nonbelligerent, assisted the Axis powers. This action intensified the diplomatic isolation into which the country was forced after the war's end—in fact, it was excluded from the United Nations until 1955.

Before his death, General Franco selected as his successor Juan Carlos de Borbón y Borbón, son of the pretender to the Spanish throne. After the 1977 elections, a new constitution was approved by the electorate and the king; it guaranteed human and civil rights, as well as free enterprise, and canceled the status of the Roman Catholic Church as the church of Spain. It also granted limited autonomy to several regions, including Catalonia and the Basque provinces, both of which, however, are still clamoring for complete autonomy.

In 1981, a group of right-wing military officers seized the Cortés and called upon Juan Carlos to establish a Francoist state. The king, however, refused, and the conspirators were arrested. The fledgling democracy overcame its first test. Its second major accomplishment—under the Socialist administration of Prime Minister Felipe González, the country's first leftist government since 1939—was to gain Spain's entry into the European Community (now European Union) in 1986.

Further proof that the new Spain had been fully accepted by the international community came in 1992. Spain was designated by the European Union (EU) as the Cultural Capital of Europe for the year; but more significant, the Summer Olympics were held successfully in Barcelona and the world's fair, Expo '92, was mounted in Seville, in Andalusia.

In March 1996, more than 78% of Spain's 32 million registered voters cast ballots and ended the 13-year rule of the scandal-plagued Socialist party of Prime Minister Felipe González. A conservative party with roots in the Franco dictatorship was swept into power, led by José María Aznar, leader of the Popular party, who pledged to represent "all Spain." González took the defeat bitterly, alleging that the vote "was a step back to the fascist dictatorship of Franco."

That dire prediction has not proved accurate, as Spain forged ahead to integrate itself more fully into the European economy, taking stringent measures to streamline its economy to meet the requirements necessary for that step.

Many time-honored traditions, such as the once-beloved siesta, are going the way of the dodo bird. "We didn't have air conditioning in the old days," Juan Alba, a Madrid businessman, told us, "and we had to sleep during the heat of the afternoon."

In the spring of 2002, Spain abandoned its age-old mode of currency, the peseta, and officially adopted the euro along with most of the other European countries. It was an epic step toward integration into "Greater Europe."

Index

See also Accommodations and Restaurant indexes below.

General Index

Accommodations: Barcelona

Accommodations: Madrid

Accommodations: Seville

Restaurants: Barcelona

Restaurants: Madrid

Restaurants: Seville

FROMMER'S® COMPLETE TRAVEL GUIDES

Alaska
Alaska Cruises & Ports of Call
Amsterdam
Argentina & Chile
Arizona
Atlanta
Australia
Austria
Bahamas
Barcelona, Madrid & Seville
Beijing
Belgium, Holland & Luxembourg
Bermuda
Boston
Brazil
British Columbia & the Canadian Rockies
Budapest & the Best of Hungary
California
Canada
Cancún, Cozumel & the Yucatán
Cape Cod, Nantucket & Martha's Vineyard
Caribbean
Caribbean Cruises & Ports of Call
Caribbean Ports of Call
Carolinas & Georgia
Chicago
China
Colorado
Costa Rica
Denmark
Denver, Boulder & Colorado Springs
England
Europe
European Cruises & Ports of Call
Florida
France
Germany
Great Britain
Greece
Greek Islands
Hawaii
Hong Kong
Honolulu, Waikiki & Oahu
Ireland
Israel
Italy
Jamaica
Japan
Las Vegas
London
Los Angeles
Maryland & Delaware
Maui
Mexico
Montana & Wyoming
Montréal & Québec City
Munich & the Bavarian Alps
Nashville & Memphis
Nepal
New England
New Mexico
New Orleans
New York City
New Zealand
Northern Italy
Nova Scotia, New Brunswick & Prince Edward Island
Oregon
Paris
Philadelphia & the Amish Country
Portugal
Prague & the Best of the Czech Republic
Provence & the Riviera
Puerto Rico
Rome
San Antonio & Austin
San Diego
San Francisco
Santa Fe, Taos & Albuquerque
Scandinavia
Scotland
Seattle & Portland
Shanghai
Singapore & Malaysia
South Africa
South America
South Florida
South Pacific
Southeast Asia
Spain
Sweden
Switzerland
Texas
Thailand
Tokyo
Toronto
Tuscany & Umbria
USA
Utah
Vancouver & Victoria
Vermont, New Hampshire & Maine
Vienna & the Danube Valley
Virgin Islands
Virginia
Walt Disney World® & Orlando
Washington, D.C.
Washington State

FROMMER'S® DOLLAR-A-DAY GUIDES

Australia from $50 a Day
California from $70 a Day
Caribbean from $70 a Day
England from $75 a Day
Europe from $70 a Day
Florida from $70 a Day
Hawaii from $80 a Day
Ireland from $60 a Day
Italy from $70 a Day
London from $85 a Day
New York from $90 a Day
Paris from $80 a Day
San Francisco from $70 a Day
Washington, D.C. from $80 a Day

FROMMER'S® PORTABLE GUIDES

Acapulco, Ixtapa & Zihuatanejo
Amsterdam
Aruba
Australia's Great Barrier Reef
Bahamas
Berlin
Big Island of Hawaii
Boston
California Wine Country
Cancún
Charleston & Savannah
Chicago
Disneyland®
Dublin
Florence
Frankfurt
Hong Kong
Houston
Las Vegas
London
Los Angeles
Los Cabos & Baja
Maine Coast
Maui
Miami
New Orleans
New York City
Paris
Phoenix & Scottsdale
Portland
Puerto Rico
Puerto Vallarta, Manzanillo & Guadalajara
Rio de Janeiro
San Diego
San Francisco
Seattle
Sydney
Tampa & St. Petersburg
Vancouver
Venice
Virgin Islands
Washington, D.C.

FROMMER'S® NATIONAL PARK GUIDES

Banff & Jasper
Family Vacations in the National Parks
Grand Canyon
National Parks of the American West
Rocky Mountain
Yellowstone & Grand Teton
Yosemite & Sequoia/ Kings Canyon
Zion & Bryce Canyon

FROMMER'S® MEMORABLE WALKS

Chicago
London
New York
Paris
San Francisco
Washington, D.C.

FROMMER'S® GREAT OUTDOOR GUIDES

Arizona & New Mexico
New England
Northern California
Southern New England
Vermont & New Hampshire

SUZY GERSHMAN'S BORN TO SHOP GUIDES

Born to Shop: France
Born to Shop: Hong Kong, Shanghai & Beijing
Born to Shop: Italy
Born to Shop: London
Born to Shop: New York
Born to Shop: Paris

FROMMER'S® IRREVERENT GUIDES

Amsterdam
Boston
Chicago
Las Vegas
London
Los Angeles
Manhattan
New Orleans
Paris
Rome
San Francisco
Seattle & Portland
Vancouver
Walt Disney World®
Washington, D.C.

FROMMER'S® BEST-LOVED DRIVING TOURS

Britain
California
Florida
France
Germany
Ireland
Italy
New England
Northern Italy
Scotland
Spain
Tuscany & Umbria

HANGING OUT™ GUIDES

Hanging Out in England
Hanging Out in Europe
Hanging Out in France
Hanging Out in Ireland
Hanging Out in Italy
Hanging Out in Spain

THE UNOFFICIAL GUIDES®

Bed & Breakfasts and Country Inns in:
- California
- Great Lakes States
- Mid-Atlantic
- New England
- Northwest
- Rockies
- Southeast
- Southwest
- Southwest & South Central Plains
- U.S.A.

Best RV & Tent Campgrounds in:
- California & the West
- Florida & the Southeast
- Great Lakes States
- Mid-Atlantic
- Northeast
- Northwest & Central Plains

Beyond Disney
Branson, Missouri
California with Kids
Chicago
Cruises
Disneyland®
Florida with Kids
Golf Vacations in the Eastern U.S.
Great Smoky & Blue Ridge Region
Inside Disney
Hawaii
Las Vegas
London
Mid-Atlantic with Kids
Mini Las Vegas
Mini-Mickey
New England and New York with Kids
New Orleans
New York City
Paris
San Francisco
Skiing in the West
Southeast with Kids
Walt Disney World®
Walt Disney World® for Grown-ups
Walt Disney World® with Kids
Washington, D.C.
World's Best Diving Vacations

SPECIAL-INTEREST TITLES

Frommer's Adventure Guide to Australia & New Zealand
Frommer's Adventure Guide to Central America
Frommer's Adventure Guide to India & Pakistan
Frommer's Adventure Guide to South America
Frommer's Adventure Guide to Southeast Asia
Frommer's Adventure Guide to Southern Africa
Frommer's Britain's Best Bed & Breakfasts and Country Inns
Frommer's Caribbean Hideaways
Frommer's Exploring America by RV
Frommer's Fly Safe, Fly Smart
Frommer's France's Best Bed & Breakfasts and Country Inns
Frommer's Gay & Lesbian Europe
Frommer's Italy's Best Bed & Breakfasts and Country Inns
Frommer's New York City with Kids
Frommer's Ottawa with Kids
Frommer's Road Atlas Britain
Frommer's Road Atlas Europe
Frommer's Road Atlas France
Frommer's Toronto with Kids
Frommer's Vancouver with Kids
Frommer's Washington, D.C., with Kids
Israel Past & Present
The New York Times' Guide to Unforgettable Weekends
Places Rated Almanac
Retirement Places Rated